THE

ROCKY MOUNTAIN SAINTS:

A FULL AND COMPLETE

HISTORY OF THE MORMONS,

FROM THE FIRST VISION OF JOSEPH SMITH TO THE LAST
COURTSHIP OF BRIGHAM YOUNG;

INCLUDING

THE STORY OF THE HAND-CART EMIGRATION—THE MORMON WAR—THE
MOUNTAIN-MEADOW MASSACRE—THE REIGN OF TERROR IN UTAH
—THE DOCTRINE OF HUMAN SACRIFICE—THE POLITICAL,
DOMESTIC, SOCIAL, AND THEOLOGICAL INFLUENCES
OF THE SAINTS—THE FACTS OF POLYGAMY
—THE COLONIZATION OF THE
ROCKY MOUNTAINS,

AND

THE DEVELOPMENT OF THE GREAT MINERAL WEALTH OF THE TERRITORY OF UTAH.

BY

T. B. H. STENHOUSE,

TWENTY-FIVE YEARS A MORMON ELDER AND MISSIONARY, AND EDITOR AND PROPRIETOR OF THE
SALT LAKE DAILY TELEGRAPH.

*ILLUSTRATED WITH TWENTY-FOUR FULL-PAGE ENGRAVINGS, A STEEL PLATE FRONTISPIECE
AN AUTOGRAPHIC LETTER OF BRIGHAM YOUNG, AND NUMEROUS WOODCUTS.*

NEW YORK:
D. APPLETON AND COMPANY,
549 & 551 BROADWAY.
1873.

Books written by thinkers—men who thought and dared to express their thoughts—are always worth reading. I care not whether their authors were Atheists or Methodists, Heathen or Mohammedan; the life's blood of the author circulates through them, and in reading you feel its pulsations. But books written by men who never saw through their own eyes, who never put out their hands, and felt the world for themselves, nor took one manly step, are the faintest echoes from the distant hills compared with the heaven-shaking thunder that produced them.—Denton.

Printing Statement:

Due to the very old age and scarcity of this book,
many of the pages may be hard to read due to the
blurring of the original text, possible missing pages,
missing text and other issues beyond our control.

Because this is such an important and rare work, we
believe it is best to reproduce this book regardless of
its original condition.

Thank you for your understanding.

Brigham Young

PREFACE.

Notwithstanding the frequency with which the American press has kept the name of the Mormons before the public, few persons have any definite idea of what Mormonism claims to be, and what it actually is.

Occupying, as the Saints do, the centre of the great highway between the Atlantic and Pacific oceans, and demanding admission into the Union as a sovereign State, Congress cannot long refuse attention to their claim. The question, therefore, of engrafting upon the Republic a Theocracy which *practices polygamy*, teaches the barbarous doctrine of *human sacrifice*, and is *in its sentiments* inimical to the constitution of the nation, demands the careful consideration of all who are interested in the honour and good name of the United States.

In the pages of this work, the politician, the preacher, the *littérateur*, and the thoughtful reader, will find abundant matter for studious reflection.

It requires no prophetic inspiration to predicate that, in spite of all the crudity and ridiculous assumption of Mormonism, the highest wisdom of the national Government may yet be required to avert scenes of conflict which would be universally deplored.

Memorials demanding the admission of Utah into the Union, under the title of "The State of Deseret," have for twenty-three years engaged the attention of Congress. Last session the demand was again made, and met with a much more favourable reception than ever before. Next Session it will be repeated, and, if not then successful, it will be again and again urged, until finally Statehood is secured.

Emboldened by the encouragement of some prominent members of Congress, the Mormon Prophet has approved of the retirement of the monogamic Delegate who served the Territory for a dozen years, and, as a test of the disposition of the national mind, sends as his successor to Washington an apostle—*the husband of four wives*. Should the nation consent to this innovation, Statehood will soon be secured for Utah, and Brigham Young's Theocracy will be triumphant over the Republic and the National laws.

Mormonism is not dead nor dying.

Until this " Utah difficulty " is settled emphatically and finally by the voice of the people, declaring that no political or domestic institution opposed to the spirit and genius of republicanism can ever be allowed to exist within the domain of the United States, Mormonism is destined to be the disturbing dream of every occupant of the chair of Washington.

CONTENTS.

CHAPTER I.

MORMONISM EXPLAINED.—The First Faith biblical—Spiritual Enthusiasm of the Elders—Establishment of a Literal Kingdom predicted—Polygamy not in the Original Programme—Mormon Errors attributable to the System and Leaders—Argument of the Miraculous Power of Healing—Difficulty experienced in leaving the Mormon Church—Assumption of Infallible Priesthood—Mormonism summed up, ... 1

CHAPTER II.

THE MORMON PROPHET—His Early Life—His Visions—His Personal Characteristics—An Angel reveals to him the Golden Plates—His Mission announced —The Story of the Stone Box, ... 8

CHAPTER III.

THE GOLD PLATES.—Joseph translates the " Reformed Egyptian "—Martin Harris acts as Scribe—Professor Anthon pronounces the Characters and Translation " a Hoax "—A Prediction of Isaiah fulfilled—Satan and Mrs. Harris bring the Prophet into Great Trouble—Oliver Cowdery replaces Harris—John the Baptist ordains Smith and Cowdery—They baptize each other, prophesy and rejoice— Witnesses are chosen to testify to the Book of Mormon, ... 21

CHAPTER IV.

ORGANIZATION OF THE CHURCH.—Disciples receive the Holy Ghost—Ancient Apostles and Prophets revisit the Earth—Newell Knight is tortured by the Devil —His Experience claimed as the first " Latter-Day " Miracle—Judge Edmonds records similar Phenomena in Spiritualism, ... 80

CHAPTER V.

THE FIRST CONFERENCE.—Parley P. Pratt and Orson Pratt converted—Missionary Enterprise begins—Elders sent to preach to the Indians—Sidney Rigdon converts his Campbellite Congregation—Saints commanded to gather in Ohio— Jackson County, Missouri, designated the " Land of Promise," . . . 86

CHAPTER VI.

SATAN THREATENS THE CHURCH.—He shakes and corrupts the Ohio Saints —The Youthful Prophet labours with Great Zeal—Missionaries evangelize the Eastern States—Smith and Rigdon behold a Great Vision—They are tarred and feathered—Go to Missouri and found a Newspaper, ... 4C

CHAPTER VII.

MEETING OF THE PROPHETS.—Brigham Young sees Joseph Smith for the First Time—They rejoice together in Kirtland—Brigham speaks in " Unknown Tongues"—Joseph predicts the Southern Rebellion—He makes an Inspired Translation of the New Testament—Troubles arise between the Saints and the " Gentiles " in Missouri—The Disciples are driven from Jackson County, . 44

CHAPTER VIII.

THE PROMISED LAND.—" The Lord " calls for " the Strength of his House " to reinstate the Exiled Saints in Jackson County—Two hundred and five Elders respond—The Prophet becomes Commander-in-Chief of " the Armies of the Lord " —A Revelation promising Restoration to the Exiles—Joseph is the Man like unto Moses to lead them to Victory, ... 48

CHAPTER IX.

ZION'S CAMP.—The Prophet's " Army " marches to Missouri—A Great Storm— The Cholera desolates the " Strength of the Lord's House "—Utter Discomfiture of the Mormons—The Promises to restore the Saints to Jackson County a Total Failure—The Army Disbanded—The Saints sue for Peace—" The Lord was only trying their Faith "—They are to curse their Enemies—Anniversary Meetings of Zion's Camp—Dancing and Rejoicing, ... 52

CHAPTER X.

TWELVE APOSTLES CHOSEN.—Quorums of " Seventies " organized—They go abroad and preach—Kirtland Temple finished—Dedication and Endowment— Joseph's Wonderful Vision of the Celestial Kingdom—A Second Pentecost— Brigham Young " Speaks in Tongues "—The Temple filled with Angels—Joseph and Cowdery are visited by Moses, Elias, and Elijah—They behold " The Lord " —Cowdery afterward apostatizes, ... 60

CHAPTER XI.

FIRST GREAT APOSTACY.—Joseph predicts about Brigham being President of the Church—British Missions projected as a Strategic Measure—One of Joseph's own Counsellors rebels against him—He is proclaimed " A Fallen Prophet "—Troubles again threaten in Missouri, ... 67

CHAPTER XII.

THE PROPHET BECOMES A BANKER.—Apostates and Capitalists bring him to Grief—Sidney Rigdon's Interesting View of a " Circulating Medium "—He assures Mr. Jones that the Bank Notes were never intended for Redemption—

The Kirtland Safety Society Bank repudiated—Joseph and Sidney fly to Missouri—Pursued by Armed Men—Extraordinary Escapes—" The Lord" protects them, ... 70

CHAPTER XIII.

CUTTING OFF APOSTATES.—Witnesses of the Book of Mormon expelled from the Church—Joseph denounces the "Lord's Chosen" as "Blacklegs, Thieves, Liars, and Counterfeiters"—More Apostles dethroned—The Prophet locates the Garden of Eden in Missouri—It was there that Adam and Eve sported in Innocence—More Trouble looming—Rigdon's famous Declaration of Independence, ... 75

CHAPTER XIV.

WAR COMMENCES.—Affidavits made against the Prophet—The Mormons and the Mob resort to Arms—The Governor calls out the State Militia—Joseph and Sidney propose to become Lawyers—The Mormon Settlements attacked—Houses burned—Women and Children forced to flee before an Infuriated Mob—Frightful Cruelties—The Saints fight and retaliate, ... 80

CHAPTER XV.

THE CHURCH IN DANGER.—Apostles apostatize—Marsh and Hyde make Affidavits against the Prophet—Charge him with aiming to be a Second Mahomet—The Danite Band—Its Name and Origin—Dr. Avard's Statements—The Doctor's Speech—Joseph denies the Paternity of the Band—Great Excitement throughout the State—A Sensational Report—More Fighting—The Apostle Patten killed—The Saints to be rooted out, ... 98

CHAPTER XVI.

EXPULSION OR EXTERMINATION.—Terrible Excitement throughout Missouri —The Country in Arms—General Clark placed in Command of the State Militia —The Governor's Order for the Expulsion of the Saints—Brutality of the Mob —Horrible Massacre of unoffending Mormons—Murder of Women and Childen —The Narrative of an Eye-witness, ... 96

CHAPTER XVII.

THE PROPHET RESOLVED TO FIGHT IT OUT.—Faith struggles with Fate—Treason in the Camp of the Saints—Joseph and the leading Mormons delivered over to General Lucas—The Prisoners tried by Court Martial—Sentenced to be shot next Morning—General Doniphan protests against their Execution—The Prophet and his Brethren sent to Jail—The Revelations contradicted by Facts, ... 103

CHAPTER XVIII.

THE MISSOURIANS TRIUMPHANT.—Grandiloquent Speech of General Clark—Mormons ordered to leave the State—Examination of the Prisoners—The Prophet not subdued—The Legislature memorialized—The Saints wavering—Joseph reviews the Situation, ... 109

CHAPTER XIX.

IN PRISON.—The New Year opens dark and dreary—The Mormons suffer—The Missouri Legislature consider the "Persecutions" of the Saints—Brigham Young flees from Missouri—Joseph indites an Epistle from Prison—The Prisoners indicted—They escape from Missouri, ... 115

CHAPTER XX.

THE EXILES FIND AN ASYLUM IN ILLINOIS.—The Prophet again at Liberty—Nauvoo selected for a new Zion—A City rapidly built—Brigham Young sent to England—The Saints importune Congress for Redress—Joseph visits President Van Buren—The Mormons still cling to the Promises of Zion in Missouri, ... 120

CHAPTER XXI.

THE PROPHET'S POLITICAL LIFE BEGINS.—New Men gather round him—A reorganization of the " Quorum of the Apostles "—Another Temple to be erected —" The Lord " commands the Saints to build a " Boarding House "—Kings are invited to the Aid of Zion, ... 126

CHAPTER XXII.

THE FICKLE FORTUNE OF POLITICS.—The Legislature liberal to the Saints —The Prophet becomes a Lieutenant-General—Foundation of the Temple laid— Grand Military Display—Joseph at the Height of his Glory—Missouri seeks to re-capture him, ... 133

CHAPTER XXIII.

POLITICAL DIFFICULTIES.—The Prophet balances between the Whigs and the Democrats—The Neighbours of the Mormons become dissatisfied—Joseph charged with Designs upon the Life of Governor Boggs—He is arrested on a Charge of Treason—Ways that are dark—Governor Ford explains—The first Budding of Polygamy—The Beginning of the End—Serious Charges are made, ... 139

CHAPTER XXIV.

JOSEPH PREDICTS THE ROCKY MOUNTAIN ZION.—He designs to found there an Independent State—Becomes a Candidate for the Presidency of the United States—Assails Clay and Calhoun—Great Trouble with Apostates—Politics and Polygamy threaten to engulf him—The Nauvoo *Expositor* founded and destroyed—Writs issued for the Arrest of the Prophet—He resolves on Flight, ... 146

CHAPTER XXV.

THE PROPHET SURRENDERS TO THE LAW.—The Governor pledges the State for his Safety—The Country intensely excited—The Destruction of the Nauvoo *Expositor* a Fatal Error—The Militia in Arms—The Murder of the Prophet planned—His Enemies resolve to kill him while Governor Ford visits Nauvoo, ... 152

CHAPTER XXVI.

LAST HOURS OF THE PROPHET.—The Presentiment of his Death—The Murderers—Their Attack upon the Jail—The Assassination of the Prophet, and the Patriarch—An Apostle shot—Thrilling Narrative of a Survivor—"Two minutes in Jail," 163

CHAPTER XXVII.

POLYGAMY IN ILLINOIS.—Its Introduction among the Mormons—The "Revelation" given by Joseph Smith—The Sons of the Deceased Prophet dispute the Polygamic Marriages of their Father—They call for the Posterity—The Promise of a "Righteous Seed" unfulfilled—Joseph without Issue by his score of Polygamic Wives—Married Women become his "Wives" without Divorce or Separation from their Husbands, ... 176

CHAPTER XXVIII.

POLYGAMY REPUDIATED.—Joseph Smith and the Mormon Leaders deny it—The Revelations of the Church condemn it—The Sons of the Prophet defend their Father's Reputation—The Evidences of his Polygamic Life, . . 190

CHAPTER XXIX.

AFTER THE PROPHET'S DEATH.—Sidney Rigdon delivered over to Satan—Brigham Young and the Twelve Apostles rule the Church—Mobocracy again rampant—The Expulsion of the Mormons demanded—The Saints agree to Expatriation, ... 204

CHAPTER XXX.

THE EXODUS FROM NAUVOO.—The Hasty Departure of the Apostles—Journey to the Rocky Mountains—The Sufferings of the Exiles—Nauvoo besieged and bombarded—An Exile's Story—Colonel Kane's Narrative, . . . 221

CHAPTER XXXI.

ON THE MISSOURI.—Enlistment of the Mormon Battalion—False Ideas about the Matter—Historical Facts—Elder Little at Washington—He is introduced to President Polk—Important Official Documents—Colonel Kane's Story—The Mormon Ball—Brigham receives the Volunteers' "Advance Pay"—Mormon Testimony in favour of Government—Brigham Young's Extraordinary Statements—The Government vindicated, ... 236

CHAPTER XXXII.

FOUNDING OF THE FRONTIER CITIES.—Brigham's first and last "Revelation"—The Departure of the Pioneers—The Discovery of Salt Lake Valley—The Return to the Missouri River, ... 250

CHAPTER XXXIII.

CHANGES IN THE CHURCH.—Brigham Young assumes Joseph's Authority and Place—The Emigration from Europe re-opened—Migration of the Saints to

x CONTENTS.

the New Zion—Brigham invites Presidents, Emperors, Kings, Princes, Nobles, etc.; to come to the Help of "the Lord"—The Pioneers *en route*, . . 262

CHAPTER XXXIV.

THE CIVIL HISTORY OF UTAH.—The "State of Deseret" created—The Crickets destroy the Crops—A Miracle performed—Territorial Government extended over Utah—Trouble with the Federal Officers, ... 268

CHAPTER XXXV.

THE IRREPRESSIBLE CONFLICT BETWEEN THEOCRACY AND REPUBLICANISM.—The Federal Officers in Utah—Some become Sycophants to the Priesthood—Some are defiant—Brigham Young a Second Time appointed Governor—Trouble with the Federal Judges—They leave the Territory, . . 279

CHAPTER XXXVI.

THE "REFORMATION" IN UTAH.—Its Extraordinary Origin—Shortcomings of the Saints—"Jeddy's" Frenzy—Sinners rebaptized—Terrible Enthusiasm—Tabernacle Teachings—Doctrine of the "Blood Atonement"—Human Sacrifices commended—Erring Saints to offer up their Blood as Incense to propitiate Deity—Brother Heber declares that Brigham Young is God to the Mormons—Strange Preaching—Confessions of the Saints—Brigham's Casuistry about rebaptizing—Extraordinary Public Meeting of the Priesthood—A "Reign of Terror"—Shocking Outrages upon Citizens—Crusade against Intellect—Results of the Reformation—An Important Letter—What Brigham and the Leaders *really* said in the Tabernacle—Apostates and Gentiles threatened, . . . 292

CHAPTER XXXVII.

EMIGRATING TO UTAH WITH HAND-CARTS.—Mr. Chislett's Narrative—The "Divine plan" for Emigrating the Poor—Outfitting in Iowa City—Organizing the Company—Journey through Iowa—The Elders prophesy a Successful Journey—Brother Savage protests—"Inspirational" Counsel followed—The Carts break down—Cattle are lost—The Apostle Richards prophesies in the Name of the God of Israel—The Elders eat the Fatted Calf—Arrival at Fort Laramie—Provisions become scarce—Great Privations—The People begin to faint by the Way—Captain Willie's Bravery—The Winter overtakes them—Snow on the Mountains—The Sweetwater—Great Privations, Disease, and Death—Envoys from Salt Lake Valley—Provisions all gone—Captain Willie goes in Search of Aid—Terrible Condition of the People—Courage and Faithfulness of the Sufferers—Arrival of Timely Aid—A Thrilling Scene—Hope revived—"Too late"—Ravages of Death—A Hard Road—An Old Man's Death—"*Thirteen Corpses all stiffly frozen*"—Fifteen buried in one Grave—The ending of the Journey—Great Kindness of the Elders and People of Utah—The Pilgrims enter Zion—Sixty-seven Emigrants dead on the Journey—Greater Losses in another Company—Folly of Modern Prophecies, ... 311

CHAPTER XXXVIII.

THE MORMON WAR.—How it was inaugurated—Isolation of Utah—Carrying the Mails—Mormon Enterprise—Senator Douglas and the Saints—Anniversary Festivities at Big Cottonwood Lake—New Official Appointments for Utah—Warlike Preparations of the Saints—Believers concentrated at Zion—Ludicrous Fears of some Elders—Major Van Vleit sent by the United States Government—Brigham receives him—Major Van Vleit's Story—Brigham's Proclamation—Defiance from the Tabernacle—Brigham's Wrath—Heber's Enthusiasm—Expedition of the United States Army—Dogberryism of Brigham—D. H. Wells instructs the Brethren to harass the Army—The Mormons burn the United States Trains— Great Suffering of the Troops—Mules and Cattle freeze on the Road—Thirty-five Miles in fifteen Days, ... 845

CHAPTER XXXIX.

THE TWO ARMIES.—The Saints rejoice, and sing their Warlike Songs—The Federal Troops in Camp Scott—Brigham sends them a Present of Salt—"The Lord" is to destroy the Enemies of Zion—Col. Kane arrives among the Mormons and converts Brigham—The Prophet concludes that he cannot "whip" the United States—He proposes Flight—Means to take Care of Himself—Col. Kane visits Gov. Cumming and arranges a Basis of Prospective Peace—He offends Gen. Johnston—A Duel imminent—The Mormons flee from their Homes, ... 371

CHAPTER XL.

PEACE RESTORED.—Gov. Cumming visits Salt Lake City—His Passage through Echo Cañon—Everywhere greeted with Honour—Brigham surrenders the Territorial Seal, and receives the new Governor with Courtesy—Commissioners arrive with President Buchanan's Pardon—Peace proclaimed—General Johnston without Opposition traverses the Streets of Zion—The Federal Troops locate Forty Miles from the City—The Saints return to their Homes—The Prophet's Boasting and the President's Folly suddenly terminate, ... 389

CHAPTER XLI.

THE JUDGES AT WORK.—The Federal Officers divided—Judge Sinclair opposed by the District Attorney at Salt Lake City—Judge Cradlebaugh holds Court at Provo—The Charges of Murder at Springville—Attention drawn to the Mountain Meadows Massacre and other Murders—The Jury find no Bills of Indictment—The Judge discharges them—Depositions of Witnesses taken— Terrible Revelations—Counterfeiting on United States Treasury—Trying to arrest Brigham—Saving the Governor's Official Head, ... 400

CHAPTER XLII.

THE EXPEDITION A FAILURE.—The Mormons enriched by the Presence of the Troops—Intercourse with the Camp forbidden to the Saints—The Assertion of Personal Liberty and the Dawning of Freedom to the bold—Brigham supplies the Military with Tithing Flour—Rowdyism and Murders in the City—The Prophet guarded Night and Day—The Desperadoes are wasted away—The Rebellion in the South a Theme of Rejoicing—The Fulfilment of Joseph's Prediction—The Expedition recalled—Great Destruction of Munitions of War—Millions of Property wasted—The Federal Troops vacate the Territory, and the Saints rejoice, ... 415

CHAPTER XLIII.

THE MOUNTAIN MEADOWS MASSACRE.—The Story of two Emigrant Trains
—The Journey across the Plains—Arrival in Salt Lake City—Denied Provi-
sions in the Mormon Settlements—The Travel to the Mountain Meadows—A
Militia Regiment follows them—Indians and Mormon Militia attack the Train—
A Fight for Four Days—Mormon Officers betray the Emigrants under a Flag of
Truce—They lay down their Arms under Promise of Protection—A Hundred
and Twenty Men, Women, and Children butchered—Seventeen Children preserved—The Story of the Massacre confirmed by the Affidavit of Bishop
Smith—The Author's Letter to Brigham Young—Superintendent Forney's Report—Names of the Little Ones saved—Judge Cradlebaugh's Speech in Congress—Sale of the Emigrants' Property—Major Carlton's Story of the Monument—" Vengeance is mine, I *have* repaid "—-" Argus " defines Brigham
Young's Responsibility—Congress deaf to the Demand for Investigation, . 424

CHAPTER XLIV.

THE SPRINGVILLE MURDERS.—The Status of the People during the Time of
Blood—Brigham's Absolute Authority—Something Personal of Lee and the
Leaders at Springville—How the Parrishes were entrapped and murdered—
Confession of the Bishop's Counsellor—" Helping those who need Help "—How
Bird " *worked* the best he could "—" A Lick across the Throat "—Paying the
Atoning Penalty—Horrible Sacrifice of an Unfaithful Wife—How John G——'s
Blood was " Spilled," 459

CHAPTER XLV.

THE FAITH OF THE SAINTS.—The Prophet's Creed given to the Public—The
Doctrines taught to the Saints—Spirits in Prison—Baptism for the Dead—Brigham Young teaches that Adam is the God of this World—Brigham and all the
Mormons are to make New Worlds and become Gods—A New Version of Paradise Lost and Paradise Regained—Origin of the Devil—The Mormon Account of
the Origin of the African Race, ... 472

CHAPTER XLVI.

THE MORMON THEOCRACY.—All Earthly Government is Rebellion—The Kingdom of God in Utah—The Gentiles to be destroyed—Why the Mormons pray
for the Overthrow of the Republic—Believers to deed all their Property to Brigham Young, " the Lord's " Representative on Earth—The Families of the Saints
to be Adopted by the Apostles—Brigham's Word equal to that of God—Orson
Hyde illustrates the Kingdoms of the " Gods," 495

CHAPTER XLVII.

THE BOOK OF ABRAHAM.—An Extraordinary Document—The Prophet buys
Egyptian Mummies—Translates Papyri found with them—Another Translation
by a Scientist—Delusion, Deception, or Folly?—Was Joseph Smith a " Spirit
Medium ?" 507

CHAPTER XLVIII.

THE BOOK OF MORMON.—Orson Pratt's Account of its Origin—Ancient Hebrew Prophecies fulfilled—First Inhabitants of America—Murder of Laban—Theft of his Plates—Migration of Israelites from Palestine to America—The Building of the "Barges"—Lehi and his Sons—Jared's Interview with "the Lord"—Difficulties of Navigation—The Wonderful Compass—Bad Ways of the Brethren—Landing in America—Nations founded and Cities built—"Christians" in America One Hundred Years before Christ was born—A Church founded—Persecutions and Preachings—Fearful Signs, Wonders, and Prophecies—Battles between the Nephites and Lamanites—Two Millions of Men slain in one Battle—The Gold Plates hid in the Hill Cumorah—Internal Evidence—Plagiarisms from the New Testament and Shakespeare—Analysis of the Book—The Folly of the Mormon Argument upon Evidence, ... 523

CHAPTER XLIX.

THE PRIESTHOOD IN ZION.—Its Organizations, Apostolic, Judicial, and Political—The Prayers of the Saints—The Surveillance of the Teachers—The Eyes of the Priesthood over all—The Missionaries abroad—The Elders travel "without Purse or Scrip"—How Mormonism is introduced among the Gentiles—Foreign Missions—His Satanic Majesty attacks the Apostles in England—"Devils" attack Brother Heber—Success in Britain—The Emigration to Zion—Baptizing Converts in the Atlantic—The Journey through the States, ... 556

CHAPTER L.

POLYGAMY IN UTAH.—Preached from the Tabernacle—A Terrible Trial to Women—Degradation of the Sex—Ancient Hebrew Examples adduced—"Living Martyrs" to a Debasing Doctrine—Brigham Young on Polygamy—Second and "following" Wives—Marriage Rites among the Mormons—The First Wife is not asked *one* Question—Impossibility of Happiness in Polygamy, . . 581

CHAPTER LI.

UTAH DURING THE REBELLION.—Change of Federal Officers—Brutal Attack upon Governor Dawson by Mormon Rowdies—Three of them shot—A Rival Prophet to Brigham—The "Morrisite" Community—They disregard a Writ of *Habeas Corpus*—The Mormon Militia acting as a *Posse Comitatus*—Three Days' Fighting—The Prophet Morris, his Counsellor Banks, and two Women, killed after the Surrender—Arrival of new Federal Officers—An early Difficulty—Arrival of the California Volunteers—Establishment of Camp Douglas—Brigham defies the Law of Congress, and takes "an Elderly Young Woman" to Wife—The Prophet afraid of Arrest—Citizens summoned to protect him—Chief-Justice Kinney arrests the Prophet for violating the Anti-Polygamic Law—Brigham gives Bail—The Grand Jury find no Evidence that Brigham had married again—Trouble with the Federal Officials—The Mormons invite them to leave the Territory—The Tabernacle and Mormon Press rejoice in the Calamities of the Union—General Connor and the Volunteers a Terror to Evil-Doers—A Midnight Scare—Another False Prophecy—Brigham predicts another Four Years of War only Four Days before General Lee surrendered, ... 591

CHAPTER LII.

AFTER THE WAR.—Grand Procession of Mormons and Gentiles—Prospective
Peace—The Federal Officers and Mormon Dignitaries wine together—The City
honours General Connor in the Social Hall—The Prophets and the Gentile
Ladies decline attending the Ball—Vice-President Colfax and Literary Friends
visit Zion—The Interview with the Prophet—The Hon. James M. Ashley sees
the Difficulty of convicting the Apostles for Polygamy—He tells Tom Corwin's
Story of the "*Eleven Jurors who had some of the Ham*"—A Gentile marries a
Mormon Elder's Second Wife—Mr. Brassfield assassinated—Great Excitement
among the Gentiles—General Sherman gives Brigham a Hint that he will send
Troops to Zion—Brigham hastens to assert his Innocence—Contention over the
Warm Springs—Dr. Robinson, the Contestant, is assassinated—A Foul and
Dreadful Murder—Brigham joins the Gentiles in offering a Reward for the Mur-
derers—No Detection—Years after, Brigham withdraws his Reward—Afraid of
tempting Men to Perjury—Three Apostates charged with stealing a Cow—
Arrested, confined, two murdered in "attempting to escape"—The Brethren
arrested for Murder, and escape—Chief-Justice Titus grossly insulted,   . 611

CHAPTER LIII.

THE DAWNING OF FREEDOM.—The Mercantile Struggle against Despotism—
"Freezing out the Gentiles"—Police Surveillance of Apostates' Stores—The
Walker Brothers—Brigham refuses a Check from them for $500—A Bishop told
to "cut away"—Handed over to the Buffetings of Satan—The Fight with Brigham—Fears of Violence—Gentile Merchants offer to sell out at a Great Loss and
leave the City—Brigham's Reply—The Gentiles and Apostates under the Ban—
Zion's Coöperative Mercantile Institution organized—Trouble among the Mormon Merchants—Ruin of the Small Traders—"The Seed of the Prophet Joseph"
go to Zion—The Reorganized Church—"Young Joseph"—Alexander H. and
David Hyrum Smith in Utah—Brigham's Jealousy—The Sons of Joseph meet
with Success—The "New Movement"—The *Utah Magazine*—Wonderful Revelations of Messrs. Godbe and Harrison—Voices from Heaven against Brigham—
The Beginning of the Great Apostacy—Godbe, Harrison and Kelsey expelled
from the Church—The *Magazine* opens its Batteries upon the Prophet—The Gentiles and Liberal Mormons encourage the "Rebels"—The "Reformers" start
a Newspaper—They preach and write themselves into Spiritualism—The Fetters burst and the Gentile Merchants triumph—Brigham's Power waning—His
Sceptre broken, ... 622

CHAPTER LIV.

BRIGHAM YOUNG.—His Father's Family—His Early Life and Occupation—Brigham's Faith—The "Gift of Tongues"—"Brother Brigham" opposed to Manifestations of the "Gift"—His Ideas of Unreasoning Obedience—The Prophet at
Home—The "Trustee in Trust"—The Prophet's Wives—His Favourites—Brigham's Domestic Life—His Habits and Traits of Character—His Hours of Business
—The Prophet in his Office—Extraordinary Influence with the People—Unheard-
of Claims to Dictation in Secular Affairs—Lovers to ask Brigham's Permission to
love—Troublesome Elders sent on Mission—Ordered to go to "Dixie"—Mission
to the Indians—How the "Lamanites" were to be made a "White and Delight-
"some People"—Heber's *Hint* to the Missionaries, and how they took it—Brigham on his Travels—The "Royal Blood of Young"—Reception of the Prophet

among the Saints—"The Lion of the Lord" in his Glory—The Saints listen
to the Prophet—His Style of Preaching—The Prophet's Successor—Brigham
the Second—Founding a Dynasty—Nepotism greater than Birthright and Priesthood—The Precedent given by Brigham—George A. Smith, Brigham's Rightful
Successor—Apostle George Q. Cannon—A Mission to Jerusalem—Influence of
the Railroad—Influx of Gentiles—Brigham's Lost Opportunities—Great Wealth
of the Prophet—How Brigham balanced his Account with the Church—How the
Prophet got rich—The Probable Future of Mormonism at his Death, .   . 646

CHAPTER LV.

THE TERRITORY OF UTAH.—Its Boundaries and Character—The Lakes—Superficial Area—The Settlements—Population—Excess of Male Inhabitants—Mules
voting for Delegates to Congress !—"Getting up" Petitions—The Militia—The
Nauvoo Legion—The Federal Governors—A Stormy Political Meeting—Governor Shaffer's Difficulties—Change of Officers—A Proclamation—Resolute Conduct of the Governor—His Last Official Act—Conflict between Mormon Officials
and Federal Officers—Delegate Hooper justifies Polygamy in Congress—Dr.
Newman discusses Polygamy with Orson Pratt—Appointment of Chief-Justice
McKean—His Legal Decisions—The Hawkins Case—Decisions reserved by the
Supreme Court—Brigham's Anxiety for a State Government,   .   .   . 671

CHAPTER LVI.

SALT LAKE CITY.—Its Situation and Beauty—Its Railway Communication—
Water Supply—Great and Increasing Improvement—The Tabernacle—Brigham
the Architect of Zion—Inspiring the Prophet with an Idea—The Great Organ
—The Tabernacle Services—Results of the Influx of Gentiles—Brigham's Com-
mercial Street—Christian Churches in Utah—Their Work and Influence—The
Episcopal Church—Christian Schools—Brigham's Opinion of Gentile Instruc-
tion—The Methodist Teacher's Difficulties—Polygamy opposed by Mr. Mc-
Leod—The Liberal Institute—Lectures in Zion—Evidences of Prosperity—
Progress of Civilization in Utah, ... 691

CHAPTER LVII.

THE MINES OF UTAH.

THE POTOSI OF THE WEST.—Early Anticipations of the Treasures of Utah—
Ore discovered in the Mountains—First Discovery of Argentiferous Galena—Enterprise of General P. E. Connor—The United States Soldiers "prospect" for
Mines—Mr. Eli B. Kelsey lectures on the Wealth of Utah—Incorporation of the
West Jordan Mining Company—First Smelting-Furnace erected at Stockton—
Rush Valley Smelting Company formed—Waiting for the Railroad—First Ship-
ments of Ore—The Utah Central Railroad—Rich Ores in Ophir District—Silver-
opolis—Valuable Mines in East Cañon—Colonel E. D. Buel's Works in Cot-
tonwood—Numerous Furnaces erected—Results of Inexperience—First Mill in
Utah—Extraordinary Success—Large Shipments of Bullion and Ores—The Emma
Mine—Formation of Veins of Ore—The Action of Water and Volcanic Force—
Statistics of the Emma Mine—Its Immense Value—*Bonanzas*—Extraordinary
Dividends to Proprietors—Southern Mines—True Fissure-Veins—Their Im-
portance—Solfataric Action—The Mineral Springs—The Staples of the Utah

Mines—Silver and Lead—Gold in Bingham Cañon—Gold in Sevier River—
Quartz Mines—Gold near Ogden—Iron and Lead Ores—Supply of Fuel—Gradual
Improvements—Scarcity of Wood—Discoveries of Coal—Building Material—
Importance of a Valid " Title "—Development of Locations—Contested Claims—
Commissioner Drummond's Decision—The Vast Mineral Resources of Utah—Im-
portance of the Territory—Its Beauty, Wealth, Capabilities, and Claims to At-
tention, ... 709

APPENDIX, ... 735
INDEX, ... 747

ILLUSTRATIONS.

 PAGE

1. BRIGHAM YOUNG—*Steel-plate Engraving*.........................[*Frontispiece.*]
2. JOSEPH SMITH'S FIRST VISION... 1
3. PREACHING IN THE HIGHWAYS... 2
4. DISCOVERY OF THE GOLD PLATES.. 19
5. MARTIN HARRIS, THE PROPHET'S SCRIBE.................................. 22
6. FAC-SIMILE OF A PORTION OF THE BOOK OF MORMON................. 23, 24
7. THE FIRST MORMON BAPTISM... 29
8. ORGANIZATION OF THE MORMON CHURCH............................... 31, 32
9. TARRED AND FEATHERED.. 42
10. "THE LORD'S" ARMY MARCHING TO THE DELIVERANCE OF ZION... 53, 54
11. THE TEMPLE AT KIRTLAND, OHIO.. 62
12. THE APOSTLE HEBER C. KIMBALL... 69
13. THE PROPHET BANKERS ON THE WING...................................... 73
14. MORMON TROUBLES IN MISSOURI BEGIN.................................. 81
15. MASSACRE OF MORMONS AT HAUN'S MILL.............................. 97, 98
16. THE PROPHET'S FLIGHT FROM MISSOURI................................... 118
17. THE HOME OF THE SAINTS IN ILLINOIS...................................... 121, 122
18. LIEUT.-GEN. JOSEPH SMITH (Prophet, Seer, and Revelator). 131, 132
19. ORRIN PORTER ROCKWELL... 141
20. THE PROPHET SURRENDERS TO THE LAW.................................... 152
21. ASSASSINATION OF JOSEPH SMITH.. 161, 162
22. THE APOSTLE TAYLOR.. 166
23. "THE END".. 168
24. "THE ELECT LADY"—MRS. EMMA SMITH..................................... 188
25. SIDNEY RIGDON.. 206
26. BURNING MORMON HOUSES.. 216
27. THE EXODUS FROM NAUVOO... 219, 220
28. RUINS OF THE TEMPLE.. 226
29. THE BATTALION BALL.. 246
30. THE PIONEERS.. 251, 252
31. MAP OF SALT LAKE VALLEY.. 257, 258
32. THE BEGINNING OF THE REFORMATION...................................... 293
33. REFORMING A HERETIC... 297
34. THE HAND-CART EMIGRANTS IN A STORM................................. 309, 310
35. PASSING THROUGH IOWA... 315

PAGE

36. "CAME TO ME AND BEGGED BREAD".......... 325
37. THE OLD MAN JAMES.. 329
38. WHAT OF THE PROMISES?... 330
39. JOHN CHISLETT... 332
40. CROSSING THE PLATTE RIVER... 335
41. THE UNITED STATES EXPEDITION TO UTAH........................... 343, 344
42. BRIGHAM'S "DECLARATION OF INDEPENDENCE"........................... 351
43. ECHO CAÑON—THE MORMON DEFENCES.................................... 363
44. LIEUTENANT-GENERAL D. H. WELLS.. 367
45. BURNING GOVERNMENT TRAINS... 368
46. THE CAMP OF DEATH... 370
47. WINTER SCENE—UNITED STATES TROOPS HAULING WOOD............. 378
48. TRIUMPHAL MARCH OF UNITED STATES TROOPS THROUGH SALT
    LAKE CITY... 387, 388
49. THE MOUNTAIN MEADOWS MASSACRE.................................. 425, 426
50. BROTHER KANOSH, THE INDIAN CHIEF.................................... 436
51. ROAD FROM FILLMORE TO MOUNTAIN MEADOWS [Map].................. 443
52. ORSON HYDE, PRESIDENT OF THE TWELVE APOSTLES.................. 483
53. THE APOSTLE ORSON PRATT... 497
54. DIAGRAM OF THE CELESTIAL KINGDOM.................................... 506
55. EGYPTIAN HIEROGLYPHICS, NO. I...................................... 511, 512
56. "   "   NO. II...................................... 514, 515
57. "   "   NO. III................................... 517, 518
58. PLATES FOUND IN KINDERHOOK, OHIO.................................. 549, 550
59. SHOOTING A RIVAL PROPHET... 589, 590
60. MAJOR-GENERAL P. EDWARD CONNOR................................... 608
61. ASSASSINATION OF DR. J. KING ROBINSON............................. 619
62. J. ROBINSON WALKER.. 624
63. JOSEPH SMITH, THE PROPHET'S SON.................................... 629
64. BRIGHAM YOUNG ON HIS TRAVELS.................................. 647, 648
65. BRIGHAM YOUNG'S HOME.. 651
66. AUTOGRAPH LETTER OF BRIGHAM YOUNG........................... 655, 656
67. THE APOSTLE GEORGE A. SMITH.. 661
68. "   "   BRIGHAM YOUNG, JUNIOR........................... 662
69. "   "   GEORGE Q. CANNON.................................. 664
70. MAP OF UTAH TERRITORY... 669, 670
71. SALT LAKE CITY.. 689, 690
72. THE MORMON TABERNACLE.. 695
73. THE SALT LAKE TEMPLE... 699, 700
74. ST. MARK'S EPISCOPAL CHURCH.. 703
75. THE FIRST NATIONAL BANK OF UTAH................................... 707
76. BINGHAM CAÑON.. 709, 710
77. LITTLE COTTONWOOD... 717, 718
78. THE PIONEER MILL.. 721, 722
79. THE EMMA MINE.. 725, 726

INTRODUCTION.

"Nothing extenuate,
Nor set down aught in malice."

THE purpose of the Author of this volume is to issue a book that will be of interest to the reading public, and of service to the people of whom it treats: the former ask for such information, and the latter cannot properly object to being understood as they really are.

In addition to his own personal experience, the works that have been previously written on Mormonism, both by friends and foes, have been carefully studied and collated. The contents of this book may, therefore, be regarded as an impartial summary of what can be said respecting the faith of the "Mormon Saints," by one who had the fellowship of the Church for over a quarter of a century, who occupied a public position in that relationship, enjoyed familiar intimacy with the apostles and leading elders, and for a dozen years had daily intercourse with Brigham Young.

The Author has no pet theories to advance, no revelations to announce, no personal animosity to satisfy. He has simply *outgrown the past*, and utterly disbelieves Brigham Young's recent claim to the possession of "a Priesthood that is Infallible," and the assumption that the Mormon Church is the exclusive and only true Church of Christ upon the earth,

and membership therein the only passport to the presence
of God.

Having contributed both by tongue and pen, from the rostrum and by the press, with the best years of his life and with
whatever talents he possessed, to teach the Mormon faith while
he believed it, he now considers it due equally to the Mormons
as to the public to exhibit what that earnest people have accomplished, and thus exemplify the ease with which a reli-
giously-disposed community may naturally mistake the legitimate results of united faith and labour for the special mark of
Divine guidance.

The change which the Author has experienced in his views
of Mormonism has not been the work of a day or a year, has
not resulted from any personal injury; neither is it due to any
special gifts or miraculous conversion. There are to-day thousands of persons in the Mormon communion in Utah, travelling
in the same direction, without that living faith in the announced mission of their Church which they once possessed.
They still cling to it with anxious solicitude, hoping for some
deliverance; knowing not what to expect, yet realizing that
"something must come." Hence the readiness with which
many have listened to those who claim to have received new
revelations and new missions among themselves.

While the tendency of the age has been to accept "revealed
"truths" on account of their own intrinsic value only, and not
from the assumption of their authority, the Mormon Church
has travelled in the very opposite direction, and has resuscitated the Jewish prophets to support the teachings of modern
apostles.

In the examination of Mormonism, the student will meet
the reproduction of nearly every principle, doctrine and usage
to be found on record from Genesis to Revelation—if not in
practice, at least in acknowledgment; and where the practice

is in abeyance, it is not its wrong but its expediency that furnishes the justification of its momentary neglect.

Before the Emancipation Proclamation of President Lincoln, slavery as well as polygamy existed in Utah.   The nation, by the stern arbitrament of the sword, settled the one, and
the other is now in controversy.   Both institutions, in the
Mormon faith, are ordinances of God.

No antiquity, however, is respected by the Mormon teacher, unless it is harmonious with the inspirations of the modern
priesthood.   This is exemplified in the unceasing use of the
Old Testament in support of polygamy, the "Blood Atone-
"ment," [i. e., shedding of the saintly sinner's blood as an
atonement for adultery or apostacy] and kindred teaching,
while the New Testament is unceremoniously set aside when
it militates against the establishment of "a literal kingdom of
"God" upon the earth.

The breathings of every anguish-burthened soul among the
Hebrews, in its longing for the restoration of monarchy and
glory to Israel, are accepted as Divine inspiration and revelation pointing directly to the times in which we live.   That
disturbing dream of the King of Babylon, interpreted by
Daniel, has been a perennial fountain of living waters to the
Mormon preacher.   The anxious monarch and the heaven-gift-
ed interpreter may not have anticipated in that hour of solicitude in the land of Shinar, that "the stone cut out of the
"mountains without hands," which was to "break in pieces
"the iron, the brass, the clay, the silver, and the gold" of the
"great image" of the king's dream, was to find its fulfilment
in the discovery of the stone box containing the plates of the
Book of Mormon, by Joseph Smith, in western New York, in
the year of grace 1820!   It requires considerable faith to accept the statement that the migrations of the Mormons from
Fayette County, New York, to Kirtland, Ohio; thence to Jackson County, Missouri; to Nauvoo, Illinois; on to the Rocky

Mountains; spreading over the Great Basin; and the Church sending thence its missionaries to the nations, was the rolling forth of the "stone" of prophecy, which was to "become a "great mountain and fill the whole earth." *

The dim light of a far distant past, added to their own revelations, preserves among the Mormons a perpetual conflict between barbarism and civilization, for the people are, in head and heart, far in advance of their religious teachings. Hence the frequent " apostacy."

No faith could well be more liberal than *written* Mormonism. In the beginning of its mission it was a beautiful ideal to those thoroughly imbued with its inspiration; yet no professors of religion in the nineteenth century could be more bitterly bigoted than the rigidly orthodox and ignorant among the Mormons to-day. Without intending it, probably, and, it may be, even without realizing it, as others do who differ from them, their profession and their practice have been the very antipodes of each other. In moments of creed-writing they are liberal and broadly cosmopolitan in sentiment, warmly inviting to "fair freedom's feast," away up in the Rocky Mountains—

> "Christian sects and pagan,
> Pope, and Protestant, and Priest,
> Worshippers of God or Dagon.† "

But when once the Plains have been traversed, there the reception of, and intercourse with, the religious stranger have been like the chilling breezes of the frigid zone. After all, this very paradox is harmonious and consistent even in its contradictions. The written invitation is the breathing of their souls' best and divinest impulses,—the Deity of their nature recognizing one common parentage in the family of man, reaching forth the hand of fellowship to humanity everywhere; but, in the practical part, in intercourse with mankind, it is the tram-

* *Divine Authenticity*, pp. 85-6.   † Hymn Book, page 103.

pled worm still in agony, the remembrance of "persecutions" that chills every forward, generous impulse and withers the soul with the baneful teaching that "he that is not for us is "against us."

Through the first twenty years of their occupancy of the Territory of Utah, the advanced and liberal minds among them hoped for a change from the ostracizing teachings of the Tabernacle, but it was almost hoping against hope. A brighter day, however, is dawning, when the barriers that have forbidden intercourse with the rest of the world, because of differences of faith, will be gently lowered and a better understanding prevail between the favoured Saints and the unbelieving Gentiles, and in some respects the former will be the greater gainers by the change. "No feud," says the shrewd and witty Sydney Smith, "can withstand social intercourse."

Throughout this work there will be found no disposition to pander to the charge of "wilful imposture" against Joséph Smith or Brigham Young. The facts of their history, to the Author's mind, do not warrant that conclusion. Men who publicly utter predictions which time must verify or prove false within the scope of their own natural lives, are entitled to the credit of honestly believing in their own mission. It is safe and sound philosophy to admit that men can be, and are frequently as zealous in the propagation of an error as of a truth; or what shall be said of the great "army of martyrs," of whom not one in a thousand ever reached the stake, the rack, or the guillotine for an absolute verity?

Whatever judgment may be passed upon the faith and personal lives of the Mormon Prophet and his successor, there will be a general recognition of a divine purpose in their history. Under their leadership the Mormon people have aided to conquer the western desert and to transform a barren and desolate region of a hitherto "unknown country" into a land that seems destined at no distant day to teem with millions of

human beings, and which promises to stand preëminent among
the conquests of the republic. It is doubtful whether any collective body of other citizens—unmoved by religious impulses
—would ever have traversed the sandy desert and sage-plains,
and have lived an age of martyrdom in reclaiming them, as the
Mormons have in Utah. But this has been accomplished, and
it was accomplished by faith. That was the Providence of the
Saints, and it must be conceded that as a means subservient to
an end, the Mormon element has been used in the Rocky
Mountain region by the Almighty Ruler for developing the
best interests of the nation, and for the benefit of the world at
large.

Should this work contribute to encourage the feeble, doubting Mormons to persevere in the domain of thought, to cultivate the reflex of the Deity within their own humanity, to
trust more to the whisperings of the "still, small voice" than
to the dogmas of men; and thus aid the downcast, sorrowing,
and oppressed, to reach the peace and happiness of true liberty
and manly independence, the Author will feel that his labour
has not been in vain.

It will be a matter of sincere regret, if, in the following
pages, any statement has been made that is incorrect in fact or
unfair in inference; but errors—should there be any—to which
attention may be called, will be carefully eliminated from a
future edition.

INCEPTION OF MORMONISM—JOSEPH SMITH'S FIRST VISION.

THE ROCKY MOUNTAIN SAINTS.

CHAPTER I.

MORMONISM EXPLAINED.—The First Faith Biblical—Spiritual Enthusiasm of the Elders—Establishment of a Literal Kingdom predicted—Polygamy not in the Origianl Programme—Mormon Errors attributable to the System and Leaders—Argument of the Miraculous Power of Healing—Difficulty experienced in leaving the Mormon Church—Assumption of Infallible Priesthood—Mormonism summed up.

THE faith of the Latter-Day Saints was in the beginning strictly confined to Biblical doctrines, and the preaching of the first elders was something like a resuscitation of the dispensation committed to the apostolic fishermen of Galilee. With the acceptance of what they deemed the new revelation of Christ, there was no sacrifice too great to make, and no self-abnegation with which they would not strive to adorn their lives. Primitive Mormonism was to the youthful disciples the fulness of the everlasting gospel, with all the blessings, gifts and powers enjoyed by the early Christian Church, and all the promises of glory and honour in the world to come that inspired the first disciples of Christ.

The first elders were peculiarly adapted for the singular work which they had to perform. They were earnest, fiercely enthusiastic, and believers in everything that had ever been written about "visions," "dreams," "the ministering of angels," "gifts of the spirit, tongues, and interpretation of tongues," "healings," and "miracles." They wandered "without purse or scrip" from village to village and from city to city, preaching in the public highways, at the firesides or in the pulpits—wherever they had opportunity—testifying and singing :

" The Spirit of God like a fire is burning!
The Latter-day glory begins to come forth;
The visions and blessings of old are returning,
The Angels are coming to visit the earth.
We'll sing and we'll shout with the armies of heaven
Hosannah, hosannah to God and the Lamb!
Let glory to them in the highest be given,
Henceforth and for ever: Amen and Amen! " *

Half a dozen such verses as these inspired with sentiments
that ranged from Adam to the time when " Jesus descends
" with his chariots of fire," sung with stentorian lungs, threw

over their audiences
an influence such as
they had never before
experienced. " The
" work was of God."
The barren, specula-
tive, carefully pre-
pared sermons of fifty
weeks in the year
chilled in the pres-
ence of the energy
and demonstration of
the Mormon elders;

Preaching in the Highways.

the latter had no dead issues to deal with; their Prophet was a
live subject. In this manner Mormonism was first announced.
It was the feeling of the soul, and not the reasoning of the mind.
It was robust believing, not calm, intellectual understanding;
and thus by natural sequence " the number of the disciples
" grew and multiplied." It was an emotional faith in both
speaker and hearer. They *felt* that God was with them, and
" feeling " at such moments sets all argument at rest.

The founder of Mormonism was naturally very impressible,
and at an early age conceived the idea that he was preëmi-
nently the subject of ancient prediction.† He soon passed

* Hymn Book, p. 268. It is claimed that this effusion was given by " the gift
" of tongues," then translated by one of the elders, by the " gift of interpretation,"
into English.

† The student of Mormonism will be struck with the similarity of experience
and claims of Joseph Smith and Mohammed. Syed Ahmed Khan Bahador, a Mo-

from faith to positive assertion, and the first men of talent who became converts—such as Oliver Cowdery, Parley P. Pratt, Sidney Rigdon, Orson Pratt, and other prominent elders—readily furnished him with the confirmation of his calling. These elders had nearly all been preachers, teachers, or exhorters, and they were not slow to ·discover that the Old Testament abounded with, to them, evidences of prediction about America, Joseph Smith, the Book of Mormon, and the reign of the Saints on earth. The Bible, that before was a sealed book, suddenly opened with living truths of the closest personal application to the new disciples and their destiny. Every verse from Genesis to Revelation was scanned with microscopic scrutiny for evidence relative to the new faith, and, with the general reverence of Christendom for the Bible and the ready credence accorded to chapter and verse, the Mormon elders were astonishingly successful with the young and piously inclined of the labouring and mechanical classes, although their teachings were not so readily accepted by the more intellectual and better taught.

From the preaching of faith in Christ, repentance, baptism, and the gifts of the Spirit as enjoyed by the primitive Christian Church, it was an easy step for the young believer to accept Joseph Smith's statement that it had been revealed to him that " the set time to restore the kingdom to Israel " had come, and that the temporal dominion of the world by an inspired prophet was not only a proper thing, but was the consistent sequence of that prophet being chosen as the recognized medium between the heavens and the earth. It had been predicted that Christ should some day return to earth in power and great glory to reign a thousand years; hence the necessity of the Saints gathering together to prepare for the day of his coming ; and in this " gathering " was laid, by the Prophet, the first stepping stone to worldly power.*

hammedan writer, in a series of Essays recently published in London, treats of the prophecies concerning the Arabian Prophet, to be found in the Old and New Testaments, precisely as Orson Pratt applies them to the American Prophet.

* As early as the second year of the Church, some of the leading elders of Zion (in Missouri) were "accusing Brother Joseph in rather an indirect way of seeking "after *monarchical power and authority*." *Vide* Orson Hyde and Hyrum Smith's *Epistle* to " the bishop, his councillors, and the inhabitants of Zion."

As the number of believers increased, the establishment of the kingdom of God as a temporal and political power became a subject of earnest discourse, and from the announcement of this literal kingdom up to the present moment there has been an unceasing warfare between the Saints and the Gentiles, wherever they have existed together, for local supremacy. All that follows in the history of Mormonism after the enunciation of temporal sovereignty is but the working out of the Prophet's conceptions of his mission which grew with his years and increased with the success of the preaching of the faith. How far his later teachings and actions, or those of his successor, have been in harmony with the original platform, may well be questioned. Let the student of history determine for himself whether there can be found in connection with the Mormon movement any defined purpose of the Ruler of the Universe, or whether it is aught else than one of those ten thousand mysterious providences which have had a work to perform in human development, and which, after performing that work, have passed away, leaving their impress upon the history of the world.

The reader will readily perceive from the following chapters that Mormonism has contained within itself the elements of a sincere faith, and has thereby captivated the simple, inquiring, religiously-traditioned minds of a certain class of persons; has held them for a time in the expectancy of greater and progressive truths; and that the abandonment of the system by many of its most devoted adherents has been but the inevitable result of growth of intellect and the acceptance of broader and more liberal views of the purposes of a beneficent Deity.

The issues which have arisen in Mormonism of late years, and which have given to it the materialistic character that it now bears, were not anticipated by the early disciples. The temporal, patriarchal government of Utah is a disappointment, not a triumph, for long ere this—according to their teachings—the wicked should have been destroyed from off the face of the earth, the elements should have melted with fervent heat, the heavens should have been rolled up like a scroll, and the elect should have been far away up in the clouds.

The Apostle Parley P. Pratt, the most eloquent and forcible

preacher of the Mormon Church, over thirty years ago, in his controversy with La Roy Sunderland, editor of *Zion's Watchman*, then published in New York, uttered the following prediction :—" Within ten years from now (1838), the people of " this country who are not Mormons, will be entirely subdued " by the Latter-Day Saints or swept from the face of the earth; " and if this prediction fails, then you may know that the Book " of Mormon is not true." During that controversy, Parley was evidently annoyed at Mr. Sunderland, and, regarding his own indignation as the inspiration of the Holy Ghost, he predicted that "within two years, La Roy Sunderland will be " struck dumb and incapacitated from speaking a loud word." At a later date, in taking farewell of New York, he penned a "Lamentation" for her citizens. In that effusion he tells the New-Yorkers : " When the Union is severed, when this mighty " city shall crumble to ruin and sink as a millstone, the mer- " chants undoing," &c., to "sing this lamentation and think " upon me."

Parley was a sincere, good meaning man, who honoured extensively the institution of polygamy, and in adding to his family circle he aroused the wrath of an outraged husband, who pursued and killed him in Arkansas, in 1856; but the Union is not severed, New York stands where it did, with no particular signs of the " millstone," and Mr. La Roy Sunderland still lives in Massachusetts, a very forcible speaker as well as writer. Mormon history abounds with innumerable predictions equally veracious.*

* The following is a specimen :—

" A PROPHECY; or an extract from the Word of the Lord concerning New York, Albany, and Boston, given on the 23rd day of September, 1832.

" Let the Bishop " (Newel K. Whitney) " go into the City of New York, and also to the City of Albany, and also to the City of Boston, and warn the people of those cities with the sound of the Gospel, with a loud voice, of the desolation and utter abolishment which awaits them if they do reject these things ; for, if they do reject these things, the hour of their judgment is nigh, and their house shall be left unto them desolate."

Sixteen years later, the *Millennial Star*, September 15, 1848, published the foregoing prophecy, supplementing it with a lengthy extract from the Albany *Express* of August 17th, giving an account of a " destructive fire " in that city. The Apostle-Editor of the *Star*—Orson Pratt—doubtless felt gratified at being able to help " the Lord " a little to the verification of the prediction. Fires in great cities and in small ones are accidents of daily occurrence all over the world, and just as much

The polygamic faith contended for to-day was not in the original programme, neither has it contributed to create the power that now reigns in Utah. It was the monogamic spiritual life and understanding of primitive Christianity that built up the organization which gave power and influence to Joseph Smith. It was the hearer's faith in Peter of Galilee, more than in Joseph of New York, that induced thousands of professing Christians to add the new prophet to their faith, and to accept his revelations. It was their confidence that the Holy Ghost had been poured out upon disciples in Judea, eighteen hundred years before, which made the promises in America possible of belief, and acceptable in the nineteenth century, and it is this reduplication of faith in the disciples to-day in Utah and throughout the world, and not the assumed genius or ability, with which he is generally credited, which clothes Brigham Young with that unchallenged authority which is a marvel to all outside the Church.

The Mormon organization is thorough and complete. It permeates every position and condition of life, and controls and governs everything from the cradle to the grave. It is a combination of iron military rule and Jesuitical penetration and perseverance, and as such in course of time it became intolerable to the very men who made it. The leading elders, the " witnesses," and the first apostles have almost all apostatized from the more recent doctrines of Joseph and Brigham, while they still cling to the original faith and believe in the ministering of angels, &c. It is this deeply rooted conviction of heavenly manifestations and their own phenomenal experience, that has held and now holds the people together, and not the personal influence of Joseph Smith, and still less that of his successor.

There is much in the first announcement of Mormonism, and its claim to divine origin through revelation, that may well be questioned; but there is little in the early faith which the Bible believer can easily assail from that standpoint. The dif-

the vengeance of " the Lord " as that in Albany for rejecting Newel K. Whitney's mission; but on such predictions and their fulfilment have the Mormons been fed by the modern apostles. Nothing was said by the Prophet about the Chicago fire. With such a terrible conflagration in fulfilment of " the Word of the Lord," Mormonism might have had a fresh lease of life.

ficulty which controversialists have experienced when in argument with Mormon casuists has been their readiness to admit
all that prophets and apostles have ever said, while they tie
themselves to none. In handling the revelations of modern
science and discovery they are never surprised. They willingly
allow all that geology may establish, and if that hurts Moses
or any one else it is nothing to them;—when science is positive,
the record has to yield. Their faith, borrowed or adopted from
the ancients, is held with a loose hand, and can be parted with
at any time; but their own faith proper, that which is given
through "the living oracles," can never be surrendered. No
authority can be accepted, or even doubtfully entertained, that
disputes Joseph Smith. To the believing Mormons, he was
"the end to all controversy," and this has not been forgotten
in the inheritance claimed by his successor.

The Mormons as a people are not justly chargeable with
the wrong-doing which has been ascribed to them. There are
bad men among them—dangerously bad men—who have committed outrages and damning deeds which would disgrace any
community. But those deeds were perpetrated by the few; the
masses were sincere and devoted to their conceptions of right
and truth, as the whole course of their lives and eventful history abundantly proves. This has been the united testimony
of all the "Gentiles" who have lived among them. The errors
of the past life of the people, whether in their treatment of
apostates or in their hostility to the nation, are attributable
to the system and to the men who direct the public mind.
Men and women who, for a religious faith, voluntarily abandon
the homes of childhood, and rend asunder the hallowed ties of
family and friends—as Mormon converts do in all parts of the
earth—traversing oceans and plains, and suffering privations
incident to creating new homes in a barren waste, are not persons devoid of the qualities of good citizens.

It was the people's love of religious truth while associated
with other churches, that induced them to listen to the Mormon elders when they proclaimed the restoration of the primitive Gospel in all its purity and power, with a Church organization of Patriarchs, Apostles, Prophets, Evangelists, Pastors,
Teachers and Deacons. This harmony in organization—the

counterpart of primitive Christianity—binds them still to Mormonism, in spite of the extravagances of their leaders against which their early teachings and innate sense of right revolt. To the mass of the Mormon people it is no simple matter to meet in argument their own teachers—men who have seldom, if ever, been vanquished in discussion when met by the most talented ministers of other religions. When to this difficulty is added the people's own personal experience of the power of healing in the Church, something more than an opponent's denunciation is required to deliver them from the thraldom of an unquestioning faith.

The educated mind takes within its range of thoughts causes and effects, and discriminates between what is general and what is special and personal, but, among the untaught masses, ninety-nine in a hundred rely upon their own experience alone. " Was I not healed by the anointing of oil, the "laying on of hands and the prayer of faith?" " Did I not " see my mother carried to the waters of baptism a poor de- " crepit invalid, and when she had been immersed for the re- " mission of sins she walked home, and has been well ever " since?" " Was not my father deaf, and did he not get his " hearing by the prayers of the elders?" " My darling child " was brought from death unto life by the prayer of faith." The unscripturalness of Brigham's " Adam Deity," the despotism of an " infallible Priesthood," and the evidence of a thousand outrages and murders are nothing to minds that cling to the personal reminiscence of miracles. The only hope, therefore, is in the education of the people to the realization that those phenomenal manifestations of healing, the influences of which they have personally experienced, are not the specialty of the Mormon Church, but are to be found to some extent everywhere, in all churches, and even among persons unassociated with any religious creed; that these manifestations which the Mormon leaders have claimed as exclusive proofs of the divinity of their mission are but the result of natural causes, conditions and circumstances, and of this fact the Mormon Church furnishes the most abundant evidence.

While healing the sick, through the laying on of hands by the elders, is a common experience in every part of the world where the missionaries have travelled, it is equally true that for one case of instantaneous healing of that character which is cited as miraculous by the Mormon writers, there have been hundreds of instances of the sick being administered to in the same way, without any beneficial results whatever, and they have been left to recover by the recuperative power of nature, or the maladies have yielded to ordinary medical treatment which the Church had actually forbidden. This "gift of heal-"ing" has also been experienced more in Europe than in America, for the young Saints in Europe have more faith than the older Saints in the very bosom of the Church. Their spiritual nature is worked up to the greatest intensity, and they are always prepared to see angels, behold visions, dream dreams, speak in tongues and prophesy. A large portion of their time in foreign countries is consumed in "rejoicing to-"gether," and "building each other up," by glowing testi-monies of their experience; but when they arrive in Utah they soon discover that another condition of affairs exists there. The hard facts of a hard life confront them, and the contemplation of heavenly things has to give place to the arduous labours for the necessaries of existence. Many, not appreciating the true causes of this change in their spiritual experience, become dis-contented, murmur, and apostatize, and those who have been the most favoured, usually become the most dejected and God-forsaken. The ignorant teacher who visits the unfortunate, disappointed, but once gifted Saint, renders his experience still worse by stating in reference to the change which he cannot explain, that "the Lord first greatly blessed him in order to "leave him without excuse for backsliding so·that He could "the better damn him when he apostatized."

The greatest dispensation of spiritual power experienced in the Mormon Church fell upon the British Saints during the Presidency of the apostle Orson Pratt, from 1848 to 1851. The other apostles are more secular than religious, and have a great deal more to do with this world's affairs than with the hopes of the next—they have all large families to provide for. Orson also has many wives, but his better education and emi-nent ability as a writer and reasoner have preserved him more a missionary than a farmer; he is, emphatically, the gospel-

apostle of the Twelve. During his mission to Europe, his pen
furnished the first logical arguments in favour of Mormonism,
and his influence spread like a consuming fire among the
Saints throughout the Old World. He aroused the ambition
and excited the zeal of young and old to spread abroad
the new faith, and, armed as they were with his arguments,
they scoured the country and invited discussion wherever they
went. They penetrated the aisles of the cathedrals, ascended
the pulpits of the meeting-houses, visited the houses of the bigoted, and stormed the haunts of vice and woe with their tracts
and pamphlets. It was a grand revival of the mission into the
highways and hedges, arousing the sinner to come to the great
marriage feast.

Controversy met these zealous missionaries, and often ston-
ing, buffeting, and even imprisonment followed. But the
Saints rejoiced the more, glorying in tribulation, and, as a
natural consequence, they grew immensely in spiritual power.

Mormonism in England, Scotland, and Wales, was a grand
triumph, and was fast ripening for a vigorous campaign in
continental Europe. There is no page of religious history
which more proudly tells its story than that which relates this
peculiar phase of Mormon experience. The excitement was
contagious, even affecting persons in the higher ranks of social
life, and the result was a grand outpouring of spiritual and miraculous healing power of the most astonishing description.
Miracles were heard of everywhere; and numerous competent
and most reliable witnesses bore testimony to their genuineness.

In whatever light this "healing power" may be regarded,
it was at the time a grand reality of the European mission, but
it has, in a great measure, passed away under the withering
teachings of the polygamous era among the Saints in Zion.
With the preaching of the simple word, the elders were powerful, the Saints were zealous, the public listened, the spirit
ran from heart to heart, and miracles were common. But the
cold logic of argument labouring to engraft a relic of barbarism
upon an age of the highest civilization, quenched the spirit and
choked the zeal which accomplished those wonders of Mormon
history.

Up to the introduction of polygamy, Mormonism was solely a " Bible-Gospel " in Europe, and differed so widely from the kingdom-building scheme of Utah, that the very sons of the apostles and prophets testify, on their return to Utah from European missions, that they never knew what Mormonism was, nor the power of God, till they went abroad to preach. This is a common admission, and a damaging testimony against Zion; but it tells a great truth, and confirms the assertion that it is especially the British mission, with latterly the Scandinavian, that has built up Utah. It is the remembrance of their first love's joy in the Church in the Old World that preserves many of the Saints now in their dreary fellowship in the Church of the New World.

It is not an easy thing to break away from a life-long hope and such early joyous experiences as most of them had in the beginning. It is not courage that is lacking. It is, in fact, easier to meet death than to live this life of anxiety and trouble; but believers dread to assume the responsibility of breaking off from shepherds whom, once they almost idolized, and making the things of eternity a matter between themselves and their Maker. Even among the greatest intellects, few have been able to leave the Church, though groaning under it for years, until some experience brought with it an issue that demanded the assertion of a personal right or a disputed truth at the expence of fellowship. The greatest of their apostles, Orson Pratt, has been a living martyr for years, and has suffered indignities which manhood would never endure outside of the Mormon communion, and all this from fear of doing a greater wrong by leaving the Church in which he had spent a long life of usefulness. This consciousness of another's scrupulous fidelity apparently emboldens Brigham Young to test every man to his utmost endurance who breathes an independent thought.

Summed up, Mormonism demands perfect submission—total dethronement of individuality—blind obedience. There is no middle path. The crowning error of Brigham Young is the claim to " a Priesthood that is infallible." No man at the head of a people ever required it less. His errors before that were all overlooked—" to err is human." It mattered not what he said or did, the people hastened to excuse him, as another in his place might be no better and might do worse; but the assertion of Infallibility was the "vaulting ambition that "o'erleaps itself." Its assertion strips the people of human charity towards him. In his counsellings and teachings they are now required to see the authority of God, failing which they are "in darkness." He recognizes no right of thought diverging from his own, and this principle, carried to its legitimate extent, makes, in fact, one great something over a community of non entities. With liberty of thought and expression protected, Mormonism could have lived on, correcting its errors as it outgrew them, but with the assumption of an Infallible Priesthood its work has seen the beginning of the end.

CHAPTER II.

THE MORMON PROPHET—His Early Life—His Visions—His Personal Characteristics—An Angel Reveals to him the Golden Plates—His Mission Announced—The Story of the Stone Box.

It is not the design of the Author to present in this place an extended biography of Joseph Smith, but a brief sketch of his career may be appropriately commenced at that period of his life when he claims to have become an object of interest to the heavenly world. Of his ancestry, little is known beyond the fact that this branch of the Smith family is of Scotch extraction, and reached the New World in the beginning of the eighteenth century. Joseph himself was born December 23d, 1805, in Sharon, Windsor County, Vermont, and was one of a family of six sons and three daughters. When he was ten years of age, the family removed to Palmyra, Ontario County (now Wayne), New York, and thence, four years later, to Manchester, in the same county, and at this place, eighteen months afterwards, the Mahomet of the West, as he has appropriately been called, began his career as the originator of the new religion.

Of young Smith's personal appearance and life preceding this time, there is little to be said. In manhood he was very handsomely formed, tall, and athletic. In his fifteenth year—the commencement of his religious experience—he was doubtless much like any other farm youth of very limited education, and remarkable for nothing, either good or bad. In his family he was considered a "good boy," and throughout his chequered career no one ever charged him with lacking that native frankness of soul which generally characterizes the country youth. The charges afterwards made against him, of being "an indolent, worthless young vagabond," are, in all probability, somewhat exaggerated, for it is hardly possible that the vast energy and benevolence of his after life could have developed from any such roots.

After Joseph's announcement of his prophetic mission, the neighbours of his parents who were opposed to his claims remembered, with wonderful facility, that the Smith family had always been "dreamers and visionary persons," and applied these terms in their most offensive meaning. In a work published after Joseph's death,* his mother tells her story in an artless, guileless way, and narrates the incidents of his boyhood as a loving, tender mother alone can speak of a darling son. Her recital leads to the conclusion that his progenitors had been highly favoured, and that the heavens had showered upon him their highest honours and choicest gifts. Whatever may be thought of the claims of the Smith family to miraculous powers, there can be no doubt that the modern prophet came of a stock which transmitted to him moral, mental, and religious qualities, well adapted to the after-work of his life. With such predisposition and support in his father's family, and from the impulses of his own singular nature,† he was fairly prepared for the "ministering of angels," with which the history of his religious life begins.

He relates in his autobiography how, introductory to his first vision, his mind had been prepared, by the accidental reading of a portion of the New Testament during the excitement of a revival, to ask for heavenly wisdom, with the expectation of receiving an answer. This revival commenced with the Methodists and extended to other denominations, and a time of general conversion ensued. While the Methodists, Presbyterians, and Baptists made a general rush among the sinners, and preached to them only Christ and Him crucified, there was harmony; but when the converts began to choose churches, discussion arose upon the relative superiority of the creeds of these denominations, and the confusion of claims perplexed the

* *Biographical Sketches of Joseph Smith, the Prophet, and his progenitors for many generations.* By Lucy Smith, mother of the Prophet.

† Before the dissenting Mormons asserted that Joseph was "nothing more than "a highly developed MEDIUM," in the spiritualistic sense of the word, Brigham Young was in the habit of saying of Joseph that " he was a *natural-born seer.*"

youthful prophet, as it has many others before and since. His mother, two brothers, and a sister were " proselyted " to the Presbyterian Church, but he experienced in his " deep and of-" ten pungent feelings " partiality for the " Methodist sect." *
He was greatly excited, and in the midst of this war of words and tumult of opinions, his mind by some influence was direct-ed to that Scripture which saith : " If any of you lack wisdom, " let him ask of God that giveth unto all men liberally and up-" braideth none, and it shall be given him." This admonition was peculiarly encouraging to one in his situation, and he re-solved to test it practically. For this purpose he retired to a solitary place in the woods, and the following is his statement of what then occurred :

" After I had retired into the place where I had previously designed to go, having looked around me and finding myself alone, I kneeled down and began to offer up the desires of my heart to God. I had scarcely done so, when I was seized upon by some power which entirely overcame me, and had such astonishing influence over me as to bind my tongue so that I could not speak. Thick darkness gathered around me, and it seemed to me for a time as if I were doomed to sudden destruction. But exerting all my powers to call upon God to deliver me out of the power of this enemy which had seized upon me, and at the very moment when I was ready to sink into despair and abandon myself to destruction, not to an imaginary ruin, but to the power of some actual being from the unseen world, who had such a marvellous power as I had never before felt in any being. Just at this moment of great alarm, I saw a pillar of light exactly over my head, above the brightness of the sun, which descended gradually until it fell upon me. It no sooner appeared than I found myself delivered from the power of the enemy which had held me bound. When the light rested upon me, I saw two personages, whose brightness and glory defy all description, standing above me in the air. One of them spake unto me, calling me by name, and said (pointing to the other), ' THIS IS MY BE-LOVED SON ; hear Him ! ' "

The original purpose of the boy's prayer being to learn which of the sects he should join—for up to that time his mind had not embraced a wider range of freedom—as soon as he was able to speak he made the inquiry with the following results :

* The historian has recorded that, in 1814, when he was only nine years of age, " he was powerfully awakened by the preaching of a Mr. Lane, an earnest Metho-" dist preacher."

"I was answered that I must join none of them, for they were all wrong, and the personage who addressed me said that all their creeds were an abomination in his sight; that those professors were all corrupt, they draw near to me with their lips, but their hearts are far from me ; they teach for doctrine the commandments of men, having a form of godliness, but they deny the power thereof. He again forbade me to join with any of them: and many other things did he say unto me which I cannot write at this time. When I came to myself again I found myself lying on my back looking up into heaven." *

From this period he relates that he became the subject of the hottest persecution and reviling ; but he continued to tell what he had seen and what had been told him, taking comfort and encouragement from the similarity of his experience with that of St. Paul, who " saw a light and heard a voice," though few believed his testimony. He continued at his farm work, and on the evening of September 21, 1823, three years after his first vision, he received another and more important communication.

" During the space of time which intervened between the time I had the vision, and the year 1823, having been forbidden to join any of the religious sects of the day, and being of very tender years and persecuted by those who ought to have been my friends and to have treated me kindly, and if they supposed me to be deluded to have endeavoured in a proper and affectionate manner to have reclaimed me, I was left to all kinds of temptations, and mingling with all kinds of society, I frequently fell into many foolish errors, and displayed the weakness of youth and the corruptions of human nature, which I am sorry to say led me into divers temptations, to the gratification of many appetites offensive in the sight of God. In consequence of these things I often felt condemned for my weakness and imperfections; when on the evening of the above-mentioned 21st September, after I had retired to my bed for the night, I betook myself to prayer and supplication to Almighty God for forgiveness of all my sins and follies, and also for a manifestation to me that I might know of my state and standing before him; for I had full confidence in obtaining a divine manifestation, as I had previously had one.

" While I was thus in the act of calling upon God, I discovered a light appearing in the room, which continued to increase until the room was lighter than at noonday, when immediately a personage appeared at my bedside standing in the air, for his feet did not touch the floor. He had

---

* His unconsciousness during the reported interview, and the position in which he found himself on awaking, closely resemble the condition of those subject to trances among the Methodists and Spiritualists, but which phenomena appear to have been unknown to Joseph at that time.

on a loose robe of most exquisite whiteness. It was a whiteness beyond anything earthly I had ever seen; nor do I believe that any earthly thing could ever be made to appear so exceedingly white and brilliant; his hands were naked and his arms also, a little above the wrist; so also were his feet naked as were his legs, a little above the ankles. His head and neck were also bare. I could discover that he had no other clothing on but this robe, as it was open, so that I could see into his bosom.

"Not only was his robe exceedingly white, but his whole person was glorious beyond description, and his countenance truly like lightning. The room was exceedingly light, but not so very bright as immediately around his person. When I first looked upon him I was afraid, but the fear soon left me. He called me by name and said unto me that he was a messenger sent from the presence of God to me, and that his name was Nephi;* that God had a work for me to do and that my name should be had for good and evil among all nations, kindreds, and tongues; or that it should be both good and evil spoken of among all people. He said there was a book deposited, written upon gold plates giving an account of the former inhabitants of this continent and the source from whence they sprang. He also said that the fulness of the everlasting Gospel was contained in it, as delivered by the Saviour to the ancient inhabitants. Also that there were two stones in silver bows (and these stones, fastened to a breastplate, constituted what is called the Urim and Thummim) deposited with the plates, and the possession and use of these stones was what constituted seers in ancient or former times and that God had prepared them for the purpose of translating the book.

"After telling me these things, he commenced quoting the prophecies of the Old Testament. He first quoted part of the third chapter of Malachi, and he quoted also the fourth or last chapter of the same prophecy, though with a little variation from the way it reads in our Bibles. Instead of quoting the first verse as it reads in our books, he quoted it thus: 'For behold the day cometh that shall burn as an oven, and all the proud, yea, and all that do wickedly, shall burn as stubble, for they that come shall burn them, saith the Lord of Hosts, that it shall leave them neither root nor branch;' and again he quoted the fifth verse, thus: 'Behold I will reveal unto you the Priesthood by the hand of Elijah the Prophet, before the coming of the great and dreadful day of the Lord.' He also quoted the next verse differently: 'And he shall plant in the hearts of the children, the promises made to the fathers, and the hearts of the children shall turn to their fathers; if it were not so, the whole earth would be utterly wasted at His coming.'

"In addition to these he quoted the eleventh chapter of Isaiah, saying that it was about to be fulfilled. He quoted also the 3rd chapter of Acts, verses 22 and 23, precisely as they stand in our New Testament. He said

* This should read, Moroni. In the "Book of Doctrine and Covenants," page 321, it is so stated. Moroni was the gentleman who is said to have " hid up " the plates, and it is very proper that he should reveal them.

2

that that Prophet was Christ, but the day had not yet come when 'they who would not hear his voice should be cut off from among the people,' but soon would come.

"He also quoted the second chapter of Joel, from the 28th to the last verse. He also said that this was not yet fulfilled, but was soon to be. And he further stated the fulness of the Gentiles was soon to come in. He quoted many other passages of Scripture, and offered many explanations which cannot be mentioned here. Again, he told me that when I had got those plates of which he had spoken (for the time that they should be obtained was not yet fulfilled), I should not show them to any person, neither the breastplate with the Urim and Thummim, only to those to whom I should be commanded to show them; if I did, I should be destroyed. While he was conversing with me about the plates, the vision was opened to my mind that I should see the place where they were deposited, and that so clearly and distinctly that I knew it again when I visited it."

After this, the light in the room immediately began to encircle the person of the angel, and " a conduit opened right up " into heaven, and the angel ascended until he entirely disappeared."

Twice more during the night the messenger appeared in the same manner, and rehearsed the same things, adding at the third visit a caution to the effect that Satan, on account of father Smith's indigent circumstances, would tempt the son to get the plates for mercenary purposes, but that no other object than the glory of God was to be entertained in obtaining them, and that if he were influenced by any other motive than a desire to build up the kingdom, they could not be obtained at all. These interviews would appear to have continued through the whole night, and at daybreak Joseph arose and went to his labour, but was so exhausted and unwell that his father insisted on his returning home. In essaying to do so, he attempted to cross a fence, but his strength failed him ; he fell helpless to the ground, and for a time was perfectly unconscious. The first thing which he recollected was hearing his name called, when he looked up and beheld the same messenger standing over his head, surrounded by light as before. All that had been related during the night was again told him, with the instruction to tell his father of the vision and the commandments that he had received. He returned and did so, and his father replied that it was of God, and bade him go and do as directed by the messenger. Joseph immediately repaired to the locality where he had been told the plates were deposited, and from the distinctness of the night's vision, he at once recognized their place of concealment.

Discovery of the Gold Plates.

Of his first view of the record, he says:

" Convenient to the village of Manchester, Ontario County, New York, stands a hill of considerable size, and the most elevated of any in the neighbourhood. On the west side of this hill, not far from the top, under a stone of considerable size, lay the plates deposited in a stone box ; this stone was thick and rounded in the middle on the upper side, and thinner towards the edges, so that the middle part of it was visible above the ground, but the edge all round was covered with earth. Having removed the earth and obtained a lever, which I got fixed under the edge of the stone, and with a little exertion raised it up, I looked in, and there, indeed, did I behold the plates, the Urim and Thummim, and breastplate, as stated by the messenger. The box in which they lay was formed by laying stones together in some kind of cement. In the bottom of the box were laid two stones crossways of the box, and on these stones lay the plates and the other things with them. I made an attempt to take them out, but was forbidden by the messenger. I was again informed that the time for bringing them out had not yet arrived, neither would until four years from that time ; but he told me that I should come to that place precisely in one year from that time, and that he would there meet with me, and that I should continue to do so until the time should come for obtaining the plates."

The autobiography is not so explicit concerning this point of the Prophet's history as the early writings of the first disci-

ples. In the latter, the Prince of Darkness is introduced at
the critical moment, surrounded by an innumerable train of his
associates, who are made to pass in review before the boy, so
that he might become acquainted with them. A renewal of
the " old dispensation " would have been incomplete without
the " wicked one."

At the end of each year, in obedience to the instructions
received, he went to this place, met with the same messenger,
and from him received further information touching " the
" Lord's purposes in the last days," and in what manner His
kingdom was to be constituted.

CHAPTER III.

THE GOLD PLATES.—Joseph translates the "Reformed Egyptian"—Martin Har
ris acts as Scribe—Professor Anthon pronounces the characters and translation
"a hoax"—A prediction of Isaiah fulfilled—Satan and Mrs. Harris bring the
Prophet into great trouble—Oliver Cowdery replaces Harris—John the Baptist
ordains Smith and Cowdery—They baptize each other, prophesy and rejoice—
Witnesses are chosen to testify to the Book of Mormon.

FORCED to earn his bread by manual labour, Joseph "hired,"
in October, 1825, to an old gentleman who lived in Chenango
county, New York, who for a month employed him along with
other men to "prospect" for a silver mine which the Spaniards
were reported to have once worked in Harmony, Susquehanna
county, Pennsylvania. From this originated the story of the
Prophet being a money digger.

During this service he boarded at the house of a Mr. Isaac
Hale, and won the affections of his daughter Emma, whom
he married on the 18th of January, 1827, and who in course of
time was designated in revelation as "The Elect Lady" * of
the Church. As the Hale family were opposed to the union,
Joseph and his young bride betook themselves to his father's
residence in New York.

The same year, on the 22nd of September, the time appointed having arrived, Joseph presented himself at the usual

---

* Mrs. Smith had an extraordinary influence over Joseph. She was to him
what Cadijah was to Mohammed. When Ayesha, a youthful beauty of his harem,
suggested that Allah had given the Arabian Prophet a better wife instead of Cadijah; in the mingled passions of grief for her loss, affection for the wife of his youth,
and indignation at the insinuation of a better, his manly soul exclaimed :—"Never
"did God give me a better! When I was poor, she enriched me ; when I was pro-
"nounced a liar, she believed in me ; when I was opposed by all the world, she re-
"mained true to me." Till polygamy came, the same might be said of Emma
Smith. She was Cadijah to Joseph, and he loved her as intensely as did the Arabian
his faithful wife.

meeting-place, and from the hands of the angel received the plates, with the charge that he was now responsible for them, and if by any carelessness he permitted them to be taken from him he should be cut off; but if he did his best to preserve them till the messenger should call for them,* he should be favoured with the Divine blessing and protection.

Joseph's former troubles were as nothing to what followed after he obtained possession of the plates. In his autobiography he says: " Multitudes were on the alert continually to "get them from me if possible," but he succeeded in maintaining possession. Embarrassments increasing, and the bride's family being more favourably disposed, the young folks returned to her father's home, carrying with them the plates. They were assisted by one Martin Harris, who from this time occupies an important position in the development of the new faith, and becomes one of the " witnesses " to the Book of Mormon.

Martin Harris, the Prophet's Scribe.

During the winter of 1827-8, Joseph copied a number of the engravings and translated them by means of the Urim and Thummim, and this copy and translation he placed in the

* To the Mormons it appeared right enough that the angel should retake possession of the plates after Joseph had translated the portion entrusted to him. Others have taken a rather different view of the transaction.

FAC-SIMILE OF A PORTION OF THE GOLD PLATES, AS SAID TO BE REPRESENTED ON THE PAPER WHICH JOSEPH SMITH GAVE TO MARTIN HARRIS, AND WHICH HE SUBMITTED TO PROFESSOR ANTHON.

hands of Harris to take to New York city for the purpose of
subjecting them to scientific scrutiny. It is probable that he
was induced to take this step on account of a desire to that
effect expressed by Harris, from whom he had already proposed
to borrow funds for the publication of the volume when completed. Be this as it may, the circumstance was afterwards
adduced as the fulfilment of a prophecy of Isaiah.* The account which Harris himself gives of his visit to New York is as
follows. He called, he says, upon Professor Anthon, a celebrated linguist, who, after examining the transcript of the characters, stated that they were Egyptian, and were correctly
translated. The untranslated copy from the plates was said
by the Professor to be Egyptian, Chaldee, Assyrian, and Ara-
bic, and that the characters of those languages were truly rendered. He gave Harris a certificate to this effect, assuring all
who might be interested in the matter, that the characters
were genuine and the translation correct; but on hearing that
young Smith claimed to have received the plates through the
ministration of an angel, he took back the certificate and tore
it in pieces, as he regarded the whole affair as an attempt to
cheat Harris of the money which he proposed to raise from the
mortgage of his farm, for the publication of the book.

Twelve years subsequently, Professor Anthon published a
very different account of this interview. He represented the
characters as a singular medley of " Greek, Hebrew, and all
" sorts of letters, more or less distorted either through unskilful-
" ness or design, and intermingled with sundry delineations of
" half-moons, stars, and other natural objects, the whole end-
" ing in a rude representation of the Mexican zodiac." The
more the man of literature denounced the affair as a mere
hoax, the more the Mormon writers saw the actual fulfilment
of the prophecy and believed that the Book of Mormon, the
Professor, Martin Harris, and all this controversy, were the subjects of Hebrew inspiration.

Notwithstanding the temporary financial aid which was
rendered to Joseph by Martin, and the fulfilment of prophecy in the person of that worthy, human weakness was destined
to interfere and the purposes of the heavens to be somewhat

* Isa. xxix.

disarranged by his instrumentality, much to the chagrin of Joseph, and the subsequent annoyance of the disciples of Mormonism.

In the autobiography published in the "Pearl of Great Price," no mention is made of this trouble, and the unsophisticated reader would naturally suppose that " the Lord" had wisely chosen fitting instruments for His work and that His purposes had been attained, when it is stated that "two days " after the arrival of Mr. Cowdery (being the 17th day of " April) I commenced to translate the Book of Mormon, and " he commenced to write for me." This, however, is not the whole truth, but it is here noticed as one of the bad features of modern revelation. Some one is for ever trying to make the relations between the heavens and the earth better than they actually are.

Preceding the advent of Oliver Cowdery, Martin Harris was Joseph's scribe while he was translating the plates. The spouse of Harris was undeveloped in her spiritual nature in the Mormon sense, and, seeing her husband devoting much of his time and not a little of his money in aid of the work, she resolved to have some satisfaction. Martin, willing to meet the demands of his wife and her abettors, importuned Joseph for permission to exhibit the translation. "The Lord" warned Joseph of Martin's weakness, and the latter was strenuously resisted for a time. But Satan, ever ready to take advantage of a woman's weakness, was powerful with Mrs. Harris, and 116 pages of the translation of the *bona fide* Book of Mormon were at length obtained from Joseph under the most sacred pledge of faithful preservation and restoration.

The manuscript, once out of the hands of the youthful Prophet, was gone for ever, and the difficulty was to replace it. Joseph was terribly humiliated, suffered intensely, and lost the " gift" by which he had been able to translate, and in this way the work was suspended from July, 1828, till the appearance of Cowdery, as stated, in 1829. Thus, through the strategy of the devil, all this important history was lost, besides nearly eighteen months of valuable time, from December, 1827, when Harris first began his work as copyist. But Satan had still greater affliction in store for the young Prophet.

The ablest scholars can rarely make two translations pre-cisely alike from any foreign language, for the idiomatic ex-pressions of one tongue often find several equivalents in an-other, and when the translation has been made from hieroglyph-ics, in which a sign represents a sentence or a paragraph, the difficulty of obtaining two perfectly similar translations is pro-portionately increased. Joseph understood this. His soul was sick, and "the Lord," ever ready to aid the penitent, came to his assistance, denounced Martin Harris as "a wicked man," and revealed to the Prophet how the difficulty could be obviated.

In the revelation which he then received,[*] Joseph was in-formed that Satan had inspired Martin Harris and his friends to get possession of the manuscript, and that they had deter-mined that, if his second translation differed from theirs, they would expose him, and say that he was an impostor and had only pretended to translate, and, should he make a perfect du-plicate of the first, they would alter their copy, and so make him contradict himself. To circumvent all this, Joseph was instructed that among the plates a "Book of Nephi" existed, and that that would serve the purpose equally as well as the lost manuscript. Joseph obeyed the heavenly oracle, and thus the sacred volume now actually commences with the Book of Nephi, instead of the Book of Mormon as originally intended. In this way was lost that narrative which had been so care-fully prepared by an ancient Judo-American prophet and engraver, under such very trying circumstances: a narrative which, according to Joseph, had been hidden up in the stone box at least twelve hundred years, until finally revealed by an angel of God for the salvation of the human family, and for the preservation of which Joseph had already suffered much perse-cution. Mrs. and Mr. Harris have much to answer for.

Some persons may have read the Book of Mormon through consecutively, but as a general thing, even among the Mor-mons, the foundation of their faith is never boasted of as being an interesting document. The substitution, therefore, of Nephi for a commencement, instead of that intended by "the Lord" but stolen by the devil, has not probably caused any irrele-vancy nor cut the thread of the story—if it ever had one.

* "Doctrine and Covenants," p. 169.

With the assistance of Oliver Cowdery as scribe, the translation went on without interruption and the character of "the "kingdom" was gradually developed. They came to a portion of the narrative that informed them that baptism by immersion for the remission of sins had been taught and commanded to the ancient inhabitants of America, and the translator, ever eager to know his "privileges," proposed, on the 15th of May, that they should retire to the woods, and "inquire of the Lord."

"While we were thus employed, praying and calling upon the Lord, a messenger from heaven descended in a cloud of light, and having laid his hands upon us he ordained us, saying unto us: ' *Upon you, my fellow-servants, in the name of the Messiah, I confer the Priesthood of Aaron, which holds the keys of the ministering of angels and of the Gospel of repentance and of baptism by immersion for the remission of sins ; and this shall never again be taken from the earth until the sons of Levi do offer again an offering unto the Lord in righteousness.*' He said this Aaronic Priesthood had not the power of laying on of hands for the gift of the Holy Ghost, but that this should be conferred on us hereafter, and he commanded us to go and be baptized, and gave us directions that I should baptize Oliver Cowdery, and, afterwards, that he should baptize me." *

This "messenger" asserted that he was John the Baptist, and that he acted under the direction of Peter, James, and John, who held the priesthood of Melchisedec, which in due time was to be conferred upon them when they would take rank—Joseph as the first elder and Oliver the second. As instructed, they went into the water together, and Joseph baptized Oliver by immersion, and he in turn immersed Joseph. The latter laid his hands upon Oliver's head and ordained him to the Aaronic priesthood, and Oliver afterwards laid his hands upon Joseph's head and ordained him to the same priesthood—"for so we were commanded."

As they came out of the water they "experienced great and "glorious blessings." "The Holy Ghost fell upon Oliver and "he prophesied," and then Joseph "stood up and prophesied." They had a happy time together, but, owing to the persecuting disposition of the unbelievers, they kept their baptism and ordination and rejoicings a secret for a time.

* " Pearl of Great Price," p. 46.

The preparatory work was now fast advancing. Joseph was rapidly developing, and Oliver was an excellent scribe. Three " witnesses " were to be favoured with a " manifestation," and, from among the personal friends of Joseph, David Whitmer was selected to join Oliver Cowdery and Martin Harris, with the assurance that if they would exercise faith they should have a view of the plates and also of the Urim and Thummim. They did exercise faith, and in their " testimony," pre-fixed to the Book of Mormon, they " de-" clare with words of " soberness that an " angel of God came " down from heaven, " and he brought

The First Mormon Baptism.

" and laid before our eyes, that we beheld and saw the plates " and the engravings thereon." * This event occurred, according to Mormon chronology, in June or July, 1829. Another " testimony" is given to the world by eight witnesses — the father and two brothers of Joseph, four of the Whitmer family, and one Page. They affirm that they had seen the original plates, " hefted" them, and that they had " the appearance of " gold, and were of ancient work and curious workmanship."

In the commencement of 1830 the translation was published under the title of *The Book of Mormon*, and thus was laid the foundation of the new faith.

* The Author entered into correspondence with one of the Whitmers to elicit from him information concerning his mental condition during the time that he affirms he saw the plates. Whitmer was asked if he was in his usual condition of consciousness and was sensible of surrounding objects while he beheld the plates ; but he refused to answer the enquiry. Harris is reported to have said that he witnessed them by " the eye of faith."

CHAPTER IV.

ORGANIZATION OF THE CHURCH.—Disciples receive the Holy Ghost—Ancient Apostles and Prophets revisit the earth—Newell Knight is tortured by the Devil —His experience claimed as the first " Latter-Day " Miracle—Judge Edmonds records similar phenomena in Spiritualism.

ON Tuesday, April 6th, 1830, the " Church of Christ " was organized in the house of Peter Whitmer, in Fayette, Seneca county, New York, an event which, according to the ingenious calculation of Orson Pratt, transpired exactly 1800 years to a day from the resurrection of Christ.

The ten years which had elapsed from Joseph's first vision had been strictly a period of preparatory work, and there were at this date but few converts to his mission ready for organization. At the appointed time these assembled, and are thus embalmed in Mormon history :

Joseph Smith [the prophet.]

Oliver Cowdery [his scribe].

Hyrum Smith [an elder brother of Joseph].

Peter Whitmer, Junr.

Samuel H. Smith [a younger brother of Joseph], and

David Whitmer.

Alternating the Smiths and the Whitmers gives a better appearance to the list than if the two families were separated. Martin Harris, though so important a personage in the preliminary work, is supposed to have been denied the honour of belonging to the first organization, in consequence of the trouble which he caused about the lost manuscript.

The chosen six " entered into covenant to serve the Lord," partook of the sacrament of the Supper, and Joseph and Oliver ordained each other as spiritual teachers to the Church. This met the unanimous approval of the two Smiths and the two

ORGANIZATION OF THE MORMON CHURCH.

Whitmers, and Joseph and Oliver laid their hands upon the others, that they might receive the " gift of the Holy Ghost." " Thus," says Orson Pratt, " was the Church of Christ once " more restored to the earth, *holding the keys of authority and* "*power to bind, to loose,* and *to seal on the earth and in heaven,* " according to the commandments of God, and the revelations " of Jesus Christ." More than this could not easily be claimed.

On the Sunday succeeding the organization, Oliver Cowdery preached the first public discourse on " this dispensation " and the principles of " the Gospel as revealed to Joseph," and from that day the " testimony " of the Mormon elders has been carried to every civilized nation.

For a time, conversions were but slowly made, but the "gifts" began to manifest themselves, and the few Saints " re- "joiced with exceeding great joy ; " the wicked raged, the devil attacked " the Kingdom," and a " miracle " was performed.

Notwithstanding so much of interest has to be but briefly stated, it seems necessary to give in detail the relation of this first miracle in the Latter-Day kingdom, and the more so from the fact of its similarity to the manifestations of modern Spiritualism. Joseph relates, in his autobiography, that a young man named Newell Knight was greatly exercised on " the " work " that he had announced to him, and attempted to pray in the woods for some enlightenment. He became unwell mentally and physically, and caused some alarm to his wife. Joseph was sent for, and thus reports what took place :—

" I went and found him suffering very much in his mind, and his body acted upon in a very strange manner, his visage and limbs distorted and twisted in every shape and appearance possible to imagine, and finally he was caught up off the floor of the apartment, and tossed about most fearfully. His situation was soon made known to the neighbours and relatives, and in a short time as many as eight or nine grown persons had got together to witness the scene. After he had thus suffered for a time, I succeeded in getting hold of him by the hand, when almost immediately he spoke to me, and with very great earnestness required of me that I should cast the devil out of him, saying that he knew that he was in him, and that he also knew that I could cast him out. I replied, ' If you know that ' I can, it shall be done,' and then almost unconsciously I rebuked the devil and commanded him in the name of Jesus Christ to depart from him, when immediately Newell spoke out and said that he saw the devil leave him, and vanish from his sight. This was the first miracle that was done in this Church, &c."

The scene changes, and Newell, overwhelmed with the good spirit, and joyous beyond expression, is lifted from the floor to the roof till "the beams would let him go no further." In subsequent gatherings of the Saints, Newell is particularly favoured, sees "the heavens opened," and "beholds the glory "of God." He was among the faithful few who endured to the end, and then quietly "fell asleep in Jesus."

It is strangely argued that this first "miracle" in the Mormon Church was an evidence of the divine mission of Joseph Smith and the truthfulness of the Book of Mormon. Elder Orson Pratt reasons thus on the subject :—

"The great miracle that was wrought upon Newell Knight, and that, too, before he became a member of the Church, and in the presence of some eight or nine of his neighbours, *must have given him the most perfect knowledge of the truth of the Book of Mormon ; and it must also have been a convincing testimony to all who saw him."* . . . "This great manifestation of the power of God, in contrast with the power of the evil one, *must have given a knowledge to those who were present that Joseph Smith was a great prophet and seer, and that the Book of Mormon was a divine revelation."* *

The Author, in searching an old file of papers, accidentally cast his eye upon a record of the experience of Judge John W. Edmonds, of New York, wherein that gentleman relates in the New York *Tribune*, some time in 1859, his experience in "casting out devils," which is so remarkably similar to the experience of Joseph Smith with Newell Knight, that it deserves the careful consideration of the Latter-Day Saints. The Judge says :—

"Casting out devils.—I take this phrase as I find it in the Scriptures, as indicating that the subject is possessed by an influence which produces violent throes, or, as it is said in Scripture, 'Straightway the spirit tare 'him, and he fell on the ground and wallowed foaming.'

"I have witnessed many instances of this when the subject was relieved simply by laying on of hands, and sometimes by a mere command to the spirit to depart.

"I was once at a circle in Troy, some twenty persons were present, when a strong man became unconscious and violently convulsed. He beat

* "Evidences of the Book of Mormon and the Bible Compared," p. 63.

the table with great force with both fists. I put my hand on his head against vehement struggles on his part to prevent it, and in a few moments he was restored to quiet and consciousness. I once had a man similarly affected in my own room, who beat his head violently on a marble-top table, and fell to the floor in convulsions. He was recovered by the same means, though more slowly. A man from Chicago called on me afflicted with convulsions of his arms and legs. He was restored by the mere exercise of will. Last year, at my own house, I found a man lying on the floor, distorted and convulsed. I lifted him up, and compelled him to sit in a chair, and then, with a few words, addressed not to him, but to the spirit who was influencing him, he was at once restored to composure."

Had Judge Edmonds known less and believed more, with such an experience, he, too, might have been presented to the world as a "prophet, seer, and revelator," and some enthusiastic Pratt might have proved that his writings were divinely inspired. Fortunately for the world, the Judge, instead of delivering a new Gospel, followed the profession of the law.

3

CHAPTER V.

On the 1st of June, 1830, the first conference was held, at which only thirty members were represented, though many others—either believers or such as were anxious to learn—were present. At this time the testimony of Joseph and his brethren did not extend far from his father's residence and the neighbourhood where his wife's family resided. About the beginning of August, the attention of Parley P. Pratt was drawn to the movement, and soon after he was converted and baptized. Parley, who had been a local preacher of some denomination, was fluent of speech and in every way calculated to be a zealous disciple of the cause. Soon after his own conversion, he visited and converted Sidney Rigdon, a very able Campbellite preacher then residing in Ohio, and Sidney immediately assumed the task of converting his flock to the new faith. Orson Pratt was also numbered among the early disciples, and Joseph soon found himself surrounded by those men of talent who gave the Biblical arguments in favour of Mormonism which it has ever since retained.

In common with all who believe themselves to be entrusted with a special mission, Joseph's faith was great and he anticipated wonderful results from his preaching. The conversion of the world was now a very urgent matter, as " the Lord " had informed him that " He was going to cut short His work " in righteousness in the last days." Consistently, therefore, with the publication of the Book of Mormon as a historical

record of the ancient inhabitants of America, the Indians on
the western frontier were the first to be honoured with a special
mission, and a number of the elders were set apart for this
work and sent forth " without purse or scrip " to preach to the
" Lamanites." *

In addition to the instruction which Joseph claims to have
received from the angels who frequently visited him, he was
also endowed with the " gift of revelation," by which he was
able to give " the word of the Lord " on every subject and to
everybody. Men were called, chosen, ordained, and sent on
missions by the commandment of revelation; they were blessed,
honoured, reproved and cursed by it—as the case might require,
and Joseph, as frequently as any one else, got his full share of
rebuke and chastisement. Jesus Christ is said to be the author
of the numerous revelations given to the Mormon Church
through Joseph Smith, and in this way the early disciples were
directed in all their affairs, whether spiritual or temporal. Joseph became, in the language of one of the hymns, " the mouth-
" piece of God," and henceforth his address to the Saints in all
matters of importance was: " Thus saith the Lord."

Sidney Rigdon was successful with many of his congregation and " the people round about," so that Ohio became the
object of the Prophet's attention. In December, 1830, Rigdon
paid a visit to the Prophet and prolonged his stay till January,
aiding him in his inspired translation of the New Testament,
after which the Prophet returned with him to Ohio. During
this visit " the Lord commanded the Saints in the State of
" New York to gather in Ohio," and instructions to that effect
were promulgated and obeyed. In a few months they were
comfortably situated in the northern portion of that State. But
all this was only temporary. Joseph had ever present in his
mind the " New Jerusalem " that was to be built up somewhere
in the last days, but where that was to be he had not yet learned.

" The Lord," who guided Joseph, would appear to have resolved to keep the locality of the New Jerusalem secret as long
as possible and therefore only spoke of it in vague terms. " In
" February, 1831, the Saints were commanded to ask the Lord
" and he would in due time reveal unto them the place where

* The designation of the Indians in modern revelation.

" the New Jerusalem should be built and where the Saints " should eventually be gathered in one." On the 7th of March they were commanded to gather up their riches with one heart and one mind to purchase the inheritance which "the Lord " would point out to them. Of this inheritance they knew nothing definite, but were told that it was somewhere on the western frontiers. In June, about thirty elders were sent out westward on a preaching tour. They were to go out by twos, and were to build up branches of the Church wherever the people would listen to them, and were eventually to meet together when the place of the New Jerusalem would be made known to them.

About the middle of July, Joseph and several of the elders met at Independence, Jackson county, Missouri, and then at length the revelation about the New Jerusalem was forthcoming. It was very explicit concerning the great things "the Lord " would do in this generation, but, as will presently be seen, that troublesome devil, who never to the moment of his tragic death forsook Joseph, was determined to thwart the purposes of " the Lord " and lead the Prophet and his brethren into fearful affliction.

By the light of facts which have since transpired, the following revelation of " the Lord " on the gathering to Missouri becomes intensely interesting, showing as it does the measure of confidence which the world can place in modern revelation, and inculcating a salutary lesson to the Mormons themselves now under the prophetic guidance of Brigham Young.

" Verily this is the Word of the Lord, that the City New Jerusalem shall be built by the gathering of the Saints, beginning at this place, even the place of the Temple, *which Temple shall be reared in this generation,* for verily *this generation shall not pass away until an house shall be built unto the Lord, and a cloud shall rest upon it, which cloud shall be even the glory of the Lord which shall fill the house."* *

" Hearken, O ye elders of my Church, saith the Lord your God, who have assembled yourselves together according to my commandments in this land, which is the land of Missouri, *which is the land which I have appointed and consecrated for the gathering of the Saints; wherefore this is the land of promise and the place for the City of Zion.* And thus saith the Lord your God, If you will receive wisdom, here is wisdom. Behold the place

* " Book of Doctrine and Covenants," p. 82, par. 2.

which is now called Independence is the centre place, and a spot for the Temple is lying westward upon a lot which is not far from the court house." *

This revelation is dated, " Zion, July, 1831." In another, given September 22, 1832, it is stated that the place was "ap-" " pointed by the finger of the Lord," and the gathering of the Saints and the building of the New Jerusalem are again assured. The succeeding history of the Mormons in Missouri exhibits anything but the fulfilment of these promises: on the contrary it relates only the overthrow of the hopes of the unfortunate believers.

The few Saints from Colesville, Broome county, New York, who had been commanded to gather to Ohio and afterwards to Missouri, had now arrived, and on the 2nd of August the foundation of the first house was laid, twelve miles west of Independence, twelve men taking part in laying that foundation in honour of the Twelve Tribes of Israel. The land of Zion on that occasion was dedicated unto the Lord by prayer, and on the following day the Temple lot was dedicated in the presence of eighteen men. Next day the first conference was held in the land of Zion. A few days afterwards, Joseph and Sidney left Independence to return to Kirtland, where they arrived on the 27th of August, and immediately afterwards Joseph had an abundant outpouring of revelation.

* " Book of Doctrine and Covenants," pp. 165–6, par. 1.

CHAPTER VI.

SATAN THREATENS THE CHURCH.—He shakes and corrupts the Ohio Saints —The Youthful Prophet labours with Great Zeal—Missionaries evangelize the Eastern States—Smith and Rigdon behold a Great Vision—They are tarred and feathered—Go to Missouri and found a Newspaper.

DURING the absence of the young Prophet in Missouri, the believers had not been doing as well as he expected. He was, therefore, immediately armed with a revelation reproving them for seeking " signs." In that revelation (August, 1831) occurs this singularly explicit statement :—" *with whom God is an-* " *gry, he is not well pleased.*" * Uninspired persons would probably consider such a declaration somewhat unnecessary ; it almost requires a second revelation to explain its meaning.

Even at that early day a few of the new converts appear to have exhibited loose notions of morality. Of these, some, charged with being " adulterers and adulteresses," were stated to have " turned away," and the others were warned to " beware and repent speedily." All through the history of the Church during the life-time of Joseph may be noticed a disposition to free-loveism. The new spirit was very affectionate, and required to be strictly guarded. It is, however, due to Joseph to add that his revelations were severe in condemnation of the lack of chastity.

Some idea may be formed of the zeal with which Joseph was building up the kingdom and preparing for the future, when it is stated that, during the year 1831, he received no less than thirty-seven revelations. In addition to the cares of the Church, preaching, testifying, and administering, he had collected the New York and Pennsylvania Saints in Ohio, had

* " Covenants and Commandments," p. 149.

commanded them to go to Missouri, went there himself, and
dedicated to " the Lord " the land " promised to believers for an
" everlasting inheritance," gave some portion of his time to
furnishing the world with an inspired translation of the New
Testament, and successfully defended himself in two lawsuits,
which were instigated by " the wicked," who " sought to per-
" secute him."

In 1832 the work extended over the States, and many converts were added to the new Church. The missionaries had no
compensation, but whenever one was required, Joseph could
with the greatest facility call an elder to labour in " the Lord's "
vineyard. It was nothing to him at what sacrifice this might
be done. It was " a day of sacrifice," and the greater that
was the nobler the reward in the world to come. The labour
that is hired is limited, but the labour of the Mormon elders
was never over. This was the secret of their successful preaching. There was no boundary to their harvest field, they were
commanded to " thrust in the sickle and reap," wherever there
was a call for help or wherever the Spirit might direct. Thus
influenced and undeterred by any difficulty the elders travelled
everywhere. They braved every danger, faced a frowning
world, rejoiced in tribulation, blessed the Saints, cursed their
enemies, and sang and shouted : " The kingdom is come, glory,
" glory, hallelujah ! "

Meanwhile Joseph was not idle. On the 16th of February,
while he and Sidney were engaged in the translation of the
Bible, they claim to have beheld a great vision. They saw
" many things unspeakable and unlawful to be uttered," and at
the same time " many great and marvellous things that they
" were commanded to write while they were yet in the Spirit."

About the end of March, Joseph and Sidney were very
roughly treated by a mob who tarred and feathered them both.
The mobbers were very cruel, and tried to force some poison-
ous liquid down Joseph's throat, but the phial was broken
against his teeth, and the contents spilt. They then leaped
on his chest and trampled him with their feet till they thought
he was dead. The Mormon historian says that Joseph's spirit
left his body during the outrage, but afterwards returned
and re-took possession. Sidney was not served quite so badly,

but he bore it worse than Joseph, and never forgot it. The
Prophet had some difficulty in getting altogether free from the
tar, and the stamping severely injured his chest, but " the Lord
" healed him up again," and next day (March 26th) it is reported that he was " acknowledged to be the President of the

" High Priesthood,"
at a General Coun-
cil of the Church. A
few days later he set
out the second time
for Missouri, and ar-
rived at Independ-
ence on the 24th of
April.

During his two
weeks' stay in Mis-
souri, it was resolved
to publish the revela-
tions in book form,

Tarred and feathered.

and to establish at Independence a journal called *The Evening
and Morning Star*, under the editorial direction of Elder W.
W. Phelps, a brother who performed a very important part in
the history of Mormonism. The career of " W. W.," as he is
familiarly styled, has been somewhat chequered, but he still
lives, and is " not to taste of death." He is about eighty years
of age, and has the promise of living till Jesus comes again.*
He is a singular genius, greatly gifted in interpreting disen-
tombed inscriptions, especially upon old coins. He is usually
credited with having furnished the political papers of Joseph
with their " highfalutin," and distorting several languages to
make the word " Mormon " mean " more good," although pro-

---

* Since the foregoing was written, the Salt Lake papers have published the following notice :

"Phelps—William Wines Phelps, born in the State of New Jersey, February,
1792, died March 7th, 1872, in Salt Lake City."

Alas, poor Phelps ! Often did the old man, in public and in private, regale the
Saints with the assurance that he had the promise by revelation that he should not
taste of death till Jesus came. The last time that the Author spoke with " Brother " Phelps, the latter was fully satisfied that the revelation of Joseph Smith could
not fail in its fulfilment.

fane opponents insist that the word is derived from the Greek, and signifies something neither pleasant nor beautiful.* At that time, however, he was well-fitted to be publisher of the journal, as he had been a practical printer, but his writings do not seem to have suited the Missourians, and doubtless contributed much to the commencement of troubles among them.

Joseph returned to Kirtland in June, and devoted his labours to the Saints of that place, but at the same time he maintained a correspondence with "Zion in Missouri," directing and controlling affairs in both places.

* Joseph Smith, when questioned on the subject, gave the following as the proper derivation of the word :

"I may safely say that the word Mormon stands independent of the learning and wisdom of this generation. Before I give a definition, however, to the word, let me say that the Bible, in its widest sense, means good ; for the Saviour says, according to the Gospel of St. John, 'I am the good shepherd ;' and it will not be beyond the use of terms to say that good is amongst the most important in use, and though known by various names in different languages, still its meaning is the same, and is ever in opposition to bad. We say from the Saxon, *good ;* the Dane, *god ;* the Goth, *goda ;* the German, *gut ;* the Dutch, *good ;* the Latin, *bonus ;* the Greek, *kalos ;* the Hebrew, *tob :* and the Egyptian, *mon.* Hence with the addition of more, or the contraction *mor,* we have the word Mormon, which means literally, *more good.*"

Notwithstanding all this pedantic parade of learning on the part of the Prophet, uninspired scholars have expressed an opinion that the word was derived from the Greek, μορμών, a spectre or hideous shape.

CHAPTER VII.

MEETING OF THE PROPHETS.—Brigham Young sees Joseph Smith for the
First Time—They rejoice together in Kirtland—Brigham speaks in " Unknown
Tongues "—Joseph predicts the Southern Rebellion—He makes an Inspired Translation of the New Testament—Troubles arise between the Saints and the " Gentiles " in Missouri—The Disciples are driven from Jackson County.

In November, 1833, Joseph first met Brigham Young, who
had been baptized in the preceding April. At that time the
latter resided in New York, following the business of a painter
and glazier ; but he had not hitherto enjoyed an opportunity
of meeting the Prophet face to face. Heber C. Kimball and
Joseph Young accompanied Brigham, and they had a high time
of rejoicing in Kirtland. During this brief visit, Brigham and
his relative, John P. Green, " spake in tongues," and this was
the first time that the " gift " had been demonstrated. The
same influence fell upon others, and they also " spake in
" tongues," and Joseph the Prophet is said to have been among
the gifted ones.

On Christmas Day he received the famous prophetic revelation relating to the rebellion in the South. On the 27th,
" the Lord " intimated his desire that a house should be built
to his name, in which " the School of the Prophets " should assemble, and everything in the shape of prayer and teaching be
done in perfect order—thus preparing the way for the Kirtland
temple.

To Joseph and the Saints, the year 1833 was destined to
be an eventful time. The general cause was advancing, but
the faithful in Missouri were doomed to suffer persecution.

Early in the year Joseph finished the inspired translation
of the New Testament, and by the beginning of July completed

the revision·of the Old Testament. In June he received the revelation giving the dimensions of the temple that " the Lord " required to be built by the Saints in Kirtland, and on the 23rd of July the first stone was laid.

From the day of trouble between the first sons of Adam there never was a controversy without a double statement of what were the contributory causes. In Mormon history, charges and recriminations concerning the hostilities in Missouri are prolific ; but it is generally admitted that at the first outbreak the anti-Mormons " were actuated much more by a fear of what " the Mormons would do when they had the power than by " what they had already done." *   On the other hand, the Mormons, proud of the promises of a glorious future, were boastful of the favours and possessions that awaited them ; and probably some of them taunted the Missourians with the coming change. But even this, however injudicious, was not likely to lead to armed hostility. Before men resort to bloodshed, there is generally something that outrages them in a personal way, and when once that is the case a very slight pretext alone is necessary to produce a collision.

At the commencement of hostilities, the country of the New Jerusalem was only sparsely settled, and the Mormons probably numbered about 1,500 souls. Whatever evidence there is to support the charges of wrong-doing which were afterwards made against some of them in other parts of Missouri, and later still in Illinois, they were, in 1833, both too few in number and too sincere in faith to assume an aggressive attitude. As a people, they could not have been very bad ; for Joseph was constantly chastening them for the slightest neglect of the revelations, and they had gathered to Missouri in the full belief that Christ was coming thither to join the faithful band. Under such circumstances, it is but fair to consider them, however chimerical in faith, intentionally right in practice, except where there is the evidence of fact to the contrary.

The other citizens of Missouri had little sympathy with the new arrivals, and saw very clearly that, with the constant accession to their numbers, it would only be a short time before the Mormons would become a political power among them—

* "Mysteries and Crimes of Mormonism," p. 41.

would control the elections in the county, and have everything their own way. According to that not very elegant expression so frequently heard in the Mormon sermons, it was destined that " Israel should be the head and not the tail." As citizens, the Mormons had political rights, and would exercise these in their own interest ; and, while no sensible person could blame them for this, the other citizens none the less felt that it was a calamity to them that these strangers had come amongst them. The only direct charge against the Mormons met with in the publications of the day is that of tampering with the slaves. The *Evening and Morning Star* had published something offensive on this subject ; for though the Mormons believed that " Ham is a servant unto his brethren," they were opposed to the general treatment of the Africans in the South.

On the 20th of July a mob tore down the office of the *Star*, tarred, feathered, and whipped a number of the brethren, and insisted upon the Mormons leaving Jackson county. Three days later a second mob assembled, and at length the leaders of the Mormons in that locality agreed to leave. Some time in October, elders W. W. Phelps and Orson Hyde carried a petition to the Governor of the State for protection, and his Excellency answered that they had a right to the protection of the law if they chose to stay in the county and fight it out.

The anti-Mormons were, however, determined that the followers of Joseph should leave the county, and they resolved to get rid of them—" peaceably, if we can : forcibly, if we must, " and believing, as we do, that the arm of the civil law does " not afford us a guarantee, or at least a sufficient one, against " the evils which are now inflicted upon us, and seem to be in- " creasing by the said religious sect, deem it expedient and of " the highest importance to form ourselves into a company for " the better and easier accomplishment of our purpose." Such was the resolution which was followed by the pledge to each other of " bodily powers, lives, fortunes, and sacred honour."

On the 4th of November this hostile organization commenced its work ; a " battle " took place, some persons were shot, and the people driven out of the county. Parley P. Pratt, in his " History of the Missouri Persecutions," presents a sad picture of personal suffering, cruelty, and outrage to men, women, and children, and the wanton destruction of property. The world has grown older since then, and, after a lapse of nearly forty years, it seems scarcely possible that such scenes could have been enacted during the present century, and in an American State.

A few of the Saints were shot, some tied up and cruelly whipped, over two hundred of their houses were burned, fences were torn down, cattle and horses stolen, and household effects, goods, and chattels destroyed or taken from them. Men, women, and children fled terrified before their enemies in every direction seeking protection. A party of about one hundred and fifty children are said to have wandered out on to the prairie, and remained there for several days without shelter, and with only the aid of half a dozen men who went with them to provide as well as they could for the helpless little ones, while their fathers and mothers were being hunted down like wild beasts.

Some of the exiles sought refuge in Van Buren (now Cass) county, but were not permitted to settle either there or in La Fayette. Most of them ultimately settled in Clay county, where they were received with some degree of kindness.

CHAPTER VIII.

THE PROMISED LAND.—" The Lord " calls for " the Strength of his House " to
reinstate the Exiled Saints in Jackson County—Two hundred and five Elders respond—The Prophet becomes Commander-in-Chief of " the Armies of the Lord "
—A Revelation promising Restoration to the Exiles—Joseph is the Man like unto
Moses to lead them to Victory.

AN eastern sage has said that " the beginning of strife is
" like the letting out of water "—it is easier to commence hostilities than to stop them—and thus it proved in the history of
the Missouri troubles, for the end has not yet come. The
Mormons were driven out of Jackson county and their enemies were now successful, but war was only begun. The
Saints never yield to wrong while life serves them. They can
be vanquished and humbled, but never conquered. The very
nature of their faith forbids the thought—" The Lord is on
" our side "—to yield is to deny the faith. When undoubted
facts are against them, they admit defeat, but then only. When
in the right, if overwhelmed, " the Lord " may counsel expediency and the point at issue may seem to be conceded ; but it
is only so in appearance and temporarily in order to gain some
greater advantage in future. It is now over thirty-seven years
since the first Missouri persecution began, but the Saints who
were then expelled from Jackson county still believe in a triumphal return to their inheritances and still expect to see the
temple built in " this generation."

In the very nature of things, the " generation " in which the
revelation and prophecy were delivered must pass away without witnessing their fulfilment, yet the last of these Jackson
county Saints will go down to his grave believing that there
has been no failure. Joseph who delivered the prophecy and

fought manfully for its fulfilment, and Brigham who has made it his principal stock in trade to raise the hopes and aspirations of his followers, will both remain as before, unchallenged in their claims to a "priesthood that is infallible." Such is faith!

While the troubles in Missouri were raging, the Prophet deemed it advisable not to provoke the fury of the mob by his presence, and therefore concluded to labour elsewhere while he still showered upon the Saints encouraging revelations. The anti-Mormons offered to buy the lands from which their antagonists had been driven and to pay them for their improvements, but negotiation was impossible. "The Lord" had commanded them to gather in Missouri and had pointed out with his own finger the place for the Temple in Independence. They could not sell their inheritances without also selling the revelations of "the Lord," his promises and the prophecies of his servant. Joseph counselled the Saints not to sell, and they obeyed, and to this day many of the faithful rejoice in the possession of their title-deeds. When Federal troops, during the rebellion, swept through those counties of western Missouri laying waste and devastating everywhere they went, the Saints in Utah saw in them the avenging angels of the Lord, and their hopes of an early return to Jackson county revived.

Joseph, during the troubles in Missouri, was closely occupied with the building of the Temple in Kirtland, and raising the means to continue that work was a herculean task. To these labours he added a mission to the Eastern States and to the Canadas. About this time it was also decided to revive the *Star*, that had been so ruthlessly dealt with in Missouri, under the designation of the *Latter-Day Saints' Messenger and Advocate*, at Kirtland. During his mission abroad, Joseph baptized many into the Church, and "his hands were "strengthened," though the people around him were poor and apostacy began to trouble him.

Up to this time Joseph had been a Prophet, Seer, Revelator, and Translator; but now another *rôle* was opened to him—he was to become a military leader and restore the Saints to their possessions in Jackson county. A lengthened revelation was given in February, 1834, to raise "the strength of the "Lord's house," and go up to Missouri to redeem Zion, and the

Prophet became, by the election of a council of elders, "Com-
" mander-in-chief of the Armies of Israel."

Revelations under the most favourable circumstances are not
always over clear to ordinary mortals, and there is often controversy about the fulfilment of a prophecy; but this revelation given through Joseph for " the redemption of Zion " is so
palpably applicable to this special period of Mormon history
that it is deserving of particular attention. The situation of
the exiled Saints from Jackson county, the gathering of " the
" Lord's hosts " to reinstate them in their possessions, the marching of those brethren a distance of 1,200 miles, and their unflag-
ging zeal and faith up to the last moment, are unequivocal facts,
yet the whole " pomp and circumstance of glorious war " accomplished nothing that was promised. Here is the revelation :

. . . "Verily I say unto you, I have decreed that your brethren
which have been scattered shall return to the land of their inheritances,
and build up the waste places of Zion, for after much tribulation, as I have
said unto you in a former commandment, cometh the blessing. Behold
this is the blessing which I have promised after your tribulations and the
tribulations of your brethren, your redemption and the redemption of your
brethren, even their restoration to the land of Zion to be established
no more to be thrown down, nevertheless if they pollute their inheritances they shall be thrown down, for I will not spare them if they pollute their inheritances. Behold I say unto you the redemption of Zion
must needs come by power, therefore I will raise up unto my people a man
who shall lead them like as Moses led the children of Israel, for ye are
the children of Israel and of the seed of Abraham, and ye must needs be
led out of bondage, by power, and with a stretched-out arm, and as your
fathers were led at the first, even so shall the redemption of Zion be.
Therefore let not your hearts faint, for I say not unto you as I said unto
your fathers, mine angel shall go up before you, but not my presence ; but
I say unto you, mine angels shall go before you, and also my presence, and
in time ye shall possess the goodly land."

. . . "Therefore let my servant Baurak Ale [Joseph Smith] * say
unto the strength of my house, my young men and the middle aged, gather
yourselves together unto the land of Zion, upon the land which I have
bought with monies that have been consecrated unto me ; and let all the
churches send up wise men with their monies and purchase land even as I
have commanded them, and inasmuch as mine enemies come against you
to drive you from my goodly land, which I have consecrated to be the

* For the purpose of protecting Joseph when the revelations were printed, in
those of a warlike character, he is designated as *Baurak Ale*, and in others he is
represented by Enoch, Gazelam, and Seth.

land of Zion, even from your own lands after these testimonies which ye have brought before me against them, ye shall curse them, and whomsoever ye curse, I will curse, and ye shall avenge me of mine enemies, and my presence shall be with you even in avenging me of mine enemies, unto the third and fourth generation of them that hate me.

"Let no man be afraid to lay down his life for my sake, for whoso layeth down his life for my sake shall find it again, and whoso is not willing to lay down his life for my sake, is not my disciple. It is my will that my servant Sidney Rigdon shall lift up his voice in the congregations in the Eastern Countries in preparing the Churches to keep the commandments which I have given unto them concerning the restoration and redemption of Zion. It is my will that my servant Parley P. Pratt and my servant Lyman Wight should not return to the land of their brethren until they have obtained companies to go up unto the land of Zion by tens, or by twenties, or by fifties, or by an hundred, until they have obtained the number of five hundred of the strength of my house. Behold this is my will; ask and you shall receive; but men do not always do my will; therefore if you cannot obtain five hundred, seek diligently that peradventure you may obtain three hundred, and if ye cannot obtain three hundred, seek diligently that peradventure ye may obtain one hundred. But verily I say unto you a commandment I give unto you that ye shall not go up unto the land of Zion until you have obtained one hundred of the strength of my house to go up with you unto the land of Zion. Therefore, as I said unto you, ask and ye shall receive; pray earnestly that peradventure my servant Baurak Ale may go with you and preside in the midst of my people, and organize my kingdom upon the consecrated land, and establish the children of Zion upon the laws and commandments which have been and which shall be given unto you."

This " revelation " is certainly very specific and direct, and evinces an unequivocal disposition on the part of " the Lord " to destroy his enemies. With such a termination to the expedition, as will be read in the following chapter, it is with pity mingled with a sense of the ludicrous that one peruses this page in the history of the Mormon Church.

4

CHAPTER IX.

ZION'S CAMP.—The Prophet's "Army" marches to Missouri—A Great Storm—The Cholera desolates the "Strength of the Lord's House"—Utter Discomfiture of the Mormons—The Promises to restore the Saints to Jackson County a Total Failure—The "Army" disbanded—The Saints sue for Peace—"The Lord was only trying their Faith"—They are to curse their Enemies—Anniversary Meetings of Zion's Camp—Dancing and Rejoicing.

THERE is no event in the history of Mormonism of such importance as that which is portrayed in the preceding chapter—it was the "call of the Lord" for "the strength of His house "to go against His enemies." The Church so understood it and the brethren answered to "the Lord's call." The Company was organized in Kirtland on the 7th of May, and as "Zion's Camp" took up their march westward. They numbered 130 men, among whom were Hyrum Smith, Brigham Young, Heber C. Kimball, George A. Smith, Orson Hyde, Orson and Parley P. Pratt, Wilford Woodruff, and many other leading elders. This little army was divided into companies of twelve men, each company choosing its own officer. The Prophet's cousin, Geo. A. Smith, was elected to be his armour-bearer.[*] Camp discipline was rigid, everything throughout the day had its appointed time, and at the sound of the evening trumpet the little "host" were called to their devotions, returning thanks for the past and invoking the protection of "the God of battles."

By the time the camp reached Missouri its numbers had increased to 205. Orson Hyde and Parley P. Pratt had been despatched in advance as delegates to the Governor of Mis-

---

[*] All through Mormonism there is a constant effort to imitate something Hebraic. Nothing can be done without some allusion to Biblical history. The above, of course, was in allusion to Saul and his faithful armour-bearer. The same may be said of the "Armies of the Lord," "the Host," and "the God of battles."

THE LORD'S ARMY MARCHING TO THE DELIVERANCE OF ZION.

souri to ask that the Mormons might be allowed to settle again in Jackson county, but Governor Dunklin refused to interfere, on the ground that it was impracticable.

On the 19th of June "Zion's Camp" reached the vicinity of Clay county, where the exiled Saints had located, and tried to effect a junction with them, but were unsuccessful. That night Joseph's, or "the Lord's," army encamped between the Little and the Big Fishing rivers, and the "mobbers," or anti-Mormons, who had learned of their coming were not far from them and ready for attack. At this important moment the elements interfered, the camp of the anti-Mormons scattered to the winds, their horses stampeded and one was killed by lightning.

On the second day (June 21st) the cholera broke out with terrible fierceness in "Zion's Camp." So sudden and overpowering was the attack that the strongest men fell to the ground with their guns in their hands. In four days, sixty-eight were attacked and fourteen of them died. Joseph went about laying on hands and "rebuking the destroyer," until he was himself prostrated. This visitation he ascribed to the disobedience of some, showed the necessity of submission, and promised that if they would "humble themselves and covenant *to obey him as* "*the Prophet of the Lord*," the plague should be stayed. The Mormon historians assert that "not another was stricken with "the cholera from that hour."

The previous "revelations" of Joseph Smith admitted of no verification beyond that of individual faith and experience; but this concerning "the redemption of Zion" revealed the revelator himself. While giving to it all the scope that the utmost devotion could claim, it must be allowed that it carries upon its surface anything but the evidence of a divine origin. The overthrow of "Zion's Camp" was a palpable failure and disappointing in every particular. There was a native honesty in Mohammed going to the mountain when the mountain would not come to him, which commands admiration, but the American Prophet lost his opportunity when, in the midst of "Zion's Camp" on the banks of the Big Fishing river, he failed to contribute to posterity a companion picture to that of his Arabian brother. Instead of that, he received another revelation:

"Behold I have commanded my servant Baürak Ale [Joseph Smith] to say unto the strength of my house, even my warriors, my young men and my middle-aged, to gather together for the redemption of my people, and throw down the towers of mine enemies, and scatter their watchmen; but the strength of mine house have not hearkened unto my words. I have prepared a blessing and an endowment for them if they continue faithful. I have heard their prayers and will accept their offering; and it is expedient in me that they should be brought thus far for a trial of their faith."

The Mormons would be very critical over such revelations if found in the history of any other religious people. The very revelation itself instructed Joseph to ask for 500 men of the Lord's house, but should he find difficulty in raising that number he was to be contented with 300; and even with 100 he was not to hesitate, but to hasten to the assistance of his brethren in Missouri, for "the Lord had decreed" the restoration of the exiles. Full of faith and hope, Joseph and "the "strength of the Lord's house" reached the place of action, preaching, praying, and exhorting each other to courage, for had not a Hebrew Prophet said that one of the chosen of the Lord should chase a thousand, and two should put ten thousand to flight? Ancient bravery and ancient miracles were thought of and descanted upon during the journey, and the "warriors" were ready for the fray; but when the moment for action arrived, "the Lord" had changed his mind. The hard-working outcasts from Jackson county, it was now said, had not learned to be obedient, they were full of all manner of evil, were not united, and did not deserve to be restored until they *had been chastised and learned obedience.* How different was the revelation of February in Ohio from that of June in Missouri! At the former date "the Lord" was determined to have a fight and restore the exiles "to their inheritances." At the latter date "the Lord" concluded that the Jackson county Saints deserved all the affliction they had got, and needed a little more of the same chastisement!

"The Lord's" reasons for refusing to restore the people to Jackson county were probably very satisfactory, for such a bad and undeserving people as they were now represented to be, could not be expected to command so great a manifestation of divine power as would have been necessary to restore them to their homes and farms. But it certainly looks a little singular, if what Joseph asserted was true, that " the Lord " had not discovered this condition of things before.

The second excuse is still worse than the first—" the " strength of mine house have not hearkened unto my words." Thus because of the dilatoriness of the Saints in the East, the Saints in the West were to remain outcasts from Jackson county, and " the Lord's " decree of the restoration of the people was to become a dead letter! What a contrast was this to the ancient story of " the sword of the Lord and of " Gideon ! " To cap the climax, the warriors in " Zion's Camp " were informed that in due time they should be properly re warded, but would have to regard the present disappointment as " a trial of their faith ! "

This Jackson county trouble has been a sad affair for the Mormon Church in many ways. It was, to say the least, very questionable instruction to declare—" ye shall avenge me of " mine enemies." There is enough of natural vindictiveness in men without elevating vengeance into a religious obligation. No people as zealous and devoted as the Mormons could receive such a commandment without partaking of its spirit and reducing it to practice. It makes it a duty for every fanatic to curse and avenge in the Lord's stead. How well it has been performed in spirit if not always in practice let the anathemas of the Tabernacle and the persecution of apostates tell.

Up to this period the Saints had no conception that they were the instruments of " the Lord's " vengeance, and it is to be regretted that they were ever enlightened upon the subject. They had already been informed that it was better to obtain Zion by purchase than by force, and they were now instructed to buy up—

————" all the lands in Jackson county that can be purchased, and in the adjoining counties. . . . and after these lands are purchased, I will hold the armies of Israel guiltless in taking possession of their own lands, which they have previously purchased with their own monies, and of throwing down the towers of mine enemies that may be upon them, and scattering their watchmen, and avenging me of mine enemies, unto the third and fourth generation of them that hate me."

To this excellent advice of purchasing all the lands and

keeping their enemies far from them, " the Lord," when en-
joining vengeance, diplomatically adds — "*but first let my
army become very great.*" In the meantime the Mormons are
to sue for peace. This is a very practical endorsement of the
First Napoleon's opinion that Providence was always on the
side of the best generalship and the strongest battalions.

Such very wholesome counsel was of course properly appreciated. The " warriors " were instructed to disperse
among the settlements or to return to their homes, and Joseph
as directed, was also to conclude some arrangement by which
the Saints who were still able to stay in Jackson county could
enjoy peace ; but the throwing down of towers, scattering the
watchmen, and restoring the people to their inheritances, were
apparently no more to be thought of. A " High Council " was
organized in Clay county, and Joseph left for Kirtland on the
9th of July.

Thus ended this extraordinary but brief campaign of two
months and two days—a period fraught with good instruction
to those who could take it.

Brigham Young annually invites the remnant of " Zion's
" Camp " to meet him in Salt Lake City—generally at the close
of the October Conference—and they have a pleasant reunion
in the Social Hall, where they with their families enjoy themselves in the dance together. The chief bishop of the Church
entertains them at dinner and supper. Usually during the
evening they are " addressed ; " they sing their songs of days
gone by, and one or two of the very aged brethren will try a
" jig " or " hornpipe," to show the others " how well they hold
" out." It is a very harmless kind of mutual admiration.
They all feel honoured in having been members of Zion's Camp,
and probably would think it very daring for any one even to
suggest a failure of that memorable campaign. Brigham
never omits at this gathering to tell how much he was *compensated* for his marching experience by the teachings he listened
to from the Prophet's lips. He seems to feel that something is
needed just there, and he furnishes the supply. The leader
says that he was " compensated "; the " remnant " then *must*
feel that *they* also were compensated ; and in two or three generations from this time their descendants will doubtless read

with great satisfaction of the trial of their ancestors' faith, and it is not at all unlikely that, in the course of time, their posterity will be fully satisfied that the Saints in Jackson county were not restored to their inheritances and were not " led out of bondage by power and with a stretched-out arm, as ' the Lord ' had decreed ! "

CHAPTER X.

TWELVE APOSTLES CHOSEN.—Quorums of " Seventies " organized—They go
abroad and preach—Kirtland Temple finished—Dedication and Endowment—
Joseph's Wonderful Vision of the Celestial Kingdom—A second Pentecost—
Brigham Young " speaks in Tongues "—The Temple filled with Angels—Joseph
and Cowdery are visited by Moses, Elias, and Elijah—They behold " The Lord "
—Cowdery afterwards apostatizes.

LAYING aside for a time the sword and buckler, the Prophet
betook himself to the olive branch, and meditated the greater
expansion of the kingdom by the preaching of the Gospel.
He had all the winter of 1834–5 in Kirtland to prepare for
the spring campaign. His Missouri mission had taught him
something. If he had not thrown down towers, he had at least
picked up a lesson. Miraculous interference was all good
enough to predict and talk about, but facts are accomplished
by organization. From that time to the day of his death his
brain was never free from an organizing scheme of some sort.
Mormonism was henceforth not to " lay around loose " and depend upon the heavens alone, it was to be a working organism.
The Christian Church began with the choosing of the Twelve
Apostles. Joseph had followed no definite plan since his
Church was organized. It was now time to choose *his*
" Twelve," * and send them to " all nations, kindreds, tongues,
" and people, to preach the Gospel of the New Covenant." On
the 4th of February, 1835, the selection was made in the fol-
lowing order:—Lyman E. Johnson, Brigham Young, Heber
C. Kimball, Orson Hyde, David W. Patten, Luke Johnson,
William E. McLellin, John F. Boynton, Orson Pratt, William

---

* In his public sermons, Brigham frequently announces that he is an Apostle of
Joseph Smith. It is his theory that " the Kingdom was *given unto Joseph.*"

Smith, Thomas B. Marsh, and Parley P. Pratt. At a later date the order of rank was determined by seniority, which gave the Presidency to Thomas B. Marsh.

During the same month Joseph introduced another organization—" The Seventies." This was to be a "Quorum" composed of seventy elders, the first seven members of which were to be seven presidents over the whole quorum, and the first of these seven to preside over all; the seventies to be auxiliaries to the twelve apostles, and to form a sort of minor apostleship. Some idea of what was working in Joseph's brain at this time, about the conquest of the world, may be drawn from his instructions to the President of the Seventies:

" If the first Seventy are all employed, and there is a call for more labourers, it will be the duty of the seven Presidents of the first Seventy to call and ordain other seventy, and send them forth to labour in the vineyard, until, if need be, they set apart seventy times seventy, and even until they are one hundred and forty-four thousand."

Joseph began the selection of the elders for the first seventy from the ranks of Zion's Camp, and since that organization (Feb. 28, 1835) others have followed, till there are now in the Mormon Church eighty-five Quorums of Seventies.

Early in May the twelve apostles started from Kirtland on their missions to the Eastern States to disseminate the new faith, and labour " wherever a door was open " during all the summer and fall, returning to Kirtland in December, to relate their success, to get fresh instructions, and to tarry till the completion of the temple, when they were to be " endowed " with great power from on high." During their absence Joseph was severely tried by " apostates and false brethren," and the return of the young apostles was very timely in strengthening the Prophet and encouraging the Saints.

The Kirtland Temple was now the object of hope, faith, prayer, and hard work. Everything depended upon its early completion. Disciples who begin their career with the experience of signs and wonders are always the slowest to comprehend facts, and are ever clamorous for a renewal of marvellous experience. " The Lord," as they believed it, thoroughly comprehended their wants, and held before them " great expectations." They contributed their mites and their labour, and by the 27th of March, 1836, " the House of the Lord " was so far finished as to admit of dedication.

It was no Solomon's Temple, but, for the few Saints who reared it, it was a commanding building. In those days " the " Lord " had to do everything, so that this house was not built up " after the manner of the world," and he commanded that " the size thereof shall be fifty and five feet in width, and let it " be sixty-five feet in length, in the inner court thereof." The Prophet having given the general outline, the Temple went up and was reported to be finished in this fashion :

The Temple at Kirtland, Ohio.*

" Outside dimensions sixty feet in width and eighty feet in length ; its height from the ground to the top of the eaves, about fifty feet ; from the basement forty-four, giving two stories of twenty-two feet each, besides an attic story in the roof for school rooms. It was lighted by thirty gothic, three venetian, two dormer, one circular, and two square gable windows. The dome of the steeple was one hundred and ten feet high, and the bell about ninety feet from the ground."

The internal divisions were arranged for the gradations of Priesthood : the west end of the lower court to the Melchise-

* The Saints, under the leadership of the eldest son of the Prophet, are now negotiating for the possession of the Temple. It has a wonderful hold upon the faith of all Saints.

dee, and the east end to the Aaronic Priesthood. The attic story was appropriated as a place for the study of Hebrew, Greek, and Latin. This curious mixture of earth and heaven was like the man himself. Had he lived to the age of Methuselah, his span of years would have been too short to have carried out all the projects that had passed through his brain. Thus early he began to study foreign languages, and stimulated the elders to do likewise before they could some of them properly write their own names, or speak their mother tongue. In the beginning of January a Hebrew professorship was established in Kirtland, and on the 21st of that month the long-promised endowment was given, and during three days in the latter part of March the Temple was dedicated.

The endowment and the dedication were very important events in Mormon history, and are, almost more than anything else in the experience of the Saints, claimed to be a divine confirmation of Joseph's mission. The narrative as given by the Prophet and his biographers is too ample to permit of being quoted at length, but can be easily comprehended from a brief statement. The "visions of eternity" were opened to the elders; angels ministered; "the power of the Highest rest-" ed upon them;" and " the house was filled with the glory of "God." It is very certain that, on the occasion stated, the Saints had a very lively time, and caused a great deal of commotion. An antagonistic writer of the period accused them of being merry from another "spirit" than that which they claimed from above. During the shouting of " Hosanna to God "and the Lamb," Joseph claims to have had a marvellous vision, in which he says:

"I beheld the celestial kingdom of God, and the glory thereof, whether in the body or out I cannot tell. I saw the transcendent beauty of the gate through which the heirs of that kingdom will enter, which was like circling flames of fire; the blazing throne of God, whereon were seated the Father and the Son. I saw the beautiful streets of that kingdom, which had the appearance of being paved with gold. I saw Father Adam,*

* Joseph does not state how he came in possession of these names. He makes some blunder here or somewhere else, for he evidently makes Adam and Michael two distinct persons, while in other revelations he sets forth that Adam is Michael. Such confusion does not tend to increase faith.

and Abraham, and Michael, and my father and mother, my brother Alvin,"* etc., etc.

This was a very great time, but it was only the forerunner of the Pentecost that was in store for them at the forthcoming dedication of the Temple. On the 27th March, 1836, a thousand Saints had assembled, and in that number were all the apostles, seventies, and elders who could possibly get there. They had come to receive great blessings, and were mentally in excellent condition for anything that the heavens might send them. A dedicatory prayer was offered by the Prophet, and the Saints were asked if they accepted the prayer dedicating the House of the Lord. They shouted affirmatively, partook of the Sacrament together, and then began to relate their experience and to testify. Brigham led off with " speaking in " tongues," and the services of the day closed with more shouting of " Hosannas " and " Amens." They were worked up to a high pitch of excitement.

In the evening Joseph met the Quorum of elders, and what then transpired and subsequently during the days of dedication is thus related by the Mormon historian :

" He gave the elders instructions respecting the Spirit of Prophecy, and called upon them to speak and not to fear, and the Spirit of Prophecy should rest down upon them. Brother George A. Smith arose and began to prophesy when a noise was heard like a rushing, mighty wind, which filled the Temple, and all the congregation simultaneously arose, being moved by an invisible power. Many began to speak in tongues and prophesy ; others saw glorious visions, and Joseph beheld that the Temple was filled with angels, and told the congregation so. The people of the neighbourhood, hearing an unusual sound within the Temple, and seeing a bright light like a pillar of fire resting upon it, came running together and were astonished at what was transpiring. . . .

" Next Sunday (April 3rd) two of the twelve apostles preached in the forenoon, and in the afternoon the Sacrament was administered ; after which Joseph retired to the pulpit, and the veils being dropped he bowed

* Joseph, in his Autobiography, expressed great surprise at beholding his brother Alvin, as Alvin when he died knew nothing of the Mormon faith, and consequently could have no title to such a lofty position in the heavens ; but the Prophet seems not to have anticipated the natural astonishment which the reader must feel that he could see his mother in Paradise, as she was not only then in the flesh, but lived long enough to write an affectionate biography of him himself after his own death.

nimself, with Oliver Cowdery, in solemn and silent prayer to the Most High. After rising from prayer, a most glorious vision of the Lord was opened to both of them. The veil was taken from their minds, and the eyes of their understandings were opened. They saw the Lord standing upon the breastwork of the pulpit before them. Under His feet was a paved work of pure gold, in colour like amber. His eyes were as a flame of fire; the hair of his head was like the pure snow; his countenance shone above the brightness of the sun, and his voice was as the sound of the rushing of great waters, even the voice of Jehovah saying—'I am the first and the last; I am he who was slain; I am your advocate with the Father.' He spoke many words of encouragement unto them, and gave them precious promises, and told them things that should come to pass.

"After that vision closed, the heavens were again opened unto them, and Moses appeared before them and committed unto them the keys of the gathering of Israel from the four parts of the earth, and the leading of the Ten Tribes from the land of the North. Elias then appeared and committed the dispensation of the Gospel of Abraham.

"After that vision had closed, another great and glorious vision burst upon them, for Elijah the Prophet, who was taken to heaven without tasting death, stood before them and said—'Behold the time has fully come which was spoken of by the mouth of Malachi, testifying that he [Elijah] should be sent before the great and dreadful day of the Lord come, to turn the hearts of the fathers to the children, and the children to the fathers, lest the whole earth be smitten with a curse. Therefore,' said he, 'the keys of this dispensation are committed into your hands, and by this ye may know that the great and dreadful day of the Lord is near, even at the doors.' " *

After such evidences of what is claimed to have been a divine attestation of the mission of Joseph, it is to be regretted that the greater portion of the witnesses of these glorious visions " fell away " and apostatized from Joseph. Within six months from that time one of his own counsellors and three of his apostles were suspended from fellowship, and in the following year this same Oliver Cowdery, who had seen, heard, and was ordained by angels, and had the most ecstatic visions, was also cut off from the Church!

At the time when these manifestations are said to have occurred in the Temple at Kirtland, few persons outside of the Mormon communion believed anything of the report; but the multitudes scattered throughout the world who now believe in

* " Autobiography of Joseph Smith."

spirit-manifestations will credit the thousand spectators and witnesses at the dedication with having had a " wonderful ex- " perience."*

* There is a great diversity of statement respecting the source of the endowment and the character of its manifestations. The orthodox Mormons claim that the angels and the Holy Spirit gave the endowments, and that, though the company had been together eight hours, everything was conducted with the greatest solemnity and the best of order preserved. Two Mormons present on the occasion, —William E. McLellin and John Corrill—the former an apostle, and the latter a high priest, publish very different statements. McLellin says: " As to the endowment in Kirtland, I state positively, it was no endowment from God. Not only myself was not endowed, but no other man of the five hundred who was present—except it was with wine!"—"True Latter-Day Saints' Herald," vol. 19, p. 437

Corrill says: " The ceremony was first performed upon the first presidency, together with the bishops and their counsellors ; after which the elders in their turn attended to the ceremony, and it was alike upon all occasions. They were to purify their bodies by washing them entirely with pure water, after which they were to wash each other's feet, and anoint each other with oil, pronouncing mutual blessings during the performance. The sacrament was then administered, in which they *partook of the bread and wine freely*, and a report went abroad that some of them got drunk ; as to that, every man must answer for himself."

Since that endowment, " bread and wine," anointings and prophesyings have often cheered the hearts of the elders.

CHAPTER XI.

FIRST GREAT APOSTACY.—Joseph predicts that Brigham will be President of the Church—British Missions projected as a Strategic Measure—One of Joseph's own Counsellors rebels against him—He is proclaimed "a Fallen Prophet"—Troubles again threaten in Missouri.

A CRITICAL period in the existence of the Church was now reached. The endowments had been given and the Temple had been dedicated, yet there was dissatisfaction among the disciples. Their anticipations had not been realized. The spirit of apostacy was abroad. But it was not the faith that so much tried the people as it was Joseph's life. Everyone had his own ideas of what a prophet should be. He was now greatly changed. The humble plough-boy had merged in the Prophet-ruler. The men who had devoted to him their best abilities in the beginning, and had contributed to shape the crude elements of his supernatural creations into form, thought that they had a right to some part in "the kingdom." Joseph saw in them only instruments subordinate to his own success—he was to be the head and front of everything. It was difficult for free-born Americans cradled in democracy to comprehend at once Joseph's theocracy. It takes time for men to strangle their truest instincts. Joseph had none of that experience himself, and he could not appreciate the cost of it in others. All the manliness of his ambitious nature found ample scope in working out what he believed to be his divine mission, and in announcements of faith. Nominally, he accorded the same privileges to his brethren, but practically, it was the very opposite. It was for him to speak; it was for them to obey. He was "the Lord's servant," and they had no right to criticise him. If he erred, "the Lord" could correct him. The man who

dared to suggest was as impious as he who in the ancient Israel-
itish story stretched forth his hand to steady the tottering ark,
and deserved the same punishment—the judgment of Heaven.

It is asserted that when Joseph first saw Brigham Young
he prophesied that " the time would come when Brother Brig-
" ham should preside over the Church." * With such a prediction ringing in his ears, it is not difficult to trace Brigham's
influence with Joseph, from the beginning of their acquaintance, and to see therein laid the foundation of that unchallenged authority which now characterizes his reign in Utah.
Nearly all the leading men during the first years of Mormon
history fell out with Joseph over his personal rule ; but Brigham was among the very few who clung to him. He never—
or, at the farthest, but once only—challenged Joseph's right to
do as he pleased, and he permits none to dispute his own.

But the Saints grew weary, and it was necessary to direct
their attention away from home. So " the Lord " revealed to
Joseph that " in order to save His Church " a foreign mission
must be improvised, and Great Britain was selected as the new
field of labour. Republicanism was at war with theocracy, and
it became necessary to seek an element that had been cradled
with kings.

The Apostles Heber C. Kimball and Orson Hyde were accordingly chosen to introduce the Gospel to Europe. On the
12th of June, 1837, they left Kirtland, and thus began the first
foreign mission. These apostles were accompanied by other
elders, and in a few months were successful in converting great
numbers in England, and in doing so saved the Church in
America.

During the summer, Joseph, accompanied by Sidney Rigdon and Thomas B. Marsh, the President of the Twelve
Apostles, made a tour through Canada, preaching and visiting
the Saints, while Brigham Young remained at home. But
troubles began to loom up again in Missouri, and apostacy
was coming to a crisis in Ohio.

On the return of Joseph from Canada, a special conference

* Some old Mormons relate that they heard Joseph also say some time before
his death : " If Brigham Young ever becomes President of the Church, he will lead
it to hell." Not a few believe the latter prediction to be as correct as the former.

The Apostle Heber C. Kimball.

was assembled at Kirtland, on the 3rd of September. Everything was in confusion; the devil was ravaging the flock. Frederick G. Williams, one of Joseph's counsellors, and the third man in the kingdom, was in rebellion; Luke Johnson, Lyman E. Johnson, and John F. Boynton, three of the Apostles, "fell away." At the same time, Brigham Young was exceedingly energetic, and attempted to neutralize the influence of the apostates. The Missourians in Clay county had also become dissatisfied with the Mormons, and asked them to leave the county. They were obliged to move, and scattered into Carroll, Davies, and Caldwell counties, founding in the latter the City of Far West.

Joseph and Sidney visited Missouri in October, and remained there some weeks, counselling and encouraging the brethren and sisters in building up Zion. At the same time it was thought best to proceed no further with the great Temple in Jackson county.

During Joseph's absence in the West, the leading "apos-"tates" in Ohio proclaimed him "a fallen prophet" and his followers heretics, and a warm time appeared to await him wherever he went.

5

CHAPTER XII.

THE PROPHET BECOMES A BANKER.—Apostates and Capitalists bring him to Grief—Sidney Rigdon's Interesting View of a " Circulating Medium "—He assures Mr. Jones that the Bank-notes were never intended for Redemption—The Kirtland Safety Society Bank repudiated—Joseph and Sidney fly to Missouri—Pursued by Armed Men—Extraordinary Escapes—" The Lord " protects them.

SOME time preceding the apostacy, the Prophet had added to his responsibilities that of being the cashier of a Safety Society Bank, of which his counsellor Sidney Rigdon was President. In connection with this some very hard stories are told about Joseph and the leading men, and Joseph is in turn as severe against the " apostates " and the Gentiles who conspired to break his bank and get him into trouble. The bank was not a success; indeed, it was altogether a failure, and Joseph and Sidney were obliged, through the operations of " apostates " and bankers, to leave very hurriedly for Missouri —" between two days." The evening of the 12th of January, 1838, found them on the wing; and Brigham had left precipitately three weeks before that. The necessity for flight was somewhat pressing, as the historian states that the cashier and president made about sixty miles the first night, and " their " enemies " continued the pursuit for about two hundred miles. The pursuers were often close upon the fugitives, and sometimes passed them on the road. On one occasion they stopped with them all night in the same road-side inn, with only a thin partition between the two parties, and once they even overtook and examined them without recognizing their features. For these wonderful escapes " the Lord " is duly credited. He protected His servants, and blinded their pursuers.

This banking episode in Kirtland clearly shows the confidence which the "outside world" placed in the integrity of the Mormon leader at that early period of his life. The notes of the Safety Society Bank were received with greater confidence than most of the bank paper then in circulation in the West. The banks in Ohio, Pennsylvania, Indiana, and Illinois no longer paid in specie, but were doing a "suspended business." The Safety Society paper obtained a wide circulation; for, however fanatical and deluded the people might be considered, their honesty had up to this time never been questioned.

"The names of Joseph Smith as cashier and Sidney Rigdon as president were signed to the beautifully engraved bank-notes. As these men professed to be prophets of the Lord, having daily communion with angels, with Christ, and even with God himself, no one supposed that they would lend themselves to a fraudulent issue of bank paper. Those who saw the notes to which their names were attached supposed the bank to be simply a savings institution in which the Saints could deposit their earnings, while they would be invested so as to pay interest, and that the notes represented actual money in bank, or the paper of good men."*

This kindly supposition was further extended, and the Safety Society Bank paper became a favourite medium of circulation with Saint and sinner. Bankers took it freely, and the people preferred it because it was "safe," while so much other paper at that period was of very doubtful character. The outfitting of the Eastern Saints for Zion in the west, the purchasing of cattle, wagons, farming and mechanical tools, and everything needed for a new home, afforded the paper, under such a favourable reception, an extensive circulation. But a crisis came which the Mormon historian charges to the wiles of the devil aided by "apostates," the bankers being the direct instruments. Joseph accused the bankers of having combined to crush him, and the bankers claimed that they only wanted to be assured of the ability of the Safety Society Bank to meet its liabilities before they received too much of its paper, which was surely not a very unreasonable precaution.

The Pittsburg bankers deputed a Mr. Jones, one of their number, to visit Kirtland, and with a well-packed satchel he found himself in due time in the presence of the inspired bankers. Mr. Jones's recital of that interview is very touching.—

* Extract from a letter by a Pittsburg banker to the Author.

He first enquired about the success of "the Lord's cause," and
how it prospered everywhere, and evinced considerable interest
in the Latter-Day religion in general. This he claims was a
matter of courtesy, but it was unfortunate, for on opening the
satchel and producing huge bundles of the Safety Society
Bank paper, the whole proceeding was regarded by brother
Rigdon, the President, as "the march of a wolf in sheep's
"clothing," which opinion Sidney unhesitatingly announced
to the astonished Jones. Brother Rigdon must have very
largely mingled humour with his severity, for he is reported to
have told the Pittsburg banker that the paper had been put
out as a "circulating medium for the accommodation of the
"people," that it would be an injury to them for the paper to
come home and be redeemed, that it could only benefit them by
remaining out. The bank redeemed nothing. Mr. Jones pleaded
for a deviation from the rule in his case, and pledged himself
never to return with Safety Society paper, if only this time
he could get the cash or convertible paper of other banks.
Sidney was, however, faithful to the programme of the bank,
exasperating Mr. Jones with the information that they "had
"never asked him or anyone else to take the paper," and referring him to that important epoch when the profession to
which Mr. Jones belonged were scourged and driven out of the
Temple at Jerusalem. Mr. Jones returned to Pittsburg, and
when the bankers heard the above report from their representative, no more of the Safety Society Bank paper was taken.
Silence was maintained for a time, and, acting out the saying
"dog eat dog," much of the unredeemed paper was put out, but
at the same time much of it was forced back into the hands
of the bankers by those who received it from them.

That Joseph Smith and Sidney Rigdon contemplated in
that experiment a deliberate swindle, is very inharmonious
with their life and programme at that period. The large
number of Saints who were looking to them for direction, suggested the bank as a protective measure against the frequent
losses by the failures of that period; and with the credit of a
good name, which is admitted on all sides to have existed, the
Prophet established the Kirtland Bank. Had not trouble
arisen among themselves, and the usual amount of detraction

ensued, which weakened the confidence of the Saints, and led them to present their own bank paper for redemption, it is very probable that Mr. Jones would have got his money. But this precautionary combination of bankers at Pittsburg, coming as it did at an untoward moment, killed the Prophet's institution. As some one must be abused, it is very natural that the responsibility of that inevitable fiasco should be relegated to the shoulders of his Satanic Majesty. It was well known to the Saints that he was the guilty party, and was trying to break up "the kingdom."

The Prophet-Bankers on the Wing.

All these troubles were spoken of by Joseph as "persecu-"tion." Of his flight from Kirtland he writes:

"A new year dawned upon the Church at Kirtland in all the bitterness of the spirit of Apostate Mobocracy, which continued to rage and grow hotter and hotter, until Elder Rigdon and myself were obliged to flee from its deadly influence, as did the apostles and prophets of old, and as Jesus said, ' When they persecute you in one city, flee ye to another ; ' and on the evening of the 12th of January, about 10 o'clock, we left Kirtland on horseback, to escape mob violence which was about to burst upon us, under the colour of legal process to cover their hellish designs, and save themselves from the just judgment of the law. The weather was extremely cold, and we were obliged to secrete ourselves sometimes, to elude the grasp of our pursuers, who continued their race more than two hundred miles from Kirtland, armed with pistols, etc., seeking our lives."

After this, the Prophet never returned to Kirtland, but he appointed an agent for the settlement of his own unfinished business in Ohio. In different parts of his autobiography he publishes cards from business men expressive of their satisfaction at the manner in which the agent had adjusted the accounts. The Prophet disclaimed any responsibility for the failure of the bank, and charged one of the brethren with dishonesty, which produced this result. He was evidently proud of a good commercial name.

Before this period, and when all was pleasant in Ohio, it was announced that " the Lord " had accepted the Saints there and had established his name in Kirtland for the salvation of the nations. But this honour was short-lived. Kirtland was soon abandoned for ever. Joseph and Sidney as fugitives took their families with them to Missouri, and overtook Brigham Young and his family before they reached the promised land. The experience of the prophets and apostles had been anything but pleasant in the East ; it was destined to be worse in the West. They arrived in Far West on the 12th of March, 1838, and in less than a month they had to cut off from the Church two of the most important witnessess of the Book of Mormon.

CHAPTER XIII.

CUTTING OFF APOSTLES.—Witnesses of the Book of Mormon expelled from the Church—Joseph denounces the "Lord's Chosen" as "Blacklegs, Thieves, Liars, and Counterfeiters"—More Apostles dethroned—The Prophet locates the Garden of Eden in Missouri—It was there that Adam and Eve sported in Innocence—More Trouble looming—Rigdon's famous Declaration of Independence.

ON the 6th of April, 1838, the eighth anniversary of that organization in which he so much rejoiced, and was so much favoured, Oliver Cowdrey was destined to find himself cast out of the Church and consigned to the tender mercies of Satan. After those extraordinary experiences with heavenly beings had all been rehearsed, Oliver still persisted in rebellion, and was formally " turned over to the buffetings of the devil." But Cowdery was not alone ; another rebel was found in the person of David Whitmer, the second witness to the Book of Mormon. Martin Harris, the third witness of this remarkable production, had already been consigned to the infernal regions, and thus the excommunication of Oliver Cowdery and David Whitmer during the conference completed the work of apostacy among those who had seen the angel, and heard the testimony about " the plates," and their translation into English. From the beginning, the devil had desired that he might possess these " witnesses," and at last " the Lord " made the transfer, with the understanding and instruction that his Sable Majesty was to heap upon the rebels all the agony under which they could wriggle.

The modern prophets trench pretty closely upon " Anathe-"ma Maranatha " of the ancient Sanhedrim, and evidently consider that it is the correct thing. A Mormon Bishop cursing

an " apostate " is a perfect realization of the prayer of Burns's
" Holy Willie : "

> " Curse thou his basket and his store,
>   Kail and potatoes.
>
> .   .   .   .   .
>
> Thy strong right hand, Lord, make it bare
>   Upo' their heads ;
> Lord, weigh it down, and dinna spare
>   For their misdeeds."

From this time Oliver Cowdery and David Whitmer are
handed down to posterity in Mormon Church history charged
with being " connected with a gang of counterfeiters, thieves,
" liars, and blacklegs of the deepest dye," and with " cheating
" and defrauding the Saints." In the formal list of charges
for Cowdery's excommunication was another : " Seeking to
" destroy the character of Joseph Smith, Jr., by falsely insinu-
" ating that he was guilty of adultery." Martin Harris had
previously been catalogued with " negroes who wear white
" skins," and he and his associates were " so far beneath con-
" tempt that a notice of them would be far too great a sacrifice
" for a gentleman to make." * Hyrum Smith, the brother of
the Prophet, after his deliverance from a Missouri prison,
charges the brothers Oliver and Lyman Cowdery with going
to his house while he was " held in durance vile," and robbing
him of his valuables under the cloak of friendship. Such were
the men whom " the Lord " had selected as witnesses to the
divinity of the Book of Mormon.

During this conference the apostles who were in rebellion
at Kirtland were formally excommunicated, viz. : Luke Johnson, Lyman E. Johnson, and John F. Boynton. Another apostle
was added to the list of apostates—William E. McLellin ; and
William Smith, another apostle, and brother of the Prophet,
had a narrow escape from expulsion. This was a trying time
to the Saints, and many left the Church, but Joseph was in-
domitable. It was during his severest trials and in the face of
approaching danger that Joseph displayed the greatest faith in
his mission. At this moment he saw the shadows of coming

* " History of Joseph Smith."

events that would try men's souls, but he would make no compromise with "the rebels." He was resolved on victory or
martyrdom. His confidence was heroic: in himself he had
unbounded faith.

Joseph saw the necessity of a new gathering place. Kirtland was gone; a few of the Saints only were conditionally
tolerated in Jackson county, and in the other counties of Missouri where they had taken refuge a continuance of peace was
very doubtful. A new city was to be laid out on the north
side of Grand River, twenty miles distant from Far West.
The brethren called the new location Spring Hill, but Joseph
had a revelation naming it *Adam-Ondi-Ahman.**

There has always been some mystery about the exact location of the Garden of Eden, the early residence of the innocent progenitors of the human race—Darwin aside—but it has
generally been supposed to have been somewhere on the eastern continent. On the occasion of naming this new gathering place, Joseph was informed that the Garden of Eden, with
all the rich incidents of the morning of creation, was localized
in Jackson county, Missouri, and that this new spot selected
for the gathering of the Saints and named Adam-Ondi-Ahman
was the identical region where Adam and Eve betook themselves after the expulsion from the historical garden. Joseph
also gives with considerable minuteness a statement about a
great gathering or conference held there of the leading men
of Adam's posterity about three years preceding the departure
of that first patriarch from this mundane sphere. In that particular valley the Saints were now commanded to gather in
the last days; but this heavenly intelligence changed in nothing the hearts of the Missourians toward the Mormons.

Governor Dunklin had advised the expelled Mormons to
seek redress in the courts for their losses in Jackson county;
and, ever ready to assert their claims, the Saints failed not to
follow the suggestion thus offered. The consequent prosecution of some of the leading "mobocrats" was a constantly-
recurring element of strife, which, added to the growing political influence of the Saints, afforded politicians and anti-
Mormons the opportunity of combining against the com-

* "The valley of God in which Adam blessed his children."

mon enemy, as they claimed to regard the followers of the
Prophet.

The Kirtland Colony was now entirely broken up, and the
eastern Saints poured into Missouri. Proud of their growing
strength, and chafing under past persecutions, Sidney Rigdon
in the Fourth-of-July oration delivered a Mormon " Declaration
" of Independence," informing the Missourians that they must
cease their oppression and persecution of " the Saints of the
" Most High God." It was the enunciation of an enthusiast's
programme, and just such a foolish speech as the Missourians
wanted to hear. It set the country on fire, and hostile action
was resolved upon. The anti-Mormons were waiting for a pretext, and Sidney furnished it. His language on that occasion
is thus reported :

"We take God and all the holy angels to witness this day that we
warn all men in the name of Jesus Christ, to come on us no more for ever.
The man, or the set of men, who attempts it does so at the expense of
their lives. And the mob that comes on us to disturb us, it shall be between us and them a war of *extermination*, for we will follow them till *the
last drop of blood is spilled*, or else they will have to exterminate us ; for
we will carry the seat of war to *their own houses* and their own *families*,
and one part or the other shall be utterly destroyed. Remember it, then,
all men ! . . . "No man shall be at liberty to come into our streets, to
threaten us with mobs, for if he does he shall atone for it before he leaves
the place, neither shall he be at liberty to vilify and slander any of us, for
suffer it we will not in this place.* We therefore take all men to record
this day, as did our fathers, and we pledge this day to one another, our
fortunes, our lives, and our sacred honours, to be delivered from the persecutions which we have had to endure for the last nine years, or nearly
that. Neither will we indulge any man or set of men in instituting vexatious law suits against us, to cheat us out of our just rights; if they
attempt it, we say *woe* be unto them. We this day, then, proclaim ourselves
free, with a purpose and a determination that can never be broken, No,
never ! No, never ! ! No, never ! ! !"

* This oration is known as " Sidney's Salt Sermon." It was inspired by vengeance, and breathed not only death to the Missourians, but also to the brethren
who, still having control of their reason, dissented from the fire-and-sword doctrine
that was preached against their neighbours. These were immediately designated ·
" apostates," and for their special edification Sidney chose the text : " If the salt
have lost its savour, it is thenceforth good for nothing but to be cast out and trodden under foot of men." That he meant this as literally as language could express,
there was no doubt. The people who heard it, and to whom it was addressed by
implication, so understood it, and in such a neighbourhood and at a time when

The elections were at hand, and the old settlers saw in the incoming Mormons from the East a repetition of the tradition-ary story of Aaron's rod, and they resolved not to be swallowed up or exterminated as Sidney threatened.*

Danitism was taught—whether by the authority of Joseph Smith or without, it matters not—the terrible dread of vengeance was all the same. The Mormons have had whispered into their ears that the story of Ananias and Sapphira " falling down dead " at the rebuke of Peter was no work of the heavens, as is generally supposed, but that " the young men " who were with Peter literally " trod them under their feet " till their bowels gushed out. Sidney's Salt Sermon had all that significance.

* Brigham Young, during the trial of Sidney, some years afterwards, said: " Elder Rigdon was the prime cause of our troubles in Missouri, by his Fourth-of-July oration."—" Times and Seasons," Vol. 5, page 667.

The Apostle Woodruff calls the oration a " flaming speech, which had a ten-dency to bring persecution upon the whole church, especially the head of it." —" Times and Seasons," p. 698.

CHAPTER XIV.

WAR COMMENCES.—Affidavits made against the Prophet—The Mormons and the Mob resort to Arms—The Governor calls out the State Militia—Joseph and Sidney propose to become Lawyers—The Mormon Settlements attacked—Houses burned—Women and Children forced to flee before an Infuriated Mob—Frightful Cruelties—The Saints fight and retaliate.

ON the 6th of August the election at Gallatin, Davies county, furnished the opportunity for a collision. A Colonel Peniston, who had headed a mob in Clay county against the Mormons, was a candidate for some office in Davies county. In the forenoon of the election he delivered an anti-Mormon speech from the head of a barrel, and " Dick " Welding, one of his admirers, just drunk enough for discussion, attacked Sam Brown, a Mormon. Perry Durphy, another Mormon, essayed the *rôle* of peace-maker, when five or six Missourians suddenly seized him, clubbed him, and sought to kill him.

Abraham Nelson, another Mormon, seeing his brethren in danger, joined in and got served as badly as Durphy. Hiram Nelson flailed around with the butt end of his whip, and did good service. Riley Stewart, another Mormon, reached the head of the redoubtable " Dick " and felled him to the ground. Riley in turn got the general attentions of the Missourians, and was badly injured, when John L. Butler joined in the free fight and brought up the scuffle to a general breathing time. Butler was an earnest man and claimed the right as an American citizen to fight for his liberty as his fathers had done before him. But the authorities of the county urged a withdrawal of the Mormon belligerents from the vicinity of the ballot boxes, as the Missourians were determined that they should not vote. Some wounds had to be dressed, and the Mormons withdrew; but the country was now aroused and the Missourians gathered with arms. Thus began the troubles in Missouri that eventually resulted in the imprisonment of the Mormon leaders, and the final expulsion of the Saints from that State.

None of the Mormons were killed, but some of them were badly wounded, while several of the Missourians "had their "skulls cracked," and two were reported dead. The Mormon historian states that "about one hundred and fifty Missourians

Mormon Troubles in Missouri begin.

"warred against from six to twelve of our brethren who fought "like lions;" to which Joseph's gushing soul ejaculated: "Blessed be the memory of those few brethren who contended "so strenuously for their constitutional rights and religious "freedom against such an overwhelming force of despera"does."

The following day, Joseph, accompanied by some of the leading Mormons, and followed by brethren from different parts of the country, rode out to learn the facts of this affray. They stopped with brother Colonel Wight over night, and next morning came up to the scene of trouble. They then called upon a Justice of the Peace, Adam Black, to learn how he stood in respect to the question of mobocracy and constitutional right. He had not given them satisfaction in his previous relations, and they now wanted to know "whether he "was their friend or enemy, whether he would administer the "law in justice; and they politely requested him to sign an

" agreement of peace." Adam handed them a satisfactory document, but they did not believe in his sincerity, and in that they were not disappointed.

Affidavits were immediately made by the orator Peniston, Adam Black, and others, charging Joseph Smith and his leading men with collecting and directing a large body of armed men in Davies county, " whose movements," according to Peniston, " were of a highly insurrectionary character . . " to take vengeance for some injuries, or imaginary injuries, " done to some of their friends, and to intimidate and drive " from the county all the old citizens, and possess themselves " of their lands, or to force such as do not leave to come into " their measures and submit to their dictation."

The country was greatly agitated, and in a few days Joseph was waited upon by a sheriff from Davies county. That official, learning that he could not act out of his own county, the writ was laid aside. Before the end of the month in which the trouble commenced, Adam Black had made affidavit before a justice of the peace of his own county, declaring that—

" A hundred and fifty-four armed men had surrounded his house and family, and threatened him with instant death if he did not sign a certain instrument of writing binding himself, as a Justice of the Peace for said county of Davies, not to molest the people called Mormons ; and threatened the lives of myself and other individuals, and did say they intended to make every citizen sign such obligation, and further said they intended to have satisfaction for abuse they had received on the Monday previous, and they could not submit to the laws."

Whether the accusations on either side were true or false, the ball was now in motion. Governor Boggs issued an order to Major-General D. R. Atchison, 3rd Division Missouri Militia, to raise immediately four hundred mounted men, armed and equipped as infantry or riflemen, as " a precautionary meas- " ure " to aid in suppressing Indian disturbances on the frontier, or to act where wanted in Caldwell, Davies, and Carroll counties.

The excitement increased, and extravagant rumours were in circulation. Joseph Smith and Colonel Lyman Wight were the particular objects of attention. It was commonly reported that they had said they would not be taken by the officers of

the law, and the whole of Upper Missouri was in an uproar
and confusion.

In the midst of this, the Prophet sent for General Atchison
to come and counsel with him.   This meeting resulted in Joseph very adroitly employing General Atchison and his partner, General Doniphan, as his lawyers and counsellors-at-law ;
and the same day Joseph and Sidney Rigdon commenced the
study of law under these distinguished gentlemen, who kindly
encouraged the Prophet and his counsellor with the hope of
being admitted to the bar in the course of twelve months if
they were diligent in application.

Acting on the advice of General Atchison, Joseph and
Lyman Wight volunteered to be tried by Judge Austin A.
King, who held them to bail in the sum of $500 each.   But
this did not satisfy the Missourians in Davies county, and the
gathering of armed men continued.

The anti-Mormon Justice of the Peace, Black, and Circuit
Judge, King, represented to the Governor that no writs could
be served on the Mormons without military assistance ; whereupon his Excellency issued orders to General Atchison to aid
the civil authorities in Davies county.   Brigadier-General
Doniphan was also called into the field, commanding the 1st
Brigade, 3rd Division, Missouri Militia.

By the presence of these Generals the mob was held in
check, and the Mormons renewed their assurances of readiness
to meet the demands of the law.   In the mean time the Saints
were everywhere preparing for defence.

General Atchison reported to the Governor, on the 17th of
September, the general condition of the county ; that there was
a great deal of excitement, but that the troops under his command would be no longer required if the mob would disperse.
The Governor, acting upon previous information from other
parties, ordered General S. D. Lucas, of the Fourth Division,
forward with an additional four hundred mounted men to the
scene of difficulty to coöperate with General Atchison.   Similar orders were issued to Major-Generals Lewis Bolton, John
B. Clark, and Thomas D. Grant.   It was evident that the
Governor had a plan of his own.

On the 20th, General Atchison disbanded the troops, with

the exception of two companies under Brigadier-General
Parks, that were deemed necessary to be retained in service
till the excitement had entirely subsided. The mob were dis-
persing and the Mormons were returning to their homes. On
hearing this, the Governor stopped the further advance of the
reinforcements to General Atchison, and everything seemed to
indicate peace. The Mormons in Davies county, where the
trouble had begun, were willing to leave that county and were
negotiating for the sale of their property. Joseph and his
associates were again at their religious duties, preaching, or-
daining missionaries, and building up Zion; and General Atchison was assuring the Governor that " he had no doubt his
" Excellency was deceived by the exaggerated statements of
" designing or half-crazy men."

Dr. Austin, of Carroll county, who was the leader of the
mob in Davies county, visited the Mormons at De Witt, a
very small settlement in Carroll county, and could not resist
the temptation to provoke a conflict.

Immediately upon hearing the report of renewed hostilities,
General Parks hastened to the scene of trouble and found on
arrival Dr. Austin with between two and three hundred men,
well armed and in possession of a piece of cannon. Colonel
Hinkle, a Mormon officer, had reached there with three or four
hundred brethren, but General Parks had to report to General
Atchison that he could do nothing. He had issued orders for
more troops, but the Missourians paid no attention to him, and
those that he had could not be relied upon. In the history of
the Church, Joseph alleges that the General was more favourably disposed towards the mob than towards the Saints. The
" notorious Bogart " was one of the captains, and the men under him were eager to join the mob. The closing paragraph
of General Parks's report to General Atchison rather favours
Joseph's impressions of unfriendliness :

" Nothing seems so much in demand here (to hear the Carroll county
men talk) as Mormon scalps ; as yet they are scarce. I believe Hinkle with
the present force and position will beat Austin with five hundred of his
troops. The Mormons say they will die before they will be driven out, etc.
As yet, they have acted on the defensive, as far as I can learn. It is my
settled opinion the Mormons will have no rest until they leave ; whether
they will or not, time only can tell."

The easy manner with which General Parks treats the demand for "Mormon scalps," and the unconcerned notice of the probability of a fight, while he knew these poor people were hemmed in and prospectively doomed to starvation, if not overwhelmed by the constantly increasing numbers of the mob, indicate anything but a lively interest in their welfare.

The Saints suffered severely. Their provisions were entirely exhausted, and several of the men perished from starvation, while the mob subsisted upon their cattle and the products of their fields. With no prospect of aid from the Governor, the Mormons listened to the proposition of the mob that they would purchase their property if they would leave the county. After ten days' siege the agreement was made, the property was appraised, and the next day the Mormons collected about seventy wagons and started for Caldwell county, and they had no sooner got ready to leave than the mob began to harass and fire upon them. On their first night's encampment one of the sisters died from exposure soon after confinement, and was buried without a coffin, by the wayside. It was a terrible time of suffering, and they reached Caldwell almost entirely destitute of everything.

The same mob hastened to Davies county to assist their friends in expediting the departure of the Mormons from that county also. It was now very evident to the lawless banditti that the authorities would not interpose in behalf of the Mormons. To the petition of the latter, the Governor replied that it was an affair between the mob and the Mormons and they might fight it out.

General Doniphan, on learning that eight hundred mobbers were marching towards a Mormon settlement in Davies county, ordered Colonel Hinkle to raise a force in Caldwell and help the Saints till the militia could be raised and reach that place.

The same cruel work that had marked the operations of the mob at De Witt was reënacted at Adam-Ondi-Ahman. The houses outside of the settlement were first attacked and some of them were burned down; the horses and cattle were driven away and stolen, and a general sacking and destruction of everything ensued. To add to the bitterness of their situation,

6

there was a snow-storm for two days, and the homeless terrified women and children had to battle with it in their flight to
their friends in Adam-Ondi-Ahman. It was a woeful sight,
for they brought nothing with them, and were only too glad
to escape with their lives. One poor woman, the wife of Joseph's brother, Don Carlos, is mentioned by the historian as
fleeing before the savage mob with two helpless babes in her
arms, and forced to wade Grand River with her sacred charge
in order to reach the settlement, while her house was being
burned down. Her husband was absent at the time on a
preaching mission in Tennessee.

At this period the Mormons were accused by the Mobocrats
of having burned some of their houses, but the former strenuously deny the accusation and charge it to the strategy of the
mob when they saw they could not drive them out from their
possessions. This it is alleged was done for the purpose of
raising "the hue and cry" that "the Mormons were burning
" and destroying all before them." Some log-houses certainly
were burned, whoever did it, and the whole country was
aroused against the supposed incendiaries.

During the 2nd Session of the 26th Congress, a document
of nearly fifty pages was published by order of the Senate
[No. 189] giving the testimony taken before the judge of the
fifth Judicial Circuit of the State of Missouri, on the trial of
Joseph Smith, Junr., and others for high treason and other
crimes against that State. This document asserts that the
Mormon leaders were guilty of the grossest outrages upon the
Gentiles. Burning their houses and stealing from them were
common occurrences; and threatenings of death to apostates,
or those who would not take part in the general fight against
the Missourians, were the teachings of the pulpit orators. With
such an array of circumstantial evidence, confirmed by a variety of persons—Mormons and anti-Mormons—it is difficult
not to believe that the few leading men around Joseph Smith,
particularly Lyman Wight and Sidney Rigdon, were not thorough fanatics and guilty of gross crimes; and if Joseph was
less culpable it was due to his greater realization of responsibility and better judgment. Lyman Wight seems to have
possessed all the characteristics of a religious "jay-hawker"—

a sort of mixture of fanatic and "Border ruffian." He was doubtless the inspiring deity of Joseph's revelation, that called into existence Zion's Camp and "the Lord's" armies. He was rightly designated "the Wild Ram of the Mountains." Sidney Rigdon was an eloquent, full-fledged fanatic, ever ready to roast heretics and annihilate all who opposed the wild flights of his imagination and ambition—a most dangerous man in the midst of such a people as he had around him in Missouri.

CHAPTER XV.

THE CHURCH IN DANGER.—Apostles apostatize—Marsh and Hyde make Affidavits against the Prophet—Charge him with aiming to be a Second Mohammed—
The Danite Band—Its Name and Origin—Dr. Avard's Statements—The Doctor's Speech—Joseph denies the Paternity of the Band—Great Excitement
throughout the State—A Sensational Report—More Fighting—The Apostle Patten
killed—The Saints to be rooted out.

AFTER the dispersion of the mob, Joseph returned to Far
West in hopes of finding rest; but there was none for him.
Troubles were gathering thickly around him, but still he was
confident that "the Lord was on his side." When he saw Far
West literally crowded with refugees, he remembered that
"the word of the Lord" had commanded the Saints to gather
into the cities some months before, but they had been slow to
obey.* He did not relish the hasty fulfilment of the commandment, but even in the midst of discomforts and sufferings
it was something to know that "the Lord" had willed it.

Affidavits of the most inflammatory kind were now made
by the leading mobocrats. Upper Missouri was on fire, and
nothing but the utter expulsion of the Saints from the State
would satisfy their enemies. At this very moment of trial,
when fidelity was but a common virtue, some of the leading
Mormons deserted Joseph, and made affidavit against him. It
is claimed that Thomas B. Marsh, the first President of the
Twelve Apostles, and Orson Hyde, another of the apostles
who made these affidavits against him, were in peril of their

* This is very characteristic of the Mormon Prophets. The people are always
in the wrong. In this particular, Brigham Young is still worse than Joseph Smith
When any of his schemes fail [and many have failed], the responsibility is always
saddled upon the people—"Had they hearkened to counsel all would have been
"right."

lives when they signed the document, and this was probably true, for it was a very unsafe time ; but there is no evidence to show that either Marsh or Hyde was in any more jeopardy than the rest of the Mormons, and could not have been spared as well as any of the brethren who bravely faced death rather than deny their faith.

As a page of history, the affidavits are interesting:

AFFIDAVIT OF THOMAS B. MARSH.

"They have among them a company, considered true Mormons, called the Danites, who have taken an oath to support the heads of the Church in all things that they say or do, whether right or wrong. Many, however, of this band are much dissatisfied with this oath, as being against moral and religious principles. On Saturday last, I am informed by the Mormons, that they had a meeting at Far West at which they appointed a company of twelve, by the name of the Destruction Company, for the purpose of burning and destroying, and that if the people of Buncombe came to do mischief upon the people of Caldwell, and committed depredations upon the Mormons, they were to burn Buncombe ; and if the people of Clay and Ray made any movement against them, this destroying company were to burn Liberty and Richmond.

"The plan of said Smith, the Prophet, is to take this State ; and he professes to his people to intend taking the United States, and ultimately the whole world. This is the belief of the Church, and my own opinion of the Prophet's plans and intentions. The Prophet inculcates the notion, and it is believed by every true Mormon, that Smith's prophecies are superior to the laws of the land. I have heard the Prophet say that he would yet tread down his enemies, and walk over their dead bodies ; that if he was not let alone he would be a second Mohammed to this generation,* and that he would make it one gore of blood from the Rocky

* It is somewhat singular that Robert Southey, the Poet Laureate of England, should, thirteen months before the organization of the Mormon Church, have in his "Colloquies " put the following words into the mouth of Sir Thomas More:

"America is in more danger from religious fanaticism. The Government there, not thinking it necessary to provide religious instruction for the people in any of the new States, the prevalence of superstition, and that perhaps in some wild and terrible shape, may be looked for as one likely consequence of this great and portentous omission. An Old Man of the Mountain might find dupes and followers as readily as the All-friend Jemima ; and the next Aaron Burr who seeks to carve a kingdom for himself out of the overgrown territories of the Union, may discern that fanaticism is the most effective weapon with which ambition can arm itself ; that the way for both is prepared by that immorality which the want of religion naturally and necessarily induced, and that camp-meetings may be very well directed to forward the designs of military prophets. Were there another Mohammed to arise, there is no part of the world where he would find more scope or fairer opportunity than in that part of the Anglo-American Union into which the older States

Mountains to the Atlantic Ocean ; that like Mohammed, whose motto in treating for peace was 'the Alcoran or the Sword,' so should it be eventually with us, 'Joseph Smith or the Sword.' These last statements were made during the last summer. The number of armed men at Adam-Ondi-Ahman was between three and four hundred.   THOMAS B. MARSH.

"Sworn to and subscribed before me, the day herein written.
                                        "HENRY JACOBS,
                                        "J. P., Ray County, Missouri.
"RICHMOND, MISSOURI, *October* 24, 1838."

AFFIDAVIT OF ORSON HYDE.

"The most of the statements in the foregoing disclosure I know to be true ; the remainder I believe to be true.   ORSON HYDE.
"RICHMOND, *October* 24, 1838.

"Sworn to and subscribed before me, on the day above written.
                                        "HENRY JACOBS, J. P."

To these affidavits is appended a "certificate" of seven persons, a "committee on the part of the citizens of Ray "county," who assure the world that Marsh was President of the Twelve Apostles, that Hyde was one of the Twelve, that they had left the Church, "and abandoned the faith of the "Mormons from a conviction of their immorality and im-"piety."

It mattered little whether there were a word of truth or not in these affidavits, they served the purpose of inflaming the Missourians, and they furnish the reader with the actual thoughts of the people about the purposes and programme of the modern Prophet. There is much in the first part of the document that sounds like truth ; for it would be very strange if the Mormons had not organized some means for making reprisals. Whatever might have been the commencement of the war in Missouri, at that date the Mormons had only the option of self-defence, butchery, or banishment. With mobocracy that had neither respected the virtue of women, the innocence of children, nor the helplessness of age, the Mormons would

continually discharge the restless part of their population, leaving laws and Gospel to overtake it if they can, for in the march of modern colonization both are left behind."

A prediction as early fulfilled as this was would have made Joseph a great Prophet.

have been despicable if they had done less. The rest of the document is such extravagant nonsense that sober people could well have afforded to laugh at it; but, to the excited populace who received it as true, it was considered to be a full justification of and incitement to the annihilation of the Saints.

Much has been written about the existence of a Danite Band among the Mormons. It is said to be composed of reliable men who are ever ready to "take off" inimical persons, and plunder or destroy the property of the offenders. Marsh makes affidavit to the fact of its existence in Missouri, but Joseph denies that the Church had any such organization. He says that at one time a certain Dr. Sampson Avard did plan the formation of such a band, and for the purposes stated by Marsh, but "when a knowledge of Avard's rascality came to the Presi- "dency of the Church, he was cut off."

At or about the time of Marsh's statement, Dr. Avard was in full fellowship with Joseph. He was with the Prophet at the house of Adam Black, the Justice of the Peace, and introduced him to that dignitary. He was unquestionably believed by the Mormons to be in the confidence of "the heads of the "Church." He organized the brethren into companies of tens and fifties, appointed captains over each company, gave "signs" and "grips" by which they should know each other by day or by night, binding themselves by the most sacred oaths to preserve in secrecy their works of darkness.

Every Mormon who realizes, as indeed nearly all of them must, the strict surveillance which "the authorities" exercise over the actions of individuals, will have difficulty in believing that Dr. Avard was alone in the organization of the Danite Band. It is very improbable that he or any other individual could impose upon the Saints to such an extent as to introduce the organizations that are admitted to have existed without some show of authoritative recognition. The historian again charges "Satan" with being in this way "busy in striving to "stir up mischief in the camp of the Saints," but Dr. Avard was more direct and avers that "he had received his authority "from Sidney Rigdon;" and as Avard's projects and Sidney's Declaration of Independence have a strong family resemblance, there is no question that the Doctor thought that he was acting harmoniously in doing as he did, even if it be denied that he was instructed to that effect.

After addressing the Danite companies about the coming glories of the kingdom, the Doctor is reported to have said:

"My brethren, as you have been chosen to be our leading men, our captains to rule over this last Kingdom of Jesus Christ, who have been organized after the ancient order, I have called upon you here to-day to teach you and instruct you in the things that pertain to your duty, and to show you what your privileges are, and what they soon will be. Know ye not, brethren, that it soon will be your privilege to take your respective companies and go out on a scout on the borders of the settlements and take to yourself spoils of the ungodly Gentiles? For it is written, 'The 'riches of the Gentiles shall be consecrated to my people, the house of 'Israel;' and thus waste away the Gentiles by robbing and plundering them of their property; and in this way we will build up the Kingdom of God, and roll forth the little stone that Daniel saw cut out of the mountain without hands until it shall fill the whole earth. For this is the very way that God destines to build up his Kingdom in the last days. If any of us should be recognized, who can harm us? For we will stand by each other and defend one another in all things. If our enemies swear against us, we can swear also. [The captains were confounded at this, but Avard continued.]* Why do you startle at this, brethren? As 'the Lord' liveth, I would swear a lie to clear any of you; and if this would not do, I would put them or him under the sand as Moses did the Egyptian, and in this way we will consecrate much unto 'the Lord,' and build up his Kingdom; and who can stand against us? And if any of us transgress we will deal with him amongst ourselves. And if any of this Danite Society reveals any of these things, I will put him *where the dogs cannot* bite him."

Joseph's explanation of the possibility of such language being addressed to his brethren, even though he says they rejected it, is plausible, but not altogether satisfactory to any one conversant with the history of those times. He charges the Doctor with being ambitious to "become the leader of the people, and "aspiring to rise a mighty conqueror at the expense of the "overthrow of the Church," and who "watched the opportu-"nity with the brethren at a time when mobs oppressed, robbed, "whipped, burned, plundered, and slew, till forbearance seemed "no longer a virtue, and nothing but the grace of God without "measure could support men under such trials."

* The Mormon historian's note—not the Author's.

The intelligent Mormon knows to-day that though there may be no *bona fide* organization called the Danites, there have been in church fellowship, from the days of Avard up to the present, men who have done the deeds charged to the Danites, ready to execute the dirtiest and most diabolical plans that ever human or demoniac vindictiveness could conceive.

Elder John Hyde, in his work upon Mormonism,* published fifteen years ago, believing in the existence of the Danite Band, gives the following suggestion as to the origin of its name:

" When the citizens of Carroll and Davies counties, Mo., began to threaten the Mormons with expulsion in 1838, a ' death society ' was organized under the direction of Sidney Rigdon, and with the sanction of Smith. Its first captain was Captain 'Fearnaught,' alias David Patten, an apostle. Its object was the punishment of the obnoxious. Some time elapsed before finding a suitable name. They desired one that should seem to combine spiritual authority with a suitable sound. Micah iv. 13 furnished the first name: ' Arise and thresh, O daughter of Zion ; for I will ' make thy horn iron and thy hoofs brass ; and thou shalt beat in pieces ' many people ; and I will consecrate their gain unto the Lord of the ' whole earth.' This furnished them with a pretext ; it accurately described their intentions, and they called themselves the 'Daughters of Zion.' Some ridicule was made at these bearded and bloody ' Daughters,' and the name did not sit easily. ' Destroying Angels ' came next ; the ' Big ' fan of the thresher that should thoroughly purge the floor ' was tried and dropped. Genesis xlix. 17 furnished the name that they finally assumed. The verse is quite significant : " Dan shall be a serpent by the way, an ' adder in the path that biteth the horse's heels so that his rider shall fall ' backward.' The ' Sons of Dan ' was the style they adopted, and many have been the times that they have been adders in the path, and many a man has fallen backward and has been seen no more."

Joseph and the Church withdrew fellowship from Avard, his Danite organizations were broken up, his teachings were disavowed ; he shook hands with the mob, and asserted that Danitism in the Church was a fact. That such an organization exists to-day is believed by many, and that such sentiments have been entertained by the fanatical, and have been in some degree executed by the desperate, there are many reasons for believing. Brigham himself contributes the following confirmation :

* " Mormonism ; Its Leaders and Designs," pp. 104–5.

" If men come here and do not behave themselves, they will not only
find the Danites, whom they talk so much about, biting the horses' heels,
but *the scoundrels will find something biting their heels.* In my plain remarks I merely call things by their own names." *

With the documents of such men as Marsh, Hyde, and
others in their possession, the people in Missouri were prepared
to believe every report against the Mormons, and the mob
leaders were not slow to supply sensational rumours. The
following is a fair specimen of the means used to rally the people :

CARROLLTON, MISSOURI, *October 24th,* 1838.

" SIR—We were informed last night by an express from Ray county
that Captain Bogart and all his company, amounting to between fifty and
sixty men, were massacred by the Mormons at Buncombe, twelve miles
north of Richmond, except three. This statement you may rely on as
being true, and last night they expected Richmond to be laid in ashes
this morning. We could distinctly hear cannon, and we know the Mormons had one in their possession. Richmond is about twenty-five miles
west of this place on a straight line. We know not the hour or minute
we will be laid in ashes—our country is ruined—for God's sake give us
assistance as quick as possible.

" Yours, etc.,   SARSHEL WOODS.
                        JOSEPH DICKSON."

Nothing of this kind occurred, nor anything out of which
to fabricate such a report. Up to the date of that communication, Captain Bogart and the Mormons had not met in hostility.

Captain Bogart with a militia company were " ranging "
the northern part of Ray county for the purpose of preventing
any invasion of that county by armed men. He had taken
three Mormon prisoners that morning, together with all the
horses and arms he could reach. News of this was brought to
Far West, and the Mormon county Judge—Higbee—ordered
Colonel Hinkle to send out a company of men to retake the
prisoners and disperse the mob. Captain David W. Patten, the
Mormon apostle, who had earned the title of " Captain Fear-
" naught," with seventy-five volunteers, left Far West at midnight and reached the camp of Bogart on Crooked River before daylight. As a portion of his company advanced, the

* *Deseret News,* vol. 7., p. 143.

picket fired and killed a Mormon. It was yet dark, but the Bogart company had the advantage of position, and the first rays of the rising sun were in their favour. Their fire was well directed, while the Mormons could only see indistinctly westward. Several of the Mormons fell; but Captain Patten rushed forward with the cry of "God and Liberty!" The enemy was routed, but at that instant one of the mob wheeled and shot Patten, who fell, mortally wounded. Three of the Mormons were killed, nine wounded. Captain Bogart lost one man only.

The news of the fight spread like wildfire and with the grossest exaggerations. One of the men under Bogart's command rushed into Lexington with the news that ten of his comrades were killed and the rest taken prisoners, and that Richmond was to be burned that night.* The women and children fled from Richmond, and the fighting men immediately rushed to arms. Runners were dispatched in every direction for men, and an express was forwarded urgently requesting assistance. The Mormons were now represented as "infuriated" "fanatics," and they were to be "exterminated or expelled" "the State en masse."

* When this Bogart first made his appearance he was the leader of a mob, but the mob was organized and became part of the militia, and Bogart became a captain. The dignity of office, however, changed in nothing the nature of the man. On one occasion "Brother" Charles C. Rich, on the part of the Mormons, volunteered under a flag of truce to convey two militia officers, who had been captured, into their own camp. They were met by Bogart, who, while receiving the prisoners, reproached Rich for being concerned in the fight at Crooked River. Rich declined discussion, as at the time his sole duty was the delivery of the officers. As he returned, however, Bogart drew his pistol, and, notwithstanding the white flag was still in Rich's hands, deliberately fired upon him when he had not gone six paces from the place of interview.

Bogart was perfectly capable of causing the circulation of just such rumours as roused the whole State to demand the expulsion of the Mormons.

CHAPTER XVI.

EXPULSION OR EXTERMINATION.—Terrible Excitement throughout Missouri
—The Country in Arms—General Clark placed in Command of the State Militia—
The Governor's Order for the Expulsion of the Saints—Brutality of the Mob—
Horrible Massacre of Unoffending Mormons—Murder of Women and Children—
The Narrative of an Eye-Witness.

On the strength of the representations made in Davies county, the Governor, on the 26th of October, issued an order to General John B. Clark of the First Division, Missouri Militia, to raise four hundred men from each of five divisions of the militia of the State, and take the field with all the trappings and paraphernalia of war. The Governor had not yet heard the story of the reported massacre of Bogart's company. The next day, when the intelligence arrived, upon no other evidence than this report, which subsequently proved to be without a particle of truth, he ordered the expulsion of the Mormons from the State. The following is the official document which he issued :

"HEADQUARTERS MILITIA, CITY OF JEFFERSON, *October 27th*, 1838.

"SIR—Since the order of the morning to you, directing you to cause four hundred mounted men to be raised within your division, I have received, by Amos Rees, Esquire, and Wiley S. Williams, Esquire, one of my *aides*, information of the most appalling character, which changes the whole face of things and places the Mormons in the attitude of open and avowed d•fiance of the laws, and of having made open war upon the people of this State. Your orders are, therefore, to hasten your operations and endeavour to reach Richmond, in Ray county, with all possible speed. The Mormons must be treated as enemies, and *must be exterminated*, or *driven from the State* if necessary for the public good. These outrages are beyond all description. If you can increase your force, you are authorized to do so to any extent you may think necessary. I have just issued orders to Major General Wallock, of Marion county, to raise five hundred men, to march

MASSACRE OF MORMONS AT HAUN'S MILL.

them to the northern part of Davies, and there to unite with General Doniphan, of Clay, who has been ordered with five hundred men to proceed to the same point for the purpose of intercepting the retreat of the Mormons to the north. They have been directed to communicate with you by express; you can also communicate with them if you find it necessary. Instead, therefore, of proceeding, as before directed, to reinstate the citizens of Davies in their homes, you will proceed immediately to Richmond, and there operate against the Mormons. Brigadier-General Parks, of Ray. has been ordered to have four hundred men of his brigade in readiness to join you at Richmond. The whole force will be placed under your command.

"L. W. Boggs, Governor and Commander-in-Chief.

"To General Clark."

The whole country was in a terrible state of excitement, and one by one the *quasi* friends of the Mormons were forced to take sides for them or against them. Some cowardly brethren followed the example of the "apostate" apostles, and that increased the conviction of the Missourians that the Mormons were unfit to live among them. Volunteers rushed to the standard of the militia generals, and mobocracy was now legalized. There were burning and destruction of property everywhere. General Atchison, in the moment of trial, also turned against the Mormons, and, with General Lucas, urged the commander-in-chief to come to the "seat of war" immediately, "for the Mormons had committed outrages which ren-"dered civil war inevitable. They had set the laws of the "country at defiance, and were in open rebellion." Such language from General Atchison, who had before done his utmost to defend Joseph and the Mormons from the attacks of the mob, confirmed more and more their enemies as to the propriety of what was being done, and increased the determination to expel them from the State. Of course the Mormons were not slow to find a reason for the defection of General Atchison —his popularity was at stake. But, if such had been the incentive, it was now too late to change. The Governor had the day before superseded him by the appointment of General Clark to the supreme command, on learning which, some days after, he resigned his command and retired from the war.

General Clark was eminently fitted to carry out the Governor's plans of extermination or expulsion; he was in perfect harmony with his Excellency from the first outbreak of the trouble. General Atchison's first reports, favourable to the Mormons, induced the conclusion that he was unsuited for the radical work that was determined upon. Atchison had seen the facts, and his personal acquaintance with the Mormon leaders had too easily impressed him.

The mob and militia, before General Clark arrived, had in-creased to about twenty-five hundred, and encamped at Rich-mond. He was on his way with about a thousand more. The work to be accomplished was now commanded by the Gover-nor, the men in arms were constituted a militia, and from them there was no mercy to be expected. The tug of war had come and the brutality of vindictiveness had full license. On the 30th of October a body of the militia under the command of Colonel Ashley, said to have been between two and three hun-dred men, began the savage work at Haun's Mills, on Shoal Creek, in the eastern part of Carroll county. This body of men was under the immediate command of Captain Nehemiah Comstock, who had given assurances the previous day that the Mormons there would be protected from the attacks of the mob that were threatening to destroy their property. Com-stock had now received a copy of the Governor's order of exter-mination from the colonel, and with that he commenced the bloody work.

A thrilling statement of this terrible butchery is made by Joseph Young (brother of Brigham), who was an eye-witness. Joseph is a truthful, honest, quiet, unoffending man, esteemed and beloved by Gentile as well as Saint. With his family and others he had just reached the home of the Saints in Missouri, from Kirtland. He had been over three months *en route*, and had not yet reached the " headquarters " of Zion. As he neared the goal of his hopes and prayers, the mob prohibited his ad-vance, and he, with others, temporarily halted at Haun's Mills the day preceding the tragedy. His statement is as follows :

" On Tuesday, the 30th, that bloody tragedy was acted, the scenes of which I will never forget. More than three-fourths of the day had passed in tranquillity as smiling as the preceding one. I think there was no indi-vidual in our company that was apprised of the sudden and awful fate that hung over our heads like an overwhelming torrent which was to change the prospects, the feelings and circumstances of about thirty families. The banks of Shoal Creek on either side teemed with children sporting and playing while their mothers were engaged with domestic employments, and their fathers employed in guarding the mills and other property, while others were engaged in gathering in their crops for their consumption. The weather was very pleasant, the sun shone clear, all was tranquil, and no one expressed any apprehension of the awful crisis that was near us—even at our doors.

"It was about four o'clock, while sitting in my cabin, with my babe in my arms, and my wife standing by my side, the door being open, I cast my eyes on the opposite bank of Shoal Creek, and saw a large company of armed men on horses directing their course towards the mills with all possible speed. As they advanced through the scattering trees that stood on the side of the prairie, they seemed to form themselves into a three-square position, forming a vanguard in front.

"At this moment, David Evans, seeing the superiority of their numbers (there being two hundred and forty of them, according to their own account), swung his hat and cried for peace. This not being heeded, they continued to advance, and their leader, Mr. Nehemiah Comstock, fired a gun, which was followed by a solemn pause of ten or twelve seconds, when all at once they discharged about one hundred rifles, aiming at a blacksmith's shop into which our friends had fled for safety; and charged up to the shop, the cracks of which between the logs were sufficiently large to enable them to aim directly at the bodies of those who had there fled for refuge from the fire of their murderers. There were several families tented in rear of the shop, whose lives were exposed, and amidst a shower of bullets fled to the woods in different directions."

The narrator and others fled and secreted themselves in a thicket of bushes till the militia had retired and darkness concealed them. Of the results of the firing, he says :

"After daylight appeared, some four or five men, with myself, who had escaped with our lives from the horrid massacre, repaired as soon as possible to the mills to learn the condition of our friends, whose fate we had but too truly anticipated. When we arrived at the house of Mr. Haun, we found Mr. Merrick's body lying in rear of the house, Mr. McBride's in front, literally mangled from head to foot. We were informed by Miss Rebecca Judd, who was an eye-witness, that he was shot with his own gun after he had given it up, and then cut to pieces with a corn-cutter by a Mr. Rogers, of Davies county, who keeps a ferry on Grand River, and who has since repeatedly boasted of this act of savage brutality. Mr. York's body we found in the house, and after viewing these corpses, we immediately went to the blacksmith's shop, where we found nine of our friends, eight of whom were already dead ; the other, Mr. Cox, of Indiana, was struggling in the agonies of death, and soon expired. We immediately prepared, and carried them to the place of interment. This last office of kindness due to the relics of the departed was not attended with the customary ceremonies or decency, for we were in jeopardy, every moment expecting to be fired upon by the mob, who we supposed to be lying in ambush waiting for the first opportunity to despatch the remaining few who were providentially preserved from the slaughter of the preceding day. However, we accomplished without molestation this painful task. The place of burying was a vault in the ground, formerly intended for a well, into which we threw the bodies of our friends promiscuously. Among those slain I will mention Sardius Smith, son of Warren Smith, about nine years old, who through fear had crawled under the bellows in the shop. where he remained till the massacre was over, when he was discovered by a Mr. Glaze, of Carroll county, who presented his rifle near the boy's head and literally blowed off the upper part of it. Mr. Stanley, of Carroll county, told me afterwards that Glaze boasted of his fiend-like murder and heroic deed all over the country.

"The number of killed and mortally wounded in this wanton slaughter was eighteen or nineteen. . . . Miss Mary Stedwell, while fleeing, was shot through the hand, and, fainting, fell over a log, into which they shot upwards of twenty balls.

"To finish this work of destruction, this band of murderers, composed of men from Davies, Livingston. Ray, Carroll, and Chariton counties, led by some of the principal men of that section of the upper country. . . . proceeded to rob the houses, wagons, and tents of bedding and clothing; drove off horses and wagons, leaving widows and orphans destitute of the necessaries of life, and even stripped the clothing from the bodies of the slain. According to their own account, they fired seven rounds in this awful butchery, making upwards of sixteen hundred shots at a little company of men about thirty in number, etc., etc."

A younger brother of the boy who was dragged from underneath the bellows, and killed, was wounded in the firing, but lay perfectly still and feigned himself dead. When the mob left, he was the only one that answered to the call of his mother. His father and brother were both lying dead beside him.* He is now in Utah, a very respectable citizen.

* The mother of this young man, at a recent meeting of Mormon women in Salt Lake City, related substantially the same story, and added that she aided to consign seventeen of the bodies into a dry, deep well, " rather than leave the dead to the fiends who had murdered them."

CHAPTER XVII.

THE PROPHET RESOLVED TO FIGHT IT OUT.—Faith struggles with Fate —Treason in the Camp of the Saints—Joseph and the leading Mormons delivered over to Gen. Lucas—The Prisoners tried by Court-Martial—Sentenced to be shot next Morning—Gen. Doniphan protests against their Execution—The Prophet and his Brethren sent to Jail—The Revelations contradicted by Facts.

On the day of the Haun's Mills massacre, the Governor's army was surrounding Far West, and camped within a mile of that place for the night. The militia of Far West (Mormons) threw up some temporary fortifications through the night, and the women gathered their most valuable effects, anticipating a fight in the morning and probably a hasty departure. The Mormons evidently concluded to fight it out, though the Gentile militia outnumbered them five to one. It was at this time that General Atchison retired from command.

With such disparity of numbers and equipments, the Mormons could not have entertained any great hopes of success. The Prophet doubtless counted upon heavenly aid as well as upon the desperation of his brethren—fighting as they were for their families and firesides. It is an ever-recurring feature in religious history that repeated evidences of defeat are never accepted as lessons of premonition. On the contrary, as failure succeeds failure and the cause seems hopelessly lost, faith rises with increased grandeur, and the believer expects every instant to witness a Red Sea victory over again. The whole spirit and genius of Joseph's life was this abounding confidence.

At this time temporary success to the Mormons was possible; but it would have demanded an unfailing series of miracles to have made it available. The whole country was in sympathy with the mob, the militia, and the Governor. Temporary

7

defeat then to the militia was certain to have insured their
ultimate success. Unless the heavens had truly decreed the
overthrow of all things that opposed the Saints, there was little chance of victory, and the "treason" of Colonel Hinkle
was from that standpoint an opportune ram in the thicket.

This officer was an elder in the Church and in the command
of the Caldwell militia. He had faced the mob when it was
purely mob, and had exhibited no lack of personal devotion.
When he saw the Governor's officers surrounding Far West, it
is due to him to suppose that his time for second sober thought
had been reached. He sought an interview with General Lucas
on the morning of the 31st. The General and the principal
officers met him. Col. Hinkle wanted to know if there could
not be some compromise or settlement of the difficulty without
a resort to arms. General Lucas made him acquainted with
the Governor's orders for extermination or expulsion from the
State, and submitted to him the following propositions:

1. To give up their [the Church's] leaders to be tried and punished.

2. To make an appropriation of their property, all who have taken
up arms, to the payment of their debts, and indemnify for damage done
by them.

3. That the balance should leave the State, and be protected out by
the militia, but to be permitted to remain under protection until further
orders were received from the Commander-in-Chief.

4. To give up the arms of every description, to be receipted for.

Colonel Hinkle asked for time to consider these propositions, and General Lucas gave him till the following morning
to decide, requiring of him in the mean time to deliver over
Joseph Smith, Junr., Sidney Rigdon, Lyman Wight, Parley P.
Pratt, and George W. Robinson, as hostages for his faithful
compliance with the terms. On his part the General pledged
himself and his officers that in the event of the Colonel declin-
ing to accept those terms, the hostages should be returned in
the morning; but in case the terms were accepted, that the
hostages would be held for trial as a part of the first stipulation. To bring the persons called for, Col. Hinkle was allowed
till "one hour by sun in the evening," and the troops were ordered to be ready to march against Far West half an hour
earlier. The afternoon was already advanced.

Colonel Hinkle waited upon the Prophet and his friends named, and informed them that the officers of the militia desired to talk with them, hoping that the difficulty which threatened would be settled without having occasion to carry into effect the exterminating orders of the Governor. Joseph and his friends immediately complied with this request, and, accompanied by Colonel Hinkle, went out to the place of rendezvous with General Lucas. They were immediately seized as prisoners.

It is asserted by the Mormon historian that Col. Hinkle, when he met with General Lucas, said : " Here are the prison-" ers I agreed to deliver to you." Henceforth he was branded as a traitor by the Mormons.

With a full knowledge of the facts occurring at the time, a modification of this charge may be entertained. Col. Hinkle was evidently satisfied that "the Lord" was not going to fight the battles of the Saints, and he was as fully convinced that General Lucas would fight those of Missouri. Aware of the numerical superiority and advantages of his enemies, with no possibility of final success on the part of his friends, there was nothing left him but to surrender. Most persons would have preferred to have acquainted Joseph and the leading Mormons with the terms submitted by the Missouri generals, and to have left the decision and responsibility with them ; Colonel Hinkle's contrary course was probably prompted by the conviction that the Saints would never consent to give up their leaders, and that within two hours the fight would commence in which helpless women and children would be slaughtered in the general vengeance with which they were threatened. Colonel Hinkle had previously exhibited no cowardice; he gained nothing by giving up the leaders, but knew well that he would lose all by doing so, and from the fact that the Mormon authorities, with all their undying hate against him, have never affixed other crime to his name, it is pretty certain that Colonel Hinkle was not corrupted by the hopes of personal advantages.

The Prophet and his associates were marched through the lines of the militia amid yells and whoopings and general rejoicing. At night they were forced to make their couch on the earth without either mattress or covering, much to their

chagrin, and correspondingly to the enjoyment of the Missourians. A Mormon of the name of Carey had "got his skull
"split" in the morning of this day; no medical attendance or
anything to assuage the sufferings of this unfortunate were permitted him, but in the evening he was taken home by his
brethren and died in a few hours.

Next morning—November 1st—Joseph's brother Hyrum
and Amasa Lyman were brought into camp, and a court-martial was immediately held, composed "of nineteen militia offi-
"cers, and *seventeen preachers of various sects*, who had served
"as volunteers against the Mormons,"[*] and the Prophet and
his associates were condemned to be shot in the public square
of Far West, in the presence of their families and friends!

While the court-martial was being held, the troops, breaking through the feeble restraint that was imposed upon them,
committed all sorts of excesses in Far West. The General commanding had previously demanded the arms of the Mormons;
they were, therefore, now helpless and unable to resist the insult and outrage of their women, or to protect their own lives.

General Doniphan opposed the decision of the court-martial to shoot the Prophet and the leaders of the Church, and
to his firmness and the determination that neither he nor his
brigade should take part in "a cold-blooded murder," the
lives of the Mormon chiefs were, fortunately for the honour of
Missouri, at that time spared.[†]

After gratifying his troops with a march through the streets
of Far West, and to let the Mormons see their force, General
Lucas ordered General Wilson to escort the prisoners to Independence, Jackson county, the headquarters of the former.
It was with some difficulty that the Mormon prisoners obtained
permission to bid good-bye to their families; and, that over,
they were hurried away from their destitute families, and from
the afflicted and sadly grieved Saints.

---

[*] Rev. Mr. Caswell's "Prophet of the Nineteenth Century," p. 178.

[†] "This is the same Gen. Doniphan who, as colonel of a regiment of Missouri
volunteers, afterwards conquered Chihuahua, and gained the splendid victories of
Bracito and Sacramento. Among all the officers of the Missouri militia operating
against the Mormons, Gen. Doniphan was the only one who boldly denounced the
intended assassination of the prisoners under the colour of law. So true it is that
the truly brave man is most apt to be merciful and just."—"History of Illinois," p. 260.

At a time of such deep affliction it would be heartless cruelty to mock the faith of any sincere people, such as the Mormons have proved themselves to be ; but in an impartial history of Mormonism it is but proper that a "revelation," given only six months and a few days preceding that event, concerning that same Far West, should be placed together with the narrative of the final expulsion of the Saints from that highly favoured land.

" Let the city, Far West, be a holy and consecrated land unto me, and it shall be called most holy, for the ground upon which thou standest is holy ; therefore, I command you to build a house unto me, for the gathering together of my Saints that they may worship me ; and let there be a beginning of this work, and a foundation, and a preparatory work this following summer, and let the beginning be made on the fourth day of July next ; and from that time forth let my people labour diligently to build a house unto my name, and in one year from this day let them recommence laying the foundation of my house ; thus let them from that time forth labour diligently until it shall be finished from the corner-stone *hereof unto the top thereof, until there shall not anything remain that is not finished." *

In their efforts at harmonizing the failures of revelation with facts, the Mormon Apostles apply that other convenient revelation that tells them how, when "the Lord" commands the Saints to do anything and their enemies hinder them, He will not require it at their hands. This explanation is good, so far as settling with whom rests the responsibility, but it changes in nothing the inference here of " the Lord's " ignorance of the forthcoming expulsion of the Saints from Missouri, and His utter inability to prevent it. At the time when this revelation was given, the Prophet Joseph was in excellent and robust faith, and his sentiments on that occasion express his sanguineness in the future. In the same revelation he calls upon the Saints to—

"Arise and shine forth, that thy light may be a standard for the nations, and that the gathering together upon the land of Zion, and upon her stakes, may be for a defence, and for a refuge from the storm, and from wrath when it shall be poured out without mixture upon the whole earth."

* " *Revelation given at Far West*, April 26, 1838, *making known the will of God concerning the building up of this place and of the Lord's House*," etc.

With all these predictions in favour of the future greatness of Far West, and the glory that awaited Independence in
the erection of the Great Temple that was to be "recom-
"menced and *continued till completion*," no ordinary men
could have been carried away prisoners from the one place to
the other without strange questionings about the predictions
of the modern Prophet; but Joseph was in no way discouraged.

On the way to Independence some of the brethren were
cast down and disheartened. On the second morning of their
travels Joseph cheered them with a revelation. "Be of good
"courage, brethren," said he; "the word of the Lord came
"to me last night, that our lives should be given to us, and
"that, whatsoever we may suffer during this captivity, not one
"of our lives shall be taken."

On their arrival at Independence they were treated kindly
by some and rudely by others. Among the strangers visiting
the Prophet and Apostles some woman asked questions. This
afforded Joseph the opportunity of preaching to her and her
companions, which the Mormon historian claims was the fulfilment of a prediction "that a sermon should be preached in
"Jackson county by one of our elders before the close of
"1838." On just as slight a foundation has the fulfilment of
many a prediction been claimed.

CHAPTER XVIII.

THE MISSOURIANS TRIUMPHANT.—Grandiloquent Speech of Gen. Clark—
Mormons ordered to leave the State—Examination of the Prisoners—The Prophet
not subdued—The Legislature memorialized—The Saints wavering—Joseph reviews the Situation.

GENERAL CLARK, entrusted with the superior command of
the militia of Missouri, arrived at Far West on the 4th of November, too late to participate in the glories of General Lucas.
But there was much yet to be done to carry out the Governor's
order of expulsion or extermination. From first to last, the
troops sent to Far West under the different commands were
probably altogether six thousand men. Before his departure
for Independence, General Lucas disbanded nearly all the militia. General Clark arrived with sixteen hundred others. The
Mormon militia here, about five hundred in number, had already given up their arms. They were now called out of their
houses and ordered into line. From a paper that had been
furnished to General Clark, the names of fifty-six of their number were read, and as they answered they were called out and
sent to Richmond jail (Ray county), without being informed of
what they were accused. Before they departed, the General
made the following speech :

"GENTLEMEN—You whose names are not attached to this list of
names, will now have the privilege of going to your fields, and of providing corn, wood, etc., for your families. Those who are now taken will go
from this to prison, be tried, and receive the due demerit of their crimes;
but you (except such as charges may hereafter be preferred against) are at
liberty as soon as the troops are removed that now guard the place, which
I shall cause to be done immediately. It now devolves upon you to fulfil
a treaty that you have entered into, the leading items of which I shall
now lay before you. The first requires that your leading men be given up

to be tried according to law ; this you have already complied with. The
second is that you deliver up your arms; this has been attended to. The
third stipulation is that you sign over your properties to defray the expenses of the war. This you have also done. Another article yet remains
for you to comply with, and that is that you leave the State forthwith.
And whatever may be your feeling concerning this, or whatever your innocence, it is nothing to me. General Lucas (whose military rank is equal
with mine) has made this treaty with you ; I approve of it. I should
have done the same had I been here. I am therefore determined to see it
executed. The character of this State has suffered almost beyond redemption, from the character, conduct, and influence that you have exerted ; and we deem it an act of justice to restore her character to its
former standing among the States by every proper means. The orders of
the Governor to me were that you should be exterminated and not allowed
to remain in the State. And had not your leaders been given up, and
the terms of the treaty complied with, before this time you and your families would have been destroyed, and your houses in ashes. There is a
discretionary power vested in my hands, which, considering your circumstances, I shall exercise for a season. You are indebted to me for this
clemency. I do not say that you shall go now, but you must not think
of staying here another season or of putting in crops, for the moment you
do this the citizens will be upon you ; and if I am called here again in
case of a non-compliance of a treaty made, do not think that I shall do
as I have done now. You need not expect any mercy, but *extermination*,
for *I am determined the Governor's order shall be executed.* As for your
leaders, do not think, do not imagine for a moment, do not let it enter
into your minds that they will be delivered and restored to you again, for
their fate is fixed, their die is cast, their doom is sealed. I am sorry, gentlemen, to see so many apparently intelligent men found in the situation
that you are ; and oh ! if I could invoke that Great Spirit, the unknown
God, to rest upon and deliver you from that awful chain of superstition,
and liberate you from those fetters of fanaticism with which you are
bound, that you no longer do homage to a man. I would advise you to
scatter abroad and never organize yourselves with bishops, presidents,
etc., lest you excite the jealousies of the people, and subject yourselves to
the same calamities that have now come upon you. You have always
been the aggressors, you have brought upon yourselves these difficulties
by being disaffected, and not being subject to rule. And my advice is
that you become as other citizens, lest by a recurrence of these events you
bring upon yourselves irretrievable ruin."

After Joseph had been with his fellow-prisoners a few
days in Independence, Colonel Sterling G. Price brought
orders from General Clark and took them to Richmond, Ray
county. There they were chained by the ankles and had

to sleep together in a row upon their backs and without any covering.

General Clark was zealous and left nothing undone. In a dispatch to Governor Boggs, dated November 10th, he reveals the complexion of his mind on the Mormon question :

" There is no crime, from treason down to petit larceny, but these people, or a majority of them, have been guilty of—all, too, under the counsel of Joseph Smith, Junr., the Prophet. They have committed treason, murder, arson, burglary, robbery, larceny, and perjury. They have societies formed under the most binding covenants in form and the most horrid oaths to circumvent the laws, and put them at defiance ; and to plunder and burn and murder, and divide the spoils for the use of the Church." *

Everything was now against the Mormons; the leaders of the first mob had triumphed, and they were now sitting in judgment over the prisoners and dictating terms to the Saints. The Governor was resolved to make a final work of it. He instructed General Clark " to settle the whole matter completely." If the Mormons as a body were disposed to voluntarily leave the State, he was to favour that course ; but upon no account to allow " the ringleaders to escape the punishment they " deserve." They were to be made an example to the others.

General Clark strained every nerve to have these prisoners tried before a court-martial ; but he had finally to remand them to Austin A. King, of the Circuit Court, and to Adam Black, that justice of the peace whose affidavit against Joseph and Lyman Wight was the commencement of their troubles. The examination lasted three days; and is reported by the Mormons to have been a mere farce, as nearly all the witnesses who might have been of service to the prisoners were thrust into prison, and those who did appear in their behalf were threatened, intimidated, and, in some cases, " actually run out

* This has always been represented by the Mormon writers as a totally unfounded charge and the work of a bitter partisan seeking the blood of the Saints ; but the perusal of the testimony taken before Judge Austin A. King, at that very time, supports General Clark in this representation. The answer of a Mormon apologist that the testimony referred to was given by men who had left the Church and apostatized, could be of no weight with him. There were doubtless exaggerations on both sides, but General Clark's letter to the Governor was a faithful reflex of what he heard ; and he witnessed enough to partially confirm it. *Vide* Senate Document.

"of the court." It was the beginning of that "border ruffianism" that afterwards so much disgraced both Kansas and Missouri. At the close of the examination sixty prisoners were "honour-ably acquitted," or held to bail; but the Prophet, his brother Hyrum, Sidney Rigdon, Lyman Wight, Alexander McRae, and Caleb Baldwin were sent to jail in Liberty, Clay county, to await their trial on the charges of treason and murder.* The "treason," says Joseph, "for having whipped the mob "out of Davies county and taking their cannon from them, "and 'murder,' for the man killed in the Bogart battle." Having "whipped" the mob, sounds as if Joseph hugely en-joyed that part of his experience. The other prisoners— Parley P. Pratt, Morris Phelps, Luman Gibbs, Darwin Chase and Normon Shearer, were placed in Richmond jail to await their trial on the same charges.

The body of the Saints were to leave the State in the spring, and their labours were devoted to preparation for that exclusively; but it was exceedingly difficult to procure the necessary means. The banditti that roamed through the coun-ties where the Mormons resided, after the militia was dis-banded, swept away everything that was valuable, and wan-tonly destroyed what they could not use.

Some of the leading Mormons sent a memorial to the State Legislature representing the terribly impoverished condition of the Saints, and asking for redress and the rescinding of the Governor's order of expulsion. The documents presented by the Mormons were fairly dealt with by many members of the Legislature who were ashamed at the course of the Governor and for the unconstitutionality of his orders for expulsion; but the majority of the Legislature were against the Mormons, and

---

* The evidence given during this examination revealed the most disgraceful con-duct on the part of some of the witnesses of the Book of Mormon, and this evi-dence, too, was given by the orthodox Mormons in fellowship with Joseph Smith. A document draughted by Sidney Rigdon, and subscribed by eighty-four Mormons, addressed to Oliver Cowdery, David Whitmer, John Whitmer, Wm. W. Phelps, and Lyman E. Johnson, exhibits these witnesses, and apostles, and their associates, to have been unmitigated scamps. "The Lord" could not well have chosen a more despicable set of thieves and liars than they were—taking the testimony of their brethren as evidence. Mormonism did little for them in the way of reformation and grace. They must have been "a hard lot" before they accepted the new revelation.

$200,000 was voted to meet the expenses of the war! To aid the people of Davies and Caldwell, $2,000 was ordered to be distributed; but of that the Mormons had a small share.

All hope of receiving aid from the State was now extinguished, and the Saints had to depend upon their own exertions during the winter to provide themselves with the necessary means of travel. Joseph, in the mean time, was busy in prison writing letters of encouragement to the Saints, and attacking with bitterness his enemies, especially the "apostates." His letter of December 16th is a curious mixture of "grace, "mercy, and the peace of God abide with you," with severe and coarse denunciation of the renegade witnesses of the Book of Mormon, and other chief men who had deserted him. It was, in fact, an exhortation to the practice of the highest morality, a general review of the charges against the Saints, a denunciation to the effect that "he or she was a liar" who "rep- "resents anything otherwise than what we now write," and a tapering off with the words:

"We commend you to God and the work of His grace, which is able to make us wise unto salvation. Amen.—*Joseph Smith, Junr.*"

Some of the Saints had been greatly shaken by the disasters in Missouri, and upon Brigham Young (then President of the Twelve Apostles) the responsibility of keeping together the Church devolved. In a meeting held at Far West, Brigham expressed himself thoroughly satisfied with the Prophet. Heber's faith was " as good as ever;" Simeon Carter " did not "think that Joseph was a fallen prophet," still he thought that "Joseph had not acted in all things according to the best wis- "dom." Thomas Grover was "firm in the faith," and believed that " the time would come when Joseph would stand before "kings and speak marvellous words." Solomon Hancock believed in all the Church books, was satisfied that " brother Jo- "seph was not a fallen prophet, but will yet be exalted and "become very high." Another brother was "stronger than "ever in the faith," thought that the scourging they had got was necessary; and another brother, following after this one, "felt ready to praise God in prisons, and in dungeons, and in "all circumstances." Such might be regarded as a representation of the faith of the people generally at this epoch of their history. They had been greatly afflicted and cast down, had some doubts of the wisdom of their leaders, and acknowledged that the brethren had brought upon themselves much of their trouble ; but, nevertheless, Joseph was still their prophet. In his autobiography he views the course of events, closing with the following pointed queries :

" But can they hide the Governor's cruel order of banishment or extermination ? Can they conceal the facts of the disgraceful treaty of the generals with their own officers and men at Far West ? Can they conceal the fact that twelve or fifteen thousand men, women, and children have been banished from the State without trial or condemnation ? And this at the expense of two hundred thousand dollars—and this sum appropriated by the State Legislature, in order to pay the troops for this act of lawless outrage ? Can they conceal the fact that we have been imprisoned for many months, while our families, friends, and witnesses have been driven away ? Can they conceal the blood of the murdered husbands and fathers, or stifle the cry of the widow or fatherless ? Nay ! The rocks and mountains may cover them in unknown depths, the awful abyss of the fathomless deep may swallow them up, and still the horrid deeds stand forth in the broad light of day for the wondering gaze of angels and men ! They cannot be hid ! . . . Thus, in a free land, in the town of Liberty, Clay county, Missouri, I and my fellow-prisoners, in chains, dungeons, and jail, saw the close of 1838."

CHAPTER XIX.

IN PRISON.—The New Year opens Dark and Dreary—The Mormons suffer--The Missouri Legislature consider the "Persecutions" of the Saints—Brigham Young flees from Missouri—Joseph indites an Epistle from Prison—The Prisoners indicted—They escape from Missouri.

THE instinctive buoyancy of feelings that ever greets a new year was little shared by the imprisoned Prophet at the opening of 1839. His first burst of awakening thought was dedicated to the nation :

"O Columbia. Columbia, how art thou fallen ! The land of the free, the home of the brave !—the asylum of the oppressed—oppressing thy noblest sons in a loathsome dungeon, without any provocation, only that they have claimed to worship the God of their fathers, according to his own word, and the dictates of their own consciences ! ! ! "

There is a charming innocence in such spurts of eloquence. Joseph never doubted the right of his own position, and expected every one to look at everything from his standpoint, failing which they were certain to be corrupt and worthy of damnation, and the world's liberty was a farce.

His youthful claims to be a prophet had in a measure withdrawn him from the ordinary experience of the world. He knew little of the diversity and wide range of human thought and the influence of circumstances upon human judgment. The sentiments of his Arabian brother—"Great is Allah ! and "Mohammed is his Prophet," was the true interpretation of his thoughts. Joseph always believed that he ought to be the first subject of interest to the whole world, as his mission was its salvation or damnation. It has ever been difficult to prevent men of his kind from drawing down fire from heaven.

During the winter the lawless and unscrupulous in Upper

Missouri were very cruel to the Saints. No Mormon's life was safe outside the settlements of that people, and any attempt to gather up the remnant of their farm property was certain to meet with fierce opposition and personal violence. A recital of barbarity is to be met with in the records of those times, such as would scarcely be credited now had not the "Jayhawk-"ing raids" in Missouri and Kansas rendered easy of belief the worst stories related by the Mormons.*

The Missouri Legislature was not at rest concerning the expulsion of the Mormons. They felt that there was something wrong. The free States were liberal in their denunciation of the slave State, and many honourable gentlemen in Missouri felt the justice of the reproach. Even Governor Boggs is reported to have acknowledged the unconstitutionality of his exterminating order, and was desirous of preventing the cruel excesses to which the remaining Mormons were subjected, and General Atchison again appeared in their defence in the Legislature.

A joint committee of two senators and three representatives was appointed to investigate the causes of the late disturbance between "the people called Mormons and other in-"habitants of this State, and the conduct of the military "operations in repressing them." This was of no service to the Mormons. The committee was to meet on the first Monday in May, and by that time the Mormons were nearly all out of the State, and the testimony could only be heard from their enemies.

* "That many of these fanatics are great scoundrels we are very well aware; but who after reading the following horrible details will have any sympathy for their oppressors? We speak of tyranny and oppression abroad, we sympathize with scoundrels, pour out our blood and money like water for graceless vagabonds, such as Keller and his *clique*, and neglect the sterner duties of humanity at home. It appears that after the Missouri mob had captured Joe Smith, Rigdon, and others, the mob entered the town of the Mormons and perpetrated every conceivable act of brutality and outrage, *forcing fifteen or twenty Mormon girls to yield to their brutal passions!!* 'Of these things,' says a respectable authority, 'I was assured by many persons while I was at Far West, in whose veracity I have the utmost confidence : I conversed with many of the prisoners, who numbered about eight hundred, among whom I recognized many old acquaintances who had seen better days. There were many young and interesting girls among them, and I assure you a more distracted set of creatures I never saw.' "—*N. Y. Herald*, Dec. 20, 1838.

Brigham Young and the other apostles and elders still at
liberty were in the mean time devoting their best energies to
prepare for a thorough exodus. The brethren covenanted to
put all their property into the hands of a committee for this
purpose so that the poor who had been plundered of everything
could leave as well as those who were more favoured.

Illinois was greatly moved by the recital of their wrongs,
and offered the exiles an asylum. In that State, land was
plentiful, offers were numerous, and terms liberal. Universal
sympathy with affliction was apparent. The citizens vied with
each other in acts of kindness to the helpless. But it was impossible as yet to decide upon a locality for their gathering-
place. Joseph was still in prison. The banks of the Mississippi,
however, seemed to be appropriate for the general rendezvous.

The persecution that had centred on Joseph now fell upon
Brigham, and in the middle of February he had to escape from
Far West to save his life. He directed his fleeting steps towards
Quincy, Illinois, whither many of the Saints had preceded him.

After some investigation in Missouri had taken place, Sidney Rigdon was released, but had for safety to return to prison
till a favourable opportunity offered for making his escape out
of the State. He also in due time reached Quincy.

Joseph protested against being tried before Austin A. King,
of the Circuit Court. In one of the early difficulties in Jackson county a brother-in-law of Judge King had been killed.
His Honour had also presided at some meeting hostile to the
Mormons, and Joseph concluding that the Judge's impartiality
would not be of the clearest stamp, resolved to get out of his
jurisdiction. A petition " to Judge Tompkins, or either of the
" judges of the Supreme Court for the State of Missouri," was
presented to the former, asking for the issue of a writ of *habeas
corpus*, that the prisoners might be heard in their defence.
This failing, Joseph resolved to escape from prison. He tried,
but did not succeed.

With the Saints fleeing from Missouri and wandering like
sheep without a shepherd, it appeared that the end of Mormonism had been reached; but it was far otherwise. There is
vitality in prophecy, and Joseph's faith rose with his difficulties.

Shortly after his failure to escape from prison he issued a

letter to the Saints which perhaps may be considered the most
interesting document of his life—one which gives the reader
ideas more characteristic of the man than anything he ever
published. When surrounded by clerks and literary men the
Prophet is not always discernible in the papers that bear his
name, but in those issued from Liberty Prison the very man
himself is visible in every word. The differences of style in this
document, his arguments in one place and the bursting forth
of the exuberance of his soul in prayer and prophecy in another
furnish the key to his revelations. At one moment he humbly
supplicates, and at another the remembrance of the wrongs
that he had suffered fires him with indignation and carries him
beyond himself.

The Prophet's Flight from Missouri.

In April, the Prophet and his fellow prisoners were indicted
in Davies county on charges of "treason, murder, larceny,
theft and stealing." The trial never occurred. The prisoners asked for a change of venue to Marion county, as the same
men who sat on the grand jury during the day acted as their
guard at night. They were granted a change of venue to
Boone county, and while being conveyed thither, the sheriff
who had them in charge gave them permission to escape. The
State authorities were evidently anxious to get rid of them, and
the prisoners longing for freedom availed themselves of the
sheriff's courtesy and fled from "the land of promise."

Joseph turned his back for ever upon the soil of the new
Jerusalem. Jackson county, with all the marvels and magnifi-

cence that had been decreed for her during " this generation," was hereafter only to be sung in song. Forty years have already passed away since the revelation was given, and there is not a single Mormon acknowledging the leadership of Brigham Young upon all the holy land.

Notwithstanding all that has transpired, many of the aged Saints in Utah have not lost their faith, and yet look for something marvellous to occur in the ever-changing wheel of time, to favour the day when the promises of the Prophet Joseph will be fulfilled! The frequency with which Brigham has alluded to the return of the faithful Saints in Utah to Jackson county has shaken a great deal the credit that has been accorded to him for sincerity of faith. For many years he held the most positive language on this point; but latterly he has prudently added—" If the Lord will." Before he goes down to his grave he will probably taper even that off with the affirmation that " the Lord " has tried the faith of his Saints, and is now satisfied, and will not require them to fulfil the prophecies in " this generation." Brigham Young's love of the wealth which he has acquired in Utah is an effectual barrier against *his* ever fulfilling that prophecy.

8

CHAPTER XX.

THE EXILES FIND AN ASYLUM IN ILLINOIS.—The Prophet again at liberty—Nauvoo selected for a New Zion—A City rapidly Built—Brigham Young sent to England—The Saints importune Congress for Redress—Joseph visits President Van Buren—The Mormons still cling to the Promises of Zion in Missouri.

THE abandonment of Missouri shook the faith of many of the disciples, but the majority were unchanged—

"They lived and spoke and thought the same."

The Missourians had been victorious they knew, but what Joseph had said about the coming glories of Zion, the New Jerusalem, and the Temple in Jackson county, was, they nevertheless believed, true and from heaven. All would yet be right.

Of those who abandoned the faith, some remained in Missouri, and others returned to their former homes in the eastern States ; and, in the language of an ancient record, " even unto "this day " they may be found—half Mormon and half nothing else — scattered throughout Ohio, New York, Indiana, Pennsylvania, and most of the New England States.

Early in the spring the citizens of Quincy saw a large increase to their numbers of poor, destitute Mormons. They were utterly helpless, and many of them bordering on starvation. Meetings were called and measures adopted for their particular benefit. At the same time, the ignorant were assured that the Mormons had no design of lowering the prices of labour, but were only seeking " to procure something to "save them from starving," and that they were, " by every "law of humanity, entitled to sympathy and commiseration." Those were humble days ; but they were soon to change.

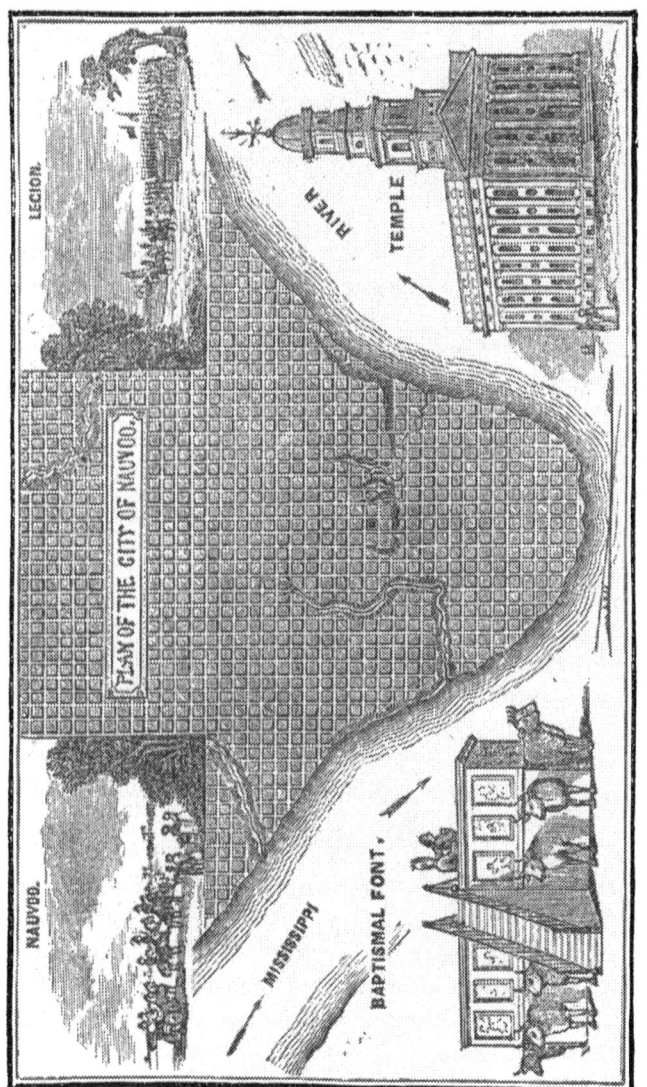

THE HOME OF THE SAINTS IN ILLINOIS.

Joseph himself, like the Angel of Deliverance, came bounding into their midst. The gloom of death that so darkly overhung their horizon vanished before the beams of the Prophet's rising sun. His chief advisers had already received and debated the offers of sections of land; it was now for him, with the guidance of Heaven, to decide.

The east bank of the Mississippi, forty miles above Quincy and twenty miles southwest of Burlington, Iowa, was the favoured spot. Here on a bend of the river, upon rising ground that commanded a magnificent view of the winding Mississippi for many miles, was to be the new home of the Saints. A group of huts and houses called Commerce was the place selected; but the name was an every-day word. The " Reformed Egyp-"tian" of the Book of Mormon supplied a better name— " Nauvoo "—the beautiful. By revelation the scattered Saints from Missouri and from all parts of the earth were now commanded to gather to this new Zion.

The apostle Parley P. Pratt, and the other leading elders who had been imprisoned in Missouri, after great suffering and privations, also made their escape and reached Illinois. They laid the foundation of new homes at Nauvoo, but " the Lord " deemed it prudent that they should not remain in the United States, and in August and September the principal apostles and elders were appointed missions to England. Among these were Brigham Young, Parley P. Pratt, Orson Pratt, and George A. Smith. Heber C. Kimball, who had already been to that country, returned in company with Brigham Young.

Nauvoo soon became an important city. The foundation of the first house was laid in 1839, and in less than two years over two thousand dwellings were erected, besides schoolhouses and public edifices. The foundation of the Temple was laid, and scores of mechanics and labourers were engaged on " the House of the Lord." Everything was going smoothly.

In the mean time, a statement of the losses of the Saints in Missouri was carefully prepared, and in October, Joseph, Sidney Rigdon, and Judge Elias Higbee visited Washington to petition Congress in their behalf, and to seek redress.

President Martin Van Buren received the petitioners courteously, and listened patiently to them; but the sovereignty

of the States was then in the fulness of its glory, and the Chief
Executive of the Republic replied : " *Gentlemen, your cause is*
"*just, but I can do nothing for you.*"

The petitioners thoroughly understood the President—the
support of Missouri could not be risked. The reply of " Matty,"
as Joseph ever afterwards contemptuously styled President
Van Buren, will never be forgotten by the Mormons. It has
served as the text for thousands of sermons at home and abroad
on " the Persecutions of the Saints," and it is to be found in
nearly every declaration of grievance against the Government.

In a statement of their sufferings, published by Orson
Pratt, Washington, January, 1854, reference is thus made to
that circumstance :

" After fifteen thousand American citizens had been driven from the
State of Missouri under the exterminating orders of Governor Boggs, having previously applied to the judicial and legislative authority of that
State in vain, they sent their delegates with a memorial to the President
and to Congress, who had the unblushing impudence to refer them for
redress to the very State whose Governor had driven them from her borders, and whose Legislature had voted two hundred thousand dollars to
pay her troops for their bloodthirsty and unconstitutional acts. Yes, they
were told to go and seek redress from their murderers, and from the murderers of their wives and children." *

At this time Sidney Rigdon, as a native of Pennsylvania,
addressed a memorial to the Senate and House of Representatives of that State, setting forth what he and his co-religionists
had suffered, and as the authorities of Missouri had refused
him redress, he asked that " the whole delegation of Pennsyl-
" vania, in both houses, be instructed to use all their influence
" in the national councils to have redress granted." Nothing
advantageous to the exiles was ever heard from either the memorial to Congress or that to the Legislature of the " Keystone
" State." By revelation, Joseph had been instructed to " seek
" redress from the least in authority even to the greatest." In
Missouri they began their petitions with the Justice of the
Peace, and then ascended in regular gradation till they reached
the Chief Executive of the State. They had finished their
task for the time being, when they had memoralized Congress

* "Seer," p. 197.

and laid their petition before the President of the United States. By their perseverance, and the official negative response that they everywhere received, it is understood by the Mormons that the whole national authority is culpable in the sight of Heaven, as participators in shedding the blood of the Saints in Missouri. This is the key to the bitterness of sentiment that may be heard in the Mormon Tabernacle, or read in the Mormon press, and the nation may be assured of this, that there never will be an end to it while Mormonism exists.* The claim to their lands in Jackson county will never be abandoned, nor will the Government be forgiven till the Mormons are restored to their " inheritances " in Missouri. They will never be silent, and when they reach the halls of Congress their senators and their representatives will be heard for ever demanding redress and restoration. It cannot be denied that there is justice in their claim.

Satisfied that compensation for the past was not to be hoped for at the seat of government, the Prophet and his friends returned to Nauvoo. Protection for the future was only to be found in their own ability to cope with their enemies, and with that conclusion they set themselves to work to provide for contingencies.

* "If the Government cannot protect citizens in their lives and property, it is an old granny, anyhow, and I prophesy, in the name of the Lord God of Israel, that unless the United States redress the wrongs committed upon the Saints in the State of Missouri, and punish the crimes committed by her officers, that in a few years the Government will be utterly overthrown and wasted, and there will not be so much as a potsherd left, for their wickedness in permitting the murder of men, women, and children, and the wholesale plunder and extermination of thousands of her citizens, to go unpunished."—*Joseph Smith's Autobiography.*

CHAPTER XXI.

THE PROPHET'S POLITICAL LIFE BEGINS.--New Men gather round him—
A Reorganization of the "Quorum of Apostles"—Another Temple to be erected
—"The Lord" commands the Saints to build a " Boarding-House "—Kings are
invited to the aid of Zion.

In Nauvoo the Prophet saw himself and his people in circumstances totally different from those in Missouri. He had
scattered the Mormons in that State in order that they might
become the possessors of the land surrounding the " New Jerusalem," and that they might preserve it as " an everlasting in-
"heritance for the Saints." In Illinois he had now to concen-
trate them. Other circumstances demanded other tactics. He
had sent off the preaching apostles to England ; he now drew
around him politicians. From this time an entirely different
class of men became prominent in Mormon history and flut-
tered around the Prophet.

A *Whig* Senator and a *Whig* Representative had introduced the memorial to Congress. The Democratic Association
in Quincy had rendered the exiles some services when they
came fleeing from Missouri. Both Whigs and Democrats realized the strength of a united vote, and that Joseph could command it, and they sought to gratify his wishes. Thus in
apparent triumph he became enmeshed in that whirlpool which
was destined to engulph him.

Release from the long imprisonment in Missouri, and from
the terrible anxieties that preceded that confinement, brought
fully back to Joseph his natural buoyancy of feeling. He
appreciated the kindly reception of the Saints in Illinois, and
the general sympathy extended everywhere to the Mormons,
on account of their recent sufferings, inspired him with the

hope of a brighter future. With the devotion of his brethren and sisters to him in the hour of their greatest trials, and the alacrity with which they rallied again at his call, he was greatly touched, and, as new men of considerable talent and social standing in the world were gathering around him, and Saints were flocking to his standard from Europe, he naturally appreciated his position.

Among the prominent men who were attracted towards Mormonism and sought alliance with Joseph at this time was one Dr. John C. Bennett, who was destined to occupy a distinguished position in the Prophet's history. Some others also about this time joined the Church, no doubt honestly hoping that it might realize their spiritual requirements, and there were others who joined from more interested motives. Among the politicians who sought his early acquaintance and political influence in Illinois was Senator Stephen A. Douglas, whose name for many years was held in reverence by the Saints.

In all his intercourse the Prophet was confiding, frank and open. He realized that he was the tallest tree in the forest, and was never afraid of being overtopped. He gave to every man the fullest scope for the development of talent or usefulness, and the heavens were never slow in sanctioning and approving of his preferments.

In a very short time Dr. Bennett was a very useful man, and soon became the mouth-piece of the Prophet. Under the *nom de plume* of "Joab, a general in Israel," he told Missouri of her evil deeds, of her wrongs to the Saints, and the retribution that awaited her.

A very lengthy revelation was received by Joseph on the 19th of January, 1841, placing every one in his proper position, reorganizing the Quorum of the Twelve Apostles, and extending a kindly word to every prominent man. Many of the first apostles had "fallen away," and it was necessary to commence again and fill up the quorum. "The Lord" made the following selection :

"I give unto you my servant Brigham Young to be a President over the Twelve travelling council, which twelve hold the keys to open up the authority of my kingdom upon the four corners of the earth, and after that to send my word to every creature ; they are Heber C. Kimball, Parley P. Pratt, Orson Pratt, Orson Hyde, William Smith, John Taylor, John E. Page, Wilford Woodruff, Willard Richards, George A. Smith; David Patten I have taken unto myself; behold his priesthood no man taketh from him; but verily I say unto you, another may be appointed unto the same calling."

Colonel Lyman Wight was elected to fill this vacancy. The members of the quorum were afterwards thus flatteringly designated by W. W. Phelps:

"Brigham Young, *the Lion of the Lord;* Parley P. Pratt, "*the Archer of Paradise;* Orson Hyde, *the Olive Branch of* "*Israel;* Willard Richards, *the Keeper of the Rolls;* John "Taylor, *the Champion of Right;* William Smith, *the Patri-* "*archal Jacob's Staff;* Wilford Woodruff, *the Banner of the* "*Gospel;* George A. Smith, *the Entablature of Truth;* Orson "Pratt, *the Gauge of Philosophy;* John E. Page, *the Sun* "*Dial;* and Lyman Wight, *the Wild Ram of the Moun-* "*tains.*"

This new revelation extended to forty-six paragraphs, and in the light of subsequent as well as of preceding events it is very interesting. It is a marvellous revelation. It heals up the wounds of the Jackson county Saints and declares for their future guidance that whatever "the Lord" may command them to do and their enemies may prevent them from doing, "the "Lord" will accept the unfinished work at their hands the same as if it had been accomplished. Another Temple was ordered to be erected "to the name of the Lord;" and, for the convenience of travellers visiting Nauvoo, "the Lord" also commanded "a boarding-house to be built!"

"And now I say unto you, as pertaining to my boarding-house which I have commanded you to build for the boarding of strangers, let it be unto my name, and let my name be named upon it, and let my servant Joseph and his house have place therein from generation to generation; for this anointing have I put upon his head, that his blessing shall also be put upon the head of his posterity after him; and as I said unto Abraham concerning the kindreds of the earth, even so I say unto my servant Joseph. In thee and in thy seed shall the kindreds of the earth be blessed. Therefore let my servant Joseph, and his seed after him, have place in that house from generation to generation, for ever and for ever, saith the Lord, and let the name of that house be called the Nauvoo House, and let it be a delightful habitation for man, and a resting-place for the weary traveller that he may contemplate the glory of Zion and the glory of this the cor-

ner-stone thereof, that he may receive also the counsel from those whom I have set to be plants of renown, etc."

This revelation excludes all " dead-heads" and speculators. The lowest amount of stock was to be $50, the highest to any one man $5,000, and none of it was to be handed over *till the money was paid down in full*, and the whole was to be kept by the posterity of the purchasers, and " not to be sold by them, " from generation to generation." These stock purchasers were also required to be believers in the Book of Mormon. Some prominent men were commanded by name to take stock in it. Dr. Isaac Galland, who was designated as " a notorious horse- "thief and counterfeiter in his early life," * is instructed to " put stock into that house," for " I, the Lord, love him for the " work he hath done, and will forgive all his sins." All the prominent moneyed men are similarly kindly instructed for the benefit of themselves and their seed after them, "from gen- " eration to generation."

Robert B. Thompson is called to help Joseph to write a proclamation after this fashion :

" Awake! O kings of the earth ! Come ye ! oh, come ye, with your gold and your silver, to the help of my people, to the house of the daugh- ter of Zion."

To this work " My servant John C. Bennett " is also called to assist Joseph " in sending my word to the kings of the peo- " ple of the earth, and [to] stand by you, even to you, my ser- " vant Joseph Smith, in the hour of affliction, and his reward " shall not fail *if he receive counsel*." Robert D. Foster is next instructed to " build a house for my servant Joseph, ac- " cording to the contract which he has made with him," and to " repent " and quit grumbling, and " *hearken unto the counsel* " of my servants, Joseph, Hyrum, and William Law," and " it " shall be well with him for ever and for ever. Even so. Amen."

To make room for the elevation of a new man at this time, Joseph retired his brother Hyrum from the Presidency of the Church, but still preserved him in rank almost equal to his own. This same revelation instructed that—

* "Mysteries and Crimes of Mormonism," p. 61.

"My servant William [Law] be appointed, ordained, and anointed as a counsellor unto my servant Joseph, in the room of my servant Hyrum; that my servant Hyrum may take the office of priesthood and patriarch, which was appointed unto him by his father, by blessing and also by right," etc., etc.

"My servant William" at this time was a wealthy merchant, and an influential man among the Mormons; but, unfortunately for the Prophet, he proved to be unprepared for the richer developments of the patriarchal relations that were "to burst from the heavens" upon the Church, and in course of time he became one of Joseph's fiercest opponents.

LIEUTENANT-GENERAL JOSEPH SMITH.

[Prophet, Seer, and Revelator.]

CHAPTER XXII.

THE FICKLE FORTUNE OF POLITICS.—The Legislature liberal to the Saints —The Prophet becomes a Lieutenant-General—Foundation of the Temple laid— Grand Military Display—Joseph at the Height of his Glory—Missouri seeks to recapture him.

THE Saints had contributed largely to the success of the Whig ticket in 1840, and the Democrats comprehended clearly the advantage it would be to them to secure their influence. When Joseph's agents presented themselves to the Legislature of Illinois, during the session of 1840-1, asking for a city charter for Nauvoo, and the incorporation of the militia into a body to be called " the Nauvoo Legion," they were very kindly received and their wishes hastily granted. The charters were passed without a dissenting voice.

The eleventh section of the city charter read thus :

" All power is granted to the city council to make, ordain, establish, and execute all ordinances not repugnant to the Constitution of the State or of the United States, or, *as they may deem necessary for the peace and safety of said city.*"

This was all that Joseph required. It was now for him to decide what was " necessary," and, had troubles not afterwards arisen in Illinois, the liberality of the charter would probably never have been regretted, for at that date Joseph was, in the sight of every law-abiding citizen, justified in seeking, by every means that had the appearance of constitutional law, to preserve himself and the people against the demands of Missouri.

The city charter provided for a mayor, four aldermen, and nine councillors, a mayor's court, with exclusive jurisdiction in all cases arising under the city ordinances ; a municipal court,

with the mayor as chief justice, and the four aldermen as associates, with power to issue writs of *habeas corpus*. The Legion
was organized, and was rendered independent of all the militia
officers of the State, save the Governor as commander-in-chief.
It established its own court-martial, and provided for everything within itself. Dr. Bennett was elected mayor of the city,
and Joseph Smith lieutenant-general of the Legion.

The city council immediately prepared for eventualities,
and passed an ordinance that no citizen could be taken from
Nauvoo by any process of law whatever, without the endorsement of the mayor as to its legality. The charter admitted of
this, and almost any construction that the city council chose to
give it. The Governor, who had signed the charter, soon afterwards perceived the blunder, and before long saw his own warrant for the arrest of Joseph set aside. In a communication,
dated September 7th, 1842, he says :

" I must express my surprise at the extraordinary assumption of power
by the board of aldermen, as contained in said ordinance ; from my recollection of the charter, it authorizes the municipal court to issue writs of
habeas corpus, in all cases of imprisonment or custody, arising from the
authority of the ordinances of said city ; *but that power was granted or
intended to be granted to release persons held in custody under the authority
of writs issued by the courts or the executive of the State, is most absurd and
ridiculous*, and an attempt to exercise it is a gross usurpation of power
that cannot be tolerated."

" Absurd and ridiculous " as the assumption of such powers
might seem twenty months after his Excellency, Governor Carlin, had attached his signature to the charter approving of it,
at the time of its passage through the Legislature, no such
language was held by any one. At a later date Governor Ford,
his successor, had to be more explicit. He, too, was embar-
rassed by the liberality of the charter, and he saddles the
responsibility of Joseph's interpretation where it justly belongs :

" The powers conferred were expressed in language at once ambiguous
and undefined, as if on purpose to allow of misconstruction. The great
law of the separation of the powers of government was wholly disregarded. The mayor was at once the executive power, the judiciary, and part
of the Legislature. The common council, in passing ordinances, were restrained only by the Constitution. One would have thought that these

charters (the city, the Legion, and the Nauvoo House) stood a poor chance of passing the Legislature of a republican people, jealous of their liberties. Nevertheless, they did pass unanimously through both houses. Messrs. Little and Douglas managed with great dexterity with their respective parties. Each party was afraid to object to them for fear of losing the Mormon vote, and each believed that it had secured their favour. A city government under the charter was organized in 1841, and Joe [Joseph]* Smith was elected mayor.

" In this capacity he presided in the common council and assisted in making the laws for the government of the city, and as mayor also he was to see these laws put into force. He was *ex-officio* judge of the mayor's court, and chief-justice of the municipal court, and in these capacities he was to interpret the laws which he had assisted to make. The Nauvoo Legion was also organized with a great multitude of high officers. It was divided into divisions, brigades, cohorts, regiments, battalions, and companies. Each division, brigade, and cohort had its general, and over the whole, as commander-in-chief, Joe [Joseph] Smith was appointed lieutenant-general. These officers, and particularly the last, were created by an ordinance of the court-martial, composed of the commissioned officers of the Legion.

" Thus it was proposed to re-establish for the Mormons a government within a government, a legislature with power to pass ordinances at war with the laws of the State ; courts to execute them, with but little dependence upon the constitutional judiciary, and a military force at their own command, to be governed by its own laws and ordinances, and subject to no State authority but that of the Governor." †

In ecclesiastical affairs " the cause " was quite as prosperous. The British mission was a grand success. The apostles and elders found " the harvest " ripe and ready for the sickle. Thousands had been converted. The Book of Mormon had been re-published, a book of hymns adapted to the new faith had been issued, and the *Millennial Star* was founded. Wealth came with the new converts, and a goodly immigration poured into Nauvoo. Under such favourable conditions the cornerstones of the " House of the Lord " in Nauvoo were laid on the 6th of April, 1841—the eleventh anniversary of the organization of the Church. This was the most pleasant season of Joseph's life ; but his happiness was of short duration. As so

* As Governor Ford thought it no condescension to address the Prophet, while living, as " President," " General," " Honourable," and " Mr. Smith," the Author assumes the liberty of correcting the appellation " Joe " wherever it appears in these quotations.

† Ford's " History of Illinois," p. 265.

long an account of his tribulations has been given, the reader
may now, perhaps, glance with interest at his short-lived
glory.

Consistent with the character of the great mission that was
ever uppermost in his mind, it was to him very appropriate
that the military on this occasion should be blended with the
ecclesiastical in laying the foundation of the Temple. As the
Church was advancing to "power and great glory," it was
proper that the Lieutenant-General should take precedence of
the Prophet. The Legion was, therefore, the first in the programme.

The *Times and Seasons*—the organ of the Church at Nauvoo—furnishes the picture of that " great day in Israel " :

" At an early hour the Lieutenant-General was informed that the Legion was ready for review, and accompanied by his staff, consisting of four
aides-de-camp and twelve guards, nearly all in splendid uniforms, took his
march to the parade ground. On their approach they were met by the
band, beautifully equipped, who received them with a flourish of trumpets and a regular salute, and then struck up a lively air, marching in front
to the stand of the Lieutenant-General. On his approach to the parade
ground the artillery were again fired, and the Legion gave an appropriate
salute. This was indeed a glorious sight, such as we never saw, nor did
we ever expect to see such a one in the West. The several companies presented a beautiful and interesting spectacle, several of them being uni-
formed and equipped, while the rich and costly dresses of the officers
would have become a Buonaparte or a Washington.

" After the arrival of Lieutenant-General Smith, the ladies, who had
made a beautiful silk flag, drove up in a carriage to present it to the Legion. Major-General Bennett very politely attended on them, and conducted them in front of Lieutenant-General Smith, who immediately
alighted from his charger and walked up to the ladies, who presented the
flag, making an appropriate address. Lieutenant-General Smith acknowledged the honour conferred upon the Legion, and stated that as long as
he had the command it should never be disgraced, and then politely bowing to the ladies, gave it into the hands of Major-General Bennett, who
placed it in possession of Cornet Robinson, and it was soon seen gracefully
waving in front of the Legion. During the time of presentation the band
struck up a lively air, and another salute was fired from the artillery.

" After the presentation of the flag, Lieutenant-General Smith, accompanied by his suite, reviewed the Legion, which presented a very imposing
appearance, the different officers saluting as he passed. Lieutenant-General Smith then took his former stand, and the whole Legion passed before
him in review."

As soon as this was ended a procession was formed with the Lieutenant-General-Prophet at its head, followed by his *aides*, brigadiers, military band, infantry, and cavalry, and " a troop " of young ladies, eight abreast." On arrival at the Temple block, the generals, with their staffs and the distinguished visitors, took their position inside the foundation ; the ladies formed on the outside next the wall, the gentlemen and infantry behind, and the cavalry in the rear. When all was ready the signal was given, and the choir burst forth with a new hymn. Sidney Rigdon was the orator, and passed in review the history of the Saints from their small beginnings, their constant persecutions, mobbings, and drivings, till now they had got where they could in peace lay the foundation of a Temple with the prospect of completing it without the interruption of mobs. Another hymn and the invocation of the blessing of the Almighty, prepared the Prophet for the ceremony of laying the " first corner-stone of the Temple of Almighty God." The entire proceeding terminated with the Prophet offering a solemn prayer, imploring the favour of Heaven for the Saints that they might be prospered and preserved to build that house in which to worship the God of their fathers. The *Times and Seasons*, inspired by the glory of the day, presaging, as the Saints believed, the beginning of a new era, gave expression to a hope of peace, which proved sadly delusive :

" It was a gladsome sight and extremely affecting to see the old revolutionary patriots, who had been driven from their homes in Missouri, strike hands and rejoice together *in a land where they knew they would be protected from mobs*, and where they could again enjoy the liberty for which they had fought many a hard battle. The day was indeed propitious ; heaven and earth combined to make the scene as glorious as possible."

Alas ! how soon this sunshine of prosperity was to be clouded, and this rejoicing in peace to be turned into mourning !

Governor Boggs was not yet through with the Prophet. He made a requisition upon Governor Carlin, of Illinois, to surrender Joseph Smith, Sidney Rigdon, and other leading Mormons, " as fugitives from justice." A writ was issued for their arrest, but the sheriff " could not find them ! " The writ was returned, and the matter for the time dropped. Public opin-

9

ion was everywhere against Missouri, and the press sustained the Mormons.

Some months afterwards Joseph was arrested on the same charge, and on a writ of *habeas corpus* the case was heard before Judge Stephen A. Douglas, of the Circuit Court, and the prisoner was discharged on the ground that the writ, having been previously returned to the Governor, was null and void.

CHAPTER XXIII.

POLITICAL DIFFICULTIES.—The Prophet balances between the Whigs and the Democrats—The Neighbours of the Mormons become dissatisfied—Joseph charged with Designs upon the Life of Governor Boggs—He is arrested on a Charge of Treason—Ways that are dark—Governor Ford explains—The First Budding of Polygamy—The Beginning of the End—Serious Charges are made.

THE people of Illinois were now becoming better acquainted with their new fellow-citizens and comprehending the inevitable political issue between a community voting as a unit and the divisional voting of promiscuous citizens. Their immediate neighbours were now as dissatisfied with their presence as were the Missourians formerly, and serious charges were preferred against them.

Joseph Smith and the Mormons had their own purposes and advancement to serve, and they used the Whigs or the Democrats as best suited them. This the politicians fully appreciated and were ready for any measure that would rid them of the power that threatened to control them. Meetings and conventions were held and an anti-Mormon organization was formed for the purpose of urging the Legislature to cancel the liberal charter that had been granted to Nauvoo, to disband the Legion and, if possible, to get rid of the Mormons altogether. Whigs and Democrats were equally hostile and equally zealous in the work, but the Prophet for a time outgeneralled them all and maintained his own.

A citizen of Nauvoo, in his narrative of those days and circumstances, groups together the facts and fears that then agitated the anti-Mormons:

" The issue was for the first time clearly drawn, the election in due time came off, and the Prophet was triumphant. He had elected everything on the county ticket. By his combinations he had completely defeated the anti-Mormon movement and had for county officers his trusty friends devoted to his interests. If his enemies chose to appeal from the decision of the polls, he was ready for them. His battalions were models of discipline, devoted to his service, numbered by thousands, and armed with an efficiency which distinguished no other troops in America. The walls of the Temple were progressing rapidly. The anti-Mormons looked upon the structure with many doubts and apprehensions. Everything the Mormons did was veiled in mystery. This structure resembled no church, its walls of massive limestone were impervious to the shot of the heaviest cannon. It had two tiers of circular windows which looked to the wondering Gentiles very much as if they were port-holes for the manœuvring of cannon. The building was near the centre of a square of four acres, to be surrounded by a massive wall ten feet in height and six in thickness. This the Mormons said was for a promenade ; the anti-Mormons would have told you, it could have been constructed for no other purpose than a fortification, and one which would have stood a heavy bombardment without being breached." *

To add to the feverish excitement, an attempt was made to shoot ex-Governor Boggs, of Missouri, at his residence in Independence. The would-be assassin in firing through the window missed the fatal aim, but the ex-Governor was severely wounded in the head. Charges were preferred against Joseph Smith and Orrin Porter Rockwell †—the former as the instigator and the latter as the instrument in this attempt at murder. An indictment was found to this effect and a requisition was made upon Governor Ford for the person of Joseph Smith.

A writ was issued in August, 1842, but the Prophet was protected by a writ of *habeas corpus*, and the matter was heard in January following before Judge N. Pope, in the United States District Court, at Springfield, which resulted in " an

* This reported enormous strength of the Temple and wall was purely imaginary.

† " Port," as he is generally termed, is commonly credited with being the chief of the Danites. He was a faithful friend of Joseph, and in moments of danger was ever near the Prophet. He was apprehended and tried on this charge, but was able to prove that he was a few miles distant from the place at the time of the attempt at assassination. The firing was probably the act of another, but he, doubtless, was no stranger to the Mormons. The Governor owed his preservation to the misdirection of the assassin's pistol, " caused by the reflection of the light upon the " window glass." It is said that Joseph promised " Port " protection to his life so long as his locks were uncut. This story smacks something of Samson and Delilah ; " Port," however, still wears unshorn locks.

"honourable acquittal;" the Judge directing "this decision
"to be entered on the records in such a way that Mr. Smith
"be no more troubled about the matter." Another demand
for Joseph soon followed from Missouri; this time on a charge
of treason, and the sheriffs of Jackson county, Missouri, and
Carthage, Illinois, stole in upon him while visiting at some distance from Nauvoo; but the sleepless vigilance of the Mor-

Orrin Porter Rockwell.

mons discovered the Prophet's critical situation in time to effect his rescue before the sheriffs could run him into Missouri.
A writ of *habeas corpus* brought Joseph and them to Nauvoo,
where the municipal court discharged the prisoner from arrest
"on the merits of the case," and upon the further ground of
substantial defects in the writ issued by the Governor of Illinois.

The sheriffs had used freely the muzzles of their revolvers
against the ribs of the Prophet to hasten his travel from the
neighbourhood of his friends, and by way of revenge, on their
arrival in Nauvoo, he made them guests at his "mansion," and
was profuse in kindness to them. Subsequently he sued them

for false imprisonment and for using unnecessary violence in his arrest, recovering damages and costs of suit.

The Missourians, still eager for the man who had so often baffled their attempts to take him back to that State, made another application to Governor Ford, asking him to call out the militia of Illinois to effect the Prophet's arrest, but the Governor refused to do so, fearing to lose the political influence of the Mormons, which just at that time was particularly valuable to the Democratic party.

In those troublous times the jurisdiction of the municipal court of Nauvoo was a constant subject of controversy, and especially in this assertion of its right to discharge Joseph from arrest upon the writ of the Governor of the State. Cyrus Walker, a leading Whig politician and able lawyer, sustained the municipal court, and was successful in securing the liberation of Joseph; in gratitude for which the latter promised the former his vote at the pending election for members of Congress. The Democratic party in the mean time were at work with others of the leading Mormons, and "the Lord" was with them—a circumstance probably unique of its kind in political experience.

Mr. Walker very naturally highly estimated the promise of Joseph's vote, and with this imagined Mormon aid he could "read his title clear" to the House of Representatives, but, in the last moments preceding the election, Joseph's brother, Hyrum, received "a revelation" commanding the Mormons to vote for Mr. Hoge, the Democrat. Here was a dilemma! Joseph kept his word to Mr. Walker and personally voted for him, but left the people to vote for whom they pleased, assuring them before the election that he "never knew his brother "Hyrum to tell a lie in his life," and thus Hoge was overwhelmingly elected.

Joseph doubtless intended, when he promised his personal vote to Walker, that the Mormons should vote the Whig ticket; but when subsequently the demand was made by Missouri that Illinois should call out the militia and take the Prophet back to Missouri, Governor Ford's refusal to so employ the militia of Illinois, and "the Lord's" revelation commanding the Mormons to vote the Democratic ticket, were plainly a very earthly negotiation. The Governor denies having been a party to this negotiation with the Mormons, but he admits that three years afterwards he learned that a prominent Democrat had given such a pledge in his name.

Politics, under the most favourable circumstances, have never been classified with the highest morality, and, to the Mormons of Hancock county, the life and liberty of Joseph Smith were of more importance than the election of Mr. Walker. Besides, the disappointed candidate could be consoled with Joseph's kindly recognition and patronage in the world to come —a promise which the Prophet Smith was never slow to make to those who served him.

This little strategy had, however, an unlooked-for and a very unpleasant issue. Governor Ford, in his " political his- " tory of Illinois," exhibits its bearing on the worldly destiny of the modern Prophet :

" It appears that the Mormons had been directed by their leaders to vote the Whig ticket in the Quincy as well as the Hancock district. In the Quincy district Judge Douglas was the Democratic candidate, O. H. Browning the candidate of the Whigs. The leading Mormons at Nauvoo having never determined in favour of the Democrats until a day or two before the election, there was not sufficient time, or it was neglected, to send orders from Nauvoo into the Quincy district to effect a change there. The Mormons in that district voted for Browning. Douglas and his friends being afraid that I might be in his way for the United States Senate, in 1846, seized hold of this circumstance to affect my party-standing, and thereby give countenance to the clamour of the Whigs, secretly whispering it about that I had not only influenced the Mormons to vote for Hoge, but for Browning also. This decided many of the Democrats in favour of the expulsion of the Mormons." *

Of Nauvoo, in its first flush of power, the Governor continues :

" No further demand for the arrest of Joe [Joseph] Smith having been made by Missouri, he became emboldened by success. The Mormons became more arrogant and overbearing. In the winter of 1843–4 the common council passed some further ordinances to protect their leaders from arrest on demand from Missouri. They enacted that no writ issued from any other place than Nauvoo for the arrest of any person in it should be executed in the city, without an approval endorsed thereon by the mayor; that if any public officer, by virtue of any foreign writ, should attempt to

* Ford's " History of Illinois," p. 320.

make an arrest in the city, without such approval of his process, he should be subject to imprisonment for life, and that the Governor of the State should not have the power of pardoning the offender without the consent of the mayor. When these ordinances were published they created general astonishment. Many people began to believe in good earnest that the Mormons were about to set up a separate government for themselves in defiance of the laws of the State."

This was certainly an extraordinary municipal jurisdiction, but remembering the expulsion of the Saints from Missouri, and the constantly recurring demands of its authorities, endorsed by the writs of the Governor of Illinois, for the person of Joseph Smith (with the view, as was generally averred, by both Saints and sinners, of murdering him), it is evident that the Nauvoo municipality fully comprehended the desperation of their situation. Add to this the sequel of the dastardly assassination of the Prophet and his brother, while in jail awaiting trial, under the promised protection of the Governor of the State, and the adoption of any means, however unconstitutional, which promised, if nothing more, temporary protection to the Prophet, can be readily understood.

But the trials of the Prophet were not only with the " out- " siders." Trouble from within was brooding over the Church. Polygamy was dawning upon the minds of the Prophet and a few of the leading elders, and preceding shadows of something resembling " affinity," and what was termed the " spirit- " ual-wife " doctrine, began to develop in the lives of some prominent men. This period of Mormon history is a perfect muddle of affirmation and denial, charge and counter-charge, oath and counter-oath. Men like John C. Bennett were charged by the Mormon leaders with the grossest corruption and marital infidelity. They, in turn, reversed the responsibility, and charged Joseph with teaching it to them. Councils were afterwards held, trials, witnesses, " confessions," and " forgiveness " were recorded, then soon after some new phase of the same kind of dark work was again revealed, the accused were " excommunicated " for their " iniquities " and " corrupt " practices," and an irreconcilable breach was made. The testimony on both sides is so perfectly bewildering that even to-day may be found, in Salt Lake City, a husband and wife in the

Mormon Church, much affected by a circumstance of these times, who are still as valiant as ever—the husband in asserting the immaculate purity of the Prophet, and the wife as stoutly asserting the opposite—from her own knowledge.

Surrounded, as Joseph Smith was at that time, with so many difficulties, it would be reasonable to expect that he would have been extraordinarily circumspect in the introduction of any proposed change in the marital relations ; but with all his caution he was unsuccessful in protecting himself from charges of the gravest description. His revelation on polygamy contains sufficient evidence that he regarded the Christian marriage as utterly wrong, and that the ceremony of any priest was valueless in comparison with his own order of priesthood ; but that he advocated, or in any way countenanced, the *promiscuous intercourse* that was charged to him by such men as Bennett, the Author has been unable to find any evidence beyond that of the one lady alluded to, and whose statement is somewhat neutralized by the fact that it is made as a counter-charge to one of Joseph's, accusing Bennett of the outrage of an absent husband. Many, however, believe the lady's statement.

Bennett made a tour through the West, lecturing on the enormities of Mormonism, and stirring up the people to mob-violence, while Francis M. Higbee had Joseph arrested for defamation of character, on a writ granted by the circuit court of Hancock county. But the municipal court of Nauvoo, ever ready at his call, protected him with a writ of *habeas corpus*, and on examination he was discharged on the ground that the suit was instituted through malice.

CHAPTER XXIV.

JOSEPH PREDICTS THE ROCKY MOUNTAIN ZION.—He designs to found there an Independent State—Becomes a Candidate for the Presidency of the United States—Assails Clay and Calhoun—Great Trouble with Apostates—Politics and Polygamy threaten to engulf him—The Nauvoo *Expositor* founded and destroyed—Writs issued for the Arrest of the Prophet—He resolves on Flight.

HARASSED by prosecutions from every side, in constant danger of being surprised and carried off to Missouri, and realizing that political jealousies were working up the State of Illinois against him and the Mormon people, the Prophet turned his eyes towards the Pacific to find there an abiding-place for Zion. As early as 1842, he prophesied that the Saints would remove to the Rocky Mountains, and in the spring of 1844, while troubles were increasing upon him, he selected a company of men to explore that unknown region, prophesying at the same time that within five years from that date, the Saints should be located there beyond the influence of mobs. In his private history he writes under date of February 20th, 1844:

"I instructed the Twelve Apostles to send out a delegation and investigate the localities, California and Oregon, and hunt out a good location where we can remove to after the Temple is completed and where we can build a city in a day and have a government of our own: get up into the mountains where the devil cannot dig us out, and live in a healthy climate where we can live as old as we have a mind to."

His design was to found an independent State somewhere west of the Rocky Mountains, and to further that end he sent a delegation to Washington seeking the countenance and, if possible, the coöperation of the Government to his scheme. The apostle Hyde,* as chief of that delegation, wrote from the

* This is the same Hyde who apostatized and left the Church in Missouri. He repented, pleaded with Joseph and the Church, and was reinstalled in full feather.

seat of government, April 25, 1844, that the Prophet's proposition to go West found great favour with leading senators, especially with Senator Stephen A. Douglas, and some members
of the Cabinet, but the Government feared that a misunderstanding might arise with England. Oregon was then by
treaty jointly occupied by both nations, and it was apprehended
that going as the emigrants would, as something like an armed
force and in such numbers, it might be regarded by England
as an infraction of that treaty, and so the Government declined
any recognition of the proposed exodus.

Inexplicable enough, as it seemed to the uninitiated, at the
very time that this proposition was made by Joseph to move
to the West, his name was put forth as a candidate for the
Presidency of the United States, and hundreds [Governor Ford
says " two or three thousand "] of the elders were sent over
the States preaching Mormonism and electioneering for Joseph.
At that time Clay and Calhoun were rival candidates, and Joseph failed not to ask them categorically what their course of
action would be towards the Mormons in case of election. The
Prophet was never without a double string to his bow—if it
were possible to have two, and when he apprehended that personally he might fail in reaching the chair of Washington, he
wanted to know what either of the other candidates would do
before he cast the Mormon vote in Illinois.

Joseph was dissatisfied with both Clay and Calhoun. He
handled them severely in lengthy communications for the indefinite answers they had sent him, and issued his own " Address
" to the American people " on the leading topics of the day.

It is difficult to believe that Joseph meant more in giving
his name as a candidate than simply to place before the public
his views upon national policy, and exhibit, as he believed, his
fitness as a statesman to become the chief executive of the
nation.

The incidents in the history of Nauvoo from this time to
the assassination of Joseph Smith, and after that to the expulsion of the Mormons from Illinois, are intensely interesting, and
as Governor Ford's record of the circumstances of those times
is in a measure official, citations from it are doubly valuable
and will be freely used. No writer on either side of a conten-

tion could well be perfectly unbiased or even strictly truthful, as he could not personally know the movements of both sides. The reader will, therefore, receive with caution even the Governor's statement, observing, however, that whatever colouring there may be here and there against the Mormons, it is more than balanced by the damaging admissions he makes against their enemies. He says:

" Soon after these institutions were established, Joe [Joseph] Smith began to play the tyrant over several of his followers. The first act of this sort which excited attention was an attempt to take the wife of William Law, one of his most talented and principal disciples, and make her his spiritual wife. By means of his common council, without the authority of law, he established a recorder's office in Nauvoo, in which alone the titles of property could be recorded. In the same manner and with the same want of legal authority, he established an office for issuing marriage licenses to the Mormons, so as to give him absolute control of the marrying propensities of his people. He proclaimed that none in the city should purchase real estate to sell again, but himself. He also permitted no one but himself to have a license in the city for the sale of spirituous liquors; and in many other ways he undertook to regulate and control the business of the Mormons. This despotism administered by a corrupt and unprincipled man soon became intolerable. William Law, one of the most eloquent preachers of the Mormons, who appeared to me to be a deluded but conscientious and candid man, Wilson Law, his brother, major-general of the Legion, and four or five other Mormon leaders, resolved upon a rebellion against the authority of the Prophet. They designed to enlighten their brethren and fellow-citizens upon the new institutions, the new turn given to Mormonism and the practices under the new system, by procuring a printing-press and establishing a newspaper in the city,* to be the organ of their complaints and views. But they never issued but one number. Before the second could appear the press was demolished by an order of the common council, and the conspirators were ejected from the Mormon Church.

" The Mormons themselves published the proceedings of the council in the trial and destruction of the heretical press; from which it does not appear that any one was tried, or that the editor or any of the owners of the property had notice of the trial, or were permitted to defend in any particular.

" The proceeding was an *ex-parte* proceeding, partly civil and partly ecclesiastical, against the press itself. No jury was called or sworn, nor were the witnesses required to give their evidence upon oath. The councillors stood up, one after another, and some of them several times, and related what they pretended to know. In this mode it was abundantly

* The Nauvoo *Expositor.*

proved that the owners of the proscribed press were sinners, whoremasters, thieves, swindlers, counterfeiters and robbers, the evidence of which is reported in the trial at full length. It was altogether the most curious and irregular trial that ever was recorded in any civilized country; and one finds difficulty in determining whether the proceedings of the council were more the result of insanity or depravity. The trial resulted in the conviction of the press as a public nuisance, the mayor was ordered to see it abated as such, and if necessary to call the Legion to his assistance.

" The mayor issued his warrant to the city marshal, who, aided by a portion of the Legion, proceeded to the obnoxious printing-office, and destroyed the press and scattered the types and other materials." *

The editor and seceding Mormons hastened to Carthage, and writs were issued for the arrest of the mayor of Nauvoo, Joseph Smith, and others engaged in the destruction of the *Expositor*. The municipal court of Nauvoo set aside the writs and discharged the prisoners. Aroused by the inflammatory reports of what the Mormons were charged with contemplating, and believing that there was an " irrepressible conflict " at hand, a committee was appointed at Carthage to visit the Governor and ask that the militia be called out to execute that writ. The Governor determined to investigate in person the complaints, and immediately visited Carthage. On his arrival he found an armed force already assembled and hourly increasing under the summons and direction of the constable of the county, to serve as a *posse comitatus*, to assist in the execution of that writ. The general of the brigade had called upon the militia of the counties of McDonough and Schuyler, and a considerable number had been gathered at Warsaw under command of Col. Levi Williams.

Governor Ford informed the mayor and council of Nauvoo of the complaint, and requested a committee to be sent to meet him, to lay before him their statement of the difficulty. Such acknowledgments were made by this committee that the Governor readily concluded what the facts really were. He says :

" Convinced that the Mormon leaders had committed a crime in the destruction of the press, and had resisted the execution of process, I determined to exert the whole force of the State, if necessary, to bring them to justice. But seeing the great excitement in the public mind, and the manifest tendency of this excitement to run into mobocracy, I was of opin-

* Ford's " History of Illinois," pp. 322-3-4.

ion that before I acted, I ought to obtain a pledge from the officers and
men to support me in strictly legal measures, and to protect the prisoners
in case they surrendered; for I was determined, if possible, the laws of
the land should not be made a cats-paw of a mob to reduce these people
to a quiet surrender, as the convenient victims of popular fury. I therefore called together the whole force then assembled at Carthage, and made
an address, explaining to them what I could, and what I could not, legally
do, and also adducing to them various reasons why they as well as the
Mormons should submit to the laws; and why, if they had resolved upon
revolutionary proceedings, their purpose should be abandoned. The assembled troops seemed much pleased with the address, and upon its conclusion, the officers and men unanimously voted with acclamation to sustain me in a strictly legal course, and that the prisoners should be protected from violence. Upon the arrival of additional forces from Warsaw,
McDonough, and Schuyler, similar addresses were made with the same
result.

"It seemed to me that these votes fully authorized me to promise the
accused Mormons the protection of the law in case they surrendered.
They were accordingly duly informed that if they surrendered they would
be protected, and if they did not the whole force of the State would be
called out, if necessary, to compel their submission. A force of ten men
was dispatched with the constable to make the arrests, and to guard the
prisoners to headquarters.

"In the mean time, Joe [Joseph] Smith, as lieutenant-general of the
Nauvoo Legion, had declared martial law in the city; the Legion was assembled and ordered under arms; the members of it residing in the country were ordered into town. The Mormon settlements obeyed the summons of their leader, and marched to his assistance. Nauvoo was one
great military camp, strictly guarded and watched, and no ingress or
egress was allowed, except upon the strictest examination. . . . .

"However, upon the arrival of the constable and guard, the mayor
and common council at once signified their willingness to surrender, and
stated their readiness to proceed to Carthage next morning at eight
o'clock. Martial law had previously been abolished. The hour of eight
o'clock came, and the accused failed to make their appearance. The constable and his escort returned. The constable made no effort to arrest any
of them, nor would he or the guard delay their departure one minute beyond the time, to see whether an arrest could be made. Upon their return they reported that they had been informed that the accused had fled
and could not be found." *

The crisis had arrived. Writs for his apprehension, and
writs of *habeas corpus* for his discharge, had in turn done their
work till the culmination had been reached. Joseph resolved

---

* Ford's " History of Illinois," pp. 332-3.

on flight. He crossed the river to Montrose, where he could conceal himself till ready for his departure for the Eastern States or the Canadas, as reported by some, or for the Rocky Mountains, as reported by others.*

* The apostle John Taylor says: "It was Brother Joseph's opinion that, should we leave for a time, public excitement, which was then so intense, would be allayed; that it would throw on the Governor the responsibility of keeping the peace; that in the event of any outrage, the onus would rest on the Governor, who was amply prepared with troops, and could command all the forces of the State to preserve order; and that the acts of his own men would be an overwhelming proof of their seditious designs, not only to the Governor, but to the world. He moreover thought that, in the East, where he intended to go, public opinion would be set right in relation to these matters, and its expression would partially influence the West, and that, after the first ebulition, things would assume a shape that would justify his return."

CHAPTER XXV.

THE PROPHET SURRENDERS TO THE LAW.—The Governor pledges the Protection of the State for his Safety—The Country intensely excited—The Destruction of the Nauvoo *Expositor* a Fatal Error—The Militia in Arms—The Murder of the Prophet planned—His Enemies resolve to kill him while Governor Ford visits Nauvoo—A Review of the Prophet's Life and Works.

MRS. EMMA SMITH, to whom Joseph was warmly devoted, notwithstanding the number of the other Mrs. Smiths, held empire in his heart, and at this critical moment was used by

The Prophet surrenders to the Law.

some "faint-hearted "brethren" to beg Joseph's return to Nauvoo. The lady is said to have written, to him and to his brother Hyrum who was with him, "a "cruel and indignant "letter," reproaching them as "coward "shepherds who had "left the sheep in "danger and fled." Joseph was anything but a "coward," and though he seemed to fully comprehend the danger of his position, he resolved at once to return to Nauvoo and give himself up to the officers of the law.

Governor Ford furnishes the incidents leading to the assassination of the two brothers:

"On the 23rd or 24th day of June, Joe [Joseph] Smith, the mayor of Nauvoo, together with his brother Hyrum and all the members of the council, and all others demanded, came into Carthage and surrendered themselves prisoners to the constable on the charge of riot. They all voluntarily entered into a recognizance before the justice of the peace for their appearance at court to answer the charge, and all of them were discharged from custody except Joe [Joseph] and Hyrum Smith, against whom the magistrate had issued a new writ on a complaint of treason. They were immediately arrested by the constable on this charge and retained in his custody to answer it. . . .

"Soon after the surrender of the Smiths, at their request I dispatched Captain Singleton with his company, from Brown county, to Nauvoo to guard the town, and I authorized him to take command of the Legion. He reported to me afterwards that he called out the Legion for inspection; and that upon two hours' notice, two thousand of them assembled, all of them armed, and this after the public arms had been taken away from them. So it appears that they had a sufficiency of private arms for any reasonable purpose.

"After the Smiths had been arrested on the new charge of treason, the justice of the peace postponed the examination because neither of the parties were prepared with their witnesses for trial. In the mean time he committed them to the jail of the county for greater security. . . . Neither they nor I seriously apprehended an attack on the jail through the guard stationed to protect it. Nor did I apprehend the least danger on their part of an attempt to escape; for I was very sure that any such attempt would have been the signal of their immediate death." *

If his Excellency's heart was void of all rancour against the Prophet, his head might possibly deceive itself respecting the better disposition of others towards the prisoners; but it required no great acumen to discover a plan and purpose to compass the death of the Smiths. In the midst of such excitement and threatenings as those which he witnessed and heard, no promises from those in arms—partly mob and partly militia—should have been asked; not the slightest confidence could be placed in them! The Governor's pledge of protection based on his own personal honour, the honour of the officers under his command and the honour of the State, was too great a trust to be committed to the hands of Captain Smith of the Carthage Grays. With such surroundings and associations while in Carthage, the Governor's repeated assurances of protection lacked evidence of that good faith which marks a resolute and reliable man.

In prison, on the 26th, Governor Ford pledged himself to

* Ford's " History of Illinois," pp. 337-8.

10

the Prophet that he would not go to Nauvoo, as he then proposed, without taking him and his brother Hyrum with him ;
but on the following morning he did set out without them for
the City of the Saints. To the Prophet and his friends this
violation of his pledge was regarded as the beginning of the
doom in store for them :

" The force assembled at Carthage amounted to about twelve or thirteen hundred men, and it was calculated that four or five hundred more
were assembled at Warsaw. Nearly all that portion resident in Hancock
were anxious to be marched into Nauvoo. This measure was supposed to
be necessary to search for counterfeit money, and the apparatus to make
it, and also to strike a salutary terror into the Mormon people by an exhibition of the force of the State. . . . .

" Two or three days' preparation had been made for this expedition. I
observed that some of the people became more and more excited and inflammatory the further the preparations were advanced. Occasional
threats came to my ears of destroying the city and murdering or expelling
the inhabitants. I had no objection to ease the terrors of the people by
such a display of force, and was most anxious also to search for the alleged
apparatus for making counterfeit money ; and in fact to inquire into all
the charges against that people if I could have been assured of my command against mutiny and insubordination. But I gradually learned to
my entire satisfaction that there was a plan to get the troops into Nauvoo,
and there to begin the war, probably by some of our own party or some
of the seceding Mormons, taking advantage of the night to fire on our
own force, and then laying it on the Mormons. I was satisfied there were
those amongst us fully capable of such an act, hoping that in the alarm,
bustle, and confusion of a militia camp the truth could not be discovered,
and that it might lead to the desired collision." *

The Governor urged these considerations upon a council of
officers, but " such was the blind fury prevailing at this time,"
that the majority of the council adhered to the first resolution
of marching into Nauvoo. This induced him to disband the
troops both at Carthage and Warsaw, with the exception of
three companies, two of which were retained as a guard to the
jail, and the other to accompany him to Nauvoo. After essaying to excuse himself from the censure of having placed the
Smiths under the guard of the Carthage Grays—their well-
known enemies—the Governor continues :

" Having ordered the guard, and left General Demming in command
in Carthage and discharged the residue of the militia, I immediately de-

* Ford's " History of Illinois," p. 332–40.

parted for Nauvoo, eighteen miles distant, accompanied by Colonel Buckmaster, quartermaster-general, and Captain Dunn's company of dragoons.

" After we had proceeded four miles, Colonel Buckmaster intimated to
me a suspicion that an attack would be made on the jail. He stated the
matter as a mere suspicion, arising from having seen two persons converse
together at Carthage with some air of mystery. I myself entertained no
suspicion of such an attack; at any rate, none before the next day in the
afternoon, because it was notorious that we had departed from Carthage
with the declared intention of being absent at least two days. I could
not believe that any person would attack the jail whilst we were in Nauvoo, and thereby expose my life and the life of my companions to the sudden vengeance of the Mormons upon hearing of the death of their leaders. Nevertheless, acting upon the principle of providing against mere
possibilities, I sent back one of the company with a special order to Captain Smith to guard the jail strictly and at peril of his life until my return." *

From the moment that the Mormon leaders arrived at Carthage it was clearly evident that there was a determination to
murder the Prophet. He and his associates went there to answer for the destruction of the Nauvoo *Expositor*, and for that
alone. On the morning of the 24th, the accused appeared before Robert F. Smith, a justice of the peace and captain of
the Carthage Grays, and, after examination, gave bail, each in
the sum of $500, to appear at the succeeding term of the Han-
cock county Circuit Court. Immediately after they were set
at liberty, a writ was sworn out against Joseph and his brother
Hyrum for " treason," by Augustine Spencer and a man named
. . . . Norton—" two worthless 'fellows." This " treason "
consisted in " levying war against the State of Illinois," and
found its interpretation in the Prophet fortifying Nauvoo and
" calling out the Legion to resist the force under the command
" of the Governor." This charge was a mere pretext and an
act of gross injustice to " Lieutenant-General " Smith—whatever his religious profession might be—for, as lieutenant-general of the Legion, he was instructed by Governor Ford on
the outbreak of the disturbances to call out the militia to defend the city against the mobocracy that threatened its destruction. For treason, no bail could be accepted ; and as neither the parties for the prosecution or the defence were ready
to go to trial, but desired a postponement of the case, the jus-

* Ford's " History of Illinois," pp. 345-6.

tice of the peace remanded both the Prophet and the patriarch back to prison.

The counsel for the accused—two very able "Gentile" lawyers—protested against the commitment of their clients without a hearing, and an appeal was made to the Governor, but—" he was sorry that the thing had occurred ; that he did "not believe the charges ; that he thought the best thing to " be done was to let the law take its course." The two brothers were now in the snare that had been prepared for their feet, and they quietly submitted to incarceration. •

In order to return to Carthage that same night, to prevent, as he claims, an attack upon the jail, the Governor halted the baggage wagons and hurried on to Nauvoo with his company. He arrived there about four o'clock in the afternoon of the 27th of June, when he assembled the citizens and reviewed the situation :

" In this address I stated to them how, and in what, their functionaries had violated the laws, also the many scandalous reports in circulation against them, and that these reports, whether true or false, were generally believed by the people. I distinctly stated to them the amount of hatred and prejudice which prevailed everywhere against them, and the causes of it, at length. I also told them plainly and emphatically that if any vengeance should be attempted openly or secretly, against the persons or property of the citizens who had taken part against their leaders, that the public hatred and excitement was such that thousands would assemble for the total destruction of their city, and the extermination of their people, and that no power in the State would be able to prevent it. During this address some impatience and resentment were manifested by the Mormons at the recital of the various reports enumerated concerning them, which they strenuously and indignantly denied to be true. They claimed to be a law-abiding people, and insisted that as they looked to the law alone for their protection, so were they careful themselves to observe its provisions. Upon the conclusion of this address I proposed to take a vote on the question, whether they would strictly observe the laws, even in opposition to their Prophet and leaders. The vote was unanimous in favour of this proposition. The anti-Mormons contended that such a vote from the Mormons signified nothing." *

In the narrative of "the martyrdom of Joseph Smith" there is a very different version given of the spirit and intent

* Ford's " History of Illinois," p. 347.

of the whole course pursued by the Governor from that which his own pen has traced.

The apostle Taylor's relation of a semi-conversation, semi-discussion between Governor Ford and the Prophet in the Carthage jail has in the light of after-acts, both Mormon and anti-Mormon, an air of strict truthfulness, and exhibits Joseph with the advantage of the argument relative to everything in Nauvoo history that was the subject of conversation, save the destruction of the press. There the Prophet doubtless realized that his action as mayor had not the support of legal form, and with that fact the Governor made his strong point against him, and treated all his statements of grievances against "apos-"tates" and anti-Mormons with ill-concealed indifference. "The press," said his Excellency, "in the United States is "looked upon as the bulwark of freedom, and its destruction "in Nauvoo was represented and looked upon as a high-handed "measure and manifests to the people a disposition on your "part to suppress the liberty of speech and of the press. "That act," added his Excellency, "together with the refusal "to comply with the requisitions of a writ were the principal "causes of the difficulty."

The Prophet at that time, however, was able to clear himself of all other charges, and while he claimed that he had acted in good faith in destroying the press "as a nuisance," and calling out the Legion to protect Nauvoo on the instructions of the Governor; he also announced himself ready to meet the legal liabilities for the destruction of the *Expositor*, if they had been in error. But it was now too late. The argument of the Prophet or that of Governor Ford could avail little; his enemies had determined that the prisoners should be murdered, and the Governor was not the man to fight and conquer the contemplated crime.

The eventful history of the Mormon Prophet is now drawing to a close. The singular commencement of his public life, his angel visits, his visions and his revelations, have been given sufficiently *in extenso* where a principle, a fact, or a link in history was necessary to elucidate his career. The insignificant number of disciples at the organization of his Church, the poverty of his family, his lack of education and social stand-

ing in society, and the barriers that crossed the path in which
he was destined to tread, have been already portrayed to the
reader.

He is seen surmounting every obstacle, treating his defi-
ciencies as Heaven's favours, and presenting to the religious
world his revelations with an impetuosity that stamps him as a
man of extraordinary faith, or the boldest of impostors. Disciples gather round him, hang upon his words as to life, and
subjugate themselves with a servile humility and obedience inconsistent with the age and the natural progress of the human race. The endearments of paternal homes, and the most
sacred associations of life are rent asunder that the faithful
may gather at his word. Intellect, aspiration, ambition,
wealth, and personality are thrown at his feet. The foundations of cities are laid, temples are erected, missions over sea
and land are undertaken at his bidding, and the rude life of
portentous war is accepted as a duty as readily as the preaching of peace and salvation.

The poor farm labourer merges in the preacher, the preacher becomes a translator, a prophet, a seer, a revelator, a banker,
an editor, a mayor, a lieutenant-general, a candidate for the
presidency of the world's greatest Republic, and last of all,
though not the least difficult of his achievements, he becomes
the husband of many wives. This variety of work, accomplished within the short space of fourteen years, exhibits a fer-
tility of brain, and a restless activity which stamps Joseph
Smith, the Mormon Prophet, as one of earth's most remarkable men.

From the beginning to the end of his public career he never
once doubted his mission—never once wavered in the belief
that he was ordained " before the world was," to lay in this
age the foundation of a kingdom whose empire should cover
the habitable globe, and reaching by doctrine, by principle, by
ordination, by endowment, by organization, by faith, from
earth to heaven, make of the posterity of Adam one grand and
universal brotherhood. Such was his dream.

He knew no sectarianism in his faith, though in his working " the Saints " alone were the favourites of Heaven, and the
objects of its peculiar and special care. There was nothing of

mysterious awe associated with him. In one hour of the day he might be found locked up in his sanctum with his amanuensis, giving to earth the secrets of the Gods;* the very next hour he was brooding over some scheme for his people's aggrandizement, or it might be that the hour which succeeded the revelation was spent in his favourite wrestling with the strongest of the brethren whom he chanced to meet. He would visit the sick, administer to them by the laying on of hands in holy ordinance, and following that, as likely as not, he was ready to kick some one out of his presence who had insulted either him or any of his brethren. He was sociable with everybody, and was convivial at times with his special friends. In brief, there was nothing about him, outside of his announced prophetic mission, to create reverence or inspire his disciples with awe. This was really the secret of his unlimited power and influence over the people. In his presence every one was at ease. His eccentricities or errors were rather virtues than defects. They loved him because he was to them so human and so like themselves, and yet, when necessary, his dignity was ready, and his mission became divine in their wondering eyes.

His success was not due to studied art ; it was the singularity of a nature that upheaves itself among the masses of humanity at but rare intervals in history. He was only suited to what he did, and following the instincts and leadings of his nature he only did what he did. Had he tried another *rôle* than that of leader of a peculiarly believing mass who needed just such a leadership, he would have failed. The world is sparsely strewn with such a people. He was their prophet. When he essayed the banker he was a failure, when he became the merchant he was muddled ; but when he talked of glory in the Temple, or on his military charger was speaking to an audience which had everything to hope for—kingdoms, thrones, dominions, principalities, powers, and universal empire were all within the range of their vision. Finance and commerce required the method and control of close calculation. Method was a burden to him, and control he never knew. In the re-

---

* " With Gods he soared in the realms of day,
    And men he taught the heavenly way."
                                    Hymn 290.

gion of the clouds, in the far-distant stars, and in the glory of Kolob, next to where " the Greatest dwells," he was perfectly at home, and knew it all. To him his priesthood was the key that unlocked the mystery of the past, made clear the present, and laid bare the future. He never assumed to be other than mortal, and taught every one to " be natural." He confessed his faults, when overtaken in public in moments of joyousness, with the simplicity of a child ; but in his projects he out-dreamed humanity, and ambitioned nothing short of peerage with the Gods.*

Such was the man, in the full-tide of his popularity, in the flush of a proud manhood, less than two-score years of age, whom the reader is now to visit in Carthage jail, on the 27th of June, 1844.

* A metrical review of the mission and greatness, past, present, and future, of Joseph, from the pen of the apostle Taylor, illustrates the Mormon idea of the Prophet's dignity :

> " Unchanged in death. with a *Saviour's* love,
> He pleads their cause in the courts above.
>
> " His home's in the sky, *he dwells with the Gods*,
> Far from the furious rage of mobs.
>
> " He died ! he died for those he loved :
> *He reigns ! he reigns* in the realms above.
>
> " Shout, shout, ye Saints ; this boon is given —
> We'll meet our martyred Seer in heaven."

ASSASSINATION OF JOSEPH SMITH.

CHAPTER XXVI.

LAST HOURS OF THE PROPHET.—The Presentiment of his Death—The Murderers—The Attack upon the Jail—The Assassination of the Prophet and the Patriarch—An Apostle shot—Thrilling Narrative of a Survivor—"Two Minutes in Jail."

WHEN he left Nauvoo, on the morning of the 23rd, the Prophet was accompanied to Carthage by a number of the leading men of the Church, in addition to those summoned to the same place for the destruction of the *Expositor*. After bail had been accepted for the appearance of the accused, they nearly all returned to Nauvoo, leaving, however, behind as many of his friends as he desired to stay with him.

Between this time and his death a number of gentlemen called upon him, who were deeply solicitous for his safety, yet hopeful of his deliverance, and it was probably not until after Governor Ford's departure for Nauvoo, on the morning of the 27th, that any conversation took place respecting the probability of murder. Had that issue been apprehended, the Mormons at Nauvoo would have delivered him, even if the whole State of Illinois had forbidden their marching to his aid. The consequences would never have been considered. His safety was to them everything.

But the hours in Carthage jail were fleeting with that ominous haste that ever marks the ebbing current of life's career. As the shadows on the prison walls announced the receding day, the approach of death was sensibly felt by the Prophet and his friends. Dr. Richards, one of the apostles, proposed to Joseph that if his life might be accepted in the Prophet's stead, he would freely give it. The apostle Taylor asked only permission, and "in five hours he would take him from his "prison." These were no idle offers. Life and deliverance were his for half a word; but at this critical moment Joseph seemed to forget all thoughts of life and of the world. It is claimed by the believing Saints that he had premonitions of his approaching end, and that on some occasions previous to the *Expositor* difficulty, he had spoken of the termination of his mission. So long had his bow been strung to its utmost tension, that this feeling of indifference can readily be appreciated without either miracle or divine manifestation ; but to him and his, impressions had special interpretations. Add to this the galling humiliation of being chided by some brethren as a " cow-" ard " when he attempted to escape on the presentation of the sheriff's writ, and then the weariness of earthly things is easy to comprehend. Life at last had lost its charm ; the charge of cowardice had stung him, and he was ready to die. It was neither want of friends nor want of ability to secure his escape. He was weary, and with his fertile faith it was easy to listen to the suggestion of those ever-ready words—" The " blood of the martyrs is the seed of the Church." Besides, a " prophet " never dies. The portals of another world hail him as the advancing conqueror, and the field of his labours becomes more extended. Joseph was ready for the change.* It is stated that on leaving Nauvoo for Carthage he said : " I

---

* Notwithstanding this apparent readiness to meet death, and the deep and clear divine impressions claimed to have been imparted to the Prophet of his forthcoming end, it is understood that he managed to send from prison a communication to the Mormon officer in military command at Nauvoo, to bring with all possible dispatch a portion of the Legion to protect him from treachery, and from that assassination which he had then so much cause to apprehend. This military commander put the Prophet's communication into his pocket and gave no heed to the call for help. No one was acquainted with the contents of the paper, and the officer was, therefore, he presumed, safe in disregarding it.

After the Prophet's death, by some accident or other, this communication was lost and was picked up on the street and read. The intelligence that Joseph had called for aid and none had been rendered him was soon bruited among the Saints, and excited their deepest indignation, as they were not only ready to march at a moment's notice, but were eager for the opportunity.

Some time afterwards, when all was quiet, this "coward and traitor" as some of the Mormons called him, or "fool and idiot" as others said, was sent on a mission to the Western frontiers, accompanied by a faithful elder. While travelling alone with his companion, he fell ill and died, *it is said of dysentery*. His companion buried him.

" am going like a lamb to the slaughter, but I am calm as a
"summer morning. I have a conscience void of offence tow-
" ards God and towards all men. I shall die innocent, and it
" shall yet be said of me ' He was murdered in cold blood.' " *

Governor Ford was at Nauvoo, haranguing the Mormons,
and reading to them homilies on obedience to law ; the Prophet
and his friends were in Carthage jail, impressed with thoughts
of treachery, abandonment, and probably coming death, while
at the same instant the murderers were preparing for their
tragic *rôle*. Death was on the wing.

To impress the Mormons with the power of his might, the
Governor had conceived the notion of parading the militia under his immediate command through the streets of Nauvoo ;
but intimations of possible danger had at the last hour counselled the abandonment of that project.

The triumph of " crowing over the Mormons," as expressed
by a Gentile writer, was a natural ambition for the class of
men who had rushed to arms in their hatred of Mormonism
and its Prophet ; but the Governor's timely abandonment of
the scheme was a fortunate decision. The march of two thousand militia through a city containing five thousand men inimical to them, with arms in their hands, in possession of every
house, and these, too, men as ready as ever fanatics were, to
fight the world for their religion and for their leader, must certainly have been a dangerous experiment. The Governor
claims for his prudence other considerations, but the disbanded
militia exclaimed bitterly against their disappointment.

Golden's Point, about six miles east of Nauvoo, was fixed
upon as the rendezvous of the troops on the morning of the
27th. Those who were in and around Carthage were at once
disbanded, with the exception of one company of the Carthage
Grays, under the command of Captain Smith, who, as justice
of the peace, had committed the Prophet and his brother for
treason. This company was to perform the double duty of protecting the prisoners and repelling any attempt at their rescue.

The regiment from the southwest part of the county, under the command of Col. Levi Williams, had not yet reached
Carthage. The Governor selected Thomas C. Sharpe, the edi-

* " Doctrine and Covenants," p. 335.

tor of the Warsaw *Signal*, who had written more inflammatory articles against the Mormons than all the others put together, to carry the orders for disbanding his regiment to
Colonel Williams.

The Prophet and his brethren in jail "felt unusually dull
"and languid, with a remarkable depression of spirits." One
by one his personal friends had left during the afternoon to
attend to some matters of business which interested the prisoners. These the guard at the jail from this time would not permit to return, and this was additional cause for alarm. One
of them was driven at the point of the bayonet out of the town,
and threatened with death if he returned. He immediately

The Apostle Taylor.

repaired to Nauvoo to raise men to protect the prisoners; but
the opportunity for such service was past. Another of the
brethren, on leaving the prison, handed his revolver to the
Prophet and this was the only weapon that Joseph, Hyrum,
and the two apostles had among them. After dinner they sent
another brother for some wine, for they "were dull and heavy;"
and he, also, was not permitted to return. The prisoners hoped
that the stimulant "would revive them," but no vinous med-
icament could elevate their spirits;—death was brooding over
them. Elder Taylor sang Montgomery's pathetic hymn:

"A poor wayfaring man of grief,"

to a plaintive air as appropriate to the occasion as Mozart's
" Dead March " in *Saul*.   " It was very much in accordance
" with our feelings at the time," wrote elder Taylor, "for our
" spirits were all depressed, dull, gloomy and surcharged with
" indefinite ominous forebodings."   After a little while, Hyrum
asked the Elder " again to sing that song."   He pled that he
" did not feel like singing," but Hyrum felt the cordiality of a
responsive soul, and they continued :

> "In prison I saw him next condemned
>   To meet a traitor's doom at morn ;
> The tide of lying tongues I stemm'd,
>   And honoured him 'mid shame and scorn."

The Elder had just got through with the last comfort he
could administer to his friend on earth, and the echoes of his
sonorous voice had hardly died away when the closing scene
of the tragedy opened.

A gentleman, a resident then and now of Nauvoo, uncon-
nected with either the Mormons or the mob, furnishes the Author with the following facts.

" The afternoon of the day was dull and quiet.   The disbanded troops
had returned to their homes, and the people of the little village of Carthage congratulated themselves on the restoration of quiet and order
about their homes.   Their joy at their deliverance was, however, of short
duration.   Near sunset an armed force, numbering perhaps one hundred
men, was seen stealthily approaching in single file upon the Nauvoo road.
Their destination was evidently the jail, as they bent their steps in that
direction.   This body of men was well armed with rifles and muskets.
Their faces were disfigured with paint, so that recognition was impossible.
Their march was silent as the grave.   The bewildered by-standers specu-
lated on the meaning of the apparition of these silent yet grim and determined soldiers.   Many supposed it was a party of armed Mormons intent on the rescue of their leaders from imprisonment : others, who were
shrewder or in possession of better means of information, thought it
meant anything but a happy deliverance for the imprisoned Saints.   The
silent and rapid approach of the intruders soon set at rest all occasion for
speculation.   On their arrival at the jail several shots were fired, and a
scuffle took place with the guard.   It apparently took but a moment to
overcome all resistance, and the triumphant mob forced their way to the
front door of the jail and burst into the lower room, which was immediately filled by a threatening mass of men with disguised and determined
faces.   They advanced up the narrow stairway which led to the room

where the prisoners were confined. Arriving at the head of the stairs, a volley was instantly fired through the door into the prisoners' apartment. One of these random shots passed through the panel with force sufficient to inflict a mortal wound on the person of Hyrum Smith, from which he instantly expired. The door was now forced, and the excited mob burst into the room, firing volley after volley. The contest was too hot and too unequal to last long. The Prophet was armed with a revolver, with which he defended himself with the haste of desperation. He discharged his weapon three times, and it is said, each time with effect. He now turned to an open window, with a view to escape, but the mob was below in the prison yard as well as around him. He hesitated; he clutched the window-sill to which he was suspended, and cast a wild and imploring look below. A volley was fired by the unrelenting mob, and the Prophet fell to the ground, if not lifeless, at least insensible.

The End.

"The mob meant sure work. The mangled and bleeding body was set up against a well-curb in the jail yard, and a volley was fired at the insensible corpse, and thus the spirit of the Prophet was released from its earthly prison-house.

"The act of the mob was at once cool, systematic, and ferocious. To plan and consummate such an act of violence coolly, in the centre of a village, in broad daylight, with the whole community looking on, required a great amount of boldness, and many bold men. But no sooner was the deed committed than they appeared to be appalled and terrified at their own bloody acts. The mob broke up in squads, and retreated in different directions. In an incredibly short space of time not a man was left who had had any connection with the bloody tragedy. Their retreat was wild and precipitate.

"The village was panic-stricken. The apprehension was universal that the news of the death of the Smiths reaching Nauvoo would instantly cause an uprising of the Mormons; that the Nauvoo Legion, numbering its thousands, would immediately march on Carthage and take complete and sanguinary vengeance upon the town and its inhabitants for the death of the Smiths. The result was that the whole population fled, with the exception, however, of one family who were persuaded at the urgent request of John Taylor and Willard Richards (who were confined in the jail with the Smiths) to remain and take care of the dead bodies. It was only after repeated pledges, and the strong assurance of these Mormon magnates, that the family in question was induced to remain."

The Governor on his return from Nauvoo met the bearers of the dismal tidings to the Saints, and afraid of the interpretation that might be put upon his part of the tragedy, he arrested their further progress. Of his fears and of the excitement in the country he gives the following picture:

" A short time before sun-down we departed on our return to Carthage. When we had proceeded two miles we met two individuals, one of them a Mormon, who informed us that the Smiths had been assassinated in jail, about five or six o'clock of that day. The intelligence seemed to strike every one with a kind of dumbness. As to myself, it was perfectly astounding; and I anticipated the very worst consequences from it. The Mormons had been represented to me as a lawless, infatuated, and fanatical people, not governed by the ordinary motives which influence the rest of mankind. If so, most likely an exterminating war would ensue, and the whole land would be covered with desolation.

" Acting upon this supposition, it was my duty to provide as well as I could for the event. I therefore ordered the two messengers into custody and to be returned with us to Carthage. This was done to get time, and make such arrangements as could be made, and to prevent any sudden explosion of Mormon excitement before they could be written to by their friends at Carthage. I also dispatched messengers to Warsaw to advise the citizens of the event, but the people there knew all about the matter before my messengers arrived. They, like myself, anticipated a general attack all over the country. The women and children were removed across the river, and a committee was dispatched that night to Quincy for assistance. The next morning by day-light the ringing of the bells in the city of Quincy announced a public meeting. The people assembled in great numbers at an early hour. The Warsaw Committee stated to the meeting that a party of Mormons had attempted to rescue the Smiths out of jail; that a party of Missourians and others had killed the prisoners to prevent their escape; that the Governor and his party were at Nauvoo at the time when intelligence of the fact was brought there; that they had been attacked by the Nauvoo Legion, and had retreated to a house where they were then closely besieged. That the Governor had sent out word that he could maintain his position for two days, and would be certain to be massacred if assistance did not arrive by the end of that time. It is unnecessary to say that this entire story is a fabrication. It was of a piece with the other reports put into circulation by the anti-Mormon party to influence the public mind and call the people to their assistance. The effect of it, however, was, that by ten o'clock, on the 28th of June, between two and three hundred men from Quincy, under command of Major Flood, embarked on board a steamboat for Nauvoo, to assist in raising the siege, as they honestly believed.

"As for myself, I was well convinced that those, whoever they were, who assassinated the Smiths, meditated in turn my assassination by the Mormons. The very circumstances of the case fully corroborated the information which I afterwards received, that upon consultation of the assassins, it was agreed amongst them that the murder must be committed whilst the Governor was at Nauvoo; that the Mormons would naturally suppose that he had planned it, and that in the first out-pouring of their indignation, they would assassinate him by way of retaliation. And that thus they would get clear of the Smiths and the Governor all at once. They also supposed that if they could so contrive the matter as to have the Governor of the State assassinated by the Mormons, the public excitement would be greatly increased against that people, and would result in their expulsion from the State at least.

"Upon hearing of the assassination of the Smiths, I was sensible that my command was at an end; that my destruction was meditated as well as that of the Mormons, and that I could not reasonably confide longer in one party or in the other." *

Besides the above statement, the act of assassination was graphically, though hastily, described by the Apostle Willard Richards, who was with the Prophet at the time of his murder, under the title of

"TWO MINUTES IN JAIL.

"A shower of musket balls was thrown up the stairway against the door of the prison in the second story, followed by many rapid footsteps. While Generals Joseph and Hyrum Smith, Mr. Taylor, and myself, who were in the front chamber, closed the door of our room against the entry at the head of the stairs, and placed ourselves against it, there being no lock on the door and no latch that was usable—the door is a common panel—and as soon as we heard the feet at the stairs' head, a ball was sent through the door, which passed between us, and showed that our enemies were desperadoes, and we must change our position. General Joseph Smith, Mr. Taylor, and myself sprang back to the front part of the room, and General Hyrum Smith retreated two-thirds across the chamber, directly in front of and facing the door. A ball was sent through the door, which hit Hyrum on the side of the nose, when he fell backwards, extended at

* Ford's "History of Illinois," pp. 348–9.

length, without moving his feet. From the holes in his vest (the day was warm, and no one had on a coat but myself), pantaloons, drawers, and shirt, it appears evident that a ball must have been thrown from without, which entered his back on the right side, and passing through lodged against his watch which was in his right vest pocket, completely pulveriz-ing the crystal and face, tearing off the hands, and smashing the whole body of the watch, at the same instant the ball from the door entered his nose. As he struck the floor he exclaimed, emphatically, '*I'm a dead man!*' Joseph looked towards him, and responded: 'Oh, dear brother Hyrum!' and opening the door two or three inches with his left hand, discharged one barrel of a six-shooter at random in the entry, from whence a ball grazed Hyrum's breast, and entering his throat, passed into his head, while other muskets were aimed at him, and some balls hit him. Joseph continued snapping his revolver round the casing of the door into the space as before, three barrels of which missed fire, while Mr. Taylor, with a walking-stick, stood by his side and knocked down the bayonets and muskets which were being constantly discharged through the door-way, while I stood by him, ready to lend any assistance with another stick, but could not come within striking distance without going directly before the muzzles of the guns. When the revolver failed we had no more fire-arms, and expected an immediate rush of the mob into the room and instant death. Mr. Taylor rushed into the window, which is some fifteen or twenty feet from the ground. When his body was nearly on a balance, a ball from the door within entered his leg and a ball from without struck his watch, a patent lever, in his vest pocket near his left breast, and smashed it into 'pie,' leaving the hands standing at five o'clock sixteen minutes and twenty-six seconds—the force of which ball threw him back on the floor, and he rolled under the bed which stood by his side, where he lay motionless. The mob from the door continued to fire upon him, cutting away a piece of flesh from his left hip as large as a man's hand; and were hindered only by my knocking down their muskets with a stick, while they attempted to reach their guns into the room, probably left-handed, and aimed their weapons so far around as almost to reach us in the corner of the room, whither we retreated and dodged, and then I recommenced the attack with my stick again. Joseph attempted, as the last resort, to leap through the same window from whence Mr. Taylor fell, when two balls pierced him from the door, and one entered his right breast from without, and he fell outward, exclaiming: '*O Lord my God!*' As his feet went out of the window my head went in, the balls whistling all around. He fell on his left side, a dead man. At this in-stant the cry was raised: '*He's leaped the window!*' and the mob on the stairs and in the entry ran out. I withdrew from the window, thinking it of no use to leap out on a hundred bayonets then around General Smith's body. Not satisfied with this, I again reached my head out of the win-dow, and watched some seconds to see if there were any signs of life, re-gardless of my own, determined to see the end of him I loved. Being

11

fully satisfied that he was dead, with a hundred men near the body, and more coming around the corner of the jail, and expecting a return to our room, I rushed towards the prison door at the head of the stairs, and through the entry from whence the firing had proceeded, to learn if the doors into the prison were open. When near the entry Mr. Taylor called out : ' *Take me.*' I pressed my way until I found all doors unbarred : returned instantly, caught Mr. Taylor under my arm, and rushed by the stairs into the dungeon or inner prison, stretched him on the floor and covered him with a bed in such a manner as not likely to be perceived, expecting an immediate return of the mob. I said to Mr. Taylor : 'This is a hard case to lay you on the floor ; but if your wounds are not fatal I want you to live to tell the story.' I expected to be shot the next moment, and stood before the door awaiting the onset."

Who committed this dastardly deed is still a mystery upon which no light has ever yet been thrown. The foregoing facts render it highly probable that the plan of assassination was devised by other men than those who carried it into execution.

It is hardly likely that Governor Ford had anything to do with the concoction of the project ; but it is impossible to dispel from the mind the idea that he was not entirely ignorant of the possibility of such an event being anticipated, if indeed not contemplated. It is quite probable that his disbandment of the troops was seized upon by greater minds than his own as a propitious circumstance that favoured the accomplishment of the desperate deed. A person of the name of Daniels, who was a private in the regiment commanded by Col. Levi Williams, made statements preceding and during the trial which afterwards took place, to the effect that when the editor of the Warsaw *Signal*, Thomas C. Sharpe, brought dispatches from the Governor, ordering the disbandment of the troops, on the morning of the 27th, the intelligence created great excitement. They were clamourous to march upon Nauvoo, and were already a few miles on their way to that place. When the order was received, the troops were formed into line, and Sharpe was invited to address them. This Daniels asserts that, in his speech, Sharpe counselled the command to march eastward to Carthage, take the jail by storm, and kill the Smiths ; that the Governor had already gone to Nauvoo ; and that the Mormons, upon hearing of the death of the Smiths, would kill the Governor, and that they would then be rid of his interference.

Other speakers on the occasion favoured the proposition; but some opposed it, maintaining as fiercely their opposition to " killing men in jail." Finally, a call was made for volunteers, whereupon William N. Grover was the first to advance, and was followed by the company that committed the murder.

The assassination of Joseph Smith was deplored by every right-thinking person. Aside from the horror and detestation naturally entertained against the crime of murder, it was readily seen that the dignity of martyrdom was the Prophet's crown of glory. It carved for him a place in history to which a natural death would never have conducted him.*

It has been difficult for public writers to agree when summing up his character. To one class he has appeared as the knave and the impostor; to others, the fanatic and self-deceived; to his own people he was the greatest of prophets; while others still have suggested that he was the victim of the extravagances of spirit-communications with an imagination crude, uncultivated, and superstitious. Knowing little and believing much, every impression was to him a revelation, and every calamity to the world an evidence that " the end " was nigh at hand. An English writer, closing a notice of the Prophet's career, says of him:

" If anything can tend to encourage the supposition that Joseph Smith was a sincere enthusiast, maddened with religious frenzies, as many have been before and will be after him; and that he had a strong invincible faith in his own high pretensions and divine mission, it is the probability that, unless supported by such feelings, he would have renounced the unprofitable and ungrateful task, and sought refuge from persecution and misery in private life and honourable industry. But whether knave or lunatic, whether a liar or a true man, it cannot be denied that he was one of the most extraordinary persons of his time, a man of rude genius, who accomplished a much greater work than he knew, and whose name, whatever he may have been whilst living, will take its place among the notabilities of the world." †

* " He is embalmed in the affectionate memory of thousands; and as time lends a halo of enchantment to encircle his name, hymns of praise and legends of his holy deeds will be sung and cherished by those who believe that the Prophet-Saint of earth is to reign a god over a brilliant world of his own creation, surrounded by happy queens and carolling children, through his own blessed eternity.'
—*Lieut. Gunnison's Work*, p. 165.

† " The Mormons," p. 165. Mackay.

The Saints in Nauvoo received the news of the assassination on the following morning. Their grief was indescribable. It was " a day of sorrow and of darkness—a day of lamenta-"tion, and mourning, and of woe."

With the news from Carthage came the recommendation from the apostles Taylor and Richards, and Samuel H. Smith (a brother of the murdered men), to the Saints to " be still—be " patient." The Governor added to that brief epistle an injunction that the Mormons should act upon the defensive until protection could be furnished them.

The Legion was called out at ten o'clock in the morning, and addressed by W. W. Phelps, Colonel Buckmaster, the Governor's *aide-de-camp*, and others. Preparations were made to receive the last remains of the murdered Prophet and his brother, the Patriarch.

When the bodies were brought to the city in the afternoon, they were met by ten thousand people of every age and of both sexes, who followed the earthly relics of the martyrs to the Mansion House, and there Willard Richards, Judge Phelps, and other prominent men, addressed the multitude. Every heart was stirred. Sorrow and indignation were mingled in every breast, and a desire for vengeance smouldered beneath the sentiments of wonder and grief.

The assembly separated peacefully, resolved to trust to the law for justice upon the assassins, and, if that failed, their implicit confidence in God for deliverance remained unshaken.*

* The interment of the mortal remains of the Prophet and Patriarch was attended to with proper solemnity, and a sorrowing multitude accompanied the mourners to the burial-place; but there was a sequel to the public services which the people never knew. The bodies of Joseph and Hyrum were not in that funeral procession : they were reserved for private interment. It was believed that sacred as the tomb is always considered to be, there were persons capable of rifling the grave in order to obtain the head of the murdered Prophet for the purpose of exhibiting it or placing it in some phrenological museum—the skull of Joseph Smith was worth money. This apprehension in point of fact proved true, for the place where the bodies were supposed to be buried was disturbed the night after the interment.

The coffins had been filled with stones, etc., to about the weight which the bodies would have been. The remains of the two brothers were then secretly buried the same night by a chosen few in the vaults beneath the Temple. The ground was then levelled and pieces of rock and other *débris* were scattered carelessly over the spot. But even this was not considered a sufficient safeguard against any violation of the dead, and on the following night a still more select number exhumed the

The Governor from this time did everything in his power for the preservation of peace, but this momentary check was only a temporary lull in the storm. Human efforts were now ineffectual to stem the tide of trouble which rolled in upon the Saints.

At the October term of the Hancock Circuit Court indictments were found by the Grand Jury against Levi Williams, Thos. C. Sharpe, M. Aldrich, Jacob C. Davis, Wm. N. Grover, John Allyer, Wm. Davis, John Willis, and Wm. Gallagher, for the murder of Joseph and Hyrum Smith. The Governor, aware of the unenviable position that he occupied in respect to the alleged charges of complicity with the mob, resolved that the prosecution should be ably and fairly conducted, and, in addition to the District Attorney, called in the aid of the Attorney-General for the State.

Out of three hundred persons summoned, and after three days' challenging, a jury was at last empanelled. Of the indicted, four only were arrested—Sharpe, Grover, Davis, and Williams. The trial lasted nine days, when the jury retired, and, after an absence of three hours, returned a verdict of " Not Guilty ;" a conclusion which surprised no one.

remains and buried them beneath the pathway behind the Mansion House. The bricks which formed the path were carefully replaced, and the earth removed was carried away in sacks and thrown into the Mississippi.

[N. B. If this last statement is true, the bodies must have been removed a third time, as, since writing the above, the Author has it on unquestionable authority that they now repose in quite a different place.]

Brigham Young has endeavoured to obtain possession of the remains of the Prophet, that they might be interred beneath the Temple at Salt Lake. It is stated by Brigham that Joseph, like the son of Jacob, made the request that the Saints when they went to the Rocky Mountains should carry his bones with them. The family of Joseph maintain that the Prophet never expressed any such desire, but said very much to the contrary. It is affirmed that, " previous to Joseph's death, he predicted that the Church would be scattered, and saw that the time might come when Brigham Young would lead the Church ; and that if he did, he would lead it to perdition. He told his wife, Emma, to remain at Nauvoo, or if she left, to go to Kirtland, and not to follow any faction."

To have given the bones of Joseph into Brigham's charge would have been to confirm the Saints in the Rocky Mountain Zion, to which the Smith family are decidedly opposed. The remains of the martyrs are destined for Zion in Missouri.

CHAPTER XXVII.

POLYGAMY IN ILLINOIS.—Its Introduction among the Mormons—The " Revelation " given by Joseph Smith—The Sons of the Deceased Prophet dispute the Polygamic Marriages of their Father—They call for the Posterity—The Promise of a " Righteous Seed " fulfilled—Joseph without Issue by his Score of Polygamic Wives—Married Women become his " Wives " without Divorce or Separation from their Husbands.

THE subject of this chapter may suitably be divided into two parts—one pertaining to the announcement of the revelation to Joseph Smith, and the other tracing its introduction among the Saints.

Without a copy of the Revelation which has played such an important part in the development of the Church, any history of Mormonism would be incomplete ; that document is therefore here given unabridged and intact, and it will doubtless prove of special interest to the historical student :

CELESTIAL MARRIAGE.

A Revelation on the Patriarchal Order of Matrimony, or Plurality of Wives. Given *to Joseph Smith, the Seer, in Nauvoo, July 12th,* 1843.*

I. " Verily, thus saith the Lord unto you, my servant Joseph, that inasmuch as you have inquired of my hand, to know and understand wherein I, the Lord, justified my servants Abraham, Isaac, and Jacob ; as also Moses, David, and Solomon, my servants, as touching the principle and doctrine of their having many wives and concubines: Behold ! and lo, I am the Lord thy God, and will answer thee as touching this matter: Therefore, prepare thy heart to receive and obey the instructions which I am about to give unto you ; for all those who have this law revealed unto them, must obey the same ; for behold ! I reveal unto you a new and an everlasting covenant ; and if ye abide not that covenant, then are ye damned ; for no one can reject this covenant, and be permitted to enter

* " Seer," p. 7.

into my glory; for all who will have a blessing at my hands shall abide the law which was appointed for that blessing, and the conditions thereof, as was instituted from before the foundation of the world : and as pertaining to the new and everlasting covenant, it was instituted for the fulness of my glory; and he that receiveth a fulness thereof, must, and shall abide the law, or he shall be damned, saith the Lord God.

II. "And verily I say unto you, that the conditions of this, law are these: All covenants, contracts, bonds, obligations, oaths, vows, performances, connections, associations, or expectations, that are not made and entered into, and sealed, by the Holy Spirit of promise, of him who is anointed, both as well for time and for all eternity, and that too most holy, by revelation and commandment, through the medium of mine anointed, whom I have appointed on the earth to hold this power (and I have appointed unto my servant Joseph to hold this power in the last days, and there is never but one on the earth at a time, on whom this power and the keys of this Priesthood are conferred), are of no efficacy, virtue, or force, in and after the resurrection from the dead; for all contracts that are not made unto this end, have an end when men are dead.

III. "Behold! mine house is a house of order, saith the Lord God, and not a house of confusion. Will I accept of an offering, saith the Lord, that is not made in my name! Or, will I receive at your hands that which I have not appointed! And will I appoint unto you, saith the Lord, except it be by law, even as I and my Father ordained unto you, before the world was! I am the Lord thy God, and I give unto you this commandment, that no man shall come unto the Father but by me, or by my word, which is my law, saith the Lord; and everything that is in the world, whether it be ordained of men, by thrones, or principalities, or powers, or things of name, whatsoever they may be, that are not by me, or by my word, saith the Lord, shall be thrown down, and shall not remain after men are dead, neither in nor after the resurrection, saith the Lord your God; for whatsoever things remaineth, are by me; and whatsoever things are not by me, shall be shaken and destroyed.

IV. "Therefore, if a man marry him a wife in the world, and he marry her not by me, nor by my word; and he covenant with her so long as he is in the world, and she with him, their covenant and marriage is not of force when they are dead, and when they are out of the world: therefore, they are not bound by any law when they are out of the world; therefore, when they are out of the world, they neither marry, nor are given in marriage; but are appointed angels in heaven, which angels are ministering servants, to minister for those who are worthy of a far more, and an exceeding, and an eternal weight of glory; for these angels did not abide my law, therefore they cannot be enlarged, but remain separately and singly, without exaltation, in their saved condition, to all eternity, and from henceforth are not Gods, but are angels of God, for ever and ever.

V. "And again, verily I say unto you, if a man marry a wife and make a covenant with her for time and for all eternity, if that covenant is not by

me, or by my word, which is my law, and is not sealed by the Holy Spirit
of promise, through him whom I have anointed and appointed unto this
power—then it is not valid, neither of force when they are out of the
world, because they are not joined by me, saith the Lord, neither by my
word; when they are out of the world, it cannot be received there, because
the angels and the Gods are appointed there, by whom they cannot pass;
they cannot, therefore, inherit my glory, for my house is a house of order,
saith the Lord God.

VI. "And again, verily I say unto you, if a man marry a wife by my
word, which is my law, and by the new and everlasting covenant, and it
is sealed unto them by the Holy Spirit of promise, by him who is anointed,
unto whom I have appointed this power, and the keys of this Priesthood;
and it shall be said unto them, ye shall come forth in the first resurrection; and if it be after the first resurrection, in the next resurrection; and
shall inherit thrones, kingdoms, principalities, and powers, of dominions,
all heights, and depths—then shall it be written in the Lamb's Book of
Life, that he shall commit no murder whereby to shed innocent blood, and
if ye abide in my covenant, and commit no murder whereby to shed innocent blood, it shall be done unto them in all things whatsoever my servant
hath put upon them, in time, and through all eternity, and shall be of full
force when they are out of the world; and they shall pass by the angels,
and the Gods, which are set there, to their exaltation and glory in all
things, as hath been sealed upon their heads, which glory shall be a fulness and a continuation of the seeds for ever and ever.

VII. "Then shall they be Gods, because they have no end; therefore
shall they be from everlasting to everlasting, because they continue; then
shall they be above all, because all things are subject unto them. Then
shall they be Gods, because they have all power, and the angels are subject unto them.

VIII. "Verily, verily I say unto you, except ye abide my law, ye cannot attain to this glory; for straight is the gate, and narrow the way that
leadeth unto the exaltation and continuation of the lives, and few there be
that find it, because ye receive me not in the world, neither do ye know
me. But if ye receive me in the world, then shall ye know me, and shall
receive your exaltation, that where I am ye shall be also. This is eternal lives, to know the only wise and true God, and Jesus Christ, whom
He hath sent. I am He. Receive ye, therefore, my law. Broad is the
gate, and wide the way that leadeth to the death; and many there are
that go in thereat; because they receive me not, neither do they abide in
my law.

IX. "Verily, verily I say unto you, if a man marry a wife according to
my word, and they are sealed by the Holy Spirit of promise, according to
mine appointment, and he or she shall commit any sin or transgression of
the new and everlasting covenant whatever, and all manner of blasphemies, and if they commit no murder, wherein they shed innocent
blood—yet they shall come forth in the first resurrection, and enter into

their exaltation ; but they shall be destroyed in the flesh, and shall be delivered unto the buffetings of Satan unto the day of redemption, saith the Lord God.

X. " The blasphemy against the Holy Ghost, which shall not be forgiven in the world, nor out of the world, is in that ye commit murder, wherein ye shed innocent blood, and assent unto my death, after ye have received my new and everlasting covenant, saith the Lord God ; and he that abideth not this law, can in no wise enter into my glory, but shall be damned, saith the Lord.

XI. " I am the Lord thy God, and will give unto thee the law of my Holy Priesthood, as was ordained by me, and my Father, before the world was. Abraham received all things, whatsoever he received, by revelation and commandment, by my word, saith the Lord, and hath entered into his exaltation, and sitteth upon his throne.

XII. " Abraham received promises concerning his seed, and of the fruit of his loins—from whose loins ye are, namely, my servant Joseph—which were to continue so long as they were in the world ; and as touching Abraham and his seed, out of the world they should continue ; both in the world and out of the world should they continue as innumerable as the stars ; or, if ye were to count the sand upon the sea-shore, ye could not number them. This promise is yours, also, because ye are of Abraham, and the promise was made unto Abraham ; and by this law are the continuation of the works of my Father, wherein He glorifieth Himself. Go ye, therefore, and do the works of Abraham ; enter ye into my law, and ye shall be saved. But if ye enter not into my law, ye cannot receive the promise of my Father, which He made unto Abraham.

XIII. " God commanded Abraham, and Sarah gave Hagar to Abraham to wife. And why did she do it? Because this was the law, and from Hagar sprang many people. This, therefore, was fulfilling, among other things, the promises. Was Abraham, therefore, under condemnation? Verily, I say unto you, Nay; for I, the Lord, commanded it. Abraham was commanded to offer his son Isaac; nevertheless, it was written, thou shalt not kill. Abraham, however, did not refuse, and it was accounted unto him for righteousness.

XIV. " Abraham received concubines, and they bare him children, and it was accounted unto him for righteousness, because they were given unto him, and he abode in my law, as Isaac also, and Jacob did none other things than that which they were commanded ; and because they did none other things than that which they were commanded, they have entered into their exaltation, according to the promises, and sit upon thrones, and are not angels, but are Gods. David also received many wives and concubines, as also Solomon and Moses my servants ; as also many others of my servants, from the beginning of creation until this time ; and in nothing did they sin, save in those things which they received not of me.

XV. " David's wives and concubines were given unto him, of me, by the hand of Nathan, my servant, and others of the Prophets who had the keys of this power; and in none of these things did he sin against me, save in the case of Uriah and his wife; and, therefore, he hath fallen from his exaltation, and received his portion; and he shall not inherit them out of the world; for I gave them unto another, saith the Lord.

XVI. "I am the Lord thy God, and I gave unto thee, my servant Joseph, an appointment, and restore all things; ask what ye will, and it shall be given unto you according to my word: and as ye have asked concerning adultery—verily, verily I say unto you, if a man receiveth a wife in the new and everlasting covenant, and if she be with another man, and I have not appointed unto her by the holy anointing, she hath committed adultery, and shall be destroyed. If she be not in the new and everlasting covenant, and she be with another man, she has committed adultery; and if her husband be with another woman, and he was under a vow, he hath broken his vow, and hath committed adultery, and if she hath not committed adultery, but is innocent, and hath not broken her vow, and she knoweth it, and I reveal it unto you, my servant Joseph, then shall you have power, by the power of my Holy Priesthood, to take her, and give her unto him that hath not committed adultery, but hath been faithful; for he shall be made ruler over many: for I have conferred upon you the keys and power of the Priesthood, wherein I restore all things, and make known unto you all things in due time.

XVII. "And verily, verily I say unto you, that whatsoever you seal on earth, shall be sealed in heaven: and whatsoever you bind on earth, in my name, and by my word, saith the Lord, it shall be eternally bound in the heavens; and whosesoever sins you remit on earth, shall be remitted eternally in the heavens; and whosesoever sins you retain on earth, shall be retained in heaven.

XVIII. "And again, verily I say, whomsoever you bless, I will bless, and whomsoever you curse, I will curse, saith the Lord; for I, the Lord, am thy God.

XIX. "And again, verily I say unto you, my servant Joseph, that whatsoever you give on earth, and to whomsoever you give any one on earth, by my word, and according to my law, it shall be visited with blessings, and not cursings, and with my power, saith the Lord, and shall be without condemnation on earth, and in heaven: for I am the Lord thy God, and will be with thee even unto the end of the world, and through all eternity; for verily, I seal upon you your exaltation, and prepare a throne for you in the kingdom of my Father, with Abraham your father. Behold, I have seen your sacrifices, and will forgive all your sins; I have seen your sacrifices in obedience to that which I have told you; go, therefore, and I make a way for your escape, as I accepted the offering of Abraham, of his son Isaac.

XX. "Verily I say unto you, a commandment I give unto mine handmaid, Emma Smith, your wife whom I have given unto you, that she stay herself, and partake not of that which I commanded you to offer unto her; for I did it, saith the Lord, to prove you all, as I did Abraham; and that I might require an offering at your hand, by covenant and sacrifice: and let mine handmaid, Emma Smith, receive all those that have been given unto my servant Joseph, and who are virtuous and pure before me; and those who are not pure, and have said they were pure, shall be destroyed, saith the Lord God; for I am the Lord thy God, and ye shall obey my voice; and I give unto my servant Joseph, that he shall be made ruler over many things, for he hath been faithful over a few things, and from henceforth I will strengthen him.

XXI. "And I command mine handmaid Emma Smith, to abide and cleave unto my servant Joseph, and to none else. But if she will not abide this commandment, she shall be destroyed, saith the Lord; for I am the Lord thy God, and will destroy her, if she abide not in my law; but if she will not abide this commandment, then shall my servant Joseph do all things for her, even as he hath said; and I will bless him and multiply him, and give unto him an hundred-fold in this world, of fathers and mothers, brothers and sisters, houses and lands, wives and children, and crowns of eternal lives in the eternal worlds. And again, verily I say, let mine handmaid forgive my servant Joseph his trespasses, and then shall she be forgiven her trespasses, wherein she hath trespassed against me; and I, the Lord thy God, will bless her, and multiply her, and make her heart to rejoice.

XXII. "And again, I say, let not my servant Joseph put his property out of his hands, lest an enemy come and destroy him; for Satan seeketh to destroy; for I am the Lord thy God, and he is my servant; and behold! and lo, I am with him, as I was with Abraham, thy father, even unto his exaltation and glory.

XXIII. "Now, as touching the law of the Priesthood, there are many things pertaining thereunto. Verily, if a man be called of my Father, as was Aaron, by mine own voice, and by the voice of him that sent me; and I have endowed him with the keys of the power of this Priesthood, if he do anything in my name, and according to my law, and by my word he will not commit sin, and I will justify him. Let no one, therefore, set on my servant Joseph; for I will justify him; for he shall do the sacrifice which I require at his hands, for his transgressions, saith the Lord your God.

XXIV. "And again, as pertaining to the law of the Priesthood: If any man espouse a virgin, and desire to espouse another, and the first give her consent; and if he espouse the second, and they are virgins, and have vowed to no other man, then is he justified; he cannot commit adultery, for they are given unto him; for he cannot commit adultery with that that belongeth unto him and to no one else; and if he have ten virgins given unto him by this law, he cannot commit adultery, for they belong to him, and they are given unto him, therefore is he justified. But if one or either of the ten virgins, after she is espoused, shall be with another man, she has committed adultery, and shall be destroyed; for they are given unto him to multiply and replenish the earth, according to my commandment, and to fulfil the promise which was given by my Father before the foundation of the world; and for their exaltation in the eternal worlds, that they may bear the souls of men; for herein is the work of my Father continued, that He may be glorified.

XXV. "And again, verily, verily I say unto you, if any man have a wife who holds the keys of this power, and he teaches unto her the law of my Priesthood, as pertaining to these things, then shall she believe, and administer unto him, or she shall be destroyed, saith the Lord your God; for I will destroy her; for I will magnify my name upon all those who receive and abide in my law. Therefore, it shall be lawful in me, if she receive not this law, for him to receive all things, whatsoever I, the Lord his God, will give unto him, because she did not administer unto him according to my word; and she then becomes the transgressor; and he is exempt from the law of Sarah, who administered unto Abraham according to the law, when I commanded Abraham to take Hagar to wife. And now, as pertaining to this law, verily, verily I say unto you, I will reveal more unto you, hereafter; therefore, let this suffice for the present. Behold, I am Alpha and Omega. AMEN."

On a matter of such grave importance as the engrafting of polygamy upon the faith of the Saints, it has always been a cause of sincere regret on the part of the intelligent Mormon elders, that nothing has ever been stated about the previous teachings which Joseph Smith received on this subject—if he ever had any.* On the introduction of the other doctrines of the Church, its principles of faith and commandments, there is a freedom of statement that carries the impression of honest sincerity, fearing no criticism; but on this there is an unpleasant silence.

In defence of this concealment it is argued that polygamy was offensive to the traditions of the people; that it had to be *stealthily* introduced, as bigamy was punishable by law, and the less that was published about it the better. There is

* Elder W. W. Phelps said in Salt Lake Tabernacle, in 1862, that while Joseph was translating the Book of Abraham, in Kirtland, Ohio, in 1835, from the papyrus found with the Egyptian mummies, the Prophet became impressed with the idea that polygamy would yet become an institution of the Mormon Church. Brigham Young was present, and was much annoyed at the statement made by Phelps, but it is highly probable that it was the real secret which the latter then divulged. The conscientious Mormon who calmly considers what is here written on the introduction of polygamy into the Mormon Church will readily see that its origin is probably much more correctly traceable to those Egyptian mummies, than to a revelation from heaven. The first paragraph of the Revelation has all the musty odour of the catacombs about it, and that Joseph went into polygamy at a venture there cannot be the slightest doubt.

weight in this statement as an argument, for no one can fail to appreciate the difficulty of introducing a practice which the civilization of a thousand years had condemned as a relic of barbarism; it was indeed necessary to be secret. But when once that silence was broken, and a lengthy revelation was given to the world, commanding all people to whom it might come to obey it, or "be damned," reticence as to its origin could be no longer needful. On a matter of such tremendous consequence as that which polygamy claims to be, the Prophet could not have been too explicit.

This revelation is dated "Nauvoo, Illinois, July 12, 1843," and was given to the Church and to the public nine years later, at a conference in Salt Lake City. Since that time, tens of thousands of sermons have been preached on its divine origin, voluminous treatises have been published in its exposition, and the Mormon press has teemed with articles in its defence; but in all of them the beginning of polygamy with the Mormons is left out.

Some of the elders who were early acquainted with the Prophet state that he was instructed by some one of his angel visitors on the marital relations of the patriarchs while he resided in Ohio, and was then informed that the time would arrive when polygamy would become the faith of all the Saints; but of this there is no evidence.

The first traceable indication of any such purpose on the part of the Prophet was in the year preceding the date of the revelation, and then so furtively was it introduced that many thousands, who at that time believed, and still believe, in the mission of Joseph Smith, as set forth by himself, deny that he ever taught such a doctrine. It was brought before the public in a quarrel between the Prophet and that shining light, Dr. John Cooke Bennett, the major-general of the Nauvoo Legion, and the mayor of the city.

With a people who subordinate their own judgment and sense of right and wrong to authoritative teaching, it was an easy matter for any doctrine to be introduced, however false and vicious it might be; and when to that disposition in the people is added their constant expectation of mysterious revelations, there is no extreme of folly or crime which may not be

easily imposed upon their credulity. Bennett's relations with
the Prophet being of the most intimate character, it was easy
for him to succeed in imposing upon silly women the "spirit-
"ual-wife" doctrine as an emanation from Heaven; and this
he is charged with doing with a success that is humiliating to
confess.

Those who have not lived under the influence of an "in-
"spired prophet" can form no idea of the facility with which a
religious people can be taught any doctrine, and be led on to lay
aside their education, or their sense of morality, and thus be cast
in the mould of a teacher's mind. It was this, and not natural
depravity, that enabled such men as Bennett to succeed in con-
taminating and debauching very respectable ladies in Nauvoo.

Bennett, it is said, taught the Mormon sisters with whom
he had acquaintance that he had been instructed by the
Prophet in this Mormon phase of "affinity;" but before the
city council he affirmed that Joseph, "as far as he knew, had
"ever been highly moral in his conduct:" and before Alderman Wells he made affidavit that he never knew him to teach
anything contrary to the strictest principles of virtue. When
Bennett got away from Nauvoo he denied these statements,
and claimed that they were made by him when his life was in
danger.* Many even of the "good Mormons" have always
believed that Joseph taught Bennett of the proposed introduction of polygamy, but that Bennett ran ahead of his teacher,
and introduced free-loveism in its broadest sense. †

* Bennett says that Joseph threatened him with half-a-dozen different kinds of
death. His narrative of "duress" is too theatrical.

† There is, no doubt, much truth in Bennett's book, "Mormonism Exposed,"
but no statement that he makes can be received with confidence. As a justification
of his separation from Joseph, and his exposure of the "mysteries" of Mormonism,
he states that he never was a believer, but only assumed the faith in order to become
thoroughly initiated, and qualify himself for its exposure. It is not unlikely that
his faith in the Prophet was very limited, but his association with "the Lord's ser-
"vant" sprang from no such consideration as that which he states. Governor Ford
gives him the following friendly notice:

"This Bennett was probably the greatest scamp in the Western country. I have
made particular enquiries concerning him, and have traced him in several places in
which he had lived, before he joined the Mormons, in Ohio, Indiana, and Illinois,
and he was everywhere accounted the same debauched, unprincipled, and profligate
character."—History of Illinois, p. 263.

Notwithstanding Bennett disclaimed that he ever had any faith in Mormonism,

Many interesting affidavits were given to the public in denunciation of Bennett and in defence of the Prophet. Everything that could be thought of was done to mislead the public as to the veritable teachings promulgated concerning marriage, and from the time of this outbreak with Bennett in 1842, until the announcement of the revelation by Brigham Young, in Salt Lake City, in 1852, it was the duty of the Mormon missionaries to prevaricate, and even positively deny, when necessary, that the Mormon Church was other than monogamic, and the extent of demoralization growing out of these denials would be incredible were the facts not incontrovertible.

The sons of the Prophet have been very restive under the imputation of polygamous practices being attributed to their father. They have laboured indefatigably in decrying polygamy, and have devoted a large share of their time, talent, ink, and paper in hostility to it, as they evidently believe it is both a great error and a great sin. But as the facts of Joseph's marital relations with "sisters" who claim to be his "wives," in the Mormon sense, are overwhelming, the sons, in denying their sire's polygamy, are driven to the alternative of silently allowing the inevitable charge of practical "free-love," "adultery," or whatever others may choose to call it. At the present time there are probably about a dozen "sisters" in Utah who proudly acknowledge themselves to be the "wives of Joseph," and how many others there may have been who held that relationship—"no man knoweth."

The defenders of the Prophet have called for the posterity of that polygamy as evidence of the claim, and the Mormons, seeing the force of the challenge, would have been glad to have accommodated the sons by presenting "the righteous seed" of the father for their recognition; but the only semblance there ever was of success was a case which once made some stir for a short time, but ended in total failure. A daughter of one of these "wives," living north of Salt Lake City, was claimed to be Joseph's; but it is said to have required more faith than

he figured extensively as a devoted believer at a conference of Mormons, under the leadership of James Strang, at Voree, Wisconsin Territory,*in October, 1846, four years after his public and scandalous denial. Governor Ford's judgment of him is too well founded.

even Brigham Young could muster to reach that conclusion,
and so that frail link failed to serve the desired end—much to
the credit of Brigham's honesty.

While the argument of the young Smiths and the friends
of the Prophet has a semblance of force, it is really very weak.
The greater portion of the Prophet's patriarchal experience
was within a few years preceding his death; and with arrests
threatening him daily, and the sleepless eye of Mrs. Emma
Smith for ever on his track, the frequent visits to the domiciles
of his unrecognized wives might find an easy physiological
explanation; while *the fact* that *the divorce did not always
precede the second matrimony* would account for much in a
very natural way.

Joseph's love was neither Platonic nor arithmetically circumscribed. He was strong in impulse, with a thorough disregard to the conventionalities of the Gentile world—he was
"a law unto himself."

It is well known in Utah that two sisters, Mrs. B—— and
Mrs. J——, were "sealed" wives to Joseph while they were
still the wives of Mr. B—— and Mr. J——. To the latter a
son was born, long after Mrs. J. had been "sealed" to Joseph,
and since these two sisters have been in Salt Lake City, the one
has added a son and the other a daughter to Joseph's family
register, through the kindness of Brigham Young and Heber
C. Kimball, who became "proxy" husbands to the widows of
the deceased Prophet. Strange and anomalous as all this may
appear, the sons of Mrs. J. take it in good part and exhibit
towards their father no lack of filial regard, while by the teachings of the faith they cling still closer to their mother with the
warmest affection—the wife of the Prophet was greater than
the wife of the elder.

There was no domestic trouble between this elder and his
wife. They were very affectionately attached to each other,
but the Prophet's eye had fallen upon his neighbour's wife, and
revelation made the acquisition easy of attainment. It was
years after the death of Joseph before the husband knew that
his wife was the wife of another. On the banks of the Missouri river, in an Indian country where redress was impossible
—had it even been desired—Brigham called up the husband

and told him that his domestic relations in that quarter were at an end: that he must not again be a husband to his wife! She whom he idolized, who had been to him the partner of his joys and cares, who had borne to him his children, and who had filled his soul with the hope of a happy future, was to be accounted his no more! Joseph had concealed the fact of his marital relations with his wife from him, and the wife, faithful to the Prophet, had for these years been reticent until silence could no longer be maintained. The Prophet's widow had chosen the Prophet's successor for her proxy husband,* and he [Brigham] could maintain no doubtful relationship towards her. The elder was cavalierly informed that he could take another wife, and soon after that he was sent on a preaching mission to England, where he could assuage his grief by a second experience of connubial bliss!

There is a temptation to add more, but where people have honestly accepted a principle of faith, as the Mormons have polygamy, and paid for it as dearly as they have, there would be no justification for adding to personal misery by the public relation of that which the parties affected would feel hurt to read. The curiosity of the reader is, however, entitled to be gratified by the statement that the sadly wronged husband is still a Mormon and that that thrice-wedded wife is practically husbandless, being kindly provided for by the excellent husband of her daughter—the offspring of Brigham in this world, but, according to the Mormon faith, the child of Joseph in the world to come. What a page of life!

It is only a few years ago that Brigham in a moment of confidence communicated to one of the leading apostles, that the wife whom he [the apostle] had cherished as the companion of his youth—a wife to him, as he supposed, for about two-score years—had actually been "sealed" to Joseph during the life-time of the latter. How many other apostles and elders

* In this confused marital relationship there is a principle of faith discernible. To have continued to live with Mr. J. and to have borne more children to him would not have added "glory" to Joseph; besides, it was very proper that Mr. J., having lost his wife, should have the opportunity of securing another wife who should be altogether his own. The general idea, therefore, that the lady was actuated solely by ambition in her choice of Brigham as a "proxy" for Joseph may perhaps be without foundation.

will "wake up in the morning of the resurrection" and find their wives the glory of a Prophet's crown, it is hard to conjecture!

Mrs. Emma Smith may feel justified in denying that her husband was a polygamist; for she may neither assent to the use of the term, nor acknowledge the principle. But there is, to the Author's mind, the most satisfactory evidence that Joseph Smith had "sealed" to him a large number of women some time before his death, many of whom have stated to the Author that they were "the wives of Joseph Smith;" that "Mrs. Emma Smith was aware of the fact," and that it was the trouble growing out of the discovery of such relationship that called forth the "Revelation." Of this the "Revelation" itself bears much internal evidence.

"The Elect Lady," Mrs. Emma Smith.*

Joseph's elder brother, Hyrum, believed at first (and well he might), that his Prophet-brother had taken counsel of his own passions, and he opposed him publicly as well as in pri-

* The above is from a recent photograph. The author regrets that he could not obtain a portrait of an earlier date. The Prophet's widow, some years after his assassination, became the wife of Major Bidamon, and continued to reside at Nauvoo, where she is the object of much attention and respect.

vate. Mrs. Smith was indignant, and rendered his life unhappy.* In those moments of gloom and deep solicitude the
Prophet realized the necessity of something to turn away wrath
and hostility from his door. There are Mormons still living
who affirm that they know from Joseph's own lips that "a
"revelation was necessary, and would be had, to satisfy Hy-
"rum, and to allay the storm that was brewing among the
"married women, and also to satisfy the young women" whom
it was desirable to convert. The Prophet went into his office
one morning, closed the door, was inspired, and his amanuensis—elder William Clayton, now in Salt Lake City—wrote
that "Revelation" as Joseph dictated to him.

In a measure, his point was now accomplished. His brother
Hyrum was converted, and took other wives himself. Peace
reigned thereafter in that branch of the Smith family. But
Mrs. Emma Smith was never truly converted to the "Revela-
"tion," though it is claimed that she "softened down" and
went so far as to acknowledge several, if she could not "re
"ceive all that have been given unto my servant Joseph."
Such were the circumstances attending the birth of this famous
"Revelation."

* "The wife of the Prophet Joseph rebelled against it, and declared if he persisted she would desert for another."—*Gunnison*, p. 72.

Mrs. Smith evidently thought something of separation, and Joseph made preparations for such an event. But "the Lord" came to his aid, and that famous
revelation on polygamy contains the following very significant menace:

"And I command mine handmaid, Emma Smith, to abide and cleave unto my
servant Joseph, and to none else. But if she will not abide this commandment, she
shall be destroyed, saith the Lord; for I am the Lord thy God, and will destroy her
if she abide not in my law."—*Revelation on Polygamy*, par. 21.

CHAPTER XXVIII.

POLYGAMY REPUDIATED.—Joseph Smith and the Mormon Leaders deny it—The Revelations of the Church condemn it—The Sons of the Prophet defend their Father's Reputation—The Evidences of his Polygamic Life.

THE storm that arose from Bennett's exposure of what he asserted to be the teachings of the Prophet suggested the publication of counter-statements. In the *Times and Seasons* there was inserted on page 939, Vol. III., an article upon "Mar-" riage," written by Oliver Cowdery, and placed as an appendix to the book of modern revelations. To this, Joseph added an editorial note in which he states :

"We have given the above rule of marriage *as the only one practised in this Church*, to show that Dr. J. C. Bennett's secret-wife system is a matter of his own manufacture, and further to disabuse the public ear and show that the said Bennett and his misanthropic friend, Origen Bachelor, are perpetrating *a foul and infamous slander upon an innocent people*, and need but to be known to be hated and despised."

A certificate from " persons of families " followed, in which it was declared that they knew of " no other rule or system of " marriage than that one published from the ' Book of Doctrine " and Covenants,' " and " that Dr. John C. Bennett's secret-" wife system is a creature of his own make." To this is appended a dozen names of leading elders, which was followed by another certificate and declaration from " members of the " Ladies' Relief Society, and married females," to the same purport and almost in the same language. The signatures were headed by Mrs. Emma Smith.

It is quite possible that those dozen elders and apostles, those nineteen "married and unmarried females" were fully justified in asserting that " Dr. John C. Bennett's secret-wife "system is a creature of his own make," and "a disclosure of "his own make, and that they knew of no such society in the "place, nor never did;" but how some of them could "certify "and declare" in October, 1842, that they knew of no other than the monogamic marriage prescribed in the " Doctrine and "Covenants," is a little more than marvellous. *Some of them did know it!*

The names appended to those certificates will be read with interest by the Mormon people. They are as follows: S. Bennett; George Miller; Alphæus Cutler; Reynolds Cahoon; Wilson Law; Wilford Woodruff; N. R. Whitney; Albert Petty; Elias Higbee; John Taylor; E. Robinson; Aaron Johnson; Emma Smith—President [Ladies' Relief Society]; Elizabeth Ann Whitney—Counsellor; Sarah M. Cleveland—Counsellor; Eliza R. Snow—Secretary; Mary C. Miller; Lois Cutler; Thyrza Cahoon; Ann Hunter; Jane Law; Sophia R. Marks; Polly Z. Johnson; Abigail Works; Catherine Petty; Sarah Higbee; Phœbe Woodruff; Leonora Taylor; Sarah Hillman; Rosannah Marks; Angelina Robinson.

Had the revelation on polygamy not followed Bennett's exposure of the Prophet's teachings, there might have been good grounds for doubting his—Bennett's—statement; but with the immediately subsequent avowal of polygamy, and the acknowledgment in the revelation itself that " the Lord " had already given wives unto his servant Joseph, the reader will readily perceive that the denials and prevarications were unfortunate for the Church.

It is easy to comprehend the statement so frequently made by the Mormon teachers that, influenced by certain notions of duty, even good men may try to " steal a march " upon their fellow-men with the purpose of doing them service; and also, that kind-hearted parents may find it inconvenient to answer directly the awkward questions of juvenile minds about marital relations and many other matters of daily life. But it seems a pity that a whole people's conceptions of the necessities of Deity should partake so much of this doubtful morality, under the name of " policy." In the early history of Mormon polygamy, it is claimed that it was the conclusion among the leading elders that " the world " should not know everything that

" the Lord " had revealed, and that evasiveness on the subject of marriage was an obligation for the protection of the Church, and to aid " the Lord " in the establishment of that institution until it became strong enough to take care of itself. Besides, great truths freely offered to the world might be like " casting " pearls before swine."

Support for this equivocal position is drawn from the report of Peter denying his acquaintance with Christ; of Abraham, who, to avoid personal injury, called Sarah his " sister ; " and of some other gentleman in Bible history who feigned imbecility in an enemy's camp until favoured with opportunity to escape. The personal evasiveness named, where the situation was accidental and not courted, is not without a certain amount of defence ; but the evasive denial of polygamy by the Mormon elders does not fare so well, as they were in no accidental position, but in one of their own choosing. With the cases cited from the Bible, the act and consequences terminated with the deliverance of the persons mentioned ; but the Mormon Church may never see the end of the denial of polygamy. It requires no profound study of human nature to comprehend to what that principle may extend. If once admitted to be justifiable, how frequently and to what other ends may it not be used ? It is indeed a dangerous doctrine.

As early as 1835, when the revelations given through Joseph Smith were compiled and published, under the title of " The Book of Doctrine and Covenants," the opportunity was seized to assure the world in an article upon " Marriage," in the Appendix of that book, that the Saints were monogamic and pure. That " Book of Covenants " was published by Joseph Smith, and contains the following passages :

"Inasmuch as this Church of Christ has been reproached with the *crime* of fornication and polygamy ; we declare that we believe that one man should have *one* wife, and one woman *but one* husband, except in case of death, when either is at liberty to marry again.

After relating the form of marriage ceremony to be used in the Church, the person officiating is to address the parties about to be united :

"You both mutually agree to be each other's companion, husband **and** wife, observing the legal rights belonging to this condition; that is, keeping yourselves *wholly for each other, and from all others* during your lives."

This very definite language was well calculated to silence those who "reproached" the Church, and to assure at least its lay members that there was no foundation for the charges against their leaders, of either "fornication or polygamy" *as a principle of faith.* Sincerely believing that there was neither a quibble in language, nor double meaning in the manner of its expression, the missionaries cited it in sermons and published it from the press in every country where Mormonism was taught. Unfortunately it is now very clearly evident that those very passages upon marriage were written purposely for the deception of the public.

From the light thrown upon the writing of this Appendix by Brigham Young—in a sermon delivered in Logan, Utah, five years ago, and which the Author listened to—it is now easy to see that the article upon marriage was published to deceive. Brigham on that occasion made the damaging avowal that the Appendix was written by Oliver Cowdery against Joseph's wishes, and was permitted to be published only after Cowdery's incessant teasing and Joseph's warning to him of the trouble which his course would create.*

According to this confession, Cowdery would seem to have had either a glimpse of polygamy at that early day, or that he was, at the very moment of receiving revelations, a profligate in morals, for he insisted, Brigham says, upon adding to his marital relations a young woman familiar with his family, and did hold the relation of husband to her. To silence the clamour and surmising that arose over this "second wife," he wrote that Appendix; and, as will be seen hereafter, it has been used by the apostles in the Mormon Church for many years—and that, too, after they well knew that its use was a direct deception and falsehood.

Throwing the responsibility of the Appendix on to Cowdery

---

* Brigham is peculiarly unctuous in confessing other men's sins to the public, but his own are never mentioned. It would have been equally proper for him on this occasion to have explained why he, for nearly a quarter of a century, had preserved that falsehood in the "Book of Covenants," notwithstanding the opportunities he had of removing it in the several editions of the book that have been published under his Presidency.

seemed to Brigham better than no defence at all, but it is certainly a very damaging confession. It places the greatest witness that the " Divinity of Mormonism " ever claimed to have, in a most unenviable position, and it opens up a budget that is exceedingly suggestive. Joseph Smith and Oliver Cowdery must as early as the first year of the Church have contemplated the introduction of polygamy at some time in the future, or Cowdery could not well have become a " practical polygamist," and still have maintained fellowship with Joseph as he did, if there were any standard of morality in the Church.

The reader in re-perusing these short extracts from Cowdery's pen will now perceive with greater force the double deceitfulness of their wording when it is observed that " crime " is only attached to the word fornication, but not to polygamy— " the *crime of fornication*, and polygamy." The Mormon apologist claims that the expression being " crime," and not " crimes," the condemnation is not attached to polygamy, but only to fornication. Grammatically, the apology is good; morally, it is very bad—a pious fraud, corrupting and degrading.

The " witness," Cowdery, is further interesting.—" We declare," says he, " that one man should have one wife, and " one woman *but* one husband." The " *but* " is here cleverly put in. He designed to deceive under the guise of fairness. " One " man should have one wife" (*at least* " *one*," is the after interpretation), and as many more as he should find it convenient to get, take, or acknowledge; and " the woman *but* one husband." She, of course, was to be the monogamist of the family.

As in every experience of falsehood, this doubly-deceitful Appendix has wrought the greater wrong the more it was believed and the longer it has lived. Nearly twenty years after it was first published, the apostle John Taylor, in a public discussion at Boulogne-sur-mer, in France, in 1850, made use of it to answer the charge brought against the Mormons of practising polygamy then. When pressed on the subject, elder Taylor answered :

" We are accused here of polygamy and actions the most indelicate, obscene, and disgusting, such as none but a corrupt and depraved heart could have contrived. These things were too outrageous to admit of belief; therefore leaving the sisters of the 'white veil,' the 'black veil,' and all the other ' veils ' with those gentlemen to dispose of, together with their authors, as they think best, I shall content myself with reading *our views of chastity and marriage*, from a work published by us containing some of our articles of faith, 'Doctrine and Covenants,' page 330." *

Elder Taylor read the entire chapter upon marriage, from which the foregoing passages from the pen of Cowdery have been cited, and he undoubtedly satisfied the audience that the Mormon Church had been vilely slandered by the accusation of polygamy. At the very time that "brother Taylor" read these pages in Boulogne-sur-mer, *he had himself, living in Salt Lake City, five wives;* one of his two companions who likewise testified during the discussion, had also *two wives* there; and the other companion had likewise *two wives in the persons of a mother and her own daughter!* In less than eighteen months after that discussion the revelation on polygamy was publicly proclaimed.

Whatever value may have been placed upon this momentary triumph in France, the victory was soon seen to be dearly purchased in England. The native elders in Britain waxed so bold in the monogamic argument after the Boulogne discussion, that they raised an almost impregnable barrier against the polygamy that was soon to be introduced. What was temporarily gained in France was a thousand times permanently lost in Britain.

That an institution so repugnant to the spirit of the age, so much at war with the natural instincts of woman, could be accepted by disciples of the Prophet's own converting, already believing in monogamy, and that also confirmed by his own teaching, must be inexplicable to all outside of Mormonism. Were the personal testimony not so abundant that Joseph Smith both taught and practiced polygamy, " or," as a Mormon lady who knew him well once said, " practiced something " else," there would be good grounds for believing that the foregoing revelation was not of his authorship—it is so inharmonious with his own preceding revelations and so distinctly condemned by his own translated Book of Mormon.

The following passages from these Mormon Church books are exceedingly forcible :

* " Public Discussion," p. 8.

"And now it came to pass that the people of Nephi, under the reign of the second king, began to grow hard in their hearts, and indulge themselves somewhat in *wicked practices ;* such as, like unto David of old, *desiring many wives and concubines,* and also Solomon his son."—Book of Mormon, p. 115.

     .   .   .   .   .   .

"And were it not that I must speak unto you concerning *a grosser crime,* my heart would rejoice exceedingly because of you. But the word of God burdens me because of your grosser crimes. For, behold, thus saith the Lord, this people begin to wax in iniquity ; they understand not the Scriptures, for they seek to excuse themselves in committing whoredoms, *because* of the things which were written concerning David and Solomon his son. Behold, David and Solomon truly had many wives and concubines, *which thing was abominable before me, saith the Lord.*"

"Wherefore, thus saith the Lord, I have led this people forth out of the land of Jerusalem, by the power of mine arm, that I might raise me up a righteous branch from the fruit of the loins of Joseph. *Wherefore, I, the Lord, will not suffer that this people shall do like unto them of old* (i. e., David and Solomon). Wherefore, my brethren, hear me, and hearken to the word of the Lord : for *there shall not any man among you have, save it be one wife ; and concubines he shall have none.*"—Book of Mormon, p. 118.

To this the Mormon polygamist answers :

"Wherefore, this people shall keep my commandments, saith the Lord of Hosts, or cursed be the land for their sakes. For if I will, saith the Lord of Hosts, raise up seed unto me, *I will command my people,* otherwise they shall hearken unto these things."—*Page* 118.

In a revelation given February, 1831, the Prophet was *very explicit in commanding monogamy :*

"Thou shalt love thy wife with all thy heart, and shalt cleave unto her, and none else."—Book of Covenants, p. 124.

A month later a revelation given to Sidney Rigdon, Parley P. Pratt, and Lemon Copley, in which occurs the following passage :

"Marriage is ordained of God unto man ; wherefore it is lawful that he should have *one* wife, and they *twain* shall be one flesh."—Book of Covenants, p. 218.

It is not a little singular that the most forcible arguments that have yet been adduced against Mormon polygamy are those furnished by the pens of the three sons of Joseph Smith. The name of the eldest son of the Prophet is found at the head of a "Memorial to Congress," protesting against Brigham Young's Church being regarded as the true "Latter-Day" Church founded by his father—principally on account of polygamy. In that memorial the following points are given:

"We, your memorialists, would therefore submit for the consideration of Congress, in its action on the Utah question, and in its legislation on the question of the right of Congress to interfere with polygamy, as being a part of the faith of the Church of Jesus Christ of Latter-Day Saints:

"1. That the law of the Church, as found in the Bible, the Book of Mormon, and the Book of Covenants, accepted by the polygamists themselves, *expressly forbids to one man more than one living wife.*

"2. That the law contained in these books is the Constitution of the Church; that no law can obtain in the Church in contravention thereof; and that therefore *the pretended revelation on polygamy* is illegal and of no force.

"3. That in the remonstrance presented to Congress by the polygamists of Utah, dated March 31, 1870, the non-publication of this pretended revelation till the year 1852, is admitted in the following language:

"'Eighteen years ago, and ten years before the passage of the Anti-Polygamy Act of 1862, one of our leading men, elder Orson Pratt, was expressly deputed and sent to Washington to publish and lecture on the principles of plural marriage as practiced by us. . . . For ten years before the passage of the act of 1862, the principle was widely preached throughout the Union and the world, and was universally known and recognized as a principle of our holy faith.'

"4. That the plea of polygamy not being at variance with the law of the land, because not expressly in violation of any law on the statute-book of the Territory of Utah, is not admissible for this reason: The polygamic revelation claims to have been given in 1843, when the Church as a body was in Illinois, in which State bigamy or polygamy was then, as now, *a crime.*

"5. That polygamy, being a crime against the law of the State of Illinois, could not have been authorized by revelation from Him who, polygamists themselves affirm, gave the revelation found in 'Book of Covenants,' Sec. 58, par. 5, which declares: 'Let no man break the law of the land; for *he that keepeth the laws of God hath no need to break the laws of the land;* wherefore *be subject to the powers that be.*'—(Old Edition, Sec. 18.)

"6. That the pretended revelation on polygamy was not published till 1852, is strong presumptive evidence that it was not in existence; but, even if it were, it would still be of no force in the Church, as it contravenes revelations previously given to and accepted by the Church, and is, therefore, precluded from becoming a Church tenet, by that clause of the Church law before quoted, which declares: 'Neither shall anything be appointed unto any of this Church contrary to the Church covenants.'"

This statement of the sons of Joseph is lucid and forcible
to the rationally thinking portion of the Mormon Church.
But while the force of the sons' argument is acknowledged,
the teaching and practice of the father silence everything.
When he secretly taught polygamy to be a divine institution,
he was right, according to the ideas of the Saints: when he
publicly denied it within the same hour, he was equally right
in their estimation. Stripping this period of Mormonism of
all the verbiage of the Tabernacle, banishing that faith which
accepts all things, and looking at the facts of its history, Mormonism was at this time a fearful tumult of contradiction and
very doubtful morality.*

One of the highest dignitaries of the Mormon Church at
that period, William Law, the principal counsellor of Joseph,
writing to the Author, November 24, 1871, says:

"I have but a faint recollection of the certificate you speak of, signed
by a number of ladies; but I presume that most of them stated the truth,
as they knew of no doctrine of the kind at that time, for it was denied
most positively by Joseph and Hyrum, at even a later date. In 1842 I
had not heard of such teaching. I believe now that John C. Bennett did
know it, for he at that time was more in the secret confidence of Joseph
than perhaps any other man in the city. Bennett was a tool of Joseph for
a time, but for some cause which I never knew, Joseph cast him off. Perhaps there was jealousy in the matter.

"I think it was in 1843 that I first knew of the 'plurality doctrine.'
I believe, however, it existed possibly as early as 1840. A great many,
like myself, were considered not strong enough in the faith to swallow
such 'strong meat;' so we were fed on milk, hoping that we should get

* The evidence is so overwhelming that Joseph Smith introduced polygamy into
the Mormon Church, that the addition of more testimony seems superfluous; but
if more were necessary, the distinct mention of polygamy in Governor Ford's "History of Illinois" [pp. 322 and 327], written only a few years after the assassination,
clearly demonstrates that polygamy did not originate, as it is asserted, with Brigham
Young after he left Illinois.

It is very probable that before long "the Reorganized Church of Latter-Day
Saints," over which Joseph Smith, junior, presides, will drop the discussion of
polygamy, and tacitly, if not explicitly, admit that the elder Joseph went astray in
affairs of love. Wm. Marks, counsellor to Joseph Smith, the son, knows full well
that Joseph Smith, the father, was a polygamist. It is said that Joseph confessed
to Marks, only a few days before his death, that polygamy was an error, authorized
him to preach against it, and intimated that he himself would make confession of
the error, and forbid its further practice. This he probably would have done had
he lived.

our strength after a time, and be able to appreciate the good gifts of heaven (or hell).

"I think Joseph's sons knew that their father taught and practiced the 'spiritual-wife' doctrine. Their mother knew all about it, and, I believe, opposed it at first. But her antagonism, or the opposition of others, availed nothing. I begged of Joseph, and pled with him, as a man might plead for the life of his best friend, to stop all these evils, and save the Church from ruin ; but he seemed determined to rush on to utter destruction, and carry all with him that he could ; and thus he met his doom."

In the *Times and Seasons*, Vol. IV., p. 143, March 15th, 1843, appears the following :

"We are charged with advocating a plurality of wives, and common property. Now this is as false as the many other ridiculous charges which are brought against us. No sect has *a greater reverence for the laws of matrimony* or the rights of private property; and we do what others do not, we practice what we preach."

Four months after this date the revelation was given, and on February 1st of the following year, it is denied again, and an elder is excommunicated for teaching the " false and cor- " rupt doctrine : " *

"As we have lately been credibly informed that an elder of the Church of Jesus Christ of Latter-Day Saints, by the name of Hyrum Brown, has been preaching *polygamy and other false* and corrupt *doctrines*, in the county of Lapeer, State of Michigan, this is to notify him, and the Church in general, that he has been *cut off from the Church for his iniquity ;* and he is further notified to appear at the special conference on the 6th of April next, to make answer to these charges.

"(Signed) JOSEPH SMITH, and HYRUM SMITH,

"Presidents of said Church."

A little more than three months before his death, Hyrum published the following letter :

NAUVOO, *March 8*, 1844.

"To the brethren of the Church of Jesus Christ of Latter-Day Saints, living on China Creek, in Hancock county, Greeting : Whereas Brother Richard Hewett has called on me to-day to know my views concerning some doctrines that are preached in your place, and states to me that some of your elders say, that a man having a certain priesthood may have as many wives as he pleases. and that doctrine is taught here, I say unto you, that that man teaches false doctrine, for there is no such doctrine taught here, *neither is there any such thing practiced here.*" †

* *Times and Seasons,* Vol. V., p. 423.   † Ibid., p. 474.

Five months after the death of the Prophet and Patriarch, there was published, in the *Times and Seasons*, a letter from " an Old Man in Israel," in which the following paragraph occurs :

——" The laws of the land and the rules of the Church do not allow *any man to have any more than one wife alive at once;* but if any man's wife die, he has a right to marry another, and to be sealed to both for eternity—to the living and the dead ! There is no law of God or man against it. *This is all the spiritual-wife* system that ever was tolerated in the Church, and they know it."

There was no parade of this polygamic revelation to the Church in Joseph's lifetime, but its purport was conveyed to a few valiant men and some excellent women, who were deemed worthy to be entrusted with the secret, and though it might be unjust to charge Joseph with seeing thus far and so planning, it was the most certain way of securing the introduction of polygamy among the people. It did a better work for " the cause " in secret than it would have done by public proclamation ; especially as bigamy was punishable by statute in Illinois ; and there is such a luxury in secretly defying the laws of men when the believers are persuaded that they do so by the commandment of God.

The favoured few could not do less than honour " the " Lord " by a return of the confidence which he had been pleased to show them. Thus, with the bewildering credulity · of a secret revelation, and the defiance of all earthly power, the *intimate* friends of Joseph Smith were " sealed up unto " eternal life," and became peers with Abraham and all the patriarchs.

To doubt a revelation through Joseph was to entertain the suspicion that he was a " fallen prophet ; " and an immediate issue between the teacher and the taught was inevitable. Some bolder spirits dared to think and question his revelations, but few indeed among them have had the courage to openly oppose them. Joseph was " the servant of the Lord ; " he was accountable to no one on earth. When his teaching was inharmonious with the age, that was nothing—the world was wrapt in midnight darkness : when it came in contact with his own preceding revelations, the ready answer was—" to "babes is given milk, to men and women strong meats." The transition, therefore, from monogamy to polygamy in the Mormon Church was only a question as to the submission and credulity of the disciples.

Had this revelation been presented to the Mormons with the "first principles" taught by the elders, not one in ten thousand among them would have accepted it as an emanation from Jesus Christ. But educated by their priesthood to regard all questioning of a revelation through the Prophet as the subtile working of Satanic influence to darken the mind and to mislead the disciple into rebellion, and with the terrible consequences of "apostacy" pictured to them and ever present in their thoughts, the Mormons could do no other than *try* to believe the doctrine of polygamy. But even under these favourable predispositions, the great majority of both men and women have fought against it, and its acceptance at all has been a terrible trial of faith and a hazardous chancing of the future.

When it was first published, the British mission was in the highest prosperity; the elders were travelling all over that island, meeting with great success; calls for preaching were everywhere heard, and large numbers were being baptized into the new faith. The Utah elders then in England, and a few only of the native elders, knew some little time before, as one of them rather coarsely expressed it in a council of the Priesthood in London, that "the cat was soon to be let out of the bag." *The Millennial Star*, the organ of the Church, had been for some months preparing the way for its *début* by the weekly publication of extracts from a work on "Marriage among the "Jews;" but almost the entire mass of the European elders, and the "Saints" there, had no knowledge of this revelation, and were constantly defending the cause in public against the charge of polygamy in Utah.

On the 1st of January, 1853, it was published in the *Star*. It fell like a thunderbolt upon the Saints, and fearfully shattered the mission. The British elders, who in their ignorance had been denying polygamy, and stigmatizing their opponents as calumniators, up to the very day of its publication, were confounded and paralyzed, and from that time to the present the avenues of preaching have closed, one after another, and the mission that was once the glory of the Mormon Church has withered and shrivelled into comparative insignificance.

The outside world misjudges the Mormon people when it imagines that polygamy was ever a favourite doctrine. Doubtless to some few it was a pleasant revelation; but it was not so to the mass of the people, for they resisted it until they were compelled to yield their opposition, or else abandon the Church in which they had faith.

The statistical reports of the mission in the British Islands —June 30th, 1853—show that the enormous number of *seventeen hundred and seventy-six persons were excommunicated there during the first six months of the preaching of polygamy.*

The entire Church then numbered, men, women, and children over eight years of age, 30,690. There were forty "seventies," and eight "high-priests," from Utah, in Britain at that time, carrying with them a powerful personal influence to help the Saints to tide over the introduction of this doctrine. These Utah missionaries were aided by a native priesthood of 2,578 elders, 1,854 priests, 1,416 teachers, 834 deacons; and yet no less than 1,776 recusants were excommunicated. That tells its own tale.

That all these persons withdrew from the fellowship of the Mormon Church on account of polygamy would be an unfair inference. Still, doubtless, polygamy was the great contributing cause of apostacy then, and more persons have left the Mormon communion on account of polygamy and Brigham's favourite deity—ADAM (which he first preached in October of the same year), than all else put together.

Few of the Mormon women have ever accepted polygamy from the assent of their judgments. They have first been led by their teachers to consider the doctrine true, and afterwards have been afraid to question it. Their fears have counselled submission. Many of them have never been able to give it a careful and deliberate reading. Some have probably never read it at all. When first placed in their hands it was, as can readily be conceived, received under the excitement and irritation of unlooked-for and unwelcome news, and hurriedly read to see what it did contain, then cast aside, in a burst of grief, and seldom if ever taken up again.

It is to be regretted that the Mormon women (and their husbands, too) have not read it more ; for the more frequently it is perused, and the horrors it threatens are faced, the more satisfied must they become that the charge of its authorship to Jesus Christ is an atrocious libel upon His name, or else the record of His life has been greatly misunderstood by the world.

From a common-sense standpoint the " revelation " is suggestive a thousand times more of Moses than of Christ. Had it been addressed by the former to the Israelites in their Egyptian bondage, in the wilderness where they, as children, were terrified and alarmed by the thunders of Mount Sinai, there might be some consistency in the oft-repeated announcement of authoritative teaching. In that one revelation—

There are ten times—" Saith the Lord ; "

Eight times—" I am the Lord thy God ; "

Six times—" Saith the Lord your God ; "

Once each—" Jesus Christ, I am He ; " " I, the Lord thy " God ; " " I, the Lord, am thy God ; "

And, finally concluding with—" I am Alpha and Omega."

It is astonishing what amount of submission and credulity can be developed when the mind is properly worked up with devotional feeling and is awe-stricken by threats of damnation. Not inaptly or without logical force has Joseph Smith been designated the Mohammed of America. Between the prophet of Arabia and the prophet of Nauvoo (each claiming divine, prophetic powers) there is a strong family resemblance and a more than singular coincidence of experience.

18

CHAPTER XXIX.

AFTER THE PROPHET'S DEATH.—Sidney Rigdon delivered over to Satan—
Brigham Young and the Twelve Apostles rule the Church—Mobocracy again
rampant—Burning the Houses of the Saints—The Expulsion of the Mormons
demanded—The Saints agree to Expatriation.

It was very natural that "the Saints" should recall to
mind the sayings of their martyred Prophet when, even in the
remotest manner, he had expressed an apprehension of early
death—such as " I am going like a lamb to the slaughter," etc.,
or when he had done anything that could be interpreted as
preparatory to " shuffling off this mortal coil." These were
now sacred reminiscences and confirmed his prophetic character in the estimation and love of the people. Unfortunately,
however, for the peace and unity of the Church, in all the multitude of his sayings and doings he made no direct and open
preparation for the presidency of the Church in case of his
death,* and thus his martyrdom wrought confusion among the
disciples. They were left " like sheep without a shepherd."

The apostles Taylor and Richards were with Joseph in Carthage jail, and all the other apostles were preaching in the
States. On hearing the news of the tragedy, most of them
hastened to Nauvoo, to counsel together upon the necessities
of the situation.

Joseph and Hyrum Smith, with Sidney Rigdon, had constituted " the first Presidency of the Church: " they were the
ruling powers of the Kingdom. The Quorum of the Twelve
Apostles had, in a conventional way, been recognized as

---

* It is claimed that " young Joseph "—eldest son of the Prophet—" was appointed through his father according to the law of lineage, by prophecy, and blessing, in Liberty jail, Missouri ; by revelation in 1841, and by a formal anointing in
a Council in Nauvoo, in 1844," to be the successor of his father.

" equal in authority to the First Presidency : " but up to this
time the acknowledgment was merely nominal. At the death
of the Smiths, Rigdon alone, of the First Presidency, remained,
while the Quorum of the Apostles was entire.

For several years preceding this period, Rigdon had been
somewhat lukewarm and unreliable. Still, he clung to the
faith, loved the Saints, and was certain to be present on the
great occasions of Mormon demonstration. Sidney had never
fairly got over the sufferings he endured in Missouri. His enthusiasm was chilled ; and, besides this, Joseph, in seeking the
hand of his daughter, Nancy, greatly offended him. At the
time of the Prophet's death, Rigdon was residing with his
family in Pittsburg, Ohio, trying to take life easily, while
Brigham Young, the Pratts, Hyde, and other apostles were
out on missions. When the news of the assassination arrived,
he set out in haste and arrived first in Nauvoo. Parley P.
Pratt, Brigham Young, Orson Hyde, Heber C. Kimball, and
other apostles arrived soon after.

Who should rule the Church was now an open question.

Rigdon—aware of the logical fact that one is the smaller
part of three, and realizing that his active fellowship with the
living Joseph had been questionable for some years back—proposed to the Saints the appointment of a " guardian " over the
Church, a sort of regency, until further development should
manifest "the will of the Lord." He had no hopes that he
would then be accepted as a " prophet, seer, and revelator,"
though he had been ordained to all those high offices. Like a
brevetted general, he had only worn his titles of glory. He
was, therefore, contented to become the " guardian "—if only
he could attain to that position.

Marsh had apostatized ; Patten had been killed ; and, by
the accident of seniority, Brigham Young was at the head of
the Quorum of the Twelve. No one questioned his fidelity to
the Prophet up to this time ; but, personally, he was remarkable for nothing — except being " hard-working Brigham
" Young " He was infinitely inferior in education and mental
development to the Pratts and Hyde, but the apostacy of Marsh
and the death of Patten, his predecessors in the ranks of the
apostles, had brought him uppermost in that Quorum.

The Church was now splitting into fragments. Many were uncertain of the future, and many more began to be doubtful of the past. In the language of Brigham, the people began to be "much every way." "Some were for Joseph and Hyrum, "the Book of Mormon, and Doctrine and Covenants, the Tem- "ple and Joseph's measures; some were for Lyman Wight: "some for James Emmett; some for Sidney Rigdon, and, I "suppose, some for the Twelve."

Sidney Rigdon.

Rigdon had been the Boanerges of the new faith, and had given it the first important aid which it received; but he was now waning in everything. He had seen Joseph revel in vis- ions, dreams, and revelations, and had witnessed their wonder- ful effect upon the bewildered minds of the Saints. To step securely into Joseph's shoes, he had to do something like him, or to be for ever overthrown—like Lucifer, for his ambition in seeking the headship of the Church. He essayed the *rôle* of Joseph and entered upon the shadowy regions of revelation. He had nightly visions about Gog and Magog, and saw wonder- ful things which were soon to take place. The great battle of Armageddon was at hand, and Rigdon was to lead on the hosts of the Lord to the slaughter till the blood flowed up to the horses' bridles. When that was all done and got through with, he, as a conqueror, was to be privileged with the honour of "pulling the nose of little Vic.!"

This mad raving before public audiences, and the familiarity of language in using the name of her most gracious majesty, the sovereign of Great Britain, render comment on such fanaticism unnecessary. In private assemblages of the brethren he announced that he held "the keys of David," and he ordained some special friends to be "prophets, priests, and kings," and made general preparation for the maintenance of his claims, by force if necessary, to the guardianship of the Church.

Rigdon was brought up for public trial before the High Council in Nauvoo, on the 8th of September, with eight of the apostles as "witnesses"—who in reality acted as principal accusers. Brigham led off with a speech about Rigdon's history, and was followed by the other apostles and all who had anything to say about the matter. He was charged with the determination to "rule or ruin the Church." Brigham was as determined that he should do neither. Rigdon was said to be sick, and failed to appear at trial; but that was no hindrance. The accusations were listened to, and the family quarrel was anything but edifying to the Saints. Finally, it was moved "that he be cut off from the Church and delivered over to the "buffetings of Satan until he repent." To this the reporter adds:

"Elder Young arose, and delivered Sidney Rigdon over to the buffetings of Satan in the name of the Lord; and all the people said, Amen."

Some ten persons voted in favour of Rigdon, and these were immediately "suspended" from fellowship.

Brigham's notions of freedom of voting are singularly amusing. He works up his audience to the affirmative of what he has to propose, and as he calls for an expression of the people's mind by a show of uplifted hands, he stands up in the congregation to watch the operation. He then asks for a negative vote, and should any unfortunates differ from him they are captured. He has more recently added to this amusement of *free* voting the instruction beforehand to the congregation: "Now, breth-

"ren, look around you, and see who are voting; we want "every one to vote one way or another." Should the voting be the "one way," all is serene; should it be "the other way," he then forces a collision which terminates with something analogous to King Richard's ejaculation — "Off with his "head! So much for Buckingham!" Brigham's *free* voting assemblies closely resemble those of the ancient parliaments of France, which were only convened to ratify the arbitrary edicts of the absolute monarchs of that kingdom.

For some time after the trial, Sidney showed considerable disposition to fight the position assumed by Brigham and the Twelve, and for that purpose he revived the *Latter-Day Saints' Messenger and Advocate*, in Pittsburg, Pa.; but it had only a short-lived existence. He is now very feeble with age and infirmity, and living in Friendship, New York. It has been generally expected that some day he would confess to having aided Joseph Smith in fabricating, from "Solomon Spaulding's "Manuscript," the Book of Mormon; but there seems to be no ground for such a hope. All through his trial those who knew him before he was a Mormon spoke of him in such a manner as leaves no room to doubt Rigdon's own sincerity in the Mormon faith, and his total ignorance of the existence of Joseph Smith and the Book of Mormon till after that work had been published.

As soon as Sidney was disposed of, the change in the government of the Church was almost magical. Joseph was always gushing over with inspiration and abounding in revelations. He had one or two men around him who aided him with counsel; but, after all, Joseph was the dominant figure throughout. Over the Church there were now twelve men, most of whom were ambitious to work. They were in new spheres of action, and set out, in the language of the conventicle, to "magnify their calling."

In entering upon a new page of history, they thought it prudent to revise the past. Joseph had trusted more to miraculous interpositions, "the Lord," and outside politicians, then had been profitable. Brigham had been a hard-working man, and he knew the superiority of practical labour over visions, dreams, and revelations. He knew, too, the uncertainty of politics. He had studied Joseph's troubles, had witnessed the terrible effect of Sidney's flighty attempts at continuing revelation, and had resolved to change the thoughts of the people.

Joseph was "a natural born seer," and had a pedestal of his own. There Brigham intended that he should remain— alone and undisturbed. With Joseph among them, the Saints had "walked by sight." With Brigham, they were now to "walk by faith." That was the safer position. Instead of vaulting to the prominence of the "Revelator," Brigham brought down the revelations to the grasp of the people, and distributed them broadcast among them. "Every member," said he, "has the right of receiving revelation for himself." This was a flattering privilege, and a great consolation ; it had to satisfy the Saints, and it saved Brigham the unpleasantness of comparison. "Let no man presume for a moment that his "[Joseph's] place will be filled by another," was the language of the hour ; "you are now without a prophet present with "you in the flesh to guide you ; but you are not without apos- "tles who hold the keys of power *to seal on earth that which* "*shall be sealed in heaven* . . . I am not a prophet, seer, or revela- "tor, *as Joseph was*," continues Brigham ; "neither do I give "revelations with 'Thus saith the Lord,' as he did, and so much "the better for the Saints, for if I did so, and they did not live "up to those revelations, they would be condemned."

This was certainly a very kind consideration. What a deal of condemnation the Saints would have been saved if Joseph had only thought of it in his time! They now, however, had only "Hobson's choice," and were obliged to accept the situation. It is a sensible axiom that "half a loaf is better than no "bread :" the Saints could not make a Joseph, they had of necessity to accept a Brigham. The soul and inspiration of Mormonism were gone. There was no successor to Joseph— there could be none. Brigham at once announced that Joseph had left enough of revelation to guide them for twenty years. To build up "the kingdom" to Joseph, and to carry out Joseph's measures, were henceforth to be ambition and glory enough. Brigham might occupy Joseph's seat on the platform, but he could never fill his place in the Church, and no one knew this better than Brigham himself. He saw before him a multitude

of people who had been gathered by revelation, and who had
fed upon it daily. There was but one thing that could be
done—make them work out an idea. "Build up the kingdom
"to Joseph: build it to Joseph!"—"He is looking down upon
"us, and is with us as much as before." The people laboured
for Joseph, and Brigham controlled and garnered the results
for himself. The past style of doing business was to be
changed; the loose ends were to be tied up, and everything
was to be put upon a strictly commercial basis. The Saints
were to gather to Nauvoo as before, but every member of the
Church was to "proceed immediately to tithe himself or her-
"self a tenth of all their property or money, and pay it into
"the hands of the Twelve," and "the members can then em-
"ploy the remainder of their capital in every branch of enter-
"prise, industry, and charity, as seemeth them good; *only*
"holding themselves in readiness *to be advised* in such manner
"as shall be for the good of themselves and the whole society."

Brigham meant to control everybody and everything; and
from the time when he signed the first epistle—"Brigham
"Young, President of the Twelve, Nauvoo, August 15th,
"1844," to the present hour, he has never lost sight of that
part of his programme.

In politics he was equally emphatic. None of the candidates for the presidential chair had "manifested any disposi-
"tion or intention to redress wrong or restore right, liberty, or
"law," and the Saints were counselled to "stand aloof from all
"men and measures till some one could be found who would
"carry out the enlarged principles of our beloved prophet and
"martyr, General Joseph Smith." In the mean time "the
"Twelve Apostles of this dispensation stand in their own
"place and always will, both in time and eternity, to minister,
"preside, and regulate the affairs of the whole Church."

The *coup d'état* that overthrew Rigdon and placed Brigham on the throne was then complete. All that remained to
be done, was to officially decapitate Rigdon and hand him over
to Satan, which, as before stated, Brigham duly attended to on
the 8th of September.

There is something strikingly characteristic of the man in
the foundation then laid of his present position. He has been

charged with inconsistency in asserting at the time of Joseph's death that "no man should stand in his place," while subsequently he filled that place himself. But to this he has a ready answer : "No one can take the place of Joseph ; he is still "in his place at the head of the Church, and will always be "there throughout time and eternity." This language is somewhat diplomatic, but it is consistent with the whole tenor of his life—"the end justifies the means."

That the people should not understand Brigham's ulterior purposes is not a matter of surprise. He understood them himself, and seized the earliest opportunity of preparing for the contemplated change as soon as the people should be ready for the experiment. On the 2nd of September an editorial appeared in the *Times and Seasons*, in which occurs the following shrewd, half-expressed anticipation of the change :

"Great excitement prevails throughout the world to know who 'shall be the successor of Joseph Smith.' In reply, we say—be patient, *be patient a little*, and we will tell you all. 'Great wheels move slowly.' At present we can say that a special conference of the Church was held at Nauvoo on the 8th ultimo, and it was carried without a dissenting voice that the 'Twelve' should preside over the whole Church, and *when any alteration in the presidency shall be required, reasonable notice shall be given ;* and the elders abroad will best exhibit their wisdom to all men by remaining silent on those things they are ignorant of."

That the Twelve should preside over the whole Church, is placed in the fore-ground to be seen of all men, and to be spoken of openly, but, " when any alteration in the Presidency shall be required," a silent reserve was to be maintained, which only the wise could understand. Discussion was imprudent— silence was wisdom. Shrewd Brigham !

From a neutral standpoint, and taking the two men and their antecedents into account, the Church, however little it may have gained, lost nothing by preferring Brigham before Rigdon ; but to a people like the Mormons, accustomed to so much revelation as Joseph had given them, and the guidance of " the Lord " in everything—even to the building of a "boarding-house"—this period of their history is singularly suggestive.—The " Revelator " was truly gone.

The distinctive feature of Mormonism was henceforth to be

implicit, unquestioning "obedience"—an utter subjugation
of will and personality to the dictates of the Priesthood.
"Religion was made up of obedience, let life or death come."
"Satan was hurled from heaven for resisting authority." *
The past troubles of Mormonism were all then traceable to
freedom of thought. The murderers of the Smiths were "a
"hundredth part" less guilty than the "apostates." "A lit-
"tle difference of feeling; a little difference of opinion; a lit-
"tle difference of spirit; and this difference has finally ended
"in bloodshed and murder." From this time the Mormon leaders have intensely hated "apostates," and to this day they have
not discovered the possibility of any person leaving the Mormon faith, without at the same time "thirsting for the blood
"of the Prophet."

While the Rigdon-Young difficulty about the succession
was going on, Lyman Wight, one of the twelve apostles, and
William Smith, another apostle and brother of the murdered
Prophet, were objects of some anxiety; but the former was
"let alone severely," and the latter, for a time, was spoken of
with patronizing kindness as "the remaining brother of the
"Prophet and the Patriarch." Wight went to Texas with a
small company to form a settlement. There they suffered a
good deal together, and finally broke up and scattered where
they could. The Prophet's brother was soon after accused of
sowing his "wild oats," without proper regard to the order of
the new revelation; and he was easily got rid of. He has since
managed to maintain a happy obscurity.† John E. Page,
another apostle, became discontented, apostatized, and was cut
off, while Gladden Bishop, Strang, Brewster, Hendrick, Cutler, Emmett, and a host of other elders were in the enjoyment

---

* "Epistle of the Twelve." *Times and Seasons*, Vol. V., page 618.

† From the beginning of Mormonism the ruling authorities have accepted defamation of character as the best weapon with which to assail the discontented.
Without challenging the Mormon charges against the Prophet's brother, it is due to
the latter to append the following from the *Clayton County* [Iowa] *Journal:*

"During the war with the South he served nearly two years as a soldier, in helping to put down the rebellion. In 1841 and '42 he served in the legislature as representative from Hancock county, in the State of Illinois. He has followed the occupation of a farmer in the vicinity of Elkader, and upon Sundays occasionally
preaching. As a man, he is candid, honest, and upright—a citizen of whom rumour
speaks no evil, and he is a faithful expounder of true Mormonism, while he depre-
cates polygamy."

of a fearful amount of new and bewildering revelation about who should succeed Joseph Smith, and all of them opposed to Brigham Young's leadership of the Church.

Unborn, yet blessed and prophetically announced, was David Hyrum Smith, to be at some future time the ruler of the Mormon Church.* David Hyrum saw the light of this vain and wicked world on the 17th of November, 1844, about five months after the death of his father, and from his birth he became an object of the deepest interest to all professors of the Mormon faith.

While the dissensions which have just been noticed stamped the history of the Church with the confusion of Babel, the Gentiles were preparing anew for hostilities. The assassination of Joseph Smith was soon discovered to be a great blunder. There was nothing about the Prophet personally, and still less, if possible, about his brother Hyrum, to justify, even in the remotest manner, the Carthage tragedy. The assassins had mistaken men for principles. Joseph was a liberal, big-hearted man, and the last person whom the world would have taken for a prophet. In Carthage jail the Prophet and Patriarch were but men: in Nauvoo they were representatives of a system. The mobbers, murderers, and assassins at Carthage could extinguish the one: the other was left intact. Brigham Young with a tragedy for his text was a more difficult man to deal with than Joseph Smith with a revelation to announce.

The excitement in Hancock county was soon renewed, and the extremists on either side felt the desperation of their situation. The one sought to justify the assassination of the Prophet, the other to revenge his death. The resolutions passed at any meeting at Nauvoo or Carthage amounted to nothing: with such an account unsettled there could be no honesty on either side. There were hostility and conflict of interests which no preambles, resolutions, or public speaking could affect. The Mormons hated the Gentiles, and the Gentiles hated the Mormons. This was the only point upon which they were agreed. They were each of them ready to believe and act upon the most exaggerated and groundless reports,

* This prediction rests upon the remembrance of the Hon. John M. Bernhisel, formerly delegate from Utah to Congress.

and there was nothing too bad for either of them to credit concerning the other. Of this time Governor Ford gives the following interesting picture :

" The Mormons invoked the assistance of Government to take vengeance upon the murderers of the Smiths. The anti-Mormons asked the Governor to violate the constitution which he was sworn to support, by erecting himself into a military despot and exiling the Mormons. The Mormons on their part, in their newspapers, invited the Government to assume absolute power by taking a summary vengeance upon their enemies, by shooting fifty or a hundred of them, without judge or jury. Both parties were thoroughly disgusted with constitutional provisions restraining them from summary vengeance ; each was ready to submit to arbitrary power, to the fiat of a dictator, to make me a king for the time being, or at least that I might exercise the power of a king to abolish both the forms and spirit of a free government, if the despotism erected upon its ruins could only be wielded for their benefit, and to take vengeance on their enemies. . . .

" In the course of the fall of 1844 the anti-Mormon leaders sent printed invitations to all the militia captains in Hancock county, and to the captains of militia in all the neighbouring counties in Illinois, Iowa, and Missouri, to be present with their companies at a great wolf-hunt in Hancock ; and it was privately announced that the wolves to be hunted were the Mormons and Jack-Mormons.* Preparations were made for assembling several thousand men with provisions for six days; and the anti-Mormon newspapers in aid of the movement commenced anew the most awful accounts of thefts, and robberies, and meditated outrages by the Mormons. The Whig press in every part of the United States came to their assistance. The Democratic newspapers and the leading Democrats who had received the benefit of the Mormon votes to their party, quailed under the tempest, leaving no organ for the correction of public opinion, either at home or abroad, except the discredited Mormon newspaper at Nauvoo. But very few of my prominent Democratic friends would dare come up to the assistance of their Governor, and but few of them dared openly to vindicate his motives in endeavouring to keep the peace. They were willing and anxious for Mormon votes at elections, but they were unwilling to risk their popularity with the people, by taking a part in their favour, even when law, and justice, and the constitution were on their side. Such being the odious character of the Mormons, the hatred of the common people against them, and such being the pusillanimity of leading men in fearing to encounter it.

" In this state of the case I applied to Brigadier-General J. J. Hardin of the State militia, and to Colonels Baker and Merriman, all Whigs, but all of them men of military ambition, and they, together with Colonel William Weatherford, a Democrat, with my own exertions, succeeded in

* A slang name applied to Gentiles who favour the Mormons.

raising about five hundred volunteers; and thus did these Whigs, that which my own political friends, with two or three exceptions, were slow to do, from a sense of gratitude. . . .

"Nauvoo was now a city of about 15,000 inhabitants, and was fast increasing, as the followers of the Prophet were pouring into it from all parts of the world; and there were several other settlements and villages of Mormons in Hancock county. Nauvoo was scattered over about six square miles, a part of it being built upon the flat skirting and fronting on the Mississippi River, but the greater portion of it upon the bluffs back, east of the river. The great Temple, that is said to have cost a million of dollars in money and labour, occupied a commanding position on the brow of this bluff, and overlooked the country around in Illinois and Iowa. . . .

"The anti-Mormons complained of a large number of larcenies and robberies. The Mormon press at Nauvoo, and the anti-Mormon papers at Warsaw, Quincy, Springfield, Alton, and St. Louis, kept up a constant fire at each other; the anti-Mormons all the time calling upon the people to rise and expel or exterminate the Mormons. . . . In the fall of 1845, the anti-Mormons of Lima and Green Plains held a meeting to devise means for the expulsion of the Mormons from their neighbourhood. They appointed some persons of their own number to fire a few shots at the house where they were assembled, but to do it in such a way as to hurt none who attended the meeting. The meeting was held, the house was fired at, but so as to hurt no one; and the anti-Mormons, suddenly breaking up their meeting, rode all over the country, spreading the dire alarm that the Mormons had commenced the work of massacre and death.

"This startling intelligence soon assembled a mob at Lima, which proceeded to warn the Mormons to leave the neighbourhood, and threatened them with fire and sword if they remained. A very poor class of Mormons resided there, and it is very likely that the other inhabitants were annoyed beyond further endurance by their little larcenies and rogueries. The Mormons refused to remove; and about one hundred and seventy-five houses and hovels were burnt, the inmates being obliged to flee for their lives. They fled to Nauvoo in a state of utter destitution, carrying their women and children, aged and sick, along with them as best they could. The sight of these miserable creatures aroused the wrath of the Mormons of Nauvoo.

"When the burning of houses commenced, the great body of the anti-Mormons expressed themselves strongly against it, giving hopes thereby that a *posse* of anti-Mormons could be raised to put a stop to such incendiary and riotous conduct. But when they were called on by the new sheriff, not a man of them turned out to his assistance, many of them no doubt being influenced by their hatred of the sheriff. Backinstos then went to Nauvoo, where he raised a *posse* of several hundred armed Mormons, with which he swept over the country, took possession of Carthage, and established a permanent guard there. The anti-Mormons everywhere fled from their houses before the sheriff some of them to Iowa and Missouri and

others to the neighbouring counties in Illinois. The sheriff was unable or
unwilling to bring any portion of the rioters to battle or to arrest any of
them for their crimes. The *posse* came near surprising one small squad,
but they made their escape, all but one, before they could be attacked.
This one, named McBratney, was shot down by some of the *posse* in advance, by whom he was hacked and mutilated as though he had been murdered by the Indians.

"The sheriff also was in continual peril of his life from the anti-Mormons,

Burning Mormon Houses.

who daily threatened him
with death the first opportunity. As he was going
in a buggy in the direction
of Warsaw from Nauvoo,
he was pursued by three or
four men to a place in the
road where some Mormon
teams were standing. But
Backinstos passed the teams
a few rods, and then stopping, the pursuers came up
to within one hundred and
fifty yards, when they were
fired upon, with an uner-
ring aim, by some one con-
cealed not far to one side of them. By this fire Franklin A. Worrell was
killed. He was the same man who had commanded the guard at the jail
at the time the Smiths were assassinated; and there made himself conspicuous by betraying his trust by consenting to the assassination. It is
believed that Backinstos expected to be pursued and attacked, and had
previously stationed some men in ambush to fire upon his pursuers. He
was afterwards indicted for the supposed murder, and procured a change
of venue to Peoria county, where he was acquitted of the charge. About
this time, also, the Mormons murdered a man of the name of Daubeneyer,
without any apparent provocation; and another anti-Mormon, named
Wilcox, was murdered in Nauvoo, as it is believed by order of the Twelve
Apostles. The anti-Mormons also committed one murder. Some of them,
under Backman, set fire to some straw near a barn belonging to Durfee,
an old Mormon of seventy years, and then lay in ambush until the old
man came out to extinguish the fire, when they shot him dead from their
place of concealment. The perpetrators of this murder were arrested and
brought before an anti-Mormon justice of the peace, and were acquitted,
though their guilt was sufficiently apparent.

"During the ascendancy of the sheriff, and the absence of the anti-
Mormons, the people who had been burnt out of their homes fled to Nauvoo, from whence with many others they sallied forth and ravaged the
country, stealing and plundering whatever was convenient to drive away.

"When informed of these proceedings, I hastened to Jacksonville, where, in a conference with General Hardin, Major Warren, Judge Douglas, and the Attorney-General, Mr. McDougall, it was agreed that these gentlemen should proceed to Hancock in all haste, with whatever forces had been raised, few or many, and put an end to these disorders. It was now apparent that neither party in Hancock could be trusted with the power to keep the peace. It was also agreed that all these gentlemen should unite their influence with mine to induce the Mormons to leave the State.

"Through the intervention of General Hardin, acting under instructions from me, an agreement was made between the hostile parties for the voluntary removal of the greater part of the Mormons in the spring of 1846." *

During the renewed contention the Mormons exerted every energy to complete the Temple. The faithful had been taught that they and all that was theirs should be consecrated to this great work, and themselves greatly blessed by aiding in it. They had learned that therein a great endowment would be bestowed upon the living, and peculiar privileges accorded to their dead. The faith and labours of the people were in an extraordinary degree stimulated by the announcement that if the Temple were not completed within a specified time "the "Lord would reject them and their dead." †

The Mormons estimated this building at about six hundred thousand dollars, and in its construction and design it exhibited " more wealth, more art, more science, more revelation, more " splendour, and more God, than all the rest of the world."

Their pride in this particular instance was pardonable, for the Temple was reared in the midst of great poverty, and, before they could complete it, the masons, carpenters, and artisans had their fire-arms lying beside their tools, while watchmen were continually on the alert to sound the alarm on the approach of any foe. Thus, in the New Zion, the Scripture story of the pains and perils of the Jewish builders of the walls of Jerusalem, under the guidance of Nehemiah, was repeated, which the Mormons failed not to remember, and from it made a pointed application.

Indictments had been found in the Circuit Court of the

---

* " History of Illinois," pp. 361–410.

† In a subsequent chapter the ordinances for the dead are treated of.

United States, for the District of Illinois, against a number of the leading Mormons, for counterfeiting the coin of the Republic, and the marshal was eager for their arrest. The Governor declined to call out the militia to support the sheriff, believing that it was better, after the calamities that had already befallen the Saints, and the promise they had given of expatriating themselves in the spring, to allow them to escape without further molestation; a conclusion which he readily reached, as he believed that none of them could be convicted.

This bogus money-making in Nauvoo has been strenuously denied by Brigham and some of the apostles, and very probably those who denied all knowledge of that business were perfectly truthful in their statements, as far as they themselves were concerned. But that bogus money was made and in circulation, in and around Nauvoo, and also was sent to a distance for circulation, can certainly not be denied. That some of "the brethren" were engaged in its manufacture seems to be well supported by facts which subsequently transpired.

No one unacquainted with the history of the Saints at this time could possibly imagine the recrimination and bitterness of feeling that existed between the Mormons and anti-Mormons of Nauvoo and the surrounding districts. It was worse than civil war, worse than a war of races; it was religious hate! It was fed by fanaticism on both sides—a fanaticism that was truly despicable. It demonstrated beyond controversy that Mormonism, and what is termed by the Saints "the world," are incompatible with each other. With the faith of the Saints that they were building up "a kingdom," it was very natural that they should act differently from the citizens of a Republic, and that they should seek to control, and not submit to be controlled. With no faith in that religion, it was as natural for "the Gentiles" to view with alarm every influence and power in the county passing into Mormon hands. The idea of subjugation was at the bottom of their thoughts, and they were determined not to submit. It was evident to every one that there could be no peace so long as the Mormons remained in the county, and for their expulsion the anti-Mormons of the neighbouring counties pledged "their lives and their sacred "honour."

THE EXODUS FROM NAUVOO.

CHAPTER XXX.

THE EXODUS FROM NAUVOO.—The Hasty Departure of the Apostles—Journey to the Rocky Mountains—The Sufferings of the Exiles—Nauvoo besieged and bombarded—An Exile's Story—Colonel Kane's Narrative.

THE year 1845 was dark and dreary, and full of painful interest to the Saints, with only now and then a momentary gleam of change for the better. There was no certainty in anything but trouble, and that rolled in upon them like the fury of the angry billows. The thought of a home in the Rocky Mountains, or "anywhere" away from the rest of mankind, where they could be by themselves, filled them with buoyant hope that the promises of the Prophet would yet be realized.

With unwavering fidelity they toiled on the building of the Temple, though they well knew that they were completing it only to leave it to the tender care of their enemies. Their resolution was a sublime illustration of the power of faith.

By the beginning of October the building had so far progressed that the semi-annual conference was held therein. It was a great and solemn gathering. All the dignitaries of the Church were present, and the exodus of the Saints was formally resolved upon, while proper committees were appointed for the conveyance of what real estate might find purchasers.

However much they may subsequently have been benefited by the change of locality, the abandonment of their homes and firesides was, for the time being, a severe trial of their temper. The following official letter, dated November 1st, expresses their feelings at that time:

" Continued abuses, persecutions, murders, and robberies, practiced upon us by a horde of land pirates with impunity in a *Christian* republic and land of liberty (while the institutions of justice have either been too

14

weak to afford us protection or redress, or else they too have been remiss), have brought us to the solemn conclusion that our exit from the United States is the only alternative; . . . we then can shake the dust from our garments, . . . leaving this nation *alone in her glory*, while the residue of the world points the finger of scorn, till the indignation and consummation decreed makes a full end."

The High Council at Nauvoo, on the 20th of January, 1846, addressed a circular to the Church throughout the world, announcing the intended departure of the pioneers, beginning in March, for the purpose of putting in early spring crops on the way, building houses, and preparing temporary resting-places for those who were to follow. But there were rumours of an intention on the part of the Government to prevent this whole-sale migration, under a plea that it was the purpose of the Mormon leaders to go to Oregon, and place themselves under the protection of the British authorities, and thus become a source of greater trouble than before.

Governor Ford admits in his history that some such rumours were encouraged, to "scare," if possible, the Mormons from lingering or returning should they faint by the way. One of the agents of Brigham Young, then in the Eastern States, professed to have received some such information from one of President Polk's cabinet, and the story is still believed by the Saints.

On the 2nd of February a council of the apostles and leading elders was held in Nauvoo, to deliberate upon a speedy departure. It was then thought that on the breaking up of the ice on the Mississippi the pioneers would be able to commence their pilgrimage, and before their enemies had any knowledge of their departure they would be some distance on their journey. Captains of hundreds and of fifties had been chosen, and these were now instructed to hold themselves in readiness to move at an hour's notice.

Three days later the first company crossed the river on the ice. On the following day the main body of the Saints began to move, and during February about 1,200 wagons were transported to the Iowa shore.

The severe inclement weather soon told upon the feeble and delicate living in their wagons and tents. They fully realized that they were homeless exiles, and that there was no rest for them until new homes were created for them in the desert. Before moving from their first camping-ground, the elders addressed a touching petition to the Governor of Iowa, in which they pictured the situation of the Saints, and asked his Excellency's protection in passing through that Territory.

"To stay," narrate the petitioners, "is death by fire and sword; to go into banishment unprepared is death by starvation. But yet, under these heart-rending circumstances, several hundreds of us have started upon our dreary journey, and we are now encamped in Lee county, Iowa, suffering much from the intensity of the cold. Some of us also are already without food, and others have barely sufficient to last a few weeks; hundreds of others must shortly follow us in the same unhappy condition."

On the 3rd of March Brigham was chosen the leader of the migrating party, and, as all was then ready, he gave the order to march on that remarkable pilgrimage which was without parallel since Moses led the Israelites from Egypt. However vain, foolish, and superstitious may have been the faith of the Saints in the judgment of others, and however arrogant and despotic the leaders of the Mormons may have since become, their exodus from the United States westward to the then unknown desert of the Great American Basin was a sublime spectacle of devotion which the most sceptical cannot regard without profound admiration.

During the most pressing preparations for the migration from Nauvoo the Temple was not neglected. In the midst of all their troubles the artistic labour of the community was directed to its last finishing touches. There was in this a sentiment of devotion creditable to their higher thoughts. They saw clearly that the Temple in all its glory would be sacrificed, but they desired that the sacrifice should be the purest and best that they could offer, and nothing therefore was left unfinished. In the beginning of May, the Temple was thus completed and dedicated, and upon it, in the front, was placed an entablature with this inscription:

"THE HOUSE OF THE LORD,

"BUILT BY THE CHURCH OF JESUS CHRIST OF LATTER-DAY SAINTS.

"HOLINESS TO THE LORD." *

* This fine building was destroyed on the 19th of November, 1848, the work of an incendiary. Two years later the French Icarians, brought to Nauvoo by Mons.

With the closing ceremonies in the Temple, the mission of the Saints among the Gentiles came to a close—their labour was over.

A controversy has arisen over the assertion of the Temple having been finished, which would of itself be unworthy of notice but that it involves a principle to the Mormons of some importance. All through the revelations the Mormon deity is represented as very exacting in his measures. He is always straining to accomplish something beyond the capacity of the people. It would be extremely difficult to apply to *that* Being the words: "My yoke is easy and my burden is light;" for he has not only demanded constant heavy sacrifices of time and labour from the Saints, but he has perpetually held over their heads threats of damnation, more like a severe taskmaster than a loving Father. In this instance a revelation had been given, stating that, if the Temple were not completed within seven years, the Mormons, as a Church, together with " their dead," should be rejected. In several of his early sermons in Utah, Brigham stated that the Saints had never been able to complete a Temple ; and this the Reörganized Church has readily seized, and argued that, if such were the case, he and the present rulers at Salt Lake, according to the revelation commanding the Temple to be built, were, therefore, " without authority." Brigham, with his usual indifference to any previous statement, hastily asserted that the Temple at Nauvoo, " through the blessing of God, it was completed and " accepted by Him." The son of Joseph Smith thus presents the case :

" It has been stated, by those whose *duty* it was to *know*, that the Temple at Nauvoo was finished—'completed as Joseph designed.' This *statement is not true.* In no sense can it be said truthfully that any part of the Temple at Nauvoo was completed, with the possible exception of the main assembly-room into which the front doors opened. The basement in which was the font was incomplete; the stairway to the left of the front was not relieved of the rough boards laid on the risings, on which the workmen went up and down; the upper assembly-room was not accessible, the floor

Cabet, the great Socialist, endeavoured to rebuild it for their own uses, but a dreadful tornado, in May, 1850, threw most of the original building to the ground, and ended that project. The rock of the Temple subsequently served as the ledges of a quarry to supply domestic building material.

not being laid, neither the doors hung, nor the walls plastered. Besides this, the inside ornamentation was by no means finished, even in those parts called completed. There are plenty of persons now living who were frequent visitors to the Temple, after the people who built it left Nauvoo, who will testify that the building was not completed; among them David Le Baron, who had charge of it for some time; Major L. C. Bidamon, for years proprietor of the Mansion House; Dr. Weld, of Nauvoo; Amos Davis, living near the Big Mound, on the Nauvoo and La Harpe road; George Edmunds, of Sonora, and the writer, with a host of others.

"It is further rumoured that, after the death of Joseph Smith, the plans and specifications were altered; and that such parts as were nearly completed were not so completed in accordance with the original design. Of this we cannot testify, never having seen the original drawings nor read the specifications. If the statements of various persons are to be relied on, there can be but little doubt that in one respect there was a *completion ;* and that respect is the *desecration* and *defilement* of the Temple, by the holding of such revels and orgies therein, as were not even thought of by the 'money changers,' who made the House of God at Jerusalem a ' den of thieves,' and against whom the righteous indignation of Jesus was so signally directed."—*True Latter-Day Saints' Herald*, Jan. 1, 1872.

Mr. Smith would have done service to the world had he been less reserved upon " the *desecration* and *defilement* of the " Temple," as he doubtless had more than vague rumour for information. It is asserted by those who had good means of knowing, that practical *polygamy* was not unknown in that edifice. A Mormon chief who had to conceal himself there from the officers of the law thought it " not good to be alone," and preferring the society of inhabitants of this lower world to those of " a higher sphere," very naturally chose to honour those with his society who had selected him as their " Lord."

By the middle of May, probably sixteen thousand souls had crossed the Mississippi and were wending their way through Iowa to rendezvous on the banks of the Missouri river in the neighbourhood of Council Bluffs. About a thousand of the Mormons were left in Nauvoo, mostly on account of their inability, from poverty or sickness, to undertake the journey with the main body of the people, while some others were left to dispose of property and settle the affairs of the Church.

Notwithstanding the departure of the Mormon leaders and

the greater portion of the community from Nauvoo during the winter and spring, the anti-Mormons professed to be doubtful of the entire evacuation of the city, and threatened the remainder with expulsion. Governor Ford says :

"It was feared that the Mormons might vote for the August elections of that year, and that enough of them yet remained to control the elections in the county and perhaps in the district, for Congress. They therefore took measures to get up a new quarrel with the Mormons."

Ruins of the Temple.

From such contemptible motives began a difficulty which ended in a three days' siege of Nauvoo, and in acts of cruelty which disgracefully stain the history of Illinois. In the month of September, under one pretext or another, the anti-Mormons, to the number of 800 men, laid siege to Nauvoo, and for several days fought against 150 of its defenders. The anti-Mormons were under the command of Thomas S. Brockman, whom the Governor describes as " a Campbellite preacher, nominally be-
" longing to the Democratic party, a large, awkward, uncouth,
" ignorant semi-barbarian, ambitious of office, and bent upon
" acquiring notoriety." The Mormons in defence of their city admit a loss of two men and a boy killed, and three or four

wounded. The anti-Mormons admit one of their number killed, and nine or ten not dangerously wounded. Each side, however, reported that they had killed between thirty and forty of their enemies.

Upon any authority less than that of the Governor of the State, the reader would scarcely credit the recital of the siege and the triumphal entrance of the anti-Mormons into Nauvoo.

" The constable's *posse* marched in with Brockman at their head, consisting of about eight hundred armed men and six or seven hundred unarmed, from motives of curiosity to see the once proud city of Nauvoo humbled and delivered up to its enemies and to the domination of a self-constituted and irresponsible power. When the *posse* arrived in the city, the leaders of it erected themselves into a tribunal to decide who should be forced away and who remain. Parties were despatched to search for Mormon arms and for Mormons, and to bring them to the judgment where they received their doom from the mouth of Brockman, who then sat a grim and unawed tyrant for the time. As a general rule the Mormons were ordered to leave within an hour, or two hours ; and by rare grace some of them were allowed until next day ; and in a few cases longer.

" The treaty specified that the Mormons only should be driven into exile. Nothing was said in it concerning the new citizens who had with the Mormons defended the city. But the *posse* no sooner obtained possession than they commenced expelling the new citizens. Some of them were ducked in the river, being in one or two instances actually baptized in the name of the leaders of the mob; others were forcibly driven into the ferry boats, to be taken over the river, before the bayonets of armed ruffians ; and it is asserted that the houses of most of them were broken open and their property stolen during their absence. . . .

" The Mormons had been forced away from their houses unprepared for a journey. They and their women and children had been thrown houseless upon the Iowa shore, without provisions or the means of getting them, or to get to places where provisions might be obtained. It was now the height of the sickly season. Many of them were taken from sick beds, hurried into the boats and driven away by the armed ruffians now exercising the power of government. The best they could do was to erect their tents on the banks of the river and there remain to take their chances of perishing by hunger or by prevailing sickness. In this condition the sick, without shelter, food, nourishment, or medicines, died by scores. The mother watched her sick babe without hope, and when she sank under accumulated miseries, it was only to be quickly followed by her other children, now left without the least attention ; for the men had scattered out over the country seeking employment and the means of living."

A Mormon writer, well known to the Author, in a communication to the *Millennial Star*, gives a paragraph of his experience on the entrance of the mob into the doomed city :

"We expected that an indiscriminate massacre was commencing, and I, with some others who were sick, was carried into the tall weeds and woods, while all who could hid themselves. Many crossed the river, leaving everything behind. As night approached we returned to our shelter, but, O God! what a night to remember!

"The next morning at nine o'clock saw me, my wife, my four children, my sister-in-law, Fanny, my blind mother-in-law, all shaking with the ague in one house; only George Wardle able to do anything for us, when a band of about thirty men armed with guns and bayonets fixed, pistols in belt, the captain with a sword in his hand, and the stripes and stars flying about, marched opposite my sheltering roof; the captain called a halt and demanded the owner of the two wagons to be brought out. I was raised from my bed, led out of doors supported by my sister-in-law and the rail fence. I was then asked if those goods were mine. I replied 'They are.' The captain then stepped out to within four feet of me, pointing his sword at my throat, while four others presented their guns with their bayonets within two feet of my breast, when the captain told me, 'If you are not off from here in twenty minutes, my orders are to shoot you.' I replied, 'Shoot away, for you will only send me to heaven a few hours quicker, for you see I am not for this world many hours longer.' The captain then told me, 'If you will renounce Mormonism, you may stay here and we will protect you.' I replied, 'This is not my house; yonder is my house (pointing to it), which I built and paid for with the gold that I earned in England. I never committed the least crime in Illinois, but I am a Mormon, and, if I live, I shall follow the Twelve.' 'Then,' said the captain, 'I am sorry to see you and your sick family, but if you are not gone when I return in half an hour, my orders are to kill you and every Mormon in the place.' But oh, the awful cursing and swearing which those men did pour out! I tremble when I think of it. George and Edwin drove my wagons down to the ferry, and were searched five times for fire-arms; they took a pistol, and though they promised to return it when I got across the river, I have not seen it to this day. While on the banks of the river I crawled to the margin to bid a sister, who was going down to St. Louis, 'Good-bye,' and while there a mobber shouted out, 'Look, look, there's a skeleton bidding Death good-bye.' So you can imagine the poor, sickly condition we were in.

"On Wednesday, 23rd, while in my wagons on the Slough opposite Nauvoo, a most tremendous thunder shower passed over, which drenched everything we had; not a dry thread left to us—the bed a pool of water; my wife and sister-in-law lading it out by basinfuls, and I in a burning fever and insensible, with all my hair shorn off to cure me of my disease. Many had not a wagon or tent to shelter them from the pitiless blast.

One case I will mention. A poor woman stood among the bushes wrapping her cloak around her three little orphan children to shield and protect them from the storm as well as she could through that terrible night, which was one continued roar of thunder and blaze of lightning, while the rain descended in torrents. The mobbers seized every person in Nauvoo that they could find, leading them to the river and throwing them in. One case I will mention. They seized Charles Lambert, led him into the river, and in the midst of cursing and swearing, one man said, ' By the Holy Saints I baptize you, by order of the Commander of the Temple,' [plunged him *backward*] and then said, ' The commandments must be fulfilled, and, God damn you! you must have another dip' [then threw him *on his face*]. They then sent him on the flat-boat across the river, with the promise that if he returned to Nauvoo they would shoot him. Such were the scenes occurring at the driving of the Saints from Nauvoo."

Colonel Thomas L. Kane,* brother of Dr. Kane, the Arctic explorer, found himself on the Western frontier at the time of the Mormon exodus, and becoming intimately acquainted with the exiles in their travels, and interested in their welfare, on his return to the East he delivered a very graphic lecture upon " The situation of the Mormons," before the Historical Society of Pennsylvania. It is to be regretted that space cannot be spared here to give this gentleman's narrative entire; but, as it

* The important *rôle* which this gentleman has played in Mormon history, and the prominence given to his diplomacy in this work, justify here a personal note. His father, the Hon. John K. Kane, of Philadelphia, was an intimate friend of President Jackson, and "Thomas L.," though then a boy, was a privileged visitor at the White House, and probably then contracted his first ideas of diplomacy. Before he was twenty years of age he was an *attaché* of legation at the court of Louis Philippe. He returned to Europe in 1846, and, as related in the succeeding chapter, he became acquainted with a Mormon missionary and agent of Brigham Young, and being compassionately moved in behalf of the Mormon exiles, he sought to aid them, and obtained from President Polk a commission to investigate the conduct of some Indian Agents in the West, and it was with this authority in his pocket that he overtook the Mormon pilgrims and rendered them his first valuable services. On his return to Philadelphia, he was appointed United States Commissioner and Clerk of the United States District Court of the Eastern District of Pennsylvania. He made a brilliant record during the war, first as colonel of the Bucktail Rifles, and subsequently as a brigade-commander. When General Lee invaded Pennsylvania, the War Department discovered that the cypher for communication with General Meade was lost or abstracted. To General Kane was entrusted the dangerous mission of passing through the enemy's lines with a new cypher. He was captured, but not recognized, and successfully accomplished his task. Had he been detected, he would have been shot as a spy. In March, 1865, he was brevetted major-general for " gallant and meritorious service " at Chancellorsville and Gettysburg. It is painful to add that he is now a great sufferer from numerous wounds received in battle.

is the only account that has been written of that episode of Mormon history, free extracts will be made.

Of his visit to the abandoned city and to the remnant of the Mormons in Lee county, Iowa, he says :

"A few years ago, ascending the Upper Mississippi in the autumn when its waters were low, I was compelled to travel by land past the region of the Rapids. My road lay through the Half-Breed Tract, a fine section of Iowa which the unsettled state of its land-titles had appropriated as a sanctuary for coiners, horse thieves, and other outlaws. I had left my steamer at Keokuk, at the foot of the Lower Fall, to hire a carriage, and to contend for some fragments of a dirty meal with the swarming flies, the only scavengers of the locality. From this place to where the deep water of the river returns, my eye wearied to see everywhere sordid, vagabond, and idle settlers; and a country marred, without being improved, by their careless hands.

"I was descending the last hill-side upon my journey, when a landscape in delightful contrast broke upon my view. Half encircled by a bend of the river, a beautiful city lay glitterir g in the fresh morning sun ; its bright new dwellings, set in cool green gardens, ranging up around a stately dome-shaped hill, which was crowned by a noble marble edifice, whose high tapering spire was radiant with white and gold. The city appeared to cover several miles ; and beyond it, in the background, there rolled off a fair country, chequered by the careful lines of fruitful husbandry. The unmistakable marks of industry, enterprise, and educated wealth everywhere, made the scene one of singular and most striking beauty.

"It was a natural impulse to visit this inviting region. I procured a skiff, and rowing across the river, landed at the chief wharf of the city. No one met me there. I looked, and saw no one. I could hear no one move ; though the quiet everywhere was such that I heard the flies buzz, and the water-ripples break against the shallow of the beach. I walked through the solitary streets. The town lay as in a dream, under some deadening spell of loneliness, from which I almost feared to wake it ; for plainly it had not slept long. There was no grass growing up in the paved ways ; rains had not entirely washed away the prints of dusty footsteps.

"Yet I went about unchecked. I went into empty workshops, ropewalks, and smithies. The spinner's wheel was idle ; the carpenter had gone from his work-bench and shavings, his unfinished sash and casing. Fresh bark was in the tanner's vat, and the fresh-chopped lightwood stood piled against the baker's oven. The blacksmith's shop was cold ; but his coal heap, and ladling pool, and crooked water-horn, were all there as if he had just gone off for a holiday. No work-people anywhere looked to know my errand. If I went into the gardens, clinking the wicket-latch loudly after me, to pull the marygolds, heart's-ease, and lady-slippers, and draw a drink with the water-sodden well-bucket and its noisy chain ; or, knocking off with my stick the tall heavy-headed dahlias and sun-flowers, hunted over the beds for cucumbers and love-apples—no one called out to me from any opened window, or dog sprang forward to bark an alarm. I could have supposed the people hidden in the houses, but the doors were unfastened; and when at last I timidly entered them, I found dead ashes white upon the hearths, and had to tread a-tiptoe, as if walking down the aisle of a country church, to avoid rousing irreverent echoes from the naked floors.

" On the outskirts of the town was the city graveyard; but there was no record of plague there, nor did it in anywise differ much from other Protestant American cemeteries. Some of the mounds were not long sodded; some of the stones were newly set, their dates recent, and their black inscriptions glossy in the mason's hardly dried lettering ink. Beyond the graveyard, out in the fields, I saw in one spot, hard by where the fruited boughs of a young orchard had been roughly torn down, the still smouldering remains of a barbecue fire, that had been constructed of rails from the fencing round it. It was the latest sign of life there. Fields upon fields of heavy-headed yellow grain lay rotting ungathered upon the ground. No one was at hand to take in their rich harvest. As far as the eye could reach, they stretched away—they sleeping too in the hazy air of autumn.

" Only two portions of the city seemed to suggest the import of this mysterious solitude. On the southern suburb, the houses looking out upon the country showed, by their splintered wood-work, and walls battered to the foundation, that they had lately been the mark of a destructive cannonade. And in and around the splendid Temple, which had been the chief object of my admiration, armed men were barracked, surrounded by their stacks of musketry and pieces of heavy ordnance. These challenged me to render an account of myself, and why I had had the temerity to cross the water without a written permit from a leader of their band.

" Though these men were generally more or less under the influence of ardent spirits, after I had explained myself as a passing stranger, they seemed anxious to gain my good opinion. They told the story of the Dead City: that it had been a notable manufacturing and commercial mart, sheltering over 20.000 persons; that they had waged war with its inhabitants for several years, and had been finally successful only a few days before my visit, in an action fought in front of the ruined suburb; after which they had driven them forth at the point of the sword. The defence, they said, had been obstinate, but gave way on the third day's bombardment. They boasted greatly of their prowess, especially in this battle, as they called it; but I discovered they were not of one mind as to certain of the exploits that had distinguished it; one of which, as I remember, was, that they had slain a father and his son, a boy of fifteen, not long residents of the fated city, whom they admitted to have borne a character without reproach.

" They also conducted me inside the massive sculptured walls of the curious Temple, in which they said the banished inhabitants were accustomed to celebrate the mystic rites of an unhallowed worship. They particularly pointed out to me certain features of the building, which, having been the peculiar objects of a former superstitious regard, they had, as matter of duty, sedulously defiled and defaced. The reputed sites of certain shrines they had thus particularly noticed ; and various sheltered chambers, in one of which was a deep well, constructed, they believed, with a dreadful design. Besides these, they led me to see a large and deep chiselled marble vase or basin, supported upon twelve oxen, also of marble, and of the size of life, of which they told some romantic stories. They said the deluded persons, most of whom were emigrants from a great distance, believed their Deity countenanced their reception here of a baptism of regeneration, as proxies for whomsoever they held in warm affection in the countries from which they had come. That here parents · went into the water ' for their lost children, children for their parents, widows for their spouses, and young persons for their lovers ; that thus the Great Vase came to be for them associated with all dear and distant memories, and was therefore the object, of all others in the building, to which they attached the greatest degree of idolatrous affection. On this account, the victors had so diligently desecrated it, as to render the apartment in which it was contained too noisome to abide in.

" They permitted me also to ascend into the steeple to see where it had been lightning-struck on the Sabbath before ; and to look out east and south, on wasted farms like those I had seen near the city, extending till they were lost in the distance. Here, in the face of the pure day, close to the scar of the Divine wrath left by the thunderbolt, were fragments of food, cruises of liquor, and broken drinking vessels, with a brass drum and a steamboat signal-bell, of which I afterwards learned the use with pain.

" It was after nightfall when I was ready to cross the river on my return. The wind had freshened since the sunset, and the water beating roughly into my little boat, I hedged higher up the stream than the point I had left in the morning, and landed where a faint glimmering light invited me to steer.

" Here, among the dock and rushes, sheltered only by the darkness, without roof between them and sky, I came upon a crowd of several hundred human creatures, whom my movements roused from uneasy slumber upon the ground.

" Passing these on my way to the light, I found it came from a tallow candle in a paper funnel shade, such as is used by street venders of apples and peanuts, and which, flaming and guttering away in the bleak air off the water, shone flickeringly on the emaciated features of a man in the last stage of a bilious remittent fever. They had done their best for him. Over his head was something like a tent, made of a sheet or two, and he rested on a but partially ripped open old straw mattress, with a hair sofa-cushion under his head for a pillow. His gaping jaw and glazing eye told how short a time he would monopolize these luxuries; though a seemingly bewildered and excited person, who might have been his wife, seemed to find hope in occasionally forcing him to swallow awkwardly sips of the tepid river-water, from a burned and battered, bitter-smelling, tin coffee-pot. Those who knew better had furnished the apothecary he needed; a toothless old bald-head, whose manner had the repulsive dullness of a man familiar with death-scenes. He, so long as I remained, mumbled in his patient's ear a monotonous and melancholy prayer, between the pauses of which I heard the hiccup and sobbing of two little girls, who were sitting up on a piece of drift-wood outside.

"Dreadful, indeed, was the suffering of these forsaken beings; bowed and cramped by cold and sunburn, alternating as each weary day and night dragged on, they were, almost all of them, the crippled victims of disease. They were there because they had no homes, nor hospital, nor poor-house, nor friends to offer them any. They could not satisfy the feeble cravings of their sick; they had not bread to quiet the fractious hunger-cries of their children. Mothers and babes, daughters and grandparents, all of them alike, were bivouacked in tatters, wanting even covering to comfort those whom the sick shiver of fever was searching to the marrow.

"These were Mormons in Lee county, Iowa, in the fourth week of the month of September, in the year of our Lord 1846. The city—it was Nauvoo. Illinois. The Mormons were the owners of that city, and the smiling country around. And those who had stopped their plows, who had silenced their hammers, their axes, their shuttles, and their workshop wheels; those who had put out their fires, who had eaten their food, spoiled their orchards, and trampled under foot their thousands of acres of unharvested bread—these were the keepers of their dwellings, the carousers in their Temple, whose drunken riot insulted the ears of the dying.

"I think it was as I turned from the wretched night-watch of which I have spoken, that I first listened to the sounds of revel of a party of the guard within the city. Above the distant hum of the voices of many, occasionally rose distinct the loud oath-tainted exclamation, and the falsely intonated scrap of vulgar song: but lest this requiem should go unheeded, every now and then, when their boisterous orgies strove to attain a sort of ecstatic climax, a cruel spirit of insulting frolic carried some of them up into the high belfry of the Temple steeple, and there, with the wicked childishness of inebriates, they whooped, and shrieked, and beat the drum that I had seen, and rang in charivaric unison their loud-tongued steamboat bell.

"They were, all told, not more than six hundred and forty persons who were thus lying on the river flats. But the Mormons in Nauvoo and its dependencies had been numbered the year before at over twenty thousand. Where were they? They had last been seen, carrying in mournful train their sick and wounded, halt and blind, to disappear behind the western horizon, pursuing the phantom of another home. Hardly anything else was known of them; and people asked with curiosity, ' What had been their fate—what their fortunes ? ' . . .

" They began their march in mid-winter ; and by the beginning of February nearly all of them were on the road, many of the wagons having crossed the Mississippi on the ice.

" Under the most favouring circumstances, an expedition of this sort, undertaken at such a season of the year, could scarcely fail to be disastrous. But the pioneer company had set out in haste, and were very imperfectly supplied with necessaries. The cold was intense. They moved in the teeth of keen-edged northwest winds, such as sweep down the Iowa peninsula from the ice-bound regions of the timber-shaded Slave Lake and Lake of the Woods ; on the Bald Prairie there, nothing above the dead grass breaks their free course over the hard rolled hills. Even along the scattered water-courses, where they broke the thick ice to give their cattle drink, the annual autumn fires had left little wood of value. The party, therefore, often wanted for good camp-fires, the first luxury of all travellers ; but to men insufficiently furnished with tents and other appliances of shelter, almost an essential to life. After days of fatigue, their nights were often passed in restless efforts to save themselves from freezing. Their stock of food, also, proved inadequate ; and as their systems became impoverished, their suffering from cold increased.

" Sickened with catarrhal affections, manacled by the fetters of dreadfully acute rheumatism, some contrived for a while to get over the shortening day's march, and drag along some others. But the sign of an impaired circulation soon began to show itself in the liability of all to be dreadfully frost-bitten. The hardiest and strongest became helplessly crippled. About the same time, the strength of their beasts of draught began to fail. The small supply of provender they could carry with them had given out. The winter-bleached prairie straw proved devoid of nourishment ; and they could only keep them from starving by seeking for the browse, as it is called, a green bark and tender buds, and branches of the cotton-wood, and other stinted growths of the hollows.

" The spring came at last. It overtook them in the Sac and Fox country, still on the naked prairie, not yet half way over the trail they were following between the Mississippi and Missouri rivers. But it brought its own share of troubles with it. The months with which it opened proved nearly as trying as the worst of winter.

" The snow and sleet and rain which fell, as it appeared to them, without intermission, made the road over the rich prairie soil as impassable as one vast bog of heavy black mud. Sometimes they would fasten the horses and oxen of four or five wagons to one, and attempt to get a-head in this way, taking turns ; but at the close of a day of hard toil for themselves and their cattle, they would find themselves a quarter or half a mile from the place they left in the morning. The heavy rains raised all the water-courses : the most trifling streams were impassable. Wood fit for bridging was often not to be had, and in such cases the only resource was to halt for the freshets to subside—a matter in the case of the headwaters of the Chariton, for instance, of over three weeks' delay.

"The frequent burials made the hardiest sicken. On the soldier's march it is matter of discipline, that after the rattle of musketry over his comrade's grave, he shall tramp it to the music of some careless tune in a lively quick-step. But, in the Mormon camp, the companion who lay ill and gave up the ghost within view of all, all saw as he stretched a corpse, and all attended to his last resting-place. It was a sorrow, too, of itself to simple-hearted people, the deficient pomps of their imperfect style of funeral. The general hopefulness of human—including Mormon—nature, was well illustrated by the fact, that the most provident were found unfurnished with undertaker's articles ; so that bereaved affection was driven to the most melancholy makeshifts.

"The best expedient generally was to cut down a log of some eight or nine feet long, and slitting it longitudinally, strip off its dark bark in two half cylinders. These, placed around the body of the deceased and bound firmly together with withes made of the alburnum, formed a rough sort of tubular coffin which surviving relations and friends, with a little show of black crape, could follow with its enclosure to the hole, or bit of ditch, dug to receive it in the wet ground of the prairie. They grieved to lower it down so poorly clad, and in such an unheeded grave. It was hard—was it right, thus hurriedly to plunge it in one of the undistinguishable waves of the great land-sea, and leave it behind them there, under the cold north rain, abandoned to be forgotten ? They had no tombstones ; nor could they find rocks to pile the monumental cairn. So, when they had filled up the grave, and over it prayed a *miserere* prayer, and tried to sing a hopeful psalm, their last office was to seek out landmarks, or call in the surveyor to help them to determine the bearings of valley bends, head-lands, or fork and angles of constant streams, by which its position should in the future be remembered and recognized. The name of the beloved person, his age, the date of his death, and these marks were all registered with care. This party was then ready to move on. Such graves mark all the line of the first year of the Mormon travel —dispiriting milestones to failing stragglers in the rear."

Under the difficulties of such travel and the labours performed in making settlements on the way, the pioneers and first companies did not advance further than the Missouri river in 1846.

CHAPTER XXXI.

ON THE MISSOURI.—Enlistment of the Mormon Battalion—False Ideas about the Matter—Historical Facts—Elder Little at Washington—He is introduced to President Polk—Important Official Documents—Colonel Kane's Story—The Mormon Ball—Brigham receives the Volunteers' " Advance Pay "—Mormon Testimony in favour of Government—Brigham Young's Extraordinary Statements—The Government vindicated.

WHEN the pioneers left Nauvoo their destination was undetermined. Very little was then known of the geography of North America west of the Missouri River. Joseph had a whispering revelation about the location of the Church in the Rocky Mountains, and Brigham was said to have had a vision about the Salt Lake Valley, but with both revelation and vision there was no certainty as to the exact locality. To give expression to a slender hope, elder Taylor furnished the poor, homeless wanderers with a song:

> " The Upper California, oh, that's the land for me ! "

which cheered many a fainting heart ; and for that much good the error of the " Infallible Priesthood " should be overlooked, even though " Towers and Temples " have not arisen

> " Along the great Pacific sea,"

as predicted.

The first company of the exiles arrived at the Missouri in the beginning of July, 1846, and a resting-place was there resolved upon, as the main body of the Saints could not reach that point till late in September. It is claimed that the pioneers would have continued westward that year but for a " demand " of the Government that the Mormons should furnish a battalion of five hundred men for the Mexican war.

As seen in the preceding chapters, the Mormons had up to

this time only charged their neighbours in Missouri and in Illinois with persecution; the Federal Government was only held guilty by implication for not affording the Saints redress and protecting them in the peaceable possession of their homes. On the banks of the Missouri begins the national crime of "persecuting the Saints of the Most High God," a crime which has ten thousand times inspired the predictions in the Tabernacle and the assemblies of the Saints that "the Republic "would be dashed to pieces like a potter's vessel, and be blot-"ted out of existence."

Of all the preaching in the Tabernacle against the nation, nothing has ever made such an impression upon the people as Brigham Young's story of the Mormon battalion, in which he charges the Government with "the design of destroying the "kingdom of God."

He asserts, unequivocally and unhesitatingly, that the Government *demanded* those five hundred men while the exiles were in an Indian country, hoping that, rather than expose their wives and children without protection in the midst of savages, they would rebel, and thus furnish the Government with a pretext for sending an army against the Saints to break them up, scatter them, and " wipe them out of existence."

This is a grave charge, and one which should not be entertained without a rigid examination of the facts of history.

One of the last official acts of Brigham Young before leaving Nauvoo was the appointment of elder Jesse C. Little, of New Hampshire, to preside over the Saints left in the Eastern States. This letter was dated—" Temple of God, Nauvoo, " January 20, 1846," and contained the following instructions :

"If our Government shall offer any facilities for emigrating to the Western coast, embrace those facilities. if possible, as a wise and faithful man."

On the same day the high council at Nauvoo issued a circular, " to the members of the Church throughout the world," announcing the forth-coming early departure of the pioneers for the Rocky Mountains, where they were to " make a resting-" place, until we can determine a place for a permanent loca-"tion." With nothing certain but a long journey westward, and that in the midst of poverty, the Mormons were ready to

15

undertake any labour that was harmonious with their own programme of travel. In this circular was the following statement:

"In the event of the President's recommendation, to build block-
houses and stockade forts on the road to Oregon, becoming a law, we
have encouragement of having that work to do; and under our peculiar
circumstances we can do it with less expense to the Government than any
other people."

With his own letter of appointment, containing the instructions to accept "any facilities which the Government might
"offer," to aid the Mormons in their migration westward, and
this public announcement in the circular, elder Little proceeded to the seat of Government. On his way thither he called a
conference of the Saints at Philadelphia on the 13th of May,
and then for the first time Colonel Thomas L. Kane became
acquainted with this Mormon elder and representative of Brigham Young. Touched by the distress of the Mormons, which
was then a matter of notoriety throughout the country, the
colonel evidently resolved to be their good Samaritan. The
high social standing of the family of Judge Kane, of Philadelphia, was a guarantee of pure philanthropy only in the good
that the colonel sought to attain for the Mormons. This gentleman introduced elder Little to the Hon. George M. Dallas,
the Vice-President, and to other distinguished gentlemen at
Washington, and finally the Elder was presented to President
James K. Polk. The President and some members of his cabinet, senators, and representatives, immediately took a lively
interest in the situation of the Mormons, then wandering beyond the confines of civilization, and they were ready to favour
any measure that would contribute assistance to them in their
distress.

Elder Samuel Brannan, the predecessor of elder Little in
the ecclesiastical charge of the Eastern Saints, had sailed in
the ship Brooklyn from New York, in January, with six hundred Mormons for San Francisco. Elder Little, during his
visit to Washington, contemplated sending another vessel with
Saints to the same destination, provided that he "could obtain
"Government freight to ship on the vessel with the people to
"assist in defraying the expenses." In his address to President
Polk he uses the following language:

" From twelve to fifteen thousand Mormons have already left Nauvoo for California, and many others are making ready to go ; some have gone around Cape Horn, and, I trust, before this time have landed at the bay of San Francisco. We have about forty thousand in the British Isles, all determined to gather to this land, and thousands will sail this fall. There are also many thousands scattered through the States, besides the great number in and around Nauvoo who will go to California as soon as possible, but many of them are destitute of money to pay their passage either by sea or land.

" We are true-hearted Americans, true to our native country, true to its laws, true to its glorious institutions ; and we have a desire to go under the outstretched wings of the American eagle ; we would disdain to receive assistance from a foreign power, although it should be proffered, *unless our Government shall turn us off in this great crisis and compel us to be foreigners.*

" *If you will assist us in this crisis, I hereby pledge my honour, as the representative of this people, that the whole body will stand ready at your call, and act as one man in the land to which we are going ;* and should our Territory be invaded we will hold ourselves ready to enter the field of battle, and then, like our patriotic fathers, make the battle-field our grave or gain our liberty."

In the first week in June the cabinet considered the situation of the Mormons. Elder Little had an interview of some hours with the President, during which his Excellency stated that " he had no prejudice against the Saints ; " " He believed " them to be good citizens ; " " was willing to do them all the " good in his power consistently ; " and " they should be protected ; " " he had confidence in the Mormons as true * " American citizens, or he would not make such propositions " as those he designed."

The news of the first battles with Mexico had just been reported at Washington, and the Government had resolved on taking forcible possession of California—then a part of Mexico ; and from the conversation with elder Little, as subsequently reported, it is very evident that President Polk and his cabinet considered the movement opportune for using the Mormons al-

* It was then generally believed that the Mormons were moving westward to throw off their allegiance to the United States Government, and but for the success of the American arms in Mexico, and the subsequent cession of Territory to the United States, the Mormons would have set up an independent Government in the Rocky Mountains, or have been forced to recognize Mexican authority. With the latter Brigham would doubtless have made very short work.

ready *en route* for "Upper California," and also facilitating the transportation of those in the Eastern States by sending them round the Cape to the Pacific coast, if they would serve the country as soldiers.

On the 3rd of June the Hon. W. L. Marcy, Secretary of War, wrote to General S. W. Kearney, then in command at Fort Leavenworth, directing the General's attention to the migration of the Mormons, and saying that the Government desired the General to use all proper means to effect a good understanding with the leaders, to the end that the United States might obtain their "coöperation" in taking possession of and holding that country, and that the General was thereby authorized to muster into service such among them as could be "*induced to volunteer*," but the number was not to exceed one-third of the force * which the General had been instructed to lead overland to California. The Mormon troops were also, as much as possible, to be allowed to elect their own officers.

The visit of elder Little to Washington, his petition for aid, the expressed sympathy of the President for the exiles, the favourable interviews of elder Little with the cabinet and influential gentlemen, the President's intimation of his confidence in the Mormons as "true American citizens," and his intention of making them a good proposition, with the prompt order of the Secretary of War to General Kearney to enlist *volunteers* among them, but *not to exceed* one-third of that officer's command—all these are so harmonious, and so like the honourable relations of a Government that sympathizes with a handful of its suffering citizens, and seeks to aid them as far as it consistently can, that the idea of duplicity or bad faith is utterly banished, and the contemplation of a design of either forcing the Mormons into rebellion, or exposing women and children to destruction by savages, is rendered perfectly absurd.

---

* The Mexican war created great popular enthusiasm everywhere throughout the Union, and the offers of volunteer regiments in many of the States far exceeded the wants of the Government. Gen. Kearney's instructions to Capt. Allen, *not to accept more than one-third of the General's entire force*, show conclusively that the instructions of the Federal Government to employ the Mormon volunteers was an act of sympathetic kindness. The Government did not require them at all, but extended as far as consistent its aid.

Seeking to set at rest this disputed subject, the Author addressed the President of the United States, and Major-General Philip St. George Cooke, who led the battalion to California, asking for information, and the following correspondence ensued:

"ASTOR HOUSE, NEW YORK, *October* 17, 1871.

"*President U. S. Grant:*

"Your Excellency will, I trust, excuse the liberty that I take in soliciting through you information from the War Department, as *your order only can procure it.*

"In 1846, when the Mormon community were upon the western frontiers, on their way towards the Pacific, 500 of their number were enrolled by a United States officer. Capt. Allen, at Council Bluffs, Iowa, into the service of the Government, then at war with Mexico. That battalion, on the death of Capt. Allen, shortly after they took up their march to the Pacific, was placed under the command of Lieut.-Colonel Philip St. George Cooke, and by him led to southern California. Their service was highly commended by their commander, and they were honourably discharged on the Pacific coast, as per terms of enlistment.

"For over twenty years Brigham Young has used his version of this Mormon Battalion very effectively in attacking the Government, by representing that it was *a cruel demand*, made with the view of crippling the expedition and leaving it exposed to the attacks of the Indians. To this, he adds that the demand was made in the hope that the Mormons would refuse, and, in so refusing, furnish the Government a pretext for preventing their further exodus, under the charge that they were going to join an enemy's country.

"Ridiculous as this may appear to your Excellency, I know of nothing in all Mormon history that has been so potential in shaping the sentiments of the Mormon people against the Government.

"I have carefully considered and traced, wherever I could, the circumstances attending this Battalion affair, and all the evidence conveys to me the very contrary of what Brigham Young asserts. It was evidently in *sympathy* for their unfortunate condition that the Government accepted that Battalion, and paid them for going to the place they had at that time upon their minds to go to.

"If your Excellency will order copies of all that pertains to the Mormon Battalion to be placed at my disposal, I am satisfied that the publication of the facts, in the history of Utah and the Mormons which I will shortly have in press, will do much to destroy the pernicious influence of the mis-statements that have been made on the subject. It is due to the national Government that the facts should be properly understood.

"Soliciting your Excellency's favourable action,

"I am, your obedient servant,

"T. B. H. STENHOUSE."

242

THE ROCKY MOUNTAIN SAINTS.

"WAR DEPARTMENT, WASHINGTON CITY, December 15, 1871.

" T. B. H. Stenhouse, Esq., Astor House, New York :

" Sir : In compliance with your request of Oct. 17, '71, addressed to the President, for copies of documents in this Department relating to the Mormon Battalion, raised for the service of the U. S. during the Mexican war, I have the honour to send you, herewith, a copy of instructions from Head Quarters Army of the West, dated June 19, 1846, for the raising of the Battalion, which comprises all the information in this Department on the subject, except subsequent occasional mention of the whereabouts of the Battalion, which would be of no service to you.

" Very respectfully, your obedient servant,

WM. W. BELKNAP, Secretary of War."

"HEAD QUARTERS ARMY OF THE WEST, FORT LEAVENWORTH, June 19, 1846.

" Sir : It is understood that there is a large body of Mormons *who are desirous of emigrating to California for the purpose of settling in that country,* and I have therefore to direct that you will proceed to their camps and *endeavour to raise from amongst them four or five companies of volunteers* to join me in my expedition to that country—each company to consist of any number between 73 and 109—the officers of the companies will be a captain, first lieutenant and second lieutenant, who will be elected by the privates and subject to your approval, and the captain then to appoint the non-commissioned officers, also subject to your approval. The companies upon being thus organized, will be mustered by you into the service of the United States, and from that day will commence to receive the pay, rations, and other allowances given to the other infantry volunteers, each according to his rank. You will, upon mustering into service the Fourth company, be considered as having the rank, pay, emoluments of a lieutenant-colonel of infantry, and are authorized to appoint an adjutant, sergeant-major, and quarter-master sergeant for the Battalion.

" The companies, after being organized, will be marched to this post, where they will be armed and prepared for the field, after which they will, under your command, follow on my trail in the direction of Santa Fé, and where you will receive further orders from me.

" You will, upon organizing the companies, require provisions, wagons, horses, mules, etc. You must purchase everything that is necessary, and give the necessary drafts upon the quarter-master and commissary departments at this post, which drafts will be paid upon presentation.

" *You will have the Mormons distinctly to understand, that I wish to take them* AS VOLUNTEERS *for twelve months, that they will be marched to California,* receiving pay and allowances during the above time, and at its expiration they will be discharged and *allowed to retain as their private property the guns and accoutrements to be furnished to them at this post.* Each company will be allowed four women as laundresses, who will travel with the company, receiving rations and the other allowances given to the laundresses of our army.

"With the foregoing conditions, *which are hereby pledged to the Mormons, and which will be faithfully kept by me and other officers in behalf of the Government of the United States,* I cannot doubt but that you will in a few days be able to raise five hundred young and efficient men for this expedition.

"Very respectfully your obedient servant,

"(Signed) S. W. KEARNY, Colonel First Dragoons.

"Capt. James Allen, First Regiment Dragoons, Fort Leavenworth."

"I certify that the foregoing is a true copy of the original on file at this office.   JOHN POTTS, Chief Clerk.

"WAR DEPARTMENT, WASHINGTON, *December 15*, 1871."

"HEAD QUARTERS DEPARTMENT OF THE LAKES, }
"DETROIT, MICHIGAN, *August* 17, 1871. }

"*T. B. H. Stenhouse, Esq., Astor House, New York:*

"SIR: I have received your communication of the 11th inst., which invites any statement I may be able to make—as commander of the 'Mormon Battalion' in the war with Mexico—of the circumstances of their enlistment and service.

"You say, 'If Brigham Young is right in the statement of intended '"persecution" on the part of the Government, I have no wish to make it 'otherwise appear, nor shall I try it; but if he is wrong, which I believe 'he is, in this work, I deem it my duty to not only defend that action of 'the Government, but to show its kindness and sympathy.

"'If the Battalion understood that the Government *demanded* their 'enlistment with the view of leaving their families unprotected and ex-'posed to the Indians, as Brigham Young has so frequently stated it since, 'it seems that the commanding officer who led them in their march through 'that severe campaign would have heard of it in their trying hour.'

"I was not at Fort Leavenworth when General S. W. Kearney sent Captain Allen, First Dragoons, to meet the migration of the Mormons from Nauvoo toward the Pacific coast, and raise a volunteer battalion, and I resigned their command prior to their discharge. I know only from frequent intercourse, subsequently, with General Kearney, and my intimate and quite friendly relations with the Battalion, that *it could scarcely have been otherwise than a friendly interest in the misfortunes of that sect in which the idea was conceived and executed, to enrol a portion of them, as volunteers,* and so assist their migration.* The usual regulations, or laws, for volunteers, regarding age, and also the number of women to be transported and fed, *were much relaxed in their favour.*

"I do not remember the dates of their payments; nor do I know if they retained their arms at discharge.

"Respectfully, your obedient servant,

"PHILIP ST. GEORGE COOKE, Brigadier-General U. S. A."

* A letter from William Wood, one of the Battalion, to his parents in England, dated Pueblo de los Angeles, Upper California, July 16, 1847, referring to their

These official documents should undeceive the Mormon people and enable them to see how grossly they have been deluded by the story of the Government " persecution."

On the 12th of June, Col. Kane left Washington for the West to overtake the Mormon camp, and was accompanied by elder Little. The colonel was the bearer of dispatches from the Government to General Kearney at Fort Leavenworth, and others in California. They were accompanied as far as St. Louis by Judge Kane, who was deeply interested, on behalf of the Mormons, in their success. On the 26th, Captain Allen had reached the Mormon camp at Mount Pisgah, but Brigham Young and the majority of the apostles were still further west, and that officer had to advance thither before he could be listened to on the subject of volunteers.

It is very unlikely that Brigham and the migrating Mormons at this time had any knowledge of the proceedings at Washington between elder Little and the Government. There were no post routes in that country in those days, and on the appearance of Captain Allen among them, it is natural to suppose that in their ignorance of the facts, the very mention of enlisting volunteers to serve the country should have produced the excitement that it did. For anything that Brigham might have said at the first sight of Captain Allen, he would be richly entitled to a hearty forgiveness. Much patriotism could not be expected in fleeing, homeless exiles. A " demand," if such had been made, for five hundred men, was enough to provoke the wrath of any Saint ; but it is his after-utterances, with a full knowledge of the facts, that give point to the charge, that Brigham designedly calumniates the Government.

Colonel Kane in his Historical Discourse tells the story of recruiting the Battalion :

"At the commencement of the Mexican war, the President considered it desirable to march a body of reliable infantry to California at as early a period as practicable, and the known hardihood and habits of discipline of the Mormons were supposed peculiarly to fit them for this service. As California was supposed to be also their ultimate destination, the long

departure from Nauvoo, says : " With this view we left, and were journeying with our teams, when the United States Government sent an *invitation* for so many men *to enlist* in the service for one year," etc.—*Millennial Star*, vol. x., p. 125.

march might cost them less than other citizens. They were *accordingly invited to furnish a battalion of volunteers* early in the month of July.

"The call could hardly have been more inconveniently timed. The young, and those who could best have been spared, were then away from the main body, either with pioneer companies in the van, or, their faith unannounced, seeking work and food about the north-western settlements, to support them till the return of the season for commencing emigration. The force was, therefore, to be recruited from among fathers of families, and others, whose presence it was most desirable to retain.

"There were some, too, who could not view *the invitation* without jealousy. They had twice been persuaded by (State) Government authorities in Illinois and Missouri to give up their arms on some special appeals to their patriotic confidence, and had then been left to the malice of their enemies. And now they were asked, in the midst of the Indian country, to surrender over five hundred of their best men for a war march of thousands of miles to California, without the hope of return till after the conquest of that country. Could they view such a proposition with favour?

"But the feeling of country triumphed. The Union had never wronged them: 'You shall have your battalion at once, if it has to be a class of our elders,' said one, himself a ruling elder. A central 'mass meeting' for council, some harangues at the more remotely scattered camps, an American flag brought out from a storehouse of things rescued, and hoisted to the top of a tree mast, and in three days the force was reported, mustered, organized, and ready to march."

The colonel's account of the ball given to the Battalion is deserving of its place in this history:

"There was no sentimental affectation at their leave-taking. The afternoon before was appropriated to a farewell ball; a more merry dancing rout I have never seen, though the company went without refreshments, and their ball-room was of the most primitive. It was the custom, whenever the larger camps rested for a few days together, to make great arbours, or boweries, as they called them, of poles and brush and wattling, as places of shelter for their meetings of devotion or conference. In one of these, where the ground had been trodden firm and hard by the worshippers of the popular Father Taylor's precinct, were gathered now the mirth and beauty of the Mormon Israel.

"If anything told the Mormons had been bred to other lives, it was the appearance of the women as they assembled here. Before their flight they had sold their watches and trinkets as the most available resource for raising ready money; and hence, like their partners who wore waistcoats cut with useless watch-pockets, they, although their ears were pierced and bore the loop-marks of rejected pendants, were without ear-rings, finger-rings, chains, or brooches. Except such ornaments, however, they lacked nothing most becoming the attire of decorous maidens. The neat-ly darned white stockings, and clean bright petticoat, the artistically clear-starched collar and chemisette, the something faded, only because too well washed, lawn or gingham gown, that fitted modishly to the waist of its pretty wearer—these, if any of them spoke of poverty, spoke of a poverty that had known its better days.

The Battalion Ball.

"With the rest attended the elders of the Church within call, including nearly all the chiefs of the High Council, with their wives and children. They, the gravest and most trouble-worn, seemed the most anxious of any to be first to throw off the burden of heavy thoughts. Their leading off the dancing in a great double cotillion was the signal which bade the festivity commence. To the canto of debonnair violins, the cheer of horns, the jingle of sleigh-bells, and the jovial snoring of the tambourine, they did dance! None of your minuets or other mortuary processions of gentles in etiquette, tight shoes, and pinching gloves, but the spirited and scientific displays of our venerated and merry grandparents, who were not above following the fiddle to the Fox-Chase Inn or Gardens of Gray's Ferry. French fours, Copenhagen jigs, Virginia reels, and the like forgotten figures, executed with the spirit of people too happy to be slow, or bashful, or constrained. Light hearts, lithe figures, and light feet had it their own way from an early hour till after the sun had dipped behind the sharp sky line of the Omaha hills. Silence was then called, and a well-cultivated mezzo-soprano voice, belonging to a young lady with fair face and dark eyes, gave, with quartette accompaniment, a little song, the notes of which I have been unsuccessful in repeated efforts to obtain since —a version of the text, touching to all earthly wanderers :

"'By the rivers of Babylon we sat down and wept:
We wept when we remembered Zion.'

"There was danger of some expression of feeling when the song was over, for it had begun to draw tears ; but, breaking the quiet with his hard voice, an elder asked the blessing of Heaven on all who, with purity of heart and brotherhood of spirit, had mingled in that society, and then all dispersed, hastening to cover from the falling dews."

With the departure of the Battalion, an agent accompanied them to Leavenworth, where he is reported to have drawn $20,000 "advance pay," and with that timely aid, Brigham Young made such outfitting purchases in St. Louis as were greatly needed. It is also understood that an agent continued with the Battalion until another draft could be made for their pay, before entering upon their march across the desert. Small as such sums were, yet in the situation and poverty of the exiles it was certainly *timely aid from the Government.* There has been much personal dissatisfaction expressed about the use made of these funds, yet the most bitter of his opponents acknowledged that Brigham showed great sagacity in at once furnishing the Battalion.*

With the presence of Col. Kane and elder Little among the apostles, the Washington proceedings were explained. On the 7th of August, the Saints assembled to choose twelve men from among the elders to act as a High Council in the new Stake of Zion, organized on the banks of the Missouri, and to transact other business pertaining to the settlement of "Winter "Quarters." After this meeting, a consultation was held with Colonel Kane, and the apostles advised together. It was then resolved that an address to President Polk should be framed, *expressive of the gratitude of the Church of Jesus Christ of Latter-Day Saints towards him for his benevolent design* " of " *arming and planting five hundred of our volunteers in Cali-* "*fornia, to take possession of that country, and for our good,*† " and also praying the President of the United States not to " appoint Governor Boggs of Missouri—the notorious enemy

---

* There are very hard stories told about the use of this money in the hands of Brigham. Affidavits have been made of his heartless indifference to the wants of the wives and families of the absent soldiers. In Mrs. Waite's "Early History of Brigham Young," pp. 6–7, the affidavit of Alexander McCord is given, relating to this affair, and bears evidence of truthfulness.

† The Mormons who remained in Nauvoo voted the Democratic ticket at the August election in 1846. Almond W. Babbitt, the agent of the Church there, as-

" of the Saints—as Governor of California and Oregon." This
is a quotation from the written language of one of the apostles,
and bears the stamp of the genuine sentiments of the Mormon
leaders at the time. The allusion to ex-Governor Boggs is
thoroughly characteristic.

Some months after the Battalion was in the service of the
country, another apostle * addressed the following language to
the British Saints :

"Although we have been inhumanly and barbarously dealt with by
the surrounding country where we dwelt, yet the President of the United
States *is favourably disposed to us*. He has sent out orders to have five
hundred of our brethren *employed* in an expedition that was fitting out
against California, with orders for them to be employed for one year, and
then to be discharged in California, and to have their arms and implements of war given to them at the expiration of the term ; and as there is
no prospect of any opposition, IT AMOUNTS TO THE SAME AS PAYING THEM
FOR GOING TO THE PLACE WHERE THEY WERE DESTINED TO GO WITHOUT.
They also had the privilege of choosing their own leaders."

Another apostle, very recently, haranguing the people in
the Tabernacle upon the persecutions of the Saints, is reported
in the Chicago *Tribune* to have uttered the following :

" The Government sent an agent who DEMANDED five hundred volunteers for the Mexican war, which was two hundred times the proportion
raised by the country. *This was done that our teams, and our women, and
our children, might be left defenceless in the Indian country, and so be killed
or perish.* They said that if we would furnish them the men, we might go
on in peace ; if not, they would cut us off on our journey."

This fruitful subject—" the Government persecution "—has
done incalculable mischief to the Saints. It has robbed them
of the natural loyalty of good citizens, and led them to curse
the Government which protects them, and to pray for the overthrow and destruction of the nation.

serted that this change in their politics was an expression of their gratitude to
President Polk. Governor Ford says they voted from the following considerations :

" The President of the United States had permitted the Mormons to settle on
the Indian lands on the Missouri river, and had taken five hundred of them into the
service as soldiers in the war with Mexico ; and in consequence of *these favours* the
Mormons felt under obligations to vote for democrats, in support of the administration ; and so determined were they that their support of the President should be
efficient, that they all voted three or four times each for member of Congress."—
" History of Illinois," p. 414.

* John Taylor, *Millennial Star*, November 15, 1846.

To say that Brigham did alone invent the story of the Government seeking the destruction of the Saints when the Battalion was recruited, would be charging him unjustly. One of the elders wrote to him from the East, stating that Senator Benton, of Missouri, disliked the Mormons, and had prevailed upon President Polk to call for volunteers, believing that they would refuse, and in that case the President pledged to the Senator that the forces of the United States should be sent against them, to annihilate the whole migrating body.

That a man of Brigham Young's hard sense should believe such a statement, is only credible upon the theory that people easily adopt what is harmonious with their own inclinations. He naturally hated Missouri, and he could, therefore, willingly accept any vicious story told him about that State, or any one from it. On such an unlikely report " Old Tom Benton " has been consigned to " his place," and now keeps company in the nether regions with " Old Zach Taylor," who in some unfortunate way had given umbrage to the Prophet Brigham. It is proper to add that in a recent conversation with Mrs. Gen. John C. Fremont, who had the pleasure of assisting her honoured father, Senator Benton, as private secretary, the Author discovered nothing that suggested confirmation of Brigham's charge, but much to the contrary. That distinguished lady claimed that Senator Benton was not the man to seek to reach the Mormons through any covert means, involving another's responsibility.

Besides this, there is such an air of good faith in the action of the Government throughout, that no sane man could believe in the diabolical scheme attributed to Senator Benton and said to have been approved by President Polk. The story was only good to tell the Saints, in order to cultivate their dislike to the Republic, and increase their endearment to " the kingdom." No other motive is apparent, and certainly no other result has been attained.

It is greatly to be regretted that a battalion recruited from the suggestions of the kindest philanthropy, responded to so promptly, at such personal sacrifice to the volunteers and their families, and with such an excellent record for faithful service, should be for ever marred in the mention of its name by such bitter vindictiveness against the national Government.

CHAPTER XXXII.

FOUNDING OF THE FRONTIER CITIES.—Brigham's First and Last Revelation—The Departure of the Pioneers—The Discovery of Salt Lake Valley—The Return to the Missouri River.

ON the banks of the Missouri, the exiles were in Indian Territory. The renowned chief of the Pottowattamies, *Pied Riche*, surnamed Le Clerc, gave them a kindly welcome on the east of the river, and *Big Elk* was as gracious on the west. The red men were liberal, extending to them the free use of their unoccupied lands, and liberty to cut all the timber they required, with which was thrown in an expression of genuine sympathy for their misfortunes. With a vivid remembrance of their recent troubles in Nauvoo, and their flight from the abodes of the " pale-faces " in the depth of winter, this warmth of human feeling made a deep impression upon the Mormons, and during their stay among the savages they returned to them manifold the favours that they received.

On the eastern side of the river, camps were formed wherever the land was good and favoured farming, and settlements sprang up near the streams and groves of timber. The main settlement was called Kanesville, in honour of Colonel Kane, and was the foundation of what is now Council Bluffs City, Iowa.

The main body of the emigrants crossed the river, and located six miles north of what is now Omaha, Nebraska. There they built up " Winter Quarters," a city of some seven hundred log-huts and " dug-outs," in the midst of which was the " Tabernacle of the congregation," where the disciples assembled for worship and instruction.

Mount Pisgah, Garden Grove, Kanesville, and Winter

THE PIONEERS.

Quarters, were necessary resting-places for the weary, where they might recruit their strength and replenish their stores of grain for the preservation of themselves and cattle. It was a hard life. The best among them had nothing too much, and many of them lacked the ordinary necessaries of life; but it was suffering for the faith, and they bore their privations with heroism.

On the 14th of January, 1847, Brigham Young issued, from his head quarters, " The Word and Will of the Lord concern- " ing the Camp of Israel in their journeyings to the West." As it is the only occasion on which Brigham has given to the Saints a written revelation, it deserves a place in history. It reads thus:

" Let all the people of the Church of Jesus Christ of Latter-day Saints, and those who journey with them, be organized into companies, with a covenant and a promise to keep all the commandments and statutes of the Lord our God. Let the companies be organized with captains of hundreds, and captains of fifties, and captains of tens, with a president and counsellor at their head, under direction of the Twelve Apostles: and this shall be our covenant, that we will walk in all the ordinances of the Lord.

" Let each company provide itself with all the teams, wagons, provisions, and all other necessaries for the journey, that they can. When the companies are organized, let them go to with all their might, to prepare for those who are to tarry. Let each company, with their captains and presidents, decide how many can go next spring; then choose out a sufficient number of able-bodied and expert men to take teams, seed, and farming utensils to go as pioneers to prepare for putting in the spring crops. Let each company bear an equal proportion, according to the dividend of their property, in taking the poor, the widows, and the fatherless, and the families of those who have gone with the army, that the cries of the widow and the fatherless come not up into the ears of the Lord against his people.

" Let each company prepare houses, and fields for raising grain for those who are to remain behind this season; and this is the will of the Lord concerning this people.

" Let every man use all his influence and property to remove this people to the place where the Lord shall locate a stake of Zion · and if ye do this with a pure heart, with all faithfulness, ye shall be blessed in your flocks, and in your herds, and in your fields, and in your houses, and in your families. . . .

" Seek ye, and keep all your pledges one with another, and covet not that which is thy brother's. Keep yourselves from evil; take not the name of the Lord thy God in vain; for I am the Lord your God, even

the God of your fathers—the God of Abraham, Isaac, and of Jacob. I am
he who led the children of Israel out of the land of Egypt, and my arm
is stretched out in the last days to save my people Israel. . . .

" Have I not delivered you from your enemies only in that I have left
a witness of my name ? Now, therefore, hearken ! oh, ye people of my
Church, and ye Elders listen together. You have received my kingdom :
Be diligent in keeping all my commandments, lest judgment come upon
you, and your faith fail you, and your enemies triumph over you. Amen,
and Amen."

With the Saints this document found peculiar favour. It
was to them " the Lord " again, after a long silence, manifesting himself as in the days of Joseph, and it foreshadowed that
his presence would go with them in their journey over the
desert, and that under his direction they would reach the promised land. This is the first time that this document has been
given to the public, and the student of Mormon revelations
will remark a striking difference between the last revelation
of Joseph Smith on polygamy, and the first of Brigham Young
on emigration. Both are stamped with the characteristics of
the men, and their peculiar situations at the moment. It is
difficult to perceive the same authorship in both, yet both are
claimed as emanations from Jesus Christ.

Accepting the phenomenal manifestation of " revelation "
in past ages, as well as that claimed by the modern spiritualists, there is nothing in Brigham's revelation, nor in those of
Joseph Smith, that is incomprehensible, except the boldness of
the assertion that they are " revelations " from " the Lord ; "
and sincerity may even be accorded to that assumption, grant-
ing that it is only a piece of folly arising from ignorance of
latent powers of the human mind which develop in certain
conditions or surroundings. The world has abounded with
notable instances of remarkable men and women who have believed themselves to be the recipients of some divine mission
in politics or in religion, and who in one department or the
other have performed prodigies of valour or miracles of faith,
which, without the impressions claimed to be " revelations,"
would never have been performed. If Joseph had kept out
" Thus saith the Lord," and the assumption of sanctity, from
his revelation on polygamy, the reader would never have suspected that document to have had any other origin than Jo-

seph Smith in the deep distress and trouble in which he was at that time. Leaving out of Brigham's revelation the few words about " the Lord," it is just such a document as any com-mander of an expedition passing through an unexplored coun-try infested with Indians would have given to his soldiers, and where it bears marks of difference from such military or-ders, it is the difference between addressing a promiscuous multitude instead of a disciplined army.

" The Lord's " style of revelation to Brigham is a great improvement upon " the Lord's " style of revelation to Joseph. It is just as much better English in Brigham's case than in that of Joseph, as Willard Richards's literary education was superior to that o William Clayton ! " The Lord's " English in the Book of Mormon, while Oliver Cowdery was Joseph's scribe, and Joseph was tenacious in clinging to his unaltered inspirations, is a remarkable specimen of English composition; but as Joseph gathered around him better scribes, and concluded that " the Lord's " revelations could be somewhat improved, they became more readable.

The annual conference of the Church was held at Winter Quarters on the 6th of April, 1847, and the people assembled from all parts of the country and prepared for moving West. On the 14th of that month a party of one hundred and forty-three picked men, with three women, two children, and seventy-three wagons, drawn by horses and oxen, left the Missouri river for the Rocky Mountains, under the leadership of Brigham Young.

As soon as the pioneers got out from camp and had bidden adieu to their families, they were organized into companies, as directed in the revelation, and put in fighting trim, lest they should be forced to try hostilities with the Indians. Every one carried his gun loaded, but uncapped, in his hand, walked by the side of his wagon, and was forbidden to leave it unless or-dered to do so. Brigham was general, and his accustomed caution was an excellent supplement to his revelation.

The Indians sometimes sallied out as the pioneers passed their villages, but when the brethren " received them in half " moon phalanx," the red-skins preferred presents to lead, and allowed the emigrants, after a brief " pow-wow," to pass on
16

Nothing of special interest occurred on the journey of the pioneers beyond what has been common to all travel over the plains ; still, it is never to be forgotten that the Saints claim to have " made the roads, bridged the streams, and killed the " snakes."

Before reaching Salt Lake City the pioneers met with the renowned " Jim " Bridger, who did anything but encourage them with hopes of finding a fruitful land in Salt Lake Basin, and, with the usual liberality of the West, " Jim " was prepared to give a thousand dollars for the first ear of corn that Brigham could raise there.

Jim had lived in wigwams with squaws for half a long lifetime, far away from the abodes of the " pale-faces," and up to that hour he had not heard of the wonders of the modern gospel. Brigham knew what faith was going to do—his kind of faith—and he prophesied liberally to Jim about what he and his squaws would yet live to see. Jim could not comprehend how that the summer-parched soil, with a rainless sky overhead, was going to sustain any body of civilized people, as those now approaching from the East, and advised the Mormons to travel on. He had " trapped " all over the country for a score of years, and knew every green sward that dotted the banks of the rivers, and had counted the verdure-clothed springs that were few and far between, and small even then. But the more that the future of Zion was doubtful in Jim's mind, the more Brigham abounded in grace and prophesied. Jim had never seen the heavens dropping rain—" only very " occasionally! " Brigham had studied irrigation. Jim was looking for favours from above. Brigham was counting on the labours of below.

Before the pioneers reached Salt Lake Valley they were met by elder Brannan, who had sailed from New York, in the Brooklyn, to San Francisco. He had made the journey overland to report to Brigham that California was a rich country and a glorious place for the future gathering of the Saints. But Brigham did not like the report. He preferred the desert. A choice and rich land would attract the Gentiles, and the Saints would soon be overwhelmed and rooted out, as they had been in Missouri and Illinois. He wanted to locate where there

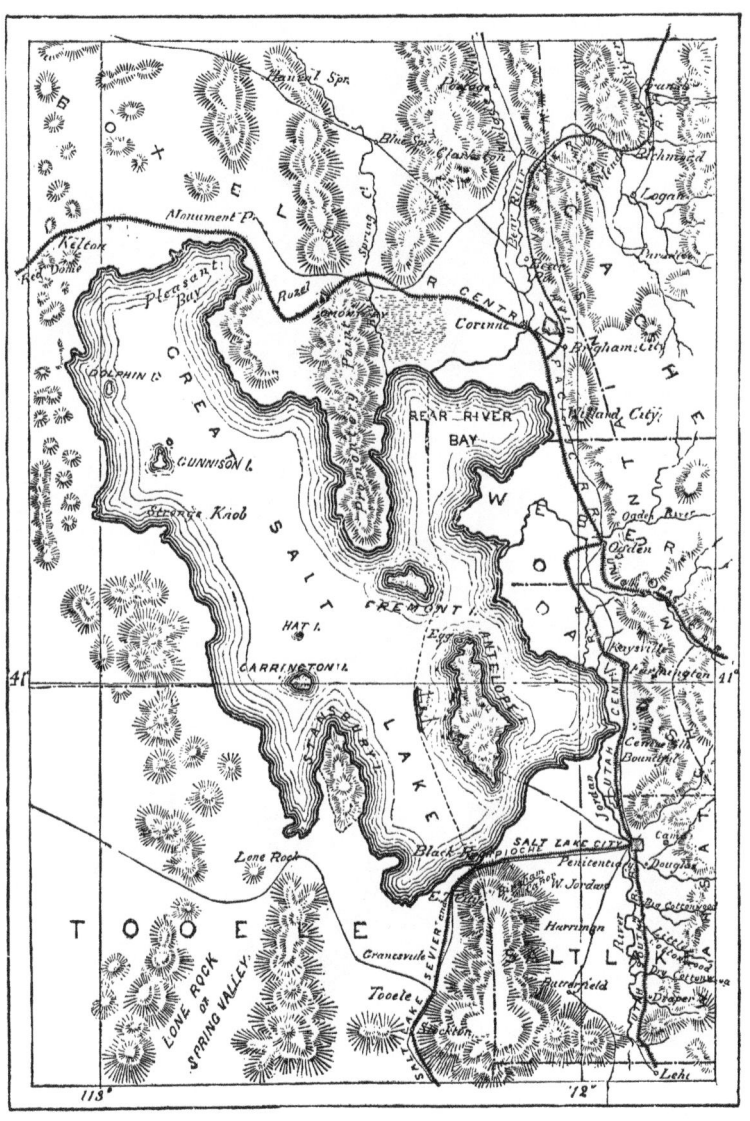

MAP OF SALT LAKE VALLEY.

was nothing to tempt the Gentile emigration.   He desired isolation, that he might build up " the kingdom." A detachment of one hundred and forty of the Battalion joined the pioneers *en route* on the 4th of July, and advanced westward with them to the Salt Lake Valley.

On the 22nd of July the apostle Orson Pratt and a few others reached the rim of the Salt Lake Basin, and the next day they rode over a portion of the valley, exploring for a camping-ground near wood and water.   They returned to the camp of the pioneers, and reported that they had found the place that Joseph had spoken of where the Church could be located, and where the Saints could increase and multiply without molestation.

On the morning of the 24th of July, 1847, when Brigham Young and the body of the pioneers first got a glimpse of the Great Basin, there was a universal exclamation—"The Land " of Promise!   The Land of Promise!—held in reserve by " the hand of God for the resting-place of His Saints!"   Thus writes the historian.   After a tedious journey over unmade roads, a distance of 1,100 miles, and passing through so many difficulties by the way, it would have been strange indeed had the weary travellers gazed upon the beautiful scenery of Salt Lake Valley without admiration and " ecstacies of joy."

From the mouth of the cañon through which the pioneers entered the valley, the view is ravishing.   In the distant west the Great Salt Lake lies glistening like a sheet of silver, and in every direction that the eye can travel lofty mountains bound the horizon.

Brigham was sick when he reached the Valley, but he was no less enthusiastic than the others, and was fully satisfied that they had reached the Zion of the Mountains, that had been the theme of ancient prediction.

On the banks of a small stream southwest of the Tabernacle block, the pioneers made their first encampment, and, as soon as their horses and cattle were unhitched and cared for, the Valley of Great Salt Lake was consecrated to the Lord.

In the same hour the ploughs were taken from the wagons and the earth was upturned to receive the seed for the autumn crops, upon which so much depended for the support of the

coming emigration. While a portion of the pioneers were
thus engaged, others were constructing a dam, by which the
waters of the creek could be controlled, and irrigation would
be secure for the dry and hitherto barren soil. No rain was
anticipated, but " providentially " a thunder-storm burst upon
them, which was accepted as an omen of the favour of " the
" Lord." The thunders and lightnings of Sinai, and the smit-
ing of the rock in Horeb while the chosen people travelled
through the desert of Zin, were not more assuring to the
wanderers of the presence of the great Hebrew lawgiver than
was the thunder-storm of the 24th of July, 1847 to " modern
" Israel."

The following day was the first of the week, and the Sabbath was to be hallowed as a perpetual institution in Zion.
Brigham, sick and peevish, invited those present who could
not keep the Sabbath as a day of rest and worship, to " leave,
" and go their own way among the ungodly."

Exploring expeditions were sent out in every direction to
gain a knowledge of the surrounding country. One party
found on the west side of Jordan about a hundred goats, sheep,
and antelopes playing about the hills, and before they returned
they made their first acquaintance with the Utah Indians. On
the north side of where Salt Lake City now stands, a party
ascended a high peak of the mountain, from which they overlooked the whole valley. Subsequently on this summit they
hoisted the national flag, and named the mountain Ensign
Peak. Brigham is credited, in Gentile traditions, with having
ascended this mountain and conversed with some angel who
made important revelations to him, and traced the laying out
of the Temple block. The orthodox are silent on this subject,
which is a pretty certain contradiction of the story. If true, it
would have been told.

On the 28th, the Temple block was selected—a plot of forty
acres ; and a city, two miles square, was laid off in lots of eight
rods by twenty, exclusive of streets, and the blocks of eight
rods each, making ten acres to the block. The streets were
laid out towards the cardinal points of the compass, eight rods
wide, with a sidewalk of twenty feet. The houses were directed to be built in the centre of the lot, twenty feet from the

front line, and shade trees were ordered to be planted in all the streets. By a foolish economy of land, the Temple block was trimmed from forty to ten acres.

After the apostles, the pioneers, and members of the Battalion had selected their inheritances in this New Zion, and had put in their autumn crops, most of them returned to the Missouri river to prepare their families for emigrating in the coming spring. On their return journey the party were exceedingly short of rations, and had to rely almost entirely upon their rifles for supplies. They endured much suffering. The Indians harassed them, and on the way stole from them fifty horses and mules. There was, however, no death among the brethren, though many of them were sick when they first started from the Missouri on the exploring expedition. On the last day of October they arrived at Winter Quarters, after an absence of eight months, and were received with great joy.

CHAPTER XXXIII.

CHANGES IN THE CHURCH.—Brigham Young assumes Joseph's Authority and Place—The Emigration from Europe re-opened—Migration of the Saints to the New Zion—Brigham invites Presidents, Emperors, Kings, Princes, Nobles, etc., to come to the Help of " the Lord "—The Pioneers *en route*.

THE grand importance and success of the mission of the pioneers to the Rocky Mountains was the beginning of a new era in Mormonism.

Up to this time Israel had been " in bondage among the " Gentiles." The laws that govern the citizens of the United States had restrained the Saints from living up to the higher laws of " the kingdom." But from this time they were to have a national existence, and in nearly every public document and in every sermon in the Tabernacle they were henceforth to be spoken of as " this people."

From the death of Joseph and the dis-fellowshipping of Rigdon, the Quorum of the Twelve Apostles had had the honour of leading the Saints, and Brigham was its senior member and President. In his opinion, however, the time had now arrived for a change.

At Winter Quarters there was a log-cabin, about fifty feet long, situated near the centre of the settlement. The roof and slanting sides and ends of the structure were covered with turf about two feet thick. It had several small windows in the roof and a door near one end. Into it none could look; from it nothing could be heard. This was " the Council-House." It was here that " the Lord " spoke unto his servants.

It is a general idea with the unsophisticated that when " the Lord " reveals his will concerning the Church, the people listen, comprehend, and obey. It had been understood in this manner with Joseph Smith ; but Brigham Young was as yet unused to the style of the heavenly world, and was extremely cautious, preparing to grope his way to the goal of his desires rather than risk the hasty announcement of "the "Lord's" programme.

As he was leading back the pioneers from Salt Lake to the Missouri river, he divulged for the first time his idea of the desirability of reörganizing the Church "as it was in the days of "Joseph," with a President and two counsellors, forming a quorum, called The First Presidency. The apostle Wilford Woodruff was taken into his confidence, and to him Brigham's purpose was first communicated as a suggestion. Brother Woodruff did not see it very clearly, for the Church and the world had been assured that the twelve apostles were to lead the Saints, and that the place of Joseph over the Church was not to be filled. Brother Woodruff, however, is a man of great faith, humble and tractable in the hands of "the Lord," and being more a follower than a leader, he soon saw the point very clearly. Brigham was successful; he had gained an apostle upon whom he could count.

The apostle Kimball, who stood next to Brigham in authority, and Willard Richards, the best scholar and secretary of the Twelve, were, if the proposed change were effected, to be elevated to the First Presidency as counsellors. These, with Woodruff and Brigham, constituted four of the Twelve already disposed of. Elder E. T. Benson had been ordained an apostle while crossing the plains going West; he could, therefore, offer no opposition to the change, had he even been capable of doing so. Amasa Lyman and Geo. A. Smith were men of excellent dispositions, and themselves free from all guile in the way of ambition—they were sure to sustain "the Lord." Lyman Wight had not followed Brigham westward, and so there was no occasion to speak of him. There remained, therefore, but four men in the Quorum of the Twelve—Orson Hyde, Parley P. Pratt, Orson Pratt, and John Taylor—to be dealt with. Each of these had retained some personal identity, and believed in the first preachings and "whisperings of the spirit" after the death of Joseph, which promised that the Twelve Apostles should lead the Church.

By the assassination of the two Smiths, Brigham Young, being the eldest of the apostles and President of the Quorum, became, *de facto*, the leader, though the Twelve were nominally the guiding " head." The elevation of Brigham and his two counsellors opened the way for Hyde, and made him President of the apostles, and in case of Brigham's death he would have become the head of the Church. " The finger of " the Lord" was clear to brother Hyde, and he heard " the " voice of the Lord " calling upon his servant Brigham to step forward and assume that position. Of course he did ; but the Pratts and Taylor were not so favoured.

On the 5th of December, 1847, in that long mud-roofed Council House which was impervious to sound from without, and from within which not the loudest wrangle could be heard by the passer-by, sat Brigham and his apostles debating on the proposed change. Elder Taylor offered a manly opposition, while Orson Pratt sternly clung to the order of the Church, its revelations, preaching, and promises ; and Parley was eloquent for the headship of the Church remaining with the Twelve. But wordy opposition availed nothing, and an appeal to the people would have divided the Church. They fully realized that no opposition to Brigham Young was possible *within* the Church, and they dared not step *without* to accomplish it. They had silently to submit, but Brigham has never forgiven that hostility.

The coming change was soon bruited among the people, and by them heard at first with astonishment. A general conference of all the Saints was convened at Winter Quarters, and there the election of Brigham took place. Soon after that council a four days' meeting was held in the Log Tabernacle near Kanesville, and there the proposed change was the subject of discourse. Faithful brethren were invited to speak on the subject, and one by one gave in their adhesion to the reorganization. When the moment for voting had arrived, every man was to be seen and to be understood. As soon as the apostles raised their hands affirmatively, the battle was over. Their example was followed, and, in their order, the High Council, the high priests, seventies, elders, priests, teachers, and deacons, and finally the vast congregation of women, raised their hands to heaven in token that they would sustain Brigham Young. Of this election he wrote to the president of the British Church : "I feel glory, hallelujah ! Nothing "more has been done to-day than what I knew would be done "when Joseph died." *

Thus Brigham became the "President of the Church of "Jesus Christ of Latter-day Saints throughout the whole "world." Kimball and Richards became his counsellors, and Hyde was made president of the apostles.

This move of Brigham's has been charged against him as an act of usurpation ; but that amounts to very little. The Mormon people have accepted the position of "unchallenged "obedience," and it would have been incompatible with their own profession of faith to question any proposition emanating from the head of the Church. Brigham's action, then, with Brigham's former teaching, is all explicable by the doctrine of "expediency."

There is a tinge of Cromwell and Napoleon about Brigham that is really charming to the very humble Mormons. Should he hereafter at any time propose to organize the United States into a kingdom, and crown himself its monarch, the Saints would be as sure to vote for him unanimously. There is no alternative. To doubt his proposition is to doubt heaven, and to leave themselves without a head to lead them.

With the Church reorganized and a new Zion to be built up, the elders were again ready for missionary work.

The Mormon emigration from Europe and all other distant countries, that had closed with the exodus from Nauvoo, was again opened. A general epistle, issued on the 23rd of December, announced the route from Liverpool to be *via* New Orleans, St. Louis, and up the Missouri to Council Bluffs, and the emigrants were to bring with them all kinds of choice seeds of grain, vegetables, fruits, trees, vines—the best stock of beasts, birds, and fowl ; the best tools and machinery, together with every interesting book, map, chart, and scientific work which they could obtain. They were to bring their treasures of precious metals and those of general utility, the curiosities of art and nature, "everything in their possession or within their

" reach, to build in strength and stability, to beautify, adorn,
" and embellish, to delight and cast a fragrance over the house
" of the Lord."

With a flourish of national feeling, Brigham, following the
time-honoured custom of the British monarch, announced in
that general epistle that the Mormons were " at peace with all
" nations, kingdoms, powers, governments, and authorities,"
save " the kingdom and power of darkness;" and invited,
" presidents, emperors, kings, princes, nobles, governors, rulers,
" and judges," and the rest of mankind, " to come and help us
" to build a house to the name of the God of Jacob."

At this period Brigham appears to have been very intent
upon building the Temple. When he was 419 miles west of
Winter Quarters, July 13, 1848, he wrote to Orson Spencer,
the President of the Church in Britain : " While you tarry
" in England I wish you would exert yourself to gather up as
" much tithing as you possibly can, and bring it with you, in
" order to prepare for glass, nails, paints, and such other arti-
" cles as will be needed to bring from the States to assist in
" building up the Temple of the Lord in the valley of the Great
" Salt Lake." Twenty-four years have since passed away, and
the Temple is but a few feet above the ground, while it is stated
that millions have been collected by tithing and contribution
for its erection !

The " day of deliverance has surely come," and the camps
of Israel on the banks of Missouri were alive in the spring of
1848 making preparations for departure. All who could,
wanted to go.

The same order of travel that " the Lord " had revealed
through his servant Brigham for the guidance of the pioneers
was again observed, and captains of tens, fifties, and hundreds
were chosen. By the beginning of June the pilgrims were *en
route.* The following inventory of the first five companies is
interesting. Altogether there were 623 wagons, 1,891 souls,
131 horses, 44 mules, 2,012 oxen, 983 cows, 334 loose cattle, 654
sheep, 237 pigs, 904 chickens, 54 cats, 134 dogs, 3 goats, 10
geese, 11 doves, 1 squirrel, and 5 ducks.

Henceforth the Mormon emigration across the plains was
" the Lord " gathering Israel home to the " chambers of the

"mountains" preparatory to the great day of wrath that was to come upon the Gentile world.

Following the pioneers to Great Salt Lake Valley, about four thousand of the Mormons arrived in September and October, taking with them a large amount of grain and agricultural implements, as well as the remnant of their property from Nauvoo, with which to commence a new home. The first winter was fortunately mild, and the emigrants suffered little, while the stock rambled about enjoying the spontaneous luxuries of a virgin soil.

The great body of the Saints from the Missouri river followed Brigham and his family in the summer of 1848, and the new settlement was greatly strengthened in numbers and with every description of labour necessary to its development.

CHAPTER XXXIV.

THE CIVIL HISTORY OF UTAH. — The "State of Deseret" created — The Crickets destroy the Crops — A Miracle performed — Great Privations of the Mormons — Territorial Government extended over Utah — Trouble with the Federal Officers.

THE troubles of the Saints in Jackson county, Missouri—if Joseph's revelations are accepted as divine communications— conveyed to "the Lord" and his Saints valuable experience in human affairs. The last revelation affecting *that* "Zion" illustrated clearly two simple propositions: First, that if the Saints purchased all the land in Jackson county, there would be no land left for the Gentiles to purchase. Secondly, that as the Gentiles had always troubled the Mormons while they were living among them, if there were no Gentiles among these the Saints would not be troubled. This logic was not lost upon Brigham, and henceforth the policy of the Church was to oc- cupy all the available lands in the county just as fast as they could do so.

What is now Davis and Weber counties, directly north of Salt Lake City, was taken possession of by the Mormons in the spring of 1848. Miles Goodyier, an Indian trader, at that time occupied the land on which is now built the city of Og- den, where the Union and Pacific Railroads form their junc- tion ; and from this trader, Captain James Brown, of the Mor- mon Battalion, purchased his shanties and a Mexican grant of land, and got him out of the way of "the kingdom." Tooele county, about forty miles to the west of Salt Lake City, and Utah county, about the same distance to the south, were taken possession of in the spring of 1849.

Up to this time there was no United States civil govern- ment in the country.

When the Mormons arrived in the valley of the Great Salt Lake, in July, 1847, the Territory belonged to Mexico; but by the treaty of Guadaloupe Hidalgo, in March, 1848, it was passed over to the United States with New Mexico and the whole of Upper California. This was unforeseen and undesirable to the Mormon leaders, for they could have dictated terms to Mexico and have worked out better the theocratic problem with the relics of the Montezumas, than with the Anglo-Saxon descendants of the Pilgrim Fathers.

The United States government was slow in extending its political jurisdiction over the newly-acquired domain, and this furnished the apostles and prophets an opportunity of creating "a provisional independent government" for themselves.

A convention of citizens was held in Great Salt Lake City on the 5th of March, 1849, at which (on the 18th) the following constitution was adopted:

"WE, THE PEOPLE, grateful to the SUPREME BEING for the blessings hitherto enjoyed, and feeling our dependence on Him for a continuation of those blessings, Do ORDAIN AND ESTABLISH A FREE AND INDEPENDENT GOVERNMENT by the name of the STATE OF DESERET, including all the territory of the United States within the following boundaries, to wit: commencing at the 33° of north latitude, where it crosses the 108° of longitude, west of Greenwich; thence running south and west to the boundary of Mexico; thence west to and down the main channel of the Gila river (or the northern line of Mexico), and on the northern boundary of Lower California to the Pacific Ocean; thence along the coast northwesterly to the 118° 30′ of west longitude; thence north to where said line intersects the dividing ridge of the Sierra Nevada Mountains to the dividing range of mountains that separates the waters flowing into the Columbia river from the waters running into the great Basin on the south, to the summit of the Wind River chain of mountains; thence southeast and south by the dividing range of mountains that separates the waters flowing into the Gulf of Mexico from the waters flowing into the Gulf of California, to the place of beginning as set forth in a map drawn by Charles Preuss and published by order of the Senate of the United States in 1848."

A glance at the map of North America will furnish some idea of the modest aspirations of the convention. Within the boundaries of that "State of Deseret" there was room enough to hold half of the monarchies of Europe.

Brigham Young was elected Governor of the new State, and, with the other officers elected, swore fidelity to the Con-

stitution of the United States. The legislative Assembly met
in July, elected Almon W. Babbitt delegate to Congress, and
sent him immediately to Washington with the constitution and
a memorial praying for the admission of "Deseret" into the
Union.

Though rejoicing in their deliverance from Gentile mobs,
and happy in the prospect of future greatness, the Saints were
not yet free from the cares and anxieties of life. Their situation in the "fat valleys of Ephraim" was for some years pre-
carious. Their first crops were abundant and timely, but those
of the following year caused them great anxiety. At one time
myriads of crickets attacked their fields of grain, till it seemed
that all would be utterly destroyed; but "the Lord" sent
flocks of gulls from the islands of the lake to devour the de-
stroyers. The gulls came in the early dawn of morning and
feasted upon the crickets all day. When full, they disgorged
them and began again their repast, and repeated their experience in eating till night closed upon their labours. The Mormons very naturally claim that the coming of the gulls was a
great miracle in their behalf. Of course the sceptical might
have something to say about who sent the crickets; but gratitude for any kind providence is better encouraged than contemned.*

The crops that escaped the ravages of the crickets exhibited
in their abundance that the virgin soil of the valleys was very
rich. Oats were reported to do better than in the States;†
wheat yielded commonly sixty bushels to the acre; and other
grains and vegetables were equally well reported in the first
year.

"One of the elders states that he had sown eleven pounds of California
wheat, on the 14th of April, and from that reaped twenty-two bushels in
the latter part of July. From half a bushel of common English wheat,
on an acre and a half of land, he reaped over twenty bushels, and one

---

* An enthusiastic Mormon writer, seeking to place divine interference beyond all
doubt, asserted that "there were no gulls in the country before the Mormons went
there!" This statement is about as facetious as that of one of the apostles who reported that no harm had befallen the pioneers, "except in two or three instances
horses were shot accidentally, or killed by not hearkening to counsel!"

† P. P. Pratt's letter [August 7, 1848] to Brigham Young, Millennial Star, Vol.
X., p. 370.

grain of seven-eared wheat produced seventy-two ears. Barley that was sowed ripened and was reaped and carried off, the land irrigated and produced from the roots a fresh crop four times the quantity of the first crop. Oats that were sown produced a good crop, were cut down and cleared, the roots again sprang up, and produced another beautiful crop. Peas, first plant, a good crop ripened, gathered, then planted the same peas, yielded another crop and again a third crop is now growing. Beet-seed planted this spring produced beets as thick as my leg, which went to seed and yielded a great quantity. Cabbage seed planted this spring produced seed again."

To this flattering story of the productiveness of the country, elder Thomas Bullock, Brigham's clerk, adds: "Above all they "report that Mother Sessions [*une accoucheuse*] has had a har- "vest of 248 little cherubs since living in the valley. Many "cases of twins. In a row of seven houses joining each other, "eight births in one week." His soul bounding with grati- tude, "brother Thomas" exclaims:

"Oh, ye hungry souls, rejoice and shout for joy! Praise the Lord, and give thanks! Oh, ye barren; ye who have been bereft of your chil- dren, praise the Lord. The place is found where you can rear your tender offspring like olive branches round your tables, where they can have plenty to be fed and clothed withal; where your souls can be lifted up unto the Lord God of Hosts, for his mercies endure for ever. The place is found where the Saints can rear another temple to the Great Jehovah; hear his word, and from whence his laws may go forth to the ends of the earth. Hosanna, Hosanna, Hosanna to God and the Lamb for ever. Amen."

However much the foreign Saints may already have rejoiced in the Latter-day faith, such a letter was worth a hundred ser- mons and epistles upon emigration. The Author well remem- bers how it caught the toiling, struggling, poor Saints of Brit- ain, and the delicate comfort extended to the spinsters was not unappreciated. Many a downcast mourning soul drank con- solation and sang with joy—" To the West, to the West, to the " land of the free!"

The large increase of emigrants in 1848, together with the destruction of the crops by the grasshoppers, rendered provis- ions very scarce in the spring of 1849. The inventory of pro- visions showed that there was only three-quarters of a pound of breadstuffs per day for each person up to the 5th of July. The people were put upon rations, and much suffering ensued.

17

Many of them went out with the Indians and dug small native roots, and ate them with anything they could get. It is related that some, in their destitution, even took the hides of animals with which they had covered the roofs of their houses, and cut them up and cooked them for their use.

" The desert to which they had come was as cheerless as their past history. From cruel foes they had fled to as unfeeling a wilderness. Renewed difficulties demanded a renewed effort from Brigham. Everything depended on him. Starvation and nakedness stared in the gloomy faces of the desponding people. Murmurs and complaints were uttered. He quelled everything; scolded, pleaded, threatened, prophesied, and subdued them. With a restless but resistless energy he set them to work, and worked himself as their example. He directed their labours, controlled their domestic affairs, preached at them, to them, for them. He told foolish anecdotes to make them laugh, encouraged their dancing to make them merry, got up theatrical performances to distract their minds, and made them work hard, certain of rendering them contented by-and-by. Feared with a stronger fear, venerated with a more rational veneration, but not loved with the same clinging tenderness that the people still felt for Joseph Smith, Brigham swayed them at his will. They learned to dread his iron hand, and were daunted by his iron heart." *

The harvest of 1849 was fortunately abundant, and all was saved.

In August of that year Captain Howard Stansbury, of the United States army topographical engineers, with his assistants, arrived in the valley for the purpose of making a government survey.

Throughout the winter of 1849–50 the Indians south of Salt Lake became very troublesome, stealing cattle, and finally firing upon the settlers. Brigham preferred peace to war with them : thought that it was cheaper to feed than to fight them, and pursued a conciliatory policy. But the red man required experience. As Governor of the State of Deseret, Brigham called out the militia, entrusted it to Gen. Daniel H. Wells, who, accompanied by a lieutenant of Capt. Stansbury's command, and a hundred of " the brethren," went after the Indians. The Mormons drove the red-skins out from the banks of the Timpanogos on to Utah lake, which was then frozen, and there killed about thirty and took over twice that number prisoners.

* " Mormonism : Its Leaders and Designs," p. 145.

The whites lost one man, and six wounded. This fight and the disposition of the prisoners * struck the Indians with terror, and their braves sued for peace.

Another change was in store for the Saints.

Three of the Battalion Mormons, upon being discharged from the United States service in California, found occupation with Thomas Marshall, of gold-discovery notoriety, and while working for him, digging Capt. Sutter's mill-race, these three " brethren " claim to have found the gold. The glory of this event is, therefore, appropriated by the Saints, and forms part of the buncombe speeches on all great occasions, when the virtues and worth of the Saints are exhibited.

The immense emigration across the plains in 1850 brought large quantities of clothing, dry-goods, and general merchandise into Great Salt Lake City. Many of the immigrants had loaded up with heavy stocks of goods, mechanics' tools, and general machinery, expecting to find a ready sale for them in the new Eldorado. Most of them had splendid outfits, and everything necessary to support themselves in a new country. Some parties, who had left the States late, had travelled fast and passed the other immigrants on the way, brought the report that steamers had sailed from New York loaded with passengers and merchandise for California, and that the new country would be flooded with both.

With such a report ringing in their ears, there was now no time to lose, and everything was to be sacrificed to expedite the journey. When they arrived in Salt Lake Valley, the Mormons obtained almost everything they wanted in exchange for grain and vegetables. Stories are related of the frantic haste with which many of the emigrants would part with wagons, cattle, and goods, for a horse or mule outfit to carry them to California. The Saints were thus suddenly prosperous, and

* It is said that the order was given to "leave neither root nor branch of them," and that it was executed to the very letter.

"A party was driven up Table Mountain, but were induced to come down and surrender. They were guarded in camp until the morning, and then ordered to give up their weapons. They refused to do this, and acting in a sullen and hostile manner, were fired upon and nearly all killed immediately. A few broke through the line of sentinels, and endeavored to escape by crossing the lake on the ice, but were chased down by horsemen, and 'ceased to breathe.' My informant was an actor in the terrible scene."—" Gunnison," p. 147.

several of the predictions of the leaders were, in this manner, claimed to be fulfilled.

In the midst of their distress in the wilderness, when leaving civilization and commerce behind, and, to all human appearance, going into a desert where the Gentiles would not follow them, Heber C. Kimball had predicted to the Saints that they "would yet buy goods as cheap in the mountains as "they could in New York city." Brigham had told them that in five years "they would be better off than ever they "were before," and thus the unlooked-for rush to California fulfilled the prediction, and "the people acknowledged the ac- "complishment of that divine inspiration." At the same time one of Joseph's predictions had its fulfilment. When the Kirtland Safety Society Bank burst in 1838, its notes were not worth the clean paper. Joseph predicted that "they would "yet be as good as gold." When the Battalion gold discoverers returned to the valley, they deposited with the Church leaders large quantities of gold-dust, and, with that as a basis, the Kirtland notes were for a little time put into circulation as a convenience, "on a par with gold," and in *that* way the prediction was fulfilled. Had the bundles of the Kirtland Safety Society notes still in Ohio been convertible and "good as gold," the holders of that paper would have seen the prediction and its fulfilment more clearly. A momentary convenience of exchange between Brother Smith and Brother Jones in Salt Lake valley (for momentary and very limited it certainly was) being the fulfilment of a prediction, requires an "eye of faith" to see.

The Congress of the United States ignored the "State of "Deseret;" and on the 9th of September, 1850, extended over the country occupied by the Mormons the Territorial organization of Utah within the following limits: "bounded on the "west by the State of California, on the north by the Territory "of Oregon, on the east by the summits of the Rocky Mountains, "and on the south by the 37th parallel of north latitude," with the proviso that Congress should be at liberty, when it might be deemed "convenient and proper," to cut it up into two or more Territories, or to attach any portion of it to any other State or Territory. On the 28th of that month, his Excellen-

cy Millard Fillmore, President of the United States, appointed,
" with the advice and consent of the Senate," BRIGHAM YOUNG,
of Deseret, Governor; B. D. HARRIS, of Vermont, Secretary;
JOSEPH BUFFINGTON, of Pennsylvania, Chief-Justice; PERRY E.
BROCCHUS, of Alabama, ZERUBBABEL SNOW, of Ohio, Associate
Justices; SETH M. BLAIR, of Deseret, U. S. Attorney; and
JOSEPH L. HEYWOOD, of Deseret, U. S. Marshal.

Mr. Buffington declined serving as chief-justice, and LEM-
UEL G. BRANDEBURY was appointed in his stead.

Snow, Blair, and Heywood were Mormons, and, with Brigham added, it gave the majority of the Federal offices to the
Saints, for which the name of President Fillmore is held in
high esteem. At once the political capital of Utah—a hundred
and fifty miles south of Salt Lake City—was designated Fillmore, and the county Millard. It is due to this statesman to
add, that the charge which has been frequently made against
him, of appointing Brigham Young governor " while he knew
" that he had eight wives," is very unfair. President Fillmore
appointed Brigham on the recommendation of Col. Thomas L.
Kane, and upon the assurance of that gentleman that the
charges against Brigham Young's Christian morality were unfounded. Col. Kane was long enough among the Mormons,
and familiar enough with them on their journey between Nauvoo and Council Bluffs, to have learned that polygamy was a
fact in Mormonism, unless the Mormons designedly kept him
in ignorance, and deceived him. The larger number of the
" eight wives" complained of were sealed to Brigham on the
banks of the Missouri. Probably, Col. Kane did not personally
know polygamy to be a fact, and certainly neither President
Fillmore nor the Senate knew it.*

On the 3rd of February, 1851, Brigham Young took the
oath of office, and was formally acknowledged governor of
Utah. He preferred Deseret under " the Lord," but with the
characteristic instinct of his nature—the love of rule—rather
than see a Gentile appointed governor of Utah, he himself accepted that office under Congress. On the 25th of March he
issued a special message to the general assembly of the State
of Deseret, notifying them of the action of Congress. On the

* The Author was so informed by letter from ex-President Fillmore.

5th of April, 1852, Deseret merged into Utah officially, but the State organization was continued and exists to-day as much as ever it did. Nominally, the civil authority is Utah : *de facto*, it is Deseret. The Government pays the Territorial legislators their *per diem* for making the laws of Utah, and hands them their mileage at the end of the session. On the day succeeding the close, Brigham, as governor of Deseret, convenes them as a State legislation : reads his message to them, and some one proposes that the laws of the legislature of Utah be adopted by the State of Deseret. In this manner, Brigham is continued governor *de facto*, and hence the tenacity with which the name of " Deseret " is preserved. To give to the State that succeeds the Territory of Utah any other name than " Deseret " would be to throw discredit upon the inspiration that named the provisional Government in 1849. Let but the Federal Congress name it " Deseret "—come when it may into the Union—and Brigham and his worshippers will see, through all the tortuous windings of its history for over a score of years, the finger of God, and the dark deeds of the past will be sanctified in their sight. They will believe that " the Lord " has been with Brigham throughout.

The Gentile Federal officers arrived in July of 1851, and very soon after their arrival concluded that Utah was not the most pleasant place in the world for unbelievers. They attended a special conference of the Church held in September, and were honoured with an invitation to sit on the platform with the prophets. On that occasion the proposition was made to send a block of Utah marble or granite as the Territorial contribution to the Washington monument at the seat of Government. Associate Justice Brocchus made a speech, and before closing it drifted on to polygamy. He spoke irreverently of that institution, going so far as to assure the ladies of its immorality, reproved the leaders for their disrespectful language concerning the Government and their consignment of President Zachary Taylor to the nether regions. This was something new in the Rocky Mountain Zion, and the " Lion of the " Lord " was in a moment aroused.

The audience was indignant at Brocchus, and when Brigham let himself loose on to the unfortunate Judge, the people would have torn that Federal functionary into shreds if the Prophet had not restrained them. When Brigham reiterated the situation and locality of the then recently deceased President Taylor, the Judge put in a demurrer, on which "brother Heber" kindly touched his Honour on the shoulder and assured him that he need not doubt the statement, for he would see him when he got there. Heber's witty endorsement of Brigham was anything but reassuring to the Judge.

It was on this occasion that Brigham immortalized the crooking of his little finger. "If," said he, "I had but crooked "my little finger, he would have been used up; but I did not "bend it. If I had, the sisters alone felt indignant enough "to have chopped him in pieces." * Since that memorable day he had not infrequently warned the troublesome of the danger of crooking that finger, and it was no idle threat when he said : "Apostates, or men who never made any profession "of religion, had better be careful how they come here, lest I "should bend my little finger." †

Judge Brocchus, failing to humble himself before "the ser-"vants of the Lord," thought that retirement from the Territory would be favoured by the Life Insurance Company, and he, accompanied by Chief Justice Brandebury and Secretary Harris, soon after bade a long farewell to Zion. Miss Eliza R. Snow's clever pen satirized the retreating Federals, in popular verse, and assured them and the world when they left the Saints that :

"They only of themselves bereft us."

This, however, was only poetic truth, for Secretary Harris, who was the custodian of the Territorial funds, retired with $24,000, which had been appropriated by Congress for the "*per diem*" and mileage of the legislature. This was a great annoyance to the Prophet-Governor, and he attempted to restrain the Secretary ; but Mr. Harris stuck to the treasure and returned it to the proper department of the Government.

The Federal officers, on their arrival in the Eastern States, published a hastily written statement of the whole occurrence, and very indiscreetly used the expression that "Polygamy "monopolized all the women, which made it very inconvenient

* " Journal of Discourses," p. 186–7.　　† Ib., p. 167.

" for the Federal officers to reside there." Loose as people
might suppose frontier life to be, no one anticipated that representatives of the Federal Government would thus express
themselves. That one sentence annihilated them.

Over the signature of Jedediah M. Grant, Brigham's counsellor, a series of letters was addressed to the New York
Herald, under the title of " Truth for the Mormons," in which
the Federal officials were turned into ridicule and fiercely
handled. The *Herald* gave the public only one letter; but
Grant, nothing daunted, published the whole series in pamphlet
form, and scattered them broadcast. The Grant letters, from
their forcible and pungent style, attracted the attention of literary men as gems of wit and vigorous English. They were
so far superior to the Mormon literature that preceded them,
and so much above Jedediah himself, that great credit was
given by the Saints to the special inspiration which controlled
him. In after years it was really painful to the Author to
learn that two of Pennsylvania's honoured sons, already alluded to in this work—one no less than an ex-Vice-President
of the United States, and the other enjoying a military title—
were the inspiration and authors of the famous letters. What
a charm there is in a mild and harmless delusion !

On the departure of the judges and secretary from Utah,
Brigham appointed his counsellor, Willard Richards, Secretary
of the Territory. Associate Justice Snow, being a Mormon,
took no offence, and remained, and the Legislature of the Territory clothed the Probate courts with " both appellate and
" original jurisdiction," and the Federal judges could thereafter be easily dispensed with. The Saints had really no use
for them.

CHAPTER XXXV..

THE IRREPRESSIBLE CONFLICT BETWEEN THEOCRACY AND RE-
PUBLICANISM.—The Federal Officers in Utah—Some become Sycophants to
the Priesthood—Some are defiant—Brigham Young a Second Time appointed
Governor—Trouble with the Federal Judges—They leave the Territory.

In his moments of calm reflection, Judge Brocchus may have
concluded that his zeal against polygamy had outstripped his
prudence. The Government took that view of it, and quietly
"dropped" the "runaway judges and secretary." Judges
Reed and Shaver, with Secretary Ferris, soon replaced Brandebury, Brocchus, and Harris. Brigham was triumphant.

The new appointees, as might be expected, received a cor-
dial welcome. The judges reciprocated, but the secretary
shared the sentiments of his predecessor. The judges delivered some favourable speeches and wrote some friendly letters,
but the secretary soon after published a book expressing sentiments the very antipodes of those uttered by his Federal associates. Thenceforth Brigham's policy was to array the Federal
officers against each other, and in doing so he has been singularly successful.

The successors of the "runaway" officials held brief tenure
of power. Judge Reed returned to New York on a visit, and
there died. Judge Shaver, apparently in good health at night,
was found the next morning dead in his bed. Secretary Ferris, after a short residence, went to California. Though Judge
Shaver had spoken very kindly of the Mormons, and was exceedingly "social" with "the brethren," his sudden death
furnished gossips with the story of his being poisoned on account of some supposed difficulty with Brigham. The Author
has never seen any ground for such a suspicion.* The judge

* Mrs. Waite says: "There was some difficulty between the judge and the

was buried with processional honours, and a discourse by one of the apostles embalmed his memory in the history of the Church.

Chief-Justice John F. Kinney, Associate Justices George P. Stiles and W. W. Drummond, and Secretary Almon W. Babbitt, were the third "batch" of officials. Judge Kinney has a very important history, and appears frequently in this work. Judge Stiles had been reared in Mormonism, but was inharmonious with the priesthood. Judge Drummond turned out a perfect Mephistopheles to the Saints. Secretary Babbitt was a full-fledged Mormon.

At this period of Utah history the Government at Washington was seemingly very kindly disposed towards the Saints, as all but two of the Federal offices were held by Mormons; but the political thermometer at Washington is always very variable.

The report of the "runaway" officials, though it accomplished nothing for themselves, stirred up the nation respecting polygamy, and what was regarded as defiance of Government. Up to the time of this report, the Church had made no public acknowledgment of polygamy as a principle of the faith. It could now no longer be concealed, and Brigham announced that he was ready to publish the revelation.

The avowal of polygamy was for a time a grave subject at Washington; but that was a question only of morals, and Congress is slow to legislate on morality. The reported speech, " Old Zachary is in hell, and I am glad of it," charged to Brigham, stirred up the political animus at the seat of government a vast deal more, and in course of time Brigham's removal from the governorship was resolved upon.

In a Tabernacle address, June 19, 1853, Brigham denied being the author of the statement about President Taylor, and said that he had only endorsed the statement of some one else: "I simply bore testimony to the truth of it." * In his denial he manifests an evasiveness that does not improve the subject.

Brigham was, however, secure as Governor. His words, "*I am and will be Governor, and no power can hinder it*," were

Prophet, the nature of which was not distinctly known. The difficulty increased, and one morning the judge was found dead in his bed. The heads of the Church took great pains to have the affair investigated, and came to the conclusion that the judge had died of some 'disease of the head!'" (Page 24.)

* "Journal of Discourses," vol. i., p. 135.

very galling to those who sought his removal. But behind that boldness there appeared in the published sermon a shrewd proviso to fall back upon in case his removal should be accomplished: " *Until the Lord Almighty says, 'Brigham, you need* " ' *not be Governor any longer.*' "

In 1854, Lieutenant-Colonel E. J. Steptoe, with about three hundred of his regiment, arrived in the Territory on their way to California. Much kind attention was paid to the colonel and his officers; social parties were frequent, and very pleasant relations existed.

Early in December, President Pierce tendered to the colonel the appointment of Governor of Utah; but before the next returning monthly mail, a memorial to his Excellency, headed by Chief-Justice Kinney, was signed, requesting Brigham's reappointment as Governor and Superintendent of Indian Affairs. The colonel's name followed that of Kinney, and the names of the officers of the regiment—three Mormons—Judge Shaver and District-Attorney Hollman.

A very romantic story is told by Mrs. C. V. Waite, in her book, in which Brigham is charged with using two sisters of easy virtue to enveigle the colonel into an unpleasant position, by which, in the language of the Tabernacle, " the Lord put a " hook in the colonel's nose." But, without that incentive to leave the Saints, the colonel doubtless preferred the profession of arms to the honour of being Governor over a handful of poor people in a desert so far removed from the rest of mankind, and after receiving such demonstrative kindness from the Mormons, could not well afford to accept an appointment which would have ousted his chief host against the wishes of the people. It is said that the colonel's letter of appointment was not hastily delivered after it reached Salt Lake City, and between the arrival of the mail that should have brought the appointment and the arrival of the mail at which the letter of appointment was delivered, dancing parties were given that secured the kind feeling of the colonel and his officers. " The Lord " had not yet concluded, " Brigham, you need not be Governor " any longer," and so, in 1855, he was reappointed by President Franklin Pierce.

In the organic act of the Territory it is provided that " the

" governor, secretary, chief justice and associate justices, attor-
" ney and marshal, shall be nominated, and by and with the
" advice and consent of the Senate, appointed by the President
" of the United States." In the list of first Federal appointments the last two important offices—those of United States
attorney and United States marshal—were filled by two Mormons, Messrs. Seth M. Blair and Joseph L. Heywood. With
the appointment of a Gentile to the office of United States
marshal as successor of Mr. Heywood, the question of jurisdiction was forced upon the attention of the court, and very singularly the most important question that has agitated Utah
during twenty years was first entertained before a Federal judge
who had himself been many years a Mormon.

The Territorial Legislature had created a Territorial marshal, and now a conflict was inevitable between him and the
marshal appointed by the United States. The United States
marshal claimed that he was the executive officer of the United
States courts, whether the business before the court was federal or territorial; the Mormon marshal claimed that he was
the officer of the United States court while it was occupied
with territorial business. It was of little consequence to any
one whether the fees of the court should pass into the pocket
of a United States marshal or a territorial marshal; but it was
a matter of great importance to every one which of these two
officials should empanel the juries and enforce the writs of
the court.

Judge Stiles favoured the claim of the United States marshal, and brought a storm of wrath about his head. Had he
been purely a Gentile judge, he would have fared better, but
being a renegade Mormon, and defying the priesthood that he
once obeyed, there was no indignity too great to offer him.
Some Mormon lawyers entered the court while the question
was pending, and, led by the best lawyer among them, insulted
and threatened the judge with personal violence unless he ruled
as they demanded. On account of these intimidations he hastily adjourned his court.*

* Though under no circumstances could there be offered any palliation for such
an offence, there is at the same time a degree of satisfaction in reading that the
outrage was reserved for the person of Judge Stiles. He was the counsel who sus-

Some of the "good brethren" had now their attention directed to the renegade judge, and while he was absent from his office they gathered up the records of the United States District Courts, placed them in safe keeping, and afterwards made a fire of books and papers found in his office. On his return, when he saw the fire, he very naturally concluded, as his office was ransacked, that *all the books, records, and papers were destroyed*. That insane and foolish outrage created a great sensation throughout the States adverse to the Saints.

Consistently with their programme, and possessing a great country in which "Israel could increase and multiply and "become a great people," the leaders were continually calling upon the Saints to "spread abroad the curtains of Zion," and as soon as it was safe to venture in advance of a settlement already made, the survey of another was immediately commenced.

North and south of Salt Lake the Mormon colonists had only the Indians to contend with, and by judiciously avoiding any conflict with the red men they experienced comparatively little trouble. But when the colonists pushed forward to the western frontier of the Territory they there met with the adventurous miner, and peace was thenceforth very doubtful.

In 1854, the western mission was given to about seventy

tained Joseph Smith and the Nauvoo Municipality in their interpretation of the city ordinance which warranted the destruction of the Nauvoo *Expositor* as a nuisance. Had the lawyer of Nauvoo set his face against the first outrage, the judge in the Rocky Mountains would probably never have been the subject of a similar experience.

The successor of Judge Stiles, the Hon. C. E. Sinclair, in the first session of the United States District Court, after the arrival of the United States troops, under Colonel Albert Sidney Johnson, pursued with determined energy those who had insulted and intimidated his predecessor. On the 14th of December, 1858, a Mormon grand jury made the following presentment:

" The grand jury find that James Ferguson, of Great Salt Lake City, U. T., did use language and threats calculated to intimidate Judge George P. Stiles, United States district judge, while in the execution of his official duties and presiding as judge of this District Court at the February term, 1857.

" Said threats and language used to George P. Stiles.

" ELEAZER MILLER, Foreman."

Mr. Ferguson was by instinct a gentleman: his actions on this occasion find interpretation in the general spirit of the times. Israel was determined not to be beaten.

families, who were directed to go out to Carson Valley—about seven hundred miles—under the supervision of Orson Hyde, the president of the apostles. Soon after that, the Legislature of Utah organized the whole of that district under the name of Carson county, appointing at the same time elder Hyde as probate judge.

It soon became evident that the Gentiles would resist all Mormon law wherever there was a hope of success. It was difficult for the miners to comprehend how the Mormons could legitimately exercise any authority over them. They had only heard of the Mormons as a religious community, and when the apostolic probate judge had assessments to make, or the officers of his court had decrees to enforce, it seemed to the "honest "miner" a huge joke, or unbearable tyranny.

Besides the occupation of the country by the mining population, enterprising men found that it was well adapted for cattle grazing and farming. Families soon settled there, and the population was about equally composed of Gentiles and Mormons. The Gentiles snapped their fingers at the Mormon lawgivers, and an anti-Mormon organization was soon established. The apostle-judge had rendered some decision that required enforcement. The officer of the court called for a *posse* to assist him, and the parties immediately arranged themselves for battle, and "for two weeks," says the Hon. James M. Crane, "their armies camped nearly in sight of each other, "without coming to a direct battle." "The Lord," ever watchful over his Saints, revealed to "brother Orson" that it was necessary to call off the brethren, and thus this bloodless war for the moment ended.

This Mormon experience in western colonization differed little in spirit and principle from that which previously existed in Missouri and Illinois. There is an instinctive feeling of dislike to civil rule being administered by any one claiming ecclesiastical authority.

The anti-Mormons appealed to Congress, and asked that the eastern boundary of California might be extended still further east, so that the settlers in Carson Valley might find themselves under the jurisdiction of citizens like themselves. In this memorial they alleged all sorts of bad things against the

Mormon rulers, and particularly objected to the probate judge taking into their midst "one of his spiritual wives for whom "he claims recognition, which the ladies petitioning indig- "nantly refuse."

Congress discountenanced the suggestion that the bound- aries of the Golden State should be extended, but sympathized with the Gentile population, and expressed an opinion that "some measure of wider scope is necessary to effect a radical "cure of the moral and political pestilence which makes Utah "the scandal of the American people."

Associate-Justice W. W. Drummond, it is asserted by the Mormons, brought with him to the Territory "a lady compan- "ion," while his wife and family were left in Illinois. After the notice of his arrival in the Mormon paper had been pub- lished, some relatives of Mrs. Drummond paid a visit to the judge's "companion," and, unfortunately for the judge, the "lady" from St. Louis did not answer to the description of the wife in Oquawkee. The discovery did not long remain a secret. The "lady" travelled with his Honour wherever he held court, and on some occasions she sat beside him on the bench.

Plurality of wives was to the Mormons a part of their re- ligion openly acknowledged to all the world. Drummond's plurality was the outrage of a respectable wife of excellent reputation for the indulgence of a common prostitute, and the whole of his conduct was a gross insult to the Government which he represented, and the people among whom he was sent to administer law. For any contempt that the Mormons exhibited towards such a man, there is no need of apology.

In the spring of 1857, Drummond went to Carson Valley to hold court in the place of Judge Stiles, who repaired to the seat of Government to make affidavit of the breaking up of his court and the destruction of the records of the District Courts.

As soon as Drummond reached the Pacific coast he made a fierce attack upon the Mormons in the papers of San Francisco. His expo ure—much of it false, and much of it exaggerated— added to the affidavit of Judge Stiles in Washington, aroused Congress to demand immediate action.

The attack upon Judge Stiles in a public court of the United States, and the subsequent outrage in his office, would be inexplicable to the reader had it transpired outside of Utah. To the people of that Territory it presented no such difficulty, for it occurred during that fearful period of fanaticism designated "The Reformation," of which an *exposé* is given in the succeeding chapter.

At no period of the history of Utah has there been a perfect *entente cordiale* between the representatives of the Government there. Some one among the Federal officers has always been found who could either be " managed " or held in submission by the threat of exposure of personal history, and in such a case the Scripture sentiment is reversed, and he who is not against us is for us. Among those friendly, the sympathy may at times have been honest ; but the adhesion to the priesthood and the services rendered to the Territory by the greater number of such officials were evidently for the attainment of a personal purpose.

Few Federal appointments have been made at Washington for Utah that some representative of the Church did not essay in some way to control, and where kindness was unappreciated and a determination evinced from the beginning by a Federal officer to keep clear from all entangling alliances, that man's history and pedigree were exceedingly useful and sure to be reached. He was a " dangerous man," and if anything could be discovered about him, from the hanging of his great-grandfather down to some recent peccadillo of his own, the pigeonhole of his alphabetical letter was soon a repository of " useful " information."

The fourth of July, and the anniversary of the arrival of the Mormon pioneers in Salt Lake Valley [July 24], have been useful institutions for ascertaining the sentiments of newly-appointed officials. What wonderful and varied developments have been made !

If the new officers arrived during the latter months of the year, " the parties " at the Social Hall furnished excellent opportunities for polite " complimentary " invitations, to which the kindly-disposed Federals failed not to respond, especially if the gentleman were a " bachelor," with "his family in the

"States," or had some pending divorce on his mind. To be
introduced by "President" Brigham Young to the assembled
Saints as "The Honourable —— Blackstone;" "The Honour-
"able —— Scratchitorum of State;" "Colonel ——, commanding the U. S. A., at Camp ——;" "Major ——, Superintendent
of Indian Affairs," was an honour to be blushingly acknowledged and indelibly imprinted upon the soul's remembrance.
To all this public attention add a personal introduction to Mrs.
A— Young; and of necessity to the other half dozen, Mrs.
B—, Mrs. C—, Mrs. D—, Mrs. E—, Mrs. F—, and Mrs. G—
Young; and the bewildered Federal was in a fair way to realize that he was "an object of interest" and a personage of
some importance. Conducting himself with the usual gallantry
of good society, there were at least these seven cotillions to be
gone through with first, and when there was added to these
the partnership in the dance of downy cheeks in the rosy bloom
of maidenhood, that Federal was ready to swear that "the
"Mormons were the best people upon the earth." To rivet
his devotion he is invited to the right hand of the Prophet at
"the first supper table" where he hears the humble invocation
upon the food, and learns that it is all due to the Lord's favour
to His peculiar people in the mountains. The heart of the
newly-arrived Federal is softened, and he pledges eternal friendship to the Patriarch.

To the inspiration of such attentions may be attributed
the numerous letters which have been hastily written from
Utah "to America," recounting the industry, the sobriety of
the people, the salubrity of the climate, the bushels of wheat
to the acre, the peace that reigned in Zion, the delicious fruit,
the Prophet's youthful appearance, and a denial of the unfounded extravagances that have always been in circulation
against the Mormons! In the fruit season that Federal could
tell of the early delicacies of the plant, the vine, and the tree,
before the market had offered them to the public. His utterances
and his compliments were reported, and the columns of his
home newspaper were watched and culled, and the first inspirations from the Territory were carefully republished for the
edification of the Saints in the mountains. Should after-ex-
perience change his first impressions, or from one cause or
18

another should his friendship chill, he was rendered powerless to act without submitting himself to the charge of inconsistency, and few men of that class have the courage to avow an error or to retrace a foolish step.

With as unjustifiable haste, other Federal officers have betrayed unmanly hostility to the Mormons, before they well knew with what they had to deal. They were ready to consign the leaders to the penitentiary, or to the nethermost regions of the bottomless pit, and were never slow to express openly the pleasure it would afford them to expedite in an official way the travels of apostles, prophets, and bishops to either destination.

One Federal chief-justice went so far in his devotion to Zion as to accept baptismal initiation into the Church. He was afterwards ordained a high priest, and was sent to Congress as delegate. His successor on the bench was as much opposed to the priesthood as he had been subservient to it, and while the delegate was operating in favour of the Church at Washington, the new chief-justice was as diligent in Utah on the opposite side, and in his antipathy denounced everything Mormon. In his view, Nature herself had stamped her curse upon the land. The very peaches were " unnatural and bas-" tard," while all know that that fruit in Utah is unsurpassed in luscious richness.

To such varied individual proclivities—from fawning and servile abasement, to the manifestation of violent antipathies —Utah owes much of the unreliableness of its history; but beneath all, and the cause of all these exhibitions, was the true difficulty—the " irrepressible conflict " between theocracy and republicanism.

The Federal officer who had nothing to ask for, saw in his government and the statutes of the nation the highest development of civilization and human liberty, and he could but seek their supremacy, and demand that they should be respected and obeyed. As naturally, Brigham Young was sincere in circumventing, by every possible means, the assertion of any human will to govern the Saints, in endeavouring to evade every Congressional statute, and prostrating the national representation at the feet of the Priesthood to accomplish the triumph of " the kingdom."

The other Federal officers, outside of the judiciary, have generally been "let alone"—collision in the exercise of their several duties was not inevitable. A Superintendent of Indians could distribute blankets and flour; a Surveyor-General could drive stakes, run lines, and make maps without hurting any one's interest or any one's inclinations; a Governor could make up his mind to "do nothing," and a Secretary could promptly pay the legislators their *per diem* and *mileage* without asking questions about the comforts or troubles of a patriarch's life. All this had been done, and the "elect of the "Lord" and the representatives of republicanism have walked together and danced together with perfect unity, but when either of these officials has "taken sides" with the hostile judiciary and given them "aid and comfort," the enchantment of the circle has been rudely broken.

An Indian Superintendent once drifted into hostility, and, among other things, exposed the "Mountain-Meadows mas-"sacre." He had quietly misappropriated Indian property, and his delinquencies were proclaimed "upon the house-tops." Two Superintendents succeeded him, who were both kindly disposed towards the Church leaders. They may not, perhaps, have stolen more abundantly, for they were judicious. They became wealthy, however, but against them nought was ever insinuated.

In a fit of discontent, an Indian interpreter, a Mormon, dictated a statement of the peculations of one of these friendly Superintendents, made due affidavits of the facts, affixed his name to the document, and all was ready for exposure. By some *legerdemain* the document disappeared, and the interpreter suddenly lost all recollection of the facts. On leaving Utah, that Superintendent was further honoured by his government, and in return for the kindness shown him in Utah he laboured for Zion at Washington.

Another Federal officer recently there was in perfect ecstacies over Zion. His wife and he travelled frequently with Brigham Young, in his annual visits to the settlements, and shared with the apostles, prophets, and bishops a place on the platform in the public assemblies. In his admiration, as he witnessed Brigham's equipage and followers on a visiting tour

north, he ejaculated to the Author : " Brigham has the best
" thing in America ! " That judgment was well founded.   In
return for all the favours of which that Federal official was the
recipient, the revenue office was conducted by Mormon assistants and clerks.

Two secretaries, and, in course of time, both acting-gov-
ernors, were vastly more serviceable than if they had been
members of the Quorum of Apostles.

The ostensible " friendship " of these Federal officials has
done a great wrong to the people of Utah.   It has clothed the
tongues of the priesthood with what they have claimed as impartial testimony from gentlemen outside of the Church, and
the mass of the people, who knew not the why and the wherefore, very naturally accepted such testimony as a corroboration
of their faith and of the rightful course of their leaders, and as
naturally prejudiced them against the men who had dared to
tell them unpleasant facts.   Whoever else has been deceived
by such testimony, there is no reason for concluding that either
the *ruling* priesthood or the officials themselves were among
that number.   Brigham's enmity against the Government is
too deeply rooted for him ever to have trusted one of its representatives beyond what he wanted the public to be told, and it
has been easily discernible in private intercourse with these
officials, that their services were nicely balanced as *quid pro
quo*.   Every one of them has discovered, sooner or later, that
Brigham was their Richelieu.

These few pliant officials have more successfully covered up
the wrongs committed in Utah—have done more to shield the
guilty and to deceive the public than all their other Federal
associates have ever been able to do in telling the truth, en-
forcing the execution of law, bringing crime to light, and reaching the guilty with punishment.

Concealment encouraged fanaticism, and crimes were committed which would never have been attempted had the vigilance of the law been a certainty.   Had the wrongs and murders in Utah been dealt with promptly at the time of their occurrence, it would have been to the honour of the Territory
to-day that the violation of law had never gone unpunished,
and that terrible fanaticism, which struck terror into the souls

of all who witnessed its influence, would have been suppressed in its infancy.

The social position of the Mormons during all this time was as trying as their political and judicial controversy and wire-pulling were bewildering. The wealth that was left in Great Salt Lake City by the passing emigration to the gold-mines of California was only temporary. Many of the inhabitants of the Territory soon became very poor. The crops had failed in 1854, and famine stared them in the face, and in some of the settlements the winters had been very severe, and the cattle ranging in the valleys died in great numbers.

All this, of course, was calculated to weaken many in the faith who had supposed that the heavens were specially propitious to Zion, and the priesthood added to the bitterness of privation the assertion that " the Lord " was punishing the Saints for their unfaithfulness. Without a hope outside of Mormonism, they took their chastisement humbly, prayed more and worked harder.

The best provided families in Utah, throughout the winter of 1855–6, had to " ration " their families to the smallest amount of bread-stuffs per day, in order to subsist until the following harvest. The condition of the poor was appalling.*

---

* In a letter from Heber C. Kimball, dated Salt Lake City, February 29, 1856, published in the *Millennial Star*, he says:

" I have been under the necessity of rationing my family, and also yours, to two-thirds of a pound of bread-stuffs per day each ; as the last week is up to-day, we shall commence on half a pound each. Brother Brigham told me to-day that he had put his family on half a pound each, for there is scarcely any grain in the country, and there are thousands that have none at all scarcely. We shall be under the necessity of eating the bran along with the flour, and shall think ourselves doing well with half a pound a day at that. So you can judge whether or not we can get through until harvest without digging roots. Still, we are better off than the most of the people in these valleys and mountains. There are several wards in this city who have not over two weeks' provisions on hand."

CHAPTER XXXVI.

THE "REFORMATION" IN UTAH.—Its Extraordinary Origin—Shortcomings of the Saints—"Jeddy's" Frenzy—Sinners re-baptized—Terrible Enthusiasm—Tabernacle Teachings—Doctrine of the "Blood Atonement"—Human Sacrifice commended—Erring Saints to offer up their Blood as Incense—Brother Heber declares that *Brigham Young is God to the Mormons*—Strange Preaching—Confessions of the Saints—Brigham's Casuistry about Re-baptizing—Extraordinary Public Meetings of the Priesthood—A "Reign of Terror"—Shocking Outrages upon Citizens—Crusade against Intellectual Societies—Results of the "Reformation"—An Important Letter—What Brigham and the Leaders *really* said in the Tabernacle—Apostates and Gentiles threatened.

In all nations, and in almost every age, something has been heard of "reform." Mormonism had also its "Reformation." But there was nothing in common between the notable reformations in the world's history and that which is inscribed in the annals of the Rocky Mountain territory in 1856.

The Mormon writers have been studiously silent about the "Reformation" in Utah, and here the Author would have gladly passed it by; but he feels that, furnishing as it does a clue to some of the worst crimes which blacken the page of American history, its tale of horrors imperatively demands a place in this volume.

While many important features in the lives of the Utah Saints will pass away and be forgotten, the "Reformation" will be remembered for ever. It was the outburst of the worst elements of fanaticism—a fanaticism at once blind, dangerous, and terrible, but at the same time the natural result of the teachings of the Tabernacle.

The Author, not being then in Utah, presents to the reader a graphic sketch—never before published—from the pen of an eye-witness, then and now a resident of Salt Lake City:

"Early in the fall of 1856, president Jedediah M. Grant went to Kaysville, about twenty-five miles north of Salt Lake City, to preach and hold a local conference meeting. He invited a few elders to meet him there, and take part in the exercises with him. To one of these elders he lent his mule to bear him thither. One of the party being a good horseman made the others keep up, going at a good pace; and on arrival at the bishop's house at Kaysville, where 'brother Jeddy' awaited them, he scanned the animals closely; they seemed to be heated, sweating, and rather jaded. No remarks were

The Beginning of the Reformation—"Jeddy's" Mule.

made just then, and the whole party, apparently with good feeling, went to the meeting together. The brethren delivered themselves in their usual style, and 'seemed good' in testifying to 'the work,' exhorting their hearers to faithfulness. Jedediah was the last speaker, and, during his remarks, he charged his brethren, the elders, in the bitterest manner with cruelty to his mule and the other animals, and with riding in such a manner as to nearly kill them. After denouncing the speakers who had preceded him for inconsistency between their preaching and practice, and accusing them of hypocrisy, he assailed the bishop and his counsellors for inactivity and carelessness, and charged the congregation generally with all manner of wickedness, calling upon them to repent and 'do 'their first works over again,' or God's judgment would overtake them speedily. Thus began the noted 'Reformation' in Utah, and 'accusation 'of the brethren' became forthwith a mania with this reformer. The same spirit was caught quickly by others, who found it easier to break and pull down than to teach, inspire, and build up, and it was quickly diffused everywhere throughout Zion.

"Another meeting was appointed to convene in a few weeks, when 'Jeddy' and most of the elders then present were again there. Accusation after accusation, more bitter than before, was hurled at the 'Saints,' and they were commanded to be *re-baptized*.* In accordance with this, after the exercises at night, numbers were re-baptized by the elders, and though the weather was cold and unfavourable, Jeddy himself remained in the water until he shivered with cold and contracted the disease from which he never recovered.

* It is a privilege accorded to the Mormons to be "baptized for the remission "of sins" not only on entering the Church, but as often afterwards as conscience may demand it.

294

ROCKY MOUNTAIN SAINTS.

"At the Tabernacle in Salt Lake City, Jedediah addressed the Saints every Sunday afterwards, charging them with sins and crimes of almost every description. The bishops were 'whipped' for dereliction of duty, for being 'old fogies,' and not being strict in making the Saints pay their tithing to 'the Lord.' All were called upon to confess their sins, and to make known to God's servant the crimes of which they were guilty. The most extravagant language and bitter denunciations were uttered against the Saints, and strict, unquestioning obedience to the priesthood was commanded in all things, with the consecration of body, soul, and property to the Church. Individuals were hinted at and sins imputed to them which they dared not deny, nor even attempt to defend themselves, however innocent they might be.

" 'I would advise some of you men here,' said Jeddy on one occasion, ' to go to President Young and confess your sins, and ask him to take you ' outside the city and have your blood shed to atone for your sins.' ' All that you have and are belong to God, and must be devoted to his Church. Not only your money, and goods, and talents, but your wives and children should be at all times ready to be devoted to his servant.'

" ' If President Young wants my wives I will give them to him without a grumble, and he can take them whenever he likes.'

" Heber C. Kimball felt only too happy to follow in the wake of Grant : he used the most disgusting vituperatives, for which he was noted, and indulged in unheard-of accusations.

" He declared to the people that Brigham Young was his God, and their God, and the only God they would ever see if they did not obey him: ' Joseph Smith was God to the inhabitants of the earth when he was 'amongst us, and Brigham is God now.' This strain was caught up and reiterated by many of the elders, from Orson Hyde, the president of the twelve apostles, down to the most ignorant teacher, and to question it openly was to be put under the ban.

" Meetings were held throughout the city, and 'missionaries' were appointed to preach in and visit every ward throughout the Territory.

" The elders returning from Europe were appointed to preach to the people, and to learn their sins. In the excitement, to which every one was expected to bend and catch 'the spirit of the work,' men—immoral, ignorant men—were sent as 'home missionaries' to keep them at work, that they might thereby gain their living irrespective of qualification or religious worth.

" Three brethren, notorious for earning their living by fiddling at the dances, and who were in every respect unqualified to teach moral principles, were ordered to go as missionaries and make their living in that capacity, as the 'Reformation' allowed no dancing. These men—H—p H——r, J—n J——s, and J—h M——y—ignorant themselves of knowing anything of religious truth, and innocent of attempting to acquire it, the laughing-stock secretly of the better informed, would shout out, ' wake up,' ' repent,' ' obey counsel,' ' pay tithing,' ' consecrate your property to the Church,' 'get more wives,' and 'give us a good collection,' and they were deemed full of 'the Spirit.'

"Elders were sent to the various settlements and stationed at certain places, whose duty it was to excite people to confess their secret sins and reveal their private conduct to them and the bishops. Teachers were appointed in every ward and for every block, whose duties were to pry into every secret and learn the private history of every family. Men, women, *and children were asked the most indelicate questions about private actions and secret thoughts.* Husbands were asked inconvenient questions about relations with their wives, and wives about their husbands, by rude and ignorant teachers, and 'counsel' was given accordingly. Girls were counselled to marry into polygamy to old men 'that they might be saved,' for young men were 'not tried' in the kingdom and could not 'save' the girls; and in many instances young women were forced to break off engagements with young men whom they loved, to gratify a bishop's preference, a missionary's feelings, or a great elder's desires.

"Meetings were held by all the 'Quorums' of 'High Priests,' 'Seventies,' and 'Bishops,' which were largely attended. The greatest zeal for the good of 'the kingdom' and unquestioning obedience were manifested, and the weak in faith, the doubting, and rebellious were, with 'Uncle Sam' and all the Gentiles, denounced without mercy.

"A catechism was printed by authority of Brigham Young, and a copy of it was put into the hands of every missionary, elder, bishop and teacher, who catechized with unblushing effrontery every member of the Church. Those refusing to answer were cursed and reported at the bishops' meetings as worthy to be disfellowshipped, and those who honestly told their feelings were likewise reported to the authorities, and became objects of attack and abuse at the public meetings, while their private characters became topics of scandal and gossip.

"The confessions of the Saints were texts for discourses, and curses were hurled on them publicly. The revelation of sins wormed out of them by the catechism and other methods adopted were astonishing, and a lower state of morals was discovered to exist than even the best informed could have suspected.

"Polygamy, notwithstanding the claims of the Utah writers, had not prevented illicit intercourse between the sexes. No houses of professional prostitution publicly opened their doors invitingly to the Saints, but secret confessions showed that private evils existed in the cities of professed Saints which were not surpassed by the inhabitants of many cities of 'Babylon' in which 'all classes and conditions of men' do congregate. Thefts, roguishness, cheating, and lying were divulged, which had been carried on for years. As illustrative of this let me recite a pretty well-known occurrence.

"On one occasion a public meeting was called at the Social Hall, which was very largely attended by the priesthood or male members only. Brigham, Heber, 'Jeddy,' and others addressed the elders. Blind and burning zeal prompted the meanest accusations and aspersions. The confessions, as before observed, were groundwork for reproofs, rebukes, and denunciations. Brigham in his speech put a motion as follows : 'All you 'who have been guilty of committing adultery, stand up.' To the surprise of some, and the chagrin of the presidency, more than three-fourths stood on their feet.* Of course, no women being present, the men only answered for themselves—the inference could only be imagined about the other sex.

"The truthful and simple replies to the questions of the catechism revealed more than was expected. Confidence and respect were lost, and society seemed to be falling in pieces. Brigham, seeing the evil results of such priestcraft and fanaticism in the hands of ignorant elders, gave general instructions, by obedience to which the Saints could evade the disgrace and publicity of their confessions. Said he : 'Repent of your sins, and 'be baptized for the remission of sins, and, as they are washed away by 'the ordinance of baptism, you can say truly that you are *not* guilty of the 'sins inquired of by the catechism, though you may have committed them.' Many easily caught at this clue and rushed to the baptismal waters to be cleansed from their iniquities, and to bury their sins from mortal eyes.

"At the meetings of the priesthood, schemes were mooted and plans adopted to remove everything obnoxious to the 'interests of the kingdom.' The reported conduct of the Gentiles was discussed and opinions were offered concerning those who were suspected of being weak in the faith, or those who were independent enough to offer opinions adverse to the course of some in authority. Extreme measures, based upon false re-

---

* "A leading bishop in Salt Lake City recently stated to the Author that Brigham was as much appalled at this sight as was Macbeth when he beheld the woods of Birnam marching on to Dunsinane. A bishop arose and asked if there were not some misunderstanding among the brethren concerning the question. He thought that perhaps the elders understood Brigham's inquiry to apply to their conduct before they had thrown off the works of the devil and embraced Mormonism ; but upon Brigham reiterating that it was the adultery committed since they had entered the Church, the brethren to a man still stood up. Brigham had evoked a spectre that he little expected.

A gentleman, who in one of the counties filled the position of "Father Confessor" in those times, frankly admits the truthfulness of the report about the meeting, but protests against it being regarded as an indication of the actual morality of the mass of the people of Utah. In that interpretation the Author fully concurs, for though the number in this assembly who confessed their guilt was, as reported, very large, the violation of morality has to be considered as occurring at some time during the whole course of their lives as Mormons. It does not seem possible that much of this could have occurred in Utah. During the twenty-five years' association of the Author with Mormonism, he never knew of more than two or three cases of this kind, and the transgressors were immediately excommunicated. Without considering the penalty of the " endowment " [death], there has always been a dreadful horror of the crime of adultery in the minds of the Mormons.

ports, were used towards many, and the victims had no time or opportunity to explain, nor any means of redress afterwards. The following are some instances in point.

"During a meeting of the faithful missionaries held in the Historian's office, presided over by Brother Brigham, when zeal ran high and testimonies were delivered, and determination of faithfulness expressed in the warmest manner, several brethren walked out to perform some mission that had been pre-arranged. That same evening the house and store of Mr. H. J. Jarvis was entered by some brethren in disguise. They walked into his store, and when he had served a customer present, they suddenly caught him by the hair of his head and dragged him over the counter,

Reforming a Heretic.

pulled him into the street, and threw him on to the snow, threatening his life if he made a noise. They reëntered his store, took what they pleased to the amount of $750, set fire to the place, besmeared the parlor furniture with their own filth, and decamped, 'breathing threatenings and slaughter.' His wives (for he had two sweetly-dispositioned, good women) rushed up stairs to save the children, and after returning with them succeeded in extinguishing the fire, which had now reached to within one foot of the powder, but not without burning their arms and hands. Mr. Jarvis and family went to a neighbour's house occupied by elder ——, the representative of 'God' in the Endowment House, for protection, but were refused shelter, Brother —— saying that they could not remain there.

" 'Why?' asked Mr. Jarvis.

" 'Because Israel is at work.'

" 'What have I done to be thus treated, and to be refused shelter for my family?' asked Mr. Jarvis.

" 'You have spoken evil of the authorities,' replied the Elder, who seemed to know the cause and to have expected the result.

" 'I have never done so,' said Mr. Jarvis.

" 'You have had Gentiles to supper in your house,' again replied the Elder.

" 'I never had; but if I had, I had a perfect right to do so if I liked,' was the honest reply.

"Mr. Jarvis was a man of unimpeachable moral character, a respectable merchant, and would be esteemed a good citizen in any community. He went to Daniel Spencer, President of the Stake of Zion, and to Bishop

Kesler in the ward in which the outrage occurred, to seek protection, as he was afraid of his life. Mr. Spencer sympathized with him very much privately, but could not obtain for him an interview with Brigham. Kesler could do nothing for him, regretted the abuse, and promised that he would see to it that he should be no further molested.

"William H. Wilson, a man of excellent character and much talent, was a clerk in General Burr's office. At a late hour at night a rap was heard at his door. He arose out of bed, slipped on his trowsers, and went to the door. There he was seized by several strong men and taken away forcibly towards Jordan river, and detained there by the ruffians till next night. He was abused and his life threatened. He inquired the cause of the seizure, and was told that he was clerking for a United States' official, and was writing articles to New York papers against the Church. This he emphatically denied.

"Their intention he believed was to kill him, but before attempting the act, one of the party who knew Mr. Wilson well and wanted to serve him, stated that they ought to be certain of his guilt before doing violence. After some deliberation it was agreed to release him upon condition that he would swear never to divulge the outrage and its perpetrators. His wife, who suffered indescribably during this time, sought to obtain an interview with Governor Young, but there was no access to his august presence for the wife of a person so weak in the faith and who was in the hands of the minions of the Church. Mr. Landon, likewise a clerk in General Burr's office, fled when he heard of the seizure of Mr. Wilson, and escaped on foot to Virginia, Nevada, report says, suffering horribly for food, and shoes, and shelter.

"Job Salter, watchmaker, a good citizen, was taken from his house by some faithful elders at night, whipped and abused because he did not enter into all the spirit of the 'Reformation' and accuse himself of sins, but was allowed to return to his family after being sworn not disclose the perpetrators of the foul deed.

"Brigham Young, who was not only president of the Church, but governor of the Territory, took no notice of these and other outrages, but by his silence gave reason to believe that he countenanced the villainy. These outrages were the legitimate result of the teaching of the elders in the Tabernacle, the doctrines set forth by Jedediah Grant, and even by Brigham Young himself.

"The sweetest words that Jesus ever uttered—' Love thy neighbour as thyself,' were commented upon by Brigham to show that a man would be loving his neighbour as himself if he killed him 'rather than he should 'apostatize.' * This terrible rendering of the Gospel of humanity is too well

* Such a perversion of the language of Jesus by any person professing Christianity might appear to the reader utterly impossible ; but that Brigham Young did so interpret these words, and fully commended his interpretation being carried into effect, the following extract from his sermon will demonstrate :

"When will we love our neighbours as ourselves ? In the first place, Jesus

remembered by many. The results of such teachings were experienced in the outrages committed during the height of the so-called 'Reformation,' in various parts of the Territory, while those alone were pronounced faithful who were most imbued with this horrid fanaticism. Many more examples might be given.

"Everything that was not ordered and presided over by the priesthood, was denounced as leading to apostacy, and all who did not take an active part in self-accusation of the meanest kind were suspected of deep sin, and treated accordingly. For example, a number of young elders of literary tastes and acquirements, some of whom were acknowledged to be

said that no man hateth his own flesh. It is admitted by all that every person loves himself. Now if we do rightly love ourselves we want to be saved and continue to exist, we want to go into the kingdom where we can enjoy eternity and see no more sorrow nor death. This is the desire of every person who believes in God. Now take a person in this congregation who has knowledge with regard to being saved in the kingdom of our God and our Father, and being exalted, one who knows and understands the principles of eternal life, and sees the beauties and excellency of the eternities before him compared with the vain and foolish things of the world, and suppose that he is overtaken in a gross fault, that he has committed a sin that he knows will deprive him of that exaltation which he desires, and that he cannot attain to it without the shedding of his blood, and also knows that by having his blood shed he will atone for that sin and be saved and exalted with the gods, is there a man or woman in this house but would say ' Shed my blood that I might be 'saved and exalted with the gods?'

"All mankind love themselves: and let those principles be known by an individual, and *he would be glad to have his blood shed. This would be loving ourselves even unto an eternal exaltation. Will you love your brothers or sisters likewise when they have a sin that cannot be atoned for without the shedding of their blood? Will you love that man or woman well enough to shed their blood?* THAT IS WHAT JESUS CHRIST MEANT. He never told a man or woman to love their enemies in their wickedness, never. He never meant any such thing; His language is left as it is for those to read who have the spirit to discern between truth and error; it was so left for those who can discern the things of God. Jesus Christ never meant that we should love a wicked man in his wickedness.

"*I could refer you to plenty of instances where men have been righteously slain in order to atone for their sins.* I have seen scores and hundreds of people for whom there would have been a chance (in the last resurrection there will be) if their lives had been taken and their blood spilled on the ground as a smoking incense to the Almighty, but who are now angels to the devil, until our elder brother, Jesus Christ, raises them up, conquers death, hell, and the grave.

"I have known a great many men who have left this Church *for whom there is no chance whatever for exaltation, but if their blood had been spilled it would have been better for them.*

"*The wickedness and ignorance of the nations forbid this principle being in full force, but* THE TIME WILL COME WHEN THE LAW OF GOD WILL BE IN FULL FORCE. *This is loving our neighbour as ourselves; if he needs help,* HELP HIM; *if he wants salvation and it is necessary to spill his blood on the earth in order that he may be saved,* SPILL IT.

"Any of you who understand the principles of eternity, if you have sinned a sin requiring the shedding of blood, except the sin unto death, should not be satisfied or rest until your blood should be spilled, that you might gain that salvation you desire. THAT IS THE WAY TO LOVE MANKIND. . . . Light and darkness cannot dwell together, and so it is with the kingdom of God.

"Now brethren and sisters, will you live your religion? How many hundreds of times have I asked that question? Will the Latter-Day Saints live their religion?"

Discourse in the Tabernacle, February 8, 1857, published in the "Journal of Discourses," Vol. IV., pp. 219, 220.

men of superior talent, organized a 'Literary and Musical Society,' a few months before the 'Reformation' began. They gave public entertainments to their friends, which consisted of original essays and poems, recitations, declamations, orations and music. They had ample talent among their own committee to occupy the evenings fully and to make them highly interesting; but as they designed to diffuse a love of literature and music throughout Zion, they called in all the talent that surrounded them. Any new arrival from the States or Europe possessed of talent was at once waited upon and requested to add to the interest of the entertainment. The society became very popular, was conducted in an interesting manner, and was governed as a thoroughly democratic institution, each member of the committee occupying the chair and keeping door in turn. This society would have done credit to any city in the world, and would have reflected honour on its originators. The meetings which were held weekly were opened and closed by singing and prayer. But they became too popular, and flourished without the president's direction, and consequently drew forth the denunciations of Brigham, Heber, and 'Jeddy.' In the public meetings at the Tabernacle the committee and society became the objects of ridicule, contempt and abuse, charging them with pride, ambition, big-headedness, conceit, and sins. A meeting was afterwards called by the society, its object being, after the exercises were concluded, to dissolve itself. Brigham, Heber, and 'Jeddy' were present, and, on being invited to speak, belittled and berated the institution, and on being informed that the society would dissolve that evening, the leaders recommended—which was equal to a command—that the members become associated with the 'Theological Institution,' a pet association that had died about three years before, but had that evening very conveniently revived. Its first death was caused by the short-sighted course characterizing many of Brigham's policies, by appointing favourites to occupy positions and hold offices who had neither ability, taste, nor education to fill them. This institution swallowed the Literary and Musical Society in one night; but it was too great a gulp, and it died again in two weeks, never to be revived.

"In order to add insult to injury and to crush the committee completely, the next Sunday, in the Tabernacle, eight of the most prominent and efficient members of the Literary and Musical Society were called to be door-keepers at the Tabernacle!

" On the motion being announced to that effect a titter passed through the vast congregation, most of whom understood the matter to be a punishment. The gentlemen, 'obedient to the heavenly call,' entered at once upon their newly appointed duties, and honoured the office, if the office did not honour them. They did their duty, and were afterwards complimented for their efficiency and punctuality by those who sought to crush them.

" The 'Reformation' wrought more evil than good, and it is now regarded by the best men in the Church as the height of folly and fanaticism. To Jedediah—a positive, impulsive, bigoted man—it became a monomania; but it brought Brigham, Heber, and others into its spirit willingly, as it is more consonant with the feelings of ignorant, untutored zealots to condemn, debase, and degrade others, than to lead them to virtue, goodness, and a higher life by noble precepts and loving teachings.

"The 'Reformation' was employed as a means to compel hundreds and thousands to engage in the practice of polygamy; and it was hinted and secretly taught by authority that women should form relations with more than one man.* Bigotry, intolerance, and tyranny were fostered by it; weakness, folly, and sins were publicly exposed; mutual confidence was destroyed; bad feelings and suspicions were engendered; self-righteousness and egotism were manifested by many; sensuousness in matters of religion, and materialism were its characteristics; spirituality and piety were condemned; and narrow, low, exclusive dogmas were received as the sublimest truths.

"When the excitement of fanaticism had died away, and calm reflection enlightened the minds of those in authority; when they had seen and learned the evil effects of the movement, they deeply regretted the part they had taken in it, and Brigham Young himself has frequently said in public that he was 'ashamed of the Reformation.'   . . . ."

With the above statement the author received the following letter:

"SALT LAKE CITY, *November* 30, 1871.

"DEAR STENHOUSE: I have read carefully the accompanying statement about the 'Reformation.' I know personally most of the particulars to be true, and the rest I am perfectly convinced are literally correct. If you want to travel wider and show the effect in the country of the inflammatory speeches delivered in Salt Lake City at that time, you can mention the Potter and Parrish murders at Springville, the barbarous castration of a young man in San Pete, and, to cap the climax, the Mountain-Meadows massacre; for although Brigham, in my opinion, never ordered these murders, they were the obviously legitimate results of the teachings of himself, Heber, 'Jeddy,' and other leaders. They taught that 'righteous'ness was laid to the line, and judgment to the plummet;' that 'the sin'ner in Zion should tremble, and fearfulness should seize the hypocrite;' that 'the tree which did not bring forth good fruit should be hewn down;'

* The Author has no personal knowledge, from the present leaders of the Church, of this teaching; but he has often heard that something would yet be taught which "would test the brethren as much as polygamy had tried the sisters." By many elders it has been believed that there was some foundation for the accusation that Joseph had taught some sisters in Nauvoo that it was their privilege to entertain other brethren as "proxy husbands" during the absence of their liege lords on mission. One lady has informed the Author that Joseph so taught her. All such teaching has never been made public, and it is doubtful if it ever extended very far, if, indeed, at all beyond the momentary combination of passion and fanaticism.

etc. [Emphasis was laid on the words '*hewn down*,' 'judgment,' 'tremble,' and others equally suggestive.] 'We must not,' it was said, 'ask
'God to punish our enemies, when we could do it ourselves.' Threats of
personal violence or death were common in the settlements against all who
dared to speak against the priesthood, or in any way protest against this
'reign of terror.'

"I was at a Sunday meeting in the spring of 1857, in Provo, when the
news of the San Pete castration was referred to by the presiding bishop
—Blackburn. Some men in Provo had rebelled against authority in some
trivial matter, and Blackburn shouted in his Sunday meeting—a mixed
congregation of all ages and both sexes—'I want the people of Provo
'to understand that the boys in Provo can use the knife as well as the
'boys in San Pete. Boys, get your knives ready, there is work for you !
'We must not be behind San Pete in *good works*.' The result of this was
that two citizens, named Hooper and Beauvere, both having families at
Provo, left the following night for Fort Bridger, and returned only after
Johnston's army came into the valley the following year. Their only offence was rebellion against the priesthood.

"This man, Blackburn, was continued in office at least a year after this,
and was afterwards taken from his bishopric and sent on a mission to
England.

"The qualifications for a bishop were a blind submission and obedience
to Brigham and the authorities, and a firm, unrelenting government of his
subjects. Strict and invariable obedience to their file leaders, 'asking no
'questions for conscience sake,' makes a good Saint. To pay tithing will
cover a multitude of sins.

"I might fill page after page in illustrating the condition of affairs, but
I presume you are posted generally on the subject. . . . .

"As ever yours, ..."

To note the hurried expressions of extempore speakers in
moments of excitement, and treasure them up as evidence
against their authors, would justly be considered by every candid person a highly censurable action. In like manner, had
the influence of the Tabernacle speeches already alluded to,
from which resulted the " Reformation," ended with their immediate effect upon the audiences present, it would perhaps be
unfair to resuscitate them. But the "discourses" were not
intended to be forgotten, neither did this occur upon one occasion only : they extended over a period of several years. The
Church organ, the *Deseret News*, carefully printed them after
they had been trimmed by a cautious secretary and super-
vised by the speakers themselves. It was the intention of the
Prophet and the apostles that their words should circulate

widely and be engraven upon the hearts of the people. They believed that they were moved by "divine inspiration" as the favour of "the gods," and could do no less than desire that all the world should benefit by it.

After these noteworthy sermons had been published in Utah, they were republished in the "Journal of Discourses," in Liverpool, in order that the European Saints might also "learn the will of God" through his servants. If ever the modern prophets and apostles could afford to challenge criticism upon their sincerity it was then. They were in earnest, even to the sacrifice of life, and a faithful historian has preserved the record of that time of zeal and devotion among the Saints.

Fortunately there was a government of the United States with a name of authority over Utah—if even no more than a name—or what might not have transpired? If men, standing at the head of the Church, could utter such sentiments as were then openly taught to the Saints and published to the world, while at the same time they were restrained by the knowledge that their words were noted by the Government and people of the United States, what would they not have said and done had their kingdom been established and they bearing unquestioned rule over the people in the mountains? Besides which, these sentiments were not the utterances of a day or a year; they were the enunciations of a programme that was sacredly believed. What Utah might have been under an unchallenged theocratic rule, what she would be with the full sway of the priesthood guaranteed under the proposed State of Deseret, is clearly shewn in the following edifying passages.

Some time before the "Reformation" had got fairly under way, this Jedediah M. Grant, the counsellor of Brigham, the third man in "the kingdom," addressing the Saints—men, women, and children—in the Tabernacle, March 12, 1854, upon the proper penalty for breaking the covenants of the Church, says:

"Then what ought this meek people who keep the commandments of God do unto them? 'Why,' says one, 'they ought *to pray to the Lord to kill them.*' I want to know if you would wish the Lord *to come down and do all your dirty work?* Many of the Latter-Day Saints will pray, and petition, and supplicate the Lord to do a thousand things they themselves would be ashamed to do. . . . .

19

" *When a man prays for a thing, he ought to be willing to perform it him-self*. But if the Latter-Day Saints should put to death the covenant-breakers, it would try the faith of the 'very meek, just, and pious' ones among them, and *it would cause a great deal of whining in Israel.*

" Then there was another odd commandment. The Lord God com-manded them *not to pity the person whom they killed*, but to execute the law of God upon persons worthy of death. *This should be done by the en-tire congregation, showing no pity.* I have thought there would have to be quite a revolution among the Mormons before such a commandment could be obeyed completely by them. The Mormons have a great deal of sym-pathy. For instance, if they can get a man before the tribunal adminis-tering the law of the land, and succeed in getting a rope around his neck, and having him hung up like a dead dog, it is all right. *But if the Church and kingdom of God should step forth and execute the law of God*, oh, what a burst of Mormon sympathy it would cause ! *I wish we were in a situation favourable to our doing that which is justifiable before God, without any con-taminating influence of Gentile amalgamation, laws, and traditions, that the people of God might lay the axe to the root of the tree, and every tree that bringeth not forth good fruit might be hewn down.*

" What ! do you believe that people would do right, and keep the law of God, by *actually putting to death the transgressors ?* Putting to death the transgressors *would exhibit the law of God, no matter by whom it was done.* That is my opinion.

" You talk of the doings of different governments—the United States, if you please. What do they do with traitors ? What mode do they adopt to punish traitors ? Do traitors to that government forfeit their lives ? Examine also the doings of other earthly governments on this point, and you find the same practice universal. I am not aware that there are any exceptions. But people will look into books of theology, and argue that the people of God have a right to try people for fellowship, but they have no right to try them on property or life. *That makes the devil laugh*, saying : I have got them on a hook now ; they can cut them off, and I will put eight or ten spirits worse than they are into their taber-nacles, and send them back to mob them."

In the midst of the excitement of the " Reformation," Brig-ham assured the Saints that these throat-cutting, blood-spilling doctrines that had been taught to them by the elders were meritorious, glorious, and soul-saving. Here are his words :

" There are sins that men commit for which they cannot receive for-giveness in this world, or in that which is to come ; and *if they had their eyes open to their true condition, they would be perfectly willing to have their blood spilt upon the ground, that the smoke thereof might ascend to heaven as an offering for their sins, and the smoking incense would atone for their sins ; whereas, if such is not the case, they will stick to them and remain upon them in the spirit-world.*

" I know, when you hear my brethren telling about *cutting people off from the earth*, that you consider it is strong doctrine ; but *it is to save them*, not to destroy them. . . . .

" It is true the blood of the Son of God was shed for sins through the fall, and those committed by men, yet men can commit sins which it can, never remit. As it was in ancient days, so it is in our day ; and though the principles are taught publicly from this stand, still the people do not understand them ; yet the law is precisely the same. There are sins that can be atoned for by an offering upon an altar as in ancient days ; and *there are sins that the blood of a lamb, of a calf, or of turtle doves cannot remit*, but *they must be atoned for by the blood of the man.* That is the reason why men talk to you as they do from this stand ; *they understand the doctrine*, and throw out a few words about it. *You have been taught that doctrine, but you do not understand it.*" *

Jedediah, ever ready to bless the Saints, urged an immediate beginning. The following is a choice piece of counsel :

" I say there are men and women here that I would advise to *go to the president immediately, and ask him to appoint a committee to attend to their case ; and then let a place be selected, and let that committee shed their blood.*" †

Believing that the reformation was to bring to pass that day of separation of " wheat and tares," " sheep and goats," the divine inspiration of Brigham, on the 2nd of March, 1856, was very emphatic and clear on the manner in which the work should be accomplished.

" The time is coming when justice will be laid to the line, and righteousness to the plummet ; when *we shall take the old broadsword, and ask, ' Are you for God ? ' and if you are not heartily on the Lord's side, you will be hewn down.*" ‡

" We have been trying long enough with this people, and I go in for letting the sword of the Almighty to be unsheathed, not only in word, but in deed." § J. M. GRANT.

The evidence that this admitted of no figurative interpretation, but meant truly all that it expresses, was furnished by Brigham as early as 1853. A Mormon elder of the name of Albert Smith, who had some leaning towards the revelations of one Gladden Bishop (a genius who figured in Nauvoo), went from St. Louis to Salt Lake. This Smith and some friends at-

---

* Tabernacle, September 21, 1856. † Ibid.
‡ " Journal of Discourses," vol. iii., p. 226. § *Deseret News*, October 1, 1856.

tempted to address the Mormons in the public street one Sunday just as Brigham was going home from the Tabernacle. On the following Sunday, March 27, 1853, Brigham was running over with " the Spirit," and revealed himself on the subject of apostacy :

" When I went from meeting last Sabbath, my ears were saluted with an apostate crying in the streets here. I want to know if any one of you who has got the spirit of Mormonism in you, the spirit that Joseph and Hyrum had, or that we have here, would say, ' Let us hear both sides of ' the question. Let us listen and prove all things.' What do you want to prove ? Do you want to prove that an old apostate, who has been cut off from the Church thirteen times for lying, is anything worthy of notice ? I heard that a certain picture-maker in this city, when the boys would have moved away the wagon in which this apostate was standing, became violent with them, saying, ' Let this man alone ; these are Saints ' that you are persecuting.' [Sneeringly.]

" We want such men to go to California, or anywhere they choose. I say to those persons, ' You must not court persecution here, lest you get so much of it you will not know what to do with it. Do NOT court persecution.' We have known Gladden Bishop for more than twenty years, and know him to be a poor dirty curse. Here is sister Vilate Kimball, brother Heber's wife, has borne more from that man than any other woman on earth could bear ; but she won't bear it again. I say again, you Gladdenites, do not court persecution, or you will get more than you want, and it will come quicker than you want it.

" I say to you, bishops, do not allow them to preach in your wards. Who broke the road to these valleys ? Did this little nasty Smith and his wife ? No. They stayed in St. Louis, while we did it, peddling ribbons, and kissing the Gentiles. I know what they have done here—they have asked exorbitant prices for their nasty stinking ribbons. [Voices, ' That's true.'] We broke the roads to this country.

" Now, you Gladdenites, keep your tongues still, *lest sudden destruction come upon you.* I say rather than that the apostates should flourish here, *I will unsheath my bowie-knife, and conquer or die.* [Great commotion in the congregation, and a simultaneous burst of feeling, assenting to the declaration.] Now, you nasty apostates, *clear out, or 'judgment will be 'laid to the line, and righteousness to the plummet.'* [Voices generally, ' Go it, go it ! '] If you say it is all right, raise your hands. [All hands up.] *Let us call upon the Lord to assist us in this and every other good work.*"

The foregoing is a literal quotation from the *Deseret News,* republished in the " Journal of Discourses," vol. i., p. 82.

These extracts, repeatedly published by the Church authorities, first in the *Deseret News*, in Salt Lake City, and afterwards in the *Millennial Star* office in Liverpool, are evidences of the sincerity of Brigham Young. No sane man—fanatic though he might be—would use this threatening and bloodthirsty language, at the same time being fully aware of his own responsibility, unless he were sincere. He assuredly believed that "life and death" were in the hands of the priesthood. He believes it still; and the exercise of such a power was " not to destroy, but to save ! "

With Judge Drummond on the Pacific coast publishing every possible charge of villainy and despotism against the leaders of the Church, asserting that law could not be administered in the Territory, and that the records of the Supreme Court had been burned ; with Judge Stiles at Washington representing to the Government that he had been intimidated and threatened, and had been forced to close his court ; and with a host of correspondents writing exciting statements to all parts of the Union about the " reign of terror," inaugurated by the " Reformation," the nation was wrought up to the highest pitch of indignation.

The administration of President Pierce was drawing to a close and did not choose to inaugurate any new measures, but this seeming indifference on the part of the Government only stirred up the opponents of Brigham Young to greater exertions, and every measure was adopted to secure some decided action.

That busy class of men who hang around Washington " waiting for something to turn up," soon saw an appropriate occasion for a display of force to bring Brigham to a realization of his obligations to the national Government. Contractors and would-be contractors became urgent for action, representatives and senators became fierce in their denunciation of the outrages in Utah, and every violent word and action of the Mormon priesthood henceforth was construed into "rebellion " against the United States."

At the organization of the Republican party, Brigham Young and the Mormons occupied too much attention to be overlooked, and in the framing of its first platform Utah was raised to a kindred association with the South, and in every

campaign procession where John C. Fremont was the standard
bearer of the party, there could be read :

> " The Abolishment of Slavery and Polygamy ; the Twin Relics of
> Barbarism."

While the affairs of Utah were thus before the nation, and
coming events, portending war, were casting forth their shadows, a sad page was added to the history of Mormon emigration.

THE HAND-CART EMIGRANTS IN A STORM.

CHAPTER XXXVII.

EMIGRATING TO UTAH WITH HAND-CARTS.—Mr. Chislett's Narrative—
The "Divine Plan" for emigrating the Poor—Outfitting in Iowa City—Organ-
izing the Company—Journey through Iowa—The Elders prophesy a Successful
Journey—Brother Savage protests—"Inspirational" Counsel followed—The
Carts break down—Cattle are lost—The Apostle Richards prophesies in the
Name of the God of Israel—The Elders eat the Fatted Calf—Arrival at Fort
Laramie—Provisions become scarce—Great Privations—The People begin to
faint by the Way—Captain Willie's Bravery—The Winter overtakes them—
Snow on the Mountains—The Sweetwater—Great Distress, Disease, and Death—
Envoys from Salt Lake Valley—Provisions all gone—Captain Willie goes in
search of Aid—Terrible Condition of the People—Courage and Faithfulness of
the Sufferers—Arrival of Timely Aid—A Thrilling Scene—Hope revived—
" Too Late "—Ravages of Death—A Hard Road—An Old Man's Death—" Thirteen Corpses all Stiffly Frozen "—Fifteen buried in One Grave—The Ending of
the Journey—Great Kindness of the Elders and People of Utah—The Pilgrims
enter Zion—Sixty-seven Emigrants dead on the Journey—Greater Losses in
another Company—Folly of Modern Prophecies.

THE story of the Hand-Cart Emigration to Utah that fills
so melancholy a page in the history of the Mormon people
could only be written properly by one who had himself passed
through the sufferings which it relates. A gentleman now in
Salt Lake City, and formerly a fellow-labourer with the Author in the Mormon missions, furnishes a graphic history equal-
ling in interest the finest pages of fiction, yet strikingly true,
and exhibiting a rare devotion that commands respect. He at
first declined to affix his name, but the Author, persuaded of
the value of his narrative, succeeded at last in inducing him to
consent.

Mr. Chislett is a gentleman who enjoys the confidence and
respect of those who know him, both in Europe and in the

United States; and this episode of his life, illustrating as it does a phase of Mormon emigration, and exploding the presumptuous folly of the predictions of modern apostles, will be read with deep interest.

MR. CHISLETT'S NARRATIVE.

PART I.

THE PILGRIMS SET OUT FOR ZION.

"For several years previous to 1856, the poorer portion of the Mormon emigrants from Europe to Utah made the overland journey from 'the Frontiers' to Salt Lake City by ox-teams, under the management of the Church agents, who were generally elders returning to Utah after having performed missions in Europe or the Eastern States. The cost of the journey from Liverpool to Salt Lake by this method was from £10 to £12. All the emigrants who were obliged to travel in this manner were, if able, expected to walk all the way, or at least the greater part of the way. The teams were used for hauling provisions, and 100 lbs. of luggage were allowed to each emigrant. Old people, feeble women and children, generally could ride when they wished. The overland portion of the journey occupied from ten to twelve weeks.

"This was a safe method of emigration, and it added to the wealth of the new Territory by increasing its quota of live stock, wagons, and such articles of clothing, tools, etc., as the emigrants brought. These were all much needed in Utah in early days, and families going to the Territory with a surplus found good opportunities for exchanging them for land and the produce of the Valley. Many families came out with their own wagons; some of the more wealthy having several well laden with necessary articles. The growth and prosperity of the Territory were slow, gradual, and natural, and as each successive company of emigrants arrived they found the country prepared to receive them. Employment could generally be obtained by the mechanics (especially of the building trades) as soon as they arrived. The wealthy could find cultivated land at fair prices without having to endure the hardship of making new homes on unbroken land, while the agricultural labourer could always find a welcome among the farmers. Artisans and men of no trade were the only class who were really out of place. They had to begin life anew and strike out fresh pursuits, suffering frequently in the undertaking. But the general condition was prosperous.

"The growth of the colony was not, however, sufficiently rapid to suit the ambitious mind of Brigham Young. Thousands of faithful devotees of the Church were waiting patiently in Europe to join the new Zion of the West, but all their faith in Brigham was practically valueless. To be of any real benefit to the Church they must gather in Zion. The question

was, how to transfer to Utah those who could not raise the necessary £10
sterling. The matter was discussed in the winter of 1855-6, in Salt
Lake City, by Brigham and his chief men. After much debate their
united wisdom devised and adopted a system of emigration across the
plains by hand-carts, as being cheaper and consequently better under the
circumstances for bringing the faithful poor from Europe.

"Whether Brigham was influenced in his desire to get the poor of
Europe more rapidly to Utah by his sympathy with their condition, by
his well-known love of power, his glory in numbers, or his love of wealth,
which an increased amount of subservient labour would enable him to
acquire, is best known to himself. But the sad results of his Hand-Cart
scheme will call for a day of reckoning in the future which he cannot
evade.

"Instructions were sent by Brigham and his chief men to their agent,
Apostle F. D. Richards, at Liverpool, and were published by him in the
Millennial Star with such a flourish of trumpets as would have done honour to any of the most momentous events in the world's history. That
apostle announced to the Saints that God, ever watchful for the welfare
of his people and anxious to remove them from the calamities impending
over the wicked in Babylon, had inspired His servant Brigham with His
spirit, and by such inspiration the hand-cart mode of emigration was
adopted. By going to Zion in this way some difficulty would be experienced; but had not the Lord said that He would have a 'tried people,'
and that they should come up 'through great tribulation,' etc. Thus
reasoned this grave apostle—declaring the plan was God's own, and of
His own devising through His servant Brigham. Thus the word went
forth to the faithful Mormons with the stamp of Divinity upon it. They
received it with gladness, believing in the assertion that 'He doeth all
things well,' and they set about preparing for their journey—at least as
many as could raise means to reach the frontiers. Those who had more
money than was necessary for this were counselled to deposit all they
had with F. D. Richards, that it might be used to help others to that
point, as all who reached there would be surely sent through.

"Many, in their honest, simple whole-heartedness, and love for their
brethren and sisters, obeyed this counsel, while many others helped their
own immediate friends and acquaintances to emigrate. The result was
that a greater number of the Saints left Liverpool for Utah that year than
ever before or since. Of this, Richards felt proud, and frequently boasted
of it, as though the success of the scheme was certain when the people
had left Liverpool.

"What his instructions from Brigham were, or whether he exceeded
them, it is immaterial now to enquire; but certain it is that the preparations on the frontiers were altogether inadequate to the number of emigrants, as indeed were the preparations throughout the entire journey
west of New York. For instance, several hundred emigrants would arrive
at Iowa City, expecting to find tents or some means of shelter, as agents

had been sent on from Liverpool to purchase tents, hand-carts, wagons, and cattle, and to prepare generally for the coming flood of emigrants. But they were doomed to disappointment. There were no wagons or tents, and, for days after their arrival, no shelter but the broad heavens. They were delayed at Iowa City for some weeks—some of them for months—while carts were being made, and this, too, when they should have been well on their way.

"The 'Divine plan' being new in this country, of course hand-carts were not procurable, so they had to be made on the camp-ground. They were made in a hurry, some of them of very insufficiently seasoned timber, and strength was sacrificed to weight until the production was a fragile structure, with nothing to recommend it but lightness. They were generally made of two parallel hickory or oak sticks, about five feet long, and two by one and a half inches thick. These were connected by one cross-piece at one end to serve as a handle, and three or four similar pieces nearly a foot apart, commencing at the other end, to serve as the bed of the cart, under the centre of which was fastened a wooden axle-tree, without iron skeins. A pair of light wheels, devoid of iron, except a very light iron tire, completed the "divine" hand-cart. Its weight was somewhere near sixty pounds.

"When we arrived at Iowa City, the great out-fitting point for the emigration, we found that three hand-cart companies had already gone forward, under the respective captaincy of Edmund Ellsworth, Daniel McArthur, and —— Bunker, all Valley elders returning from missions to England. These companies reached Salt Lake City in safety before cold weather set in.* No carts being ready for us, nor indeed anything necessary for our journey, we were detained three weeks at Iowa Camp, where we could celebrate the Fourth of July.

"A few days after this we started on our journey, organized as follows: James G. Willie, captain of the company, which numbered about five hundred. Each hundred had a sub-captain, thus: first, Millen Atwood; second, Levi Savage; third, William Woodward; fourth, John Chislett; fifth, —— Ahmensen. The third hundred were principally Scotch; the fifth, Scandinavians. The other hundreds were mostly English. To each hundred there were five round tents, with twenty persons to a tent; twenty

---

* One of the hand-cart emigrants, writing of the arrival of the first two companies in Salt Lake City, says:

"On that occasion Brigham took one of the brethren by the hand, and said in a tone that showed he was begging the question: 'This *experiment* is a success.' The brother thought: 'So, after all that we have heard of divine plan, etc., *you, the Prophet* '*of the Lord, the originator of the scheme*, acknowledge it only an experiment! An 'experiment in human life, human misery! Can we imagine anything more cold-'hearted than that? Human nature, kindness, brotherhood, all forgotten, all sacri-'ficed to feed ambition! An ambition to do what? To establish a despotism more 'complete than that of the Vatican!'"

hand-carts, or one to every five persons; and one Chicago wagon, drawn
by three yoke of oxen, to haul provisions and tents. Each person was
limited to *seventeen pounds of clothing and bedding*, making eighty-five
pounds of luggage to each cart. To this were added such cooking utensils
as the little mess of five required. But their *cuisine* being scanty, not
many articles were needed, and I presume the average would not exceed
fifteen to twenty pounds, making in all a little over a hundred pounds on
each cart. The carts being so poorly made, could not be laden heavily,
even had the people been able to haul them.

"The strength of the company was equalized as much as possible by
distributing the young men among the different families to help them.
Several carts were drawn by *young girls* exclusively; and two tents were
occupied by them and such females as had no male companions. The
other tents were occupied by families and some young men; all ages and
conditions being found in one tent. Having been thrown closely together
on shipboard, all seemed to adapt themselves to this mode of tent-life without any marked repugnance.

Passing through Iowa.

"As we travelled along, we presented a singular, and sometimes an
affecting appearance. The young and strong went along gaily with their
carts, but the old people and little children were to be seen straggling a
long distance in the rear. Sometimes, when the little folks had walked as
far as they could, their fathers would take them on their carts, and thus
increase the load that was already becoming too heavy as the day advanced. But what will parents not do to benefit their children in time of
trouble? The most affecting scene, however, was to see a mother carrying
her child at the breast, mile after mile, until nearly exhausted. The heat
was intense, and the dust suffocating, which rendered our daily journeys
toilsome in the extreme.

"Our rations consisted of ten ounces of flour to each adult per day, and half that amount to children under eight years of age. Besides our flour we had occasionally a little rice, sugar, coffee, and bacon. But these items (especially the last) were so small and infrequent that they scarcely deserve mentioning. Any hearty man could eat his daily allowance for breakfast. In fact, some of our men did this, and then worked all day without dinner, and went to bed supperless or begged food at the farm-houses as we travelled along.

"The people in Iowa were very good in giving to those who asked food, expressing their sympathy for us whenever they visited our camp—which they did in large numbers if we stopped near a settlement. They tried to dissuade us from going to Salt Lake in that way, and offered us employment and homes among them. A few of our company left us from time to time; but the elders constantly warned us against 'the Gentiles,' and by close watching succeeded in keeping the company tolerably complete. Meetings were held nearly every evening for preaching, counsel, and prayer; the chief feature of the preaching being, '*obey your leaders in all things.*'

"I do not know who settled the amount of our rations, but whoever it was, I should like him, or them, to drag a hand-cart through the State of Iowa in the month of July on exactly the same amount and quality of fare we had. This would be but simple justice. The Scripture says: 'What-'soever measure ye mete shall be measured to you again.'

"When we travelled in this impoverished manner through Iowa, flour was selling at three cents per pound, and bacon seven to eight cents. The Church agents were, no doubt, short of money; but, where was the wisdom in sending forward so many people when the preparations were altogether inadequate for them? Would it not have been better to have brought over fewer emigrants with some small degree of comfort, than to have brought so many and have deprived them of the merest necessities of life?

"A little less than four weeks' travelling brought us to the Missouri river. We crossed it on a steam ferry-boat, and encamped at the town of Florence,* Nebraska, six miles above Omaha, where we remained about a week, making our final preparations for crossing the plains.

"The elders seemed to be divided in their judgment as to the practicability of our reaching Utah in safety at so late a season of the year, and the idea was entertained for a day or two of making our winter quarters on the Elkhorn, Wood river, or some eligible location in Nebraska; but it did not meet with general approval. A monster meeting was called to consult the people about it.

"The emigrants were entirely ignorant of the country and climate—simple, honest, eager to go to 'Zion' at once, and obedient as little children to the 'servants of God.' Under these circumstances it was natural

* Formerly "Winter Quarters."

that they should leave their destinies in the hands of the elders. There were but four men in our company who had been to the valley, viz. : Willie, Atwood, Savage, and Woodward; but there were several at Florence superintending the emigration, among whom elders G. D. Grant and W. H. Kimball occupied the most prominent position. These men all talked at the meeting just mentioned, and all, with one exception, favoured going on. They prophesied in the name of God that we should get through in safety. Were we not God's people, and would he not protect us? Even the elements he would arrange for our good, etc. But Levi Savage used his common sense and his knowledge of the country. He declared positively that to his certain knowledge we could not cross the mountains with a mixed company of aged people, women, and little children, so late in the season without much suffering, sickness, and death. He therefore advised going into winter quarters without delay; but he was rebuked by the other elders for want of faith, one elder even declaring that he would guarantee to eat all the snow that fell on us between Florence and Salt Lake City. Savage was accordingly defeated, as the majority were against him. He then added: 'Brethren and sisters, what I have said I know to 'be true; but, seeing you are to go forward, I will go with you, will help 'you all I can, will work with you, will rest with you, will suffer with you, 'and, if necessary, I will die with you. May God in his mercy bless and 'preserve us. Amen.'

"Brother Savage was true to his word; no man worked harder than he to alleviate the suffering which he had foreseen, when he had to endure it. Oh, had the judgment of this one clear-headed man been heeded, what scenes of suffering, wretchedness, and death would have been prevented! But he was overwhelmed with the religious fanaticism and blind faith of others who thought the very elements would be changed or influenced to suit us, and that the seasons would be transposed for our accommodation because we, forsooth, were 'the people of God!'"

PART II.

THE JOURNEY ACROSS THE PLAINS.

"We started from Florence about the 18th of August, and travelled in the same way as through Iowa, except that our carts were more heavily laden, as our teams could not haul sufficient flour to last us to Utah; it was therefore decided to put one sack (ninety-eight pounds) on each cart in addition to the regular baggage. Some of the people grumbled at this, but the majority bore it without a murmur. Our flour ration was increased to a pound per day; fresh beef was issued occasionally, and each 'hundred' had three or four milch cows. The flour on the carts was used first, the weakest parties being the first relieved of their burdens.

"Everything seemed to be propitious, and we moved gaily forward full of hope and faith. At our camp each evening could be heard songs of joy, merry peals of laughter, and *bon mots* on our condition and prospects. Brother Savage's warning was forgotten in the mirthful ease of the hour. The only drawbacks to this part of our journey were the constant breaking down of carts and the delays caused by repairing them. The axles and boxes being of wood, and being ground out by the dust that found its way there in spite of our efforts to keep it out, together with the extra weight put on the carts, had the effect of breaking the axles at the shoulder. All kinds of expedients were resorted to as remedies for the growing evil, but with variable success. Some wrapped their axles with leather obtained from boot-legs; others with tin, obtained by sacrificing tin-plates, kettles, or buckets from their mess outfit. Besides these inconveniences, there was felt a great lack of a proper lubricator. Of anything suitable for this purpose we had none at all. The poor folks had to use their bacon (already totally insufficient for their wants) to grease their axles, and some even used their soap, of which they had very little, to make their carts trundle somewhat easier. In about twenty days, however, the flour being consumed, breakdowns became less frequent, and we jogged along finely. We travelled from ten to twenty miles per day, averaging about fifteen miles. The people felt well, so did our cattle, and our immediate prospects of a prosperous journey were good. But the fates seemed to be against us.

"About this time we reached Wood river. The whole country was alive with buffaloes, and one night—or, rather, evening—our cattle stampeded. Men went in pursuit and collected what they supposed to be the herd; but, on corralling them for yoking next morning, thirty head were missing. We hunted for them three days in every direction, but did not find them. We at last reluctantly gave up the search, and prepared to travel without them as best we could. We had only about enough oxen left to put one yoke to each wagon; but, as they were each loaded with about three thousand pounds of flour, the teams could not of course move them. We then yoked up our beef cattle, milch cows, and, in fact, everything that could bear a yoke—even two-year old heifers. The stock was wild and could pull but little, and we were unable, with all our stock, to move our loads. As a last resort we again loaded a sack of flour on each cart.

"The patience and faith of the good honest people were shaken somewhat by this (to them) hard stroke of Providence. Some complained openly; others, less demonstrative, chewed the bitter cud of discontent; while the greater part saw the 'hand of the Lord' in it. The belief that we were the spiritual favourites of the Almighty, and that he would control everything for our good, soon revived us after our temporary despondency, and in a day or two faith was as assuring as ever with the pilgrims. But our progress was slow, the old breakdowns were constantly repeated, and some could not refrain from murmuring in spite of the general trustfulness. It was really hard for the folks to lose the use of their milch cows, have beef rations stopped, and haul one hundred pounds more on their carts. Every man and woman, however, worked to their utmost to put forward towards the goal of their hopes.

" One evening, as we were camped on the west bank of the North Bluff Fork of the Platte, a grand outfit of carriages and light wagons was driven into our camp from the East. Each vehicle was drawn by four horses or mules, and all the appointments seemed to be first rate. The occupants we soon found to be the apostle F. D. Richards, elders W. H. Kimball, G. D. Grant, Joseph A. Young, C. G. Webb, N. H. Felt, W. C. Dunbar, and others who were returning to Utah from missions abroad. They camped with us for the night, and in the morning a general meeting was called. Apostle Richards addressed us. He had been advised of the opposition brother Savage had made, and he rebuked him very severely in open meeting for his lack of faith in God. Richards gave us plenty of counsel to be faithful, prayerful, obedient to our leaders, etc., and wound up by prophesying in the name of Israel's God that 'though it might storm on our ' right and on our left, the Lord would keep open our way before us and ' we should get to Zion in safety.' This assurance had a telling effect on the people—to them it was 'the voice of God.' They gave a loud and hearty ' Amen,' while tears of joy ran down their sunburnt cheeks.

" These brethren told Captain Willie they wanted some fresh meat, and he had our fattest calf killed for them. I am ashamed for humanity's sake to say they took it. While we, four hundred in number, travelling so slowly and so far from home, with our mixed company of men, women, children, aged, sick, and infirm people, had no provisions to spare, had not enough for ourselves, in fact, these ' elders in Israel,' these ' servants of God,' took from us what we ourselves so greatly needed and went on in style with their splendid outfit, after preaching to us faith, patience, prayerfulness, and obedience to the priesthood. As they rolled out of our camp I could not, as I contrasted our positions and circumstances, help exclaiming to myself: '*Look on this picture, and on that!* '

" We broke camp at once and turned towards the river, the apostle having advised us to go on to the south side. He and his company preceded us and waited on the opposite bank to indicate to us the best fording place. They stood and watched us wade the river—here almost a mile in width, and in places from two to three feet deep. Our women and girls waded, pulling their carts after them.

" The apostle promised to leave us provisions, bedding, etc., at Laramie if he could, and to secure us help from the valley as soon as possible.

" We reached Laramie about the 1st or 2d of September, but the provisions, etc., which we expected were not there for us. Captain Willie called a meeting to take into consideration our circumstances, condition, and prospects, and to see what could be done. It was ascertained that at our present rate of travel and consumption of flour, the latter would be exhausted when we were about three hundred and fifty miles from our destination ! It was resolved to reduce our allowance from one pound to three-quarters of a pound per day, and at the same time to make every effort in our power to travel faster. We continued this rate of rations from Laramie to Independence Rock.

"About this time Captain Willie received a letter from apostle Richards informing him that we might expect supplies to meet us from the valley by the time we reached South Pass. An examination of our stock of flour showed us that it would be gone before we reached that point. Our only alternative was to still further reduce our bill of fare. The issue of flour was then to average ten ounces per day to each person over ten years of age, and to be divided thus: working-men to receive twelve ounces, women and old men nine ounces, and children from four to eight ounces, according to age and size.

"This arrangement dissatisfied some, especially men with families; for so far they had really done better than single men, the children's rations being some help to them. But, taken altogether, it was as good a plan as we could have adopted under the circumstances.

"Many of our men showed signs of failing, and to reduce their rations below twelve ounces would have been suicidal to the company, seeing they had to stand guard at night, wade the streams repeatedly by day to get the women and children across, erect tents, and do many duties which women could not do.

"Our captain did his utmost to move us forward and always acted with great impartiality. The sub-captains had plenty of work, too, in seeing that rations were fairly divided, equally distributing the strength of their hundreds, helping the sick and the weakly, etc.

"We had not travelled far up the Sweetwater before the nights, which had gradually been getting colder since we left Laramie, became very severe. The mountains before us, as we approached nearer to them, revealed themselves to view mantled nearly to their base in snow, and tokens of a coming storm were discernible in the clouds which each day seemed to lower around us. In our frequent crossings of the Sweetwater, we had really 'a hard road to travel.' The water was beautiful to the eye, as it rolled over its rocky bed as clear as crystal; but when we waded it time after time at each ford to get the carts, the women, and the children over, the beautiful stream, with its romantic surroundings (which should awaken holy and poetic feelings in the soul, and draw it nearer to the Great Author of life), lost to us its beauty, and the chill which it sent through our systems drove out from our minds all holy and devout aspirations, and left a void, a sadness, and—in some cases—doubts as to the justice of an overruling Providence.

"Our *seventeen pounds of clothing and bedding* was now altogether insufficient for our comfort. Nearly all suffered more or less at night from cold. Instead of getting up in the morning strong, refreshed, vigorous, and prepared for the hardships of another day of toil, the poor 'Saints' were to be seen crawling out from their tents looking haggard, benumbed, and showing an utter lack of that vitality so necessary to our success.

"Cold weather, scarcity of food, lassitude and fatigue from over-exertion, soon produced their effects. Our old and infirm people began to droop, and they no sooner lost spirit and courage than death's stamp could be traced upon their features. Life went out as smoothly as a lamp ceases to burn when the oil is gone. At first the deaths occurred slowly and irregularly, but in a few days at more frequent intervals, until we soon thought it unusual to leave a camp-ground without burying one or more persons.

"Death was not long confined in its ravages to the old and infirm, but the young and naturally strong were among its victims. Men who were, so to speak, as strong as lions when we started on our journey, and who had been our best supports, were compelled to succumb to the grim monster. These men were worn down by hunger, scarcity of clothing and bedding, and too much labour in helping their families. Weakness and debility were accompanied by dysentery. This we could not stop or even alleviate, no proper medicines being in the camp; and in almost every instance it carried off the parties attacked. It was surprising to an unmarried man to witness the devotion of men to their families and to their faith, under these trying circumstances. Many a father pulled his cart, with his little children on it, until the day preceding his death. I have seen some pull their carts in the morning, give out during the day, and die before next morning. These people died with the calm faith and fortitude of martyrs. Their greatest regret seemed to be leaving their families behind them, and their bodies on the plains or mountains instead of being laid in the consecrated ground of Zion. The sorrow and mourning of the bereaved, as they saw their husbands and fathers rudely interred, were affecting in the extreme, and none but a heart of stone could repress a tear of sympathy at the sad spectacle.*

"Each death weakened our forces. In my hundred I could not raise enough men to pitch a tent when we encamped, and now it was that I

---

* A letter from one of the hand-cart emigrants of a later company found its way into the London *Times*. This emigrant relates his apprehension of the company starting too late from the Missouri river, and of the resolution of himself and relations to defer their journey to Zion; but, being instructed and cheered up by the preaching of elders Richards and Wheelock, they resolved to go forward, "let the consequence be what it would." After he had travelled part of the journey, he writes: "We pushed on; my mother walking sixteen, eighteen, or twenty miles a day for weeks, without a ride or any assistance, until she was exhausted, with no convenience to ride. This brought on disease, and I had to haul her in my hand-cart for two days; and after a month's journey from Florence she was quite worn out, wished to give up, and died one morning before we started out. We buried her by the roadside, without a coffin. We mourned her loss, knowing she was one of our best friends. The time rolled on for eight or nine days, and my sister Mary caught the same complaint. I hauled her in my hand-cart for some days, and she then died. We went on our journey for another fortnight, when my youngest child, Ephraim, died likewise. My father kept pushing and pulling the hand-cart, with sore feet, until he was worn out and had to go to the wagons to ride. My wife pushed at the hand-carts until she fell sick, was worn out, and had to go to the wagons to ride. My son William fell sick of the fever and ague, and his mother was ill of the same

20

had to exert myself to the utmost. I wonder I did not die, as many did who were stronger than I was. When we pitched our camp in the evening of each day, I had to lift the sick from the wagon and carry them to the fire, and in the morning carry them again on my back to the wagon. When any in my hundred died I had to inter them; often helping to dig the grave myself. In performing these sad offices I always offered up a heartfelt prayer to that God who beheld our sufferings, and begged him to avert destruction from us and send us help.

PART III.

FEARFUL SUFFERINGS : THE RAVAGES OF STARVATION, DISEASE, AND DEATH.

"WE travelled on in misery and sorrow day after day. Sometimes we made a pretty good distance, but at other times we were only able to make a few miles' progress. Finally we were overtaken by a snow-storm which the shrill wind blew furiously about us. The snow fell several inches deep as we travelled along, but we dared not stop, for we had a sixteen-mile journey to make, and short of it we could not get wood and water.

"As we were resting for a short time at noon a light wagon was driven into our camp from the west. Its occupants were Joseph A. Young* and Stephen Taylor. They informed us that a train of supplies was on the way, and we might expect to meet it in a day or two. More welcome messengers never came from the courts of glory than these two young men were to us. They lost no time after encouraging us all they could to press forward, but sped on further east to convey their glad news

complaint. We pushed on to Fort Laramie, where I was completely exhausted with hunger and fatigue, and stayed behind with another young man from Manchester (John Barlow). If I had gone on another week, I should have been a dead man. I cannot say whether my father is dead or alive."

* "Joseph A.," as the Prophet's eldest son is familiarly termed, was the last of the returning missionaries to leave the emigrant camp on the banks of the Platte river. Though ignorant of the apprehension that he felt for their welfare, and the presentiments he had of the inevitable suffering that awaited them, many of the emigrants clung to him with more than ordinary affection, and detained him till the warning of approaching night urged him to follow his companions. When he bade them good-by, he could scarcely say more than 'You shall see me again soon.' All speed was made by him and his companions, and immediately on arrival in Salt Lake City he reported to his father how far the emigrants were yet behind. Brigham comprehended their situation in a moment. Though his son had been absent two years from his home, he ordered him instantly to make ready to return to the assistance of the emigrants and gave him authority to take all the provisions, clothing, and vehicles that he could find on the way and press them forward to the rescue. Brigham Young on that occasion earned the good opinions of foes as well as friends.

to Edward Martin and the fifth hand-cart company who left Florence about two weeks after us, and who it was feared were even worse off than we were. As they went from our view, many a hearty ' God bless you ' followed them.

" We pursued our journey with renewed hope and after untold toil and fatigue, doubling teams frequently, going back to fetch up the straggling carts, and encouraging those who had dropped by the way to a little more exertion in view of our soon-to-be improved condition, we finally, late at night, got all to camp—the wind howling frightfully and the snow eddying around us in fitful gusts. But we had found a good camp among the willows, and after warming and partially drying ourselves before good fires, we ate our scanty fare, paid our usual devotions to the Deity and retired to rest with hopes of coming aid.

" In the morning the snow was over a foot deep. Our cattle strayed widely during the storm, and some of them died. But what was worse to us than all this was the fact that *five persons* of both sexes lay in the cold embrace of death. The pitiless storm and the extra march of the previous day had been too much for their wasted energies, and they had passed through the dark valley to the bright world beyond. We buried these five people in one grave, wrapped only in the clothing and bedding in which they died. We had no materials with which to make coffins, and even if we had, we could not have spared time to make them, for it required all the efforts of the healthy few who remained to perform the ordinary camp duties and to look after the sick—the number of whom increased daily on our hands, notwithstanding so many were dying.

" The morning before the storm, or, rather, the morning of the day on which it came, we issued the last ration of flour. On this fatal morning, therefore, we had none to issue. We had, however, a barrel or two of hard bread which Captain Willie had procured at Fort Laramie in view of our destitution. This was equally and fairly divided among all the company. Two of our poor broken-down cattle were killed and their carcasses issued for beef. With this we were informed that we would have to subsist until the coming supplies reached us. All that now remained in our commissary were a few pounds each of sugar and dried apples, about a quarter of a sack of rice and a small quantity (possibly 20 or 25 lbs.) of hard bread. The brother who had been our commissary all the way from Liverpool had not latterly acted in a way to merit the confidence of the company ; but it is hard to handle provisions and suffer hunger at the same time, so I will not write a word of condemnation. These few scanty supplies were on this memorable morning turned over to me by Captain Willie, with strict injunctions to distribute them only to the sick and to mothers for their hungry children, and even to them in as sparing a manner as possible. It was an unenviable place to occupy, a hard duty to perform ; but I acted to the best of my ability, using all the discretion I could.

" Being surrounded by snow a foot deep, out of provisions, many of

our people sick, and our cattle dying, it was decided that we should remain in our present camp until the supply-train reached us. It was also
resolved in council that Captain Willie with one man should go in search
of the supply-train and apprise its leader of our condition, and hasten
him to our help. When this was done we settled down and made our
camp as comfortable as we could. As Captain Willie and his companion
left for the West, many a heart was lifted in prayer for their success and
speedy return. They were absent three days---three days which I shall
never forget. The scanty allowance of hard bread and poor beef, distributed as described, was mostly consumed the first day by the hungry, ravenous, famished souls.

"We killed more cattle and issued the meat; but, eating it without
bread, did not satisfy hunger, and to those who were suffering from dysentery it did more harm than good. This terrible disease increased rapidly amongst us during these three days, and several died from exhaustion.
Before we renewed our journey the camp became so offensive and filthy
that words would fail to describe its condition, and even common decency
forbids the attempt. Suffice it to say that all the disgusting scenes which
the reader might imagine would certainly not equal the terrible reality.
It was enough to make the heavens weep. The recollection of it unmans
me even now—those three days! During that time I visited the sick,
the widows whose husbands died in serving them, and the aged who could
not help themselves, to know for myself where to dispense the few articles that had been placed in my charge for distribution. Such craving
hunger I never saw before, and may God in his mercy spare me the sight
again.

"As I was seen giving these things to the most needy, crowds of famished men and women surrounded me and begged for bread! Men whom
I had known all the way from Liverpool, who had been true as steel in
every stage of our journey, who in their homes in England and Scotland
had never known want; men who by honest labour had sustained themselves and their families, and saved enough to cross the Atlantic and trav-
erse the United States, whose hearts were cast in too great a mould to
descend to a mean act or brook dishonour; such men as these came to me
and begged bread. I felt humbled to the dust for my race and nation,
and I hardly know which feeling was strongest at that time, pity for our
condition, or malediction on the fates that so humbled the proud Anglo-
Saxon nature. But duty might not be set aside by feeling, however natural, so I positively refused these men bread! But while I did so, I explained to them the painful position in which I was placed, and most of
them acknowledged that I was right. Not a few of them afterwards
spoke approvingly of my stern performance of duty. It is difficult, however, to reason with a hungry man; but these noble fellows, when they
comprehended my position, had faith in my honour. Some of them are
in Utah to-day, and when we meet, the strong grip of friendship over-
comes, for the moment at least, all differences of opinion which we may

entertain on any subject.* May the Heavens ever be kind to them, whatever their faith, for they are good men and true. And the sisters who suffered with us—may the loving angels ever be near them to guard them from the ills of life.

"Came to me and begged Bread."

" The storm which we encountered, our brethren from the Valley also met, and, not knowing that we were so utterly destitute, they encamped to await fine weather. But when Captain Willie found them and explained our real condition, they at once hitched up their teams and made all speed to come to our rescue. On the evening of the third day after Captain Willie's departure, just as the sun was sinking beautifully behind the distant hills, on an eminence immediately west of our camp several covered wagons, each drawn by four horses, were seen coming towards us. The news ran through the camp like wildfire, and all who were able to leave their beds turned out en masse to see them. A few minutes brought them sufficiently near to reveal our faithful captain slightly in advance of the train. Shouts of joy rent the air; strong men wept till tears ran freely down their furrowed and sun-burnt cheeks, and little children partook of the joy which some of them hardly understood, and fairly danced around with gladness. Restraint was set aside in the general rejoicing, and as the brethren entered our camp the sisters fell upon them and deluged them with kisses. The brethren were so overcome that they could not for

* Without a note this remark would be misunderstood by the general reader. When any one outgrows the Mormon faith, the orthodox generally are averse to the recognition of " an apostate." Mr. Chislett wishes to express in his remark that the friendship created in that trying hour has been proof against even the bitterness of Church discipline.

some time utter a word, but in choking silenced repressed all demonstration of those emotions that evidently mastered them. Soon, however,
feeling was somewhat abated, and such a shaking of hands, such words
of welcome, and such invocation of God's blessing have seldom been witnessed.

" I was installed as regular commissary to the camp. The brethren
turned over to me flour, potatoes, onions, and a limited supply of warm
clothing for both sexes, besides quilts, blankets, buffalo-robes, woollen
socks, etc. I first distributed the necessary provisions, and after supper
divided the clothing, bedding, etc., where it was most needed. That
evening, for the first time in quite a period, the songs of Zion were to be
heard in the camp, and peals of laughter issued from the little knots of
people as they chatted around the fires. The change seemed almost miraculous, so sudden was it from grave to gay, from sorrow to gladness,
from mourning to rejoicing. With the cravings of hunger satisfied, and
with hearts filled with gratitude to God and our good brethren, we all
united in prayer, and then retired to rest.

" Among the brethren who came to our succour were elders W. H.
Kimball and G. D. Grant. They had remained but a few days in the Valley before starting back to meet us. May God ever bless them for their
generous, unselfish kindness and their manly fortitude! They felt that
they had, in a great measure, contributed to our sad position; but how
nobly, how faithfully, how bravely they worked to bring us safely to the
Valley—to the Zion of our hopes!

PART IV.

THE PILGRIMS ENTER THE CITY OF THE SAINTS.

" THE next morning the small company which came to our relief divided : one half, under G. D. Grant, going east to meet Martin's company,
and the other half, under W. H. Kimball, remaining with us. From this
point until we reached the Valley, W. H. Kimball took full charge of us.

" We travelled but a few miles the first day, the roads being very heavy.
All who were unable to pull their carts were allowed to put their little
outfits into the wagon and walk along, and those who were really unable
to walk were allowed to ride. The second day we travelled a little farther, and each day Brother Kimball got the company along as far as it
was possible to move it, but still our progress was very slow.

" Timely and good beyond estimate as the help which we received from
the Valley was to our company generally, it was too late for some of our
number. They were already prostrated and beyond all human help. Some
seemed to have lost mental as well as physical energy. We talked to them
of our improved condition, appealed to their love of life and showed them
how easy it was to retain that life by arousing themselves; but all to no
purpose. We then addressed ourselves to their religious feelings, their

wish to see Zion ; to know the Prophet Brigham ; showed them the good things that he had sent out to us, and told them how deeply he sympathized with us in our sufferings, and what a welcome he would give us when we reached the city. But all our efforts were unavailing ; they had lost all love of life, all sense of surrounding things, and had sunk down into a state of indescribable apathy.

" The weather grew colder each day, and many got their feet so badly frozen that they could not walk, and had to be lifted from place to place. Some got their fingers frozen ; others their ears; and one woman lost her sight by the frost. These severities of the weather also increased our number of deaths, so that we buried several each day.

" A few days of bright freezing weather were succeeded by another snow-storm. The day we crossed the Rocky Ridge it was snowing a little —the wind hard from the north-west—and blowing so keenly that it almost pierced us through. We had to wrap ourselves closely in blankets, quilts, or whatever else we could get, to keep from freezing. Captain Willie still attended to the details of the company's travelling, and this day he appointed me to bring up the rear. My duty was to stay behind everything and see that nobody was left along the road. I had to bury a man who had died in my hundred, and I finished doing so after the company had started. In about half an hour I set out on foot alone to do my duty as rear-guard to the camp. The ascent of the ridge commenced soon after leaving camp, and I had not gone far up it before I overtook a cart that the folks could not pull through the snow, here about knee-deep. I helped them along, and we soon overtook another. By all hands getting to one cart we could travel; so we moved one of the carts a few rods, and then went back and brought up the other. After moving in this way for a while, we overtook other carts at different points of the hill, until we had six carts, not one of which could be moved by the parties owning it. I put our collective strength to three carts at a time, took them a short distance, and then brought up the other three. Thus by travelling over the hill three times—twice forward and once back —I succeeded after hours of toil in bringing my little company to the summit. The six carts were then trotted on gaily down hill, the intense cold stirring us to action. One or two parties who were with these carts gave up entirely, and but for the fact that we overtook one of our ox-teams that had been detained on the road, they must have perished on that Rocky Ridge. One old man, named James (a farm-labourer from Gloucestershire), who had a large family, and who had worked very hard all the way, I found sitting by the roadside unable to pull his cart any farther. I could not get him into the wagon, as it was already overcrowded. He had a shot-gun which he had brought from England, and which had been a great blessing to him and his family, for he was a good shot, and often had a mess of sage hens or rabbits for his family. I took the gun from the cart, put a small bundle on the end of it, placed it on his shoulder, and started him out with his little boy, twelve years old. His wife and two daughters older than the boy took the cart along finely after reaching the summit.

"We travelled along with the ox-team and overtook others, all so laden with the sick and helpless that they moved very slowly. The oxen had almost given out. Some of our folks with carts went ahead of the teams, for where the roads were good they could out-travel oxen; but we constantly overtook some stragglers, some with carts, some without, who had been unable to keep pace with the body of the company. We struggled along in this weary way until after dark, and by this time our 'rear' numbered three wagons, eight hand-carts, and nearly forty persons. With the wagons were Millen Atwood, Levi Savage, and William Woodward, captains of hundreds, faithful men who had worked hard all the way.

"We finally came to a stream of water which was frozen over. We could not see where the company had crossed. If at the point where we struck the creek, then it had frozen over since we passed it. We started one team to cross, but the oxen broke through the ice and would not go over. No amount of shouting and whipping could induce them to stir an inch. We were afraid to try the other teams, for even should they cross we could not leave the one in the creek and go on. There was no wood in the vicinity, so we could make no fire, and were uncertain what to do. We did not know the distance to the camp, but supposed it to be three or four miles. After consulting about it, we resolved that some one should go on foot to the camp to inform the captain of our situation. I was selected to perform the duty, and I set out with all speed. In crossing the creek I slipped through the ice and got my feet wet, my boots being nearly worn out. I had not gone far when I saw some one sitting by the roadside. I stopped to see who it was, and discovered the old man James and his little boy. The poor old man was quite worn out.

"I got him to his feet and had him lean on me, and he walked a little distance, but not very far. I partly dragged, partly carried him a short distance farther, but he was quite helpless, and my strength failed me. Being obliged to leave him to go forward on my own errand, I put down a quilt I had wrapped round me, rolled him in it, and told the little boy to walk up and down by his father, and on no account to sit down, or he would be frozen to death. I told him to watch for teams that would come back, and to hail them when they came. This done I again set out for the camp, running nearly all the way and frequently falling down, for there were many obstructions and holes in the road. My boots were frozen stiff, so that I had not the free use of my feet, and it was only by rapid motion that I kept them from being badly frozen. As it was, both were nipped.

"After some time I came in sight of the camp fires, which encouraged me. As I neared the camp I frequently overtook stragglers on foot, all pressing forward slowly. I stopped to speak to each one, cautioning them all against resting, as they would surely freeze to death. Finally, about 11 P. M., I reached the camp almost exhausted. I had exerted myself very much during the day in bringing the rear carts up the ridge, and had not eaten anything since breakfast. I reported to Captains Willie and Kimball the situation of the folks behind. They immediately got up some horses, and the boys from the Valley started back about midnight to help the ox-teams in. The night was very severe and many of the emigrants were frozen. It was 5 A. M. before the last team reached the camp.

"I told my companions about the old man James and his little boy. They found the little fellow keeping faithful watch over his father, who lay sleeping in my quilt just as I left him. They lifted him into a wagon, still alive, but in a sort of stupor. He died before morning. His last words were an enquiry as to the safety of his shot-gun.

"There were so many dead and dying that it was decided to lie by for the day. In the forenoon I was appointed to go round the camp and collect the dead. I took with me two young men to assist me in the sad task, and we collected together, of all ages and both sexes, *thirteen corpses, all stiffly frozen.* We had a large square hole dug in which we buried these thirteen people, three or four abreast and three deep. When they did not fit in, we put one or two crosswise at the head or feet of the others. We covered them with willows and then with the earth. When we buried these thirteen people some of their relatives refused to attend the services. They manifested an utter indifference about it. The numbness and cold in their physical natures seem to have reached the soul, and to have crushed out natural feeling and affection. Had I not myself witnessed it, I could not have believed that suffering would have produced such terrible results. But so it was. Two others died during the day, and we buried them in one grave, making *fifteen in all buried on that camp ground.* It was on Willow creek, a tributary of the Sweetwater river. I learned afterwards from men who passed that way the next summer, that the wolves had exhumed the bodies, and their bones were scattered thickly around the vicinity.

"What a terrible fate for poor, honest, God-fearing people, whose greatest sin was believing with a faith too simple that God would for their benefit reverse the order of nature. They believed this because their elders told them so; and had not the apostle Richards prophesied in the name of Israel's God that it would be so? But the terrible realities proved that Levi Savage, with his plain common sense and statement of facts, was right, and that Richards and the other elders, with the 'Spirit of the Lord,' were wrong.

The Old Man James.

"The day of rest did the company good, and we started out next morning with new life. During the day we crossed the Sweetwater on the ice, which did not break, although our wagons were laden with sick people. The effects of our lack of food, and the terrible ordeal of the Rocky Ridge, still remained among us. Two or three died every day. At night we camped a little east by north from the South Pass, and two men in my hundred died. It devolved on me to bury them. This I did before breakfast. The effluvia from these corpses were horrible, and it is small matter for wonder that after performing the last sad offices for them I was taken sick and vomited fearfully. Many said my 'time' had come, and I was myself afraid that such was the case, but by the blessing of God I got over it and lived.

"It had been a practice among us latterly, when a person died with any good clothes on, to take them off and distribute them among the poor and needy. One of the men I buried near South Pass had on a pair of medium-heavy laced shoes. I looked at them and at my own worn-out boots. I wanted them badly, but could not bring my mind to the 'sticking-point' to appropriate them. I called Captain Kimball up and showed him both, and asked his advice. He told me to take them by all means, and tersely remarked: 'They will do you more good than they will him.' I took them, and but for that would have reached the city of Salt Lake barefoot.

"Near South Pass we found more brethren from the Valley, with several quarters of good fat beef hanging frozen on the limbs of the trees where they were encamped. These quarters of beef were to us the handsomest pictures we ever saw. The statues of Michael Angelo, or the paintings of the ancient masters, would have been to us nothing in comparison to these *life-giving pictures*.

"After getting over the Pass we soon experienced the influence of a warmer climate, and for a few days we made good progress. We con-

"What of the Promises?"

stantly met teams from the Valley, with all necessary provisions. Most of these went on to Martin's company, but enough remained with us for our actual wants. At Fort Bridger we found a great many teams that had come to our help. The noble fellows who came to our assistance invariably received us joyfully, and did all in their power to alleviate our sufferings. May they never need similar relief! From Bridger all our company rode, and this day I also rode for the first time on our journey. The entire distance from Iowa City to Fort Bridger I walked, and waded every stream from the Missouri to that point, except Elkhorn, which we ferried, and Green river, which I crossed in a wagon. During the journey from Bridger to Salt Lake a few died of dysentery, and some from the effects of frost the day we crossed the fatal Rocky Ridge. But those who weathered that fatal day and night, and were free from disease, gradually regained strength and reached Salt Lake City in good health and spirits.

" When we left Iowa City we numbered about five hundred persons. Some few deserted us while passing through Iowa, and some remained at Florence. When we left the latter place we numbered four hundred and twenty, about twenty of whom were independent emigrants with their own wagons, so that our hand-cart company was actually four hundred of this number. Sixty-seven died on the journey, making *a mortality of one-sixth of our number.* Of those who were sick on our arrival, two or three soon died. President Young had arranged with the bishops of the different wards and settlements to take care of the poor emigrants who had no friends to receive them, and their kindness in this respect *cannot be too highly praised.* It was enough that a poor family had come with the hand-carts, to insure help during the winter from the good brethren in the different settlements. My old friend W. G. Mills and his wife received me and my betrothed most kindly, so I had no need of Church aid.

" After arriving in the Valley, I found that President Young, on learning, from the brethren who passed us on the road, of the lateness of our leaving the frontier, set to work at once to send us relief. It was the October Conference when they arrived with the news. Brigham at once suspended all conference business, and declared that nothing further should be done until every available team was started out to meet us. He set the example by sending several of his best mule teams laden with provisions. Heber Kimball did the same, and hundreds of others followed their noble example. People who had come from distant parts of the Territory to attend conference volunteered to go out to meet us, and went at once. The people who had no teams gave freely of provisions, bedding, etc.—all doing their best to help us.

" We arrived in Salt Lake City on the 9th of November, but Martin's company did not arrive until about the 1st of December. They numbered near six hundred on starting, and *lost over one-fourth of their number by death.* The storm which overtook us while making the sixteen-mile drive on Sweetwater, reached them at North Platte. There they settled down to await help or die, being unable to go any farther. Their camp-ground became indeed a veritable grave-yard before they left it, and their dead lie even now scattered along from that point to Salt Lake. They were longer without food than we were, and being more exposed to the severe weather their mortality was, of course, greater in proportion.

" Our tale is their tale partly told ; the same causes operated in both cases, and the same effects followed.

" Immediately that the condition of the suffering emigrants was known in Salt Lake City, the most fervent prayers for their deliverance were offered up. There, and throughout the Territory, the same was done as soon as the news reached the people. Prayers in the Tabernacle, in the school-house, in the family circle, and in the private prayer circles of the priesthood were constantly offered up to the Almighty, begging Him to avert the storm from us. Such intercessions were invariably made on behalf of Martin's company, at all the meetings which I attended after my arrival. But these prayers availed nothing more than did the prophecies of Richards and the elders. It was the stout hearts and strong hands of the noble fellows who

John Chislett.

came to our relief, the good teams, the flour, beef, potatoes, the warm clothing and bedding, *and not prayers nor prophecies*, that saved us from death. It is a fact patent to all the old settlers in Utah, that the fall storms of 1856 were earlier and more severe than were ever known before or since. Instead of their prophecies being fulfilled and their prayers answered, it would almost seem that the elements were unusually severe that season, as a rebuke to their presumption."

THE STORY OF MARTIN'S COMPANY. — TERRIBLE SUFFERING AND PRIVATION.

MR. CHISLETT's thrilling narrative should properly have been supplemented by a relation of the sad experience of the last hand-cart company, under the guidance of elder Martin. The story already told is too deeply interesting to allow the listener to leave the last company struggling with the winter's fury, without a feeling of sympathy, and a very natural desire to know the fate of the poor emigrants. It could not be expected that elder Martin himself would furnish such a history, as its authorship would have cost him his membership in the Church.

A gentleman, however, in the ox-train that followed the last of the hand-carts, and closed that year's emigration to Zion, and who was himself an eye-witness and sufferer, has furnished the Author with the following picture of endurance, sacrifice, and heroism that fitly closes the story of the "experiment"* of the divine plan for gathering the poor from Europe :

"Iowa City was selected that year for an outfitting point for Salt Lake Valley—the haven of rest for the travel-tired Saints. The apostle John Taylor had charge of the emigration in New York, the apostle Erastus Snow at St. Louis, the apostle Franklin D. Richards in Liverpool, and elder Daniel Spencer at Iowa City. There was some trouble among them as to who was chief, which occasioned much delay, and was probably never settled. To this difference are attributable the suffering and death of so many persons which occurred later in the season.

"Elder Chauncey G. Webb bought the wagons—the first of the Chicago make that subsequently became so popular in Utah—and also the material for making hand-carts, and shipped them to Iowa City, to which point the railroad had just been completed. The artisans were selected

---

* The Author at first thought that the use of the phrase "divine plan" was only an expression of the ironical feeling of the emigrants who had suffered and had become disgusted with Mormonism, but there is abundant evidence that such was the language of the elders in Europe when they were urging the poor to emigrate. The following is one of the songs that the unfortunate Mormons sung on their journey before their hearts were benumbed by suffering :

HAND-CART SONG.

TUNE—*A Little More Cider.*

CHORUS : Hurrah for the Camp of Israel!
Hurrah for the hand-cart scheme!
Hurrah! hurrah! 'tis better far
Than the wagon and ox-team.

Oh, our faith goes with the hand-carts,
And they have our hearts' best love ;
'Tis a novel mode of travelling,
Devised by the Gods above.
Hurrah! etc.

And *Brigham 's their executive,*
He told us the design ;
And the Saints are proudly marching on,
Along the hand-cart line.
Hurrah! etc.

Who cares to go with the wagons?
Not we who are free and strong ;
Our faith and arms, with a right good will,
Shall pull our carts along.
Hurrah! etc.

from among the emigrants, and were required to work without wages, and this they did faithfully if not cheerfully. While thus working they were insufficiently rationed, which caused great dissatisfaction, resulting in a refusal to continue their labours unless they were properly supplied. Their demand was complied with.

" The hand-carts were fitted up on the most economical plan, and so far was parsimony carried that the wheels had no tires, and to preserve the felloes the emigrants wound them with raw-hide while *en route*. This defect was afterwards partially remedied by putting on a rim of hoop-iron and rivetting where it lapped. Elder John Van Cott was deputed to buy and bring up cattle and mules, which he did, I believe, from Missouri. The trouble before named as to who was the " big chief " occasioned delays in branches of the outfitting, so that company after company arrived on the camping-ground, and had to stay there a long time before they could commence their journey, but I cannot say how long.

" When the cattle arrived they were entrusted to the hand-cart emigrants to herd, and this part of the business was very badly managed. The hand-cart folks had no interest whatever in the oxen, besides which they were new to the business, and were inefficiently directed. The consequence was that lot after lot of the stock was lost, and a proportionately greater price was put on what was left to cover the deficiency, the good Saints being forbidden to buy from settlers. The independent companies wanted to purchase their own stock, with the privilege of taking care of it themselves, but this was not allowed. From the above causes the cattle ' increased in value '—I think, three times—and were finally delivered to the emigrants at much higher prices than they could have been bought for in the neighbourhood. In this way the independent companies were kept back in order that they with their teams might relieve the hand-carts, if needed.

" I will say nothing about the percentage collected from the emigrants on passage, railroad, wagons, hand-carts, and provisions—it is perhaps unnecessary.

" Florence, some six miles above Omaha, was chosen as a final outfitting depot for the Great Plains, and pulling the hand-carts from Iowa City to the Missouri river demonstrated the weak places both in carts and men. On arrival there they were without delay outfitted for their long journey, supplies having been sent up in quantity from St. Louis. James McGaw was in charge at Florence; he was a capable and indefatigable man.

" The last hand-cart train, under Tyler and Martin, arrived at Florence towards the middle of August, and many of the people were discouraged at the prospect ahead, but they were cheered by the elders preaching and telling them that a testimony would be given them that they were the chosen people of God, for they would go through safe and unharmed. ' The Indians, the seasons, nay, the very elements, would be controlled for ' their benefit, and after they got through they would hear of storms on the

'right and on the left, of which they in their travelling would know noth-
'ing.' Notwithstanding this encouragement, some remained behind for
that season—and for many seasons, for aught I know; others begged
hard for permission to do so, but this was refused; others offered their
personal effects and promises to pay after arrival in Utah to any one who
would take them in wagons. One lady offered all her jewellery, worth a
considerable sum, for that purpose.

" The last ox-team—of which John A. Hunt had charge—was despatched soon after. It was a sort of Church train; that is, it consisted
of wagons belonging to the returning missionaries, viz., Daniel Spencer, C.
H. Wheelock, C. G. Webb, Captain Dan. Jones, F. D. Richards, James
Linforth, and others. The wool or cotton machinery brought by George
Halliday was in this train, and also the harp belonging to the poor old
blind man Giles, which, as he was unable to pay freight upon it, he had
'donated' to Brigham Young. He was afterwards accorded the privilege
of going to Brigham Young's mansion and playing upon his own instrument sometimes, of which privilege he gladly availed himself. It is said
that the poor, afflicted old man would play there for hours at a time, while
the hot tears streamed down his face as thoughts that would not be controlled rose unbidden in his mind. He afterwards got possession of his
much loved instrument: he may have bought it or Brigham Young may
have given it to him, as no one of his household could play on it then.

Crossing the Platte River.

In this last train there were also several young girls; some of whom
had a wagon fitted up for their comfort, and others had still better accommodation in the way of ambulance or carriage. The wagons belonging
to Mr. Tenant—whose property soon melted away in Zion—were also in
this train. Mr. Tenant died on the plains at O'Fallon's Bluffs. Mr. Hunt

had instructions on no account to pass Tyler's hand-cart train—a pretty conclusive proof that what the elders had told the Saints with so much earnestness about the Heavens protecting them against the storms was an assurance they did not themselves believe.

"The wagons overtook the hand-carts at the Platte crossing, west, I think, of Laramie, and the poor hand-cart folks were thoroughly worn out and weak alike in body and mind. Under all circumstances they were regularly called up to prayers, and it was remarked that the shorter the rations the longer were the prayers. At this time great numbers of the emigrants died. I do not know how many, and will not attempt to conjecture, for a general account is sufficiently painful without particularizing. The wagon and hand-cart train camped together at the crossing of the river—and such a crossing ! The men from the ox-train made each several trips across the Platte, sometimes pulling a hand-cart, and sometimes carrying on their backs a sick or weak man, woman, or child. Then, after all were over, there followed more long prayers and lengthened exhortations, to which the poor emigrants listened in their wet clothes and shivering with the cold. These prayers were succeeded by the distribution of their scanty rations.

"Next morning one of the men was found close to camp, dead and partly eaten by the wolves. He had gone out and was perhaps too tired or too careless of life, or possibly was unable to return. It was at this place that Tyler, when asked to lend his riding mule for the purpose of helping to take the sick and the aged men and women across, refused, assigning as a reason that he did not want his mules worn out. The mortality at this camp was greater than usual.

"The first snow which overtook the emigrants was on the east side of the river at the last Platte crossing, about sixty or seventy miles below Devil's Gate, near Red Buttes. Several trappers and traders lived there, among whom were Reichau, Seminole, Baptiste, Pappau, and others. The river was forded and camp made some two or three miles up on the other side. Here there was a very heavy snow-storm, and the train was unable to move at all. It was at this camp that Joseph A. Young and Steve Taylor met the disheartened emigrants and infused into them new energy. The grass was covered with snow, and cottonwood trees were cut down so that the cattle might feed upon the bark and small branches.

"The toilsome march was again renewed under increased difficulties, and when we had advanced as far as Sage creek we met some more of the returned missionaries sent out by Brigham Young at the October conference to help the people through the difficulties caused by the foolish and fatal delay at the starting-point. C. H. Wheelock and John Van Cott were among this relief party. Too much praise cannot be given to those who thus came out from Salt Lake to help us : they worked like heroes, and their moral influence accomplished perhaps as much as their bodily efforts, for they were full of stamina, while the emigrants were utterly worn out.

" The toilsome march was immediately resumed, and to give you an idea of how low the oxen were, I may mention the fact that the pulling of the wagons up Prospect Hill killed several of them—perhaps fifteen.

" On arrival at Devil's Gate on the Sweetwater, where we found five or six log-houses in a dilapidated condition, it was concluded that the hand-carts should go no farther. A temporary halt was therefore made, and a remodelling of both trains was made. The wagons were unloaded and the contents stored in two of the log-houses; the hand-carts were unloaded and the people were put into the wagons, as many being placed in each wagon as the teams could move, and the remainder were left. Assistance was constantly arriving from Salt Lake, and those fresh teams helped wonderfully.

" The weather now set in so cold that in two days the Sweetwater river was frozen thick enough to bear the wagons and teams, and they crossed on the ice. Several more people died and were buried at Devil's Gate. Twenty men were detailed to remain there all winter to take care of the property left, and also a lot of young stock that was too poor to drive through at that time. D. W. Jones, Ben. Hampton, and F. M. Alexander—three men from Salt Lake—were appointed to this charge; the other seventeen were emigrants. A small quantity of flour was left with them—some five or six sacks, I should think—and the rest of the people moved on.

" The track of the emigrants was marked by graves, and many of the living suffered almost worse than death. One sick man there, who was holding by the wagon-bars to save himself from the jolting, had all his fingers frozen off. Men may be seen to-day in Salt Lake City, who were boys then, hobbling round on their club-feet, all their toes having been frozen off in that fearful march.

" It is a noticeable fact that, as a rule, the men failed first: the poor fellows toiled on until they could do so no longer. They have been accused of a lack of consideration, and of being devoid of all manhood, to let women and girls slave as they did. It is true that a fearful amount of selfishness, not to say brutality, was brought to the surface; but perhaps the above few words of explanation may serve to temper the opinion which might otherwise have been formed respecting the conduct of some of them. It may possibly be said that the men should have worked until they died on their tracks, rather than see wives and mothers engage in that terrible toil. Some certainly did so, and for those who did not, it may be urged that humanity is frail at best, and that hunger and hard work, endured hundreds of miles from any hope of relief in the full bitterness of a most inclement season, not only destroy all romance but deaden the natural feelings of the most manly and affectionate.

" What remained of the last hand-cart and ox-train companies for that season were got into Salt Lake by the exercise of almost superhuman exertions, and numbers died after their arrival.

" The twenty left at the Devil's Gate were at once put on rations of

21

flour, but of meat they had enough, such as it was. The weather was intensely cold ; the snow fell deep, and the wolves soon began to make sad havoc among the poor stock, and what the wolves spared the season threatened to kill. The remainder was therefore driven up, killed, and the meat frozen. A United States mail came up from the East, but could take their mud wagons no further, so the men left them and started again with packed mules, but they could not travel, and returned to the Platte Bridge. This I mention to show that no provisions could reach the Devil's Gate.

"The flour was soon consumed, and meat without salt was the only article of food, and even that began to run short. About this time Jones and another man took the only two horses that were left—all the rest had died—and started for Platte Bridge to try and obtain some supplies. The first night out the wolves killed one horse, and the other was not seen until spring; so they returned empty-handed and on foot. There was very little game, and only a buffalo, a deer, and a few rabbits were shot. Finally the meat was consumed ; then the hides were eaten, as also all the hide wrapped round the wheels of the hand-carts, and every scrap about the wagons and the neck-piece of the buffalo-skin, which had already done service as a doormat for two months. In the spring they subsisted on thistle roots, segoes, and a species of wild garlic, until flour came down from Salt Lake. But, to cut a long story short, the twenty men eventually got safely through ; terribly emaciated it is true, but still safely.

"Such was the ending of the 'divine plan' for emigrating the poor in the year 1856."

The story of the hand-cart expedition has now been partially told, and that for the first time, to the public, for no pen can ever fully trace nor pencil picture the sufferings of that poor, devoted people. It would melt the hardest heart to listen to the personal recitals of that horrible journey which in moments of confidence the sufferers relate to their friends. One of the elders, whose pen was the most potent in England in urging the poor to emigrate by hand-carts, and who in the honest sincerity of his faith confided implicitly in the inspiration of apostles and prophets, was destined to witness and share in the deepest of that suffering. Of the intensity of the cold which the last company endured, his story is almost incredible. Men and women sitting on a wagon-tongue, on the ground, or leaning against their fragile carts while eating their scanty fare would in an instant die without an evidence of coming change. With a morsel of bread or biscuit in their hands, bearing it to their mouths, could be seen men, hale-looking and apparently strong, stiff in death. Such scenes can hardly be imagined by those who did not witness them, but to the hundreds of men and women who had fled from "merry "England" to escape the destruction which they were taught was coming upon the Gentile nations, what a commentary was there upon the predictions of men who claimed to be the inspired servants of the most high God, in that bitter struggle for life.

But the reader will justly inquire—What was the sequel to the hand-cart story, and how was it understood in Utah?

When the news reached Brigham Young, as already stated, he did all that man could do to save the remnant and relieve the sufferers. Never in his whole career did he shine so gloriously in the eyes of the people. There was nothing spared that he could contribute or command. In the Tabernacle he was "the Lion of the Lord," and "his fierce anger was kin- "dled" against those whom he supposed were the cause of the calamity.

The apostle Richards was at once chosen as the victim of his wrath, and upon him and his counsellor, elder Daniel Spencer, he spent the fury of his soul. When Brigham is aroused he thinks of nothing but the annihilation of his enemy. A more humble, devoted worshipper of Brigham never breathed than the apostle Richards had been; at Brigham's word he would have licked the dust of his feet, and to carry out the purposes of his prophet he would have travelled to the ends of the earth, or would have joyfully given his life to shield him from harm. By nature F. D. Richards is a kind, good man, with more love and devotion than are good for him, and it was in his pride to make Brigham great in carrying out the "divine plan" that he had aroused the poor Mormons in Europe to emigrate in greater numbers than he had at last the capacity to control and direct. He counted upon the aid of a brother apostle—John Taylor—then at New York, which he appears not to have received in the way that he expected, and, that failing him, the doom of the hand-cart scheme became a certainty.

Blinded, it is charged, by pride and selfishness, neither of these apostles foresaw the distant results of this misunderstanding, or neither of them would have risked the consequences; but there was a valuable lesson in store for both, and still more important instruction for the Mormons.

The agency of the Mormon emigration at that time was a very profitable appointment. With this department attached to the Liverpool publishing office, the presidency of the British mission was always coveted by the apostles. It afforded many " opportunities " * of replenishing the family purse.

By arrangement with ship-brokers at Liverpool, a commission of half a guinea per head was allowed the agent for every adult emigrant that he sent across the Atlantic, and the railroad companies in New York allowed a percentage on every emigrant ticket, and some abatement was also made on the freight of extra baggage in favour of the agent. But a still larger revenue was derived from the outfitting on the frontiers. The agents purchased all the cattle, wagons, tents, wagon-covers, flour, cooking utensils, stoves, and the staple articles for a three months' journey across the plains, and from them the Saints supplied themselves. Many a good editorial was written and sermon preached upon the blessings of unity and accumulative purchases, and " no one could be regarded as in "good standing in the Church " who would sail by other ships, or travel by other direction than that prescribed by the Church.

At the date of the hand-cart expedition, the apostle Richards was president of the Church throughout all Europe. He was also a director of the Perpetual Emigration Fund Organization, and to him was entrusted the financial management of the entire European emigration of that year from Liverpool to Salt Lake. The apostle Taylor was at that time presiding over the Mormons in the Eastern and New England States, with New York for his head-quarters. By ordination, the apostle at New York took precedence of the apostle at Liverpool, and it is presumed entertained the idea that the arrangements for the

* One of the sons of an apostle facetiously replying to an enquiry respecting his father's ability to provide for so many wives and children, when he was without salary or compensation for services rendered to the Church, answered: "He has a "good many *opportunities*."

passage of the emigrants through the States on to the frontiers
should be under his direction. The apostle at Liverpool could
not see things in that light—he only wanted the influence and
assistance of the apostle at New York, but nothing more, and
thus each misunderstood the other's position. Even inspired
apostles may fail in attaining unity of purpose when the subject under consideration is the " almighty dollar."

The early months of 1856 passed away while the two apostles stood upon their dignity and arrived at no understanding,
though each doubtless thought that he was right. New York
waited for some request from Liverpool, and Liverpool waited
with great anxiety for items of information from New York;
" brother Franklin " was nearly crazy because he could not
hear from " brother John," and " brother John " was perfectly
innocent of thinking that " brother Franklin " wanted to hear
from him at all.

After so many promises being made " in the name of the
" Lord " for the success of the " divine plan," it seems strange
that it did not occur to Franklin to get " the Lord " to touch
the intellect of John and bring them to an understanding.
How contemptible appear all the promises that " the Lord "
would still the winds and the waves, would change the seasons
and cause the snow to fall on the right hand and on the left
for the safety of the emigrants going to Zion, while the same
" Lord," whose words had been pledged thousands of times to
the poor Saints, was powerless to touch either of his own apostles and bring them to comprehend that the precious lives of
thousands of persons were placed in jeopardy by their selfishness or pride !

The apostle Taylor got back first to Zion and explained his
action in the matter, which then appeared satisfactory. On
the arrival of the apostle Richards, Brigham attacked him in
the Tabernacle, held him up to ridicule and contempt, and
cursed him in the name of Israel's God. Elder Daniel Spencer,
who had been the counsellor of Richards, came in for his share
of the contempt and anathemas. For years after, the apostle
could scarcely lift up his head; he absented himself from the
public meetings and was rarely seen in times of rejoicing. His
heart was crushed. He could not defend himself, for when

once Brigham has spoken no man who values his favour dares to contradict him. For ten years Richards and Spencer were under a cloud, and silently bore their heavy grief. At length it told upon the riper years of elder Spencer, and he went to his grave a broken-hearted man, the object of much sympathy in the community. Elder Edward W. Tullidge, then one of the editors of the *Utah Magazine*, resolved in that periodical to tell the facts of the hand-cart story, and exonerate the apostle Richards and elder Spencer. Mr. Tullidge was in the Liverpool office editing the *Millennial Star*, under Richards, at the time of outfitting the emigrants, and knew that it was humanly impossible for the apostle Richards to have done more than he did, and that the whole calamity which befell the emigrants was due to the misunderstanding between the Liverpool and New York offices, as here narrated.

Brigham, by the merest accident, heard of the intended revelation in the *Magazine*. He sent for Mr. Godbe, the principal owner of that periodical, and, though one side of the whole edition had been worked off, the order was given to destroy it, and it was destroyed: not a copy saw daylight. It would not then do to show that Brigham had ruined an innocent man; besides, it would have been dangerous to have attacked the other.

To the apostle Richards, favours have since been shown, and he is working up again to his former prominence among the apostles; but Brigham retracts nothing, and the anathemas are left in the minds of the people. What a commentary upon Brigham's claim to the possession of " a priesthood that is in-" fallible ! "

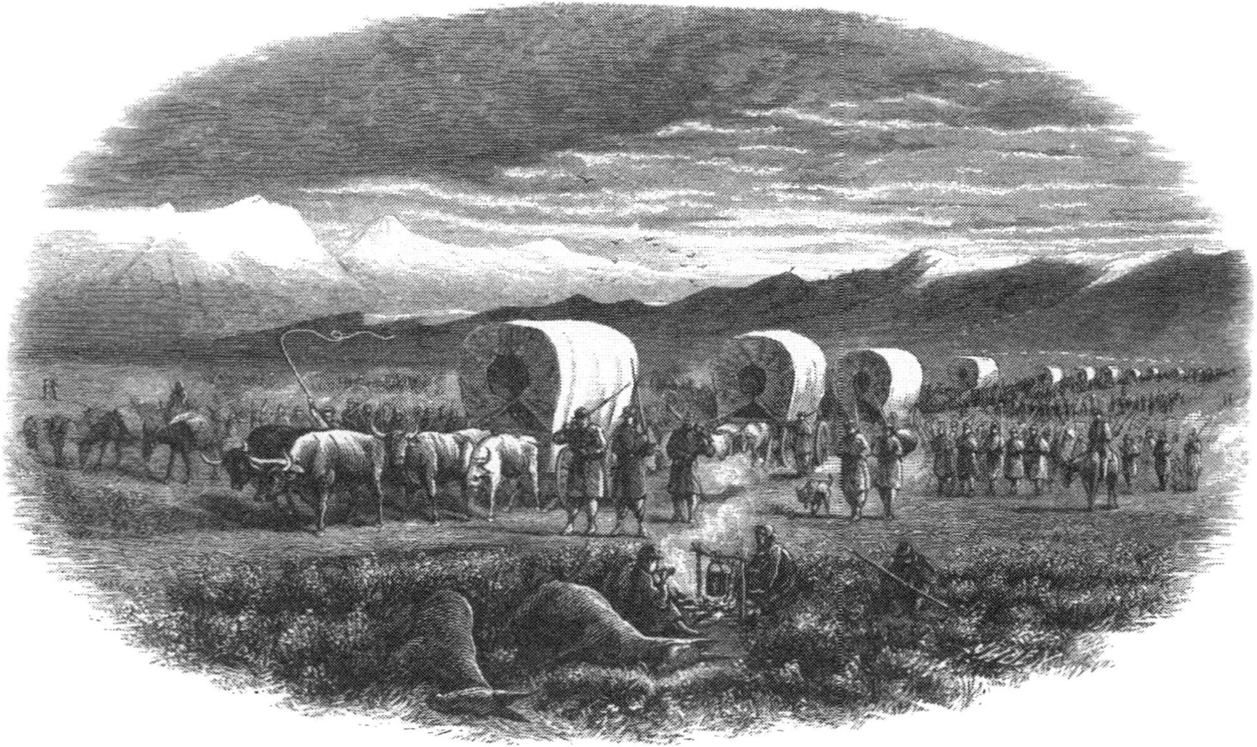

THE UNITED STATES EXPEDITION TO UTAH.

CHAPTER XXXVIII.

THE MORMON WAR.—How it was inaugurated—Isolation of Utah—Carrying the
Mails—Mormon Enterprise—Senator Douglas and the Saints—Anniversary Festivities at Big Cottonwood Lake—New Official Appointments for Utah—Warlike
Preparations of the Saints—Believers concentrated at Zion—Ludicrous Fears of
some Elders—Major Van Vleit sent by the United States Government—Brigham
receives him—Major Van Vleit's Story—Brigham's Proclamation—Defiance from
the Tabernacle—Brigham's Wrath—Heber's Enthusiasm—Expedition of the United
States Army—Dogberryism of Brigham—D. H. Wells instructs the Brethren to
harass the Army—The Mormons burn the United States Trains—Great Suffering
of the Troops—Mules and Cattle freeze on the Road—Thirty-five miles in fifteen Days!

WHILE the Mormons were locked out by deep snows on the
mountains from nearly all intercourse with the Eastern States,
and were almost as destitute of news from the Pacific, they had
little idea of the stir which Utah had created everywhere
throughout the Union.

Perfectly unconscious of having disturbed the tranquillity
of any one, and never suspecting that the great sermons of the
Tabernacle would be taken for more than buncombe, the Mormon leader began in early spring to carry out his projects at
home and his missions abroad.

One of the citizens of Utah had obtained the contract from
the Post-Office Department for the transportation of the United
States mails across the plains between Leavenworth, Kansas,
and Salt Lake City. In this Brigham saw the foundation for a
grand carrying company, and bent all his energies to organize
a "B. Y. Express." He gathered around him the most in-
trepid men of the mountains, pressed the brethren who had
"stock" to join in the enterprise, and succeeded in controlling
all that was necessary to make the company successful.

The winter snows of 1856-7 had tarried long on the mountains and the plains, and this rendered the stocking of the road and the building of stations over the long distance of 1,200 miles a very severe task. But there was every incentive to more than ordinary diligence. The Government had never exhibited much favour to any Mormon citizen, and delay in commencing the new mail contract might be seized as a pretext for repudiating the new contractor. With this fully impressed upon their minds, the most daring and hardy of the mountaineers were called to assist, and in an incredibly short space of time, and in the midst of very severe weather, stations were built and relays of horses and mules were strung all the way along the travelled route from the mountains to the river. There was a fair prospect then that the " B. Y. Express Carrying Company " would have grown into a gigantic enterprise, conveying all the merchandise and mails from the East, and have placed Utah, by means of express messengers, in daily intercourse with the rest of the world, a decade before that desired end was accomplished by the railroad. This was to all appearance the most sensible enterprise that Brigham ever attempted ; but, alas !

> " The best laid schemes o' mice an' men
> " Gang aft a-gley."

The correspondence from Utah, the serious charges of the judges, the wire-pulling of contractors, and the deep-laid schemes of politicians,* were too much for any government to resist ; but the unkindest cut of all was the desertion of the Mormon interest by their long-tried friend, Senator Stephen A. Douglas.

As circuit judge in Illinois, that honourable gentleman had befriended the founder of Mormonism, when he was the victim of an erring interpretation of the law, or the subject of

---

* It is difficult to resist the conclusion that the opportunity afforded by the U. S. military expedition to Utah in 1857 was not eagerly seized by Mr. Floyd as favourable to the long-cherished scheme for the rebellion of 1861. At all events, as will be seen in the succeeding chapter, placing " the flower of the American army " so far away from rail and water, with such a huge mass of munitions of war—which were wholly lost to the nation—was not inharmonious with the general plan of Mr. Buchanan's Secretary of War preparatory to the declaration of secession.

unwarrantable interference. The Mormons looked upon the judge very kindly, and in after-years, when he became senator, every delegation from Utah to Congress was certain to consult and listen to his suggestions and counsels.

His "squatter-sovereignty" was their political creed, and while they sought his influence at the seat of government, he found in them the living exponents of the sovereignty doctrine to which he devoted his life. But the time had come when this harmony was to be disturbed.

In the spring of 1856 Senator Douglas delivered a great speech at Springfield, Illinois. It was the announcement of his platform before the assembling of the conventions that were to nominate the successor of President Pierce. In that speech the senator characterized Mormonism as "the loathsome ulcer "of the body politic" and recommended the free use of the scalpel as the only remedy in the hands of the nation. The Author well remembers that speech and its effect upon the Mormons. He was then engaged as assistant editor of *The Mormon*, a weekly paper published in New York city. His first impulse was to notice the speech, but a careful examination of it rendered the expediency of such a course very doubtful. There were so many "ifs" and so often "should it be," that it was at last concluded to leave it alone, for the senator might after all have only said what he did from the necessity of sailing with the popular tide against the Mormons, while at the same time he might in the Senate demand evidence of the criminality of the Mormons before any action was taken against them. Brigham alone could determine what course, if any, should be adopted in respect to the Springfield speech.

Before long the *Deseret News*, Brigham's official organ, presented to the world a reply to Senator Douglas. The priesthood's phials of wrath were poured out without stint or mercy upon the head of their quondam friend and defender. All the good that he had ever done was in a moment forgotten, and all their obligations were in an instant cancelled for ever. An irreconcilable breach was made, and the spirit of prophecy was rampant. The predictions of Joseph that had been embalmed in the catacombs of history were dragged forth from their long and silent slumbers, and the Illinois statesman was reminded

of the time when he was "but a county judge " and when
the Prophet Joseph patronizingly told him that he would yet
be an aspirant for the chair of Washington, that, if he continued
the friend of the Mormons, he should live to be President of
the United States, but if he ever lifted his finger or his voice
against them his plans should be frustrated and his ambitious
hopes utterly disappointed. All this Brigham circumstantially
related to the senator in reply to his Springfield speech, and
closed with the anathemas of the priesthood and the prediction
that the senator should fail in his attempt and never attain to
the goal of his ambition. The Democratic Convention met
in Cincinnati soon after, and Senator Douglas was a candidate
for the Presidency of the United States. The Hon. James
Buchanan was nominated, the Illinois senator was defeated,
Brigham was a prophet, and the faithful rejoiced.[*]

During that campaign, in the fall of 1856, Republicans
carried the banner hostile to polygamy, and Democrats made
speeches against the same institution: the Mormons had no
friends anywhere.

On the 4th of March, 1857, Mr. Buchanan was inaugurated
chief magistrate of the republic, with a cabinet that soon
proved itself hostile to Utah and ready to obey the behests of
the nation in bringing Brigham Young and the Mormons
"into subjection to the laws."

The Mormons had hardly got to the Missouri river with
the first mail from the mountains before the noisy preparations of war were heard. The new mail contractor received
at Leavenworth but one monthly mail to carry across the

---

[*] Senator Douglas was again a candidate for the Presidency in 1860, and received
the nomination of the convention. His chances of success were not unfavourable,
and the Utah Mormons had some anxiety about the prediction. Fortunately the
split in the Democratic party and the candidature of Senator John C. Breckinridge
helped "the Lord " and his people. Mr. Lincoln received of the popular vote
1,857,610; Mr. Douglas was next in order, and received 1,365,976. There was even
then another chance for the prophecy to be defeated, but " the Lord " had the elec-
toral college fairly in his hands, and Mr. Douglas only received twelve votes, while
Mr. Lincoln received 180 ! That was a Red Sea defeat ; and, to add to the dismay
and humiliation of the enemies of " the kingdom," Mr. Douglas was more than
three times distanced by Mr. Bell, and Mr. Breckinridge was six times ahead of the
Illinois senator. Nothing could have been more satisfactory to the Saints. " The
Lord," Joseph, and Brigham had triumphed.

plains, and, when he presented himself for the second, it was denied him. The Government had concluded on a change; an act of bad faith which "military necessity" alone might perhaps justify; but the ground upon which the contract was said to be annulled was discreditable to the Government and tended to impress the Mormons more and more with dislike to the representatives of the nation.

Brigham's representative in the East, A. O. Smoot, then mayor of Salt Lake City, a discreet and honourable man, hastened back to the mountains bearing with him evidence of the appointment of a new governor and new Federal officers for Utah, who were to be escorted thither by "the flower of "the American army."

Utah had passed through severe trials in 1856. There had been Indian troubles, the destruction of the crops by crickets, the Reformation, the unfortunate hand-cart experiment, and the troubles with the judges. The summer of 1857 was promising a rich harvest, the judges had left the Territory, there was no one to disturb or annoy, and nothing could be more appropriate than a grand celebration on the return of "the "anniversary of their deliverance"—the 24th of July, the day when the pioneers entered Salt Lake Valley. It was a great anniversary and a day to be celebrated with great rejoicing.

To avoid the enervating effects of processional display in the city, Brigham invited those who had the means of transportation to join him in an excursion to Big Cottonwood Lake, distant about twenty-four miles from Salt Lake City, and nearly ten thousand feet above the level of the sea. It was a kind of three days' jubilee. One day was given to getting up a steep, narrow, and rugged cañon, fixing tents, and preparing for enjoyment; the second was a day of festivity, and the last was devoted to a quiet return home, under the pleasant influences of the rejoicings of the previous day.

On the 24th of July, 1857, there were probably gathered at the lake about two thousand persons—men, women, and children—in the fullest enjoyment of social freedom. Some were fishing in the lake, others strolling among the trees, climbing the high peaks, pitching quoits, playing cricket, engaging in gymnastic exercises, pic-nicking, and gliding through the boweries that were prepared for the mazy dance. It was a day of feasting, joy, and amusement for the silver-haired veteran and the toddling child. The welkin rang with the triumphant songs of Zion, and these, accompanied by the sweet melody of many-toned instruments of music, thrilled every bosom with enthusiastic joy. Their exuberance was the pure outgushing of their souls' emotion, and owned no earthly inspiration, for their only beverage was the sparkling nectar of Eden, while their sympathies were united by a sacred and fraternal bond of affectionate love, which for the time rendered them oblivious of the artificial distinctions of social life. The highest and the lowest rejoiced together, rank and authority were set aside ; it was a day in which the dreary past could be favourably contrasted with the joyous present, and hearts were made glad in the simple faith that the God of their fathers was their protector, and that they were his peculiar people.

When Brigham, ten years before, had addressed the pioneers at their first halting-place in the Valley, he spoke to them of the mobs that had driven them from their homes in Missouri and in Illinois, and of the Government that deserved its share of condemnation for affording them no redress. In winding up that speech, he expressed the confidence that he felt in the future, and the assurance that, if the Saints had ten years of peace from that time, " he would ask no odds of " Uncle Sam or the devil ! "

With a full realization of the weight and importance of the news of which he was the bearer, elder Smoot lost no time on the plains, and, knowing well that the tenth anniversary would be celebrated, he strained every nerve to be present—not to mar the happiness of the occasion, but to afford his chief the best opportunity for instructing the people before they separated to all parts of the Territory.

The weary journey from the States was at length accomplished, and, before the sun had crimsoned the snowy peaks that surrounded the worshipping, rejoicing Saints, Brigham was in possession of the news, and the people were listening with breathless attention to the most stiring, important address that ever their leader had uttered, for upon his decision depended peace or war.

Brigham was undaunted. With the inspiration of such surroundings—the grandeur of the Wahsatch range of the Rocky Mountains everywhere encircling him, the stately trees whose foliage of a century's growth towered proudly to the heavens, the multitude of people before him who had listened to his counsels as if hearkening to the voice of the Most High

Brigham's Declaration of Independence.

—men and women who had followed him from the abodes of civilization to seek shelter in the wilderness from mobs, prattling innocents and youths who knew nothing of the world but Utah, and who looked to him as a father for protection—what could he not say?

"God was with them, and the devil had taken him at his "word. He had said ten years before, and he could but repeat "it, he would ask no odds of Uncle Sam or the devil." He preached to them; and he prophesied that in twelve years from that time he himself should be President of the United States, or would dictate who should be.*

* It is extremely difficult to persuade men who claim to be governed by "a "priesthood that is infallible" that their utterances have any other origin than the natural inspiration of antagonistic convictions. Parley P. Pratt's prediction about La Roy Sunderland, already alluded to (page 5), is an example in point. He says:

"And furthermore, as Mr. La Roy Sunderland has lied concerning the truth of heaven—the falness of the Gospel, and his blasphemed against the Word of God, except he speedily repent and acknowledge his lying and wickedness and obey the

With such glory before their wondering eyes, the simple-hearted people sang again their songs of joy, and he blessed them over and over again. They renewed their dancing in the boweries, and when the day was fully spent they returned happily to their tents, more than ever satisfied that the angels had charge concerning them. Sublime spectacle of faith!

Before the news reached elder Smoot's ears that the newly installed administration had resolved upon a thorough change in Utah, President Buchanan and his Secretary of War, John B. Floyd, had already made an entirely new list of Federal appointments, and issued orders for the march of the army. Alfred Cumming, of Georgia, was the new Governor; D. R. Eckles, Chief-Justice; John Cradlebaugh and Charles E. Sinclair, Associate Justices; John Hartnett, Secretary; and Peter K. Dotson, Marshal.

It is an understood thing among the Saints that nothing of this kind should take place without "the Lord" previously notifying the Prophet of what was about to transpire; but it is very evident that the evil one, who is always "seeking to "destroy the kingdom," did get *a little* the start of the Prophet on this occasion. Long before elder Smoot reached the scene of rejoicing at Big Cottonwood Lake, the United States army was on the march. Brigadier-General W. S. Harney was appointed commander of the expedition, and Major Stew-

---

message of eternal truth which God has sent for the salvation of his people, God will smite him dumb that he can no longer speak great swelling words against the Lord; and trembling shall seize his nerves, that he shall not be able to write, and *Zion's Watchman* shall cease to be published abroad; and its lies shall no longer deceive the public; and he will wander a vagabond on the earth, until sudden destruction shall overtake him; and, if Mr. La Roy Sunderland inquires when shall these things be? I reply, It is nigh thee—even at thy doors; and I say this in the name of Jesus Christ. Amen."—*P. P. Pratt's " Zion's Watchman Unmasked," New York, 1838.*

Parley's expression, "Nigh thee, even at thy doors," is very slow of fulfilment. Thirty-four years have passed away, and Mr. Sunderland still persists in speaking and writing, and awkwardly refuses to " wander about a vagabond on the earth un-"til sudden destruction shall overtake him," and to this day his opinion of Parley's fanaticism is unchanged, and he still regards Mormonism as a gross delusion. He won't repent!

The "twelve years," and a few more, have passed away since Brigham uttered the prediction that he should be President of the United States, and he is to-day further away from its fulfilment than he was when he announced to the following Saints in Cottonwood cañon this and others of his seed.

art Van Vleit had been selected as Captain Assistant Quarter-Master, to repair immediately to Utah in advance of the army to make the necessary purchases of lumber for their quarters, forage for the animals, and such provisions as might be required for the subsistence of the troops.

The Saints had no time now to lose; the enemy was approaching their homes. War was then everything in Utah. The leaders preached war, prayed war, taught war; while saintly poets scribbled war, and the people sang their ditties. " The God of Battles " was the deity of the hour, and his influence was everywhere seen and felt. Public works and private enterprise were alike suspended, while every artist who had sufficient genius for the manufacture of revolvers, repairing old guns, or burnishing and sharpening rusty sabres and bayonets, was pressed into service for the defence of Zion. The sisters, too, were seized with the war-fever, and their weaving and knitting talents were fully exercised in preparation for the coming campaign. It was a great time for rejoicing in the Lord, cursing Uncle Sam, and keeping powder dry.

Two apostles, Amasa M. Lyman and Charles C. Rich, had successfully established a colony of Mormons at San Bernardino, in Southern California. Orders were immediately dispatched to them, and to Orson Hyde's colony in Carson Valley, to " break up " and come home for the defence of Zion.* A special messenger was sent to Europe to direct the apostles Orson Pratt and Ezra T. Benson to send home immediately all the Utah elders, and to return themselves the best way they could. The elders who were on missions in the Atlantic and Pacific States were all " called in " to protect their families in the coming struggle.

When " the Lord " called upon Joseph to go up and re-

* The property then abandoned by the Mormons in Southern California is now worth millions, and the claims of the others in Carson, Washoe, and Jack's valleys in one year after their evacuation of the country became immensely valuable through the discovery of the celebrated mines of Nevada. The Mormons had taken up the whole of the land on both sides of the Carson river in Eagle valley. Carson City the capital of Nevada, was the property of a Mormon, and the site of what is now Dayton was sold by one of the brethren for " a plug of a pony " to help him back to Zion. For all their property the six hundred persons did not receive, probably, more than $5,000. Brigham's decision for a fruitless war cost something.

deem Zion in Missouri, the Prophet could only muster two
hundred and five "warriors," but the times were changed.
Israel had grown and multiplied, and in numbers was not now
to be despised. The republic was a great nation, but Zion was
greater. The prophecies were about to be fulfilled, and what
the Saints wanted in cannon and munitions of war they could
make up in faith. Not only were the missionary elders eager
to return to the mountains for the protection of their families,
but, could it have been accomplished, thousands of the Saints
in Europe and the States would have rallied round the standard
of the Prophet. There was no fear, no hesitation anywhere;
every one believed that "the Lord" would come out of his
hiding place and vex the nation.

The *Western Standard*, the Mormon organ then published
in San Francisco, and *The Mormon*, published in New York,
were ordered to be discontinued—the world was to be left without light. The missionary elders returning from Europe landed
at New York as secretly as possible, and made their way westward to the frontiers by various routes, so that they should not
be recognized or hindered by any action of the Government as
they journeyed home, or be delayed by any annoyances on the
part of the citizens as they passed by.

The Utah elders are by no means cowards, but many of
them when returning had formed the idea that Uncle Sam was
ready to devour them, and that the devil was always at their el-
bow ready to denounce them as they passed along. If a person
chanced to look twice at any of them, or ask a question about their
destination or object in travelling, he was instantly regarded as a
spy or some Government officer in disguise, who meant mischief and peril to them. A number of elders returning from
their missions to Europe, while passing through Chicago, met
with a little difficulty which did serious damage to the cause
of human enlightenment. An officer in blue, with eagle buttons, chanced to put up at the same hotel, and one of the chief
brethren at sight of him was instantly demoralized. Visions
of a terrible fate troubled his mind; he and his brethren were
certainly going to be thoroughly overhauled, and, it any papers
were found upon them that would establish their identity as
Mormons, detection was a certainty. He communicated his

apprehensions to the others, and counselled the immediate destruction of all the books and papers that any of the brethren chanced to carry about their persons or in their satchels. One of the elders had been for years the "private secretary of "Brigham Young," and had kept a pocket-journal in which he had jotted down the inspired droppings of the sanctuary. It was to him then a priceless treasure, and undoubtedly would one day have become a valuable contribution to the historian's office. It was brimful of choice sayings, bits of some rare revelations and interpretations of others, dates, memoranda, "bless- "ings," and receipts for money paid. In it, too, were tracings of the names of his forefathers and foremothers, for whom he was yet to be baptized in the Temple, in order to aid their salvation and deliverance from the hands of the devil. It was one of those priceless bijous that no one can ever part with, and "brother Thomas" held on to it as a fond mother to her only child. But obedience to "counsel" was insisted on, and this rich treasure, this priceless journal, was tearfully consigned to the dark caverns of a Chicago third-class hotel sewerage! Poor Thomas! Years later, with tears in his eyes, he narrated to the Author his grief and the annoyance which he suffered from the loss of his treasured volume. Thomas probably may not have quite so much faith to-day, and may fret less.

The apostles from Europe, and a few elders who attended them as a body-guard, crossed the Atlantic *incognito*, preserved themselves secretly in New York till the Pacific steamer sailed for San Francisco, preferring the long sea journey and the western route, *via* Southern California, rather than the risk of following the usual route of the Saints to Zion through the Atlantic States, and across the plains where the troops were journeying.

A high priest, who was presiding over the Saints in the Atlantic States at the outbreak of the Mormon war, was so terror stricken that, if he saw a sergeant or captain of police in a street car in which he chanced to be riding, he would become perfectly nervous. He it was who had first in New York given the Utah elders counsel to store away their books and papers where they would be safe till they could send for them, and it was the private secretary's attachment to his journal and dis-

22

obedience to this counsel that terrified the chief elder in Chicago, till he could see nothing in the memoranda but a veritable Jonah that would sink the whole ship.

The high priest while in New York would have died from sheer fright, had he not been stimulated to live by the kindly glances of a sweet Connecticut maiden, who in time became his second wife. Before the war, while he was a brave preacher and defiant of all earthly powers, he had worn what was called a Kossuth overcoat, but that was now too conspicuous, and all the braid and filligree-work had to come off lest it should lead to his identity. A coloured barber, who had long dyed the high priest's locks, in a moment of gushing kindness and with his blandest smile exclaimed to him : "Massa, I knows who "you was ! Yah, yah !" That ebony acquaintance was cut for ever. The Author well remembers the last time that he was chatting with "the judge" on the affairs in Utah, at a new boarding-house where he had hoped that no one would recognize him as a Mormon. He could scarcely speak above a whisper, and feared that some one might hear through the keyhole. Very different was the Author's own experience. He was known and seen daily in the offices of the New York press, and treated with more respect and attention by those who knew that he was a Mormon than he would probably have been had he been a Gentile ; he saw no signs of the nation's vindictiveness, and witnessed and heard nothing that could possibly be construed into "persecution of the Saints" on the part of the republic.

Major Van Vleit arrived in Salt Lake City in the beginning of September. He was politely received by Governor Young, but was informed with great frankness that they had abundance of all he required, but they would sell nothing to the Government, and were determined that the United States troops should not enter Salt Lake Valley. Through the politeness of Major-General Van Vleit, the Author is able to give portions of that officer's report to the commanding general of the army, which throw great light upon this period of Mormon history :

"He [Brigham] stated that the Mormons had been persecuted, murdered, and robbed in Missouri and Illinois, both by the mob and State authorities, and that now the United States were about to pursue the same course, and that, therefore, he and the people of Utah had determined to resist all persecution at the commencement, and that the *troops now on the march for Utah should not enter the Great Salt Lake Valley.* As he uttered these words, all there present concurred most heartily in what he said. . . . In the course of my conversation with the Governor and the influential men in the Territory, I told them plainly and frankly what I conceived would be the result of their present course. I told them that they might prevent the small military force now approaching Utah from getting through the narrow defiles and rugged passes of the mountains this year, but that next season the United States Government would send troops sufficient to overcome all opposition. The answer to this was invariably the same : ' We are aware that such will be the case ; but when those troops arrive, they will find Utah a desert, every house will be burned to the ground, every tree cut down, and every field laid waste. We have three years' provisions on hand, which we will *cache*, and then take to the mountains, and bid defiance to all the powers of the Government.'

" I attended their service on Sunday, and in course of a sermon delivered by elder Taylor he referred to the approach of the troops, and declared *they should not enter the Territory.* He then referred to the probability of an overpowering force being sent against them, and desired all present, who would apply the torch to their own buildings, cut down their trees, and lay waste their fields, to hold up their hands ; every hand in an audience numbering over four thousand persons was raised at the same moment."

The Major further reported that he anticipated that the Mormons would burn the grass on the plains, stampede the cattle, and hinder the advance of the expedition till the snow rendered it impossible for the army to force a passage through the cañons, and suggested that Fort Bridger should be selected for winter-quarters.

At the very moment when this representative of the Government was listening to the harangues of Brigham Young and the Mormon leaders against the advance of the army, and protesting their innocence of the charges preferred against them, there was perpetrated, two hundred and fifty miles south of Salt Lake City, the darkest crime on record in American history—the Mountain Meadows massacre, in which over one hundred and twenty men, women, and children were butchered by Indians and Mormons ! A fouler deed of treachery was

never known in any nation professing the Christian faith.
Had Mormonism up to that hour been stainless, had its principles been as pure as the breathings around the throne of Jehovah, that one cursed deed unatoned for was alone sufficient
to shut against it for ever the portals of heaven. The historian's pen will yet record that the hand of an avenging angel
has been uplifted in retributive justice ever since against the
shedders of that innocent blood, and the withering curse of the
Almighty has followed that priesthood who had not the manhood to rise up and demand that the cause of which they were
the exponents should not be blighted by the bloody work of
savages who claimed to be their brethren in Christ and the
anointed of the Lord. The people were horrified at the deed,
and it has been the canker-worm of their souls ever since.

On the 14th of September Major Van Vleit left the city
and returned to the East. The next day Brigham issued the
following document :

" PROCLAMATION BY THE GOVERNOR.

" *Citizens of Utah :* We are invaded by a hostile force, who are evidently assailing us to accomplish our overthrow and destruction.

" For the last twenty-five years we have trusted officials of the Government, from constables and justices to judges, governors, and presidents,
only to be scorned, held in derision, insulted, and betrayed. Our houses
have been plundered and then burned, our fields laid waste, our principal
men butchered while under the pledged faith of the Government for their
safety, and our families driven from their homes to find that shelter in
the barren wilderness, and that protection among hostile savages which
were denied them in the boasted abodes of Christianity and civilization.

" The Constitution of our common country guarantees to us all that we
do now, or have ever, claimed.

" If the Constitutional rights which pertain unto us as American citizens were extended to Utah according to the spirit and meaning thereof,
and fairly and impartially administered, it is all that we could ask—all
that we ever asked.

" Our opponents have availed themselves of prejudice existing against
us because of our religious faith, to send out a formidable host to accomplish our destruction. We have had no privilege, no opportunity of defending ourselves from the false, foul, and unjust aspersions against us before the nation.

" The Government has not condescended to cause an investigating
committee or other person to be sent to enquire into and ascertain the
truth, as is customary in such cases.

" We know those aspersions to be false, but that avails us nothing. We are condemned unheard, and forced to an issue with an armed mercenary mob, which has been sent against us at the instigation of anonymous letter-writers, ashamed to father the base, slanderous falsehoods which they have given to the public; of corrupt officials who have brought false accusations against us to screen themselves in their own infamy; of hireling *priests* and *howling* editors, who prostitute the truth for filthy lucre's sake.

" The issue which has been thus forced upon us compels us to resort to the great first law of self-preservation, and stand in our own defence, a right guaranteed to us by the genius of the institutions of our country, and upon which the Government is based.

" Our duty to ourselves, to our families, requires us not tamely to be driven and slain without an attempt to preserve ourselves. Our duty to our country, our holy religion, our God, to freedom and liberty, requires that we should not quietly stand still and see those fetters forging around which are calculated to enslave, and bring us in subjection to an unlawful military despotism, such as can only emanate (in a country of constitutional law) from usurpation, tyranny, and oppression.

" *Therefore* I, Brigham Young, Governor, and Superintendent of Indian Affairs for the Territory of Utah, in the name of the people of the United States in the Territory of Utah:

" 1st. Forbid all armed forces of every description from coming into this Territory, under any pretence whatever.

" 2d. That all the forces in said Territory hold themselves in readiness to march at a moment's notice to repel any and all such invasion.

" 3rd. Martial law is hereby declared to exist in this Territory from and after the publication of this proclamation, and no person shall be allowed to pass or repass into or through, or from the Territory without a permit from the proper officers.

" Given under my hand and seal at ,Great Salt Lake City, Territory of Utah, this 15th day of September, A. D. 1857, and of the Independence of the United States of America the 82nd.

(Signed)   " BRIGHAM YOUNG."

On the following day (Sunday) the Tabernacle discourses were overflowing with inspiration. For years the Saints had been listening to predictions which promised them national independence. They had been looking forward to the time when the Government by some act of folly should rise up against the Lord's anointed and force an issue that would justify the Saints in throwing off their allegiance and verify the inspiration of the apostle Taylor:

" We'll burst off all our fetters, and break the Gentile yoke,
"For long it has beset us, but now it shall be broke :
    " No more shall Jacob bow his neck ;
    " Henceforth he shall be free
" In Upper California—oh, that's the land for me! " *

When the congregation in the morning had got well seated,
and prayer had been offered, in an unctuous tone Brigham
spoke of his confidence in the future, and then bursting out
revealed himself in this fashion :

" This people are free ; they are not in bondage to any government on
God's footstool. We have transgressed no law, and we have no occasion
to do so, neither do we intend ; but as for any nation's coming to destroy
this people, God Almighty being my helper, they cannot come here. [The
congregation responded a loud ' Amen.'] . . .

" We have borne enough of their oppression and hellish abuse, and we
will not bear any more of it, for there is no just law requiring further forbearance on our part. And I am not going to have troops here to protect
the priests and hellish rabble in efforts to drive us from the land we possess ; for the Lord does not want us to be driven, and has said, ' If you
will assert your rights, and keep my commandments, you shall never again
be brought into bondage by your enemies.' . . . They say that their
army is legal ; and I say that such a statement is as false as hell, and that
they are as rotten as an old pumpkin that has been frozen seven times, and
then melted in a harvest sun. Come on with your thousands of illegally-
ordered troops, and I will promise you, in the name of Israel's God, that
you shall melt away as the snow before a July sun. . . .

" You might as well tell me that you can make hell into a powder-
house, as to tell me that you could let an army in here, and have peace ;
and I intend to tell them and show them this, if they do not stay away.
. . . And I say our enemies shall not slip ' the bow on old Bright's neck '
again. God bless you. Amen."

"Brother Heber," Brigham's first counsellor, an eccentric,
good-natured, jocular Saint, wanted to have a hand in the fight,
and gushing over with " the Spirit " he set forth his views of
the situation :

" Is there a collision between us and the United States ? No ; we have
not collashed ; that is the word that sounds nearest to what I mean. But
now the thread is cut between them and us, and we will never gybe again
—no never, worlds without end. [Voices, 'Amen.'] . . .

" Do as you are told, and Brigham Young will never leave the governorship of this Territory, from this time henceforth and for ever. No,

* Hymn Book, p. 353.

never. And there shall no wicked judge with his whore ever sit in our courts again ; for all who are against Israel are an abomination to me and to our God. The spirit that is upon me this morning is the spirit of the Lord, that is, the Holy Ghost—though some of you may think the Holy Ghost is never cheerful. Well, let me tell you, the Holy Ghost is a man ; he is one of the sons of our Father and our God, and he is that man that stood next to Jesus Christ—just as I stand by Brother Brigham. . . . You think our Father and our God is not a lively, sociable, and cheerful man ; he is one of the most lively men that ever lived. . . . Brother Brigham is my leader, he is my Prophet and my Seer, my Revelator ; and whatever he says, that is for me to do, and it is not for me to question him one word, nor to question God a minute." *

Between sermons, Brigham had leisure for further reflection, and as, doubtless, many of the brethren had cordially shaken hands with him on his way to and from home, and blessed "the Lord" for his favour to his servant, he felt that all had not yet been said. With such encouragement, in the afternoon assemblage, after partaking of the sacrament, he again addressed the Saints :

"There cannot be a more damnable, dastardly order issued than was issued by the administration to this people while they were in an Indian country in 1846. Before we left Nauvoo, not less than two United States senators came to receive a pledge from us that we would leave the United States ; and then, while we were doing our best to leave their borders, the poor, low, degraded curses sent a requisition for five hundred men to go and fight their battles ! That was President Polk ; and he is now weltering in hell, with old Zachary Taylor, where the present administration will soon be, if they do not repent.†

"Liars have reported that this people have committed treason, and upon their lies the President has ordered out troops to aid in officering this Territory ; and if those officers are like many who have previously been sent here—and we have reason to believe that they are, or they would not come where they know they are not wanted—they are poor, miserable blacklegs, broken-down political hacks, robbers, and whoremongers ; men

---

* This is an excellent specimen of the compound of blasphemy and ridiculous twaddle to which the audiences in Utah have had to listen. Opposition to such tirades was designated "the Spirit of Apostacy." Were the subject not sacred, what fund of amusement could be found in the apostolic sermons of the Tabernacle. Fancy the Holy Ghost as "a man performing the same offices to Jesus "Christ as Heber did to Brigham !" God himself " is one of the most lively men that "ever lived," and naughty things " are an abomination *to me and* to our God."

† This language ill comports with Brigham's denial, seen on page 280, of having used this language only as " an endorsement " of some one else's statement.

that are not fit for civilized society; so they must dragoon them upon us for officers. I feel that I won't bear such cursed treatment, and that is enough to say—for we are just as free as the mountain air. . . .

"I have told you that if this people will live their religion, all will be well; and I have told you that if there is any man or woman who is not willing to destroy anything or everything of their property that would be of use to an enemy if left, I wanted them to go out of the Territory. And I again say so to-day; for when the time comes to burn and lay waste our improvements, if a man undertakes to shield his, he will be sheared down; for 'judgment will be laid to the line, and righteousness to the plummet.'

"Now the faint-hearted can go in peace; but should that time come, they must not interfere. Before I will suffer what I have in times gone by, there shall not be one building, nor one foot of lumber, nor a stick, nor a tree, nor a particle of grass or hay that will burn, left in reach of our enemies. I am sworn, if driven to extremity, to utterly lay waste, in the name of Israel's God." *

With such sermons and with such threats of death to the lukewarm and rebellious, what could the dissenting among the people do but bend before the storm? The masses were, in the language of the Tabernacle, but "clay in the hands of the "potter," to be shaped and fashioned according to the dictates of a ruler's mind. Brigham's declaration to Major Van Vleit, that "he *and the people* of Utah had determined to resist," is interpreted by his Sunday sermon, wherein he informs the faint-hearted who would not destroy their property that if the troops advanced into the city they should "be sheared down." The reader has but to imagine himself in a sparsely settled desert country, "a thousand miles from everywhere," from which there was no possibility of escape without the loss of everything, and the risk of life itself, and his indignation against the Mormon people for their rebellion will soon change to sympathy.

The brethren made but rough soldiers, although they had been drilled as well as their situation, arms, and the ability of their instructors permitted. They were immediately sent out into Echo Cañon, a narrow defile between the mountains about twenty-five miles in length, through which the troops were expected to pass. There, on the east side, the high rocks were swarming with men engaged in building dry stone walls as a

* *Deseret News*, November 18, 1857.

protection for the riflemen, and on the sloping sides of the
western mountains trenches were dug for the same purpose.
On the east side, at the base of the overhanging mountains,
was the ordinary road through the cañon. The Mormon
engineers had constructed dams for the purpose of throwing a
great body of water on to the west of the road, among the willows and scrub-trees, so that the army would be forced to take
the east side of the cañon, where the Saints were prepared for
them.

On the overhanging rocks large quantities of boulders and
masses of rocks were placed, so that, as the army passed by, a
small leverage would be amply sufficient to hail them down
upon the soldiers. It may be hardly fair to smile at this primitive arrangement, but in these days of rifles and long-range

Echo Cañon—The Mormon Defences.

shells the critical unbeliever can hardly refrain from comparing such defensive operations to the process of "catching birds
"by putting salt on their tails!" As the traveller in the luxurious Pullman cars of the Union Pacific Railroad passes through
that cañon to-day, it is edifying to raise the eyes and see still
standing the dry stone walls—the "bulwarks of Zion."

The officers of the "invading army" had little conception
of the importance of their mission, and were taken by surprise
when, for the first time, they learned what kind of a reception

awaited them. Instead of lead and bullets they anticipated a
repetition of the hospitable reception extended to Col. Steptoe
and his command three years before, and had supplied themselves with lavender and "cream kids" for the parties in the
Social Hall. The little trinkets that speak of thoughtfulness
for the fair sex, and the kindly interchange of social courtesies,
were not forgotten by the younger aspirants to fame and ladies'
graces. In brief, they started West on the best of terms with
themselves and the acquaintances they expected to make.

Major Van Vleit reached Washington in the middle of November, and made the following report to the Secretary of War:

"In explaining to Governor Young the object which the Government
had in view in sending troops to Utah, I told him that the Territory of
Utah had been organized into a separate military department the same as
Florida, Texas, Kansas and other portions of the United States had been,
and the troops crossing the plains had been simply ordered to take post
in it. I told him further that I had seen the orders which were to govern
the commanding officers of the troops, and that they contained no intimation whatever that the troops would or could be used to molest or interfere with the people of Utah. I explained that the troops could only be
called upon to interfere when the authority of the Government was set at
defiance, and only then as a *posse comitatus* on the requisition of the Governor of the Territory, the same as then obtained in the Territory of Kansas.

"I also told them that I was convinced that the intentions of the Government towards the people of Utah were of the most pacific nature, and
that the past was forgotten, and that as the Constitution of the United
States guaranteed to each one entire freedom in religious matters, I was
certain that Governor Cumming would have no instructions that could
in any way interfere with the Mormons as a religious people. I stated
that I had seen Governor Cumming just before I left the frontiers, and
had he had any such instructions I would have been made acquainted
with them.

"In making these statements to Governor Young and other citizens of
Utah, I was governed by a desire to allay if possible the hostile feeling
which I plainly saw existed towards the United States, and to place before them the action of the Government in its true light. I was soon convinced, however, that Governor Young had decided upon the course he
intended to pursue, and could I have laid before him the most pacific intentions of the Government, over the signature of the President himself,
it would not have turned him from it.

"At present Governor Young exercises absolute power, both temporal
and spiritual, over the people of Utah, both of which powers he and the
people profess to believe emanate directly from the Almighty. Hence the

opposition of the people to a new Governor, and the remark of Governor Young that, should Governor Cumming enter the Territory, he would place him in his carriage and send him back.

"I heard elder John Taylor, in a discourse to a congregation of over four thousand Mormons, say that none of the rulers of the earth were entitled to their positions unless appointed to them by the Lord, and that the Almighty had appointed a man to rule over and govern his Saints, and that man was Brigham Young, and that they would have no one else to rule over them."

When the order was given for the march of the troops to Utah, no one could have divined that such terrible misfortunes were in store for them as those which they experienced before the close of the year. The force consisted of two regiments of infantry—the Fifth and Tenth; one regiment of cavalry—the old Second Dragoons; and two batteries of artillery—Reno's and Phelps's. There was nothing forgotten in the equipment of the expedition, and the chief officers were gentlemen of thorough military education and eminently qualified for the position which they held. The probabilities then were all against Brigham, should he conclude to oppose the advance of the army; but, before the end of 1857, a more unfortunate expedition could not well be conceived. The troubles originated at the beginning of the march. Kansas at that moment was supposed to require the presence of General Harney and the Second Dragoons. The General, therefore, never took command of the Utah expedition, and the dragoons were absent from the Plains at the time when they were most required.

General Persifer F. Smith was assigned to the command in place of General Harney, but he fell ill and died at Fort Leavenworth. The infantry and artillery, with all the quarter-master and commissary stores, were then on the plains, and the command of the expedition, by seniority of rank, devolved upon Colonel Alexander, of the Tenth Infantry. The expedition was, therefore, without any instructions from the Government; all that its commander knew was its destination.

As the army passed the boundary line of Utah, Brigham's declaration of September 15th was forwarded, together with another missive, dated September 29th, for the perusal of "the "officer commanding the forces now invading Utah Territory," the gist of which was that Brigham was still Governor, as the

Act of Congress organizing the Territory provided that the
chief executive should hold his office for four years, or " *until*
" *his successor should be appointed and qualified*, unless sooner
" removed by the President of the United States." Brigham
asserted that no one had been legally appointed and qualified
to succeed him, that he himself had not been removed by the
President, and hence he was still Governor and Superintendent
of Indian Affairs, and Commander-in-chief of the militia of
the Territory. The remainder of the document, as a gem of
Dogberryism, is worthy of notice :

"By virtue of the authority thus vested in me, I have issued and forwarded you a copy of my proclamation forbidding the entrance of armed
forces into this Territory. This you have disregarded. I now further direct
that you retire forthwith from the Territory by the same route you entered.
Should you deem this impracticable, and prefer to remain until spring in
the vicinity of your present position at Black's Fork or Green River, you
can do so in peace and unmolested, on condition that you deposit your
arms and ammunition with Lewis Robinson, Quarter-Master-General of the
Territory, and leave in the spring as soon as the condition of the roads
will permit you to march. And should you fall short of provisions, they
can be furnished you upon making the proper applications therefor."

The Mormon "warriors" now set to work vigorously to
fulfil the instructions of their leaders, to hamper and impede
the advance of the army, and the detention of the Second Dragoons in Kansas was now felt to be not only a serious blunder,
but an irreparable loss, for there was no proper force to prevent
the Mormon cavalry from plundering the supply-trains, or doing whatever else they pleased.

Meanwhile, a new commander had been appointed at Washington in the person of Col. Albert Sidney Johnston. He was
a brilliant soldier, but at the date of Brigham's proclamation
was still at Leavenworth, twelve hundred miles from the army
to which he was appointed. His command had as yet heard
nothing from him, and, without instructions and fearing everything, Col. Alexander concentrated his forces at Ham's Fork,
until some course could be resolved upon by a council of the
officers. It was then the latter part of September ; winter was
approaching, the stock of forage was rapidly decreasing, and
the country was altogether unfitted for winter-quarters. Every
day's delay was disastrous, and threatened the very existence

of the expedition, for the mountains were already draped with snow, and the Mormons were constantly harassing the supply-trains. The troops began to show signs of demoralization;

Lieut.-General D. H. Wells.

they were in a bleak and barren desert, with an enemy surrounding them that knew every inch of the ground, and who to all appearances could easily destroy them without shedding a drop of their own blood.

On the 4th of October, Brigham's counsellor, D. H. Wells, issued the following order:

"On ascertaining the locality or route of the troops, proceed at once to annoy them in every possible way. Use every exertion to stampede their animals, and set fire to their trains. Burn the whole country before them and on their flanks. Keep them from sleeping by night surprises. Blockade the road by felling trees, or destroying the fords when you can. Watch for opportunities to set fire to the grass on their windward, so as, if possible, to envelop their trains. Leave no grass before them that can be burned. Keep your men concealed as much as possible, and guard against surprise. Keep scouts out at all times, and communication open with Colonel Burton, Major McAllister, and O. P. Rockwell, who are operating in the same way. Keep me advised daily of your movements, and every step the troops take, and in which direction.

"God bless you and give you success.

"Your brother in Christ,

(Signed) "DANIEL H. WELLS.

" P. S.—If the troops have not passed, or have turned in this direction,
follow in their rear, and continue to annoy them, and stampede or drive
off their animals at every opportunity.   D. H. WELLS."

These instructions were carried out to the letter. One of
the Government supply-trains was burned at Simpson's Hollow, ten miles east of Green river, and two trains were burned
on the Sweetwater ; in all seventy-five wagons containing provisions, tents, tools, and clothing. At the same time those
who burned them ran off a large number of cattle.

Burning Government Trains.

The Prophet had given orders that no blood was to be shed
under any temptation or provocation, save only in the extremity of self-defence, but the army was to be "wasted away."
The teamsters, wagon-masters, and *attachés* of the trains were
corralled, furnished with an outfit of provisions, and their faces
turned eastward. Of that entire host of civilians it is stated
that not a dozen of them reached the frontiers. They perished
by the way, from exhaustion, cold, and the attacks of Indians.

On the 10th of October the officers of the expedition held
a council of war and determined that the army should advance
from Ham's Fork, but to change the route of travel and make
Salt Lake Valley, if they could, *via* Soda Springs, a distance
of nearly three hundred miles, and at least a hundred and fifty

miles farther than the route through Echo Cañon. The order was issued, and next day the troops commenced a dreary march.

Early in the morning the sky was surcharged with dark, threatening clouds, and as they started the snow fell heavily. A few supply-trains were kept together and guarded by the infantry, but the travel was slow, vexatious, and discouraging. The beasts of burthen were suffering from want of forage, as, in anticipation of this movement, the grass had been burned all along that route. The animals were completely exhausted, and, before they were a week on the new route, three miles a day was all the distance that could be made.

Another council of war was held, but the only topics of discussion were the suffering, disaster, and heavy losses of the company. The soldiers were murmuring, and dissatisfaction reigned everywhere. Some gallant officers were desirous of forcing an issue with the Mormons, cutting their way through the cañons, and taking their chances of what might come. This course might have afforded some gratification to individuals, but to the company at large it was impracticable: every effort was necessary to save the expedition from total ruin.

In this forlorn condition the new commander was heard from, and the troops were instantly inspired with new life. Colonel Johnston comprehended the situation and ordered the expedition to retrace its steps. The snow was six inches deep, the grass all covered, the animals starving. The advance had been slow, the retreat was simply crawling. On the 3rd of November they reached the point of rendezvous, and next day Colonel Johnston joined them with a small reinforcement and the remainder of the supply-trains.

The *morale* of the army was restored by the presence of an efficient commander with instructions in his pocket, but the difficulties of the expedition were increasing every hour. The supply-trains were strung out about six miles in length, the animals worrying along till, thoroughly exhausted, they would fall in their tracks and die.

All this long line of wagons and beef cattle had to be guarded to prevent surprise and the stampede of the animals.*

* About the middle of October, the Mormon "boys" drove 800 oxen from the rear of the army into Salt Lake Valley. On the 5th of November they made another

The snow was deep on the ground and the weather was bitterly cold. Many of the men were fatally frost-bitten and the
cattle and mules perished by the score. In Colonel Philip St.
George Cooke's command fifty-seven head of horses and mules
froze to death in one night on the Sweetwater, and from there
to Fort Bridger, where the expedition finally wintered, the road
was literally strewn with dead animals. The camp on Black's
Fork, thirty miles from Bridger, was named "The Camp of
"Death." Five hundred animals perished around the camp on
the night of the 6th of November. Fifteen oxen were found
huddled together in one heap, frozen stiff.

The Camp of Death

In this perilous situation the expeditionary army to Utah
made the distance to Bridger—thirty-five miles—in fifteen
days! Often the advance had arrived at camp before the end
of the train had left. On the 16th of November, the army
reached their winter-quarters, Camp Scott, two miles from the
site of Fort Bridger and one hundred and fifteen from Salt
Lake City.

successful drive of 500 oxen, and literally fulfilled the words of the popular song,
"Du dah," which the Mormons had adapted to their own views, and which had received the approval of "the Prophet of the Lord."

"There's seven hundred wagons on the way,
        Du dah!
And their cattle are numerous, so they say,
        Du dah! Du dah day!
Now, to let them perish would be a sin,
        Du dah!
So we'll take all they've got for bringing them in,
        Du dah! Du dah day!
CHORUS.—Then let us be on hand,
        By Brigham Young to stand,
        And if our enemies do appear,
        We'll sweep them off the land."

CHAPTER XXXIX.

THE TWO ARMIES.—The Saints rejoice, and sing their Warlike Songs—The
Federal Troops in Camp Scott—Brigham sends them a Present of Salt—"The
Lord" is to destroy the Enemies of Zion—Col. Kane arrives among the Mormons and converts Brigham—The Prophet concludes that he cannot " whip"
the United States—He proposes Flight—Means to take Care of Himself—Col.
Kane visits Gov. Cumming and arranges a Basis of Prospective Peace—He offends Gen. Johnston—A Duel imminent—The Mormons flee from their Homes.

WHILE these misfortunes beset the Government troops, the
Mormons were the happiest of mortals. The calamities that
had befallen their own hand-cart emigrants only the year before were instantly forgotten, and the sufferings and privations
of the soldiers were regarded as the immediate and direct
judgments of the Almighty against those who would " fight
" against Zion."

As the snow had closed the passage through the mountain
cañons, there was no longer any necessity for " defence," and
the brethren returned to the settlements to be greeted with
songs of victory. One of the pæans of the time was a " Wel-
" come to the returned warriors of Zion : dedicated to Lieuten-
" ant-General Wells and his co-champions in arms," which expresses the view that the enthusiastic took of their situation :

> "Strong in the power of Brigham's God,
>   Your name 's a terror to our foes ;
>   Ye were a barrier strong and broad
>   As our high mountains crowned with snows.

> " Fear filled the myrmidons of war,
>   Their courage fell in wordy boast ;
>   The faith and prayers of Israel's host
>   Repelled the tyrant's gory car.
>   Then welcome ! sons of light and truth,
>   Heroes alike in age and youth."

23

That was the gayest winter ever known in Utah, and dancing and theatrical representations were everywhere encouraged,
while the songs of the Mormon camps, adapted to the popular
negro melodies of the day, were brought into the city and were
heard in all the assemblies. The Sunday worship was enliv-
ened with the jovial chorus of "Du dah,"* and the "sweet
"singers of Israel" discoursed Mormon patriotic sentiments to
the air of "The Red, White, and Blue." To fire the souls of
the Saints, one of the brethren, who is now an "apostate," made
a most excellent translation of the "Marseillaise Hymn," while
another of the elders sang the praises of the "warriors" in
verse that has immortalized him among the poets of the Tabernacle. Nor were the sisters wanting in enthusiam. Sister
"E—— M——"—a delicate, *petite* English lady, whose heart
would have been moved at the violent death of a spider,
aroused with her eloquence "the defenders of Zion" to "gird
"on for the fight." She was "inspired."

* This Mormon "Du dah" is a remarkable composition, but it is too lengthy to be
given entire. Two verses, however, will suffice to show the breathings of the Tabernacle, and the extent of the enthusiasm which then prevailed. After partaking of
the Sacrament of the Lord's Supper, such a song as the following seems hardly in
harmony with the place and occasion:

> "Old Sam has sent. I understand,
>   Du dah!
> A Missouri ass to rule our land,
>   Du dah! Du dah day!
> But if he comes, we'll have some fun,
>   Du dah!
> To see him and his juries run,
>   Du dah! Du dah day!
>
> CHORUS—Then let us be on hand,
>   By Brigham Young to stand,
>   And if our enemies do appear,
>   We'll sweep them from the land.
>
> "Old Squaw-killer Harney is on the way,
>   Du dah!
> The Mormon people for to slay,
>   Du dah! Du dah day!
> Now if he comes, the truth I'll tell,
>   Du dah!
> Our boys will drive him down to hell,
>   Du dah! Du dah day!"
> CHORUS.

From such lyrical effusions as these, sung during "divine worship" in the Tabernacle, the elevated tone of the sermons can be imagined. It is due to the better
taught of the people to add that they had no alternative but to submit to the
infliction.

The following verses are illustrative of the warlike enthusiasm to which the preaching of the leading elders had brought
the people :

"Up, awake, ye defenders of Zion !
   The foe 's at the door of your homes ;
Let each heart be the heart of a lion,
   Unyielding and proud as he roams.
Remember the wrongs of Missouri,
   Remember the fate of Nauvoo :
When the.God-hating foe is before ye,
   Stand firm, and be faithful and true.

"By the mountains our Zion 's surrounded,
   Her warriors are noble and brave ;
And their faith on Jehovah is founded,
   Whose power is mighty to save.
Opposed by a proud, boasting nation,
   Their numbers, compared, may be few ;
But their union is known through creation,
   And they've always been faithful and true.

"Shall we bear with oppression for ever ?
   Shall we tamely submit to the foe ?
While the ties of our kindred they sever,
   Shall the blood of the Prophets still flow ?
No ! The thought sets the heart wildly beating ;
   Our vows at each pulse we renew,
Ne'er to rest till our foes are retreating,
   While we remain faithful and true !

"Though assisted by legions infernal,
   The plundering wretches advance,
With a host from the regions eternal,
   We'll scatter their hosts at a glance !
Soon 'the Kingdom' will be independent ;
   In wonder the nations will view
The despised ones in glory resplendent ;
   Then let us be faithful and true ! "

Brother C. W. Penrose, the author of this effusion, at this
date had nothing of the mountain bluster and boasting in his
disposition. He was a young man of very pleasant manners, a
missionary, with a more than average mental cultivation. His
poetry only expressed the heart-felt convictions to which the

teachings of the priesthood had led him. He fully and unquestioningly believed, as indeed did all the Mormons, what Brigham Young taught. With " the Lord " to fight their battles, the few Saints were a match for the whole world. They knew no fear ; they only awaited the word to arise and conquer, and every mile that the United States troops advanced towards their homes, only brought the hoped-for consummation more pleasantly near to their longing souls. Many, doubtless, shared the sentiments of Brigham, and his hatred of all authority outside of himself ; but the masses have nothing of blood-thirstiness in their character. As the United States army approached, they saw only the fulfilment of predictions, and naturally longed to be the witnesses of the Lord's power.

From the pen of that same " C. W. P." flowed the sweetest song that the Mormons ever sang. At all great gatherings a little Scotchman with a warbling voice is certain to be invited to sing " O Zion," in which the whole audience, contrary to the usages of the Tabernacle services, burst forth in the chorus. This effusion is sung to the sweet air of " Lily Dale " :

" In thy mountain retreat, God will strengthen thy feet ;
    On the necks of thy foes thou shalt tread ;
And their silver and gold, as the prophets have told,
    Shall be brought to adorn thy fair head.
O Zion ! dear Zion ! home of the free,
    Soon thy towers will shine with a splendour divine,
And eternal thy glory shall be.

" Here our voices we'll raise, and we'll sing to thy praise,
    Sacred home of the prophets of God ;
Thy deliverance is nigh, thy oppressors shall die,
    And the Gentiles shall bow 'neath thy rod.
O Zion ! dear Zion ! home of the free,
    In thy temples we'll bend, all thy rights we'll defend,
And our home shall be ever with thee."

No words can express the electrifying influence of this song upon a Mormon audience. As the sound of the last words dies away, an outburst of enthusiasm is certain to follow. If the occasion is a religious ceremony, a loud and long-continued " Amen " is heard like " the voice of many waters." If the occasion is political, the hand-and-heel applause is given with a vim that tells how well the poet has touched the soul of his auditory.

The orators of the Tabernacle waxed bold and spoke of the Government and the army in terms of supreme contempt. With such an inevitable issue before their eyes, the leaders must either have been sincere in their faith that the end of national rule had been reached, or they were most unaccountably foolish in speech. A questioning voice was never heard : there was one current of unvarying boast of independence and victory for Israel, and of defeat and disgrace for the nation.

For years previous, the people had been taught to look forward to the time when "the kingdom" should throw off its allegiance to all earthly power, and now they naturally concluded that "the long-expected blessed day" had arrived, when they beheld on the one side of the mountains the national army advancing to their homes, and on the other side the Prophet with the armies of Israel determined to dispute their entrance into the valleys.

It had been a favourite pulpit expression that "the gates "would be let down between the Saints and the rest of the "world." and now it was that Brigham announced that he would regard the present as "the set time to favour Zion," and that the will of the Almighty was "that the thread should be cut" between them and the Gentiles when he saw armed men coming to shed his blood and that of his brethren. Heber, who was Brigham's favourite prophet, did not require to wait for the shedding of blood to be assured of the will of the Almighty. He was already fully advised and knew that the Saints and the Gentiles were separated for ever and "never would gybe "again."

Men clothed with the inspiration of an "infallible priest-"hood" must needs be positive in their assertions, and it is only with such a faith that the leaders could demand unquestioning allegiance, and the people render the service of "blind "obedience." Yet running all through the defiant speeches of those times, and the wordy assertion of "the Lord's com-"mands," it is easy to discern the expression of stray thoughts which would have told any free-thinking people that the very men who claimed to be the inspired of "the Lord" and His

mouth-piece to them, were themselves in grave doubt about
the truthfulness of what they uttered, although they exacted
unswerving faith and obedience from others. Those who dared
to think saw this position clear enough, but to divulge such a
discovery was impossible.

Nothing could better illustrate the incompatibility of theocracy with republicanism than the stormy days of "the Utah
"Rebellion;" and argument is unnecessary to demonstrate that
abject slavery is the inevitable condition of a people who accept the despotism of "the one-man-power." Brigham Young,
in Utah, in the year of grace 1857, rendered unintentionally by
his own example, this service to his generation.

But Heber could see nothing to hurt his faith or to discourage him in the slightest degree. To him everything was perfectly delightful to contemplate. Brigham was to become
President of the United States, he was himself to be Vice-
President, and Brother Wells the Secretary of the Interior.*
In the mean time the Saints were "just as sure to go to hell as
"they live, and I know it, if they consent to dispossess Brother
"Brigham as our Governor."† To avoid such a destination,
the Saints very properly, with uplifted hands, voted that the
troops should never come through the cañons, and that Brigham should for ever be their Governor! The thoughtful Legislature, too, resolved that the officers appointed for Utah by the
National Government should "neither qualify for, or assume
"and discharge within the limits of this Territory the func-
"tions of the offices to which they have been appointed, so
"long as our Territory is menaced by an invading army."‡
Such was the spirit and such the letter of the teaching of the
apostles during the first six months of the Utah war.

With the genial breath of spring and the melting of the
snows, one of two things was certain: the Mormons would
have to conquer the United States army, or they would have
to retreat from their defiant position of resistance.

At Camp Scott, near Fort Bridger, where Colonel Albert
Sidney Johnston wintered his troops, the Governor and Federal
officers had pitched their tents and entered upon the discharge

* Tabernacle, September 6, 1857.   † Ibid., August 30th, 1857.
‡ "Resolutions adopted and signed," December 21st, 1857.

of their official duties. On the 21st of November, Governor
Cumming issued a very temperate proclamation to " the peo-
" ple of Utah Territory," informing them that they were in a
state of rebellion, and commanding them to disband. Chief-
Justice Eckles opened court, empanelled a grand jury, took
the burned trains into consideration, and found indictments
against Brigham and the leading Mormons for treason, at the
same time assessing the damages to the Government for goods
burned and cattle stolen at a round million of dollars.

The winter of 1857–8 at Camp Scott was not quite so gay
as that enjoyed by the Saints on the western side of the Wahsatch range of mountains. The burning of the three trains by
the Mormons had greatly reduced the commissariat of the
troops. Rations were short, and many articles of daily necessity were altogether unattainable.

Enterprising suttlers, who had ventured out with the expedition, taking the usual stock of extras, found the necessities
of the civil and military officers and the wants of the camp followers a mine of wealth. The miserable whiskey that was pois-
onous enough at less than a dollar a gallon was eagerly purchased at twelve times that price, while tobacco was sold at $3
a pound, and coffee and sugar at about the same rate.

The greatest privation, however, was caused by the absence
of salt, and Brigham in his " magnanimity " sent a present of
that needful article to Colonel Johnston ; but the gallant soldier
ordered the messengers from his camp with every expression
of contempt for the "rebel" prophet.* The Indians, however,
soon settled the question of patriotism and necessity, and hurried through the snow into Camp Scott with all the salt they
could pack, and sold it readily at five dollars per pound. The
commercial principle of supply and demand, however, soon
reduced by one-half the price of that indispensable condiment
during the remainder of the winter. Flour for a time was a
luxury at a very high figure, and the possession of a good supply with no other protection than the covering of a tent was

---

* How mutable are human affairs ! Five years later, that same Colonel Johnston was himself designated " a rebel," and became one of the most distinguished
generals in the Confederate army. The Colonel Johnston of Utah became the General Albert Sidney Johnston of Shiloh !

as dangerous to its owner as a well-filled purse is to a pedestrian in a first-class city after sunset.

The beef-cattle had been run off by the hundred, and the poor, thin, worn-out, emaciated work-cattle were consigned to the butcher, partly as a substitute for the better-conditioned which had been stolen, but quite as often " to save the critturs " the trouble of dying," and to furnish the soldiers with something like mocassins, which the needy but industrious men manufactured from their hides. From these necessities resulted the most galling phase of the expedition to Utah. Every day, all through that winter, bands of fifteen or twenty men might be seen hitched to wagons, trailing for five or six miles to the mountain-sides to get loads of fuel for the use of the camp. It will readily be credited that under these circumstances there was little kind feeling for the Mormons entertained at Camp Scott.

Winter Scene.—United States Troops hauling Wood.

The unpleasant situation of the troops and any incidents of interest were duly reported by scouts at the Mormon headquarters, and added greatly to the faith of the disciples that " the Lord " was with them. The following letter from a lady in Salt Lake City to her children in Providence, Rhode Island, breathed the true Mormon spirit that characterized those warlike times :

" I expect you have heard the loud talk of Uncle Sam's great big army coming to kill the Saints. Now, if you did but know how the Saints rejoice at the folly of the poor Gentiles. There are about four thousand on the border of our territory, and six hundred wagons—one naked mule to draw them—all the rest having died. The men are sitting in the snow, about a hundred and fifteen miles from us, living on three crackers a day, and three-quarters of a pound of beef a week. Thus you see the old Prophet's words are fulfilled—whoever shall fight against Zion shall perish. The time is very near when one man shall chase a thousand, and ten shall put ten thousand to flight ! Zion is free ; she is hid in one of the chambers of the Lord. We are a free people. We do not fear 'Uncle Sam's' soldiers. We only fear our Father in heaven. We are learning His commandments every day from His prophet, and I am determined to keep them. If you were here, and could hear the Prophet's voice as I do, and could hear the Lion of the Lord roar from the mountains, as I do, and know how near the scourge of the Lord is upon the Gentiles, you would flee to the mountains with haste. The time has come when the Lord has called all the elders home, and commanded them to bind up the law and seal the testimony. They are now coming home as fast as possible. What comes next ? The judgment, hail-storm, thunder, lightning, pestilence, war ; and they that will not take up the sword against their neighbour must flee to Zion for safety. Will you come, oh ! my dear children ? "

That letter was a truthful reflex of the Mormon mind in 1857, and exhibits how grossly ignorant that people were of the progress of the world and the might of the Government against which they were arrayed. The people did honestly believe that the time had fully come when the Government of the United States would be broken to pieces, and that the little handful of Mormons in the valleys of the Rocky Mountains was " the kingdom," and was indeed that stone which should grind into powder all upon whom it fell.

" The whole United States and the whole world could not " prevail against the Saints." As for the army at Camp Scott, " a swarm of long-billed mosquitoes could eat them up at a " supper spell." * Heber, full of rollicking fun, fire, and fagots, announced that he had himself alone " wives enough " to whip the United States," " but he did not want to shed " the blood of his brothers and sisters, neither did the Saints " want to see these things "—" unless the Holy Ghost dictates

* Bishop L. D. Young, Tabernacle, December 13, 1857.

" for us to shed the blood of our enemies, and then it is as just
" and right as it is for us to partake of the sacrament." For
himself, however, he would prefer that the army would go
some other way, and not try to come into the city, for " we do
" not want to hurt them; but if they come down upon us and
" we have to repel them by the force of arms, God Almighty
" will give us the power to do it, now mark it." *

The Mormons had another lesson to learn.

Notwithstanding the difficulty experienced at that time of
travelling across the plains in winter, an express occasionally
carried to the Government the unwelcome news of the disaster
that had befallen the expedition and the sufferings and privations that ensued. At one time there were grave fears of its
ultimate success, but brave men and the unlimited resources
of the Government were destined to overcome every obstacle.
Captain Marcy with a company of picked men undertook a
perilous journey from Fort Bridger to Taos, New Mexico, to
obtain provisions, cattle, and mules for the relief of the expedition, and after most terrible suffering and heavy loss of animals, and many disabled men, he reached the point of supply,
and was eminently successful.

The misfortunes that had befallen the troops aroused the
Government to a realization of the necessity of rendering every
aid, both in men and material, to save the expedition and
make it successful. Lieut.-Gen. Scott was summoned to Washington to consult with the Secretary of War, and at one time
the project of entering Utah from the west was seriously entertained. The intimation that two regiments of volunteers
would probably be called for in the spring met with a ready
response from all parts of the Union. It was very evident
that the nation was thoroughly dissatisfied with the state of
affairs in Utah, and wanted to bring the Mormons to a settlement.

Ready to take advantage of anything which promised
wealth, there were multitudes of solicitous contractors seeking
to supply the army in the West; and, with a prodigality beyond
all precedent, the War Department was perfectly reckless.
The Sixth and Seventh regiments of infantry, together with

* Tabernacle, September 20th, 1857.

the First Cavalry, and two batteries of artillery—about three thousand in all—were ordered to Utah, and every arrangement made for speedy and colossal warfare with the Prophet. Political writers charged to the administration of Mr. Buchanan an utter recklessness of expenditure, intended more for the support of political favourites and for the attainment of political purposes in Kansas than for the overthrow of the dynasty of Brigham. It was estimated in Washington that forty-five hundred wagons would be required to transport munitions of war and provisions for the troops for a period of from twelve to eighteen months, besides fifty thousand oxen, four thousand mules, and an army of teamsters, wagon-masters, and employés, at least five thousand strong. It was very evident that the Government was playing with a loose hand, and the consideration of cost to the national treasury was the last thing thought of. The unanimity, however, that prevailed throughout the Union exhibited the wide-spread detestation of " the " rebellion " of Brigham Young. The transportation item for 1858 provided for the expenditure of no less than four and a half millions, and that contract was accorded to a firm in western Missouri, without public announcement or competition.

While all this was occupying the attention of the public, and the Government seemed determined that the war against the Mormons should be carried out with vigour, there was another influence at work to bring " the Utah rebellion " to a peaceful termination.

Among the passengers who, in the first week of January, 1858, steamed out of New York harbour for San Francisco, was a gentleman registered as Dr. Osborne. On reaching the Pacific coast the said " Doctor " hastened overland to Southern California, and there overtaking the Mormons from San Bernardino, who were returning home for the defence of Zion, he was readily provided with the necessary escort through the Indian country, and in the latter part of February he reached Salt Lake City.

The presence of the stranger in the city was soon known, but to Brigham Young and his associates only was the reputed Dr. Osborne known as their whilom friend Col. [now General] Thomas L. Kane, of Philadelphia.

What was communicated from President Buchanan to
·Brigham Young through Col. Kane has never been published,
nor is there a soul in Utah to-day who claims to be in possession of that information ; but whatever the nature of this intelligence may have been, if any communication at all, it is
very certain that President Buchanan was particularly careful
to have it understood that there was nothing like yielding contemplated on the part of the Government before the predic·
tions of the Prophet. In his annual message to Congress, on
the 5th of December, 1858, Mr. Buchanan made honourable
mention of the services of Col. Kane, but he went out of his
way to assure Congress that the Colonel went to Utah " with-
" out any official character or pecuniary compensation ; " that
it was solely " from motives of pure benevolence," and· " that
" the Colonel had only sought to contribute to the pacification
" of the Territory." In a letter furnished to Col. Kane on the eve
of his departure for Utah, Mr. Buchanan was very particular
in defining their relative positions, and addressed him thus :

"MY DEAR SIR : You furnish the strongest evidence of your desire to
serve the Mormons, by abandoning the comforts of friends, family, and
home, and voluntarily encountering the perils and dangers of a journey
to Utah, at the present inclément season of the year, at your own expense,
and without official position. . . . Nothing but pure philanthropy,
and a strong desire to serve the Mormon people, could have dictated a
course so much at war with your private interests." *

After the Colonel's arrival in Salt Lake City, it is very clear
that he impressed Brigham Young with the determination of

---

* Some writers have essayed to represent that Col. Kane was a Mormon, and
they state that he was baptized at Council Bluffs in 1847. The Colonel himself,
however, has not seen fit to confess such a relationship with the Saints. and it can
be of little consequence to the world whether he was so or not. There is no doubt
in the Author's mind that Col. Kane acted, in 1847, on the Missouri River, and in
1858, at Salt Lake City, in the interest of the Mormons, just as Mr. Buchanan
states, "from motives of pure philanthropy."

The Colonel was very sick when with the Mormons in 1847, and but for the excellent nursing and care that he then received he would probably have died. The
debt of gratitude for those services he has sought to fully repay, and no man stands
higher in Brigham Young's favour to-day than General Thomas L. Kane. This fact
alone is sufficient to set at rest all questions of the Colonel's Mormonism. Had the
Colonel been a Mormon, Brigham would have treated him with less respect. To the
Prophet, adhesion to the faith inevitably entails servile obedience. Instead of
courting Gen. Kane, as he now does, he would have commanded him.

the Government to subdue all opposition, and satisfied him that in the coming spring the troops would force a passage through the cañons, and would occupy the city if any resistance were offered to the instalment of the new Territorial Governor and the Federal officers.

On the 12th of March an exhausted traveller was seen plodding his way from the west through the snow towards the military lines of Camp Scott. When challenged by the picket, he requested to be conducted to the tent of Governor Cumming, whom he desired to see without delay. This enfeebled young-looking gentleman was Col. Thomas L. Kane. With the natural politeness of a thorough gentleman, Governor Cumming bade him welcome, and did everything that he possibly could to make his guest feel at home.

In the relations of Col. Kane with the Mormons at that time, there was exhibited evidence of the highest Christian charity and personal heroism of character. He must have well known that in entering the encampment of General Johnston at Camp Scott, his second, if not his first, duty was to make known to the commander something of the nature of his business within the lines of the army. His silence wounded General Johnston and his officers, and everywhere in the camp the Colonel was spoken of as " a spy." In course of time an invitation to dine at the General's head-quarters was sent to the Colonel by the hand of an orderly ; but, instead of delivering the invitation, by some unaccountable mistake, the orderly forgot his instructions, and proceeded to place the Colonel under arrest. The Governor instantly extended his protection over his guest, and immediately a challenge from the Colonel to General Johnston was dictated ; but by the timely interference of Chief-Justice Eckels, who threatened to arrest the whole party, the affair of honour was nipped in the bud.

Governor Cumming warmly espoused the cause of his guest, and felt himself also personally insulted, and from that moment the *entente cordiale* between the civil Governor and the military commander of the Utah expedition was for ever broken. Brigham was now safe—the military could only act as a *posse comitatus* on the call of the Governor, and the latter was for peace. Was this the settled diplomacy of Colonel Kane from the beginning? Was it to accomplish this that he risked his life in a long, weary journey over sea and land, that almost proved fatal to him, passed under a fictitious name, and bore the epithet of "spy" in Camp Scott—to serve the Mormon people and save them from certain death? Such would appear to have been the fact. It was the noblest heroism.

Soon after the departure of Col. Kane for Fort Bridger, a "special council" was held in the Tabernacle—on the 21st of March—at which "a series of instructions and remarks" was delivered by Brigham for the edification of the leading men around him. The "instructions and remarks" were never published in any of the organs of the Church, but for the use of the bishops and chief men they were printed in a pamphlet form. It is a most singular document, and one that few persons have seen. The gist of the "remarks" was the forced confession of Brigham that the Saints were not prepared to fight the United States, and that he was resolved on flight. In it he tells the "special council" that if Joseph Smith had given heed to the whisperings of the Spirit, he never would have given himself up to the marshal and gone to Carthage, and he then avows his determination not to be taken, and speaks at random, like a man utterly in the dark respecting the future, notwithstanding his previous boasting of continuous "revela-"tion," and the guidance of "the Lord." To that special council he said:

"I do not know precisely in what manner the Lord will lead me, but were I thrown into the situation Joseph was, *I would leave the people and go into the wilderness, and let them do the best they could.* Will I run from the sheep? No. Will I forsake the flock? No. But if Joseph had followed the revelations in him he would have been our earthly shepherd to-day, and we would have followed his voice and followed the shepherd instead of the shepherd's following the sheep. When the shepherd follows the sheep, it reverses the natural order, for the sheep are to follow the shepherd. I want you to understand that if I am your earthly shepherd, you must follow me, or else we shall be separated."—pp. 3–4.

The idea of a shepherd leading his flock to greener and richer pasture is known the world over, but that a faithful shepherd should flee before his sheep and tell them to follow him, when those sheep were surrounded and threatened by ravenous beasts seeking to devour them, is a picture which has yet to spring from the artist's pencil.

As he had seen the winter approaching, and knew that a handful of men could defend the narrow defiles of the cañons, Brigham was bold and threatening; but when the balmy breath of spring was felt on the deep snow that intervened between the national army at Fort Bridger and the city of the Saints, and told as certainly as the returning season itself that that army would soon advance, the Prophet comprehended the desperate situation in which he was placed. It was then that he stumbled upon this, to him, logical method of escaping from the difficulties which surrounded him. To the council already spoken of he continued his address:

"A great many parents follow off their children, and men follow their women. *For a man to follow a woman is, in the sight of Heaven, disgraceful to the name of a man.* It is a disgrace for parents to follow their children. I am your leader, Latter-Day Saints, and you must follow me; and if you do not follow me, you may expect that I shall go my way, and you may take yours, if you please. I shall do as the Spirit dictates me. What does it now direct me to dictate to you? Our enemies are determined to blot us out of existence if they can." [p. 4] . . . "Should I take a course to waste life? We are in duty bound to preserve life—to preserve ourselves on the earth—consequently *we must use policy* and follow in the counsel given us, in order to preserve our lives. Shall we take a course to whip our enemies? or one to let them whip themselves? or shall we go out and slay them now? We have been preparing to use up our enemies by fighting them, and if we take that course and shed the blood of our enemies, we will see the time, and that, too, not far from this very morning, when we will have to flee from our homes and leave the spoils to them.—That is as sure as we commence the game." [Excellent second sober thought: thanks to Colonel Kane.] "If we open the ball upon them by slaying the United States soldiery, just so sure they would be fired with anger to lavishly expend their means to compass our destruction, and thousands, and millions if necessary, would furnish the means, if the Government was not able, and turn out and drive us from our homes, and kill us if they could. [p. 6.] [How strange "the Lord" did not whisper that before!] . . 'Where are you going?' To the deserts and the mountains. There is a desert region in this Territory larger than any of the Eastern States, that no white man knows anything about. Can you realize that? What is the reason you do not know anything about that region? It is a desert country with long distances from water to water, with wide sandy and alkali places entirely destitute of vegetation and miry when wet, and small, scattering patches of greasewood, and it is a region that the whites have not explored, and where there are but few Indians. There are places here and there in it where a few families could live.

25

"Four years ago this spring we sent Bishop David Evans and a company to go to that desert, for we then had too long neglected to explore it. We wanted to plant settlements there in preparation for this day, for we have had foreshadowings and a promise of the scenery now before us. That company did not accomplish the object of their mission; they were absent a few weeks, and went to the first mountain, but they did not go to the mountain where they were sent, and made no settlement. Now we are going to try it again. Probably there is room in that region for 500,000 persons to live scattered about where there is good grass and water. *I am going there*, where we should have gone six or seven years ago. *Now we are going to see whether the sheep will follow the shepherd. I do not care whether they follow me or not.*"—p. 7.

Brigham wound up his remarks, extending over thirteen pages, with the following words: "My mind is too full this "morning to come to close points"—that the reader could easily believe. The tone of the "defenders of Zion" was now to be changed. *Flight*, and not fight, was to be the watchword. The safety of Brigham and the leaders was the salvation of the people. The "game of bluff" was over.

The Hon. John M. Bernhisel, the Mormon delegate, had gone East with Major Van Vliet, and in his very quiet and unobtrusive way he laboured faithfully at Washington with Colonel Kane to arrive at an understanding with President Buchanan. Mr. Buchanan, dreading to saddle his administration with the responsibility of domestic warfare, if it could be avoided, gladly accepted the assurance that a settlement could easily be effected without compromising the Government, and in that spirit did he favour the unofficial services of Colonel Kane, and furnished that gentleman with letters to Governor Cumming and other officers of the Federal Government in order to facilitate and protect him in his travels.

Efforts have been made to charge Mr. Buchanan with "backing down." That the initiatory steps for the settlement of the Utah difficulty were made by the Government, as it is so constantly repeated among the Saints, is not true. The Author at the time of Colonel Kane's departure from New York for Utah was then on the staff of the New York *Herald*, and was conversant with the facts, and confidentially communicated them to Frederic Hudson, Esq., the distinguished manager of that great journal, to be used as he thought proper.

TRIUMPHAL PASSAGE OF UNITED STATES TROOPS THROUGH SALT LAKE CITY.

CHAPTER XL.

PEACE RESTORED.—Gov. Cumming visits Salt Lake City—His Passage through Echo Cañon—Everywhere greeted with Honour—Brigham surrenders the Territorial Seal, and receives the new Governor with Courtesy—Commissioners arrive with President Buchanan's Pardon—Peace proclaimed—General Johnston without Opposition traverses the Streets of Zion—The Federal Troops locate Forty Miles from the City—The Saints return to their Homes—The Prophet's Boasting and the President's Folly suddenly terminate.

THE visit of Col. Kane to Governor Cumming was eminently successful. On the 3rd of April his Excellency informed Gen. Johnston that he was ready to proceed to Salt Lake City to assume the duties of his office; and two days later, accompanied by Col. Kane, he set out from Camp Scott.

After all the violent speeches against the advance of the troops, and the repeatedly expressed determination of Brigham that he would never permit them to enter the city, and that he would send back Governor Cumming, it is interesting to note the facts as they actually transpired.

As soon as the Governor passed beyond the Federal military lines he was met by a Mormon escort, and was the recipient of all the honours the militia could heap upon him. His passage from Camp Scott to Salt Lake City was one grand ovation of loyalty and profession of respect for the person of the chief representative of the Government.

The country was in a condition of war, and as no official steps had been yet taken to bring it to a close, his Excellency was too much of a gentleman to think of travelling through Echo Cañon during the day, as it was obvious that he would then have every facility for taking notes of the enemy's fortifications! Travelling by night afforded "the boys" every op-

24

portunity for showing the Governor what a formidable place
the United States troops would have to pass through, and that
would certainly not fail to impress him still more favourably
with the advantages and necessity of peace.

From one end of the cañon to the other great fires could
be seen at night on the hill-sides and on the mountain-tops,
representing the works and bivouacks of a great army, while
the lurid flames of the pine-tree fires rendered the darkness
still more impressive, and conveyed to the bewildered Govern-
or the idea that near at hand there was a mighty host under
arms.

The military chieftains managed to keep his Excellency in a
continued strain of feverish expectation. At every important
bend of the road the Governor and his escort would be suddenly challenged by the pickets, and the countersign demanded. On one occasion there was a call to arms, and a mock effort at hostility, but some of the principal officers arrived just
in time to save his Excellency's life, and to call off the pugna-
cious militia, and hinder them from taking him prisoner! At
several of the principal posts the Mormon troops would be
called together to salute the Governor as he passed, and to listen to his kindly words. Soon after that he would again be
detained by other pickets, while the militia which he had addressed but a few minutes before had an opportunity, in the
darkness of the night, of passing by unobserved, and were
ready to salute him again, and listen to another address at a
succeeding stage of the journey. In this way the new Governor of Utah was impressed with the idea that the men under
arms numbered several thousands, while probably at that time
there was not more than a couple of hundreds.

In course of time he discovered how the Mormon leaders
had imposed upon him and amused themselves with his credulity, and he was ever afterwards unpleasantly reticent when
the affair was mentioned. Although subsequently upon friendly terms with Brigham, he could not forget the incidents of his
passage through the cañon by night, and to the last hour that
he was in the Territory he felt annoyed at having been so ab-
surdly deceived, and held Brigham responsible for the mortify-
ing joke.

On the 12th of April, Governor Cumming reached the city, where he was kindly welcomed by the leading men of " the " kingdom," and escorted to the most comfortable quarters in the city—the residence of elder Wm. C. Staines, an intelligent gentleman and faithful disciple of the Prophet. Among the first to salute the new Governor and to do him honour was his Excellency Governor Young.* Governor Cumming was perfectly delighted, and " the Utah war " was practically at an end.

From the time that the Federal troops left the States, all mail communication with Salt Lake across the Eastern plains was entirely stopped ; but by a singular inadvertence, the mail service to and from the Pacific Coast was continued uninterruptedly, and through this channel the success of the mission of Colonel Kane was communicated to the Government.

On the very day that Governor Cumming entered Salt Lake City and Brigham had remitted to him the executive seal of the Territory, President Buchanan appointed Gov. L. W. Powell, of Kentucky, and Col. Ben. McCulloch, of Texas, commissioners to repair to Utah as bearers of a pardon from Washington for all offences committed during the rebellion, if those in arms would accept of the clemency of the President, and return to their allegiance to the Government.

The course of Governor Cumming was a great annoyance to the other Federal officers, but to that his Excellency was perfectly indifferent. He was fully conversant with the programme that had been traced out in Washington, and after-events in the adjustment of the Utah difficulty verified the correctness of his judgment. The movements of Col. Kane in Utah, and the action of President Buchanan at the seat of Government, were perfectly harmonious, and coincided with an accuracy which was altogether remarkable.

Chief-Justice Eckels tried to reach something by his court against the Mormon elders, and General Johnston was fast

* John Hyde, in his work published July, 1857, nine months previous to the entrance of Governor Cumming, predicted of this event : " The new Governor, all " Brigham's vapouring to the contrary notwithstanding, will be courteously received " at Salt Lake City."—p. 320. The Mormon Elders thoroughly understand the Mormon Prophet.

completing the preparations for his advance upon the enemy, but it was all to no purpose. Three days after his arrival in the city his Excellency notified General Johnston that he had been fully recognized as the Governor of the Territory, and was in the full and unmolested discharge of his duties, and that therefore the presence of the army in Salt Lake City was altogether unnecessary.

The commander of the army fully comprehended that as a *posse comitatus* at the call of the Governor, no requisition was ever likely to be made. He had, however, direct instructions from the Secretary of War about establishing military posts in Utah, and with these the Governor could not interfere.

On the first Sunday after the Governor's arrival among the Saints a great meeting was convened in the Tabernacle, and Brigham Young introduced Governor Cumming to the congregation. Another feature of the "Utah rebellion" was now to be developed.

It was ridiculous to expect Brigham Young to publicly back down and eat the humble pie of submission. He was a Prophet in the eyes of the Saints, and the position in which he stood was one of world-wide notoriety. It was absolutely necessary that some plan should be adopted whereby he might escape the difficulties which surrounded him. President Buchanan, too, was before the world, and he had to be saved from the appearance of folly in the beginning and weakness in the ending of "the Utah rebellion." Diplomacy was again the order of the day.

The proceedings in the Tabernacle were all an understood thing. An apostle reviewed Mormon history and pictured "the persecutions of the Saints," from the tarring and feathering of Joseph Smith in 1830 to the annulling of the mail contract in 1857. The Government was denounced and berated for sins of omission and commission, the last of which was the appointment of "a Missourian" to govern the Mormons.

The new Governor was almost beside himself at the indignity offered to him after all he had done to bring about peace. He called out in the congregation that he was *no Missourian:* "I am a Georgian, sir, a Georgian, sir." The error was immediately corrected and the ruffled Governor was gently soothed and pacified. After that, one speaker after another arose in the congregation and in a state of excitement denounced the Government and the Federal officials who had been in the Territory. There was, in fact, a general denunciation of the enemies of the Saints and a reiteration of their determination, if need be, to fight for their rights. One of the most amusing features of that well-arranged comedy was the speech of a very eloquent Irishman who had been but a few years in the new world, who, with a "brogue" which was in every way most marked and distinguishable, contended for his "rights." His forefathers had, he said, fought and bled for American liberty, and he would be an unworthy scion of such illustrious sires did he not contend for the right to worship God according to the sacred birthright of every American freeman.*

Brigham was seated beside the Governor on the platform, and tried to control the unruly spirits who were clamourous for their "rights." Governor Cumming may for the moment have been deceived by this apparent division among the Mormons, but three years later he told the Author that it was all of a piece with the incidents of his passage through Echo Cañon. He fully comprehended it. In his characteristic brusque way he said: "It was all humbug, sir; all humbug; but never mind, "it is all over now. If it did them good, it did not hurt me. "Brigham Young is a smart man—smart man, but he may yet "find out that other people are not so blind as he may think "they are. Smart man! but he doesn't know everything."

The Governor's report to President Buchanan, in the light of the facts stated, is very amusing. Of his journey he says:

"I left camp on the 5th, *en route* for this city, accompanied by Colonel Kane as guide, and two servants. . . . I was escorted from Bear River Valley to the western end of Echo Cañon—the journey through the cañon being performed, for the most part, in the night. It was about eleven o'clock when I arrived at Weber Station.

"I have been everywhere recognized as the Governor of Utah, and, so far from having encountered insults and indignities, I am gratified in being

* This eloquent orator, whose "forefather" was a brushmaker in Liverpool, three years later, with two wives and several children, was glad to escape from the "liberty" he was once contending for, and continued his flight by the overland stage until he reached the Pacific Coast, and has never since returned to Utah.

able to state that, in passing through the settlements, I have been universally greeted with such respectful attentions as are due to the representative of the executive authority of the United States. . . . .

"When it was arranged with the Mormon officer in command of my
escort that I should pass through Echo Cañon in the night, I inferred that
it was with the object of concealing the barricades and other defences. I
was therefore agreeably surprised at the illumination in honour to me.
The bonfires kindled by the soldiers, from the base to the summit of the
hills, completely illuminated the valley, and disclosed the snow-covered
mountains which surrounded us."

Before anything was learned upon which to base a well-
grounded hope of a peaceful adjustment of the difficulty between Brigham Young and the Government, "counsel" had
been given to the Saints to vacate the city and to move southward. Obedient to this "counsel," the people gathered all
that they could take with them "upon wheels"—personal
property and effects, household goods, and articles of daily use,
and leaving all their possessions as best they could, they prepared for another exodus.

Before turning the key of the outer door for the last time,
straw, wood, shavings, and everything combustible, were
massed in heaps and placed throughout the houses, so that if
it became necessary to burn the city, the work of destruction
would be so speedily executed that there would remain no
shelter for the advancing enemy, or their camp-followers. Less
than a score of men were left behind to apply the torch, and
repeat upon a small scale the tragedy of Moscow, should it become necessary.

Such a "sublime illustration of faith" has been frequently
descanted upon, and it is really a very pretty subject to talk
about; but when the threatening language of Brigham about
"shearing down" all who would not commit their homesteads
to the flames is remembered, the heroic devotion said to be displayed is not so clearly visible. This episode in Mormonism
exhibits at least how easily the people can be manipulated by
their rulers, whether from convictions of faith, from fears of
violence, or from both.

On the 7th of June, the Peace Commissioners Powell and
McCulloch arrived in the city. Previous to this, Brigham was
advised of the nature of their mission, and was in possession

of a copy of President Buchanan's proclamation of pardon. Notified of their presence, he returned from the southern country, whither he had gone with the fleeing Saints, and met the Commissioners in conference on the 11th and 12th in Salt Lake City. Speeches similar to those first listened to by Governor Cumming were made in the hearing of the Commissioners, and were duly reported by them in the following language :

"They denied that they had ever driven any officials from Utah, or prevented any civil officer from entering the Territory. They admitted that they burned the army trains, and drove off the cattle from the army last fall, and for that act they accepted the President's pardon. All the charges that had been made against them, except the one last named, they denied. . . . . We are pleased to state that the conference resulted in their agreeing to receive, quietly and peaceably, all the civil officers of the Government, and not to resist them in the execution of the duties of their offices ; and to yield obedience to the authorities and laws of the United States.

"That they would offer no resistance to the army ; that the officers of the army should not be resisted in the execution of their orders within the Territory. *In short, they agreed that the officers, civil and military, of the United States, should enter the Territory without resistance, and exercise, peaceably and unmolested, all the functions of their various offices."* *

Unable now to prevent the advance of the army, the Mormon leaders requested that the troops should not be permitted to camp within the city, nor near to any of the settlements. The Commissioners were non-committal in promises, but used their good offices with General Johnston to meet the wishes of the Mormons, and prevent the army from committing any injury to the property of the citizens.

Immediately on learning that it was feared the troops might retaliate for their sufferings during the winter, the General issued a proclamation assuring the people that no one should be " molested in his person or rights, or in the peaceful " pursuit of his avocations." On the same day the Governor

* The "inspired" sermons, songs, and legislative resolutions of resistance were probably only intended by "the Lord" to scare "Uncle Sam," and again "try the faith of the Saints." Joseph had a similar experience with "the Lord's army" in Missouri. It is to be hoped that the next prophet will not deem it necessary to follow in the wake of his predecessors. These unpleasant affairs might be repeated once too often.

officially announced "the restoration of peace to the Ter-
"ritory."

Captain Marcy had arrived at Camp Scott on the 8th of
June with about fifteen hundred horses and mules, and an
escort of five companies of infantry and mounted riflemen,*
and, with the addition of the animals which he brought to
what had been preserved during the winter, the expedition
was soon ready for marching orders.

On the 13th, General Johnston's army began to move forward in three columns. They passed through that much
talked-of Echo Cañon, and were greatly amused with the Mormon defences. On the morning of the 26th the United States
troops emerged from the Emigration Cañon into Salt Lake
Valley, directly east of Salt Lake City, and, despite of the numerous predictions of " the servants of the Lord " to the contrary, the national standard was unfurled to the breeze, and
under its starry folds, with full equipment of arms and munitions of war, the Federal army, in all the glory and pride of
unconquered warriors, marched through the streets of Zion,
and passed before the mansion of the " Lion of the Lord."

A correspondent with the army thus pictures the occurrence:

"It was one of the most extraordinary scenes that have occurred in
American history. All day long, from dawn till after sunset, the troops
and trains poured through the city, the utter silence of the streets being
broken only by the music of the military bands, the monotonous tramp
of the regiments, and the rattle of the baggage-wagons. Early in the
morning the Mormon guard had forced all their fellow-religionists into
the houses, and ordered them not to make their appearance during the
day. The numerous flags that had been flying from staffs on the public
buildings during the previous week were all struck. The only visible
groups of spectators were on the corners near Brigham Young's residence, and consisted almost entirely of Gentile civilians. The stillness
was so profound, that, during the intervals between the passage of the
columns, the monotonous gurgle of the city-creek struck on every ear.
The Commissioners rode with the General's staff. The troops crossed
the Jordan and encamped two miles from the city, on a dusty meadow by
the river-bank."

* The expedition undertaken and accomplished by Captain [now General]
Marcy is one of the brightest pages of our military annals. In his "Thirty Years
of Army Life on the Border " the General tells his thrilling story. He was the
subject of honourable commendation by Lieutenant-General Scott, and was named
by the Secretary of War in terms of the highest praise.

The permanent location of the camp was a matter of deep concern to the Mormon leaders. Afraid that General Johnston would choose Cache Valley—eighty miles north of Salt Lake City—and concluding that he was certain to refuse what they commended, they were very urgent in representing the desirability of that place. Cedar Valley, forty miles west of the city, was chosen, and their camp was named after Mr. Floyd, the Secretary of War, and as there were few settlements in that direction and very few improvements in the immediate locality, the Mormons were fully satisfied with Camp Floyd.

After resting three days on the banks of the Jordan while the permanent camp was being selected, the army again took up its march, and moved slowly southward from the city to the ridge of the basin called "The Point of the Mountain," and then moving westward, crossed the Jordan and a low range of the Oquirrh Mountains, reaching camp on the 6th of July. Notwithstanding all the vandalism, death, and destruction that was ascribed to the mission of the army, their march through the settlements was unmarked by the first act of violence. " Not a field was encroached upon, not a house molested, not " a person harmed or insulted by troops that had been so har- " assed and vituperated by a people now entirely at their mer- " cy. By their strict subordination they entitled themselves to " the respect of the country, as well as to the gratitude of the " Mormons."

What an eventful year this had been to the Saints! On the 24th of July—less than a year before—Brigham at Big Cot- tonwood Lake had hurled defiance at the Government, and de- clared " the kingdom " independent. The Tabernacle for months resounded with great swelling words. The promises of " the Lord " that victory should be for " Israel " had been reiterated in the pulpit and from the press and sung in rhyme, times without number! Predictions of defeat, disgrace, and destruction had been hurled at the army. The nation was ridiculed and its rulers anathematized, while the thread was severed for ever between the Saints and the Gentiles. " The " Lord " was to come out of his hiding-place to vex the nation, and to make bare His arm in the overthrow of those arrayed against Zion. The Federal army was to waste away and per-

ish, and on no account was it ever to enter the sacred city—the
Prophet's habitation. By the end of twelve months all this
was falsified by facts, and Brigham who uttered and the people
who listened to these glorious predictions were unhappily fleeing from their homes, and seeking the " dens and caves of the
" mountains." What a lesson !

The flight of the Mormons from Salt Lake City and the
neighbouring settlements was heart-rending to witness. The
poor people—and the great mass of them were very poor indeed—were utterly destitute. There had been for years but
very little money in the country, and that little reached only
the hands of the few who could trade and speculate.

For many years in Utah a coin of any kind was seldom
seen by the farming and labouring classes. Labour was exchanged for labour, and " store-pay " was the best that the
produce of the field and garden could command. When
" counsel " was given to " move south " the people were reduced to the greatest extremity to furnish themselves with the
means of transportation. Fraternity is beautiful in Sunday
sermons, but in a time of flight that sentiment is too frequently exchanged for *sauve qui peut*, for those from whom most
might have been expected, by way of generous aid, too often
take advantage of the necessities of others to " drive very hard
" bargains." One very prominent gentleman to-day in Salt
Lake City owes the foundation of his fortune to the high prices
that he obtained for old wagons " at the move."

Governor Cumming was greatly touched at the sight of the
fleeing Mormons. The sad impression made upon his mind
was often revived—especially when his Excellency was a " lit-
" tle happy." Then he would tell the story of poverty and
rags, of " the poor women and innocent children " travelling
barefooted and covered with dust, till they looked more like
Indians than Caucasians. The old gentleman's eye would fill
with tears, his lips compress, his head nod, and he would mut-
ter : " Terrible sight !—hope never to see the like again—Brig-
" ham Young, imprudent man—must never do it again—but it
" is all over now ! "

The Governor followed his " constituents " fifty miles south,
beseeching them to turn back, and representing to them that

there was no danger to be apprehended from the troops; that their homes would be preserved, and that they would be unmolested; but it was to no purpose. As well say to the tidal-wave: "Hitherto shalt thou go, but no further." The Governor and the Peace Commissioners spoke in vain. The power that led away the Mormons from their firesides alone could send them back again.

At Provo, on the 5th of July, Brigham announced his intention to return to Salt Lake City, and left the people at liberty to do as they pleased. In a few hours afterwards the greater number were on the march home. Many who had exhausted their resources in going south were unable to return immediately, and some remained permanently where the flight had landed them.

In this memorable flight there were probably no less than 30,000 persons on "the move south," from the latter part of March till the beginning of August.

CHAPTER XLI.

THE JUDGES AT WORK.—The Federal Officers divided—Judge Sinclair opposed by the District Attorney at Salt Lake City—Judge Cradlebaugh holds Court at Provo—The Charges of Murder at Springville—Attention drawn to the Mountain Meadows Massacre and other Murders—The Jury find no Bills of Indictment—The Judge discharges them—Depositions of Witnesses taken—Terrible Revelations—Counterfeiting on United States Treasury—Trying to arrest Brigham—Saving the Governor's Official Head.

WITH the arrival of the new Federal officers a thorough work of investigation into the charges made against the Mormon leaders was expected. The few Gentiles and the dissatisfied Mormons immediately realized that there was another influence than that of the priesthood dominating; but every sensible looker-on could readily see that though Brigham had been brought to terms, he was very far from feeling that his reign was over. " The Lord " was still with him, and the Prophet could afford to bide his time. With that accommodating faith which sees in every opposition and change but the stepping-stone to something better and greater, Brigham could comprehend that " the Lord " had made him stoop only to conquer. Could the troops have been kept out of " the Valleys of the Mountains " it would have been the work of " the Lord " for the protection of his people; but as the troops were now in the midst of the Saints, that was " the Lord " trying the faith of his people. It was necessary that the Saints should exhibit their inclinations, and that those who might incline to " the kingdom of dark- " ness " should have the opportunity of abandoning their faith.

When Governor Cumming first entered Salt Lake City, and appeared in the Tabernacle, he announced that he was prepared to extend protection to all who desired to leave the Territory, and invited all such persons to communicate to him their names and addresses. One of the accusations against the Mormon leaders was that they prevented persons who had become dissatisfied from leaving the Territory. On the other hand, the Mormons indignantly denied that any one was ever intimidated or his liberty circumscribed,* and that on this occasion when the Governor afforded them such an excellent opportunity of leaving, only a very few persons—probably less than a score—availed themselves of it. Other sources of information, however, tell a very different story. †

The machinery of the courts was soon set in motion. The Chief Justice preferred the military camp for his residence. Associate-Justice Sinclair was assigned to the district embracing Salt Lake City; and Associate-Justice Cradlebaugh had within his district all the southern country.

Up to this time the Governor of the Territory had also been Superintendent of Indian Affairs, but on the appointment of Governor Cumming, the office of Superintendent was conferred upon Jacob Forney, of Pennsylvania. Alexander Wilson, of Iowa, was appointed District Attorney of the Territory, and thus was completed the full list of Federal officials.

---

* Much of this feeling of fear about leaving the Territory was due more to apprehension of what might take place, than to any direct action of the Church leaders. Some persons had left the Territory without opposition or annoyance, but the opinion always prevailed that there was a great risk to life in leaving the Church. Some "apostates" had fallen by the way, and "the Indians" were charged with their "taking off." There is a strong impression among even "good Mormons," as well as among the Gentiles and those in opposition to the priesthood, that some of the murders of "apostates" were committed by "white Indians," and in justification of much of that impression the Tabernacle sermons may be cited. There is, besides, much circumstantial evidence to justify the accusation.

† A responsible correspondent of the New York *Tribune*—Albert G. Browne, Esq.—in a communication to the *Atlantic Monthly*, April, 1859, writing of the Governor's offer of assistance, says:

"During the ensuing week nearly two hundred persons registered themselves in the manner he proposed, and a greater number would undoubtedly have been glad to follow their example, but were deterred by the surveillance to which they were subjected by certain functionaries of the Church before being admitted to his presence. Those who were registered were organized into trains, with the little movable property they possessed, and dispatched toward Fort Bridger. They arrived there in the course of May—as motley, ragged, and destitute a crowd as ever descended from ..he deck of an Irish emigrant ship at New York or Boston. The only garments which some possessed were made of the canvas of their wagon covers. Many were on foot. For provisions they had nothing but flour and some fresh meat. It is a fact creditable to humanity, that private soldiers, by the score, shared their own abridged rations and scanty stock of clothing with those poor wretches, and in less than a day after their arrival they were provided with much to make them comfortable."

The Governor's policy from the beginning was "peace, if "that were possible;" and though he and Brigham concluded that it was better that they themselves should refrain from personal intercourse, the leading men around the latter were closely intimate with the official party, and for all practical purpose were as friendly as need be desired. Superintendent Forney was personally intimate with the Governor, and was for a time of some little service to the Mormons in that relationship; the District Attorney also supported the Governor's policy, and sought by every means in his power the peace of the Territory. The Secretary was unreliable.

The three judges and the marshal were united for a vigorous prosecution of past offences, and powerful aid was rendered them by the *Valley Tan* *—the first Gentile paper published among the Mormons.

Judge Sinclair convened the Third Judicial District Court in Great Salt Lake City in November, 1858, and in his charge to the grand jury he exhibited an anxiety upon three particular points—treason, the intimidation of the courts, and polygamy. President Buchanan's pardon, the Judge admitted, was "a public fact in the history of the country," but, "like any "other deed, it ought to be brought judicially before the court "by plea, motion, or otherwise." In brief, he wanted to bring before his court Brigham Young and the leading Mormons to make them admit that they had been guilty of treason, and make them humbly accept from him the President's clemency. The District Attorney would not present to the jury bills of indictment for treason, pleading that the commissioners had presented the pardon, and the people had accepted it, and the Governor had proclaimed that peace was restored to the Terri-

---

* Among the first efforts at home manufacture in the mountains was shoe leather, and this article was so successfully produced that kindly critics on examining it gave preference to the leather *tanned in the Valley*. Ever afterwards the home-made leather, to distinguish it from the imported article, was designated " *Valley Tan*." As other home-made articles were produced, with very pardonable pride this general term was affixed, and the name of everything manufactured was prefixed with the words "Valley Tan." Even the very poteen was designated in commerce "Valley Tan Whiskey." The publisher of the first paper appropriated the popular term, and called his weekly four-paged sheet *Kirk Anderson's Valley Tan*. The first issue of the paper is dated Nov. 5th, 1858.

tory. The jury required no further instruction, and the charge of treason was for ever ended.

But "the young judge" was more successful in his efforts in bringing forward the charge of intimidating the courts, as already noticed, and with the grand jury's presentment of Mr. Ferguson that subject was also dropped. It could not be expected that the charge to the jury on polygamy would secure much attention. It was regarded little better than a grand farce to ask a Mormon jury to find indictments against their brethren for polygamy. The term of Judge Sinclair's judicial service was a failure, only memorable for one thing—he sentenced the first white man who was ever hanged in Utah, and he was a Gentile, to be executed *on a Sunday !*—Of course the day had to be changed.

Judge Cradlebaugh had a larger field of operation, and a still more interesting experience, but it was an experience that ended in much the same way as that of Judge Sinclair. Judge Cradlebaugh was a brave man, and he undertook the unpleasant and herculean task of investigating the charges of murder that had been committed in the Territory. It was, undoubtedly, his purpose to saddle upon the parties really guilty the responsibility of the murders committed during the said " re-" bellion in Utah," especially those commonly known as the Potter and Parrish murders at Springville, and the Mountain Meadows Massacre in southern Utah. He failed in his effort, but he gained a mass of valuable evidence that is held in reserve for the day of reckoning that has yet to come.

So much of a contradictory character has been stated concerning the proceedings of Judge Cradlebaugh at this time, and so little is clearly known of the murders which he essayed to bring to light, and which are almost daily alluded to in the public press, that it is due to the people of Utah as well as to the people of the United States that the facts should be freely stated in this work, and the sources of information given.

On the 8th of March, 1859, at Provo, Judge Cradlebaugh addressed to the grand jury the following language :

"I will say to you, gentlemen of the grand jury, that, from what I learn, it has been some time since a court, having judicial cognizance in your district, was held. No person has been brought to punishment for some two years ; and from what I have learned I am satisfied that crime after crime has been committed.

"There is no such effectual way of stopping crime, no means has been found so effectual and sure as the speedy punishment of the offender ; and therefore, so far as you are concerned, and your community, it is a very important matter, if you desire innocent and unoffending persons to be protected, that you vigilantly and diligently prosecute all persons who are violators of the law. . . . .

"I said to you in the outset that a great number of cases had come to my knowledge of crimes having been committed through the country, and I shall take the liberty of naming a few of them. The persons committing those offences have not been prosecuted, the reasons why I cannot tell, but it strikes me that those outside influences have prevented it. If you do your duty you will not neglect to inquire into those matters, or allow the offenders to go unpunished. I may mention the Mountain Meadows murders, where a whole train was cut off, except a few children who were too young to give evidence in court. It has been claimed that this offence was committed by Indians, but there is evidence that there were others who were engaged in it besides.

"When the Indians commit crimes they are not so discriminate as to save children ; they would not be so particular as to save the children and kill the rest. I say that you may look at all the crimes that have been committed in the western country by the Indians, and there is no case where they have been so careful as to save the innocent children. But, if this be not enough, we have evidence to prove that there were others there engaged in it.

"A large body of persons leaving Cedar City, armed, and after getting away were organized, and went and returned with the spoil. Now there are persons who know that there were others engaged in the crime ; I brought a young man with me who saw persons go out in wagons with arms, others on horseback, were away a day or two and came back with the spoil. The Indians complain that in the distribution of the property they did not get their share, they seem to think that the parties engaged with them kept the best and gave them the worst. The chief there [Kanosh] is equally amenable to law, and liable to be punished, and I suppose it is well known that he was engaged in assisting to exterminate the hundred persons that were in that train. I might name to you persons who were there ; a great number of them I have had named to me. And yet, notwithstanding this crime has been committed, there has been no effort made to punish those individuals. I say then, gentlemen, it is your duty to look after that, and if it is a fact that they have been guilty of that offence, indict them, send for them, and have them brought before this court.

"I might bring your attention to another case near here, at Springville ; that is the case of the Parrishes and Potter. Springville is a vil-

lage of several hundred inhabitants. There was one young man whom it
was intended to kill. He ran to his uncle's, and was followed to his uncle's house. Here are three persons killed, and the criminal goes unpunished.

"There can be no doubt but by the testimony of young Parrish that
you will be able to identify those persons who were connected with it.
He can tell you who was engaged in it, and who followed him to the
house of his uncle. Here are three persons who were butchered in a most
inhuman manner, and the offenders have not been brought to justice.
This is sufficient to shew that there has been an effort to cover up instead
of to bring to light and punish.

"At the same place there was another person killed, Henry Fobbs,
who came in from California and was going to the States, but got in here
when the difficulties arose between this community and the general Government, and was detained. When Henry Fobbs was here he made his
home at Partial Terry's, stayed there a few weeks; during that time his
horse and revolver were stolen; he made his escape, tried to get to Bridger, was caught, brought back, and murdered; and that is the last of
Henry Fobbs. No investigation has been made; his body has been removed several times so that now, perhaps, it could not be found. Shortly afterwards his horse was traded off by Terry. Here is a man said to be
killed by the Indians, and then his horse is taken by Mr. Terry and traded
for sheep. It seems to me that these are matters that you ought to investigate. Fobbs, I believe, lived in the State of Illinois; he had a wife and
children, and was anxious to get back; and I suppose his wife is still
anxious about him; but as to what has become of him she cannot tell.
I say this case ought to come under your notice and be investigated, and
the offenders punished; don't let them go unpunished.

"Then there was Henry Jones that was murdered up here; I believe
he was first castrated up in the city, then went to Payson, was chased to
Pond Town and was shot there. It is said that he committed some offence. But if persons do commit offences, the public have no right to
take the law into their own hands; they have no right to take persons and
punish them. I understand that he was castrated; that he came down
here, and the house in which he and his mother lived was pulled down.

"There is another matter to which I wish to call your attention. A
few days before the matter of the murder of the Parrishes and Potter, the
stable of Parrish was broken into, and his carriage and horses were taken
out; this was done in the night. These horses have never been returned.
That woman, the wife of Mr. Parrish, told me that since then at times she
had lived on bread and water, and still there are persons in this community riding about on those horses. Mr. Lysander Gee has those horses;
he says that a few days after they were stolen they were given to him, and
that he was directed to give them to no person whatever.

"Now, it is a strange kind of matter that persons should go to Parrish's, break open his stable and rob him, and then take the horses to Mr.

25

Lysander Gee and tell him to keep them. It does not look reasonable.
It would look more reasonable to suppose that Mr. Lysander Gee was engaged in it himself, and it is an outrageous thing that this woman, one of
whose children was killed with her husband, has been obliged to live in
the very dregs of poverty. I say, bring that man up and compel him to
restore those horses, and give the property back to her, and do not allow
her to live in poverty, while others are riding about the country here with
her husband's property.

"Young Mr. Parrish is here ; if the grand jury desire to have him, they
can use him as a witness.

"It is not pleasant to talk about these things, but the crimes have been
committed, and, if you desire, you can investigate them. My desire is that
the responsibility shall be with the grand jury, and not with the court ;
all the responsibility shall be with you, and the question is with you,
whether you will bring those persons to trial.

"I have hereby named some few things ; there has been a great deal
of crime committed, and there is a way to punish those who have committed them.

"I hear every day of cases of larceny, and an officer is now after a number who are engaged in committing depredations. A great many cases
have been committed near Camp Floyd, such as I shall call the attention
of the Territorial Attorney to, such as buying soldiers' clothes. Unless
you faithfully discharge your duty, I cannot see how you are to escape
from the influence of these cases of larceny that have been committed. I
therefore present these for the purpose of having you promptly discharge
your duty.

"When you retire, you will elect your clerk ; and as it is the desire of
the court to expedite business, you will therefore be permitted to meet
upon your own adjournment. If time is required, the court will adjourn
from time to time to give it to you.

"To allow these things to pass over, gives a colour as if they were
done by authority. The very fact of such a case as the Mountain Meadows shows that there was some person high in the estimation of the
people, and it was done by that authority ; and this case of the Parrishes
shows the same ; and, unless you do your duty, such will be the view that
will be taken of it.

"You can know no law but the laws of the United States and the laws
you have here. No person can commit crimes and say they are authorized by higher authorities, and if they have any such notions they will
have to dispel them.

"I saw something said in that paper [the *Deseret News*] of some higher
law. It is perhaps not proper to mention that, but such teachings will
have their influence upon the public mind."

These extracts are taken from the *Deseret News* report.
During the session of the court, the judge made a requi-

sition upon General Johnston for troops to act as a protection to the witnesses, and also, in the absence of a jail, to serve as a guard over the prisoners. The mayor of Provo protested that the presence of the military was an infringement upon the liberties of his fellow-citizens; but the judge answered that he had well considered the request before he had made it. A petition was sent to Governor Cumming, and he asked General Johnston to withdraw the troops, asserting that the court had no authority to call for the aid of the military but through him. The judges interpreted General Johnston's instructions from the War Department adversely to the statement of the Governor, and the troops were continued at Provo. On the 27th of March, the Governor issued a proclamation protesting against the continuance of the troops at Provo, and exhibited to everybody the hostility which existed between himself and the military commander.

After Judge Cradlebaugh had waited for two weeks for some action on the part of the grand jury against the murderers, his patience was exhausted, and he discharged them, assigning as his reason the folly of trying to bring any of the murderers to justice with a Mormon jury. He narrated how the officers of the court had sought to apprehend criminals in Springville, and how, when they got to that settlement, a trumpet was sounded, and the persons sought were secreted until the departure of the officers, when the trumpet was again sounded, and the accused came out of their hiding-places and went about their ordinary business.

After the jury was discharged, the judge continued to take the affidavits of witnesses, which revealed the existence of a Reign of Terror in the country settlements wherever there were "apostates," beyond all credibility.

Governor Cumming was a head-strong, positive man, and to his personal repugnance to General Johnston was justly attributed his official protest against the presence of troops, while evidence in possession of the court was most positive that the witnesses testifying of the murders in Springville believed themselves to be in constant jeopardy, and that their lives were insecure but for the protection afforded by the troops.

The Governor's interpretation of his instructions was afterwards sustained by Jeremiah S. Black, the Attorney-General,
but it has always been a matter of regret with those who
sought the punishment of crime and the overthrow of fanaticism, that his Excellency's private animosity prevented
him from acting in concert with his Federal associates. That
was certainly a time when the representatives of the Government ought to have been united. Still, there is little room for
regret, as the members of the grand jury at that session of
the court were themselves accused of participation in the very
crimes they were instructed to investigate.*

In summing up the evidence in the case of the murders at
Springville, the judge concluded with the following address :

" Until I commenced the examination of the testimony in this case, I
always supposed that I lived in a land of civil and religious liberty, in
which we were secured by the Constitution of our country the right to
remove at pleasure from one portion of our domain to another, and also
that we enjoyed the privilege of ' worshipping God according to the dictates of our own conscience.' But I regret to say, that the evidence in
this case clearly proves that, so far as Utah is concerned, I have been
mistaken in such supposition. Men are murdered here. Coolly, deliberately, premeditatedly murdered—their murder is deliberated and determined upon by church council-meetings, and that, too, for no other reason
than that they had apostatized from your Church, and were striving to
leave the Territory.

" You are the tools, the dupes, the instruments of a tyrannical Church
despotism. The heads of your Church order and direct you. You are
taught to obey their orders and commit these horrid murders. Deprived
of your liberty, you have lost your manhood, and become the willing instruments of bad men.

" I say to you it will be my earnest effort, while with you, to knock off
your ecclesiastical shackles and set you free."

The grand jury would not have listened to such language
had there been no foundation for the accusations. Murders

* By legislative enactments, the County Court and the Territorial Marshal have
the empanelling of juries in Utah. With a community that was at that time almost
wholly of the Mormon faith, it was impossible to have anything but a Mormon jury,
and a discreet marshal is not supposed to make distinctions between citizens.
Whether any of those jurors were themselves guilty or not is not proven, but it is
certain that, immediately after they were dismissed, several of them betook themselves to concealment, and Judge Cradlebaugh expressed his sorrow that he did not
keep them when he had them.

of an atrocious character had been committed in that neighbourhood, and the evidence was clear and pointed as to who
the murderers were. The grand jury could do nothing without doing too much. Had they ever moved in earnest, the
whole net-work would have been exposed; but that jury owed
allegiance to "a higher court," and could therefore do nothing
but pocket silently the most offensive language that could be
addressed to honest men.

With the military supporting him, Judge Cradlebaugh was
determined to reach the guilty, if that were possible, without
the aid of the grand jury. Before any intimation of his purpose could possibly be known to the Mormons, he had furnished the marshal with writs for the apprehension of those
accused of murder, and before daylight in the morning the
marshal and his *posse* reached Springville. The troops accompanied the *posse*, and surrounded the settlement so that flight
was impossible. The houses were searched, but no one could
be found. The " ten wives " of the bishop received the *posse*
kindly enough, and seemed to enjoy the disappointment of the
gentlemen who were hunting their liege lord. Everywhere it
was about the same experience. A company of the soldiers
sought to penetrate the neighbouring cañon, whither it was reported the accused had fled; but the snow was too deep for the
cavalry, and the search was abandoned.

Chagrined and annoyed at his inability to reach the guilty,
the Judge entered upon the docket of his court: " The whole
"community presents a united and organized opposition to the
"proper administration of justice." Two or three Indians
were held as prisoners, and, with a few Gentiles, would have
come up before his Honour for trial during that session of his
court, but the hostility which he met with on the part of the
community when in pursuit of Mormon criminals decided him
to close his court altogether. He therefore dismissed the prisoners, and adjourned his court " without day." This was the
first and last effort to reach the Springville murderers.

The affidavits taken by Judge Cradlebaugh were given to
the public through the *Valley Tan* immediately afterwards,
and they vividly reveal the terrible condition of Utah in 1857.
The " Reformation " of the preceding year had borne fearful

fruit. Had the United States army not entered the Territory
in 1858, and had the work of " Reformation " continued, it is
difficult to conceive what the condition of the people might
have been. It is charitable to conclude that the leading
preachers who advocated the sacrifice of human beings as an
atonement for their sins were absolutely crazy. To believe less
is to charge them with something worse.

Judge Cradlebaugh was appointed to the Western Judicial
District of the Territory and made Carson City his official residence. After the Territory of Nevada was created, his Honour
was sent to Washington as delegate, and while at the seat of
Government he was not unmindful of the Mormon leaders.
On the 7th of February, 1863, he made a lengthy speech on the
murders in Utah, and gave what is considered a fair representation of the Mountain Meadows massacre, an account of which
will be given in a succeeding chapter.

While the contention between General Johnston and Governor Cumming concerning the action of the military continued, there was a constant expectation of a collision. Governor
Cumming was beset by influential men among the Mormons who
complained that the military was a menace to them, and that
the action of the judges and the General was a personal insult
to him. The fanatical longed for an opportunity of seeing the
Territorial militia called out by the Governor to resist the
Federal troops, and at one time their suggestions appeared to
be favourably received.

A clever artist among the Mormons had been engaged by
smarter men than himself to engrave a counterfeit plate similar to that used by the quarter-master at Camp Floyd for
notes drawn upon the assistant treasurers of the United States
at St. Louis and New York, and the artist had been so successful that it was difficult to tell the counterfeit from the original.
When the fraud was discovered, the principal in the transaction was arrested at Camp Floyd, and a few hours after he
agreed to become State's evidence. In his confession he pan-
dered to the prejudices of the locality, and implicated some one
in the office of Brigham Young as having furnished the paper,
and it was hoped that possibly the Prophet himself might
prove to be not quite guiltless. The latter suspicion was, how-

ever, entirely without foundation, but it served the purpose of the moment, and in what consequently ensued the anticipated collision between the troops and the militia seemed at one time imminent.

It was proposed that a writ should be issued for the apprehension of Brigham as well as the artist, and calculating upon the Prophet's resistance to the marshal, the military was to be ordered into the city.

The officers from camp entrusted with this little business arrived and presented themselves at the Governor's office to request his coöperation. His Excellency entertained them as gentlemen and as friends, and was ready to grant them every proper assistance. The writ for the arrest of the artist was shown to him, and met with his approval. With a suspicion of something in reserve, and a consciousness of the fullest coöperation on the part of the Mormons, the Governor called a messenger, sent a note to a Mormon official, and " in fifteen " minutes," as he afterwards related, "I placed their man be-" fore them."

"They had 'got the dead wood on Brigham Young this " ' time,' so they said as they unfolded to me their plans. If " Brigham resisted, General Johnston's artillery was to make a " breach in the wall surrounding his premises, and they would " take him by force and carry him to Camp Floyd.

" I listened to them, sir, as gravely as I could, and exam-" ined their papers. They rubbed their hands and were jubi-" lant they ' had got the dead wood on Brigham Young.' I was " indignant, sir, and told them, ' By ——, gentlemen, you can't " ' do it! When you have a right to take Brigham Young, " ' gentlemen, you shall have him without creeping through " ' walls. You shall enter by his door with heads erect as be-" ' comes representatives of your government. But till that " ' time, gentlemen, you can't touch Brigham Young while I " ' live, by ——! ' "

Such was the story told by the Governor to the Author a few years later, and as he related it all the fire of his nature was depicted on his countenance and told unmistakably that he would have made good every word with his life.

The officers returned to Camp Floyd discomfited, and immediately the news was circulated that General Johnston would send two regiments and a battery of artillery to enforce the writ for the apprehension of Brigham. A Mormon correspondent, writing to the New York *Herald*, April 23rd, 1859, stated that the Governor had ordered General Wells to be in readiness with the militia to repulse the Federal troops.*

The engraver's tools and paraphernalia were all seized by the marshal, and in afterwards visiting his regular workshop where he had done work for Brigham Young on the " Deseret " Currency," the plates of that institution were also taken possession of and carried to Camp Floyd. The marshal's zeal had carried him too far. The plates of the Mormon currency got scratched and damaged. Brigham brought suit against the marshal for the illegal seizure and injury of his plates, and after a long and tedious trial the marshal was fined heavy damages, for payment of which his house was seized. It is now a valuable piece of property adjoining the theatre, and is of much more value to Brigham than the unscratched plates of the " Currency " would have ever been.

On the 17th of May, an official letter from Washington decided that the military could only be issued as a *posse* on a call from the Governor, and thus ended the contention between the Governor, the Judges, and the General on this subject. †

* " An express from Camp Floyd arrived here on Sunday night with the intelligence that two regiments were coming to the city to make arrests, and it was expected that they would have orders for forced marches, to come in upon us unawares. *Immediately* on Governor Cumming being made acquainted with the report and circumstances, which leaves no room to doubt of the plans of the judges, he notified Gen. D. H. Wells to hold the militia in readiness to act on orders. By two o'clock on Monday morning five thousand troops were under arms. Had the United States troops attempted to enter the city, the struggle must have commenced, for the Governor is determined to carry out his instructions. What has deferred their arrival here we know not ; but now that this plan is known, a watchful eye is kept on the camp, and the shedding of blood seems inevitable."

† It should be stated that General Johnston succeeded General Harney in the command of the Utah expedition, and to General Harney were given instructions differing from those which were afterwards given to Gov. Cumming. General Harney was appointed early in the spring, when Washington was feverish with the news from Utah, and it was not till the 6th of July that Cumming was appointed Governor. Had there been no personal difficulty between the military chief and the chief executive of the Territory, their instructions would doubtless have been harmoniously interpreted.

This victory on the part of the Governor, and with it the end of prosecution for past crime, was very satisfactory to the Mormons; but there was a moment when all this joy was seriously threatened. The Gentile influence everywhere was invoked to support the Judges, and to have Governor Cumming removed. For a time this was under consideration in the Cabinet, and the probabilities were all against the Governor being retained, but an excellent piece of strategy saved him.

Soon after the return of Col. Kane to the eastern States, that gentleman was invited to deliver a lecture before the Historical Society of New York upon "the situation of Utah." Though in very feeble health, and unprepared for such a lecture, his devotion to what he no doubt sincerely believed to be the welfare of the Mormons and the honour of the Government overcame all impediments, and the lecture was delivered. In that audience were two Mormon elders listening eagerly for a sentence that might help "the cause" in the West. By previous arrangement the agent of the Associated Press was to be furnished with a notice of the lecture, and thus a despatch next morning was read everywhere throughout the Union to the effect that there was a division among the Mormons, that some were eager for strife, others for peace, but that Brigham Young was on the side of peace and order, and was labouring to control his fiery brethren. This was a repetition of a part of the diplomacy of the Tabernacle. Governor Cumming was complimented by the gallant Colonel as a clear-headed, resolute, but prudent executive, and the very man for the trying position.

Before such an endorsement, sent broadcast over the Republic, coming from the lips of the gentleman who had warded off the effusion of blood, and saved the nation from the expense and horror of a domestic war, the Cabinet of Mr. Buchanan silently bowed, but they were terribly chagrined.

A mass convention of Gentiles was held at Camp Floyd on the 23rd of July, at which the Judges and the Indian agent—Dr. Garland Hurd—were present, and in which they took a prominent part. An address was penned, rehearsing all the crimes charged to the Mormons, asserting that they were as disloyal after the President's pardon as when they were in arms in Echo Cañon, that the President was deceived and badly advised, and had done a great wrong in withdrawing the protection of the military from the courts.

In perusing the lengthy report of this convention, and comparing statements then and accusations since, the reader is struck with the unanimity of the opponents of the Mormon leaders, and the clearness with which results were anticipated years before their accomplishment.

CHAPTER XLII.

THE EXPEDITION A FAILURE.—The Mormons enriched by the Presence of the Troops—Intercourse with the Camp forbidden to the Saints—The Assertion of Personal Liberty and the Dawning of Freedom to the bold—Brigham supplies the Military with Tithing Flour—Rowdyism and Murders in the City—The Prophet guarded Night and Day—The Desperadoes are wasted away—The Rebellion in the South a Theme of Rejoicing—The Fulfilment of Joseph's Prediction—The Expedition recalled—Great Destruction of Munitions of War—Millions of Property wasted—The Federal Troops vacate the Territory, and the Saints rejoice.

THE social position of many of the Mormons was much improved by the entrance of the army into the Valley. However much they were prepared to fight the troops before they saw them, there were few indeed who did not afterwards thank a kind Providence for their arrival. The people had been utterly destitute of almost everything necessary to their social comfort. They were poorly clad, and rarely ever saw anything upon their tables but what was prepared from flour, corn, beet-molasses, and the vegetables and fruits of their little gardens. They were alike destitute of implements of industry, and horses, mules, and wagons for their agricultural operations. Utah was truly very poor.

The presence of the army soon changed the condition of those who were bold enough to seek directly the intercourse of trade with the Gentiles, and the more timid, who were afraid to be known as having themselves any dealings with the camp, in course of time found out ways of supplying those who dared to risk the anathemas of the Tabernacle. In this way money was gathered in freely by the Gentiles and the bold Mormon traders, and the people generally were thus indirectly clothed, and supplied with the delicacies of tea, coffee, and sugar, in return for the produce of the field, the dairy, and the chicken-coop.

It was a certain indication of "apostacy" for any of the people to deal with the camp; but as the heavens have always been very complaisant towards "Brother Brigham," he was not held to such strict accountability. It has been argued in defence of some of his dealings which eventually came to light, that if he had utterly refused to supply the camp with flour, the Government might have charged him with hostility! While the Tithing-office clerks, who had the handling of the flour, found it necessary for the preservation of their own confidence in the Prophet to adopt this convenient philosophy, the "Chief" himself has never deemed it expedient to make any allusion to the circumstance. He, however, was kind enough not to parade the transaction before the eyes of the people, and the wagons which took the wheat of the people's contributions from the Church Tithing-office, were not necessarily employed in the blaze of noonday!

Among the rascalities of those times, contracts were awarded to certain "political hucksters" at Washington for an enormous quantity of flour to be supplied at $28.40 per 100 lbs., which, in course of time, was furnished by the Prophet at $6 in the City of the Saints. That contractor also managed to get an order from the Secretary of War for the specie at Camp Floyd, failing which he was to be paid in mules, and of these he had his choice, at figures ranging from $100 to $150 each. Great bands of these animals were driven to California, and sold on the Pacific at nearly six times their Camp Floyd prices. With such and many other more flagrant facts, it is not surprising that the Prophet and the apostles designated Mr. Buchanan's expedition to Utah, in 1857, "a Contractors' War!"

But the army was the Republican entering wedge to Theocracy, and the isolation of the prophets. Men of sober thought and of resolute purpose saw clearly enough that, however well adapted might be the revelations of Mount Sinai to the wandering Israelites in Zin, the prohibitive teachings of Brigham Young were a compound of folly and duplicity.

They burst the chains that bound them to the Prophet's chariot, and began that struggle for freedom in Utah that has eventuated in the present freedom of the press and the platform.

Unable to throw off at once allegiance to the priesthood, some merchants lightened the oppressive weight by compounding with the Prophet, and paying grudgingly a tithe of all their income to the Church. Foremost, and nearly alone, as pioneers in the grand work of personal freedom in Utah were the Messrs. Walker Brothers and Mr. John Chislett, the latter of whom, in the hand-cart expedition, has already been presented in these pages, and the former will be spoken of at greater length in a future chapter.

With such a large body of troops there were, as usual, numerous camp-followers plying their *petit industries*, gambling, thieving, and drinking. General Johnston, with strict surveillance and severe military punishment, had been able to control them on the march and at Camp Scott; but when they found in the valleys of the Saints a wider and safer field for operations, they gave rein to their vilest passions, and a worse set of vagabonds never afflicted any community with their presence than did the followers of Johnston's army the inhabitants of the chief city of Zion. Quite a number of young Mormons—and some not so young—became as reckless and daring as any of the imported Gentiles, and life and property for a time were very insecure in Salt Lake City.

The programme of the police authorities seemed to be to give the desperadoes the largest liberty, so that they might, in their drunken carousals, "kill off each other," and what they left undone invisible hands readily accomplished. During the summer and fall of 1859 there was a murder committed in Salt Lake City almost every week, and very rarely were the criminals brought to justice.

The Mormon leaders taught the people to attend to their fields and work-shops, keep out of "Whiskey Street," and let "Civilization"* take its course. They had plenty of hard

* The conclusion being accepted that all Christian nations are totally corrupt, and are hurrying on to final dissolution and ruin, every wrong-doing is represented by the Mormon leaders to be the result of "Christian civilization," which the Gentiles are unceasingly striving to force upon the faithful.

work to engage their attention, and no money, so that the
business street was seldom visited by them, and they saw little
of what was transpiring in their midst. The Church weekly
paper took pride in reporting, as it occurred, " another man
" for breakfast," and with that " the people of God " were satisfied that " the good work was rolling on." Israel would one
day be free from his oppressors.

The rioting and killing that were traceable occupied little
more than passing attention, but the midnight work of invisible hands created a sensation of terror in the minds of all who
were inimical to the priesthood. The *Valley Tan*, notwithstanding its true boldness, felt the danger of the hour, and in
one of its doleful wails ejaculated : " How long, oh ! how long
" are scenes like this to continue ? . . . . It would seem as if
" the insatiable demon and enemy of man must himself be
" gorged with the flow of human blood in our midst." . . . . .
" No man's life is secure as long as the scenes of violence
" and bloodshed, which have been of such frequent occurrence
" among us for months past, continue to be repeated, and the
" perpetrators escape unpunished or not detected."

The bloody work continued, and finally terminated with
the murder of Brewer and Joaquin Johnston,* two intimate
friends, who were shot at the same instant as they were walking home together. The Author well remembers seeing very
early the next morning the marshal of the city and the chief
of police, who gravely informed him of the " sad news."—
" Johnston and Brewer had quarrelled, and killed each
other ! " This story was feeble enough, but no one cared to
question it : the people had got used to the record of scenes of
blood.

In the " swift destruction " that fell upon the desperadoes,
there was no mitigation of punishment on account of faith or
family relationship, and very respectable Mormon families had

* Brewer was the principal in the matter of counterfeiting the Quarter-Master's
cheques, and turned States' evidence against the Mormon artist. Johnston was a
notorious gambler, and had, on the preceding day, threatened to shoot a Mormon
editor. He was a handsome scoundrel, and princely in his attire. On the day before his murder he put on a magnificent suit of buck-skin, elaborately ornamented
with flowers and figures worked in coloured silk. The buttons of his vest were
$2.50 gold coins.

to mourn the untimely end of boys who, before the entrance of the army, gave promise of lives of usefulness and honour. All the bad and desperate Mormons were not brought to judgment, but the pretext alone was wanting for carrying more extensively into execution the general programme. Resistance to an officer, or the slightest attempt to escape from custody, was eagerly seized, when wanted, as the justification of closing a disreputable career, and in more than one case of this *legal* shooting, there is much doubt if even the trivial excuse was waited for. The Salt Lake police then earned the reputation of affording every desperate prisoner the opportunity of escape, and, if embraced, the officer's ready revolver brought the fugitive to a "halt," and saved the county the expenses of a trial and his subsequent boarding in the penitentiary. A coroner's inquest and cemetery expenses were comparatively light.

With the troops themselves there was no collision. The Governor had requested General Johnston to withhold furlough from the soldiers, and few of them ever had the opportunity of visiting the City of the Saints. With some officers there had been, in the city, slight difficulties, which were, however, easily settled. Only one serious affair occurred, ending in the death of Sergeant Pike. This person was charged with violently assaulting a young Mormon and cracking his skull with a musket. During the sergeant's trial in Salt Lake City, while on the public street at noon, passing to his hotel, a young man shot him down, and shortly afterward he died. The young man, with the aid of others, escaped, and was never arrested. There was great excitement at Camp Floyd, but the sergeant's comrades were too far away to retaliate.

From the time of the arrival of the troops in the valley, Brigham was personally very cautious, and never exposed himself to attack. For a long time he absented himself from the public assemblies, kept an armed door-keeper at the entrance of his residences, and by night was protected by an armed guard of the faithful. Every ward in the city took its turn in watching over the Prophet, and the floor of his offices was nightly covered with a guard, armed and equipped, and ready at a moment's notice to repulse the imaginary foe.

During the day, when Brigham ventured beyond the outer

walls of his premises, half a dozen friends always accompanied him wherever he went.   It is pleasing to add that no one ever so much as said to him an unbecoming word.

But there was soon to be a change in Zion.

In Congress the political excitement over slavery was rapidly travelling to a culmination.   The news from the East was cheering to the Prophet's soul, and he felt assured of the early departure of the troops.   The horizon began to lighten up.

The experiment of the Pony Express from the Missouri River to the Pacific Ocean had been undertaken just in time to make early news a necessity.   From the East the constant rumours of secession were too good for the pony to be permitted to pass by without its rider dropping a duplicate of the despatches which he was conveying for the Pacific press.

"The Lord" was again to be seen.   He was about to comfort Zion, and to exchange her mourning for joy.   What a wonderful buoyancy there is in human nature, and how readily it asserts itself after a long season of depression!   The Tabernacle was again to be blessed with the presence of the Prophet, and the Saints were to rejoice in the fullest freedom.   Sitting under vines and fig-trees and none daring to make them afraid, was no longer a prophecy which awaited a distant realization. The happy time was at their doors, and Uncle Sam was to be visited with the wrath of the Almighty, and the words of the Prophet Joseph were now to be fulfilled.   Joseph, long years before, had had a remarkable revelation, which all the Saints believed, and the time of its accomplishment was at hand:

REVELATION GIVEN DECEMBER 25, 1832.

"Verily thus saith the Lord, concerning the wars that will shortly come to pass, beginning at the rebellion of South Carolina, which will eventually terminate in the death and misery of many souls.   The days will come that war will be poured out upon all nations, beginning at that place ; for behold the Southern States shall be divided against the Northern States, and the Southern States will call on other nations, even the nation of Great Britain, as it is called, and they shall also call upon other nations in order to defend themselves against other nations; and thus war shall be poured out upon all nations.   And it shall come to pass, after many days, slaves shall rise up against their masters, who shall be marshalled and disciplined for war.   And it shall come to pass, also, that the remnants who are left of the land will marshal themselves, and shall become exceeding angry, and shall vex the Gentiles with a sore vexation; and thus with the sword, and by bloodshed, the inhabitants of the earth shall mourn; and with famine and plague and earthquakes, and the thunder of heaven and the fierce and vivid lightning also, shall the inhabitants of the earth be made to feel the wrath and indignation and chastening hand of an Almighty God, until the consummation decreed hath made a full end of all nations; that the cry of the Saints, and of the blood of the Saints, shall cease to come up into the ears of the Lord of Sabaoth, from the earth, to be avenged of their enemies. Wherefore stand ye in holy places, and be not moved, until the day of the Lord come; for behold it cometh quickly, saith the Lord. Amen."

At a conference held in Nauvoo, April 6, 1843—the year preceding the Prophet's death—he reiterated the prediction:

" I prophecy in the name of the Lord God, that the commencement of the difficulties which will cause much bloodshed, previous to the coming of the Son of Man, will be in South Carolina (it probably may arise through the slave question); this a voice declared to me, while I was praying earnestly on the subject, December 25, 1832."

When the reader takes into consideration the Alabama arbitration at Geneva, and the peaceable adjustment of Britain's difficulties with the United States, the hasty fulfilment may not be very evident of that part of the prediction which states that Great Britain is to "call upon other nations in order to " defend themselves against other nations; and thus war shall " be poured out upon all nations." Equally obscure and improbable is the prediction of the time when the "remnant" [Indians] " who are left of the land will marshal themselves " and become exceeding angry, and shall vex the Gentiles with " a sore vexation."

The Saints at the outbreak of the war, however, saw none of these difficulties; they were filled with joy, resulting from the fact that South Carolina had flung to the breeze the Palmetto flag and " fired the first gun." Joseph was now worthy of national recognition as a prophet, and the horizon of the Saints was radiant with glory.

The Federal troops at Camp Floyd were ordered to the Potomac. That movement brought great joy to " Israel."

The expedition to Utah had cost the treasury at least fourteen millions of dollars. An enormous quantity of munitions
26

of war had been accumulated at Camp Floyd. It was impossible to re-transport this back again to the States, and with the
settled fear that the Mormons could not be entrusted with the
means of successful rebellion, the order was given to destroy
the best equipped military post ever established in the West. *

Before the evacuation and the destruction of arms, public
sales were announced of provisions and army stores of every
kind. The Mormon people who had religious scruples about
visiting the camp stayed at home ; but those who went made
fortunes. Brigham had his agents there and bought enormously for a mere song.

Mr. H. B. Clawson, Brigham's son-in-law and agent, during
the sale became familiarly acquainted with quarter-master Col.
H. G. Crossman and other officers. The army now, instead of
being threatening and a terror to the Saints, as had been predicted, was to them and their prophet a source of wealth and
prosperity. It was, therefore, very proper for Mr. Clawson to
extend to the officers a courteous invitation to visit President
Young before their departure from the Territory. They politely accepted, and seized the opportunity to present to the
Prophet the flag-staff which had borne aloft the national
banner at Camp Floyd. It was afterwards transplanted to the
brow of the hill on the east of Brigham's mansion, and, singularly enough, that flag-staff on which were hoisted the "stars
"and stripes" to rally the troops that had come to overthrow
"the kingdom," was subsequently used to assemble the Mormons for the defence of Brigham against the Californian volunteers, who for months were expected to arrest him.

After the sales were over, the arms and amunition were
taken to a distance and piled up in pyramids ; long trains of
powder were then properly arranged, and at a given signal the
fusee was touched, and away up in the air went the missiles of
death that had been prepared to trouble the " Saints of the
" Most High." Could the faithful do other than rejoice and

* For years after, the " regulation blue pants " were more familiar to the eye, in
the Mormon settlements, than the Valley Tan Quaker gray, and there was scarcely
an officer in the Mormon militia who was not proud to sport Uncle Sam's blue
overcoat, ornamented with the fur that the Territory produced! How often that
which is at first most abhorred becomes subsequently an object of respect !

see in the ruin and desolation that covered the military reserve the workings of a kind Providence that over-ruled all things for their good ?

Several pieces of ordnance that could not be exploded were consigned to deep wells ; but the bishop of that region, with the aid of the faithful, brought them from their watery graves and gave them a glorious resurrection. They now do excellent service on the Fourth and twenty-fourth of July, when the city rejoices in the National birthday, and in the greater day of the arrival of the pioneers in the Great Basin of the Mountains.

In the early autumn of 1861 the troops marched from Zion, and thus ended the military expedition of "King James" Buchanan against the Prophet Brigham.

CHAPTER XLIII.

THE MOUNTAIN MEADOWS MASSACRE.—The Story of two Emigrant Trains
—The Journey across the Plains—Arrival in Salt Lake City—Denied Provis-
ions in the Mormon Settlements—The Travel to the Mountain Meadows—A
Militia Regiment follows them—Indians and Mormon Militia attack the Train—
A Fight for Four Days—Mormon Officers betray the Emigrants under a Flag of
Truce—They lay down their Arms under Promise of Protection—A Hundred
and Twenty Men, Women, and Children butchered—Seventeen Children preserved—The Story of the Massacre confirmed by the Affidavit of Bishop
Smith—The Author's Letter to Brigham Young—Superintendent Forney's Report—Names of the Little Ones saved—Judge Cradlebaugh's Speech in Congress—Sale of the Emigrants' Property—Major Carlton's Story of the Monument—" Vengeance is mine, I *have* repaid "—" Argus " defines Brigham
Young's Responsibility—Congress deaf to the Demand for Investigation.

A FEW weeks in advance of the United States Expedition
to Utah in 1857, there were two trains of emigrants crossing
the plains with the purpose of going to southern California.
The one was from Missouri, the other from Arkansas. The
former was composed chiefly of men who named themselves
" Missouri Wild-cats ; " the other train was a company of
highly-respectable persons, sober and orderly, and in their associations seemed like a large gathering of kindred, or very
near friends. The first were probably venturous spirits seeking fortune ; the others, citizens seeking new homes.

The latter company was wealthy, and there were around
them every indication of comfort, and everything in abundance
for pleasant travelling. In addition to the ordinary transportation wagons of emigrants, they had several riding carriages, which betokened the social class of life in which some
of the emigrants had moved before setting out on the adven-
ture of western colonization.

THE MOUNTAIN MEADOWS MASSACRE.

They were in no hurry, but travelled leisurely, with the view of nursing the strength of their cattle, horses, and mules, in order to accomplish successfully the long and tedious journey which they had undertaken. In that company there were men, women, and children, of every age, from the venerable patriarch to the baby in arms. It was a bevy of families related to each other by the ties of consanguinity and marriage, with here and there in the train a neighbour who desired to share with them the chances of fortune in the proposed new homes on the golden shores of the Pacific.

One of their number had been a Methodist preacher, and probably most of the adults were members of that denomination. They were moral in language and conduct, and united regularly in morning and evening prayers.

On Sundays they did not travel, but observed it as a day of sacred rest for man and beast. At the appointed hour of service, this brother-preacher assembled his fellow-travellers in a large tent, which served as a meeting-house, within their wagon-circled camp, for the usual religious exercises, and there, on the low, boundless prairies, or in higher altitudes at the base of snow-capped mountains, he addressed them as fervently, and with as much soul-inspiring faith, as if his auditory had been seated comfortably within the old church-walls at home, and they too sang their hymns of praise with grateful, feeling souls, and with hearts impressed with the realization that man was but a speck in the presence of that grand and limitless nature that surrounded them, and of which they were but a microscopic part.

Those who passed the company *en route*, or travelled with them a part of the way, were favourably impressed with their society, and spoke of them in the kindest terms as an exceedingly fine company of emigrants, such as was seldom seen on the plains.

Though utterly unlike themselves in character and disposition, the "Wild-cats" contracted for them much respect, and came as near to them in travelling as was convenient for the grazing of the cattle and the purposes of the camp at night. Within sight of each other they would form their corrals, but, while the one resounded with vulgar song, boisterous roaring,

and "tall swearing," in the other there was the peace of domestic bliss and conscious rectitude.

A gentleman, a friend of the Author, travelled with this
Arkansas company from Fort Bridger to Salt Lake City, and
speaks of them in the highest terms : he never travelled with
more pleasant companions. Hearing the nightly yells of the
"Wild-cats," he advised the Arkansas company to separate
from them as much as possible while passing through the settlements, and in going through the Indian country. At that
time it was easy to provoke a difficulty ; the whole country
was excited over the news of the "invading army ;" and so
much was this gentleman impressed with the necessity of great
prudence on the part of the emigrants that, after he had left
them on his arrival at Salt Lake City, he afterwards returned
and impressed upon the leading men the urgency of refusing
to travel further with the Missouri company so near to them.
The kindly suggestions were appreciated, and they expressed
their desire to act upon them. Up to this time the journey of
the emigrants had been prosperous, and everything bade fair
for a pleasant termination of their travels. Like all other pilgrims, they had counted upon replenishing their stock of provisions at Salt Lake City, and to do this, and to rest their
cattle, they concluded to camp awhile by the Jordan.

In early times of overland travel, the arrival of a Gentile
emigrant train was usually a pleasant season for trade and
barter, and those who thought proper to visit the camp could
readily exchange the fruits of the garden and the produce of
the dairy or the field for tea, coffee, sugar, and similar useful articles, which the emigrants had in greater abundance.
Many a sister in Salt Lake City has bedecked herself with
apparel advantageously purchased from the passers-by with
the eggs and butter she had accumulated for just such an opportunity.

But a change had come over the spirit of the people in
1857. The Federal troops were advancing upon Zion, and the
Saints were preparing for the defence of their homes. The
Indian is not the only human being who fails to discriminate
between the innocent and the guilty.

Since that date it has been frequently asserted by the Mormon preachers that some of the Missouri company had boasted on the way that they had taken part in driving the Mormons from that State, and they are also said to have expressed their joy at the approach of the United States army to " wipe out the Mormons," and adding to that folly that they themselves would willingly assist in such a pleasant work. The alleged animus against the other company can be briefly told.

About twelve months preceding that time one of the Apostles, Parley P. Pratt, had been arraigned at Fort Smith, Arkansas, on a charge of abducting the children of one Hector McLean, of New Orleans, and trying to run them off to Utah. The mother of the children had years before become converted to the Mormon faith in California, and subsequently became one of the Mrs. P. P. Pratt in Utah. This apostle had not, at this time, been to New Orleans, and he personally did not abduct the children : of the act direct he was guiltless, but he was to meet with Mrs. McLean Pratt in Arkansas while she was *en route* from New Orleans to Utah. Of that Hector McLean became assured, and he started " upon their trail."

At the examination before a magistrate, Mrs. McLean Pratt assumed all the responsibility for the abduction of the children, and the apostle was honourably discharged. His friends, however, apprehended danger, and advised him to escape, if he could, for McLean was a violent man. Those who proffered this advice also offered him a brace of revolvers for his defence, but the apostle refused the carnal weapons, and preferred, on this occasion, to leave " his life in the protection of the Lord."

In such a sparsely-settled country the escape of the apostle was impossible. In a few hours McLean was certain to overtake him wherever he went. At length he came within sight of his enemy, as he regarded the apostle, and hotly pursued him with a thirst for blood. Hoping for some possible shelter, Mr. Pratt made some *détour* from the public road, but it served him nothing, for McLean reached him before he could arrive at the house where he thought to take refuge. Following him closely, he emptied his revolver at the apostle, but failed to touch him. He became much enraged, urged forward his horse, and, as he rode past him, made a lunge with a bowie-knife, and gave him a fatal thrust in the side. The wounded man instantly fell from his horse, and McLean, with a Derringer that he obtained from one who accompanied him, fired again at his victim as he lay bleeding on the ground. That ball penetrated his breast, and in a few hours later the apostle Parley P. Pratt was dead.*

McLean returned to Fort Smith, walked through the town with his friends, and in the evening took the passing steamer for the South. No one seemed to think that he should be arrested; Mormonism and apostles were unpopular. Whether with justice in this case or not, there is always a feeling of sympathy for the injured when domestic intrusions are before the public.

A contributor to the Corinne *Reporter*, a Gentile paper published about sixty miles north of Salt Lake City, recently published a series of "open letters" addressed to Brigham Young, in which there is much light thrown upon the terrible fate of the two emigrant companies from Missouri and Arkansas. The writer of the letters signed himself "Argus," † and, for prudential reasons, has withheld his name from the public.

As this gentleman relates with minuteness of detail the circumstances preceding the massacre, and also gives a thrilling picture of that dreadful deed, the Author avails himself of the courtesy by which he has been permitted to make such extracts as were necessary to tell the story of the Mountain Meadows Massacre: only prefacing these extracts with the statement that the charges as to the author of the order for

---

* It has often been charged to Parley that he seduced Mrs. McLean from her husband. Mrs. McLean asserts to the contrary.

† As no statements of such importance as those made by this writer could possibly be cited in a work of this kind without knowing who he was, and whether he was likely to be in possession of the information that he claimed to know, for some months the Author sought anxiously, but ineffectually, to discover the writer's name; the publisher very properly concealed it. At an unlooked-for moment the thread was accidentally found, and "Argus" frankly avowed that he wrote the "open letters," and assured the Author that before a Federal court of justice, where he could be protected, he was prepared to give the evidence of all that he had asserted. It need only be added that "Argus" has probably been for thirty years a Mormon, has resided many years in Utah, has been a high-priest in the Church, and has held responsible civil positions in the Territory.

the massacre, and the deductions of the writer against Brigham
Young, have been nearly all left out: first, and principally,
for brevity's sake, and secondly, from the consideration that,
on so serious a charge as wholesale murder, the unconvicted
should have, as before expressed, the benefit of whatever uncertainty there is about the matter. There is, however, sufficient extracted to make it very desirable for Brigham Young
to encourage the investigation of these charges before a competent tribunal, to clear his name of the imputation—if he is
innocent.

EXTRACTS FROM "OPEN LETTERS FROM 'ARGUS' TO BRIGHAM
YOUNG."

"SIR: The company of emigrants slaughtered on the 15th of September, 1857, at the Mountain Meadows, and within your jurisdiction, was
one of the wealthiest, most respectable and peaceable that ever crossed
the continent by the way of Salt Lake City. They were American citizens—were within the territory of the United States, and when they
encamped by the Jordan river, upon the free, unenclosed and unappropriated public domain, and by the laws of Utah, their stock were 'free com-
moners' on that domain. The most of those emigrants had unquestionably been farmers, all of them rural in their habits of life; and from the
fact that you did not charge them with being thieves, or robbers, or of
trespassing upon the rights of others, or disturbing the public peace, or
with behaving themselves unseemly, it is fair to infer that they were as
upright and virtuous in their habits of thought, and as honest and honourable in their intercourse with others as people from country parts generally
are. They came from Arkansas.*

"When they encamped by the Jordan they were weary and foot-sore,
their supply of food was wellnigh exhausted, and their work-cattle nearly
'used up' by the labours of the long and toilsome journey. The necessity rested upon them of tarrying in Utah sufficiently long to rest and recruit their teams and replenish their store of provisions. The harvest in
Utah that year, then gathering, was abundant, and mountain and valley
were covered with rich and nutritious grasses. What was there to hinder
this company from staying as long as they pleased, recruiting their stock,
and pursuing their journey when they got ready? And, besides, what
had they done that the protection of the law, represented in your person,
should be worse than withdrawn from them? that they should be ordered
to break up camp and move on? and, worse than all, that a courier should
be sent ahead of them bearing your written instructions to the Mormons
on said company's line of travel to have no dealing or intercourse with

* Mrs. McLean Pratt is said to have recognized one or more of the emigrants as
being present at the murder of the apostle.

them; thus compelling them to almost certain death by starvation on the deserts? You were at that time the Governor of Utah. Commander-in-Chief of the militia, and Superintendent of Indian Affairs, a sworn officer of the United States and of the Territory, upon whom devolved, and with whom were intrusted grave and important responsibilities, affecting the liberties of the people, the rights of persons and property, and the welfare and happiness of all within the pale of your authority without regard to sect, creed, name, or nativity, or differences between individual opinions. In addition to your magistrature, you were the chief high-priest of almost the entire body of the people, assuming to yourself extraordinary heavenly powers and an unusual amount of spiritual excellence. Without any modification of the term, you were professedly the earthly Vicar of the heavenly Saviour—of Him who divinely discoursed on earth of mercy and of love, and whose last words were, 'Father, forgive them!' . . .

"Not being allowed to remain, this weary, unrested company 'broke camp' and took up their line of travel for Los Angeles. Their progress was necessarily slow. Arriving at American Fork settlement they essayed to trade off some of their worn-out stock for the fresh and reliable cattle of the Mormons, offering fine bargains; and also sought to buy provisions. What must have been their surprise when they found they could do neither? Notwithstanding that flour, bacon, vegetables in variety, poultry, butter, cheese, eggs, etc., were in unusual abundance, and plenty of surplus stock, not the first thing could be bought or sold! They passed on through Battle Creek, Provo, Springville, Spanish Fork, Payson, Salt Creek and Fillmore, attempting at each settlement to purchase food and to trade for stock, but without success. It is true that occasionally some Mormon more daring than his fellows would sack up a few pounds of provisions, and under cover of night smuggle the same into the emigrant camp, taking his chances of a severed windpipe in satisfaction for such unreasonable contempt of orders; but otherwise there was no food bought by this company thus far. And here it is worthy to remark that up to this time no complaint had been made against these travellers. They had been accused of no crime known to the laws, and, undeniably, it had been a point with them to quietly and peaceably pass through Utah, in the hope of reaching some Gentile settlement where their gold and cattle could buy them something to eat.

"The query arises here, What caused so strange and unprecedented a proceeding towards this particular company? The custom of the overland emigration at that time was well known; which was, to provision their trains for Salt Lake City, and refit at that place for California. If other trains could rest and recruit, could buy, sell and refit in Utah, why not this? . . . These people were from Arkansas, a State in which Parley P. Pratt, one of your fellow-apostles, had been killed . . . But to return. This ill-fated company were now at Fillmore. They had left their camp at the Jordan with almost empty wagons, they had been unable to purchase provisions, as before stated, they had but three or four settle-

ments yet to pass through; and then their way would pass over the most
to be dreaded of all the American deserts, where there would be no possibility of obtaining a pound of food. What their prospects, feelings and
forebodings were at that time, I leave for your consideration; but, sir, I
beg to call your attention to the fact that, at the capture of their train at
the Mountain Meadows, their stores were found to be inadequate for the
journey in contemplation. They were, indeed, wellnigh exhausted, with
the exception of two purchases which I shall describe presently, which purchases were made after they had left Fillmore. There cannot be a reasonable doubt that they were already on short allowance when they reached
that settlement. . . . There have been times, as in late occurrences in
Paris, when men's passions have been aroused and excited, especially upon
religious differences, and still more especially when associated with the
idea of caste or race; outrages and wholesale butcheries have occurred;
but here we have in free America a peaceable company of emigrants who
were forced untimely into a journey, then half-starved, and finally slaughtered in cold blood! And this was the result of the apparent action of
an entire people. Do you expect the world to believe that action to have
been spontaneous with them? That the whole people from the Jordan to
Fillmore should, of their own free will, uninfluenced, uninstructed, unco-
erced, should all as one unite in denying these strangers the right even
of buying food? Impossible! This company of Arkansas farmers, travelling with their wives and little ones, had now travelled through and by
fifteen different settlements, large and small, peopled by Mormons under
your absolute control in all things, and had not been able to buy food.
Oh! what a falling off was there from the words of Him who said. ' If
thine enemy hunger, feed him!'   .   .   .   .

"At Fillmore their store of provisions was too scanty to allow of delay; and so soon as they found they could do no trading there they
moved on, and in due course reached Corn Creek. Here they saw the
first kindly look and heard the first friendly word since they left the Jordan. And, strange to say, those friends were Indians! They sold the
emigrants 30 bushels of corn—all they had to spare—and sent them away
in peace.

"The company passed on from Corn Creek, and, reaching Beaver, they
found the same order of non-intercourse, the same prohibition as to trading as before; and, passing on, they came to Parowan, *but were not permitted to enter the town.* Now be it known, and the books will show, that
the General Government had paid twenty-five thousand dollars in gold
coin for the surveying and opening of this road which passed directly
through the town of Parowan, and upon which this company was travelling and had travelled all the way from Salt Lake City, passing through
American Fork, and all the principal settlements on the route. They had
passed through those settlements without let or hindrance; but here they
were forced to leave the public highway and pass around the west side
of the fort wall. When they reached the stream abreast of the town

they encamped, and tried, as before, to trade for food and fresh cattle, but failed. There was a little Englishman who was determined to sell them some provisions; but Bishop Lewis's son and Counsellor advanced before him, and, pressing the edge of a bowie-knife against his throat, compelled him to retreat without realizing his humane intentions. There was a grist-mill at Parowan, the first the company had 'struck' since they left Corn Creek. They made application to have the corn ground which they had bought of the Indians, but were flatly refused.

"Now, sir, why were these emigrants refused permission to enter and pass through Parowan? However unpleasant it may be to you, this question will probably yet be asked in such form and by such authority that you will feel constrained to answer. You are quite competent to give the answer, so is your aide-de-camp and Brigadier-General, George A. So is Wm. H. Dame, the colonel of the regiment forming a part of the militia under your supreme command—that same regiment that afterwards fell upon that same unoffending company at Mountain Meadows and destroyed them. But you will not answer until compelled. Then let me suggest that Parowan was the legitimate headquarters of that particular regiment; that it was the place of residence of Colonel Dame; that there was a certain military appearance inside the walls that it would not be prudent for the emigrants to see or suspect, for their destruction had been decreed, and they must be taken at a disadvantage. And, further, the emigrants hitherto had encountered only a passive hostility, now it was to be active; and they must not be permitted to enter the town where their unoffending manners and quiet deportment might win upon the sympathies of the people.

"The emigrants made their way to Cedar City, at that time the most populous of all the towns in Southern Utah. Here they were allowed to purchase fifty bushels of tithing wheat, and to get the same, and also the corn, ground at John D. Lee's mill. No thanks, however, for this seeming favour; for the authorities that pretended to sell that wheat knew that they would have the most of it back in less than a week; at least they knew that it would never leave the Territory. But, waiving that, still this company of one hundred and twenty souls, or thereabouts, had not to exceed forty-nine hundred pounds of provisions, less than forty days' rations, all told, to take them to San Bernardino, in California.

"Now, sir, I have consulted with one of the old pioneers of the road from Cedar City to the Mojave river, one whose judgment and experience are worthy of respect; one who saw that company in Utah as they were passing along on the Territorial road, and knew the condition of their teams. I asked him how long it would have taken them to go from Cedar to the Mojave? He reflected, then answered, 'Sixty days.' From there to San Bernardino would have taken six to ten days. Here was a company made up of men, women and children, with at least one child to be born on the road, whose mother would require a little rest and at least some comfort, forced to undertake this journey under circumstances beyond their control, but altogether under *yours*, who were obliged to put themselves on short allowance on the start. . . . .

"The Arkansas company remained at Cedar City but one day, and then started on that fatal trip which was but too soon to come to a tragic and sanguinary end. And here I will state a fact well known at Cedar City and Pinto Creek, to prove that I have not overdrawn the picture when speaking of the jaded and worn-out condition of their teams. It took them three days to go to Iron Creek, a distance of only twenty miles. The distance from Iron Creek to the Meadows, about fifteen miles, was made in two days. The morning they left Iron Creek, the fourth after leaving Cedar, your militia took up their line of march in pursuit of them, intending to make the assault at the ' Clara Crossing '—*your* militia ! you, Brigham Young, were at that very time Governor of Utah, and Commander-in-Chief of the military forces of the Territory, and were drawing your salary as such from the treasury of the United States.

"These soldiers did not come together by chance. Indeed, sir, it is on oath, and witnessed by the seal of the court, that the calling out of those troops ' *was a regular military call from the superior officers to the subordinate officers and privates of the regiment.*' And said sworn testimony further states that ' *said regiment was duly ordered to muster, armed and equipped as the law directs, and prepared for field operations.*' I am fully aware, sir, of the fearful import of these quotations. . . . . The call to arms was the result reached by a regular military council, held in the town of Parowan, at which were present, President Isaac C. Haight (the Mormon High-Priest of Southern Utah), Colonel Dame, Major John D. Lee, and your fat Aide-de-Camp.

"The regiment camped at Cedar City—was commanded by its major, John D. Lee (who was also your Indian Agent for Southern Utah), and marched from that place in pursuit of the emigrants. It was accompanied by baggage-wagons, and, with the exception of artillery, the other necessary ' make-up ' of a military force in the field. Lee had extended an invitation to the Piede Indians to accompany him ; and with these auxiliaries he had a force which the poor, hungry emigrants could not hope to resist.

"The emigrants were overtaken at the Mountain Meadows. Being entirely ignorant of the danger so near them, they ' rolled out' from camp in a careless matter-of-course way, on the morning of the 12th of September, and, as soon as the rear wagon had got a safe distance from the spring, the Indians, unexpectedly to Lee, commenced firing. The emigrants were taken completely by surprise. It is conclusive beyond a doubt, from the loose and unguarded manner of their travelling, that they had no idea of the military expedition sent against them until they saw and felt it. Yet, unguarded as they were at the moment of the attack, they had travelled too far over roads infested with Indians to become confused. They immediately corralled their wagons and prepared for defence, fortifying as best they could ; but, alas, they were too far from water !

"They fought your troops all that day and all the next. Major Lee, beginning to think that he had waked up the wrong passengers, sent to Cedar City and Washington for reënforcements, which were at once raised and forwarded, forming a junction with the main body on the morning of the fourth day's fight. This call for reënforcements took every able-bodied man from Washington, and all but two from Cedar City.

"During the third day's battle it became a necessity with the emigrants to get water. They were choking with thirst, and without water they could hold out but little longer. There it was in abundance, in plain sight, but covered by the rifles of your troops. They made several desperate but fatal and unsuccessful efforts, and finally, hoping there might be some little of humanity remaining with the Mormons, they dressed two little girls in white, and started them with a bucket toward the spring. *Your soldiers shot them down!*

Brother Kanosh, the Indian Chief. p. 494.

"On the next morning, the reënforcements having arrived, Major Lee massed his troops at a point about half a mile from the emigrants' fort, and there made them a speech, during which he informed them that (I quote from a sworn statement) his orders from headquarters were, ' *To kill the entire company except the children.*' Now, sir, as to whether those ' headquarters' were located in your office at Salt Lake City, or at Parowan, is a matter to be settled between you and Colonel Dame ; and, if I am not mistaken, you will yet have to settle it. If Colonel Dame shall ever confess before a proper tribunal that he issued that extraordinary order on his own responsibility, and independently of you, I shall be very much mistaken. But, of the fact that such an order was actually made, there can be no doubt. There had been two military councils held in

Parowan—one before or about the time the emigrants passed that place, and one on the day they left Cedar. Haight and Lee were at both these councils, and from the last returned together to Cedar—the latter to take command of the troops, and the former to stand prepared to render him any service which might be needed.

" It is on oath, sir, that it was at Cedar City, two days after the emigrants had left, that President Haight said to certain parties (who shall be nameless here), 'that he had orders from headquarters to kill all of said company of emigrants except the little children!' This fixes the fact beyond dispute that Lee and Haight were professedly acting under orders from headquarters; and to suppose that such profession was false —that two subordinates should take upon themselves the responsibility of such a bloody affair, professedly in your name, and yet without your authority—is out of the question. It is equally absurd to suppose that said order originated with Colonel Dame. All the reasons are against such a supposition. Besides, no colonel of a regiment would have the right or the authority to do anything in such premises, except to promulgate and enforce the order of his superior officer. To do otherwise would be to subject himself to the eventualities of a military court ; and it is certain that neither Colonel Dame nor Major Lee was ever court-martialled for his action in the military operations at the Mountain Meadows.

" After Major Lee had announced that fatal order to his troops, and instructed them as to how he intended to carry it out, ' he sent a flag of truce into the emigrants' fort, offering to them that if they would lay down their arms he would protect them.' This was on the 15th day of September, and the fourth since the battle, or, rather, siege had begun. You will not forget that the little band of Arkansans were not ' whipped.' Though well-nigh exhausted with fatigue and loss of sleep, and burning up with thirst, they were not conquered. They were fighting for their wives and little ones more than for themselves, else, at any time, under cover of the darkness, they could have formed in solid column, broke through your lines and escaped. But to their honour, be it said, they refused life when associated with the condition of deserting their families.

" But the flag of truce came into their little fort—that white flag held by all civilized nations and peoples, from time immemorial, as an emblem at once of peace, of truth, of honour. By the message accompanying this flag, they were promised protection. Alas, that it should prove to be ' such protection as vultures give to lambs!' But the message was not from Indians, it was from Major Lee, a regularly constituted officer of the military forces of the Territory of Utah, one of the Territories of the United States. What should they do but believe its promise? They marched out of their little fort, laid down their arms, marched up to the spring where Lee stood, and placed themselves under his protection; and his promises of protection were yours.

" But now was to be enacted one of those scenes which the pen is inadequate to describe, and the horrors of which it is impossible for one not

then present to realize. Here were unarmed, unresisting men, innocent
and inoffensive women, and helpless children, none of which had ever
harmed you, or offended the majesty of the laws of Utah. They had every
possible claim not only to Lee's protection, but to life, liberty, and their
property. Their right to be treated truthfully, honourably, and humane-
ly was perfect. But, sir, your order was practically as irrevocable as it
was terrible. And it would not do for the troops to think long about it,
lest conscience should assert rights which even the thought of you could
not overcome. There must be no time for parleying between obedience
to you and duty to humanity. So, without allowing these famishing
prisoners time even to refresh themselves, the women and children were
separated from their husbands and fathers, and started on ahead towards
Cedar City, the men following immediately in their rear, and all guarded
by the entire command, with Lee at the head of the column. There is no
reason to suppose that, up to the moment of the massacre, the emigrants
thought they were going to be shot down. After they had been marched
about a half mile, Lee gave the word to 'halt;' then immediately the command to 'shoot them down' was passed down the column, and before the
poor emigrants could realize their situation the first volley was delivered!
Then from the survivors went up such a piercing, heart-rending scream!—
such a shriek of blank despair!—then the flight of all except one young
woman, who sprang to Lee, and clung to him for protection—then the
chase—then another volley—and then another—and still another, and
then—all was still! save the last death-strugglings of the unhappy victims, the cries of the remnant of little ones who had been left behind in
the flight, and the heavy breathings of the soldiers, pale, trembling and
aghast at the horrid scene before and around them!

"Another scene was now to be enacted so utterly revolting to our sense
of modesty, so grossly at variance with all our ideas of propriety, so altogether repulsive to the better qualities of human nature, that it vies even
with the massacre itself in damnable wickedness. This remark is not intended to apply to all of the troops, for it is just and fair to understand
that many a man was mustered in that regiment sorely against his will.
But apparently a majority of them took to the whole work of the campaign with willing earnestness, and finally returned home seemingly
without remorse. And, as good Utah Mormons, why should they not?
Why should they not slay upon the right hand and upon the left, until
they could wade in the gore of apostates and Gentiles, and then return
home singing hosannas to God and the Lamb? They had been taught
from your pulpits to expect and to do just such things. The carnage
around them was simply a matter of course. It was but an episode in
what was yet to be the gory history of the Kingdom of God. It was but
a faint realization of those glorious campaigns when they should go
through the United States 'like a lion among the flocks of sheep, tread-
ing down, breaking in pieces, with none to deliver, leaving the land desolate and without an inhabitant.' It was for these (your) soldiers, these

demons to commit the last outrage upon their victims. Among the slain there was the nursing babe which the mother could not forsake, even in death ; there were females of all ages, from budding girlhood to the prime of life ; there was also the youth and the strong man. Those females were not abandoned characters ; they had not unsexed themselves by whore- dom ; they were the chaste, the modest, virtuous and pure-hearted daugh- ters, sisters and wives of the emigrants. Well, sir, your soldiers, with many a coarse, ribald, vulgar jest, with many an obscene, beastly remark, stripped them entirely of their clothing, and the whole company were left nude and stark, and without burial ! Even the young maiden, who had implored Lee for her life, was found among the sage-brush with her throat cut, and stripped naked !

"The *order* had been given to spare the *little* children ; but in the ex- citement of the massacre some were killed. Seventeen, however, were saved. They were taken care of by Bishop Smith, who had been detailed by Major Lee before the massacre for that purpose. In this labour of mercy he was voluntarily assisted by John Willis and Samuel Mardy. The hap- less orphans were put into two regimental baggage-wagons and taken to Jake Hamlin's ranche, and the next day to Cedar City, where they were distributed among the Mormon families. Two of these children afterward made some remarks which were thought dangerous, and they were pri- vately taken out and—buried ! After the administration in Utah had changed hands, they were gathered up by the Government and sent to St. Louis. The troops at the Meadows, having stripped the bodies of the dead, gathered the stock, and Lee took possession of the wagons and their contents, and also the stock."

While these sickening details of this terrible chapter were being sent to the press, unlooked-for confirmation comes from Salt Lake City in the following affidavit from Bishop Philip Klingon Smith. It is proper to remark that " Argus " could have no possible knowledge of the Bishop's affidavit, nor could the Bishop know of " Argus's " letters. The affidavit was made in April, 1871, and was secretly preserved in the hands of a Federal officer : the " Argus Letters " were written in July and August. It is singularly strange that both writers should give so harmonious and clear a statement.

" *State of Nevada, County of Lincoln,* ss. :—Personally appeared before me, Peter B. Miller, Clerk of Court of the Seventh Judicial District of the State of Nevada, Philip Klingon Smith, who being duly sworn, on his oath, says : My name is Philip Klingon Smith ; I reside in the County of Lincoln, in the State of Nevada ; I resided at Cedar City, in the County of Iron, in the Territory of Utah, from A. D. 1852 to A. D. 1859 ; I was re- siding at said Cedar City at the time of the massacre at Mountain Meadows,

27

in said Territory of Utah; I had heard that a company of emigrants was on its way from Salt Lake City, bound for California; said company arrived at said Cedar City, tarried there one day, and passed on for California; after said company had left Cedar City, the militia was called out for the purpose of committing acts of hostility against them; said call was a regular military call from the superior officers to the subordinate officers and privates of the regiment at Cedar City and vicinity, composing a part of the militia of the Territory of Utah; I do not recollect the number of the regiment; I was at that time the Bishop of the Church of Jesus Christ of Latter-Day Saints at Cedar City; Isaac C. Haight was President over said church at Cedar City and the southern settlements in said Territory; my position as Bishop was subordinate to that of said President; W. H. Dame was President of said Church at Parowan in said Iron County; said W. H. Dame was also colonel of said regiment; said Isaac C. Haight was lieutenant-colonel of said regiment, and said John D. Lee, of Harmony, in said Iron County, was major of said regiment; said regiment was duly ordered to muster, armed and equipped as the law directs, and prepared for field operations; I had no command nor office in said regiment at the time, neither did I march with said regiment on the expedition which resulted in said company's being massacred in the Mountain Meadows, in said County of Iron; about four days after said company of emigrants had left Cedar City, that portion of said regiment then mustered at Cedar City took up its line of march in pursuit of them; about two days after said company had left said Cedar City, Lieutenant-Colonel I. C. Haight expressed, in my presence, a desire that said company might be permitted to pass on their way in peace; but afterward he told me that he had orders from headquarters to kill all of said company of emigrants except the little children; I do not know whether said headquarters meant the Regimental Headquarters at Parowan, or the Headquarters of the Commander-in-Chief at Salt Lake City; when the said company had got to Iron Creek, about twenty (20) miles from Cedar City, Captain Joel White started for Pinto Creek settlement, through which said company would pass, for the purpose of influencing the people to permit said company to pass on their way in peace; I asked and obtained permission of said White to go with him and aid him in his endeavours to save life; when said White and myself got about three miles from Cedar City we met Major John D. Lee, who asked us where we were going; I replied that we were going to try to prevent the killing of the emigrants; Lee replied, 'I have something to say about that;' Lee was at that time on his way to Parowan, the Headquarters of Colonel Dame; said White and I went to Pinto Creek; remained there one night, and the next day returned to Cedar City, meeting said company of emigrants at Iron Creek; before reaching Cedar City we met one Ira Allen, who told us 'that the decree had passed, devoting said company to destruction;' after the fight had been going on for three or four days, a messenger from Major Lee reached Cedar City, who stated that the fight had not been altogether successful, upon which Lieutenant-Colonel Haight ordered out a reënforcement; at this time I was ordered out by Captain John M. Higbee, who ordered me to muster, 'armed and equipped as the law directs;' it was a matter of life or death to me to muster or not, and I mustered with the reënforcing troops; it was at this time that Lieutenant-Colonel Haight said to me that it was the orders from headquarters that all but the little children of said company were to be killed; said Haight had at that time just returned from headquarters at Parowan, where a military council had been held; there had been a like council held at Parowan previous to that, at which were present Colonel Dame, Lieutenant-Colonel I. C. Haight, and Major John D. Lee; the result of this first council was the calling out of said regiment for the purpose already stated; the reënforcement aforesaid was marched to the Mountain Meadows, and there formed a junction with the main body; Major Lee massed all the troops at a spring, and made a speech to them, saying that his orders from headquarters were to kill the entire company except the small children; I was not in the ranks at that time, but on the side talking to a man named Slade, and could not have seen a paper in Major Lee's hands; said Lee then sent a flag of truce into the emigrant camp, offering said emigrants that 'if they lay down their arms, he would protect them;' they accordingly laid down their arms, came out from their camp, and delivered themselves up to said Lee; the women and children were then, by the order of said Lee, separated from the men, and were marched ahead of the men; after said emigrants had marched about a half mile toward Cedar City, the order was given to shoot them down; at that time said Lee was at the head of the column; I was in the rear; I did not hear Lee give the order to fire, but heard it from the under officers as it was passed down the column; the emigrants were then and there shot down, except seventeen little children, which I immediately took into my charge; I do not know the total number of said company, as I did not stop to count the dead; I immediately put the little children in baggage-wagons belonging to the regiment, and took them to Hamlin's ranche, and from there to Cedar City, and procured them homes among the people; John Willis and Samuel Murdy assisted me in taking charge of said children; on the evening of the massacre, Colonel W. H. Dame and Lieutenant I. C. Haight came to Hamlin's, where I had the said children, and fell into a dispute, in the course of which said Haight told Colonel Dame that, if he was going to report of the killing of said emigrants, he should not have ordered it done; I do not know when or where said troops were disbanded; about two weeks after said massacre occurred, said Major Lee (who was also an Indian Agent), went to Salt Lake City, and, as I believe, reported said fight and its results to the commander-in-chief; I was not present at either of the before-mentioned councils, nor at any council connected with the aforesaid military operations, or with said company; I gave no orders except those connected with the saving of the children, and those, after the massacre had occurred, and said orders were given as bishop and not in a military sense ; at the time of the firing of the first volley I discharged my piece ; I did not fire afterward, though several subsequent volleys were fired ; after the first fire was delivered I at once set about saving the children ; I commenced to gather up the children before the firing had ceased. I have made the foregoing statement before the above-entitled court for the reason that I believe that I would be assassinated should I attempt to make the same before any court in the Territory of Utah.* After said Lee returned from Salt Lake City, as aforesaid, said Lee told me that he had reported fully to the President, meaning the commander-in-chief, the fight at Mountain Meadows, and the killing of said emigrants. Brigham Young † was at that time the commander-in-chief of the militia of the Territory of Utah ; and further deponent saith not.

(Signed)   PHILIP KLINGON SMITH.

" Subscribed and sworn to before me, this 10th day of April, A. D. 1871.

(Signed)   P. B. MILLER, County Clerk.

" District Court, Seventh Judicial District, Lincoln County, Nevada. (Copy of seal.) "

" *Utah Territory, County of Salt Lake, ss. :*—I, O. F. Strickland, Associate Justice of the Supreme Court of Utah Territory, hereby certify that I have carefully compared the foregoing copy of affidavit with the original of the same, and that the foregoing copy is a true literal copy of said original, and that such comparison was made this 4th day of September, 1872."

(Signed)   O. F. STRICKLAND."

" *Territory of Utah, Salt Lake County, ss. :*—I, James B. McKean, Chief Justice of the Supreme Court of said Territory, do certify that I have carefully compared the above copy of an affidavit with the original of the same, and know the same to be in all particulars a true copy thereof.

(Signed)   JAMES B. McKEAN, Chief Justice, etc.

" Dated *September* 5, 1872."

The following map throws much additional light upon the statements of both " Argus " and Bishop Smith. The latter states that while he and Captain Joel White were travelling

---

* Since this affidavit was made, great changes have taken place through the influx of Gentiles, and Bishop Smith now expresses his readiness to " return to Utah and give testimony in person."

† The Mormons, who seek to exonerate Brigham Young from all complicity with the murderers of the emigrants, relate that, when Lee offered to pay him a tithing of the ill-gotten gear, he refused it, and threw it from him. Be the latter part of the statement true or false, the acknowledgment of the former shows that Brigham Young had the opportunity of knowing who were the guilty parties, even if he himself did not direct them, and could have brought them to justice. But there is no necessity to argue from any disciple's admissions, for it is a fact, of which there is evidence, that *John D. Lee did make a report of the Mountain Meadows Massacre to Governor Brigham Young, Superintendent of Indian Affairs, etc*, and that report

southward from Cedar City to Pinto Creek, they met Lee three miles south of Cedar, who had something to say about " trying to prevent the killing of the emigrants." The subject of attacking them had evidently been spoken of among the Mormons ; but as yet, not by authority, at least so far as White and Smith knew, or they would not have undertaken the journey to Pinto Creek to dissuade the people from " killing the " emigrants." Lee was then *en route* to headquarters at Parowan. On the return of the Bishop and Captain White from Pinto Creek, the next evening, before they reached Cedar City,

he says, " We met Ira Allen, who told us that ' the decree had " ' passed devoting said company to destruction.' " In a letter dated August 10, 1871, " Argus," without any knowledge of Bishop Smith's affidavit, incidentally accounts for the information in the possession of Allen, and says :

"Had the original order to assault the emigrants in Santa Clara Cañon been carried out, not one of them would have been living in fifteen minutes after the head teams had been shot down. They would have been

was written in the house of the apostle Ezra T. Benson, in Salt Lake City, within two hundred yards of the official residence of the Governor and Prophet of the Lord!

covered by the rifles of your troops from every possible direction. But ample provision was made to cut off any that might escape. *For this purpose a party, headed by one Allen, was sent to watch the road between the train and the Muddy,* and Ira Hatch and a fellow-missionary (!) were sent to the crossing of the Muddy. These good brethren were instructed to shoot down any who should chance to escape the attack of Lee. On the night of the second day of the battle, two men, on horseback, left the emigrants' camp, and started cautiously toward California. They had, probably, been sent. As they were passing Allen's ambush, one of them was shot— the other got away. Word was dispatched to Parowan, and armed parties were immediately sent out to hunt down and kill him. They did not find him—he had returned to camp, and was recognized after the massacre."

It is further stated by this writer, that

" . . . a man named Boyle was sent on a mission to the Mojave Crossing well armed and with a key [mail-sack key], to prevent any suspicious mail-matter from reaching San Bernardino, and to kill off any one who by any possibility might have escaped and got along that far. These particulars are given to show how thoroughly planned and cold-blooded was everything connected with the war of extermination made upon the Arkansas emigrants," . . . .

and to further show that some other mind than that of John D. Lee had concocted the plan of the massacre.

It was with the knowledge of these facts that Judge Cradlebaugh delivered that extraordinary charge to the Grand Jury at Provo.* The Judge had with a Federal escort visited the scene of the massacre within eighteen months of the perpetration of the deed, and had seen the bones of that Arkansas company bleaching on the Meadows.† With the actors all

* *Ante*, p. 404.

† While Judge Cradlebaugh was in Cedar City, on his return from the Meadows, a number of persons made affidavit against the leading Mormons there who had taken prominent part in the massacre, and several of the actors in it came to him by night and expressed their readiness to testify to the facts whenever they had the assurance of protection. On the information obtained from these parties the Judge issued warrants for the arrest of the following persons :

"*Isaac C. Haight*, President of the Cedar City Stake ; Bishop *John M. Higbee* and Bishop *John D. Lee :* Columbus Freeman, *William Slade, John Willis,* William Riggs, —— Ingram, Daniel McFarlan, William Stewart, *Ira Allen* and son, Thomas Cartwright, E. Welean, William Halley, Jabez Nomlen, John Mangum, James Price, John W. Adair, —— Tyler, Joseph Smith, Samuel Pollock, John McFarlan, Nephi Johnson, —— Thornton, *Joel White,* —— Harrison, Charles Hopkins, Joseph Elang, Samuel Lewis, Sims Matheney, James Mangum, Harrison Pierce, Samuel Adair, F. C. McDulange, Wm. Bateman, Ezra Curtis, and Alexander Loveridge." The names in italics are specially mentioned in the reports both by Bishop Smith and " Argus."

While the Judge was so occupied, the captain commanding the Federal troops around him, and the people horrified at the enormity of the crime, he would have held his court at Cedar City, and could have brought to light the truly guilty authors of that atrocious deed, but for the interference of Governor Cumming, whose confiding nature trusted in the promises of his predecessor to make a full investigation of the matter " without the presence " of the troops." On that promise Governor Cumming relied, and on his representation to the Government at Washington that the United States troops were unnecessary to sustain the Federal Judges, the Government immediately ordered General Johnston to furnish no troops except on the requisition of the Governor alone.

" Argus," from personal conversation with the Governor, affirms that he felt keenly his failure to investigate those murders, and relates that before he left the Territory he visited Brigham Young and upbraided him with " having purposely " lied to and deceived him." Such was no doubt the feeling of the Governor expressed to " Argus "—whether he ever said so to Brigham or not—for he used about the same language to other persons. The opportunity and duty of bringing the guilty to justice were those peculiarly belonging to the governorship of Alfred Cumming: the crime had been committed after he was appointed to Utah, and he was the fitting person to have made the investigation. But the diplomacy that brought him into collision with the military commander at Fort Bridger tied him hand and foot, and he afterwards could only move as Brigham moved him.* The strength of his right arm was gone when he broke with General Johnston, and his left leaned on a bruised reed that was destined to fail him; and no man saw this more clearly than Cumming did himself.

that had escorted his Honour to the Mountain Meadows informed him that he " had received orders for his entire command to return to Camp Floyd ; the General having received orders from Washington that the military should not be used in protecting the courts, or in acting as a *posse* to aid the marshal in making arrests."

* A day or two before the Governor left the Territory, the Author, in familiar conversation with him about the then near future, asked : " How will Wootton [the " Secretary in his absence became Acting Governor] get along ? " " Get along ? " replied he ; " well enough, if he will do nothing. There is nothing to do. Alfred " Cumming is Governor of the Territory, but Brigham Young is Governor *of the people.* " By ——, I am not fool enough to think otherwise. Let Wootton learn that, and he " will get along, and the sooner he knows that the better. This is a curious place ! "

There was no "public opinion" in Utah at that time, nor for years after could any expression of condemnation be heard; but among those who could utter free words within their own circle of friends, the Mountain Meadows Massacre has been branded with a condemnation as burning as was ever expressed by the Gentiles. The dominant theory among the intelligent Mormons was that Brigham Young had not himself ordered the massacre, but that he feared its investigation, as the men who did the deed were his brethren in the faith, and were in official relations with him, and that the massacre being brought before a court it would doubtless lead to the execution of men who might plead that it was the teachings of the Tabernacle that had rendered them capable of the perpetration of such a terrible crime. Further, an investigation would have revealed the despotism of a system that constrained men to imbrue their hands in the blood of unoffending, innocent men, women, and helpless children, in order only to save themselves from the charge of disobedience and the fatal consequences of rebellion at such a moment.

Believing, with many others in Utah, that it was possible that Lee and his confederates had been tempted by the wealth of the passing emigrants, and had availed themselves of the excitement of the people to attack the train, the Author addressed the following communication to the Prophet, in hopes that he would avail himself of this opportunity, however insignificant it might be in his estimation, of putting himself right with at least a portion of the public:

"ASTOR HOUSE, NEW YORK, July 10, 1871.

"<i>President Brigham Young—</i>

"SIR: Being engaged in preparing a work for publication that will notice prominent incidents in Utah history, and desirous of doing no injustice by misstatement, I think it proper to ask information such as, in the quality of Governor of Utah and Superintendent of Indian Affairs, you probably possessed at the date referred to, and may not think it improper to impart now.

"What Indians committed what is generally termed the Mountain Meadows Massacre? What number of Indians were engaged in it? Were any of them ever punished; if so, how, and by whose order? Did any person by the Governor's order take charge of the property of the emigrants? What became of it?

"It is generally understood that you sent an express to the leading white men in that neighbourhood to allow the emigrants to pass along unmolested. I should be pleased to publish*such an order if you would furnish a copy. I have heard of the recent excommunication from the Church of John D. Lee, Isaac C. Haight, and others, for being participators in that horrible crime. If this is correct, I should be gratified with this and such other information on this point as you might feel disposed to furnish me. I shall of course make use of the intelligence which I may receive in the book in a manner to place your statements fairly before the public, recommending at the same time that the guilty be brought to justice. Very respectfully, etc. T. B. H. STENHOUSE."

To this letter no reply was vouchsafed.

Whatever differences of opinion may exist between former members of the Church and the Prophet, no proper-minded person among them desires to see any wrong imputed to Brigham Young of which he is innocent; and of the responsibility of this massacre, above all other things, his bitterest enemy should be pleased to see him exonerated.

The apostles who have spoken and written upon this painful subject, have endeavoured to fasten the guilt solely upon the Indians, but this was a grave error, as well as being directly and palpably false.

There is implanted in the human breast an instinctive horror of the act of murder, and a large number of the Mormons who took part in the massacre were too good men to rest in peace after the commission of a dreadful deed that was forced upon them. It has unmistakably withered and blasted their happiness, and some of them have suffered agonizing tortures of conscience, equal to those of Shakespeare's Thane of Cawdor. Two of them are said to have lost their reason entirely, and others have gone to early graves with a full realization of the terrible crime upon their souls. To expect silence among the living while such a deed was consuming them was a great folly, and the exposure in detail now coming to light is what every sensible man might have expected some time or other.

In his speech to Congress, already referred to, Judge Cradlebaugh thus relates what he had personally and officially ascertained of the massacre:

" During our stay there [Santa Clara] I was visited by the Indian chiefs of that section, who gave me their version of the massacre. They admitted that a portion of their men were engaged in the massacre, but were not there when the attack commenced. One of them told me, in the presence of the others, that after the attack had been made a white man came to their camp with a piece of paper, which he said *Brigham Young had sent*, that directed them to go and help to whip the emigrants. A portion of the band went but did not assist in the fight. He gave as a reason that the emigrants had long guns, and were good shots. He said that his brother [this chief's name was Jackson] was shot while running across the Meadow, at a distance of two hundred yards from the corral where the emigrants were. He said the Mormons were all painted. He said the Indians got a part of the clothing; and gave the names of John D. Lee, President Haight, and Bishop Higbee, as the big captains. It might be proper here to remark, that the Indians in the southern part of the Territory of Utah are not numerous, and are a very low, cowardly, beastly set, very few of them being armed with guns. They are not formidable. I believe all in the southern part of the Territory would, under no circumstances, carry on a fight against ten white men.

" From our camp on the Santa Clara we again went back to the Mountain Meadows, camping near where the massacre had occurred. The Meadow is about five miles in length and one in width, running to quite a narrow point at the southwest end. It is the divide between the waters that flow into the Great Basin and those emptying into the Colorado river. A very large spring rises in the south end of the narrow part. It was on the north side of this spring that the emigrants camped. The bank rises from the spring eight or ten feet, then extends off to the north about two hundred yards, on a level. A range of hills is there reached, rising perhaps fifty or sixty feet. Back of this range is quite a valley, which extends down until it has an outlet, three or four hundred yards below the spring, into the main meadow.

" The first attack was made by going down this ravine, then following up the bed of the spring to near it, then at daylight firing upon the men who were about the camp-fires—in which attack ten or twelve of the emigrants were killed or wounded; the stock of the emigrants having been previously driven behind the hill and up the ravine.

" The emigrants soon got in condition to repel the attack, shoved their wagons together, sunk the wheels in the earth, and threw up quite an intrenchment. The fighting after continued as a siege; the assailants occupying the hill, and firing at any of the emigrants that exposed themselves, having a barricade of stones along the crest of the hill as a protection. The siege was continued for five days, the besiegers appearing in the garb of Indians. The Mormons, seeing that they could not capture the train without making some sacrifice of life on their part, and getting weary of the fight, resolved to accomplish by strategy what they were not able to do by force. The fight had been going on for five days, and no aid was received from any quarter, although the family of Jacob Hamlin, the Indian Agent, were living in the upper end of the Meadow, and within hearing of the reports of the guns.

" Who can imagine the feelings of these men, women, and children, surrounded, as they supposed themselves to be, by savages ? Fathers and mothers only can judge what they must have been. Far off in the Rocky Mountains, without transportation—for their cattle, horses, and mules, had been run off—not knowing what their fate was to be—we can but poorly realize the gloom that pervaded the camp.

" A wagon is descried far up the Meadows. Upon its nearer approach it is observed to contain armed men. See! now they raise a white flag ! All is joy in the corral. A general shout is raised; and in an instant, a little girl, dressed in white, is placed at an opening between two of the wagons, as a response to the signal. The wagon approaches; the occupants are welcomed into the corral—the emigrants little suspecting that they were entertaining the fiends that had been besieging them.

" This wagon contained President Haight and Bishop John D. Lee, among others of the Mormon Church. They professed to be on good terms with the Indians, and represented the Indians as being very mad. They also proposed to intercede and settle the matter with the Indians. After several hours of parley, they, having apparently visited the Indians, gave the *ultimatum* of the Indians; which was, that the emigrants should march out of their camp, leaving everything behind them, even their guns.* It was promised by the Mormon bishops that they would bring a force, and guard the emigrants back to the settlements.

" The terms were agreed to—the emigrants being desirous of saving the lives of their families. The Mormons retired, and subsequently appeared at the corral with thirty or forty armed men. The emigrants were marched out, the women and children in front, and the men behind, the Mormon guard being in the rear. When they had marched in this way about a mile, at a given signal, the slaughter commenced. The men were most all shot down at the first fire from the guard. Two only escaped, who fled to the desert, and were followed one hundred and fifty miles before they were overtaken and slaughtered.

" The women and children ran on, two or three hundred yards farther, when they were overtaken, and, with the aid of the Indians, they were

---

* At first, it baffled every one in Utah to account for the emigrants giving up their arms, and to this fact there is but one feasible solution. The Arkansas company was composed of persons of high moral character, and devotedly religious. They were worshippers of the Christian Deity, and when they saw the faces of white men they believed themselves secure. They confided in the fidelity of those who professed to believe in the teachings of " the greatest name given among men," and as those who came to their succour claimed the direction of a still later revelation of the will of God to man, what else could the honest, truthful, simple-hearted emigrants do but confide in men of their own race, who assumed to be nearer than themselves to the guidance of the Supreme Being? What a terrible lesson awaited them !

slaughtered. Seventeen only of the small children were saved, the eldest being only seven years. Thus, on the 10th day of September, 1857, was consummated one of the most cruel, cowardly, and bloody murders known in our history. Upon the way from the Meadows, a young Indian pointed out to me the place where the Mormons painted and disguised themselves."

Mr. Jacob Forney, the first Superintendent of Indian Affairs after Brigham Young, gathered up sixteen of the children, made orphans by that foul, treacherous deed, and gives the names and ages, eighteen months after the occurrence, as follows :

"John Calvin, now seven or eight years old; does not remember his name ; says his family lived at Horse Head, Johnston Co., Arkansas. Ambrose Mironi, about seven years, and William Taggit, four and a half years, brothers; these also lived in Johnston Co. Prudence Angeline, six years, and Annie, about three years ; these two are said to be sisters. Rebecca, nine years ; Louisa, five years ; and Sarah, three and a half years ; from Dunlap. Betsy, six years, and Anna, three years, said to be sisters ; these know nothing of their family or residence. Charles Fancher, seven or eight years, and his sister Annie, three and a half years. Sophronia or Mary Huff, six years, and Elisha W. Huff, four years. A boy; no account of him ; those among whom he lived call him William. Francis Hawn or Korn, four and a half years old.

"I have come to the conclusion, after different conversations with these children, that most of them come from Johnston Co., Arkansas. Most of them have told me that they have grandfathers and grandmothers in the States. Mr. Hamlin has good reasons for believing that a boy about eight years, and belonging to the party in question, is among the Navajos Indians, at or near the Colorado river."

No human soul can read the list of those helpless, destitute children of such tender years without experiencing a harrowing feeling of grief for the sad beginning of their lives, and a burning indignation against the " Saints " who committed the atrocious crime which bereft them of their natural protectors.

Superintendent Forney reports in a letter to the Commissioner of Indian Affairs, dated from Provo City, March, 1859, that—

"Facts in my possession warrant me in estimating that there was distributed a few days after the massacre, among the leading Church dignitaries, $30,000 worth of property."

In August of the same year, to the the same Commissioner, he writes :

" I am justified in the declaration that this massacre was concocted by white men, and consummated by whites and Indians. . . . . The children were sold out to different persons in Cedar City, Harmony, and Painter [Pinto] Creek, and bills are now in my possession from different individuals, asking payment from the Government, but I cannot condescend to become the medium of even transmitting such claims to the Department."

In his Annual Report, September, 1859, he continues:

" Mormons have been accused of aiding the Indians in the commission of the crime. I commenced my inquiries without prejudice or selfish motive, and with the hope that, in the progress of my inquiries, facts would enable me to exculpate all white men from any participation in this tragedy, and saddle the guilt exclusively on the Indians; but, unfortunately, every step in my inquiries satisfied me that the Indians acted only a secondary part. . . . White men were present and directed the Indians. John D. Lee, of Harmony, told me in his own house, last April, in presence of two persons, that he was present three successive days during the fight, and was present during the fatal day. . . . I gave several months ago to the Attorney-General, and several of the United States Judges, the names of those who I believed were not only implicated, but the hell-deserving scoundrels who concocted and brought to a successful termination the whole affair.

" The following are the names of the persons most guilty : Isaac C. Haight, Cedar City, president of several settlements south ; Bishop Smith, Cedar City ; John D. Lee, Harmony ; John M. Higbee, Cedar City ; Bishop Davis, David Tullis, Santa Clara ; Ira Hatch, Santa Clara. These were the cause of the massacre, aided by others. It is to be regretted that nothing has yet been accomplished towards bringing these murderers to justice.

" I remain, very respectfully, your obedient servant,

" J. FORNEY, Superintendent of Indian Affairs, Utah Territory.

" Hon. A. B. GREENWOOD, Comr. Indian Affairs, Washington, D. C."

Whatever sympathy one would naturally feel for the men who were forced into the massacre, much of that kindly sentiment is greatly modified, when the statement is made that after the fathers and mothers of those little children had been cruelly butchered and all their worldly wealth had been appropriated by their murderers, a portion of that same people, calling themselves " Saints " did so debase themselves as to claim of the Government a remuneration for sheltering the helpless innocents ! To this should be added that wives and daughters of some of those murderers wore the apparel of the massacred women and maidens, while their polygamic husbands and fathers wore the masculine garments of their victims, ploughed the fields with their cattle, and drove to their religious assemblies with the horses that they had stolen from the Arkansas train, *and no one called them to account!*

It has been repeatedly asserted that the best carriage was taken to Salt Lake City and was there seen rolling through the streets of that place for years after, and the jewellery of the murdered victims is said to have adorned the persons of some distinguished women; but all this seems too incredible. Lee and his marauders could steal and murder—that has been demonstrated; but surely no one in fellowship with the Prophet at the chief city of Zion, could either afford the luxury of such a carriage nor yet the glitter of such gold at so fearful a price.

Of the actual property of the emigrants no definite statement can be made, for those who knew would not tell; but it is as near the truth as will ever be reached, till a court of justice shall compel a full divulgence of the facts, that " the train " consisted of 40 wagons, 800 head of cattle, and about 60 " horses and mules." *   " The property," says Mr. Beadle, " was divided, the Indians getting most of the flour and ammu- " nition; but they claim that the Mormons kept more than " their share.   Much of it was sold in Cedar City *at public* " *auction;* it was there facetiously styled, ' Property taken at " ' the siege of Sevastopol;' and there is legal proof that the " clothing stripped from the corpses, spotted with blood and " flesh and shredded by bullets, was placed in the cellar of the " tithing-office and privately sold.   As late as 1862, jewellery " taken at Mountain Meadows, was worn in Salt Lake City, " and the source it came from not denied. " †

Major [now General] Carlton, in 1859, with a company of United States cavalry, escorted from California to the southern settlements of Utah the United States paymaster of the troops at Camp Floyd.   On his return the Major passed through the Mountain Meadows and gathered the whitened bones of the emigrants and erected over them a large cairn of stones.

" It was constructed by raising a large pile of rock, in the centre of which was erected a beam, some twelve or fifteen feet in height.   Upon one of the stones he caused to be engraved, ' Here lie the bones of one hundred and twenty men, women, and children, from Arkansas, murdered

* The Mormon Prophet, p. 65.   † Life in Utah, p. 184.

on the 10th day of September, 1857.' Upon a cross-tree, on the beam, he caused to be painted: 'Vengeance is mine, saith the Lord, and I will repay it.' This monument is said to have been destroyed the first time that Brigham visited the Territory." *

It is reported by one who stood at Brigham's side as he read aloud the inscription, that the Prophet with unfaltering voice changed the purport of its language and said to those who were around him that it should read thus: " Vengeance " is mine, saith the Lord, *and I have* repaid ! "

" Argus " closes his series of letters with the following discussion of Brigham's supposed justification :

"That an entire company of peaceful families, as at the Mountain Meadows, should be butchered in cold blood, anywhere in the United States, upon the public highway, and within the easy reach of the arm of the civil power created expressly for the protection of life and property, is a mystery which the purely American mind finds very hard to understand. And the marvel is only increased by the fact that no inquest was held over the remains of those slaughtered ones—that no arrests were made of the murderers, although they were well and notoriously known, and that no official notice was taken of the matter (except as I have heretofore stated) during the remainder of your term as Governor, and no apparent authoritative notice since, except to gather up, by soldiers of the United States, what bones the wolves had left, and giving them respectable sepulture. Based upon American ideas, and, indeed, upon the more general notions of civilization, the whole story becomes incomprehensible. In order to understand this matter, it will be necessary for the reader, first, to mentally segregate Utah geographically from the United States—to consider it as absolutely a foreign State and nation, with a civilization such as existed thirty-five hundred years ago, and a religion as antagonistic to Christianity as Moslemism itself, including within its creed a tenet more cruel and bloody than the Thuggism of India. Second, to consider this Deseret nation as incensed to the last degree against the Government and people of the United States, for a series of wrongs committed against them, including exile and the loss of life and property. Third, to take into the account, that the American Government at that time had actually proposed to extend its jurisdiction over said Deseret (otherwise called Utah), and an army was then on its way to occupy said Utah for the purpose of maintaining the sovereignty of said Government there, and that a state of war was apparently existing between said two nations. Fourth, that you were, at the very time of the massacre at the Mountain Meadows, mustering and putting into the field an army of one thousand two hundred men, which was known in Utah as 'The Standing Army,' and that said army was designed for active operations against the forces

* WAITE, p. 71.

of the United States, under Colonel Johnston, then *en route* for Salt Lake. Fifth, that *you* were the 'Sovereign' lord of Deseret—that your rule was an absolute and unmitigated despotism—that your word was the only recognized law—that it was within your imperious nature to rule with a high hand and a stretched-out arm over all your subjects, and with fury poured out against your enemies. If the reader can grasp the ideas contained in the above items, and arrange them into one compound proposition, he will be able to form some idea of the causes which made the aforesaid massacre possible.

"But the misfortune is, that said proposition being based upon falsehood and not upon the truth, affords you no justification whatever; for, first, Utah was a part of the United States, and not a foreign State; second, your intense hatred of Americans and their Government was without adequate cause; third, the occupation of Utah as a Military Department was altogether a friendly act, and in strict accordance with the known military policy of the Government; fourth, that all your acts in relation to the State of Deseret were and are treasonable in their intent, and therefore illegal and of no binding force. For these reasons, the American people will refuse to look upon that massacre from your stand-point. They will and do hold you to your responsibility as a citizen of the Republic. And as you were at that time the Chief Magistrate of Utah, they have the right to demand why you took no official steps to inquire into that sanguinary affair which is *the shame and damning disgrace of your administration*. They have the right to demand why you took no official action in the case of Dame, Haight, and Lee; and how it is that you have so far persistently and successfully screened those murderers from the officers and the action of the law. It is a foul blot upon the workings of the system of American jurisprudence that the Mountain Meadow Massacre should having been committed nearly sixteen years ago, and to this present writing you, and Lee, and Dame, and Haight, are at large, and come and go unquestioned by the proper authority. The blush of shame should mantle the cheeks of the Governor of our Territory so long as that bloody affair remains uninvestigated, now that such investigation is possible. The judges of our courts should not have the courage to look a law-abiding man in the face so long as anything remains undone which they can legally do to bring those murderers to justice.

"It appears to have all along been the opinion that the investigation of the Mountain Meadow Massacre must originate in the criminal courts. With that view, and the Grand Jury subject to your dictation, and under your complete control, what could be done? Nothing, absolutely nothing, but to wait. Murder is shielded by no statute of limitations. But I will here suggest, that such investigation should be made by a military court, for the reason that the operations of Lee were purely and undeniably of a military character. Such a court would officially determine the military character of those operations, would collect all necessary facts in the case, and those facts would fix the responsibility where it justly belongs. Then such ulterior proceedings could be had as the case would seem to demand. If there are not Gentile officers enough in the Utah militia to constitute such a court, enough can soon be commissioned. But no Mormon should be allowed to constitute a part of that court, nor any Gentile who could be allured from duty by your sirens or be purchased by your ill-gotten gold.

"And now, in conclusion, as a Mormon, I demand of the proper authorities that this long-neglected affair be investigated, in order that the innocent may no longer suffer that reproach which belongs to Brigham Young and others only. In this connection it is proper to state that there is a strong and growing feeling in Southern Utah against Lee and his co-labourers on that bloody mission, and against their confederates, apologists, and protectors. Even in Cedar City those characters are now known as 'Mountain Meadow Dogs.' As a citizen of the United States, I demand that the veil of mystery so long covering that butchery be rent asunder, and the foul deed exposed in all its repulsive hideousness, bringing to the light those latent agencies which superinduced its commission, in order that justice may be meted out to the guilty parties, thus wiping out a foul blot upon the American name. In the name of Justice I demand it, that it may no longer be said that in Utah the direst of felonies may be committed with impunity. In the name of Truth, I demand that the facts concerning the Mountain Meadow Massacre be ascertained and stated in official form by competent authority, in order that the people of the United States may know that said massacre, even to its most sickening details, was only too true."

There are many incidental circumstances in the story of this massacre, and events which have occurred since its perpetration, that keenly touch the souls of those who are capable of appreciating the facts of that horrible tragedy.

Judge Cradlebaugh speaks of the joy which he witnessed among the children when they found themselves together again, and under the protection of American citizens:

"I recollect," he says, "one of them, John Calvin Sorrow, after he found he was safe, and before he was brought away from Salt Lake City, although not yet nine years of age, sitting in a contemplative mood, no doubt thinking of the extermination of his family, saying: 'Oh, I wish I was a man; I know what I would do; I would shoot John D. Lee; I saw him shoot my mother.' I shall never forget how he looked."

Poor boy! What terrible anguish must have been in the reflections that found such expressions in a child of his years!

There is represented in the engraving preceding this chapter a maiden of sixteen summers, cruelly murdered while pleading for life. The Author's friend, who travelled with

28

the company from Fort Bridger, speaks of her as a lovely
sweet creature, with dark flowing curls, who had been the
life and joy of the camp, and the companion of the venerable
patriarch of the company. When the first volley of rifles had
strewn the ground with the dead, she flew into the arms of
young Lee, and begged protection of her life. The manly instinct of the youth was instantly aroused by the supplicating
look of that pure and innocent being, in her defence, and he
sheltered her by his person. In an instant his father seized
him by the collar, and by greater force bending his son's head,
fired his revolver, and shot the maiden in the forehead. She
fell lifeless at his feet. This incident, and the forced part which
he played in the massacre, has blighted for ever the life of the
young man, and to his confidants he has sorrowfully related his
poignant grief.

Three of the men who escaped from the massacre were pursued for a long distance. One of them is said to have perished
in the desert, after a flight of one hundred and fifty miles ; and
of the disposition of the other two, the band under the captaincy of Ira Hatch could probably tell a thrilling story.

There is, too, a legend that the written order for the massacre of the emigrants has been preserved, and is to-day in safe-
keeping. If such a document does exist, it can only be in the
hands of some one who means to use it at a proper time, but
to acknowledge now the personal possession of such property
would be dangerous folly. There are, however, persons in
Utah who are fully confident that the document is a reality.

Wherever the story of this treacherous massacre has gone
forth, a curse has been muttered by the lips of honest men and
women, and a demand for retribution has lingered on their
tongues, while, humiliating as it is to confess, in the Forty-
second Congress there were gentlemen to be found in the
Committees of the House, and in the Senate, who were bold
enough to declare their opposition to all investigation of these
murders. One who had a national reputation during the war,
from Bunker's Hill to New Orleans, was not ashamed to say
to those who sought the legislation that was necessary to make
investigation possible, that it was " too late." To the petition-
er he said :

" Have any murders been committed in Utah during twenty years ? "

" Yes.'

" Have any been committed during the last fifteen years ? "

" Yes."

" Have any been committed within ten years ? "

" Yes."

" Have any been committed within five years ? "

" Perhaps not."

" Well, then," was the reply, " if there have been none within five years, I am opposed to meddling with the past. There are murders in New York nearly every day."

To that representative from the proudest State in the Union, the answer of the fatherless should be, that one single murder resulting from religious hatred, systematically shown, is more damning than ten thousand murders, the casual offspring of the vile passions of the most debased of men.

Moreover, that a sedate, honourable Senator, also one who has not deemed the Presidency of the United States beneath his ambition, should make a similar announcement, and ask that the past might be buried in oblivion, is passing strange.*

To this lengthy statement, and circumstantial detail of facts, the Mormon apostles may continue, as they have done before, to allege that the emigrants put poison on the body of a dead ox, that some Indian chiefs partook of the poisoned meat and died, and that the rest of the Indians became enraged, and " wiped them out." They may, perhaps, also add

---

* In addition to the labours of the regular delegate from Utah to Congress during the winter of 1871-2, there was another delegation from Utah, composed of two Gentiles and an apostle who enjoyed the freedom of the House, and whose business it was to secure the admission of Utah into the Union and thereby end all interference of Congress with the bloody record of that Territory. The apostle was but doing his duty to " the Lord ; " the two Gentile gentlemen were to be rewarded, the one with senatorial honours and the other with the position of Representative of the " State of Deseret."

On one occasion the Author visited that assembled body of honoured gentlemen, and was chatting with some of them on the proposed legislation for Utah which was to bring up and investigate the Utah murders, and expressing surprise at the evident intention of some parties to prevent all legislation, the answer was made unreservedly by a number of gentlemen, with ill-disguised contempt : " It is very evident, Mr. Stenhouse, that Brigham Young has a financial agent in Washington."

that the emigrants poisoned a spring, and that for doing so the Indians attacked them.   To those who can accept such statements, in the light of the facts stated in this chapter, as a solution of the Mountain Meadows Massacre, they are perfectly welcome; but upon the Government of this great Republic, that massacre will ever be a stain until the fullest investigation has been made, and the guilty ones brought to justice.

Fifteen long years have passed away since that dark tragedy was enacted, and yet the nation slumbers, and the representatives of the Government are deaf to the cries of the slaughtered!   How well did Britain, a few years ago, earn the admiration of the world for the proud march of her army into the heart of Abyssinia, to demand from the infatuated Theodorus the release of British subjects!   Other nations, too, have disregarded distance, time, and money, when the cries of injured citizens have been heard calling for protection.   But here, in the very heart of "the Great Republic," on the highway between the seas, the darkest deed of the nineteenth century is passed by in silence!   The cries and prayers of the orphans have been heard in vain in free America!

CHAPTER XLIV.

THE SPRINGVILLE MURDERS.—The Status of the People during the Time of Blood—Brigham's absolute Authority—Something Personal of Lee and the Leaders at Springville—How the Parrishes were Entrapped and Murdered—Confession of the Bishop's Counsellor—"Helping those who need Help"—How Bird "*worked* the best he could"—"A Lick across the Throat"—Paying the Atoning Penalty—Horrible Sacrifice of an Unfaithful Wife—How John G——'s Blood was "Spilled."

THE Mormon newspapers very properly declaim against "the people" of Utah being branded as murderers, because murders have been committed within their Territory, and, further, they protest against the great crimes being charged to Brigham Young. Unfortunately for these defenders, no sane person, in or out of the Territory of Utah, ever did hold "the "people" responsible for the black deeds of their history, and if the Prophet is selected by the universal judgment of mankind to bear the charge of crimes, his own teachings may have had something to do with inducing that conclusion.

When a public teacher utters a thousand times the statement that it is his right to dictate, direct, and control the affairs of a whole people, from the building of a temple down "to the ribbons that a woman should wear," or to "the set- "ting-up of a stocking," and that his influence over the passions of men and women in a religious assembly was so potential that, if he "had but crooked his little finger" they would have torn a United States judge to pieces, neither he nor his friends can righteously complain when violence is done among such a people, without personal cause being visible, that a suspicion should follow that "the ruling priesthood" may have been the cause.

That the citizens of Cedar, Parowan, Pinto, Harmony, and Washington settlements, south of Fillmore, were any more

wicked than the citizens of the settlements north of Fillmore,
no one believes—yet the Mountain Meadows Massacre was
committed by the militia from those southern settlements.
When the news of that deed was heard, the people north were
terror-stricken, and shuddered with horror at the thought of
the barbarous crime, and the recital of the bloody work is harrowing to them to-day. Had the massacre been committed in
the north, the people of the south would have experienced the
same sentiments of abhorrence, yet they in the south committed the crime, and served themselves with the spoils of their
victims.

The Mormon people in Utah are not the offspring of a barbarous race, neither were they raised and nurtured in uncivil-
ized nations. Apart from the spitefulness of religious controversy—which, by-the-by, is nothing peculiar to them—a kinder
and more simple-hearted people is not upon the face of the
earth. Had the Mountain Meadows Massacre occurred in any
of the neighbouring Territories, and that crime was clearly the
work of white people, the Mormons would have despised them,
hated them, and in all probability would have refused all intercourse with them.

That Brigham Young is by his natural instincts a bad man,
or that his apostles and his bishops are men of blood, is not
true. Here and there among them a malicious man is met
with, but, apart from religion, the ruling men in Utah would
be considered good citizens in any community.

Without the consideration of the question of personal divinity, the high moral teaching and unspotted life of the Naza-
rene have been the greatest blessings to mankind, and have,
through the varied channels, and slow, tortuous, and muddled
windings of progressive civilization, made the nineteenth century what it is. Under the influence of that Christianity, the
Mormons were second to no people of their class; but once
from under it, and with headlong rush flying back to the habits, customs, and morality, of the ages of the world's childhood,
Mormonism is consistently just what it is. Moving in the light
of past ages, the hatred of the Gentile and the apostate has
made the history of Utah what it has been. The more they
have approximated in situation to the nomadic Israelites, the

more have they been able to reproduce their works. It is with this understanding that the Mountain Meadows Massacre is explicable, and the subject-matter of this chapter can be comprehended.

John D. Lee, who has been selected as the chief scapegoat upon which to pile the responsibility of the Mountain Meadows Massacre, is not, in his own estimation, without defence. That his instincts are, in the judgment of others, low and brutal, is unquestioned, but he probably prays as much as the most refined Mormon in Utah, and doubtless pays his tithing with as great regularity. The Author wrote to a gentleman, who had visited Lee and had been with him some time, to ask what his personal opinion was about this man now so notorious. His answer was : " Lee is a good, kind-hearted fellow, who would " share his last biscuit with a fellow-traveller on the plains, but " at the next instant, if Brigham Young said so, he would cut " that fellow-traveller's throat."

It is not intended to infer here that Lee, in the Mountain Meadows Massacre, was but the tool of Brigham Young. Lee has refused to divulge anything on the subject, but he has said that the order was not given by the Prophet, and though there has been but little done that was not, either directly or indirectly, ordered or countenanced by Brigham, it is due to the latter that he should have all the advantage of Lee's disclaimer, till evidence shows that Lee has spoken falsely. The arguments and statements of " Argus " are very forcible to all who have lived in Utah, and they point logically to Brigham, but there is not yet before the public the evidence of direct communication between Brigham Young, in Salt Lake City, and Col. W. H. Dame, in Parowan. That the communication was possible, is true, but that it was had is as yet "not proven," and Brigham Young has a right to the benefit of that fact.*

The chapter on the " Reformation " must have satisfied the reader that the commission of the massacre was possible in

---

* Many respectable persons in Utah, who have free intercourse with the apostles and leading men of the Mormon Church, do not believe that Brigham Young had anything to do with this massacre. It would be very gratifying to see him exonerated from the charge. Should it yet turn out that it was the work of another, and that Brigham has patiently borne the imputation for so many years, he will richly deserve respect where he now is condemned.

1857, for the Tabernacle had been preaching a "reformation" by blood for a period of three years. The provocation to violence was all that was required. The advance of the troops and the passage of the emigrant trains were only the accidents. Before either of them was heard of, the teachings of the "Reformation" had begun to bear their fruits among the Mormons themselves, particularly in the very notable case known as the Parrish Murders at Springville.

The family of Parrish had at one time been very devoted to the Church. In the controversy that occurred between Sidney Rigdon and the Twelve Apostles at Nauvoo for the ruling supremacy of the Church, Parrish's name figures in one of the documents, and he is reported to have said that "he would fol-"low the Twelve if they led him to hell." Ten years later his zeal had cooled considerably, and he had resolved to leave the Territory. It is not likely that the consideration of the influence abroad of a man of his calibre could have weighed much with the Mormon leaders, yet he was brutally and foully murdered, as also was one of his sons, and the other son was seriously wounded, on the evening that they were preparing to start for California. This particular case is probably the best illustration of how men are "killed to save them."

The facts of this deed of blood clearly exhibit that it was a religious murder. The major part of the men charged with compassing the death of the Parrishes never would have soiled their hands with the blood of these or any other persons on their own account. They are not men of bad habits; not riotous, nor drunkards. Bishop Johnson, for whose apprehension Judge Cradlebaugh issued a warrant on the charge of this murder, is a very quiet, inoffensive man. He has a well-regulated and, for aught the public know, a peaceable home, with ten excellent wives and a long string of children. Mayor McDonald is a thorough Scotchman, a Gaelic Highlander, born and reared with the best surroundings of Presbyterianism, a man of unfailing honesty, strict integrity, and truthfulness, and blessed with as sweet a wife as ever honoured man with her love. Though great and powerful physically, he was by nature docile as a lamb. There could be nothing possibly in the "apostasy" of Parrish, and the proposed departure of his family from Utah, to tempt such men as these to harbour thoughts of deadly violence or to countenance it in others, yet they are charged with other persons with deliberating in a council of elders against this man Parrish, and with having put the machinery to work that brought about his death. It is to be hoped that of all this they are innocent, for it is painful to see men who have every quality calculated to command respect dragged into such frightful positions.

According to the affidavits made under oath of persons who had been actors in the Parrish tragedy, the first move against the "apostate" was made in a council of elders that was convened on the 1st of March of that same bloody 1857. Two of that council—Abraham Durfee and Duff Potter—were appointed to play the part of spies upon the Parrish family and to assume that they also were dissatisfied with the condition of things in Utah, and thereby ingratiating themselves with the Parrishes and winning their confidence, worm out of them when they intended to leave for California, and all their plans.

On the 14th of March, the evening of the departure of the Parrishes, Potter and Durfee were with them and professed to aid them in leaving without observation, while in reality they were leading them to the place where they were to be killed. In the darkness of the night, Potter, who decoyed the elder Parrish, was accidentally shot and killed. The old man Parrish seems to have rallied from his surprise and struggled with his assailant, and was finally stabbed to death. His eldest son fell dead upon the road, and the younger son, though severely wounded, escaped and got back into Springville. He and Durfee were arrested and examined to see whether they had committed the murders!! The farce of an inquest was gone through with before the public, and some of the men who were afterwards charged with being privy to the murder sat as jurors: the details are sickening, and leave no room for questioning why the deed was done—they were "apostates." After the affidavits taken by Judge Cradlebaugh had been published (as referred to in a previous chapter), one J. M. Stewart, who at the time of the murder was counsellor to Bishop Johnson, made confession of the whole matter, and in it implicates Brigham Young as the author of the order for that deed also; but of Brigham's guilt there has been no other evidence given to

the public, and the caution on misjudging him already expressed is again suggested to the reader. The following is the

CONFESSION OF STEWART.

"SAN BERNARDINO, *July* 4, 1859.

. . . .

"At a certain time during the notable 'Reformation,' I think in the
winter of 1857, I was, as one of the Bishop's counsellors, presiding and
speaking at a ward meeting in the house of G. G. (Duff) Potter, where a
brother counsellor, N. T. Guyman, came to the door and said, 'Brother
Stewart, please to cut your remarks short; the Bishop wishes to see you.'
I did so, and went with him to the Bishop's council-room, an upper room
in his dwelling-house. As this was in the night, our movements were
perhaps observed by but very few. The Bishop (Johnson), Guyman, and
myself, and some few others, whom I cannot now identify, composed this
council. After all had assembled, and were orderly seated, the Bishop
stated the object of the meeting, which was that we might hear a letter
which he had just received from 'President Young.' He there read the
letter, the purport of which was about this:

"He, Brigham, had information that some suspicious characters were
collecting at the 'Indian Farm' on Spanish Fork, and he wished him
(Bishop Johnson) to keep a good lookout in that direction; to send some
one out there to reconnoitre and ascertain what was going on, and if they
(those suspicious characters) should make a break and be pursued, which
he required, he 'would be sorry to hear a favourable report;' 'but,' he
wrote, 'the better way is to lock the stable-door before the horse is stolen.'
He then admonished the Bishop that he (the Bishop) understood these
things, and would act accordingly, and to 'keep this letter close.' This
letter was over Brigham's signature, in his own peculiarly rough hand,
which we all had the privilege of seeing. About this matter there was
no counselling. The word of Brigham was the *law*, and the object was
that we might hear it.

"Early one morning during the week succeeding the council, Parrish
and Durfee called at my house (or office), for I was the precinct magistrate, when Parrish, under oath, said his horses were stolen the night before from his stable, and asked for a search-warrant. I could find no law
in Utah making it the duty or the privilege of a justice or any other officer to grant a search-warrant, yet I considered that there could be no
harm in it, and therefore granted it, directing it to the sheriff, his deputy,
or any constable of Utah County, requiring him to search diligently Utah
County for such property. Parrish wished me to deputize Durfee to
search, but I refused. It was at this time that Durfee aimed, as I understood it, to give me a hint of his situation. 'In private,' he said, 'you
know how I stand.' I replied 'yes,' supposing that he alluded to his
apostasy, which he had made as public as he dare, when he replied, 'All's
right in Israel!' I did not understand him.

"The next Saturday night there was a council which I attended by special invitation. In the council were, as well as I remember, Bishop A. Johnson, J. M. Stewart, A. F. McDonald, N. T. Guyman, L. Johnson, C. Sanford, and W. J. Earl. I am pretty certain there were others present, but I cannot now name them. Oh, yes! Potter and Durfee were present. They came in with blankets wrapped around them. In this council there was a good deal of secret talking, two or three individuals getting close together, and talking in suppressed tones, which I, being dull of hearing, did not wholly understand. I understood, however, when Potter requested of the Bishop the privilege to kill Parrish wherever he could find 'the damned curse,' and the Bishop's reply, 'Shed no blood *in* Springville.'

"During this council, to the best of my recollection, I scarcely spoke a word. I understood that blood would probably be shed, not *in* Springville, but *out* of it. I did in my heart disapprove of the course, but I was in the current and could not get out, and policy said to me: 'Hold your tongue for the present.' This was Saturday night, and, as well as I remember, I heard no more of the affair till the next (Sunday) night one week; that is, eight days after.

"I knew nothing of the plan nor of the deeds until near midnight, when I was awakened and requested to go and hold an inquest over some dead bodies. W. J. Earl, one of the city aldermen, and my predecessor in the magisterial office, made this requirement of me, and undertook to dictate to me in selecting a jury. I considered my position for a moment, and concluded to suffer myself to be dictated to, unless an attempt should be made to lead me to the commission of crime. In that case I felt that I would try mighty hard to back out.

"I obeyed my manager, W. J. Earl, in selecting the jury. Having summoned a part of the number requisite, and being told by Earl that the jury could be filled out after we got there, we proceeded along the main road, south, about one mile from the public square, to the corner of a field, known as 'Child's Corner.' Here lay the bodies of William R. Parrish and G. G. Potter (Duff Potter). They had evidently been killed in the road, and dragged to the place where they lay. I proceeded to fill up and qualify the jury. The examination took place under my own observation. It was a protracted one—a minute record being kept by A. F. McDonald, foreman. Before we got through with young Parrish, Beason (so called) was discovered dead, about fifteen rods southeast of the other bodies. The verdict was, 'That they came to their deaths by the hands of an assassin or assassins to the jury unknown.'

"The bodies were hauled to the school-house by George McKinzie, who, by somebody's direction, I suppose, was on the ground with his team and wagon. The bodies were guarded through the night by the police.

"The next morning the Bishop sent word to me to bury the bodies, which I did, and made out the bill according to the charges of the men employed. I was told to take charge of the goods, chattels, and clothing of the murdered men, which I did, and in due time delivered every article to their families, except a butcher-knife, claimed by Mrs. Parrish, which I did not suppose belonged to her, and which I would not give to her (professing ignorance of its whereabouts) till I could get directions from the Bishop. She never got the knife ; it was subsequently lost in my family.

"Some considerable time—I don't know how long—after the murder, I spoke to Bishop Johnson concerning the above-named knife. I suppose, from the fact that when the knife came into my possession it was all over blood, that it had been used by the assassin ; but the Bishop thought differently. During our chat about the knife and the murder, the Bishop asked :

" ' Do you know who done that job ? '

" I replied, ' No.' He then asked ·

" ' Have you any idea ? '

" ' No.'

" ' Can't you guess ? '

" I answered, ' I guess I could.'

" He then said, ' Well, guess.'

" ' I guess William Bird.'

" He replied, ' You are pretty good at guessing.'

" I know nothing which would naturally have caused me to suspect William Bird, even as much as some others; but there was an internal prompting right at the moment, and I spoke accordingly.

" I suppose I had as well say something about the notorious ' court ' in which Durfee and O. Parrish were tried for the murder of Potter and the Parrishes. H. H. Kearns, Captain of the Police, came to me on Monday, the next day after the murder, and told me that I must hold court some time that afternoon, and examine Durfee and young Parrish in regard to the murder, as he had them prisoners on that account. I understood that it was only to be done as a show or kind of a · put-off.' I ordered the prisoners before me, and, as I was directed, swore them to tell the truth in the case then under consideration. Durfee made his statement first, which was about what has hitherto been revealed. He, of course, told what he had been instructed to tell. Parrish, as might have been expected, chose not to know anything of consequence. It was certainly wise in him to be ignorant.

" It would have been in order, while on the subject of the ' knife,' to state that which I will now state. Before the Bishop and I had got through our chat, Bird came in sight, and the Bishop called to him. He came to us, and, during our conversation, coolly and deliberately made the following statement :

" ' When Potter fell, I clinched Parrish and killed him with my knife.'

" I know that Parrish was killed with a knife. Potter was killed with what appeared to be one load of four balls from a shot-gun, entering just under his left breast. Beason Parrish was also killed by one or two shots in his body, the particular locality not now remembered.

" Thus I have written all that I can think of of that tragical affair.

I am perfectly aware that that portion of the community, who have no knowledge of the undercurrents and wire-workings of Mormonism, will consider me a 'poor concern' for suffering myself to be swayed in my official duties by ecclesiastical dignitaries, for suffering myself, in the case above mentioned, to be governed by the Bishop. But I perfectly understood that, to act without counsel, or to disobey counsel, was to transgress; and, if I had never understood it before, I could not but understand it then, by the example of the three dead bodies right before my eyes, that 'the way of the transgressor is (was) hard.'

" I might make some revealments, but they would not be very important, concerning the case of Mr. Forbes. I may make them at some future time.

" I will now close.   I am, etc., your humble servant,
" J. M. STEWART." *

That all this was the work of the " Reformation," and its teaching about killing apostates " to save them," there can be no doubt ; but, in making this assertion, it is also right to say that it is extremely difficult to believe that the actuating spirit of those murders sprang from " loving one's neighbour " as oneself," after the fashion of the Tabernacle teaching already quoted. The surroundings of the philosophy and logic of Brigham about " helping those who need help," and shedding the blood of those who " want their blood to be shed," is all wanting in the Springville, Payson, Pondtown, and other murders.

There is lacking all the beautiful romance, the heroism, the martyrdom, about the manner in which Parrish took his " cut-" ting-off ; " and Bird, instead of severing his windpipe with a sweetly-scented penknife, seems to have hacked him to death with a more fatal weapon which butchers are wont to use.

Mrs. Parrish affirms, on affidavit, that her husband " was " no believer in the doctrine of *killing to save*, as taught by " the teachers." There is, also, in the after-confession of Dur-fee, the revelation of a very strong suspicion that, notwithstanding he was employed to bring about the death of Parrish, he too might have been included in that scheme of " salvation " and exaltation with the gods."

The Japanese have preserved among them, from very remote ages, a romantic way of redeeming one's name from the

* *Valley Tan*, August 24, 1859.

stain of dishonour, by the unpleasant practice of "hari-kari."
On such occasions, the unfortunate, who is to expiate his offence by the instruments of death within his own hands, invites his friends to witness the event, and the highest functionaries in the land honour him with their presence, and go there
to testify that the transgressor died nobly and without the un-
dignified squirming of a muscle of his frame.

But the modern Mormon has not reached that degree of
Oriental refinement in seeking for himself dignity in the heavens. To that ancient illustration of heroism in the East a contrast is presented in the Rocky Mountains:

"Bird was lying in the corner of the fence; as Parrish and Potter
walked along the fence, he, Bird, said he shot Potter, whom he supposed
to be Parrish; that after he, Bird, had shot, he got up and stepped out to
where Parrish stood, and Parrish spoke and wanted to know if it was him
that had shot; he said that Parrish had his gun in his hand, and laid it
down, and they, Parrish and Bird, clinched together. As they clinched,
Bird drew his knife, and *worked* the best he could in stabbing Parrish.
Bird said after Parrish was down *he gave him a lick which cut his throat.*
He never said anything about any other person being there helping him.
Bird said after he *got through with the old man* he took Potter's gun and
his own, and got in the corner of the fence again to be ready for us. He
said he lay there till we came up—the two Parrish boys and myself. Then
he said he fired, and he saw one fall; he said he was afraid that the person he had shot would run off, and he fired at him again.

"When Orrin and I started, he said he came out from the fence and
shot at Orrin; he said he saw me, or he supposed it was me, when I ran
into the hollow; he asked me if I heard him call for me, I told him I
did; he wanted to know why I did not come to him. I told him *I did
not like to,* that I did not know what it meant in regard to their shooting.

"The next morning after the murder, I heard Bishop Johnson and
Bird talking together, and he blamed Potter and Bird for not going farther
away with them; the Bishop said he wanted I should be satisfied about
the affair, and not tell who was in it, that if I did *they would serve me the
same way.*" *

In the introduction of new doctrines and practices in the
Mormon Church there has always been more or less of confusion, which in time has been better arranged. Perhaps "the
"gods" will yet fix out this "killing to save," and render it,
at least in appearance, if in nothing else, better than the
crudest cannibalism, as illustrated by Bird.

* Durfee's confession.

The italicized portions of that confession are very refreshing. Fancy that kind of business meeting with the approval
of the God of Christendom ! Imagine Bird, with his coat off, his
sleeves rolled up, and a great butcher-knife, "*working his best*"
at the poor old Mr. Parrish, giving him a "*lick across his*
throat," and when he "*got through*" with that affectionate,
soul-saving work, taking up the gun of the assassinated man
for the purpose of using it to murder his sons !

Durfee had certainly good reasons to get out of the way
when invited by Bird to stay. He was not so very certain that
his sands of life had not run out. That was a fearful period in
Utah history. "Judgment had begun at the House of the
" Lord," and sinners were closely looked after.*

A month after the Parrish murders at Springville, one
Henry Jones and his mother, living at Payson (only a few
miles from Springville), were both killed. They were accused
of an unnamable offence, and both were shot. The mother
was killed in the house, and the son was pursued and killed in
a neighbouring settlement. There was no attempt at concealment about it. The Parrishes, too, were properly " laid out,"
arrayed in " the robes of the priesthood," and were the subjects of a sermon. They are to come forth in the first resurrection, for they paid the atoning penalty, and are, therefore,
entitled to the honours of the immortalized Saints !

There are a few notable cases in Utah history, but only a
few, that have properly illustrated the blood-atonement doctrine, as taught by Brigham.

In one instance, it is related that one of the wives of a
polygamist was unfaithful during his absence when he was on
a mission. On his return, the " Reformation " was in full
blast, and the unhappy wife believed that, from this *faux pas*,

* On affidavit, Joseph Bartholomew related before Judge Cradlebaugh that repeated efforts were made to kill him and Durfee, as they had been indiscreet in speaking of this Springville murder, and were evidently apostate in spirit. There can be
very little sympathy for such men, even when their story is true. In the Mountain
Meadows Massacre, when men were called out as a militia, without knowing their
destiny and the work to be done ; and when, as in some instances, even knowing
the work, men were afraid of their lives if they refused, there can be honest sympathy ; but, for such men as would deliberately decoy an unsuspecting friend to the
shambles, there can be no honest tears shed. If Bird had " got through " with a
few more of his assistants, the world would have wagged quite as well.

she was doomed to lose her claim to motherhood over the children which she had already borne; that she would be cast aside in eternity as well as in time, by her husband; that, in fact, she would only " be an angel, and with the angels stand;" * and that she could not reach the circle of the gods and goddesses unless her blood was shed. She consented to meet the penalty of her error, and while her heart was gushing with affection for her husband and her children, and her mind absorbed with faith in the doctrine of human sacrifice, she seated herself upon her husband's knee, and after the warmest and most endearing embrace she had ever known—it was to be her last—when the warmth of his lips still lingered about her glowing cheek, with his own right hand he calmly cut her throat and sent her spirit to the keeping of the gods. That kind and loving husband still lives near Salt Lake City, and preaches occasionally with great zeal. He seems happy enough.

One of the elders at Council Bluffs, in a dispute over some trifling matter, warned one of the brethren not to cross a certain boundary-line in his field or garden. He braved the threat, and the other shot him dead. The murderer offered to expiate his crime, but for years no one was found willing to " help " him," and he lived on miserably under the influence and teaching of the " blood atonement." He seemed to be unhappy when living with the Saints, and was equally so when among the Gentiles; finally he returned to Zion, and engaged in business in Salt Lake City. One evening he was walking quietly home, the firing of a pistol was heard, and the dead body of a man was soon after picked up. A report was circulated that John G. . . . n had committed suicide. But another, and probably more correct account, was believed by those who knew of his " sin unto death." †

* The Saints, arguing from the words of St. Paul, " Know ye not that ye shall " judge angels," place those celestial beings much lower in the " Kingdom of heaven " than the souls of redeemed and sanctified men and women. The Mormon revelations clearly define that Gentiles if they behave themselves in the next world may be permitted to occupy the position of servants or " angels " to the Saints. Brigham and Heber used to calculate that some Presidents of the United States would yet be their " boot-blacks," and might be otherwise honoured to do the " chores " for the apostolic families in the Millennium and afterwards.

† " Verily, verily I say unto you, if a man marry a wife according to my word " (that is, in polygamy and by virtue of the requirements of this revelation), " and

Though John was no coward beyond the consciousness of guilt, he probably had an aversion to getting "a committee "appointed," as the apostle Grant recommended, and going to an appointed place and there having his "blood shed" by that kindly committee. A specified time and place and executioners could not well be pleasant to think of, and John was supposed to have arranged with some friend who "loved him "as himself," to take him unawares and "spill his blood." John was properly conveyed to the cemetery, and the veil fell upon his career.

In this and in preceding chapters, phases of Utah history, illustrative of very doubtful principles promulgated by the Mormon priesthood, have been freely dealt with; but the numerous charges of murder in Utah could not possibly be investigated here, and are very properly remitted to the labours of some future prosecuting attorney. Enough, however, has been shown to exhibit to the Mormon people the disaster that must inevitably ensue to any people who make murder an auxiliary of their faith, and it is to be hoped that the Government of the United States will yet take such action in these murders as will teach the guilty that this vile wrong, and the standing threat against the unpopular Gentile and the "apos- "tate," will not go unpunished.

they are sealed by the Holy Spirit of promise, according to mine appointment." (that is, at the Mormon altar), "and he or she shall commit any sin or transgression of the new and everlasting covenant whatever, and all manner of blasphemies, and if they commit no murder wherein they shed innocent blood, yet shall they come forth in the first resurrection, and enter into their exaltation, BUT THEY SHALL BE DESTROYED IN THE FLESH, and shall be delivered unto the buffetings of Satan, unto the day of redemption, saith the Lord."—"Revelation" on Polygamy, Section IX.

CHAPTER XLV.

THE FAITH OF THE SAINTS.—The Prophet's Creed given to the Public—The Doctrines taught to the Saints—Spirits in Prison—Baptism for the Dead—Brigham Young teaches that Adam is the God of this World—Brigham and all the Mormons are to make New Worlds and become Gods—A New Version of Paradise Lost and Paradise Regained—Origin of the Devil—The Mormon Account of the Origin of the African Race.

THE most devoted of the intelligent adherents of the cause of Brigham Young, who dare to look calmly at facts, will hardly dispute that the vitality of the Mormon faith, introduced by its founder Joseph Smith, had reached its climax within the first quarter of a century from the date of its organization, and that from that period onward the Mormon Church has subsisted upon its organization and not upon lifegiving principles.

The believers in the new faith were organized in 1830: they were only six in number, but they were full of their mission, and, in their way, wholly devoted to Christ. Their heroism in the proclamation of their doctrines never was surpassed in any age or in any country, by any other disciples or missionaries of any faith. They were pure in thought, and burned with zeal for the redemption of mankind. The results were a grand increase of numbers of disciples begotten in their own faith, for in nothing probably more than in religious enthusiasm does " like beget like."

As the reader has seen in this review of history, Joseph Smith had ambition enough for temporal aggrandizement and rule, but the people who surrounded him and his were strong enough to resist and repulse the power that insidiously sought to crush them. What Joseph might have done with the better "opportunities" of his successor, may be open to question ; but it is asserted by the defenders of Brigham that the former would have, in the love of power, which isolation in the Rocky Mountains has so signally favoured in the latter, done more outrageous things than are even charged to the name of Young. Such might have been the case. Joseph Smith had within himself, doubtless, all the ambition for greatness with which his religious fancies clothed his mind, but there was nothing instinctively cruel and remorseless in him. He could personally err, he could repent, confess his wrong-doing, and sue for forgiveness. With such qualities the force of circumstances would have taught him better ways ; but the isolation that favoured the weak with protection from " persecution " was equally provident in furnishing the opportunity for the development of whatever was dormant of the quality of aggressiveness.

Mormonism, therefore, may be said to have exhibited in the preceding chapters, commencing with that upon the " Refor-"mation," followed by the dark ways of murder, then rebellion against the Government, what were the first demonstrations of the change from the " love of Christ shed abroad in the "heart " to the mad ambition of a temporal, absolute "king-"dom " that should crush every opposing power.

Nine-tenths of the Mormons who slaughtered the Arkansas emigrants in 1857, would, ten years before that time, have started on a mission to preach to these same persons at their own firesides in Arkansas, and would have sought by every possible labour and personal sacrifice to imbue them with the faith of Jesus Christ and the blessings which the heavens were pouring out upon the Latter-Day Saints. These Mormon preachers would have suffered hunger and every kind of privation while preaching " without purse and scrip " in order to save those very people of Arkansas, and deliver them from " the wickedness of the Gentiles." How these same men, capable of having been formerly missionaries of peace, were able ten years later to butcher them in Utah, is the evidence of the pernicious teachings of the Salt Lake Tabernacle. With such a reversion in their practical religion, a summary of the original faith and the after-work of the leaders seems here to find a place preparatory to a further statement of the development of theocracy in the mountains.

Fully believing in the divinity of his mission, Joseph Smith, in 1842, furnished for publication a sketch of "The Rise, "Progress, Persecutions and Faith of the Latter-Day Saints." After threading together the chief incidents of his life, he closes his statement with the following points of faith:

" We believe in God, the Eternal Father, and in His Son, Jesus Christ, and in the Holy Ghost.

" We believe that men will be punished for their own sins, and not for Adam's transgression.

" We believe that through the atonement of Christ all mankind may be saved by obedience to the laws and ordinances of the Gospel.

" We believe that these ordinances are : First, Faith in the Lord Jesus Christ; second, Repentance ; third, Baptism by immersion for the remission of sins; fourth, Laying on of Hands for the Gift of the Holy Ghost.

" We believe that a man must be called of God, by ' prophecy and by laying on of hands ' by those who are in authority to preach the Gospel and administer in the ordinances thereof.

" We believe in the same organization that existed in the primitive Church, viz. : apostles, prophets, pastors, teachers, evangelists, etc.

" We believe in the gift of tongues, prophecy, revelation, visions, healing, interpretation of tongues, etc.

" We believe the Bible to be the Word of God, as far as it is translated correctly ; we also believe the Book of Mormon to be the Word of God.

" We believe all that God has revealed, and that He does now reveal, and we believe that He will yet reveal many great and important things pertaining to the Kingdom of God.

" We believe in the literal gathering of Israel and in the restoration of the Ten Tribes. That Zion will be built upon this continent. That Christ will reign personally upon the earth, and that the earth will be renewed and receive its paradisaic glory.

" We claim the privilege of worshipping Almighty God according to the dictates of our conscience, and allow all men the same privilege, let them worship how, where, or what they may.

" We believe in being subject to kings, presidents, rulers, and magistrates, in obeying, honouring, and sustaining the law.

" We believe in being honest, true, chaste, benevolent, virtuous, and in doing good to *all men ;* indeed, we may say that we follow the admonition of Paul, ' We believe all things, we hope all things,' we have endured many things and hope to be able to endure all things. If there is anything virtuous, lovely, or of good report, or praiseworthy, we seek after these things.   Respectfully, etc., JOSEPH SMITH." *

* *Times and Seasons*, vol. iii., p. 706.

To preach this doctrine he adds :

"Proud of the cause which they have espoused, and *conscious of their innocence* and of the truth of their system, amidst calumny and reproach have the elders of this Church gone forth and planted the Gospel in almost every State in the Union. It has penetrated our cities, it has spread over our villages, and has caused thousands of our intelligent, noble, and patriotic citizens to obey its divine mandates, and be governed by its sacred truths. It has also spread into England, Ireland, Scotland, and Wales ; in the year 1840, when a few of our missionaries were sent, over five thousand joined the standard of truth; there are numbers now joining in every land.

"Our missionaries are going forth to different nations, and in Germany, Palestine, New Holland, the East Indies, and other places, the standard of truth has been erected; no unhallowed hand can stop the work from progressing. Persecutions may rage, mobs may combine, armies may assemble, calumny may defame, but the truth of God will go forth boldly, nobly, and independently, till it has penetrated every continent, visited every clime, swept every country, and sounded in every ear, till the purposes of God shall be accomplished, and the great Jehovah shall say the work is done."

While the Prophet presented these articles of faith for the edification of the general public, he held in reserve " higher " truths" which the Saints at that time alone were entitled to know, and, as it is the privilege of every prophet to receive revelation, Brigham has in some material points greatly added to the original creed promulgated by Joseph.

The Mormon understanding of salvation, glory, and immortality, embraces a general series of compliances with certain laws, and obedience to certain ordinances.

Shortly before Joseph's death he revealed to the faithful that a great work devolved upon the living Saints for their kindred who had gone before them to the other world, and, as the Prophet has laid it out, it was indeed no small undertaking.

First, all men and women must have faith in redemption wrought out by Jesus Christ, and MUST BE BAPTIZED BY IMMERSION " in the name of the Father, Son, and Holy Ghost," in order that their own individual sins may be washed away. This being the happy condition of mind, and the ordinances complied with, the hands of the elders are laid upon the heads of the disciples that " they may receive the Holy Ghost."

In due time every man is also to receive the priesthood of
Aaron and Melchisedec, and thereby become entitled to com-
mune with the heavens, and, when they have accepted the
" Celestial Law" of Marriage — i. e., polygamy — and have
passed through the ordinances of the "Endowments," they
are presumed to be fairly started for "honour, glory, and eter-
"nal lives with the gods"—a progression which the apostle
Orson Hyde illustrates, as shown in the following chapter.

In all this profession of faith, sincerely entertained by the
modern Saint, there is associated the obligation of the substitutional labour of "the living for the dead," in order that the
latter, who knew not Joseph Smith and Mormonism, may yet
be taken out of the clutches of the devil, and be finally redeemed and glorified with the believing Latter-Day Saints.

All the Mormon elders who leave this mundane sphere, instead of "entering into the rest prepared for the righteous,"
are understood to go on a preaching mission, on the other side
of the veil, in order to wake up all their relatives who have
been held for long ages "in prison," because they "obeyed not
" the Gospel in the flesh."

As the Mormon law takes no account of faith by itself, the
spirits of the dead who in that shadowy region accept and believe in the mission of Joseph Smith, from the preaching of
these dead elders, are all still accounted to be unbaptized, and
consequently cannot be admitted into "the kingdom." To
obviate that inconvenience, Joseph received a revelation instructing him that, if the living Saints would go forth into the
water and be immersed for their dead relatives and friends,
that act, being recorded on the books of the priesthood here
below, the transfer of the names to the other world would immediately affect the condition of the converted spirit.

That revelation had a very pleasing effect upon the Saints
in Nauvoo. It was very gratifying to be able to help out of
"prison" parents, brothers, sisters, relatives of every degree,
and near and dear friends who had lived and died before the
great Latter-Day work had begun. In their transports, before
they had well considered the seriousness of the business, there
was an eagerness for the waters of the Mississippi that flowed
so majestically past their loved Nauvoo, and there by the

banks of that river the brethren and sisters gave the names of the dead whom they loved, and by the elders were led into the stream and immersed in their behalf.

Under the most pleasing circumstances of life, difficulties will sometimes occur, and the baptisms in the river were soon discovered to be premature and incomplete. Maidens had gone forth and been baptized for their grandfathers; youths had exhibited an equal affection and interest for grandmothers; widows were baptized for departed husbands; and living husbands were equally delighted to "deliver from their prison-"house" those with whom they had had earlier enjoyments in life.

It took but little reflection for Joseph to perceive that that mode of proceeding would work confusion. To say the least of it, there was some awkwardness in laying hands upon Mary Jane to ordain her an elder in the stead of her Uncle James! and sealing upon Mary Jane all the rights and privileges belonging to the manhood of James—embracing therein the addition of other wives, the power to continue lives in spirit, and to become "the *father* of generations!" It was equally inconvenient to baptize Richard in the name of Martha, and for the former using her name to receive on his head the laying on of hands, and the blessings of the priesthood, conferring upon him, for her, the favours of the heavens—including the greatest of all earthly blessings for a lady who loves her lord. It was confusing for a young man to be appointed to be "a "*mother* in Israel."

Joseph was soon armed with another revelation, and from one of his places of concealment he announced that the work of baptism for the dead should be done in a more perfect way: he had "had a few additional views in relation to the matter." He began to comprehend that it was a task of some magnitude for the living to be baptized for all the dead; and, small as Nauvoo was, in point of population, in 1842, there was too much work for one recorder to do correctly, and as a transcript of the book kept in Nauvoo was to settle the question of imprisonment or glory and salvation in the other world, the machinery of record-keeping ought to be more extensive. Instead of one of the brethren noting imperfectly by the light

of the moon, or a lantern-candle, who had come to the Mississippi to be baptized that the dead might be delivered, there
was to be a recorder appointed in every ward of the city, not a
bungling, careless brother, but one "who is well qualified to
"take accurate minutes, and let him be very particular and
"precise in taking the whole proceedings." Again, he says:
"Let all the records be had in order, that they may be put in
"the archives of my Holy Temple, to be held in remembrance
"from generation to generation, saith the Lord of Hosts."
Thus, whatsoever the priesthood "record on earth shall be
"recorded in heaven," and whatsoever the priesthood "do not
"record on earth shall not be recorded in heaven." In reference to these books he says:

"And, further, I want you to remember that John the Revelator was
contemplating this very subject in relation to the dead when he declared,
as you will find in Revelation xx. 12: 'And I saw the dead, small and
great, stand before God; and the books were opened; and another book
was opened, which was the book of life; and the dead were judged out
of those things which were written in the books, according to their
works.'"

In support of the general principle of this baptizing the
living for the dead, he adduced that passage from St. Paul,
which has puzzled so many commentators [1 Corinthians xv.
29]: "Else what shall they do which are baptized for the dead,
"if the dead rise not at all? why are they then baptized for
"the dead?" He also quotes the fifth and sixth verses of the
last chapter of Malachi: "Behold, I send you Elijah the
"Prophet, before the coming of the great and dreadful day of
"the Lord; and he shall turn the heart of the fathers to the
"children, and the heart of the children to their fathers, lest
"I come and smite the earth with a curse;" and from this
passage he argues:

"It is sufficient to know in this case that the earth will be smitten
with a curse, unless there is a welding-link of some kind or other, between the fathers and the children, upon some subject or other, and behold, what is that subject? It is the baptism for the dead. For we
without them cannot be made perfect; neither can they without us be
made perfect. Neither can they or us be made perfect without those who
have died in the gospel also; for it is necessary in the ushering-in of the
dispensation of the fulness of times; which dispensation is now begin-

ning to usher in, that a whole and complete and perfect union, and weld·
ing together of dispensations, and keys, and powers, and glories should
take place, and be revealed from the days of Adam even to the present
time."

With such a task before them, the Mormons are to trace
back all the families of their own names, evidently guided by
the adage that "blood is thicker than water," and in due time,
under the better registration, brothers will go forth to be baptized for the remission of the sins of all their male progenitors
bearing the same name. Each one will also be ordained for
all his deceased relatives, that they all, separately and distinctly, may bear the priesthood; and as plurality of wives is the
marital condition of "the gods," the living Saint will also have
a proper number of wives sealed to him, for each one of his
deceased kinsmen, that they may abound in good works as
well as in grace. The living sister-Saint has also to pass
through all the same ordinances in the same order, and is to
go on from the first step at the baptism for her sisterly ancestry, till she has climbed the ladder of salvation, and been
blessed and sealed to one of the living brothers, in order that
the redeemed sister in the spirit-world may become one of the
wives of somebody in eternity.

The magnitude of this work naturally suggested that, while
fathers, mothers, grandsires, and grandames, kind uncles and
aunts, and promising brothers and sisters, might easily be remembered and traced, there was a great probability of some
good souls converted to Mormonism in the other world being
left out in the cold from lack of remembrance. The uncertainty, too, as to who would consent to be converted in the
other world, and accept all these substitutional ordinances, was
very naturally a question for consideration. But Joseph
could cut any Gordian knot, and here he gives the trenchant
blow:

"The great and grand secret of the whole matter, and the *summum
bonum* of the whole subject that is lying before us, consists in obtaining
the powers of the Holy Priesthood. For him to whom these keys are
given, there is no difficulty in obtaining a knowledge of facts in relation
to the salvation of the children of men, both as well for the dead as for
the living."

Joseph was equal to any emergency, and his people were ready to believe all that he announced.

But the Temple had to be built within a certain time, in order that the baptisms and ceremonies for the dead might be properly administered; and as " the Lord " had announced that, if the Nauvoo Temple was not completed within a specified time, the living Mormons, and their dead also, " would be rejected," the poor, sickly, half-starved, ill-clad citizens of Nauvoo worked like beavers on that Temple, and donated everything they could to rush up the structure; and yet, after all their toil, it is claimed by the Mormons, under the guidance of the son of the Prophet Joseph, that Brigham Young and the people did not finish the Temple, and, as a consequence, the Mormon chief and all the Rocky Mountain Saints, and all the converted in the other world, are directly and unmistakably " rejected." That is pretty hard!

The literal resurrection of the bodies of the Saints, and the after-inhabiting of this world, when purified by fire and celestialized, was also a favourite doctrine among the Mormon preachers for a long period of years. At first, they seemed to know all about these matters to the minutest details, but of late years the subject has been rarely mentioned. The last reference to it was the enunciation of Brigham that " Joseph Smith was " to be the first person resurrected," and after his framework was knit together again, and was clothed with immortalized flesh, he was to proceed to " resurrect " those who had laboured valiantly, and died for the Latter-Day faith, each one according to his rank in the priesthood, and then he would, doubtless, at an early day, proceed to " resurrect " all his wives, beginning with the best beloved one, of course, and continuing to the last, " each one in her order," according to the degree of favour with which the suggestive mind of the " resurrected " Prophet regarded her. The children of each of these wives would come next " in their order." The Prophet is to give to the first elders whom he clothes with immortality " the keys of the res- " urrection." and they will in turn proceed to the pleasant labour of calling forth from the long-silent tomb their own households and particular favourites; and thus the power to " resurrect " is to be handed down from one person to another

till the grave has given up its dead for "the first resurrec
tion."

After all the Saints have been "resurrected," the best Gentiles will next be attended to, and they will be leisurely brought
from their graves. There will, however, be an order for their
moving "bone to bone, and sinew to sinew" according to
merit. The Gentiles who aided the Prophet in the hour of his
trial, as some few did with financial assistance, will be first on
the baptismal record, and will be favoured with priority in
coming from the tomb; and this is the fulfilling of that text
which saith: "Make to yourselves friends of the mammon
" of unrighteousness, that when ye fail they may receive you
"into everlasting habitations." Such men as the Honourable
Senator of Illinois, who had so long been the friend of the
Prophet, would have been early and well cared for in some
of Joseph's everlasting habitations, had he not delivered the
Springfield speech; and that President of the United States
who made Brigham Governor of Utah is certain to be received
with the greatest kindness in the kingly domain of the successor of Joseph.

It will be gratifying to the American nation to learn that
General George Washington has already been kindly remembered by the Saints, and that he is no longer in "the prison-
"house" with Hamlet's father—

> "Doomed for a certain time to walk the night,
> And, for the day, confined to fast in fires."

The "Father of his Country" is now happy in sweet communion with Joseph Smith and the Latter-Day elders.*

The distinguished dead of all nations are thus certain to be
awakened early from "their last long slumbers," as the disciples are gathered to Zion from all the kingdoms of the world;

---

* At a mass-meeting of sisters in the Tabernacle, January 13, 1870, to resolve
and admonish Congress against the passage of the Cullom bill, punishing the practice of polygamy, an aged sister, rejoicing in the Revolutionary blood that flowed in
her veins, made allusion to her father fighting "beside General Washington."
"How old are you, sister McMinn?" inquired the "presidentess." "I am eighty-
four," was the reply. Then, by way of comfort to the kind old lady, that she might
know that her father's commander was in a good place, sister Kimball added: ' I
"would observe that General Washington is a member of this Church and kingdom.
" I was present when Judge Adams, of Springfield, was baptized for Washington."

and, as each nation has its "idols," there will be no possible chance of forgetfulness.

Fully believing in this literal resurrection of the body, the Saints are carried to their graves "clothed with the robes of "the priesthood," such as they hope to be seen in when they burst the bands of the tomb, and exclaim: "O grave, where "is thy victory?"

About ten years ago, an assistant grave-digger, Jean Baptiste, an Italian by birth, threw the people of Salt Lake City into terrible confusion and excitement. Tempted by the carefully prepared clothing of the interred, he carried on for a long time the disrobing of the dead. The discovery of this fact produced the most painful sensation that any community ever experienced. The fearful grief of mothers at the thought of their sweet little ones lying naked in their graves is beyond description. No language could depict their heartfelt mourning. When Baptiste's house was searched, and the clothing of the dead was taken to a public place for identification, all business was suspended in the city. Nothing was spoken of but the sad outrage. The women in their poignant grief would have torn Baptiste into shreds had he not been protected by the iron bars of a prison. Brigham preached a timely sermon, and assured the heart-bruised and weeping mothers that all would be right, that the power of "the Lord" was equal to everything, and that, in the morning of the resurrection, the mothers would greet their little ones arrayed in suitable garments—all would be well. The people were soothed, though their faith was seriously tried, and in the current of events this painful incident was forgotten. Jean Baptiste was taken somewhere—no one knows whither. Romantic stories of his ears being cut off, of his being branded on the forehead "Robber of the "dead," and of his being sent to wander on an island of the Lake, were put in circulation; but the probabilities are that he "ceased to breathe." He was to the community "a monster," and none have cared to ask what had become of him.

A grave difficulty at one time arose as to whether the superficial crust of the earth would be sufficiently extensive for all the inhabitants of the world, when "resurrected," to find standing-room upon it; but that astute philosopher and apostle, Orson Pratt, went to work and solved the question. He levelled all the mountains, and raised all the valleys, according to the promise of the ancient Hebrew prophet, who foretold that the hills should be laid low, the valleys exalted, the rough places made smooth, and the crooked places straightened. Without the slightest difficulty he arranged a magnificent and more extended globe, freed from mountains, deserts, and waste-places, and then, to his own satisfaction, demonstrated that there would be ground enough to allow an acre and a quarter for each " resurrected" Saint who had ever lived, from the morning of creation to the day of doom ; so that each might be provided with a snug little farm. The best argument, how-ever, was that which was actually advanced by a Mormon elder at a public discussion in England. The Elder was non-plussed by a great array of figures, which his opponent had produced to prove that the surface of the earth was incapable of becoming the everlasting habitation of the " resurrected." While the elder's fingers were trying to " resurrect" an argu-ment from the roots of his hair, another elder gravely whis-pered to him: " Tell your opponent that if, after all this work " of reconstruction, the world is not large enough to contain " the teeming myriads which sprang from its bosom, *the Lord* " *will build a gallery around it*, and thus supply the deficien-" cy." That ended the discussion.

But, with all these beautiful thoughts of a materialized body resurrection, Orson Hyde once well-nigh made sad havoc. This apostle broke in upon the reveries of the resurrection with an argument in favour of a " baby resurrection."

Brother Orson is troubled with a dreamy, speculative mind, and, though he could not comprehend the materialistic philoso-phy of the decayed particles of the human body, after they had evaporated, and had in turn amalgamated with the earth, the grass, the vegetation, and had been in these forms partaken of by the cow, the ox, and the ass, and in the air had been inhaled by all sorts of mortals—coming together again in human form —he concluded that it was at least within his comprehension that babies were born.

The physical nature of the President of the apostles was altogether harmonious with the practicabilities of this latter philosophy; and, besides, he saw in the "baby resurrection" an additional argument in favour of polygamy. But Brigham hastened after Orson and speedily squelched his "baby resur- "rection." It is very doubtful, however, if Orson does not still believe that David, king of Israel, Moses, Elijah, and other distinguished folks may not yet find a resurrection somewhere within the extensive folds of his numerous family.

Orson Hyde, President of the Twelve Apostles.

The modern Saints' views of Deity were at this time re- duced to the greatest simplicity. The "God" of the Universe, in the language of one of the apostles, is "*like a well-to-do* "*farmer!*" Doubtless, an English farmer—

"A fine old English gentleman,
One of the olden time—"*

ruddy in health, with a good roast-beef appetite, and not at all averse to "prime old malt," or, patterned from an earlier day, he might be fond of "sack"—the charm of Falstaff's life.

Consistent with this, the modern apostle has no difficulty in accounting for the second person in the Trinity. The "im-

* Solomon says there are certain persons who should only be answered in their own style, and the prophet Elijah had no delicacy in ridiculing the prophets of Baal. The amusing nonsense of the Mormon faith needs not, therefore, be an- swered by weeping.

"maculate conception" is rudely dispensed with as an unnecessary doctrine. God the Father is credited with being as directly the Father of Jesus Christ as Brigham Young, senior, claims to be the father of Brigham Young, junior.* While no one in the whole Christian world has ever before ascribed to Jesus marital relations, the Mormons have sought in His life for a support for their own plural marriages, and to their satisfaction they have discovered that He had both wives and children. The fruitful apostle Hyde says:

"If at the marriage at Cana of Galilee, Jesus was the bridegroom and took unto him Mary, Martha, and the other Mary whom Jesus loved, it shocks not our nerves. If there were not an attachment and familiarity between our Saviour and these women highly improper, only in the relation of husband and wife, then we have no sense of propriety, or of the characteristics of good and refined society. Wisely then was it concealed; but, when the Saviour poured out his soul unto death, when nailed to the cross, he saw his *seed of children*, but who shall declare his *generation?* "

In another part of this work, a quotation has already been made from the apostle Heber C. Kimball, who materialized the Holy Ghost into the person of a man, holding to Jesus the same relation of Counsellor as Heber did to Brigham Young.

With such doctrinal conclusions in his mind, it was easy for Brigham Young to announce:

"Now hear it, O inhabitants of the earth, Jew and Gentile, Saint and sinner! *When our father Adam came into the Garden of Eden,* HE CAME INTO IT WITH A CELESTIAL BODY, *and* BROUGHT EVE, ONE OF HIS WIVES, WITH HIM. He helped to make and organize this world. He is Michael the Archangel, the Ancient of Days! about whom holy men have written and spoken. HE IS OUR FATHER AND OUR GOD, AND THE ONLY GOD WITH WHOM WE HAVE TO DO. *Every man upon the earth, professing Christians or non-professing, must hear it,* AND WILL KNOW IT SOONER OR LATER." †

At a later date, he repudiated the Bible narrative of Creation:

"*You believe Adam was made of the dust of this earth.* THIS I DO NOT BELIEVE. . . *You can write that information to the States if you please—that* I HAVE PUBLICLY DECLARED THAT I DO NOT BELIEVE THAT PORTION OF THE BIBLE AS THE CHRISTIAN WORLD DO. I NEVER DID, AND I NEVER WANT TO. *Because I have come to understanding, and*

* The details and arguments are better confined to Mormon publications than cited here.   † Tabernacle, April 9, 1852.

BANISHED FROM MY MIND ALL THE BABY-STORIES MY MOTHER TAUGHT
ME WHEN I WAS A CHILD."*

One step more was wanted, and the apostle Heber C. Kimball took it when he announced that Brigham himself was " God " to the people.

Brigham very considerately told his audience only a part of the story of the new deity which he then introduced to the world for worship, as there were terrible consequences following any one's unbelief. He says :

"Let all who hear these doctrines pause before they make light of them, or treat them with indifference, *for they will prove their* SALVATION OR DAMNATION ; "

and, with a consciousness of the estimate that would be placed on such a revelation, he adds :

"Were I to tell you the whole truth, *blasphemy* would be nothing to it, in the estimation of the superstitious and over-righteous of mankind."

Growing out of this materialized Adam deity of " flesh and " bones,"† springs the other doctrine of the Mormons that they are all yet to be gods ; for, when this earth is celestialized and is made the home of the resuscitated Saints, it becomes a sort of nursery for the peopling of other worlds.

The marital relation of the Saints existing in the celestialized world is, to the very fullest extent, unrestricted polygamy, and the offspring of the celestialized Saints furnishes the spiritual life of embryo men and women. Brigham in his theory of the Saints making worlds, peopling them, and in due time becoming gods, has entered very clearly into all particulars,

---

* Tabernacle, October 23, 1853.

† The Mormons believe in three distinct states of existence. The first is a purely spiritual existence before people come into this world. The second is a mortal existence in this world—the flesh-and-*blood* arrangement. The third is a " resurrected " existence and is identically the same as the earthly existence, only the blood is drained out of the system, and the arteries of the life-giving fluid are supplied with spirit, and thus Jesus said to his affrighted disciples : " Handle me and see, for a spirit hath not flesh *and bones* as ye see me have." Jesus afterwards partook of some " broiled fish and an honeycomb ; " therefore the Mormons believe in a very tangible heaven where there shall be eating, drinking, and the usual enjoyment of the pleasant things of this life, which will last for ever, as blood, the source of mortality, is dispensed with.

and taking his own life and progress as an illustration it is very easily comprehended.

Passing over his infantile joys and sorrows, and the brief period of "eleven days and a half" at school, he chose the honest profession of a painter and glazier: in due time he became a Mormon, a preacher, and a prophet. He takes unto himself many wives, and begets many children. If the world holds out long enough, he will probably be "gathered to his "fathers," when—like Moses—he has attained the ripe age of one hundred and twenty years. He then goes to the "spirit-"world," and engages anew in the missionary business. After a time Joseph Smith becomes "resurrected"—how, when, and by whom this is to be done, is not yet understood, or, if understood, it is preserved among "the mysteries"—he will then "resurrect" Brigham Young, with others, as already stated in a preceding portion of this chapter. When Brigham's wives are resurrected, having been "married to him for eternity" as well as "married for time," their family relations with the Prophet will be renewed, and they will beget millions and myriads of "spirits." Whether these ethereal young folks have apartments with their parents, or float about in space without any particular local habitation, is not of great present importance: they have, however, to themselves, a very tangible existence and opportunities of developing into very excellent men and women, or otherwise, as they may kick up rows, quarrel, and the worst of them be sent to "hell."

In course of time Brigham sees that he has begotten a very respectable family, numbering probably myriads of spirits, and, during that period of family increase, he has himself been progressing extensively in the "knowledge of the gods;" he has been learning how to control the elements, and how to command them to come together and take the shape and form which he may desire. When he has sufficiently mastered this education and become sensible of his power, he will say to some one: "Let us go to, and make a world, upon which the "spirits of my family may find the opportunity of living in "bodies of grosser matter, and thereby gain valuable experi-"ence." The command is given to the elements, and they, obedient to the word, gather together in a globular form, and

30

a new world is created. Brigham and his friends who have
assisted him to create this world find it rather unfinished in
the first stage of its formation, but they continue to make improvements, and in course of time succeed in beautifying and
adorning it. They take with them the seeds of trees of every
kind, from the celestialized world on which they dwell, and
plant them in the soil of the new world, together with the
seeds of grasses and of flowers, and of everything that grows
which is pleasing to the eye, agreeable to the smell, etc. They
control the waters, and direct them where to flow; they place
in the rivers and in the seas fish of every kind. Fowls of the
air, beasts of the field, and all things and creatures which are
necessary to make a world and furnish it—these are brought
from the celestialized world upon which Brigham dwells.

The supposition now is, that the task of this new-world-
making comes to an end, and those who were engaged in the
labour are fully satisfied with it, and pronounce it " all very
" good."

Then Brigham says to his favourite wife: " Let us go down
" and inhabit this new home;" and they do so. And in this
way some future Moses will call them Adam and Eve. For a
time the noble pair will get along very well and comfortably ;
but the " old serpent," or a monkey as some may have it, will
creep along and insinuate kindly mischief to Eve, and with the
sweetness of her sex she will innocently partake of some forbidden fruit and be expelled from their garden of Eden. Adam
[Brigham] up to this time will have done nothing to offend or
to incur any one's displeasure, and he very naturally will be
troubled about Eve's unpleasant position. The penalty of
Eve's transgression will entail her expulsion from the garden,
and as a consequence there would be a separation, for Adam
[Brigham] has, as yet, done nothing to deserve being driven
out of the garden. The situation will be very awkward, but
Adam [Brigham] will comprehend it at a glance, will see that
it will never do for " man to be alone;" that the object in creating the new world would thus be frustrated; that, if Eve
leaves, there will be no possibility of any terrestrial bodies
being made for his myriads of spirits that will then be waiting
to come down and " tabernacle in the flesh." After mature

reflection, he will express to Eve how much he loves her, and how much he desires to carry out the original programme for the benefit of their little ones in the celestial world, who were anxiously waiting for earthly tabernacles. The conclusion reached will be that Adam [Brigham], in order to enjoy Eve's society and be driven out of the garden, must also partake of the forbidden fruit. Adam [Brigham] will then taste of it, and share Eve's destiny. The first Adam did taste of it ; hence the meaning of that remarkable passage in the Book of Mormon—" Adam fell, that men might be." In other words, if Adam had stopped in the garden, and Eve had been driven out, the chances of family increase would have been very unsatisfactory—men would never have been born ; and in this strain argues the American prophet Nephi :

" Now, behold, if Adam had not transgressed, he would not have fallen, but he would have remained in the garden of Eden. And all things which were created must have remained in the same state which they were after they were created; and they must have remained for ever, and had no end. And they would have had no children ; wherefore they would have remained in a state of innocence, having no joy, for they knew no misery ; doing no good, for they knew no sin." *

The lucidity of this passage is not very remarkable, but the deduction to be made from it in connection with the peopling of worlds, is that when Brigham gets on to the new world which he has yet to make, and his wife eats the forbidden fruit, he will do so also—this is all previously arranged †—and

* Book of Mormon, page 58.

† Everything about this programme may not be entirely sequent and consistent, but grains of allowance here and there will enable the reader to comprehend the gist of the argument, and see how readily certain minds could take in this story. The prophet Nephi conveys the idea that everything would have remained *stationary*, had Eve not partaken of the forbidden fruit, and there would have been no one born ; therefore the very purpose of creating the earth as a habitation for others besides Adam and Eve would have been frustrated. To get out of that little difficulty, and to afford Adam ever after the reflection that it was his own voluntary act that drew down upon him and creation the curse of toil and strife, he is placed in a position where the charms of Eve, and the hope of children, overcome the prospective aches and pains of transgression, and he consents to carry out the original programme of the " gods." It seems hardly fair to abuse Adam for this original sin, as the consequences to follow were " joy," " good ; " and " misery " and " sin " were but the shading of the picture. From this statement it will be readily concluded that Adam " fell upward ! "

as a curse falls upon him, upon her, and upon everything
around them, in the course of a thousand years the "cursed"
character of their food will tell upon their systems, and they
will go down into their graves. They will then, however,
have had a lengthened opportunity of preparing numerous
earthly tabernacles, and of seeing their spirit-children come
from the other world. Brigham by some means will get back
to his celestial abode, and will ever afterwards keep an eye
upon his children in the new world. They will in process of
time forget all about him, whence they came, and whither
they are going. He will send messages to some of them occasionally, and keep up as much relationship with them as they
will permit. Finally a scheme will be laid to bring them all
back again into his presence. The eldest son of the family
will be intrusted with the mission, and faith in his name only
will secure the favour of the " father."

Brigham, by this time in his progressive life, has become a
" god," and is the " Being " whom all the children born on his
created world should worship. This is his logic in giving now
to the Latter-Day Saints the man Adam of the garden of Eden
for their deity.

What has here been stated of Brigham's progressive life,
from the dawn of his childhood till he reaches the godhead, is
equally the programme of "the least of the Saints." Every
one of them is destined, some time or other, to make a world,
to go down with an Eve and people it, and pass through all the
routine that has here been traced. The Mormon faith is, as
the reader will perceive, quite extensive.

To account for the existence of " Lucifer, Son of the Morn-
" ing," and the variety of races of men upon the earth, springing from the same parents, the Mormon Prophet relates that
" the spirits " in their " first estate " held a grand convention
to arrange about how they were best to manage the proposed
mundane education while in corporeal form. As the story
goes, everything in this lower world was to be much as it has
been. Jesus, being " the first-begotten of the spirits," was by
seniority permitted the leading speech in that convention. He
proposed to have Adam his father, and Eve his mother, come
down as before related, and do as they did ; and that then he

also would come down among his brothers and sisters, in the fulness of time, and teach them the truths that would elevate and redeem them from their errors, "save them *from* their "sins," and bring them back to his father's presence, purified by the experience of affliction. Lucifer was one of the princes of Adam's spirit-race—the second son of Adam in that world. He was jealous of the popularity which Jesus, his brother, had acquired on account of the scheme proposed by him, and he himself proposed to "save men *in* their sins." Lucifer appears to have been a jovial but proud personage, who thought that the acquisition of experience and pleasure might go hand-in-hand. His proposition was immensely satisfactory to about one-third of the spirits, and they set to work to oppose the scheme of Jesus. Ultimately a fight ensued; the most determined on either side "nailed their colours to the mast," and fought on bravely and without any disposition to surrender. During this contest there were a number of spirits who would not fight on either side, but looked on as *neutrals*. When the contending parties came to the closing struggle, Lucifer was whipped, and with "a third of the host of heaven" he was driven out of that blessed region and was forced to take up his abode in a place that has since become familiarly known as "hell."

There is no attempt made in this mythological Mormon story to account for all the numerous races of men upon the globe, for that was too great a task even for Joseph's mind. But the modern prophet settled the origin of the Caucasian and the African races. The white race comprises all who fought with or for Jesus in heaven, when Lucifer rebelled and was cast out, and therefore they merited an honourable body. The Africans are the neutrals who did not perform quite enough in the fight to necessitate their being driven into the "nether "regions" with Lucifer; neither were they for anything they had done entitled to an honourable body; hence, they came into this world through the lineage of Ham, the son of Noah—for he was a wicked youth.* Africans can enter the Mormon

---

* The Mormons, to account for persons being "possessed of devils," and for the "devils," on one occasion, possessing a herd of swine and running into the sea, allege that the spirits "who kept not their first estate" are so anxious even for mo-

Church and can be baptized like white people, but they " are
" not worthy to receive the priesthood." With such a faith, it
was very consistent that slavery and polygamy should exist together in Utah. From this theory of existence, it is very easy
to perceive how Brigham Young has made Mormonism a religion hostile to all earthly governments and professions of faith.
The following chapter on "the Kingdom of God" brings this
subject to its practical results.

The grandeur of the universe, and the infinity of its wonderful and glorious organizations, that have filled the noblest
minds with veneration and awe, never disturbed the soul of
Brigham Young. The arrogance of unchallenged authority
grows rapidly upon its flattered possessor, and easily carries
him from the level of human beings. How near must Brigham Young have imagined himself to deification when he announced that Adam was God! And what a humiliating spectacle has the Mormon Church presented to the world, in resting
quietly and submissively for nearly twenty years under such
threats of damnation! while, to the credit of the Saints, be it
said, they have as a people refused to abandon their faith in
" the God of their fathers." The mass of the Mormon people
do not believe the doctrine of the Adam deity, but of them
all, one only, Orson Pratt, has dared to make public protest
against that doctrine.

No community of people in Christendom, no church organization upon earth, could have listened to the dogmatic enunciation of a new god for the people's worship, without remonstrance. In Utah some pricked up their ears, but the masses
were unmoved.

Orson Pratt, for presuming to teach a deity contrary to
Brigham's Adam, was for years upon the point of being severed from the Church; at last, ten years ago, he was tried
for rebellion. On that occasion—the Author well remembers
it—Orson Pratt showed a manliness and Christian determination to cling to the truth, that earned for him the admiration

mentary occupation of bodily powers that they were even ready to occupy the
bodies of the swine. These "devils" seem to be very short-sighted, for, if they had
turned into the mountains instead of into the sea, they could have longer enjoyed
their habitations.

of every soul that dared to think and love the God-given liberty of an untrammelled mind. His defence, his mien, his attitude, when, before Brigham and the apostles, he lifted up his
hand, and with upturned face called God and angels to witness that he was ready to meet the doom of his opposition,
rather than violate his conscience and his faith, was the sublimest spectacle of humanity in its noblest phase that the Author ever witnessed. It was the grandeur of the martyr's soul
made manifest. As the apostle stood in Brigham's little office, surrounded by the other apostles of his quorum, not a
voice was heard in his support, not a word was whispered
either to encourage him or relieve his racked and harrowed soul
as he keenly realized the fact that he risked his apostleship and
fellowship with the Church.

When he had expressed his thorough comprehension of the
responsibility of his position, he told, in words of unmistakable earnestness, that when the teachings of the Bible, together
with the revelations of the Prophet Joseph, came into collision
with the teachings of Brigham Young, it was the decision of
his soul that, whatever the cost might be, he " would cling to
" the former."

It was before a small assembly that he was tried, and it was
for some a favour to be there ; but, small in number as the auditory was, there were hearts moved with admiration for the
man who dared to announce, under such circumstances, that
truth was to him greater than Brigham, and that his self-re-
spect was nobler than his apostleship. Galileo before the bar
of the Inquisition was no grander sight.

Poor Orson ! what a sad future was near him.

Brigham branded him with natural stubbornness and told
him that he had always been ungovernable, and had given
trouble to Joseph in his day, and to that he added that the
brave apostle would yet supplicate for forgiveness at his feet.
Poor Orson ! it was martyrdom to him. One soul, at least, in
that auditory felt keenly for him, and, when the council closed,
one person rushed after him, to clasp his hands and bless him
for his God-fearing independence of soul.

But alas ! within thirty-six hours that brave, honest, truthful apostle stood in the Tabernacle before an assembly of thou-

sands, and confessed the error of his ways in opposing the head
of the Church! Ever afterwards he would keep silence upon
the subject! Yet, Orson Pratt is no coward; for his conceptions of truth he would gladly give his life, if duty called for
an assertion of that truth; but he had not the faith to sacrifice
others. Six or seven wives, a score or more of children, dependent for bread on his apostleship and his relationship with
the Church—a long life's labour in the cause of Mormonism,
dearer to his soul than all else, all to be thrown to the winds,
and for him himself to be branded with the stigma of "apos-
"tacy," was more than he could then bear. Those who believed with him in the falsity of Brigham's doctrine, honoured
him for displaying the heroism that bearded the lion in his
den, and probably some have accepted his Galileo-like submission as a dire necessity, for Orson still clings with unchanging
devotion to the faith of the God of his youth.

Orson's submission was painful to his friends, but the
thoughtful hoped for the growth and development of his soul
outside the iron cast of infallible priesthood. From the hour
of that trial he was silently accounted an "Apostate," and for
years there was considered to be no temerity in "digging" at
him from the pulpit. He was sent to Europe on mission, and
treated with marked neglect by the ruling authorities—men
far beneath him in moral and intellectual qualities. He bore
it all in silence, and returned to Utah determined to stand by
his convictions of truth against the Adam deity. His associate
apostles tried to shake him out of their Quorum, and in their
councils they did everything to bring his "stubbornness" to
the point of disfellowship. After two weeks of nightly councils—while Brigham and his twelve were journeying through
the northern settlements in 1868—the point was reached.
Orson would not, however, recant, even before the threat of
disfellowship, but Brigham, at the last moment, entered the
council, and arrested the final action. Brigham needs Orson's
sermons on the Book of Mormon, Polygamy, and the prophecies, and he fears his influence with the people.

CHAPTER XLVI.

THE MORMON THEOCRACY.—All Earthly Government is Rebellion—The Kingdom of God in Utah—The Gentiles to be Destroyed—Why the Mormons pray for the Overthrow of the Republic—Believers to deed all their Property to Brigham Young, "the Lord's" Representative on Earth—The Families of the Saints to be Adopted by the Apostles—Brigham's Word equal to that of God—Orson Hyde illustrates the Kingdoms of the "Gods."

EVERYWHERE among the Saints "the Kingdom" is a household word. It figures in every sermon, is read of in every epistle, and in every business of life it has some bearing. In adversity and in success, in poverty and in wealth, in every position and sphere of action, "the Kingdom" is credited with something. When refractory members of the Church are threatening to "take their own way," the Saints are taught obedience to "the Kingdom" as the highest duty, and are instructed that to secure salvation it must be "the Kingdom of God or nothing."

A coöperative dry-goods and grocery stock-holders' meeting could not well be held in Utah without some mention being made of "the Kingdom." Even in the opening prayer preceding a dance, "the Kingdom" is delicately remembered. Breaking ground for a canal or railroad is an exceedingly appropriate occasion to descant upon its expansion. The arrival of an emigrant train was, in former years, an important time for unfurling its banner. An agricultural fair is considered particularly suitable for holding up "the Kingdom" for admiration; and Brigham's travels through the settlements are truly Pentecostal showers of joy and rejoicing for the processional youngsters who are yet to "carry off the Kingdom."

The visitor in Utah may have difficulty in discovering any

special characteristics of "the Kingdom of Heaven" in the
streets of Salt Lake City, or in the other cities and settlements
of the Territory of Utah, but the Saints none the less honestly
believe that "the Kingdom" spoken of by all the prophets
since the world began is there and nowhere else. In this prevailing sentiment is to be found the explanation of their contempt for all earthly governments—"theirs is the Kingdom."

The apostle Orson Pratt is on this point very lucid and
forcible, and expresses clearly the faith of the Mormons. He
says:

> "The Kingdom of God is an order of government established by di-
> vine authority. It is the only legal government that can exist in any part
> of the universe. All other governments are illegal and are unauthorized.
> . . . . Any people attempting to govern themselves by laws of their own
> making, and by officers of their own appointment, are in direct rebellion
> against the Kingdom of God. . . . . For seventeen hundred years the na-
> tions upon the Western Hemisphere have been entirely destitute of 'the
> Kingdom of God'—entirely destitute of a true and legal government, en-
> tirely destitute of officers legally authorized to rule and govern. All the
> emperors, kings, princes, and presidents, lords, nobles, and rulers, during
> that long night of darkness have acted without authority. . . . . Their
> authority is all assumed—it originated in man. Their laws are not from
> the Great Lawgiver, but the productions of their own false governments;
> their very foundations were laid in rebellion, and the whole superstruc-
> ture, from first to last, is a heterogeneous mass of discordant elements in
> direct opposition to the Kingdom of God, which is the only true Govern-
> ment which should be recognized in earth or in heaven." *

Forty pages are devoted by elder Pratt to this subject, setting forth everything about "the Kingdom" that he could
group together under that designation. After establishing to
his own satisfaction that "the Kingdom" had been given to
the Saints, he concludes his argument with the important announcement:

> "The Almighty has decreed to rend and break in pieces all earthly
> governments, to cast down thrones, to turn and overturn, and break up
> the nations, to send forth his messengers and make a way for the estab-
> lishment of the everlasting Kingdom, to which all others must yield, or
> be prostrated—never more to rise. Awake! then, oh, ye nations, for with
> you the Lord hath a controversy! His Kingdom is now for the last time
> organized upon the earth. All nations are invited to become citizens—it

* "The Kingdom of God," part i., p. 1.

is the only government of safety or refuge upon all the earth. *It hath its seat in the everlasting mountains* * [Utah]—its dreadful majesty shall strike terror to the hearts of kings in the day of His power," etc. †

After these quotations, the reader should be apprised that elder Pratt is a remarkably quiet, retiring, modest man, and one of the advanced mathematicians of the age. His language is not intended to be that of the firebrand or the revolutionist, for he is neither. His sentiments are the offspring of modern revelation, and the eloquence of an inspired priesthood.

The Apostle Orson Pratt.

A faith founded upon such sentiments as these is trained to read in the political revolutions of earthly powers the preparatory workings of " the Lord" for the overthrow of all stable governments, in order to make way for the advancement and growth of the Mormon Kingdom :

> " Thrones shall totter, Babel fall,
> Satan reign no more at all ;
> Saints shall gain the victory,
> Truth prevail o'er land and sea ;
> Gentile tyrants sink to hell ;
> Now 's the day of Israel ! " *

Every malignant and corrupting influence, every disaster—political and natural—which tends to the disintegration of society, is regarded as a sign of the coming end. A desolating plague abroad, the ghastly cholera at home, the earthquake in its throes engulfing cities and holocausts of human victims, the raging tempests of the ocean—drowning in their wild roar the dying shriek of multitudes, the fierce tornado, the stormy thunderbolts of heaven, the warring of the elements, and the conflict of human passions — all, according to the Mormon teaching, tend but to one great purpose—the establishment of " the Kingdom." Nor are the minor details of life less significant. A railway catastrophe, a steamboat explosion, a desolating fire, or any other calamity which may bring tribulation to the hearts of men—one and all are, to the Saint, so many cheering confirmations of his faith, and intimations of the triumphant recognitions of that same " Kingdom."

The mass of the Mormon people would shudder at witnessing these calamities, and could their energy save their fellow-creatures, they would as hastily fly to the rescue as any other people, but their instincts would then be at war with the teachings which they had accepted. This very Orson Pratt, the eloquent exponent of the Mormon faith, apart from Mormonism, never would cherish the fiendish delight of rejoicing in the tribulation of others ; but when he believes that God is punishing the nations for the rejection of Joseph Smith, he is perfectly consistent. The peroration to his tract on " the King- " dom of God " is a perfect gem :

" Awake, for troublous times are at hand ! Nations shall no longer sit at ease ! The troubled elements shall foment, and rage, and dash with tremendous fury ! A voice is heard unto the ends of the earth ! A sound

* Hymn Book, p. 85.

of terror and dismay! A sound of nations rushing to battle—fierce and dreadful is the contest—mighty kingdoms and empires melt away! The destroyer has gone forth—the pestilence that walketh in darkness. The plagues of the last days are at hand, and who shall be able to escape? None but the righteous—none but the upright in heart—none but the children of the Kingdom. They shall be gathered out from among the nations—they shall stand in holy places, and not be moved! But among the wicked, men shall lift up their voices and curse God because of his sore judgments, and die. And there shall be a voice of mourning and lamentation unto the ends of the earth; for *the cup of the indignation of the Almighty shall be poured out without mixture of mercy*, because they would not receive his messengers, but hardened their hearts against the warning proclamation—against *the gospel of the Kingdom*—and against the great preparatory work for the universal reign of the King of kings and Lord of lords."

When the fratricidal war between the Northern and Southern States filled the nation with mourning, Utah alone rejoiced. Every flash that thrilled along the telegraph wires announcing a terrible battle and the immolation of tens of thousands, was welcome to the Saints, and inspired the Tabernacle orators with higher flights of eloquence, and clothed them with greater prophetic power. Though the Northern representatives in Congress had not offered as much opposition to the affairs of Utah as those from the South, the sympathy of Brigham and the apostles was wholly with the Confederates. Brigham wanted to see the Union severed. The Prophet Joseph had predicted it, and, very consistently, Brigham desired to see the fulfilment of the prophecy; besides, had secession from the Union been successful in 1861, it would have been seized upon by Brigham as a precedent for the withdrawal of Utah from the Federacy whenever he deemed it safe to run up his independent bunting, and verify the poet's dream:

> " High on the mountains the ensign we see ;
> Fall'n is the Gentile power,
> Soon will their reign be o'er,
> Tyrants must rule no more,
> Israel is free ! " *

The inspiration of building up this literal kingdom has not only been demoralizing and pernicious in sentiment, but it has

* Hymn 77.

literally robbed the Mormons of the blessings of Christianity,
and sent them back to the worst ages of Hebrew barbarism to
collect the materials of their faith. For one sentiment of peace
towards all mankind uttered by Christ, to be heard from the
lips of modern apostles in the Mormon Tabernacle, the audiences there have listened to ten thousand from the men of
blood and war who revelled in the destruction of the enemies
of ancient Israel. In the written faith Christ is the head of
the Mormon Church ; in its practical, every-day history " the
" God of Battles " is the inspiring deity. The " Lamb of God "
is displaced by " the Lion of the Lord," and the Throne of
Grace is forgotten in " the might of the Kingdom."

To build up this theocracy every effort has been made, and
ingenuity has been taxed to the uttermost for the furtherance
of this idea, even at the sacrifice of the most sacred principles
of individual honour and happiness.

This frenzied lust of power, more, perhaps, than passion,
was the foundation of Brigham Young's vehement advocacy of
the practice of polygamy. That he could build up " the Kingdom " faster at home by the natural increase of the Saints than
he could by the proselytizing of the missionaries abroad, was
his favourite expression. All were urged from the pulpit to
the discharge of their duties to " the Kingdom," and on silver-
haired, tottering age was this obligation placed, as much as
upon the man of early or middle life, while, incredible as it may
seem, the Legislature provided for the legitimate marriage of
boys at fifteen and girls at twelve years of age ! Nothing was
to stand in the way of the increase of " the Kingdom." A
son might, if he preferred it, marry his half-sister, and a father
might take unto himself the daughter of his wife ; it was all
right—if for " the Kingdom." Nothing seemed so meritorious
in the eyes of the leaders as a loving, youthful pair beginning
life's journey in a tent, or in a wagon-bed, if they were not
fortunate enough to possess the shelter of adobe walls and a
shingle roof, and thrice blessed and honoured was he who had
faith to take a Rachel and a Leah to the altar at the same moment, and be for ever indifferent to the injunctions that " these
" *twain* shall be one flesh."

" Build up the Kingdom, build up the Kingdom," has

been the unceasing call of the priesthood, and "the Lord" has blessed the labours of the faithful till Utah is swarming with the lambs of the flock in every settlement, from Bear Lake in the north to the sunny regions of the Colorado in the south.

But all this preaching and marrying were but the preliminaries, the stepping-stones that all the world could see and comprehend. Beyond these were found greater supports to "the Kingdom" in "consecration" and "adoption."

The Saints are taught that "the Lord" requires of them a tithing of all they possess in this world, and after that an annual tenth of their increase. But that is only preliminary to greater blessings that "the Lord" has in store for them, for when they have increased in faith "the Lord" will afford them the opportunity of "consecrating" to Him all that they possess. Their houses and lands, their chairs and tables, their horses and pigs, their hammers and saws, their buggies and wagons, and all and everything that they own or hope to own, to be deeded over to "the Lord's" Trustee in Trust—Brigham Young; and thereafter the bishops will sit in judgment to assign to Jones one talent, to Smith five, to Young ten, and so on, according to their necessities, and their several abilities to use and increase that over which "the Lord" has made them stewards. All this is for "the Kingdom's sake."

Illustrative of the systematic manner in which "the Lord" manages earthly affairs, the following *bona fide* consecration document is valuable.

"BE IT KNOWN BY THESE PRESENTS that I, JESSE W. FOX, of Great Salt Lake City, in the County of Great Salt Lake, and Territory of Utah, for and in consideration of the sum of One Hundred ($100) Dollars, and the good will which I have to the CHURCH OF JESUS CHRIST OF LATTER-DAY SAINTS, give and convey unto BRIGHAM YOUNG, Trustee in trust for said Church, his successor in office, and assigns, all my claim to and ownership of the following described property, to wit:

One house and lot, being lot 6, block 60, plat C., G. S. Lake City; value of said house and lot........	$1,000
One city lot, as platted in plat E, being lot 2, block 6, value..........	100
East half of lot 1, block 12, five acres, plat G., S. L. Co., value........	50
Lot 1, block 14, Jordan plat, containing nine acres, value..........	75
Two cows, 50, two calves 15 dollars........	65
One mare, 100 dollars, one colt, 50 dollars..........	150
One watch, 20 dollars, one clock, 12 dollars..........	32
Clothing, 300 dollars, beds and bedding, 125 dollars..........	425
One stove, 20 dollars, household furniture, 210 dollars..........	230

Total amount, Twenty-one hundred and twenty-seven Dollars.................$2,127

—together with all the rights, privileges, and appurtenances thereunto belonging or appertaining ; I also covenant and agree that I am the lawful
claimant and owner of said property, and will warrant and for ever defend
the same unto the said TRUSTEE IN TRUST, his successor in office,
and assigns, against the claims of my heirs, assigns, or any person whomsoever.   JESSE W. FOX.

Witnesses : { HENRY McEWAN,
             { JOHN M. BOLLWINKEL.
TERRITORY OF UTAH, COUNTY OF GREAT SALT LAKE.

"I, E. Smith, Judge of the Probate Court for said county, certify that
the signer of the above transfer, personally known to me, appeared this
second day of April, A. D. 1857, and acknowledged that he, of his own
choice, executed the foregoing transfer.   E. SMITH."

The transfer by deed of all personal property and estate to
the Church is designated in modern revelation " The Order of
"Enoch." To have called it " The Order of Joseph Smith,"
or by the name of any modern apostle or prophet, would have
aroused no enthusiasm in the devotional mind ; but associating
it with Enoch lent to the " Order " the enchantment of distance. Enoch had been distinguished for devotion and piety,
and had been triumphantly translated from this wicked world
and vale of tears. The inference was clear—those who " con-
"secrated" were entitled to Heaven's choicest favours when
" the Kingdom " was triumphant.

The preaching in the Tabernacle and in the ward meetings
throughout Utah, at the date of Mr. Fox's consecration, was
almost wholly devoted to the Order of Enoch, and many believing souls placed all they possessed for ever beyond their
own personal control and robbed their children of their rightful inheritances.* But the majority of the Saints could not be
brought to consign themselves to the tender mercies of the

* In an unguarded moment of inspiration, Brigham declared that " The Order
"of Enoch " was an excellent barrier to Apostacy. " Tie the calf at home," said he,
" and the cow is sure to return." " Where a man's treasure is, there will his heart
"be also." Let but a man's property be " consecrated," and it is not only alienated
from his heirs, but is beyond the recall of the donor himself should he ever regret
his " consecration " or apostatize from ' the Kingdom." He has tied himself up
for ever, and over his own property he becomes a steward or mere " tenant at will."
To leave the Territory was an impossibility : he had nothing to sell. He *must* remain, or go forth a beggar. There are now several cases in the courts of Utah in
which children are seeking to recover from the " Trustee in Trust " the title to
their deceased father's property.

priesthood, and thus the purposes of " the Lord " had to be deferred.

Had the Saints accepted this " Order of Enoch," and transferred into the hands of Brigham Young all that they possessed, the slavery of Utah would have been without parallel in the history of the world. Mediæval serfdom and the tyranny of feudal barons and feudal kings might be harmonious with their times; but to entertain the wild dream of reversing the order of progress and civilization and establishing, in the free Republic of America, in the nineteenth century of the Christian era, the basest degradation of the human intellect would be beyond all conception were it not, in the Mormon theory of " consecration," proved indeed too true.

To effectively establish this great " Kingdom," Brigham Young, after the death of Joseph Smith, introduced among the Mormons the " law of adoption," which for shrewdness challenges all comparison.

This law of adoption assumes that Joseph Smith was appointed and ordained from before the creation of the world to be the head and ruler of " the Last Dispensation." Adam, Noah, Abraham, Moses, Elijah, and Jesus had each their place in the world's history as great men to whom special dispensations had been accorded; but to Joseph was given " the Dis- " pensation of the Fulness of Times," which, by bringing into harmony the labours of the prophets and apostles of all ages should be the crowning work of the heavens above and of the earth beneath.

The declaration—" No man cometh to the Father but by " me " was applied by modern apostles to Joseph Smith, and now to Brigham Young, and should he have a thousand successors, it would be considered as equally applicable to them all. Rome never dreamed of a completeness of mental subjugation which might be compared with the actualities of the Mormon Temple.

Of Brigham's relation to the people, his second counsellor—Grant—said :

" He holds the keys of life and salvation upon the earth ; and you may strive as much as you please, but *not one of you will ever go through the straight gate into the Kingdom of God, except those that go through by that*
31

man and his brethren, for they will be the persons whose inspection you must pass." *

Heber, the first counsellor, was, if possible, still more emphatic :

"I have often said that *the word of our leader and Prophet is the Word of God to this people.* We cannot see God, we cannot hold converse with Him, but He has given us a man that we can talk to, and *thereby know His will, just as well as if God himself were present with us.* I am no more afraid to risk my salvation in the hands of this man, than *I am to trust myself in the hands of the Almighty.* He will lead me right if *I do as he says* in every particular and circumstance." †

Before leaving Nauvoo these assumptions took practical shape in the "sealing," by the law of adoption, of heads of families to Brigham and the apostles in the Temple. This doctrine was first whispered by one person to another as a great mystery, just as polygamy had previously been silently introduced. After this whispering had done its work in a confused way, the apostles met with the Quorums of priesthood and taught them that "the Kingdom" had been given unto Joseph, and it was necessary, in order to obtain salvation, that all the Saints should be sealed to one another, and finally to him.

The marriages of the Gentile world being utterly unauthorized, it becomes necessary for married persons, on accepting Mormonism, to come before the altar and be sealed by the Mormon high priesthood as husband and wife—the previous relationship being without the sanction of "the Lord." Until this initiation, the children born in Gentile wedlock are "aliens from "the commonwealth of Israel:" children born after the sealing of the father and mother at the altar are the rightful heirs with Isaac to all the blessings of "the Kingdom." To place the former children on an equality with the latter, they must be sealed before the altar by the rites of the priesthood to their own fathers and mothers. That family contract being quite satisfactory, the father and mother now find that they themselves are without legitimate parentage; for the same logic that made their children aliens places them also in the same awkward predicament. To extricate, therefore, the husband

---

* *Deseret News*, December, 1856.   † *Ibid.*, October 1, 1856.

and wife from this dilemma, Brigham taught that it was the
privilege of the Saints to be adopted into the families of the
twelve apostles, and they were all to be sealed to Joseph, and
Joseph was to be sealed to Christ. This was the briefest way
of reaching a full salvation.

For the attainment of this object, the building of the Temple at Nauvoo was hastened, and the faithful Saints were invited to receive " endowments," and those who were worthy
and desired it, to be sealed to the apostles. This was not
simply a ceremony; a proper filial care for the parents was
enjoined, and the adopted son of Brigham was to be as obedient and devoted to his adopted father's interest as the offspring of his own loins.

At this time Brigham exhibited his usual weakness for a
favourite. A very handsome lady, who had forsaken a luxurious home at Boston, to dwell among the Saints in Nauvoo,
was at that period the idol of his eyes. His faithful and devoted wife—the companion of his youth and the mother of his
children—was overlooked for the educated and attractive Mrs.
C——. This lady became for a time the Queen of " the Kingdom." *

When the believing Saint approached the altar, and Brigham became his father by adoption, Mrs. C—— at the same
time, and by the same ceremony, became his mother: the wife
of the adopted son in like manner vowed fealty to Brigham as
her father, and to Mrs. C—— as her mother.

To impress the idea of this ladder of salvation and exaltation in the kingdom in this world, and in that which is to
come, upon the minds of the British Saints, the apostle Orson
Hyde published, in 1846, in the *Millennial Star*, the following
illustration :

" The above diagram shows the order and unity of the Kingdom of
God. The Eternal Father sits at the head, crowned King of kings and
Lord of lords. Wherever the other lines meet, there sits a King and Priest
unto God, bearing rule, authority, and dominion under the Father. He is

* To-day that queenly lady lives in Salt Lake City, left " severely alone : "
a sad picture of deserted greatness. Another took her place in the Prophet's affections, and again a third has supplanted the favoured second, and she also lives in
painful neglect.

one with the Father, because his kingdom is joined to his Father's, and becomes part of it.

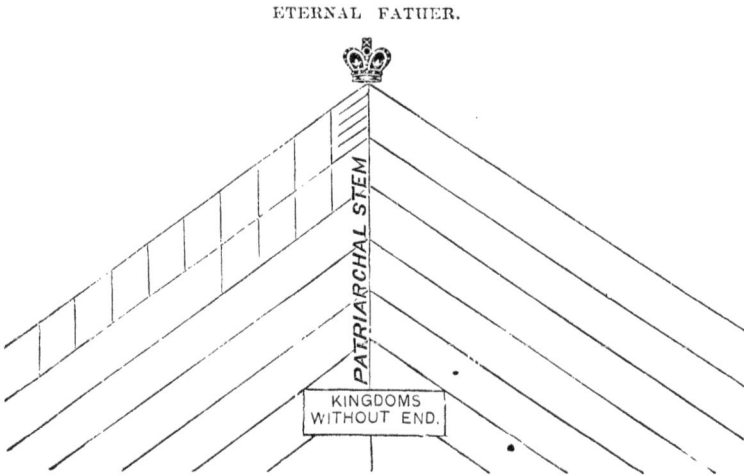

ORSON HYDE'S DIAGRAM OF THE CELESTIAL KINGDOM.

"The most eminent and distinguished prophets, who have laid down their lives for their testimony (Jesus among the rest), will be crowned at the head of the largest kingdoms under the Father, and will be one with Christ, as Christ is one with the Father, for their kingdoms are all joined together; and such as do the will of the Father, the same are his mothers, sisters, and brothers. He that has been faithful over a few things will be made ruler over many things : he that has been faithful over ten talents shall have dominion over ten cities, and he that has been faithful over five talents shall have dominion over five cities, and to every man will be given a kingdom and dominion according to his merit, powers, and ability to govern and control. It may be seen from the above that there are kingdoms of all sizes, and an infinite variety to suit all grades of merit and ability. The chosen vessels unto God are the kings and priests that are placed at the head of these kingdoms. These have received their washings and anointings in the Temple of God on this earth ; they have been chosen, ordained, and anointed kings and priests, to reign as such in the resurrection of the just. Such as have not received the fulness of the priesthood (for the fulness of the priesthood includes the authority of both king and priest), and have not been anointed and ordained in the Temple of the Most High, may obtain salvation in the celestial kingdom, but not a celestial crown. Many are called to enjoy celestial glory, but few are chosen to wear a celestial crown, or are worthy to be rulers in the Celestial Kingdom."

CHAPTER XLVII.

THE BOOK OF ABRAHAM.—An Extraordinary Document—The Prophet buys Egyptian Mummies—Translates Papyri found with them—Another Translation by a Scientist—Delusion, Deception, or Folly?—Was Joseph Smith a "Spirit Medium?"

DURING the lifetime of the Mormon Prophet much importance was attached to his "translation" of the papyri found with some Egyptian mummies, which he designated "The "Book of Abraham." The translation has been extensively published in the Mormon papers, both in England and America, and has probably been translated into different languages in Europe where the elders have found converts. In addition to its newspaper publicity it formed the chief attraction of a pamphlet published in Liverpool in 1851, by the apostle Richards, under the title of "The Pearl of Great Price"—a title which, by the way, the profane regarded as more applicable to its cost than its quality.

The Mormons were taught to regard the finding of the mummies, the papyri, and the translation, as a manifestation of "the Lord" working indirectly in a providential way with "his servant Joseph;" thus corroborating his claim to be an inspired translator, and confirming the faith of the Saints by the supposed harmony of his teaching with that of Abraham. The apostle-editor, Richards, was himself so impressed with the stamp of divinity apparent, as he thought, in the contents of the "Pearl of Great Price," including the Book of Abraham, that he conceived it impossible for any one to carefully peruse the revelations, "translations," and narratives therein "without being deeply impressed with a sense of the divine "calling of the man through whom they have been communi- "cated to the world."

When Joseph, according to his statement, translated the
Book of Mormon from the gold-plates, no one was ever permitted to see him at his work : he sat at the other side of a
blanket,* which served as a curtain to separate him from his
amanuensis, and in that position he dictated to the latter the
contents of the book. The *fac-simile* of the original characters on the plates, found in another chapter, was not accompanied with its English translation, nor was it sufficiently extensive of itself to engage the attention of the *savants* who
might have expressed an opinion concerning its genuineness ;
but in the Book of Abraham which has confirmed so much the
faith of the Saints in the Book of Mormon, Joseph furnishes
the learned with an opportunity for testing his claim to the
gift of interpretation.

The correctness or incorrectness of his so-called translation
of the gold-plates admitted of neither corroboration nor detection. These men, " because of their great faith," were permitted to see the plates, and " an angel " told them that the translation was correct. Eight other men of Joseph's acquaintance
were chosen " to witness " to the world that they had seen the
plates, and " hefted " them, and that the engraved characters
had the appearance of ancient workmanship. Beyond this, all

---

* The critics state that Joseph had on his side of the curtain the " lost manu-
"script " of Solomon Spaulding, which he interpolated with extracts from the Old
and New Testaments, adding to them his own crude knowledge of Methodism, and
thus palmed upon his credulous scribes, Harris and Cowdery, the Book of Mormon.
This is the prevailing view of the opponents of Mormonism as to the origin of that
book. But it may yet be accepted that Joseph's seclusion behind the curtain with
his crystal " interpreters " answers to the dark *séances* so common in the experience
of modern Spiritualism. There is much in Joseph's history to confirm such a theory. He has frequently been charged with pretending to give revelations through
" a peep-stone " which he placed in his hat, then putting his face against the hat
and excluding all light therefrom, in that manner is said to have read the language
of the heavens. The Author is acquainted with a gentleman who, when he was a
boy, was frequently in the company of Joseph at Nauvoo, as his father was very
intimate with the Prophet. This gentleman is what is now called clairvoyant, and
relates that Joseph frequently put his " Urim and Thummim," " interpreters," or
" peep-stones," or whatever else they might be called, into his hat when the boy
was visiting him, and by looking upon them as Joseph did, he claims to have had
wonderful panoramic visions. There are multitudes of persons throughout the
world—many in Utah now—who claim perfect familiarity with this " peep-stone "
business, and the better Joseph Smith is known, the nearer he approaches those
" gifted " persons, and the easier is he understood.

is faith. In the publication of the hieroglyphics and their translation in the Book of Abraham it is quite otherwise.

Hundreds of scholars have made the science of hieroglyphics a special study, and without difficulty can read the inscriptions on the tombs of the Ptolemies and Pharaohs and decipher the picture-writing upon the walls of the ruined temples at Thebes. Impressed with the interest of a corroboration or a contradiction by science of Joseph's inspired translation of the papyri found with the mummies, two French travellers, MM. Remy and Brenchley, during a visit to Utah in 1855, gathered up the Prophet's story, and in the work published by these gentlemen in 1860, in Paris, two translations are given.

Some time in July, 1833, these mummies, with other curiosities, were on public exhibition at Kirtland, at that time the headquarters of the Prophet. When the proprietor of the mummies exhibited to Joseph the papyri found with them, he unhesitatingly gave an interpretation of them, and in return the showman handed to the inspired man the following certificate :

" This is to make known to all who may be desirous concerning the knowledge of Mr. Joseph Smith, junr., in deciphering the ancient Egyptian hieroglyphic characters in my possession, which I have in many eminent cities shown to the most learned, and from the information that I could ever learn or meet with, I find that of Mr. Smith, junr., to correspond in the most minute matters.

" MICHAEL H. CHANDLER,
" Travelling with and Proprietor of Egyptian mummies.

The reader will not fail to remark the impudence of such a document. What possible value could be attached to the statement of an ignorant showman about the " deciphering" of a language of which he had not the slightest knowledge ? But Chandler wanted a customer for his mummies, and the Saints purchased them for Joseph a few days afterwards, " and " much to our joy," says the Prophet, " we found that one of "these rolls contained the writings of Abraham, another the " writings of Joseph," etc. . . . " Truly we can say that the " Lord is beginning to reveal the abundance of truth," etc. In 1842, the inspired translation was first published in the *Times and Seasons*, with the accompanying preface :

"Who these ancient inhabitants of Egypt were I do not at present say. The record of Abraham and Joseph, found with the mummies, is beautifully written on papyrus with black, and a small part red ink, or paint, in perfect preservation. The characters are such as you find upon the coffins of mummies, hieroglyphics, etc., with many characters and letters like the present [though probably not quite so square] form of the Hebrew without points. The records were obtained from one of the catacombs in Egypt, near the place where once stood the renowned city of Thebes, by the celebrated French traveller Antonio Sebolo in the year 1831. He procured a license from Mehemet Ali, then viceroy of Egypt, under the protection of Chevalier Drovetti, the French consul, in the year 1828, and employed 433 men four months and two days—if I understand correctly, Egyptian or Turkish soldiers—at from four to six cents per diem for each man, entered the catacombs, June 7th, 1831, and procured eleven mummies. There were several hundred mummies in the same catacomb. . . . . On his way from Alexandria he put in at Trieste, and after ten days' illness expired in 1832. Previous to his death he made a will of the whole to his nephew, Mr. Michael H. Chandler (then in Philadelphia), whom he supposed to have been in Ireland. Accordingly the whole were sent to Dublin, and Mr. Chandler's friends ordered them to New York, where they were received at the custom-house in the spring or winter of 1833. In the month of April of the same year Mr. Chandler paid the duties and took possession of his mummies. Mr. Chandler, who expected to find diamonds or other valuables, was disappointed. He was immediately told, while yet in the custom-house, that there was no man in the city who could translate the roll; but was referred by the same gentleman to Mr. Joseph Smith, junr., who, continued he, possesses some kind of power or gifts by which he had previously translated similar characters. I was then unknown to Mr. Chandler, neither did he know that such a book or work as the Records of the Nephites had been brought before the public. He took his collection on to Philadelphia, where he obtained his certificate of the learned (see *Messenger and Advocate*, p. 235), and thence came on to Kirtland. Thus I have given a brief history of the manner in which the writings of Abraham and Joseph have been preserved, and how I came into possession of the same —a correct translation of which I shall give in its proper place." *

When the travellers, Messrs. Remy and Brenchley, returned to Paris, they placed the hieroglyphics in the hands of a young *savant* of the Museum of the Louvre, M. Théodule Devéria, whose translation is here placed parallel with that of the Prophet Smith :

* "Autobiography of Joseph Smith."

A Fac-Simile from the Book of Abraham.

No. 1.

No. I.

HIEROGLYPHICS REPRESENTING THE RESURRECTION OF OSIRIS.

INTERPRETATION

By the Mormon Prophet.	By the Hieroglyphists.
FIG. I. The angel of the Lord.	FIG. I. The soul of Osiris, under the form of a hawk (which should have a human head).
II. Abraham fastened upon an altar.	II. Osiris coming to life on his funeral couch, which is in the shape of a lion.
III. The idolatrous priest of Elkenah attempting to offer up Abraham as a sacrifice.	III. The god Anubis (who should have a jackal's head) effecting the resurrection of Osiris.
IV. The altar for sacrifice by the idolatrous priest standing before the gods of Elkenah, Libnah, Mahmackrah, Korash, and Pharaoh.	IV. The funereal-bed of Osiris, under which are placed the four sepulchral vessels called canopes, each of them surmounted by the head of the four genii.
V. The idolatrous god of Elkenah.	V. Kebh-son-iw, with a hawk's head.
VI. The idolatrous god of Libnah.	VI. Tioumautew, with a jackal's head.
VII. The idolatrous god of Mahmackrah.	VII. Hâpi, with a dog's head.
VIII. The idolatrous god of Korash.	VIII. Amset, with a human head.
IX. The idolatrous god of Pharaoh.	IX. The sacred crocodile, symbolic of the god Sebet.
X. Abraham in Egypt.	X. Altar laden with offerings.
XI. Design to represent the pillars of heaven as understood by the Egyptians.	XI. An ornament peculiar to Egyptian art.
XII. Raukeeyang, signifying expanse, or the firmament over our heads; but in this case, in relation to this subject, the Egyptians meant it to signify Shaumau, to be high, or the heavens, answering to the Hebrew Shaumahyeem.	XII. Customary representation of ground in Egyptian paintings. (The word Shauman is not Egyptian, and the Hebrew word שָׁמַיִם is badly copied.

M. Devéria observes, with respect to this papyrus, that he never saw the resurrection of Osiris represented in funerary MSS. He is of opinion that, if it exists, it must be extremely rare, and that if the present figure be not a modern imitation of the great bas-reliefs in which this mythological scene is represented, it has at all events been altered, for Anubis should have a jackal's head.

No. II.

INTERPRETATION

By the Mormon Prophet.	By the Hieroglyphists.
Fig. I. Kolob, signifying the first creation, nearest to the celestial, or the residence of God. First in government, the last pertaining to the measurement of time. The measurement according to the celestial time signifies one day to a cubit. One day in Kolob is equal to a thousand years, according to the measurement of this earth, which is called by the Egyptians Jah-oh-ch.	Fig. I. The spirit of the four elements (according to Champollion), or rather of the four winds, or the four cardinal points; the soul of the terrestrial world. This god is *always* represented with four rams' heads, and his image has certainly been altered here.—They have also evidently made a very clumsy attempt at copying the double human head of the god figured above, fig. 2, instead of the four rams' heads. The word Jah-oh-ch has nothing Egyptian in it; it resembles the Hebrew word יהוה badly transscribed.
II. Stands next to Kolob, called by the Egyptians Oliblish, which is the next grand governing creation, near to the celestial, or the place where God resides; holding the key of power, also, pertaining to other planets; as revealed from God to Abraham, as he offered sacrifice upon an altar which he had built unto the Lord.	II. Ammon-Ra, with two human heads, meant probably to represent both the invisible or mysterious principle of Ammon, and the visible or luminous principle of Ra, the sun; or else the double and simultaneous principle of father and son; which characterizes divinity in the religion of ancient Egypt.—The word *Oliblish* is no more Egyptian than those already met with, nor than those which are to be found in the Mormon explanation.
III. Is made to represent God, sitting upon his throne, clothed with power and authority: with a crown of eternal light upon his head: representing, also, the grand key-words of the Holy Priesthood, as revealed to Adam in the Garden of Eden, as also to Seth, Noah, Melchizedek, Abraham, and all to whom the Priesthood was revealed.	III. The god Ra, the sun, with a hawk's head, seated in his boat. In the field the two symbolical figuring, according to M. de Rougé, the fixed points of an astronomical period.

HYPOCEPHALUS, OR FUNERARY DISK, TO WHICH THE EGYPTIANS ASCRIBED THE VIRTUE OF PRESERVING THE PRINCIPLE OF LIFE OR VITAL HEAT IN THE MUMMIES, AND OF DEVELOPING ITSELF IN THE DAY OF THE RESURRECTION.

By the Mormon Prophet.

IV. Answers to the Hebrew word *Raukeeyang*, signifying expanse, or the firmament of the heavens; also a numerical figure, in Egyptian, signifying one thousand; answering to the measuring of the time of Oliblish, which is equal with Kolob in its revolution, and in its measuring of time.

V. Is called in Egyptian Enish-go-on-dosh; that is, one of the governing planets also; and is said by the Egyptians to be the sun, and to borrow its light from Kolob through the medium of Kae-e-vanrash, which is the grand Key, or in other words, the governing power, which governs fifteen other fixed planets or stars, as also Floeese, or the moon, the earth, and the sun, in their annual revolutions. This planet receives its power through the medium of Kli-flos-is-es, or Hah-ko-kau-beam, the stars represented by numbers 22 and 23, receiving light from the revolutions of Kolob.

VI. Represents the earth in its four quarters.

VII. Represents God sitting upon his throne, revealing through the heavens the grand Key-Words of the Priesthood; as, also, the sign of the Holy Ghost unto Abraham in the form of a dove.

VIII. Contains writing that cannot be revealed unto the world; but is to be had in the Holy Temple of God.

IX. Ought not to be revealed at the present time.

X. Also.

By the Hieroglyphists.

IV. The Hebrew word רָקִיעַ, Roki'a, expansum, solidum, cœlum, firmamentum, besides being badly described, has no relation whatever to this figure, which represents a mummified hawk, called in Egyptian Ah'em. It is the symbol of the divine repose of death; its extended wings have reference to the resurrection.

V. The *mystic cow*, the *great cow*, symbolizing the inferior hemisphere of the heavens. It is called the *virgin cow* at ch. 162 of the funerary ritual, which particularly enjoins that its image be painted on the hypocephalus, and another image of it in gold on the throat of the defunct. It is the form of Hathor, who figures on several monuments under the name of *noub*, gold. Behind the cow is a goddess, whose head, represented by a mystic eye in a disk, is incorrectly copied.

VI. The four funerary genii, the sons of Osiris, Amset, Hâpi, Tioumautew, and Kebhsoniw.

VII. The form of Ammon, with a bird's tail, or Horammon (?). An ithyphallic serpent, with human legs, offers him a symbolical eye. This last figure has certainly been altered in the hypocephalus of the Mormons.

VIII., IX., X., XI. Four lines of the linear hieroglyphic text, which are numbered from bottom to top, instead of from top to bottom. The meaning is: *O great God in Sekhem ; O great God, Lord of heaven, earth, and hell. . . . Osiris S'es'enq.* These

By the Mormon Prophet.

XI. Also.—If the world can find out the numbers, so let it be. Amen.

XII. to XX, will be given in the own due time of the Lord.

The above translation is given as far as we have any right to give, at the present time.

By the Hieroglyphists.

last words inform us that the personage in whose mummy this hypocephalus was found was called S'es'enq or S'esonchis, a name written *Sesak* in the Bible, and of which there is no known example anterior to the twenty-second dynasty; that is, to the ninth century before our era, but which may be much posterior to it.

XII.–XV. Four lines of writing similar to the former, of which they are the pendant. They appear to be numbered upside down, and are illegibly copied.

XVI. – XVII. Two more lines which cannot be deciphered in the copy. It begins above the god with two human heads, fig. 2; and there is in it twice mention made of a sacred dwelling-place in Heliopolis.

XIX.–XXI. These columns of writing, illegible in the copy. It is evident to me that several of the figures to be found in these various MSS. have been intentionally altered.   T. Devéria.

No. III.

Initial painting of a funerary MS. of the Lower epoch, which cannot be anterior to the beginning of the Roman dominion.

INTERPRETATION

By the Mormon Prophet.

Fig. I. Abraham sitting upon Pharaoh's throne by the politeness of the king, with a crown upon his head, representing the Priesthood, as emblematical of the grand Presidency in Heaven; with the sceptre of justice and judgment in his hand.

By the Hieroglyphists.

Fig. I. Osiris on his seat.

4

By the Mormon Prophet.

II. King Pharaoh, the first person on the left of our engraving, whose name is given in the characters above his head.

III. Signifies Abraham in Egypt; as before in the interpretation of No. I., fig. 10.

IV. Prince of Pharaoh, King of Egypt, as written above the hand.

V. Shulem, one of the king's principal waiters, as represented by the characters above his hand.

VI. Olimlah, a slave belonging to the prince. Abraham is reasoning upon the principles of astronomy in the king's court.

By the Hieroglyphists.

II. The goddess Isis. The star she carries in her right hand is the sign of life.

III. Altar, with the offering of the deceased, surrounded with lotus flowers, signifying the offering of the defunct.

IV. The goddess Ma.

V. The deceased led by Ma into the presence of Osiris. His name is Horus, as may be seen in the prayer which is at the bottom of the picture, and which is addressed to the divinities of the four cardinal points.

VI. An unknown divinity, probably Anubis; but his head, which ought to be that of a jackal, has been changed.

The English text of the "Book of Abraham," published with these rude engravings, covers ten pages in the "Pearl of "Great Price," entitled "A translation of some ancient rec-"ords that have fallen into our hands from the catacombs of "Egypt, purporting to be the writings of Abraham, written "by his own hand upon papyrus." *

In all probability, many of the Mormons will be staggered by the translation of M. Devéria, but many more will treat it with indifference. Those who devote some consideration to this subject will be very apt to carry their thoughts to the translation of the Book of Mormon, where their confidence in its divinity and truthfulness is not likely by this circumstance to be much increased. Brigham Young has been in possession of the two translations for several years, but the Mormon press has been silent on the opposition of science to inspiration.

With the Prophet's story of the supposed Book of Abraham placed side by side with the translation of the papyrus by the scientist, the reader may possibly conclude that Joseph

* *Times and Seasons*, vol. iii., p. 704.

Smith imposed upon the credulity of the Saints, and hence
that the claim throughout this work that Joseph was sincere is
here unsupported. The Author, notwithstanding, still clings
to the assertion that Joseph believed sincerely that he was inspired, and the pride with which he gave this translation to
the world supports that conclusion. Had he ever doubted the
correctness of his translation, he never would have given to
the public the *fac-simile* of the characters and his translation
of them. Joseph Smith at this time was over thirty years of
age, and had passed through too rough an experience to have
risked his reputation upon anything about which he had the
slightest doubt. If the translation of the scientist is correct,
and it bears upon its face evidence to that effect, then Joseph
was as much deceived as many others have been before and
since, who have laid claim to the possession of divine and supernatural powers, and the receiving of revelations. A noticeable case is given elsewhere in this work, where it is related
how Joseph Morris gave to a handful of his people, in a moment of extreme peril, a revelation from God that " not a hair
" of their heads should be injured," and the very next minute
two women were killed and the jaw of a little girl blown off, and
before that difficulty terminated the very revelator himself lay
stiff in death among his own people, many of whom *still* believe him to have been a prophet and revelator! The revelations of Joseph Smith concerning the throwing down of towers,
scattering the watchmen, and the restoration of the exiles to
Jackson county, Missouri, were as signally unfulfilled, yet the
Mormons believe them still to have been divine, and Joseph a
revelator! In the face of such palpable failures no rational interpretation can be given to what is called " the faith of the
" Saints," than that that faith being attested in some instances
within their own experience by positive truths, they dread to
harbour a doubt of anything that comes to them with the
same authority, lest in doing so they should " doubt the
" Lord." *

---

* Since the foregoing was written, the Author has received the following communication from a gentleman who has been about thirty years associated with Mormonism, and who personally knew well the Prophet :

" Joseph Smith was no more and no less than a ' spirit-medium '—more *impres-
sional* than clairvoyant or clairaudient. Being the first of the age operated upon

During one of the periods of Joseph's concealment from
the officers of the law he indited an "Address to the Church
"of Jesus Christ of Latter-Day Saints," dated Nauvoo, September 6th, 1842, in which he gives the names of his visitors
from the other world, which tends to confirm the supposition
that the Mormon Prophet was nothing more than a "medium"
through whom it is claimed the spirits of the dead communicated. Joseph says:

"And again, what do we hear? Glad tidings from Cumorah! *Moroni*,
an angel from heaven, declaring the fulfilment of the prophets—the books
to be revealed. *A voice of the Lord* in the wilderness of Fayette, Seneca
county, declaring the three witnesses to bear record of the book. *The
voice of Michael* on the banks of the Susquehanna, detecting the devil when
he appeared as an angel of light. *The voice of Peter, James*, and *John* in
the wilderness between Harmony, Susquehanna county, and Colesville,
Broome county, on the Susquehanna river, declaring themselves as possessing the keys of the kingdom, and of the dispensation of the fulness
of times.

"And again, *the voice of God*, in the chamber of old father Whitmer,
in Fayette, Seneca county, and at sundry times, and in divers places,
through all the travels and tribulations of this Church of Jesus Christ of
Latter-Day Saints. And *the voice of Michael* the archangel; *the voice of
Gabriel and of Raphael*, and of *divers angels*, from *Michael* or *Adam* down
to the present time, *all declaring each one their dispensation, their rights,
their keys, their honours, their majesty and glory, and the power of their
priesthood*; giving line upon line, precept upon precept; here a little, and
there a little—giving us consolation by holding forth that which is to
come, confirming our hope."

To the reader unacquainted with the phenomena of spiritualism the claims of the founder of Mormonism to revelation
and the gift of interpretation must bear the stamp of craziness
or imposture, but the believer in such manifestations experiences
no difficulty in comprehending the position which he occupied.

Probably all the writers on these phenomena, from the
days of Emanuel Swedenborg to the present hour, would admit that there was some ground for the assertion of the Mormon Prophet that he had received and communicated with
visitors from the unseen world, who represented themselves to

by spiritual power, he was very crude in his conceptions, both of the character and
modus operandi of spiritual communications, and gave them all the weight of divine
revelations, while they were really no more than the opinions of the spirits of men
who had once lived on the earth."

be the personages he named—save the highest. But while they would admit the probability of such representations, they would condemn the use made of their communications by Joseph Smith; for while modern psychomancists seek for intelligence by means of communication with the spirits of the dead, they deny to those spirits any right to dictate to them any peculiar system of faith or any direction of their actions. In this way the modern spiritualist asserts that he moves in harmony with the general intelligence and science of his age, while, on the contrary, Joseph Smith became the slave of every spirit that assumed a great name, and following without a question their dictum, travelled back to the barbaric ages in which they lived, reviving the institution of their times—such as slavery, polygamy, and theocratic sovereignty—and thus placed himself in direct opposition to the intelligence of the present day.

CHAPTER XLVIII.

THE BOOK OF MORMON.—Orson Pratt's Account of its Origin—Ancient Hebrew
Prophecies fulfilled—First Inhabitants of America—Murder of Laban—Theft of
his Plates—Migration of Israelites from Palestine to America—The Building of
the "Barges "—Lehi and his Sons—Jared's Interview with " the Lord "—Difficulties of Navigation—The Wonderful Compass—Bad Ways of the Brethren—
Landing in America—Nations founded and Cities built—" Christians " in America One Hundred Years before Christ was born—A Church founded—Persecutions and Preachings—Fearful Signs, Wonders, and Prophecies— Battles between
the Nephites and Lamanites—Two Millions of Men slain in one Battle—The
Gold Plates hid in the Hill Camorah—Internal Evidence—Plagiarisms from the
New Testament and Shakespeare—Analysis of the Book—The Folly of the Mormon Argument upon Evidence.

THE circumstances under which this singular work was
brought to the knowledge of the public, together with its claims
to a divine origin, as believed by the Latter-Day Saints, have
been given in the first chapters of this work. Of the book itself, something may now be stated.

" The Book of Mormon claims to be the sacred history of ancient
America written by a succession of ancient prophets who inhabited that
vast continent. The plates of gold containing this history were discovered by a young man named Joseph Smith, through the ministry of a holy
angel. . . . With the plates were also found a Urim and Thummim.
Each plate was not far from seven by eight inches in width and length,
being not quite so thick as common tin. Each was filled on both sides
with engraved Egyptian characters ; and the whole was bound together
in a volume as the leaves of a book, and fastened at one edge with three
rings running through each. This volume was something near six inches
in thickness, a part of which was sealed. The characters or letters upon
the unsealed part were small and beautifully engraved. Mr. Smith, by
the Urim and Thummin, and by the gift and power of God, translated
this record into the English language." *

* " Divine Authenticity," p. 49.

Controversial writers against Mormonism are unanimous in discarding this whole story of angel visits and gold plates as a pure invention, and they characterize Joseph Smith as an impostor.

The statement of the modern Prophet as to the origin of the book cannot, however, well be invalidated. What he says may be sheer falsehood, and as such the world regards his statement, but of itself it furnishes no opportunity for disproof. He asserts that an angel visited him and instructed him where to find the plates; that he went to the place designated on several occasions during a period of four years, saw and handled the plates, and finally took them as instructed. This is a simple assertion and admits of no argument.

That Joseph had at one time in his possession metallic plates of some kind, with engraved characters upon them, there appears no reason to doubt, if human testimony is to be accepted as evidence; but where and how he got the plates which he exhibited to a number of persons, and whether the Book of Mormon is a veritable interpretation of the characters on those plates, and whether or not the narrative presented is true and of any importance to the world, are subjects purely of faith.

It is claimed by the Mormon preachers that both Joseph Smith and the Book of Mormon were objects of inspired prediction about three thousand years ago. The unromantic name of Smith is not said to be a biblical subject, nor is that of Mormon stated; but one of the Hebrew prophets,* relating his vision of matters interesting to the scattered Israelites, narrates that, while an angel talked with him, another angel came forth and said : " Run, speak to *this young man*, saying, Jerusalem " shall be inhabited as towns without walls," etc., and another inspired prophet † tells of something that " shall speak out of " the ground . . . . and thy speech shall whisper out of the " dust." Joseph Smith was a young man, and the golden plates were taken out of the ground; hence the argument.

* Zech. ii. 4.
† Isaiah xxix. 4.
Isaiah is the favourite prophet of the Mormons, and is said to have been greatly gifted with comprehensive views of the Western continent, the mission of Joseph Smith, the location of Salt Lake City, and the building of the Pacific Railroad!

By referring to these passages of Scripture, and taking into account the subjects occupying the attention of Zechariah and Isaiah, the reader may have difficulty in seeing the relevancy of the predictions to the Book of Mormon. These were, however, favourite passages in the dawn of the Mormon movement, and served the excellent purpose of exercising the faith of the young converts! There is nothing so powerful in the founding of a sect as large doses of obscure Scripture, and a plentiful supply of mystery, and of the abundance of both the first Mormons might well have proudly boasted.

Of the evidences of the " Divine Authenticity " of this book, Orson Pratt furnishes the student with ninety-six octavo pages, and with much satisfaction asserts that " the witnesses of the " Book of Mormon are not only equal in number, but supe- " rior in certainty to those which this generation have of " Christ's resurrection." He concludes a long series of elab- orate arguments with the statement that " this generation " have more than one thousand times the amount of evidence " to demonstrate and for ever establish the divine authenti- " city of the Book of Mormon, than they have in favour of the " Bible."

Elder Pratt has three grand sermons : the Fulfilment of prophecy in the mission of Joseph Smith, Polygamy, and the Book of Mormon, and, whenever he ascends the rostrum, he is certain to launch out with one of the three. He ignores all thought of opposition to the last named, and announces " that " the Book of Mormon is a divine revelation, for the voice of " the Lord hath declared it unto me." He further asserts that there are " many thousands of witnesses to whom God has " revealed the truth of the Book of Mormon by heavenly vis- " ions, by angels, by the revelations of the Holy Ghost, by His " own voice and by the miraculous gifts and powers of His " kingdom."

With the burden of such a revelation upon his soul, this apostle bears his " humble testimony to all the nations of the " earth," and warns " all mankind to repent," and enter into the Mormon Church; failing which they " shall be damned," and shall in no wise enter into the kingdom of God, for this message shall condemn them at " the last day." In the mean

time there are terrible visitations to be looked for among those
who refuse to believe, and no one is to escape.

The Book of Mormon forms a large-sized volume consisting
of between five and six hundred pages of closely printed matter. It is divided into fifteen books, some of which are again
divided into chapters. The Author has read most of the arguments for and against the genuineness and authenticity of this
remarkable production. He does not desire to combat or support any theory, but as, of course, the reader will expect to
learn something of the groundwork of the Mormon faith, he
presents without unnecessary comment a brief abstract of the
whole work, together with a few quotations which will help the
truth-seeker to arrive at a correct conclusion of his own.

The plates from which the book is said to be " translated "
are stated by Nephi, the author of the first two books, to be
written " in the language of my father, which consists of the
" learning of the Jews and the language of the Egyptians "
[Nephi, p. i.]. Nephi possibly understood better than the
reader can be expected to, how " the learning of the Jews "
added to the " language of the Egyptians " could form the
speech of any people, and also how Nephi, himself a Hebrew,
came to call the tongue of the bitterly-hated Egyptian " the
" language of my father."

The whole work is supposed to contain, besides a large
amount of incidental doctrinal matter, the record of the ancient
inhabitants of the American continent.

According to the Book of Mormon, America was first peopled by the family of one Jared, who after the confusion of
tongues at Babel set out for this hemisphere. Here they grew
and multiplied, but in course of time became sinful and finally
exterminated one another in battles, in one of which *two millions* of men are said to have been slain. This took place six
hundred years before Christ.

The second emigration consisted of the family of Lehi of
the tribe of Manasseh, who left Jerusalem during the troubles
of Zedekiah's reign and came over in eight " barges." Here
they flourished and became exceedingly numerous, but, like
their predecessors, falling into evil ways, dissensions and exterminating wars ensued, ending tragically about A. D. 420.

Besides these a third migration is mentioned of certain Jews who came over about eleven years after Lehi, with whose descendants they mingled and whose fate they shared. The period by these transactions, reckoning from Jared's migration, is about 2,500 years, or 1,000 years from the migration of Lehi to the putting-up of the gold plates by Moroni in the hill Cumorah. The details of the immigration of Jared and that of Lehi are both given *in extenso*, and are of an extraordinary description. A brief outline will interest the reader, as throwing Mormon light upon that vexed question—the original peopling of America.

Jared, who lived just after the flood, left the Tower of Babel when the confusion of tongues took place, and made for the sea-shore. The reader is told [p. 517] that " Jared and his " brother were not confounded." Jared and his brethren with their servants and followers remained near the coast about four years, and, " at the end of four years, the Lord came again " unto the brother of Jared, and stood in a cloud and talked " with him "—[p. 519].

The time at last arrived when the Jared family should leave the Eastern Continent, and seek for homes in the New World, and they began to build a navy. They accordingly made eight " barges," in which they proposed to cross the ocean. The following is a description of the outfit "—[pp. 519, 520] :

" And the Lord said, Go to work and build after the manner of barges which ye have hitherto built. And it came to pass that the brother of Jared did go to work, and also his brethren, and built barges after the manner which they had built, after the instructions of the Lord. And they were small, and they were light upon the water, like unto the lightness of a fowl upon the water; and they were built like unto a manner that they were exceeding tight, even that they would hold water like unto a dish ; and the bottom thereof was tight like unto a dish, and the ends thereof were peaked ; and the top thereof was tight like unto a dish ; and *the length thereof was the length of a tree ;* and the door thereof when it was shut was tight like unto a dish. And it came to pass that the brother of Jared cried unto the Lord, saying : O Lord, I have performed the work which thou hast commanded me, and I have made the barges according as thou hast directed me. And behold, O Lord, in them is no light, whither shall we steer? And also we shall perish, for in them we cannot breathe, save it is the air that is in them ; therefore we shall perish. And the Lord said unto the brother of Jared, Behold thou shalt make a hole in the top thereof, and also in the bottom thereof; and when thou shalt suffer for air, thou shalt unstop the hole thereof and receive air. And if it be so that the water come in upon thee, behold ye shall stop the hole thereof, that ye may not perish in the flood. And it came to pass that the brother of Jared did so, according as the Lord commanded."

The eight air-tight barges of the emigrants were totally destitute of light, a fact which it appears the Lord had as yet not provided for. Jared stated the matter to him [p. 520], and the Lord said, " What will ye that I should do that ye may have " light in your vessels ? " at the same time informing Jared that ordinary windows [!] would be dashed to pieces by the waves. Jared does not appear to have continued the conversation, for, without making any reply to the Lord's question, he " went forth into the mount " and " did *moulten* out of a rock " sixteen small stones; and they were white and clear even as " transparent glass ; and he did carry them in his hands " to the Lord, who " touched " " one by one with his finger " [p. 521], and they miraculously gave forth light of themselves. Jared then placed one at each end of every barge.

As the Lord was touching these wonderful stones, Jared saw visibly the divine finger, and, not only so, but, after some little preliminary conversation, was more highly privileged than ever was seer before or since. Moses is recorded to have seen the " back parts " of the Almighty, but might not see His glory ; three Apostles saw Christ transfigured, and even Joseph Smith saw " the Lord " in a vision. But Jared excelled them all, for, although previous to his interview, it is said [p. 521], "he knew not that the Lord *had flesh and blood*," yet now the Lord showed Himself unto him, saying at the same time, " I " am Jesus Christ—I am the Father AND the Son !!! Behold " this body which *ye* now behold is the body of my spirit; and " even as I appear unto thee to be in the spirit, will I appear " unto my people in the flesh "—[p. 521].

In these " barges," after they " did also lay snares " to catch fowl and wild beasts, they placed pairs of all created animals, after the fashion of Noah—" all manner of that which " was upon the face of the land "—every kind of seed, with

" *deseret* " [which by interpretation is a honey-bee], " swarms " of bees," and "*fish of the waters*," and "*flocks* and *herds* " [p. 525]. In addition to all these, food and fodder were also stored up for man and beast [including the *wild* ones] for nearly a year! Yet, all this enormous burthen was placed, as before stated, in eight barges, " *small*," and " *like unto the light-* " *ness of a fowl upon the waters ! !* "

The dish-like barges were without sails or rigging, but were miraculously driven through the sea by a " furious wind," which " did never cease to blow towards the promised land " while they were upon the waters ; and thus they were driven " forth before the wind " [p. 526], and " no monster of the sea " could break them, neither whale could mar them." The voyage occupied 344 days—very nearly a year—and when they had reached the promised land, they bowed themselves in worship before the Lord.

On the American Continent they grew and multiplied, founded mighty cities, and became a great people ; but, becoming exceedingly sinful, great divisions and strife sprang up among them, and they separated into various nations. Devastating wars depopulated the country,* and finally the contending parties utterly exterminated each other.

The second migration occurred just about the time when the descendants of the Jaredite emigrants were annihilated— i. e., 600 years before Christ. According to the Book of Mormon, Lehi, an Israelite of the tribe of Manasseh, with his family, left Jerusalem early in Zedekiah's reign. His son, Nephi, a pious young man, according to his own testimony [p. 6], desired to possess certain plates of brass, upon which were engraved the records of his family, the law of Moses, the prophets, etc., which were in possession of Laban, his kinsman. Laban refused to sell them and tried to obtain the property of the emigrants without any transfer of the plates [p. 7]. Nephi went up to Jerusalem to see what could be done in the matter,

---

* In one of these battles, in which the two millions of men were slain, we are told : " And it came to pass that when they had all fallen by the sword, save it were Coriantumr and Shiz, behold Shiz had fainted with loss of blood. And it came to pass when Coriantumr had leaned upon his sword, that he rested a little, he smote off the head of Shiz. And it came to pass that, after he had smote off the head of Shiz, that Shiz raised upon his hands and fell ; and after he had struggled for breath, he died."—" Book of Mormon," p. 549.

and found Laban in the street near his own house, where "he "had fallen to the earth, for he was drunken with wine." The good Nephi appears to have had some little compunction about attacking his kinsman while he was in that helpless condition, but after a little equivocation he resolved to seize the opportunity, and "constrained by the Spirit" [p. 8], and arguing "it "is better that one man should perish, than that a nation "should dwindle and perish in unbelief," he "took Laban by "the hair of his head, and smote off his head with his own "sword." He then took Laban's sword, garments, and armour, and, arrayed in them, set out for the dead man's "treasury." On his way he met with Laban's servant, and, passing himself off for his master, obtained the objects of his visit—viz., the plates, records, etc.—and enticed the servant himself away to the outside of the city, where he made him prisoner. For all these exploits, Lehi and the emigrant party gave God thanks.

They then "did travel and wade through much affliction in "the wilderness," and "did slay wild beasts," and in this manner subsisted. "So great," says Nephi, "were the blessings "of the Lord upon us, that, *while we did live upon raw meat* "in the wilderness, our women did give plenty of suck for "their children, and were strong, yea, even like unto men." Yet as they journeyed some of the brethren "did rebel against "us; yea, against I Nephi, and *Sam!*" p. 12.—[I. Neph. v., par. 17.]

Regardless of all difficulties, Nephi and his brethren travelled towards the sea-shore, but what sea it was can only be conjectured, as he calls all the rivers, mountains, and other prominent landmarks, which they passed, by other names than those generally known either in ancient or modern geography. On their way they made a great discovery, which Nephi thus relates:

"It came to pass that as my father arose in the morning and went forth to the tent door, to his great astonishment he beheld upon the ground a round ball of curious workmanship; and it was of fine brass. And within the ball were two spindles: and the one pointed the way whither we should go into the wilderness."

This "ball" elsewhere described as a "compass" [p. 314] did not point to the pole, but "if they had faith to believe that

" God could cause that those spindles should point the way
" they should go, behold it was done." This was a marvellous
and convenient ball ; it served alike to direct them to good
hunting-grounds and to indicate their way, and afterwards it
was their guide overland and across the ocean. It also had another quality and served as a divine instructor, for upon the
" pointers " were written from time to time, as their spiritual
necessities demanded, various divine counsels and directions.
One only of the pointers served as a guide : the use of the
other is not stated.

Nephi in course of time began to build a ship, and " did
" make tools of the ore which I did molten out of the rock ; "
and his brethren said : " Our brother is a fool, for he thinketh
" that he can build a ship : yea, he also thinketh that he can
" cross these great waters," and they said to him, " we knew
" that ye could not construct a ship, for we knew that ye were
" lacking in judgment, wherefore thou canst not accomplish so
" great a work " [p. 37]. Nephi, however, argued with them,
and " they were confounded." The Lord also promised to
" shock " them [p. 41], which he did so effectually that they
fell down before their brother and were about to worship him.
The " shock " greatly improved them, and they then assisted him
in the preparation of his ship, of which he says that he did not
build it " after the manner of men," but " after the manner
" which the Lord had shown unto me." Ill-feeling was for a
time forgotten ; they accomplished their task, took in ample
stores, and then set sail in Nephi's vessel, and in due course
arrived near the American coast.

The Jaredites had been driven to this country on the surface and beneath the water propelled by the " furious wind "
which the Lord caused to blow upon their bare " barges ; " but
this was not the case with the Nephite migration. They had
sails, etc., and needed guidance which they obtained by means
of the before-mentioned interesting brass ball. After they
" had been driven forth before the wind for the space of many
" days," the brothers of Nephi went back to their old ways again
" and began to make themselves merry, insomuch that they be-
" gan to dance and sing and to speak with much rudeness." The
result was that when Nephi interrupted their merriment they

were angry with him, and he says: "It came to pass that "Laman and Lemuel did take me and bind me with cords." They kept him bound prisoner for four days, during which time he states that they were "driven back" [p. 43], though how he knew it, as "the compass did cease to work," he does not state. A tempest arose and the hard-hearted brethren released Nephi, who says: "It came to pass that after they had loosed "me, behold I took the compass, and *it did work whither I* "*desired it.*" After this performance the emigrants arrived safely in "the promised land," and there settled as their predecessors had done before them.

As far as can be conjectured from the story of the Book of Mormon, the journey of the emigrants, after travelling by land along the coast of the Red Sea, was through the Gulf of Aden, and by way of India and Australasia over the Pacific eastward to America, landing a little north of what is now called the Isthmus of Panama.

On reaching this "*isle* of the sea" [p. 78] they tilled the ground and erected habitations. They also found in the forests "both the cow and the ox, and the ass and the horse, and "the goat and the wild goat, and all manner of *wild* animals "that were for the use of man" [p. 44]. In another place it is stated [p. 533] of the Jaredites that they had "all manner "of cattle, of oxen and cows, and of sheep and of *swine*, and "of goats, and also many other kinds of animals which were "*useful for the food of man ;* and they had also horses and "asses, and there were elephants and *cureloms* and *cumoms.*" What the latter beasts were it is impossible to determine, but scientific men are unanimously agreed that elephants never existed on this continent, and that horses, asses, oxen, and swine, were introduced by the European settlers within the last three hundred years. Had they existed at the times alluded to by the Mormon writer, some vestiges of them would certainly ere this have been discovered. Theologians will stand aghast at *swine* being spoken of among Hebrews as "*use-* "*ful for the food* of man.*" But in all things these wandering Israelites appear to have had a taste for repudiating their nationality. It has been already seen how they rejected their beloved Hebrew tongue which they believed sacred, and adopted the language of their detested Egyptian oppressors. In one place they defile themselves with swine's flesh, and in another place break the holiest commandments and commit murder in God's service [p. 8], and elsewhere they are spoken of as building temples and consecrating priests [p. 208], and even in domestic affairs forgetting the weights and measures of their fathers, the omer, the ephah, the hin, the bath, the cab, and the shekel, and using the "seon, the senine, the senum, "the onti, limnah, ezrom, shum, shiblon, shiblum, leah, antion, "shublon, etc."

Soon after their arrival in this country they increased and multiplied exceedingly and became a great nation. They were, however, constantly divided among themselves and engaged in fierce warfare with each other.

Like the Jews, they had their prophets and teachers to whom they sometimes listened, but whom they more frequently persecuted and put to death. The great mission of these prophets appears to have been to foretell the coming of Christ. This they did, not in that shadowy and mystic fashion common to the Hebrew prophets of Palestine, but in the plainest words which could be used. On page 335, it is stated that "all those "who were true believers in Christ took upon them gladly the "name of Christ or Christians, as they were called, because of "their belief in Christ who should come." This was *a century before* the coming of Christ! This, however, is not more strange than another passage where an angel speaks of "the "mouth of *a Jew*" when speaking of an Israelite of the ten tribes, and that too before the Babylonish captivity when the remnant of the Israelites were first called Jews, or on the other hand to talk of the "Gospel" and "Churches" as long as 600 years before Christ! These singular pre-historic American Christians experienced much the same difficulties as the early converts of Peter and Paul in Europe, and were persecuted much after the fashion described in Fox's "Book of Martyrs" [p. 179].

At the time when Christ was born the people had "dwin-"dled away in unbelief" [a favourite expression in the Book of Mormon, apparently meaning the reverse of what it says]. Many of them doubted whether Christ would ever really come [p. 450.]. They were informed that "the kingdom of "heaven was *soon* at hand," and on the plates which formed their sacred records the exact time was minutely foretold. Five years before the birth of Christ, it was predicted that "the night before he cometh there shall be no darkness. "There shall be one day and a night and a day, as if it were "one day, and there shall be no night" [p. 426]. And thus it is represented to have been. On that night, the land being full of unbelievers in the coming of Christ. and many saying, "It is not reasonable that such a being as a Christ shall come" [p. 431], "Nephi cried mightily unto the Lord," and in return was told, "On the morrow come I into the world." The prophet announced this to his people, and "at the going down "of the sun there was no darkness, and the people began to be "astonished, because there was no darkness when the night "came". . . . and "there was no darkness in all that night, "but it was as light as though it was mid-day" [p. 434]. It is to be regretted that all the ancient European historians of those times, who must have known of such an extraordinary occurrence, even if they did not witness the phenomenon themselves, have all without exception preserved a profound silence respecting it.

As might be expected, the people were "so exceedingly "astonished that they fell to the earth . . . . and began to "fear because of their iniquity and unbelief" [p. 434]. "A "new star also did appear." Nephi made the most of the occasion, and preached and baptized, and many were "converted "unto the Lord."

This good work, however, did not continue very peaceably, and wars, disputes, and fightings, followed until the thirty-fourth year [p. 450], when there arose a storm such as was never heard of either in ancient or modern times. Cities were swallowed up, mountains sunk, multitudes were carried away in a whirlwind, and "the whole face of the earth became *de-* "*formed*," while "behold the rocks were rent in *twain*." After this "behold there was darkness upon the face of the "land. . . . Thick darkness. . . . The inhabitants could *feel* "the *vapour* of darkness. . . . No light. . . . Neither candles "nor torches. . . . Neither could there be fire kindled with "their fine and exceeding dry wood. . . . Neither fire nor "glimmer, neither the sun, nor the moon, nor the stars. . . . "*It did last for the space of three days.* . . . There was great howling" [p. 451]. During the three days of darkness the people heard voices which are stated to have proceeded from Christ, attendant upon whose crucifixion these signs are supposed to have been [p. 451].

After this a great assemblage met "in the land bountiful" [p. 455]; and while the people talked over the marvellous events which had just transpired they heard a voice, and they "saw a man descending out of heaven." This "man" was Christ, who announced himself to them and they fell down and worshipped him [p. 456]. He then told the whole multitude to "Arise and come forth unto me that ye may thrust your "hands into my side, and also that ye may feel the prints of "the nails in my hands and in my feet, that ye may know that "I am the God of Israel, and the God of the whole earth, and "have been slain for the sins of the world" [p. 456]. Then "the multitude went forth and did thrust their hands into His "side, and did feel the prints of the nails in His hands and in "His feet; and this they did do, going forth one by one, until "they had all gone forth." The multitude in another place [p. 469] is said to have numbered 2,500 souls! Now, even allowing the time occupied by each individual to have been only one-quarter of a minute (a calculation far too low, when arrangements for order and precedence, and some degree of decent respect for his person are considered), the time occupied must have been over ten hours and a quarter, and, after all, it is difficult to see what proof this thrusting of hands into the side of Christ and seeing the print of the nails would afford that he was Christ. Thomas *a* Didymus refused to believe that his Master was raised from the dead unless he saw and touched him; but Thomas knew Christ personally, and the evidence that he sought was not at all inconsistent, for he believed that such demonstration would convince him that what he saw was the real body of Christ with which he was familiar, and not a phantom. How touching Christ's body could convince the multitude in America who had never before seen him that He was indeed the "God of Israel," is not so plain. Thomas when he *saw* Christ was more than satisfied, but the vast multitude in America, it is said, actually *did* "thrust their hands into His side, and felt the nail-prints "in His hands and feet," and this, too, not by proxy, but personally, for "this they did do, going forth *one by one*, until they "had all gone forth" [p. 457].

Nephi then states that "the Lord" explained to him and to the whole multitude the office of baptism with the most minute details, for, in order that "there should be no disputa-"tions," He told them that they should be *immersed after* repentance and expressing a desire to be baptized in His name. He then repeated his sermon on the mount with numerous additions, enlargements, and quotations, from the New Testament [p. 465], and afterwards "their sick, and their afflicted, and "their lame and their blind, and their dumb, and all they "that were afflicted in any manner," were brought before him, and "he did heal them every one" [p. 468]. Then "it came "to pass that he commanded that their little children should "be brought." The people were then commanded to kneel "down," and "he prayed unto the Father, and the things "which he prayed cannot be written;" he wept, and "he took "their little children one by one and blessed them." "And "as they looked to behold, they cast their eyes towards heaven, "and they saw the heavens open and they saw angels descend-"ing out of heaven as it were, in the midst of fire; and they "came down and encircled those little ones about and they "were encircled about with fire; and the angels did minister "unto them." He then re-instituted the Sacrament and "when "the multitude had eaten [i. e., of the bread] and were filled," he explained the nature and administration of the rite, and gave the wine to the multitude, and they "did drink of it *and* "*were filled*" [p. 469]. His address was then continued at considerable length, after which "he departed from them and "ascended into heaven" [p. 472].

The next day the multitude re-assembled, and the twelve apostles who had previously been appointed "did pray unto "the Father" and angels came down and "did minister unto "them," and "Jesus came and stood in the midst and ministered "unto them" [p. 473]. The Sacrament was then again partaken of, and the multitude "were filled with the Spirit." Christ then began a new sermon, which is related on pp. 475 to 483. "And he did expound all things, even from the begin-"ning until the time when he should come in his glory." "And now there cannot be written in this book even a hun-"dreth part of the things which Jesus did truly teach unto "the people. . . . Behold I *were* about to write them all . . . . "but the Lord *forbid* it."

After this came a repetition of the old scenes in this marvellous history. The prophets and apostles taught with such effect that a Church was again formed, and by the year 36, after Christ, "the people were all converted unto the Lord," had all things in common, were blessed with miracles and wonders [p. 492], and "did multiply exceeding fast, and became an ex-"ceeding fair and delightsome people." But the evil spirit returned among them. They became luxurious and proud, and began to be divided into classes; division and strife arose among them; the righteous decreased in numbers, while the wicked increased; and "all dwindled in unbelief from year "to year" [p. 494]. Robbers spread over all the land, and fearful battles were fought between the Lamanites and Nephites. At last the Nephites, who were the more righteous people, gathered for a final struggle with the Lamanites [the wicked] round the hill Cumorah, between what is now called Palmyra and Manchester, in the State of New York, and there encamped in readiness for the foe. It was then that Mormon received from his father the plates of Nephi, which contained the sacred records of his people, and which had been religiously transmitted from father to son. These he "hid up in the hill "Cumorah," after he had written an abridgment of them which he gave to his son Moroni. After this the "tremendous "battle" [p. 507–9] was fought, upwards of 230,000 men were slain, and the Nephites were utterly destroyed. Only twenty-four escaped, besides Mormon, and perhaps a few of whose fate he says he was uncertain. Moroni having, as has been seen, received the abridged plates from his father Mormon, who was soon after slain, added to them a short account of his own, together with an abridged account of the Jaredite expedition, and then buried the whole in Cumorah, about the year 400 [p. 510].

Moroni soon after died, the last of his nation, and with him the Nephites became extinct, and descendants of the successful but wicked Lamanites, who were distinguished [p. 66] by the peculiar colour of their skin, are now known as the North American Indians.

The plates remained in their hiding-place over 1,400 years, until finally discovered to Joseph Smith, through "the ministry of an angel," on the 22d of September, 1823.

After such a remarkable history of the peopling of the American Continent, it is proper that the reader should have placed before him a few extracts from the Book of Mormon, exhibiting how singularly the people in the New World were familiar with, and used the same religious sentiments as, the people of the Old World! For convenience of comparison the following extracts from the Book of Mormon are placed side by side with similar passages from the Old and New Testaments. These extracts are taken from speeches, exhortations, and sermons, said to have been delivered by American prophets and apostles, who, of course, never saw, or could see, the English Bible as it now exists in its modern translations. The reader will probably be struck with the very close resemblance of these expressions to texts with which most persons are familiar, but which were first written in the shape of translation many centuries after they are claimed to have been spoken by the prophets of America; and still more strange is the reproduction in the Book of Mormon of the errors of translation existing in the English edition, which was produced twelve hundred years after the death of the last of the American seers.

From the Book of Mormon.	*From the Bible.*
"Behold the axe is laid to the root of the tree, therefore every tree that bringeth not forth good fruit, shall be hewn down and cast into the fire."—B. of M., p. 224.	"Now also the axe is laid unto the root of the trees: therefore every tree which bringeth not forth good fruit is hewn down, and cast into the fire."—Matt. iii. 10.
"Wrest them [the Scriptures] to their own damnation."—B. of M., p. 247.	"They that are unlearned and unstable wrest, as they do also the other Scriptures, unto their own destruction."—II. Peter iii. 16.
"Cursed is he that putteth his trust in man, or maketh flesh his arm."—B. of M., p. 64.	"Cursed be the man that trusteth in man, and maketh flesh his arm."—Jer. xvii. 5.

From the Book of Mormon.	From the Bible.
"Be ye separate, and touch not *their* unclean things."—B. of M., p. 225.	"Be ye separate, saith the Lord, and touch not the unclean thing."—II. Cor. vi. 17.
"Yea, it is the love of God which sheddeth itself abroad in the hearts of the children of men."	"The love of God is shed abroad in our hearts."—Rom. v. 5.
"They shall be thrust down into hell."—B. of M., p. 74.	"Shalt be thrust down to hell."—Luke x. 15.
"Therefore remember, O man, for all thy doings thou shalt be brought into judgment."—B. of M., p. 18.	"Rejoice, O young man, in thy youth; . . . . walk in the ways of thine heart, and in the sight of thine eyes: but know thou, that for all these things God will bring thee into judgment."—Eccl. xi. 9.
"Blood, and fire, and vapour of smoke."—B. of M., p. 52.	"Blood, and fire, and *pillars* of smoke."—Joel ii. 30. [Quoted] "*Vapour* of smoke."—Acts ii. 19.
"And behold the heavens were opened, and they were caught up into heaven, and saw and heard unspeakable things, . . . whether they were in the body or out of the body they could not tell."—B. of M., p. 489.	"I knew a man in Christ, above fourteen years ago (whether in the body, I cannot tell: God knoweth), such a one caught up to the third heaven. And I knew such a man . . . How that he was caught up into paradise, and heard unspeakable words, which it is not lawful for a man to utter."—II. Cor. xii. 2.
"All the proud and they who do wickedly shall be as stubble, and the day cometh when they must be burned." B. of M., p. 41.	"Behold the day cometh that shall burn as an oven; and all the proud, yea, and all that do wickedly, shall be stubble; and the day that cometh shall burn them up."—Mal. iv. 1.
"I say unto thee, woman, there has not been such great faith among all the people of the Nephites."—B. of M., p. 263.	"I say unto you, I have not found so great faith, no, not in Israel."—Luke vii. 9.
"And it came to pass that I looked and beheld the whore of all the earth, and she sat upon many waters; and she had dominion over all the earth, and among all nations, kindreds, tongues, and people."—B. of M., p. 29.	"The great whore that sitteth upon many waters. . . . The inhabitants of the earth have been made drunk with the wine of her fornication. . . . The waters which thou sawest, where the whore sitteth, are peoples and multitudes, and nations and tongues."—Rev. xvii. 1, 2, 16, etc.

33

From the Book of Mormon.	*From the Bible.*
" Those who stand in that liberty wherewith God had made them free." —B. of M., p. 382.	" Stand fast, therefore, in the liberty wherewith Christ hath made us free."—Gal. v. 5.
" The house of Israel was compared unto an olive-tree, by the Spirit of the Lord which was in our fathers," etc.—B. of M., pp. 30–1, see also p. 18.	" And if some of the branches be broken off, and thou, being a wild olive-tree, were graffed in among them, and with them," etc.—Rom. xi. 17, *et seq.*
" Behold I am born of the Spirit." —B. of M., p. 202.	" Born of the Spirit."—John iii. 6.
" Redeemed from the gall of bitterness, and the bonds of iniquity." —B. of M., p. 202.	" Thou art in the gall of bitterness, and in the bond of iniquity." Acts vii. 23.
" They shall judge the twelve tribes of Israel."—B. of M., p. 27.	" And sit on thrones judging the twelve tribes of Israel."—Luke xxii. 30.
" The last shall be first, and the first shall be last."—B. of M., p. 27.	" Many that were first shall be last, and the last shall be first."— Matt. xix. 30.
" Awake, my sons, put on the armour of righteousness, and come forth out of obscurity, and arise from the dust."—B. of M., p. 55.	" Put on the whole armour of God, . . . the breastplate of righteousness."—Eph. vi. 11, 14. " Awake, put on thy strength, O Zion; put on thy beautiful garments, O Jerusalem, the holy city. . . . Shake thyself from the dust; arise, and sit down."—Isa. lii. 1, 2.
" He is not dead; but he sleepeth in God. . . . He shall rise again. . . Believest thou this?—B. of M., p. 263.	" She is not dead, but sleepeth." Luke viii. 52. " Thy brother shall rise again. . . Believest thou this? "—John xi. 23, 26.
" And twice were they cast into a den of wild beasts, and behold they did play with the beasts as a child with a sucking lamb, and received no harm."—B. of M., p. 489.	" They brought Daniel, and cast him into the den of lions. . . . My God hath sent his angel, and hath shut the lions' mouths, that they have not hurt me," etc.—Daniel vi. 16, 22 [see also Apocrypha].
" The fiery furnace could not harm them."—B. of M., p. 511.*	" I see four men loose, walking in the midst of the fire, and they have no hurt."—Daniel iii. 23.

* This apparently refers to Daniel's three companions, but, as their miraculous preservation occurred some years after Lehi and his sons left Asia for America, it is difficult to see how Mormon obtained his information on the subject.

From the Book of Mormon.

" In them shall be written my gospel, saith the Lamb. . . . And whoso shall publish peace, yea, tidings of great joy, how beautiful upon the mountains shall they be."—B. of M., p. 26.

" He spake also, concerning a prophet who should come before the Messiah, to prepare the way of the Lord, and make his paths straight; for there standeth one among you whom ye know not; and he is mightier than I, whose shoe's latchet I am not worthy to unloose. . . . He should baptize in Bethabary, beyond Jordan. . . . He should baptize the Messiah with water. And after he had baptized the Messiah with water, he should behold and bear record, that he had baptized the Lamb of God, who should take away the sins of the world."—B. of M., p. 17.

" Charity suffereth long, and is kind, and envieth not, and is not puffed up, seeketh not her own, is not *easily* † provoked," etc.—B. of M., p. 556.

" They shall be saved, even if it so be as by fire."—B. of M., p. 52.

" To be carnally minded is death,

From the Bible.

" How beautiful upon the mountains are the feet of him that bringeth good tidings, that publisheth peace; that bringeth good tidings of good, that publisheth salvation, that saith unto Zion, Thy God reigneth ! "—Isa. lii. 7.

" Prepare ye the way of the Lord, make straight in the desert a highway for our God."—Isa. xl. 3. " There standeth one among you whom ye know not . . . . he is preferred before me, whose shoe's latchet I am not worthy to unloose. These things were done in Bethabara beyond Jordan, where John was baptizing. The next day John seeth Jesus coming unto him, and saith, Behold the Lamb of God, which taketh away the sin of the world."—John i. 26-29.*

" Charity suffereth long and is kind; charity envieth not, charity vaunteth not itself, is not puffed up, doth not behave itself unseemly, is not *easily* provoked."—I. Cor. xiii. 4.

" But he himself shall be saved ; yet so as by fire."—I. Cor. iii. 15.

" To be carnally minded is death,

* The parallel passage from the Book of Mormon would appear to have been compounded from the above Scripture quotations. The Mormon writer is supposed to have uttered his prophecy six hundred years *before* Christ came, and it is extraordinary how minutely he predicts events and expressions, even to a word, as recorded in the New Testament, while those prophecies given through the ancient Hebrew seers to " His own " to whom He came in the flesh, and " to whom were the promises," were so vague, even to the wisest, until they were accomplished. It must not, however, be overlooked that these singularly clear American prophecies, although supposed to be delivered so long before Christ came, were unknown to the world until Joseph Smith discovered the plates, eighteen hundred and twenty-seven years *after* they were fulfiled !

† The word " easily " *is not in any Greek MS.* It is (incorrectly) in the Eng-

From the Book of Mormon.	*From the Bible.*
and to be spiritually minded is life eternal."—B. of M., p. 75.	but to be spiritually minded is life and peace."—Rom. viii. 6.
"For *do we not read* that God is the same yesterday, to-day, and for ever; and in him there is no variableness nor shadow of turning."—B. of M., p. 513.	"Jesus Christ the same yesterday, and to-day, and for ever."—Heb. xiii. 8. "With whom is no variableness neither shadow of turning." James i. 17.
"And behold, he [the Son of God] shall be born of Mary, *at Jerusalem.*" —B. of M., p. 227.	"Jesus was born *in Bethlehem* of Judea, in the days of Herod the king."—Matt. ii. 1.
"In the city of *Nazareth.*" —p. 21.	

Any person acquainted with the history of the "camp" "meetings" in rural districts fifty years ago, and the peculiar expressions of the preachers, will be somewhat astonished at reading in the Book of Mormon so many of those familiar phrases from the mouths of the fathers of the Indians. The following are a few examples :

"I am encircled about eternally in the arms of his love," p. 55. [About 570 years *before* Christ.]*

"Have ye spiritually been born of God ? " p. 222. [80 years before Christ.]

"If ye have experienced a change of heart," p. 222.

lish translation ; but how did the Mormon prophet, inspired by "the gift of God," come to make the same blunder ? The following is also a case in point :

"The Lord God, and His Spirit, hath sent me."—B. of M., p. 47.	[English version] : "The Lord God, and His Spirit, hath sent me."—Isa. xlviii. 16. [Bishop Lowth's version] : "And now the Lord Jehovah hath sent me, and His Spirit."

This passage in the English translation, and also the quotation in the Book of Mormon, would appear to assert that "The Lord God and His Spirit" had sent the speaker. Bishop Lowth and most other learned commentators have pronounced that the sentence is incorrectly rendered in the English version, and that it ought to read : "The Lord Jehovah hath sent me, and His Spirit"—i. e., "God the Father," as Celsus says, "sent both Christ and the Holy Spirit." How strange it is that both Nephi, an inspired Prophet, who is supposed to have quoted direct from the original, and Joseph Smith who translated by "the gift and power of God" should have made, identically and to the letter, the same mistake as the uninspired translator of King James's time ! This is the more extraordinary when it is considered that according to learned philologists, "in the Hebrew manuscripts of the Old Testament there have been counted 800,000 different readings, as to consonants alone." [*Vide* Stuart on the Canon of the Old Testament, p. 192.]

* The dates used in *this* chapter are taken from the "Compendium of the Faith of Doctrines," by F. D. Richards, Liverpool, 1857.

" Ye shall awake to a sense of your awful situation," p. 531.

" For the arms of mercy are extended towards you," p. 222.

"Many died firmly believing that their souls *were* redeemed by the Lord Jesus Christ," p. 337. [About 70 years *before* Christ.]

" Have they not revealed the plan of salvation ? " p. 136. [More than 400 years *before* Christ.]

" The own due time of the Lord," pp. 102, 17, etc. [600 years *before* Christ.]

" Or otherwise, can ye imagine yourselves brought before the tribunal of God with your souls filled with guilt and remorse ? " p. 221. [80 years *before* Christ.]

" Thus mercy can satisfy the demands of justice," p. 304. [About 75 years *before* Christ.]

" If ye have *felt to sing* the song of redeeming love," p. 222. [About 80 years *before* Christ.]

In another place [p. 18], Nephi tells of his father speaking "by *the power of the Holy Ghost ; which* power he received by *faith on the Son of God ; and the Son of God was the Messiah.*" This was very nearly *six centuries before Christ !*

Nephi, writing 545 years *before* Christ, says: "I glory in my Jesus, for he *hath* redeemed my soul from hell " [p. 113]. "Enter into the narrow gate, and walk in the straight path, which leads to life ; " and of the Gentiles he writes : "For none of these can I hope, *except they shall be reconciled to Christ.*"

But perhaps the best point in the book is the plagiarism of Hamlet's well-known speech, " To be, or not to be." Five hundred and seventy years *before* Christ, Lehi, in his last hours, addressing his sons, spoke of " the cold and silent grave "*from whence no traveller can return* " [B. of M., .p. 55]. Two thousand two hundred years later, Shakespeare, who had never read Lehi's writings, spoke of " the undiscovered "country *from whose bourn no traveller returns.*" Hamlet, Act iii., scene i.

The Scripture story of Joshua commanding the sun : " Sun, " stand thou still upon Gibeon, and thou moon in the valley " of Ajalon," has always been a subject of grave dispute among the learned, and upon it unbelievers have based many arguments against the veracity of the Scriptures. According, however, to the Book of Mormon, the words of Joshua admit of a very easy explanation, and were understood ages ago to have a very different interpretation from what is commonly supposed. Not only so, but the fact that the earth revolves round

the sun, of which the ancients are supposed to have been ignorant, was not only a matter of common knowledge here, but was
used as an argument which every one was sure to understand.
The prophet Helaman says: " According to his word, the earth
" goeth back, and it appeareth unto man that the sun standeth
" still ; yea, and behold this is so; for sure it is the earth that
" moveth, and not the sun."—[B. of M., p. 421.]   On this subject, Elder John Hyde says: " Here are all the prophets tran-
" scended ; Ptolemy refuted ; Copernicus and all his discoveries
" anticipated 2,000 years before he was born.   The only pity
" is, that this was not published, however, *until* 200 *years af-*
" *ter he was dead!* "   It is an undoubted fact that the astro-
nomical system of Ptolemy was universally received by the
ancients.   The earth, they believed, was the stationary centre
of the system, and round it sun, moon, and stars revolved.
All the Scripture allusions to the heavenly bodies support this
statement, for the distinction between the planets [the word
" planet " itself] and the fixed stars was then utterly unknown.
The prophet Alma, however, wiser, even in scientific matters,
than Joshua and David, Solomon, Job, the captive of Patmos,
and all the sages of antiquity, says : " The Scriptures are laid
" before thee, yea, and all things denote there is a God ; yea,
" even the earth, and all things that are upon the face of it,
" yea, and *its motion ;* yea, and also *all the planets* which move
" in their regular form."

The simplicity of many portions of the Book of Mormon
is very touching; witness the following :

" And when Moroni had said these words, he went forth among the
people, *waving the rent* of his garment in the air, that all might see *the
writing which he had wrote upon the rent ! ! !* " *—[page 334.]

" I *beheld* wars and *rumours* of wars."—[p. 21.]

" I *saw* wars and *rumours* of wars. . . . And in wars and *rumours* of
wars I saw many generations pass away."—[p. 23.]

" There were no robbers nor murderers, neither were there Lamanites,
or any manner of *ites ! ! !* "—[p. 493.]

" Now the joy of Ammon was so great, even that he was full ; yea, he

* That a " rent " can be visible—sometimes *too* visible—is an undoubted fact,
but how a man could *write upon a rent* is not so easy of demonstration.   Possibly
corroborative evidence of the practicability of this performance might have been
given by the Irishman who gave as a recipe for making a cannon : " Take a round
hole and pour melted iron around it."

was swallowed up in the joy of his God, even to the exhaustion of his strength ; and he fell again to the earth. Now was not this exceeding great joy ? "—[p. 285.]

" The Lord provided for them. . . . He also gave them strength that they *should suffer no manner of *afflictions*, save it were swallowed up in the joy of Christ ! "—[p. 298.]

" They all did swear unto him . . . that whoso should vary from the assistance which Akish desired should *lose his head*, and whoso should divulge whatsoever thing Akish should make known unto them should *lose his life*."—[p. 530.]

Many opponents of the faith of the Saints have devoted considerable time to the discussion of the origin of the Book of Mormon, and the general conclusion reached has been that Joseph Smith had before him the manuscript of a religious novel, written by one Solomon Spaulding, and that he interpolated all through it the portions which bear evidence of his own lack of education, while the body of the story remained intact.

There is evidence that this Spaulding actually did write something about the ancient inhabitants of America, and it is asserted by one of his brothers, from his recollection of the portions of the manuscript, that it was identical with the Book of Mormon, and that the latter was indeed the *bona-fide* work of his deceased brother. It is further said that several of Mr. Spaulding's personal friends sustain this statement from their remembrance of the readings to which they had frequently listened.

Those who accept such statements as the true solution of the origin of this book must necessarily conclude that Joseph Smith was " a deliberate falsifier and wilful impostor." There is no avoiding this. The most incisive writer on this subject— John Hyde, formerly an elder in the Church—unhesitatingly announces this as his own conclusion. His " Analysis of the " Book of Mormon," and its " Internal Evidences," is a masterly work, to which no Mormon elder has attempted a reply. The only man among the Mormons capable of the effort is Orson Pratt, and, by an attempt at refutation, he would only exhibit common honesty, for he is morally under obligations to that long-suffering people in the Tabernacle to do so.

At the moment of writing this, there is before the Author

" brother Orson's " last discourse on the Book of Mormon, delivered in the Tabernacle on the 22d of September, 1872. It
is undoubtedly the best sermon that could be preached on
" the forthcoming " of that notable book, but, by the side of
the unanswered " Analysis " of Elder John Hyde, it is very unsatisfactory. But, while the Author frankly admits the unan-
swerable and powerful arguments of Mr. Hyde, he dissents
from his conclusion that Joseph Smith was a *wilful* impostor.

To conclude that there was " wilful " imposture in the
origin of Mormonism is, in an argumentative sense, to " take
" arms against a sea of troubles " to which there is no limit.
There is, however, an easy solution of the difficulty respecting
the origin of the book—i. e., to admit honest credulity in Joseph Smith, in the persons who " witnessed unto the world " of
that which they saw, and in all that follows in the history of
the Mormon movement. Probably, if Mr. Hyde were now to
write on the subject, while he would undoubtedly preserve the
same powerful arguments against the divinity of the book he
would conclude that Joseph Smith was after all only an extraordinary " spirit medium," and had been subjected to all the
vagaries and caprices of that peculiar condition.

In this solution of the difficulty respecting Joseph's claims,
there is a perfect consistency, and it harmonizes completely
with the testimony, both of the orthodox and the heterodox.
It admits the claim of honesty in Joseph Smith, and in his
" witnesses," and equal honesty in those who have rejected
their testimony, and denounced the folly of their assertions.
In brief, when Joseph Smith said that he had visions, dreams,
and revelations, it is best to allow that he probably had all
that experience ; but when he clothed his communications with
the sanctity of absolute and divine truth, the acceptance or rejection of which was to be " the salvation or damnation of the
" world," it was simply the operation and assertion of that yet
uncomprehended mysterious influence that has been experienced by both good and bad men in all ages and in all countries within the historical ken of man.

With the developments which have followed, the life of the
Mormon prophet is easily understood. He was but the vehicle of " spirit communication," and when he erred it was *not in-*

tentional imposture or *deliberate fraud,* but in the native honesty of his simple nature he believed too much.* Than that he was imposed upon or ignorantly imposed upon himself in the " translation " of the Book of Mormon, nothing seems more certain to those who have fully studied his career, while his assertion that the English " translation " of the plates is the history of the ancient inhabitants of the country, of the people who built the temples and palaces of Central America, and constructed the gigantic works, the mounds and ruins which are met with all over this continent, is assuredly untrue. The American Indians never descended from those builders, nor did Jared or Lehi give that posterity birth. With faith, any thing, however extravagant or unreasonable, can be accepted; but no rational being, looking upon the past as he does upon the present, can behold the evidences of the existence of a great and civilized people upon this continent long ages ago, and believe that the Book of Mormon story of Jared and Lehi is the true record of the buried past. That history has yet to be written.

Calmly regarding the plagiarisms from the New Testament in the Book of Mormon, the frequent use of the expressions and thoughts of Methodists in the nineteenth century, and the use of republican political sentiments, all of which Joseph Smith, notwithstanding his youth and lack of education, did know, there can be no doubt that the title-page of the first edition of the Book of Mormon stated something near the truth when it bore the announcement : " Joseph Smith, *Author* and Proprietor."

Singularly enough, no Mormon authority has ever related how Joseph Smith claimed to translate the plates, and what is still more strange of the hundreds of men who personally knew Joseph, and who could have very properly asked him that question, the Author, to his inquiries addressed to them,

* One of the Mormon elders called upon a spirit-medium in New York, and in seeking communion with the dead the medium immediately became entranced, and to this Elder, Heber C. Kimball is reported to have said: " The difficulty with brother Joseph was that he kept a spiritual hotel and entertained all comers." The reader can take such a professed report from the dead for what it is worth, but in the light of Mormonism this statement from whatever personage, in the flesh or out of it, is exceedingly suggestive of the truth.

never got an answer. One man only acknowledged that he had asked the Prophet, but forgot what the answer was.

The reader may long ere this have arrived at the conclusion that the whole story is a stupendous fraud, and a wicked fabrication, but, to the Author's mind, Joseph is still defensible against the charge of *wilful* imposture. It does not seem possible that he could have borne up through his whole life of persecution, and have lived and died maintaining the truth of his story, if the book had been a fraud.

At the time of its professed translation he was not capable of dictating the whole of it without aid. Though it all passed from his tongue to the ears of his scribes, and bears throughout in its language the impress of his scanty education, whatever there is of plot in the book was far beyond him. Ridiculous as may be the story of the Jaredite " barges," the spindle-compass, the traversing of three oceans from the Red Sea to the southern portion of North America, and the many other grotesque stories about the first inhabitants of the Western Hemisphere, yet there is pervading the whole book another mind than that of young Joseph Smith.

The ruins found in Central America, the great mounds in the valley of the Mississippi, and in several States of the Union, establish beyond the possibility of a doubt that a great population once existed on this continent, which has long ages ago passed away. They who built the colossal temples, the magnificent palaces, and the great aqueducts, have left, in the ruins that now meet the gaze of the explorer, the evidences of a civilization that astonishes the student. That some of those ancient inhabitants may have made and engraved plates, and that they did so for a purpose—whatever that might be—is very possible. The relics of sculpture and painting suggest also the probability of engraving. Other persons besides Joseph Smith have discovered in the ground similar plates,* bearing evidence of a great antiquity, and, as time rolls on, there may yet be many similar discoveries. There need be no difficulty, then, in accept-

---

* On the opposite page is an engraving of two (out of six) bell-shaped plates, which were *actually* and unquestionably discovered by one Mr. R. Wiley, in April, 1843, while excavating an ancient mound in the neighbourhood of Kinderhook, Ohio. They have never been translated.

PLATES FOUND IN KINDERHOOK, OHIO.

ing Joseph's story of finding the plates; it is what is claimed to be the contents of the plates that is incredible.

If no living person fabricated for Joseph Smith the Book of Mormon, and if Joseph did not use the manuscript of Solomon Spaulding, the Mormon may very properly ask : " Who, " then, was the author of the book ? " To this query, the Book of Abraham is the answer. In the preceding chapter, the Prophet's " translation " of the papyrus, found with the Egyptian mummies, is evidently untrue ; yet Joseph Smith sat with his amanuensis, and, by " the gift of God," believed he was giving a truthful translation. The scientist says that the whole story is untrue, that the Prophet's version of the hieroglyphics is a perfect romance, that the hieroglyphics had no more allusion to the Abraham of Mosaic history, than they had to do with Abraham the martyred President of the United States.

When Joseph Smith translated the Book of Mormon by the means of his Urim and Thummim, the " reformed Egyptian " was evidently not transformed before his eyes into the translated text, or " the gift and power of God " used peculiarly bad English. He gazed upon that Urim and Thummim until his mind became psychologized, and the impressions that he received he dictated to his scribe. With such a conclusion, the anachronisms of the book, the quotations from the Old and New Testaments, and the language of modern preachers and writers, are accounted for.

That there is such a mental condition in human life as clairvoyance, in which persons are strangely operated upon, and can mentally perceive what to the natural eye is unseen, is a belief as old as the history of man, and that, when the mind is psychologized by a condition of its own, or by the operation of external influences, singular impressions or revelations are had, few people to-day dispute. That Joseph Smith was in these experiences one of the most remarkable men that ever lived, those outside of Mormonism altogether, who knew him intimately, testify. He believed that his gifts were divine, and his impressions were revelations from the Almighty Creator.

To insist that there were deliberate imposture and deliberate falsehood at the origin of Mormonism is to challenge the vera-

city and honesty of the hundreds and thousands of persons who
accept that faith and who testify that *they know* of its truth.
It is more rational and consistent to admit that what such a
body of people allege that they have experienced is probably
true in statement, than to deny it and brand it as imposture,
but it does not follow that the interpretation which any of
them put upon their experience is itself true. They may be fully
persuaded that they have had visions, dreams, the ministering
of angels, and have heard the " voice of God," all witnessing to
the truth of the divinity of Mormonism, for all this has been
asserted again and again by very many others besides Joseph
Smith—men, and women too, who have claimed to have received divine missions. Outside of all religious enthusiasm,
also, there are tens of thousands of men and women, sober,
reliable, and truthful in every relation and business of life,
with as unchangeable convictions as ever the Mormons had
that they have personally experienced all these extraordinary
phenomena.

The trouble with the Mormons and with all this class of
believers is, not in what they have experienced, but the after-
interpretation that they may have put upon it. If the reader
turns to pages 33-35 of this volume, he will find the key to the
Mormon testimony and the explanation of the whole movement. There it is illustrated by this very Orson Pratt, the
champion expounder of the evidences of the Book of Mormon.

Joseph Smith relates that he cast a devil out of Newell
Knight in the name of Jesus. Judge Edmonds innocently
relates that he too "cast out devils " frequently without any such
invocation. Orson Pratt, in commenting upon Joseph's "first
" miracle," flies to the conclusion that those persons who witnessed the experience of Newell Knight, tortured with an evil
influence and afterwards " overwhelmed with the good spirit,"
had from these circumstances " a knowledge" that "Joseph
" Smith was a great prophet and seer, and that the Book of
" Mormon was a divine revelation ! " Nothing could be more
preposterous. The experience of Newell Knight had its cause
and its issues, but these had no more bearing upon the seer-
ship of Joseph Smith and the divinity of the Book of Mormon
than upon any and all of the assumptions of his life.

On just such statements and arguments have the Mormons been fed for over forty years, till "hundreds of thousands of "witnesses," as Elder Pratt boasts, can testify that to them "God has revealed the truth of the Book of Mormon."

A great man once said : "Let me write the songs of the "people, let others make their laws." The apostle Orson Pratt has written the testimony of the Book of Mormon, and the "Saints" have reiterated his statements, and no one has had better opportunities than he of knowing the worthlessness of such evidence and the fallacy of such arguments as he has adduced from the devil in Newell Knight.

Of the "hundreds of thousands of witnesses to whom God "has revealed the truth of the Book of Mormon," he knows full well that comparatively few indeed have ever read that book, know little or nothing intelligently of its contents, and take little interest in it. He has written and spoken extensively of the "divine evidence" respecting it, to the Mormons ; and they have read and listened to his arguments. They have, of course, been pleased with his display of "testimony." With the "eye of faith" everything was clear to them, and to them it was "The Holy Ghost witnessing of the divinity of the "'book.'" Some "brother" or "sister" is "possessed by "devils" and thrown into convulsions, and an "apostle" or "elder" "lays hands" upon the possessed, "conjures" the evil spirit to depart from the troubled soul, and it becomes tranquil—*ergo*, the Book of Mormon is divine, and Joseph Smith is "a great prophet and seer." Such is the argument !

Brigham Young has "cast out devils," yet, for all that, it is well known that Orson Pratt himself is not over-strong in the belief that Brigham is "a great Prophet and seer," and all the devils that Brigham has ever cast out have never convinced Orson of the divinity of Brigham's Adam-deity ! If the whole world is to be "damned" for rejecting the claims and assertions of Joseph about himself and his Book of Mormen, while it has had no opportunity of seeing him "cast out "devils," Orson Pratt is certain to find himself at "the bottom "of the lowest hell," to use Tabernacle language, for rejecting Brigham's "Adam," after all the evidence before him of Brigham "casting out devils."

Intelligent people in Utah, who have rejected Mormonism, can trace their first awakening to reason and common-sense to the first consideration of such assumptions of the evidences of divinity set forth by the Mormon apostles.

While the time and attention of the masses are wholly absorbed in procuring the bare means of existence, and their only time for reflection is demanded for the Tabernacle and the ward meetings, the " evidences " of divinity upon anything may pass unchallenged. But, the moment the mind is awakened and stretches beyond Mormonism, the acceptance of such evidences is very doubtful.

There have been multitudes of persons in the world who have believed and asserted that to them, and to them only, God gave visions, dreams, angel-visits, the power of healing the sick and " casting out devils "—and they have declared that these were proofs of the heavenly origin of the faith which they proclaimed, and this it is that the Saints have been taught by the modern apostles to regard as special and particular to them, while it has been a peculiarity common to the religious experience of all the world, and is an evidence of nothing more than a certain condition of mind that renders such manifestations possible with persons adapted naturally to receive them.

Probably no enthusiast ever left the Mormom Church without a rich experience in the shape of visions, angels, and " miracles ; " and seldom are such persons found without " the voice " of God " whispering something to them. The " Reorganized " Church," at the head of which is the eldest son of Joseph Smith, is peculiarly " favoured " with " visions," and " visits " of angels " and " gifts of tongues," " interpretations " and " powers of healing ; " and these worshippers " cast out " all the " devils " that come in their way. It is undeniable that the great " evidences " that are adduced by Orson Pratt in favour of the truth of the Book of Mormon and the mission of Joseph Smith are more abundantly manifest to-day in " Young Joseph's church " than among the Rocky Mountain Saints. Yet " Young Joseph " and his " Saints " denounce Brigham Young as a " usurper " and a " fraud " upon the Mormon people.

Brigham Young and his apostles, backed up by visions, dreams, revelations, miracles, and "the voice of God," preach and teach to the Mormons in Utah that "Young Joseph" in Illinois is an aspiring, ambitious youth, an emissary of the devil, seeking to lead away the faithful from the "true fold." Joseph Smith—the *young* man—sustained by as credible witnesses as Orson Pratt can produce, supported by "angel reve-"lations," the "voice of God," and any amount of "miracles," is with his apostles now praying earnestly, long, and loud, and sending missionaries all through Utah Territory, warning the people against that ruin of soul and body to which they assert Brigham Young and his apostles are leading them. The claim, therefore, of such a host of witnesses testifying to the truth of the Book of Mormon because of visions, dreams, revelations and miracles, is unworthy of a moment's consideration.

That Joseph thought Moroni and some of those ancient personages whom he mentions in his biography appeared to him, is, no doubt, true ; that they used him for their purposes Spiritualists all believe, and, when the origin of some of the great religions of the world is considered, there is not much cause for wonder that those persons who have accepted Mormonism, with all its crudities, should have honestly believed it. Millions have accepted Mohammed and his visions; many millions more have lived and died in the faith of Buddha ; Confucius has swayed a spiritual empire from ages long before the Christian era ; and by these and other founders of religious systems, and by many of their disciples, visions and revelations, gifts and miraculous powers, have all been claimed.

CHAPTER XLIX.

THE PRIESTHOOD IN ZION—Its Organizations, Apostolic, Judicial, and Political—The Prayers of the Saints—The Surveillance of the Teachers—The Eyes
of the Priesthood over all—The Missionaries abroad—The Elders travel "without Purse or Scrip"—How Mormonism is introduced among the Gentiles—Foreign Missions—His Satanic Majesty attacks the Apostles in England—"Devils"
attack Brother Heber—Success in Britain—The Emigration to Zion—Baptizing
Converts in the Atlantic—The Journey through the States.

In the Mormon Church there are two priesthoods, the Melchisedec and the Aaronic—the latter an appendage to the former. The lowest rank in the Priesthood is the office of "Dea-
"con:" his duties, without anything sentimental, are somewhat menial. In all "the branches" of the Church, outside of
Zion, the deacon is expected to look after the public halls or
places of preaching; he "keeps the door," sees that no disorder-
ly persons enter to disturb the meeting, takes up the collections,
and is the treasurer on a small scale for "the branch:" besides
which he inquires into the necessities of the widows and the
fatherless, and renders them what aid he can. The deacon
should physically be a strong man, not on account of the
weight of the pennies that he carries home, but on account of
the practical manner in which he has frequently to "cast out
"devils." The Author well remembers attending a "council
"meeting" of the Mormon priesthood, in Birmingham, England, when one of the brethren proposed that a number of the
heaviest men among the Saints should be that evening ordained
deacons. The proposer of that motion set forth that they
were all strong men; one of them used a forge-hammer in a
smithy, another was a drayman, a third had been on the police
force, and there were two carpenters. Others were also named
whose strength was equal to the office. The presiding officer

over the conference, who had but newly arrived among the
Birmingham Saints, wanted to learn what necessity there was
for so many ordinations, and why the quality of strength was
dwelt upon. His predecessor had been a great preacher, and
had attracted a great deal of attention, and persons of a certain
class, not afraid to go anywhere, were his attendants. Every
Sunday night Father Crooke was unhappy without " a row."
His attacks upon other religionists were sure to bring up some
of the audience on their feet in opposition, and then the deacons were called for: " Deacons, this man challenges me to
" show him a miracle, and asks me to cast out devils. We
" can do it. Deacons, cast *him* out!" That unfortunate opponent was in a moment clutched by the neck and hands, and
hurried to the door. If he was resolute and opposed the
rough handling, he went quickly down the stairs without
touching all the steps. Father Crooke gazed upon the operation with undisguised satisfaction, and the audience was
equally delighted. On the return of the deacons, the old man
would recommence his sermon with a prefatory word of approval to the deacons and the announcement to the audience
that they had had demonstrated that they could " cast out
" devils."

The " Teacher " is the second round in the ladder of priesthood. His duties are to visit the Saints and to inquire into
their faith and life. Without challenging the design, the Mormon leaders find a powerful auxiliary to their influence over
the people in " the prayers of the Saints." Every household
is instructed to have morning and, evening prayers. The father
gathers his children around him, and all kneeling, he prays for
revelation, the gifts of the Spirit for himself and family; then
in turn comes every order of priesthood. " Bless Brigham
" Young, bless him ; may the heavens be opened unto him,
" angels visit and instruct him ; clothe him with power to de-
" fend thy people and to overthrow all who rise up against
" him ; bless him in his basket and in his store, multiply and
" increase him in wives, children, flocks, and herds, houses and
" lands—make him very great," etc.

After Brigham has been properly remembered, then come
his counsellors, the apostles, the high-priests, the seventies, the

elders, the priests, the teachers, the deacons, and the Church universal. Another divergence is made in remembrance of the President of the Conference, and the president of that particular " branch " where the family resides, and every officer in it. All are prayed for—if the father does his duty. The power and the greatness of the "kingdom," that is to roll on till it fills the whole earth and subjugates all earthly and corrupt man-made governments, are specially urgent. All nations are to weaken and crumble to pieces, and Zion is to go forth in her strength conquering and to conquer till the priesthood shall

> " . . . . reign and rule and triumph,
> And God shall be our King."

The teacher's duty is to visit every house once a week, and inquire if the Saints there pray regularly ; that there are no contentions among them ; that there are no doubts arising in their minds ; and, finally, ascertain that they pay their tithing and are regular in their contributions. After the teacher is through with his inquiries, he kneels with the family and prays —and angels are to succeed him and the gifts are to flow in upon their patient souls if they " weary not in well-doing."

That teacher's next duty is to report the spiritual life of the family at the " council meeting," and wherever he discovers the dawning of a doubt in the form of a question, that family is watched with solicitude and " laboured " with. If the doubt disappear, 'tis well ; if it grows, it is fought ; if it becomes unconquerable, " apostacy " ensues, the untamable is " cut off " and consigned to the tender mercies of his Majesty of the nether regions, to be " buffeted " in the flesh.

With such a system of supervision, and the moulding of the disciple's mind by the habit of special prayer for the priesthood, asking that all that the prophet aims to be and to do may be favoured by the heavens—who cannot comprehend the power of the Mormon leader ? The Gentile world need not wonder at the submission of the Mormon people—they have prayed themselves into it. " Apostasy " from such a system must necessarily be of slow growth, and can only be reached by the men and women who *dare* to be free.

The " Priest " is the head of the Aaronic or Levitical priesthood, whose privilege it is to preach from the rostrum, and he can baptize by immersion "for the remission of sins," and, when wanted, he can act with the teachers and the deacons. The greater can always officiate with the less, but the less cannot officiate for the greater.

The Melchisedec priesthood commences with the "Elder." It is his privilege and calling to preach and administer in all the ordinances of the Church. He lays on hands to confirm all the baptized persons members of the Church, and they receive "the gift of the Holy Ghost" through the laying on of his hands upon their heads. When the Mormons are sick, they send for the elders and they anoint the afflicted with oil by pouring it upon their heads, and internally, if required by the sick, the Elder administers at the same time a tablespoonful of consecrated olive-oil, then lays hands upon his or her head, prays and "seals" upon him or her the blessing of health, commands the disease to depart, and the patient is healed—or should be.

There is no priesthood higher than that of an "elder," "after the order of Melchisedec;" but there are orders of rank above the elder—"seventies," "high-priests," and "apostles"—with special duties attached to their offices. The "Quorum" "of Apostles" is confined to twelve members, who are the chief presiding and ruling authorities wherever they are in the Churches abroad. They have all authority to regulate the affairs of the Saints, to appoint and displace presiding officers when necessary, and to direct the missionaries, and assign new fields of labour to the elders. They are the powerful men who "bind on earth that which is bound in heaven." They send the Gospel to the nations, or they withdraw the elders from the vineyards, shake the dust off their feet, and "seal up" the rebellious Gentiles to damnation.

The Seventies claim the rank next to the twelve apostles, and assume for themselves that they also are apostles, or special messengers to the nations. Each "Quorum of Seventy" is composed of seventy elders, and has an organization of its own, with a president and six counsellors. Over all the "Quorums of Seventies" there is a president and six counsellors. The number of these "quorums" is unlimited.

The high-priest's "quorum" is not numerically limited, and the nominal duty of the high-priest is to preside over the Saints wherever they are located in a collective body; but the callings of the high-priest and "seventies" have hitherto been more sounding in titles than distinctive in duty. The high-priest goes on missions as well as the "seventies," and the "seventies" preside as well as the high-priest.

Over the whole Church is the "First Presidency," a "Quo-"rum of Three," and these three are harmonious in representation upon the earth with "the Father, the Son, and the Holy "Ghost" in heaven. That first presidency is at present Brigham Young, George A. Smith, and Daniel H. Wells—the successors of Peter, James, and John.

Throughout all Mormondom the highest rank of the priesthood is sacred, and all counsellors are but aids. The theory is that a president is nearer to "the Throne" than his counsellors, and, though the latter may speak and diffuse their measure of light, at the moment the president is ready to decide * what should be done, "the Lord" will give him direction.

* This authoritative teaching silences all opposition when Brigham speaks. Whatever views may be entertained by any one in the Mormon Church, these must change, and an opinion by any one expressed before Brigham has spoken is immediately afterwards set aside. Elder Hyde gives two excellent illustrations in the cases of Elder Dunbar and Brother Heber. The former had spoken in one of "the Schools for the Prophets," and made himself clearly understood. He says:

"He proved his position, I thought, satisfactorily; an American elder, however, told him that 'Brigham taught the contrary doctrine.' Said this mental Colossus, 'If he said so, he must be right, and I withdraw my argument!'"

A still more absurd example is related. Elders Bullock, Hawkins, and others, were one day discussing with Heber about the resurrection, and the question was, whether, when the body came out of the grave, any visible hole would be left in the earth. "No," said Kimball, "not at all, the atoms will be reunited, and *they won't leave no hole.*" He began to explain his reasons for this opinion, when Brigham came in, and the question was referred to him. "Yes, certainly *it will,*" he replied; "Christ is the pattern, you know; he had to have the stone rolled away from the sepulchre, and that left the hole visible, for didn't the soldiers see it?" "Brother Brigham," cried Kimball, "*that is just* my opinion!"

One of the recently-made apostles was for many years Brigham's private secretary, an excellent scholar, and, taken "all in all," a very pleasant gentleman, but a perfect "echo." It mattered not what was under discussion before Brigham entered the office. If the Prophet expressed judgment to the contrary of what "Albert" had been arguing, in a moment he would express, in the presence of those who knew better, "Exactly, Brother Brigham, I was just saying so!" Who can

Each "quorum" has its own meetings. Any of the higher orders can visit and take part, if invited, in any "quorum" of a lesser priesthood; but no member of a lesser "quorum" is invited to take part in a higher "quorum." The "inspira-"tion" cometh from above, and flows like water downwards. It would never do for the knowledge or understanding of any principle or doctrine to seek shelter in the cranium of any member of the priesthood, till it had permeated the brain of the president. "Brother Heber," being an eccentric genius, did sometimes make unlooked-for announcements before Brigham had spoken, but Heber always dressed them in his own peculiar drollery, and they were permitted to be heard without censure. It is in consequence of this rigid discipline and order of teaching that Brigham Young is very properly held responsible for the utterances of the Tabernacle. Jedediah M. Grant's Reformation "blood-atonement" speeches did not, and could not, have originated with himself. He only uttered and amplified what were the conclusions of his chief. No false doctrine can, therefore, *creep in* among the Saints; it must come forth primarily, like the "Adam-deity," from the head of the president.*

The reader unacquainted with the Mormons might fall into the error of supposing that the priesthood was a body of learned men, and that the highest offices were filled by men of greater attainments in education. The male Mormons all receive the priesthood—all but the Africans.

There can be no "earthly" qualifications for rank in the priesthood—"the wisdom of the world is foolishness." Those who are elected and hold "position" in the Church are "en-"dowed from on high." Some few well-educated persons have held high office, but "learning" in general has been considered a dangerous element to its possessor. Very few of this class have been humble enough for "the Lord" to work with

wonder that Brigham Young has a good opinion of his own judgment, when no one ever ventures to differ from it?

* Brother Heber had considerable pride in relating to his intimate friends that he was the source of Brigham's revelation on the "Adam-deity." In a moment of reverie, Heber said: "Brother Brigham, I have an idea that Adam is not only our father, but our God." That was enough: Brigham snapped at the novelty, and announced it with all the flourish of a new-made revelation.

them long.   Heber had some acquaintance with the business
of a potter, and in his eloquent moments he delighted to instruct the people about the manipulation of clay—they were
all " clay " in the hands of the " potter," and if they expected
ever to be " vessels of honour " they had to be *ground very
fine*.   The application was clear, and in the experience of
many of the Mormons it has been terribly truthful.   The official in the Mormon Church must be as " limber as a tallowed
" rag." *

On the 6th of April, the anniversary of the organization of
the Church, a general conference is held in Salt Lake City, and
a semi-annual conference is held on the 6th of October.   During these conferences the people vote with uplifted hands to
sustain all the presiding authorities.   One of the apostles rises
on the platform, and moves that Brigham Young be " sus-
" tained " as " President of the Church of Jesus Christ of Lat-
" ter-Day Saints," and as " prophet, seer, and revelator."   The
motion is seconded, the show of hands is called for, and the
vote is unanimous.

All the other officials are reëlected in the same manner.   A
negative vote is called, but no hand is ever lifted in opposition.
Only two remarkable cases of negative voting have taken
place since the death of Joseph Smith—the one in Nauvoo, in
1844 (when Sidney Rigdon was tried); the other in Salt Lake
City, in 1869, when elders W. S. Godbe and E. L. T. Harrison
were disfellowshipped.   In both cases all these negative voters
were cut off from the Church, and in that there was perfect consistency.   The only possible use of brains in a theocracy is to
support " the chosen of the Lord ; " in this, the " unity of the
" Saints " is manifest.   Elder Amos M. Musser, the general
agent of Brigham, has been ridiculed for exhorting the Saints
to "go it blind; " but brother Musser was philosophic.   A
simple-hearted missionary—an Italian—who had long served
in Brigham's household, once addressed the Saints in Liverpool ; and, after " bearing his testimony " to the joy of living
in " Zion," he exhorted his hearers to " obey the authorities,"
as there was great happiness in obedience.   He said that he
had no trouble in getting along: " I puts my head in de bag,

* A favourite expression among the inspired.

"and I goes along, and I sees nothin'." Everywhere "blind
" obedience " is the mark of the highest virtue.

In the organization of the priesthood there are three distinct lines of power, *viz.* : the apostolic, the judicial, and the
political. The first is seen in the " kingdom "-building and
missionary labours, and embraces the " first presidency," the
twelve apostles, the " seventies," and elders. These are " the
" saviours of the world." The judicial organization embraces
the " first presidency," the high-council, the bishop and counsellors in each ward, and the visiting teachers—they decide all
questions of litigation among the Saints. The political branch
of the Church is little known, even among the Saints themselves, and is but seldom used. But there is in reality a resemblance to the Sanhedrim in a " council of fifty," composed
of the apostles and leading men. In Nauvoo this council was
more frequently used than it is in Utah.

Another very important order of the priesthood is that of
the " Patriarchs." The chief is designated " The Presiding
" Patriarch *over* the Church ; " the others are patriarchs *in* the
Church. These brethren have power to bless the people, and
to tell them from what particular branch of " Jacob " they have
sprung, and in this way the Saints learn what is the lineage
through which their blessings are to come.

The present chief Patriarch is still a young man, and inherited his office. He was the eldest son of Hyrum Smith,
who was assassinated at Carthage jail. " Uncle John " [Young],
the eldest brother of Brigham, was for many years the best
illustration of the Patriarch *in* the Church, and was very
earnest in his labours in " blessing " the people. This good
man had wives and children, and was properly enough entitled
to charge for his " blessings "—his family had to be supported.
Before money was known in Utah, the Patriarch had, of necessity, to be paid for his blessings in the produce of the country.
At times, this unwieldy payment entailed considerable inconvenience, but " Uncle John " was persevering, and managed
to get along comfortably. When paid in butter or flour—if
either of those articles was scarce and difficult to obtain—
" Uncle John " was certain to give " *a good* blessing "—at the
rate of two dollars apiece, and, when there were several to be

" blessed " in one family, there was some slight reduction. He travelled all over the Territory, and when he arrived in a settlement, announcement was made of his head-quarters, and all the " unblessed " were invited and urged to " get a blessing." As produce rose or fell in value, the exact amount of flour, butter, eggs, beef, and potatoes, would be specially designated, and those who possessed the requisite articles were " blessed." " Uncle John," doubtless, gave many " blessings " in his lifetime without any reward; but, as a rule, the " Patriarchal " blessing " was strictly a matter of trade. One of the brethren, west of Salt Lake, tells that he was once very anxious to have the Patriarch lay his hands upon his head, but he had only vinegar wherewith to pay for it. " Uncle John " could not receive such remuneration, and the " brother " returned home sorrowing; but after a time he was able to present an " acceptable " offering, and then he got a " first-class blessing." These blessings are singular documents—they are all written by the Patriarch's scribe, and are preserved in the family of the recipient with great reverence.

The judicial department of the priesthood is very valuable to the Saints; it is the best institution connected with Mormonism. It has saved the brethren and sisters all the trouble and expence of lawsuits when differences have arisen among them, and, following the closing of a controversy, reconciliation of the contestants is insisted upon.

If John Smith has any difficulty with John Jones, it is immediately discovered by the teachers. The contending parties are visited, and the grievance is investigated. The offender is instructed to go to the offended, and make confession of his error, and obtain forgiveness. Should Smith, the offender, refuse to make confession, and be reconciled to his brother, Jones, the offended man, makes complaint, and the teachers " labour " with Smith. Should the latter remain obstinate, the teachers summon him to appear at the council-meeting of his ward, and before the bishop, his counsellors, and the members of the priesthood who attend the council-meeting, the difficulty is stated; both parties are heard, and, when the evidence is all weighed, the bishop sums up the whole matter, and gives his decision. In most cases that decision is accepted, the matter ends, and the contending brothers are reconciled, and agree to live together again in "good fellowship as becometh Saints." Should either of the contestants, however, be still dissatisfied, an appeal can be made for a hearing before the chief bishop of the whole Church and his counsellors, or to the High Council.

This latter organization is composed of fifteen elders, not specially the greatest men in the community, nor yet selected for any legal acumen. The absence of a critical mind is no detriment to a member of the High Council, for "the spirit" is more valuable than schooling with Chitty or Blackstone. The head of this council is the President of the Stake of Zion and his two counsellors: the twelve others are appointed like the members of any other "quorum."

When any important case comes before the council for trial, six members are assigned to each side—the odd numbers taking the prosecution, and the even numbers taking the defence, or *vice versa*. Till the case is brought into the council-room, neither prosecutor nor defendant knows who will represent him in the debate. The object of the council is to reach facts—to decide according to equity. The judgment of the council is reached by the vote. Should it be a tie-vote, the president casts his own, and that ends it. From this council there is also an appeal to the "quorum" of the "First Presi-"dency," and from that, if desired, to the Church collectively in General Conference. Such trials, however, are very rare. Sidney Rigdon's trial, in Nauvoo, was the last.

Should either of the contestants before the High Council refuse to accept its decision, and make no further appeal to a Church tribunal, if the subject in dispute is property, and the adjudged guilty one will not abide by "the judgment" and make "restitution," he will be "cut off" from the Church, and the injured party can then sue him before a court of law, like any Gentile.

But it is not only between brothers in faith that the Church adjudicates. Into every relation of life the teachers have a right to inquire. Between parents and children, husband and wife, and between wife and wife, the "faithful teacher" has the right to step in. He is the all-seeing eye of "the Lord," and knows everything. Many a man has been surprised to know how intimate Brigham Young was with his family affairs, and when Brigham has thought him worthy of his wrath, he has been surprised to hear the Prophet relate, with minute precision, acts of his life, the knowledge of which he thought was confined to the walls of his own "castle." To the superstitious, the fulness of the Prophet's intelligence upon any subject has often been credited to revelation; to those better acquainted with the machinery of the priesthood and its influence, the visit of the teacher, or that of a wife, to the Prophet's office, was the truer solution of the mystery. There is nothing concealed from Brigham; he sees everything and hears everything.

This great net-work of priesthood which covers everything, and the influence of which permeates everything, is the key to the power of Brigham Young over the Saints in Zion. Through this priesthood he can sway them as he will. Once, by his decision, they expatriated themselves from the United States, and sought Mexican soil for a future home, and every notable feature of Mormon history since has sprung from the same source. As seen in all the Conference minutes, the people are, by their own free voting, made responsible for everything that is done, and when once they have, by uplifted hand before heaven, expressed their wish, it becomes their duty and obligation to sustain it.

At the last Conference, on Wednesday, October 9, 1872, the following were reëlected the presiding authorities of the Mormon Church:

"Elder George Q. Cannon presented the authorities of the Church to the Conference, in the following order, the vote to sustain them being unanimous:

"Brigham Young, Prophet, Seer, and Revelator, and President of the Church of Jesus Christ of Latter-Day Saints in all the world.

"George A. Smith, Prophet, Seer, and Revelator, and first Counsellor to President Young.

"Daniel H. Wells, Prophet, Seer, and Revelator, and second Counsellor to President Young.

"Orson Hyde, President of the Quorum of the Twelve Apostles, and Orson Pratt, Sen., John Taylor, Wilford Woodruff, Charles C. Rich, Lorenzo Snow, Erastus Snow, Franklin D. Richards, George Q. Cannon, Brigham Young, Jr., Joseph F. Smith, and Albert Carrington, members of said Quorum.

"John Smith, Patriarch of the Church.

"John W. Young, President of this Stake of Zion, and George B. Wallace and John T. Caine his counsellors.

"William Eddington, John L. Blythe, Howard O. Spencer, John Squires, Wm. H. Folsom, Thomas E. Jeremy, Joseph L. Barfoot, John H. Rumell, Miner G. Attwood, Wm. Thorn, Dimick B. Huntington, Theodore McKean, and Hosea Stout, members of the High Council.

"Elias Smith, President of the High-Priests' Quorum, and Edward Snelgrove and Elias Morris his counsellors.

"Joseph Young, President of the first seven Presidents of the Seventies, and Levi W. Hancock, Henry Herriman, Albert P. Rockwood, Horace S. Eldridge, Jacob Gates, and John Van Cott, members of the first seven Presidents of the Seventies.

"Benjamin L. Peart, President of the Elders' Quorum; Edward Davis and Abinadi Pratt, his counsellors.

"Edward Hunter, Presiding Bishop; Leonard W. Hardy and Jesse C. Little, his counsellors.

"Samuel G. Ladd, President of the Priests' Quorum; Wm. McLachlan and James Latham, his counsellors.

"Adam Spears, President of the Teachers' Quorum; Martin Lenzi and Henry I. Doremus, his counsellors.

"James Leach, President of the Deacons' Quorum; Peter Johnson and Chas. S. Cram, his counsellors.

"Brigham Young, Trustee-in-Trust for the Church of Jesus Christ of Latter-Day Saints.

"Truman O. Angel, Architect for the Church.

"Albert Carrington, Historian and General Church Recorder, and Wilford Woodruff, his assistant." *

These are the presidents, and as every sane man in the Mormon Church "holds the priesthood," and can be instantly reached by his superior, the reader cannot fail to comprehend that the "one-man-power" in Utah is a reality, and no myth or "phantom of a Gentile brain." Those who have estimated Joseph Smith, the founder of Mormonism, "as a fool," have greatly mistaken the man. With him originated this order of priesthood, and his tongue enunciated every principle or doctrine believed and practised by the Mormons. Brigham Young received the Church in its entirety as an inheritance, as probably in a few years his successor will inherit it from him.

But the reader has only seen the priesthood at home: an-

* _Deseret News_, October 9, 1872.

other, and still more interesting page of history is the missionary priesthood abroad.

From the youth in his teens, to the elder in hoary age, all the brethren are subject to be " called on mission " at any time, and in such calls no personal conveniences are ever consulted. Should a merchant be wanted for a " mission," his business must be left in other hands, and his affairs can be conducted by other brains: so with the artisan, the mechanic, the farmer, and the ploughboy—they must in their way do the best they can. Seed-time or harvest, summer or winter, pleasure or important work—nothing in which they are engaged is allowed to stand in the way. If poor, and the family is dependent upon the outgoing missionary, that must be no hinderance—the mission is given, he has to go, and the family " trusts in the " Lord," and in the tender mercies of the bishop !

There is no missionary fund to defray the expenses of him who is sent; he travels onward " without purse and scrip," and makes his way from Utah to the " Gentile " nations in the best manner he can. Of late years, the missionaries have been permitted to take money with them to defray their expenses—if able to do so ; but in the beginning it was considered that there was glory in literally travelling without money to do " the " Lord's " work, and trusting to His providence for daily bread, shelter, and clothing. The only qualification demanded was a good stock of faith, and, ever-powerful as money is, with such a task before him faith is far more essential, and far more potential, with the missionary, than solid cash, worldly influence, or " green-backs."

Preceding the completion of the Pacific railroad, the departure of the missionaries was an important epoch among the Saints. The April Conference was looked forward to with great interest. It was then that the missionaries were called. Many a man was nervous when the hour of appointment arrived. No previous intimation was given, not a word whispered, and the man who thought that he could not be spared a week or a day from his business heard, without warning, his name proposed for a foreign mission. He could object, certainly, but to do so was to question " the Lord," and to bear ever after the brand of " weak in the faith."

The elders who are called on mission are invited to meet in the evening in the Historian's Office, to be "set apart for their "missions." Brigham and the apostles meet with them, and lay their hands upon them, and bless them, and "consecrate" them to the work of "the Lord," and predict upon their heads that they will do "wonderful works." The eager ears of the missionary catch every word, and he treasures up in his heart what he has to accomplish. No salary, no question of paltry gold, is anything when compared with a prediction. The one "perishes with the using," the other is the "day-star of hope," that brightens more and more as the clouds of adversity thicken and lower, and the weary soul is ready to faint. The missionary is now fully qualified, and the one of whom least is expected often accomplishes the most.

It was usually arranged that the day of departure should be at the beginning of May. Salt Lake City was the general rendezvous, and there the missionaries would organize to travel together for economy and mutual protection. Usually they would travel by mule-teams; but many a missionary band has crossed the plains with ox-teams in common covered wagons, and on one occasion a company made the whole distance to the Missouri river dragging hand-carts.

None of these missionaries would ever have undertaken that experiment for money, nor in any business of their own; but with them it was an act of faith to be illustrated, and they did it "for the work's sake." Brigham and the apostles were just at that time particularly "exercised" about the calamities that were coming upon the outside world, especially about great troubles that were to arise between Great Britain and the United States. "The Lord" was whispering to them of a coming war, and it was essentially necessary that the Saints should be "delivered" before the struggle began. Fortunately for two great nations, as well as for the Mormon immigrants, "the Lord" of the Saints was on that occasion, as he had frequently been before, slightly incorrect in his calculations.*

* With so many failures of prediction as are manifest in Mormon history, ordinary persons would be likely to suspect that there was something wrong about these "whisperings of the Spirit." Brigham never would trust a man an hour who failed him as frequently as "the Lord" has failed the modern apostles. There is a growing suspicion in the minds of intelligent persons that Brigham has for some years

When the missionaries arrived on the Missouri river, they would sell their outfits, and, with the money received, some of them would hurry onward and hasten to their fields of labour; others would send back what they could get to Utah, to comfort their wives and children, and they themselves would proceed eastward, trusting in "the Lord."

What a history the Mormon elders could write of their experience! Without a claim upon a soul for support, without knowing where to procure the necessities for life and travel, they would start out to evangelize the world. The only document the missionary would carry would be his "elder's certifi-"cate," a brief, plainly-written note, setting forth that he "is "in full faith and fellowship with the Church of Jesus Christ "of Latter-Day Saints," and inviting "all men to give heed to "his teachings and counsels, as a man of God, sent to open to "them the door of life and salvation." The reader is asked to "assist him in his travels, in whatsoever things he may need," and the Lord is invoked to bless "all who receive him, and "minister to his comfort." That document is signed by Brigham Young and his two counsellors, and with that alone the missionary travels.

All that the Mormon missionary asks is, to be heard, to be listened to, and his poverty forces him to seek an auditory among the poor. He begins at the lowest round of the ladder and works upwards. He is familiar with the text of the Bible, and he fails not to say "Blessed are the poor," to them "the "Gospel is preached." Had its advocacy been entrusted to men of education and wealth, Mormonism never would have troubled the world. The Mormon net is adapted to its own peculiar fish, and the fishermen are to go "without purse and "scrip." Poor themselves, they can go anywhere, and among the poor they are certain to find sympathy:

"One touch of nature makes the whole world kin."

Nine-tenths of the elders who have preached Mormonism would

concluded that he and "the Lord" were one and the same person. Many of Brigham's most trusted men begin to show their doubting, and hint, *in a quiet way*, that if Mormonism, after all, should not be the thing they thought it was, they will be no worse off than others who have been deceived, and in the mean time they are sure of the "life that now is."

be uncomfortable if walking, as the poet has it, in "silver slip-"pers." They despise the world and all its glory.

In religious experience personal indiosyncrasy has much to do with the faith that a person embraces, and circumstances more frequently than "grace" contribute to the intensity of a new belief. In the narratives of the experience of the Mormon missionary it is almost universally one and the same story : "Persons were found discontented with the established forms of "religion, they were longing for something that had more soul-vi-"tality," something that warmed the instinctive heroism of the heart, something that could make them "rejoice in tribulation" and be willing to "forsake all for the Gospel's sake." The world is not overcrowded with persons of this condition of mind, but to a certain extent they are to be met with every-where among people of all religions.

The announcement of the Mormon missionaries that angels were again visiting the earth, and that elders were once more being sent forth "without purse or scrip" to gather the lost sheep of the house of Israel, was the very tidings that such per-sons had longed to hear. It is a pleasant thing to believe one's self miraculously visited. The faith of such a missionary is "a live coal from off the altar," it touches the hearts of hearers. His very impoverished condition stamps him with honesty of purpose even if his doctrine may be unpalatable ; he is with-out a home, is wholly dependent upon invitation to the domes-tic board ; his helplessness, as "a stranger in a strange land," awakens sympathy, and admiration of his courage is drawn even from those who may oppose him. He is invited home. Curiosity is aroused, and inquiry follows. He relates his travels, how he has left his family in a far-distant country, and "forsaken all"—to bring to them the glad tidings of a "New "Dispensation." He feels his dependence on "the Lord;" he is grateful for the moment's providential care, and his words are humbly and fitly chosen to touch the soul of his entertainer.

In all this he certainly is not acting a part; he is not en-snaring, but is ever believing that the heavens are operating with him, and using him for the attainment of a great purpose ; he aims to be "wise as a serpent and harmless as a dove." The Mormon missionary is by no means a Tartuffe.

This fireside preaching is a new experience to his hearers. The minister and the people are drawn together closer than they ever were before ; and he, fully charged with chapter and verse for the new doctrines, and thoroughly acquainted with the predictions of the remotest ages, bearing on his interpretation of the Latter-Day kingdom, skilled also in wayside polemics, knows how to use them ; and though in his mien he appears to be but the humble mechanic or labourer, he is soon discovered to be no ordinary man. The more he stumbles in speech and shows a lack of education, the more forcible the argument : the Scriptures all seem to apply to him. He sees the force of a personal application of the words " the " Lord hath chosen the weak things of the earth to confound " the mighty." He claims little for himself, but he adds to his own personal importance by asserting more for others. There is " one mightier than he "—" The Lord " hath raised up a prophet to whom He hath revealed the secrets of His will. The Prophet is absent in Zion, he is far distant, and the farther the distance the greater the faith. Under these circumstances the hearer becomes dazzled with the complexity of the statements of the missionary and the mental struggle which his arguments induce. New thoughts are born, wonder and amazement are let loose, and what is not said by the missionary himself is inferred by the hearer, till the most extravagant pictures are created in their minds, and angels descending to hold communion with men seems perfectly natural ; and, if so, why should *they* not also be among the favoured whom angels may visit ? Abraham, Isaac, Jacob, and the ancient prophets, were thus blessed ; and why, then, should not mortals now receive similar heavenly visits ? The road is smooth from what has been to what may be. Thus the Mormon missionaries have touched the very souls of their hearers, and found believing hearts all over the earth—one here, and another there, ready waiting for their testimony.

In this undemonstrative way, Mormonism was first disseminated throughout the United States and introduced into Britain and Continental Europe. As the number of converts increased, tracts and pamphlets were profusely circulated, and halls rented for preaching.

In the summer of 1837, the Mormon Elders first preached in England, and at their April Conference, in 1841, there was represented a total of 5,184 persons baptized. Of these, 106 were ordained elders, 303 priests, 169 teachers, and 63 deacons. Besides these, eight hundred souls had emigrated to "build " up Zion at Nauvoo." This was a rapid work for the few elders engaged in it.

In some parts of England "the fields were very ripe" when the elders arrived there; they had only to thrust in their sickles and reap a bountiful harvest of souls. It was very difficult to introduce the faith into London; and in large cities generally the task was onerous; but in some of the inland counties, "the Spirit" was poured out in great abundance. The apostles went into Herefordshire, and their preaching resulted in a perfect "pentecost" of conversions. They swallowed up the entire "United Brethren," people, preachers, meeting-houses and almost all they had got. It was the Hereford disciples who rendered the success of Mormonism in England easy. They furnished the money to publish the Book of Mormon, were liberal to the mission, and many of them became themselves valiant preachers. Seven of the apostles, including Brigham and Heber, were all labouring in Herefordshire at one time. The might of the priesthood was there concentrated, and great numbers were baptized in that and in the neighbouring shires.

Manchester and other manufacturing towns in Lancashire listened early to the "glorious news," and many were baptized. The first initiatory rite was administered in the British kingdom at Preston, and the first candidate was a lady, but "brother George D. Watt was more fleet of step, and he ran "some distance to the water's edge," got up to Heber before the lady, and "was the first British subject who entered the king-"dom of God!" By way of dividing the honours, however, the sister was the first confirmed.

Before this could be accomplished, Heber and Orson Hyde relate that they had a terrible tussle with a host from the infernal regions. The "devils" came into their bedroom in Preston, the night before they were to make their *début* in the streets as preachers, and they had a fearful time together.

One of the brethren, who had accompanied these elders from America, was the first seized by the invisible powers, and, to relieve him of his torture, Heber and Orson proceeded to " lay "hands" upon him. While in the performance of that " ordi-"nance," the " devils " struck Heber a powerful blow on the head and he fell senseless to the floor. Hyde and the other elder raised him to the bed, laid hands upon him, and he gradually recovered and sat up.

But the fight was not over. The " devils," after a little time, became visible, and tried to clutch the brethren with their hands as if they wanted to tear them to pieces. All night this was continued, but the elders were able to keep them at a respectable distance by commanding them " in the name of " Jesus Christ " to depart. The departure, however, was not very rapid, as they stopped all night within a few feet of the three elders and swore fearfully at them and " old Joe Smith," and threatened to do dreadful things to them.

These three elders believed all that has been here related, and many a time and oft Heber and Orson have publicly told the story, and described the hideous visages of their visitors and how they gnashed their teeth at them and " swore like " troopers," and used awfully vile and dirty language all night. There were no horns, hoofs, or other appendages to the visitors, but they looked ugly enough without. Hyde adds to his narrative that one of them was " a sneaking fellow ; " he was about the last of the crowd, and stepped back as they retired to make friends with the apostle, or at least to soften his wrath. He was anxious that the apostle should know and remember that he had acted no violent part on this occasion, as he was merely an on-looker. All this has been repeatedly told to the Saints, and the inference derived from the story is, that Satan was mad because the apostles had been sent by Joseph Smith to preach the gospel to the British, and thereby disturb the devil's kingdom—ergo Mormonism is divine, and the time will come when the modern apostles will be able to " serve out " the devils, for into the hands of the priesthood the judgment will be given of " the quick and the dead."

In 1841 the apostle Orson Hyde undertook a mission to Judea to bless that land for the return of the Jews. Early in the morning he ascended to the Mount of Olives and constructed an altar from a pile of loose rock, and with pen, ink, and paper, there offered up a dedicatory prayer consecrating the land to "the Lord," and asking for favours and blessings upon scattered Israel.

In 1843, missionaries were sent to the Pacific Isles; and for a time, owing to the troubles in Nauvoo and the exodus to the mountains, new missionary enterprises were held in abeyance.

In 1850, three of the apostles were sent to "open up the "gospel to Europe." Scandinavia, France, and Italy, were selected, and the Book of Mormon was translated into Danish, French, Italian, and German. Switzerland and Germany heard the "gospel" about the same time. In that year missionaries were sent to the Sandwich Isles, and there the Book of Mormon was also translated into the Hawaiian language.

A grand missionary enterprise was undertaken in 1852. The revelation on polygamy had been given to the public about a month before the October Conference, and a host of elders—about eighty—were sent to the nations to help through the new doctrine and to defend Zion. The elders went to Australia, Hindostan, China, Siam, Ceylon, South Africa, the West Indies, British Guiana, Gibraltar, and Malta—but very little was accomplished. Many of the elders endured great privations and suffered more than words can tell; they made a few converts and returned to Zion. In 1853 an effort was made to introduce Mormonism into Prussia, but the elders were ordered to leave that kingdom. In the following year, a similar attempt was made to conquer Austria in the cause of the faith, but nothing was accomplished.

After the British mission, the Scandinavian has been the most successful; Germany and Switzerland have contributed a considerable number of converts; a few of the Protestants of Piedmont and a still less number from Paris and Havre-de-Grâce have accepted the new faith. Between 1840 and 1854, of all the converts, 17,195 emigrated from Liverpool. Of that number over a thousand were from Scandinavia. Up to 1860, about 30,000 Mormons emigrated from Europe, and from that time to the present there have probably been 25,000 more, making a contribution to America of a round 55,000 souls.

But this number of emigrants gives no idea of the aggre-
gate of those who have, at one time or another, been baptized
into the Mormon Church in Europe. Probably not one person
in twenty who receives the faith "endures to the end," and
many of those who are "faithful" are so very poor that they
are unable to pay the expenses of their emigrating to Zion, and
they linger on in the old homes of their fathers. Brigham has
made a vigorous effort to gather all the foreign Saints, and has
laid the Rocky Mountain Saints under very heavy contributions to that end. To some of the foreign disciples emigration
has been a great blessing; to others it has been the ruin of
everything of earthly value.

The reader, however, must not suppose that Brigham has
heedlessly distributed the wealth of the disciples in Utah for
the suffering poor among the Saints. The prophet thinks
himself a financier, and he loves to boast of that qualification.

A resolution was taken by the Mormons in Nauvoo, who
had wealth enough to lead the van in the exodus to the Rocky
Mountains, that they would never cease their efforts to assist
the poor whom they had left behind, till every deserving soul
was gathered to the body of the Church. The exiles honoured
their word, and, as the pioneers found resting-places in the
West, teams were sent back to Iowa and Illinois, and the poor
were assisted forward to the Missouri river.

During this exodus, the emigration from Europe to the
States was entirely closed; but, stimulated by the apostles,
the British Saints memorialized her Majesty the Queen to provide them transportation to Vancouver's Island or Oregon, and
to grant them the means of subsistence till they could produce
it from the soil. The memorial has been severely criticised by
those who charge the Mormon leaders with disloyal sentiments
to the Republic, and there is a paragraph in it that quite admits of that construction; but Brigham has enough sins to account for without being responsible for that. In 1846 the distress in England among the poorer classes was sorely felt by
the Mormons, and justified their seeking deliverance at the
hands of royalty, even though their presence, 30,000 strong, in
the Territory of Oregon, might have been prejudicial to American interests during the boundary debate. The British treas-

ury, however, was represented at the time as unable to favour
the prayers of the thirteen thousand persons who signed the
memorial, and the Saints had no alternative but to " bide their
" time."

In the spring of 1848 immigration was reopened, *via* New
Orleans, up the Mississippi river to St. Louis, thence by the
Missouri to Council Bluffs and Winter-Quarters on the opposite bank of the river. During the October Conference of the
following year, the resolution for gathering the poor from Nauvoo was extended to the poor of all countries, and a " Perpet-
" ual Fund " was created. A liberal contribution was made,
and some of the leading elders, under the direction of the chief
bishop, were sent East to first gather up the Saints left on the
Missouri river, and from that time the operation of the fund
was to be extended to Europe.

The funds, of course, like everything else, were, and are
under the direction of the First Presidency, and the immigrants
assisted were usually met by the clerks of the Trustee-in-Trust
one day before they entered Salt Lake City, and signed their
obligations to refund the money with ten per cent. per annum
added till paid. Contributions have been continually called for,
and the fund has increased to a pretty large sum. During the
present summer Brigham announced that the immigrants owed
the fund nearly a million of dollars! As the fund is a general
receptacle for contributions, loses nothing, and gains annually
ten per cent. upon its entire capital, it is destined to be a great
institution, and a rod in pickle for the disobedient.

The opponents of Brigham are usually very severe upon
him for " the bondage " in which he holds his poor debtors;
but he has his defence. Many of those immigrants can never
return the funds unless they apostatize, and if that dreadful
deed is done, his agent is instantly after the rebel. One
of the elders who had been on mission for several years in
England, and who had, in addition, been a liberal contributor
with his pen to the Church organ there, had to be assisted to
Zion by the fund. He thought they had no right to expect
his " obligation " after all those years of service ; but he was
obliged to give it. Three years ago he apostatized, and gave
promise of being a magnificent rebel. He was tried before the

High Council, condemned, consigned to the buffetings of Satan, and, before he left the Council room, or his Satanic Majesty had well got hold of him, one of Brigham's clerks placed before his bewildered eyes his obligation to the Perpetual Fund, and demanded settlement. He was, like all poets and great martyrs, without the ready cash. It was spiteful and undue haste, on the part of Brigham, and provoked a measure that promises to be to the Prophet

" A Roland for an Oliver." *

The Mormon immigration in general has been very orderly conducted. The Saints are very obedient and give no trouble on shipboard. In former years, when they crossed the ocean in sailing-packets, the captain who could get the Mormon immigrants was considered fortunate for that voyage. " The Lord " was with His people, and of course " the prayers of the Saints " prevailed and the ship was safe † and made a speedy voyage. After they got over the effects of the first rolling of the vessel they were summoned morning and evening to prayers; they sang their hymns, and the elders gave them instructions about their daily duties. On Sundays, if the weather was favourable, they had preaching between-decks, and rejoiced together in the deliverance they had gained from " Babylon," and spoke of the bright future that lay before them. Even when several hundreds were on board, there was no rush or confusion to get first to the cooking galley. The whole ship was nominally partitioned off into wards, and a member of the priesthood placed over each. These presidents arranged the order and time for each ward to see to their cooking, and every day the

* There are numbers of men in Utah who would be pleased for the Trustee-in-Trust to take action in a civil court against them for such indebtedness. They have preserved their tithing receipts for every pound of butter, tenth pig, gosling, eggs, apples, and scores of other things paid into the Tithing-office, and on such a trial *they could compel the Trustee-in-Trust to bring his books into court, and show what he has done with the tithing !* That would be a lengthy trial, and the rebels threaten it.

† The ships conveying the Mormon immigrants have been so free from accident, that it is not strange that the Saints should believe that the peculiar favour of " the Lord " is extended over them. The hand-cart disasters and an unfortunate steamboat explosion, on the Missouri, in March, 1852, in which many of the Saints were killed, temper such enthusiasm.

order was changed. Thus they realized, there, if nowhere else, that "the first shall be last and the last shall be first." Everything on board ship was done by order; no smoking or drinking was allowed, and the sailors or other passengers were not permitted to make love to the young sisters. It is fair to add that on shipboard, as well as on *terra firma*, love *would* break through bolts and bars, and some of the sisters, who had less grace than others, "forgot their covenants."

On several of the trips, the returning missionaries were successful in converting passengers and sailors. On one occasion nearly the whole crew were baptized. A canvas raft was soon made and hoisted over into the sea, and there the elder would stand and with uplifted hand would announce his authority, and immerse his convert in the briny deep "for the "remission of his sins." That sailor or that passenger could then associate with the Saints, and rejoice in salvation; but even that pleasant reminiscence is tainted with the reflection that, in some cases, the conversion did not last long, and more than one trusting maiden had to suffer the consequences of a hasty marriage.

Now everything in connection with emigration is changed, and the nine months' travel by sea and land is a work of days. Brigham's agent at Liverpool sees the emigrants on board a steamship of the Guion line, and another of his agents meets the Saints on arrival in New York. Everything is prepared; there is nothing to ask. The officer who has charge on board knows before he leaves Liverpool the exact amount of fare that every family has to pay for the remainder of the journey; he collects their gold and silver, and the agent at New York, without a moment's loss of time, knows where to make his exchange. The railroad tickets are already in his office, and if the steamer has arrived early in the day, the immigrants are whirled out of the city in the evening on a special train, and onward they travel over the Pennsylvania, Pittsburg & Fort Wayne railroad, to Chicago. A baker is telegraphed when the train will arrive at that city, and he is ready with "the staff of life." A brief rest, and permission to get the extra cheese or sausage, and off they are again, the engine steaming and snorting over the Chicago & Northwestern line

for Omaha.   Another baker with supplies, a few hours' rest, or
it may be half a day, to stretch their limbs, and then they
make the final change of cars that carries them over that magnificent national highway, the Union Pacific railroad, to the
Zion of the latter-days, the goal of their hopes, and the land
of their inheritance.

CHAPTER L.

POLYGAMY IN UTAH—Preached from the Tabernacle—A Terrible Trial to Women—Degradation of the Sex—Ancient Hebrew Examples adduced—"Living Martyrs" to a Debasing Doctrine—Brigham Young on Polygamy—Second and " following " Wives—Marriage Rites among the Mormons—The First Wife is not asked *one* Question—Impossibility of Happiness in Polygamy.

In two preceding chapters the history of the introduction of Polygamy among the Saints is given *in extenso*, illustrating the dubious path in which the Prophet Joseph had to tread in order to establish in his Church the usages of the Orientals. The reader has now presented to his consideration the " pecul- " iar Institution " in the fulness of its glory in Zion ; where there is nothing to hinder " the Lord " from manifesting His favour to Israel, and where the faithful can sit under their own vines and fig-trees, none daring to make them afraid.

Joseph had been persecuted, but Brigham was now beyond the reach of the oppressor. The former had the statute of big- amy before his eyes in Illinois ; the latter was master of the situation in Utah, and was determined there should be no stat- ute on the subject. Marriage was no longer a civil contract ; it was to be a sacrament of the Church, and a sacred tenet of the faith. But Utah nevertheless was a portion of the United States domain, and it was uncertain what Congress might wish to do with this innovation upon Christianity. Joseph had only risked the faith of a few of the Saints, and his communica- tions were confidential. Brigham had to cope with a govern- ment, and his mind grasped the conclusion that there was power in numbers. To punish individuals for an infraction of law was an easy matter ; to deal with a whole people was quite another thing. The utmost publicity had now to be given to

" Celestial Marriage," and an open parade of a " plurality of " wives" was a virtue, and not an indiscretion.

The Tabernacle in winter, and the Bowery in summer, were to resound with arguments in favour of Polygamy. The world was rapidly hastening to a close, and there were multitudes of spirits in the other world anxiously waiting for honourable bodies in which they could tabernacle in the flesh. The Gentiles were corrupt, and those ethereal spirits would rather anxiously wait for the favours of the Saints than come down to the palaces of the unbelieving, accursed Gentiles. The argument was lucid, and it appealed to the grandest sentiment of humanity —self-abnegation. The woman who viewed with the most searching jealousy the wandering of her idol's love, could in time listen to argument and could reproach her suffering soul with selfishness if it refused to endure for the weal of another. She loved herself, and her soul's idol was beyond price, but it was *her duty* to make her life a sacrifice ! The Greatest of all the human family had given His life to redeem; why could not she help to save ? Such was the argument in Utah, on the public recognition of Polygamy, and, if not in the words of the preacher, it was at least in the soul of the woman.

Whoever has read debasement in the women of Utah, has done them injustice. Some there may be who are devoid of refined sentiment and the nobler instincts of their sex; but no women in history ever deserved more respect and sympathy than the true women among the Mormons. They have not only made the sacrifice of the most vital principle of their souls, but they have voluntarily submitted to a life of daily affliction, for the sake of an article of faith.

Could the same judgment be passed upon the teachers as upon the taught, the people of Utah could rank with the highest martyrs of history ; but the opposite has been the fact, and, while the women have endured the most heart-piercing woes, the men have been taught that he was the noblest who valued the companionship of soul the least—that his wife was but the mother of his children. Following this inspiration, she has been often degraded to the level of the inferior animals; and, in the familiar language of one of the most elevated of the apostles, they thought " no more of taking another woman " than they did of "buying another cow." Whatever there has been and is higher than this conception of ownership in and the ability of women among the Mormon men, it is traceable to their better instincts and to their reminiscences of a Christian motherhood. The tendency of the matrimonial teachings of inspired tongues has been degrading to the sexes, placing the domestic circle on a level with the farm-yard.

The philosophy of nomadic ancient Israel is glorified in Utah :

"Lo, children and the fruit of the womb are a heritage and gift that cometh of the Lord.

"Like as the arrows in the hand of a giant; even so are the young children.

"Happy is the man that hath his quiver full of them; they shall not be ashamed, when they speak with the enemies in the gate."—Psalm cxxvii.

Harassed, despoiled, and driven in Missouri and Illinois by superior numbers, long years of isolation in the mountains were prayed for that Israel might grow and multiply, and cover the earth with cities, and become a great people that no man could number. Now the glories of the faith are artistically portrayed, and weepingly the women of Utah promise to obey; and from the moment that promise is given the woman lives in constant dread of the coming day when her husband has to become a practical polygamist.

The hallowed love, the sacred reminiscences of their happy years of undivided union, confront the threatened intrusion of another's presence at the home fireside. The wifely heart revolts at the invasion of the privacy of her domestic empire, and she maddens at the thought that he who was to her " sacred in person," and " all her own," was one day to become to another what he has been to her. Peace flies from her bosom, and in her soul commences a fearful struggle between obedience to the supposed commandment of Deity, taught by the Mormon priesthood, and the assertions of a nobler deity within her own nature. These contending influences wage unceasing warfare, and " the faith " slowly but surely gains the ascendancy over " the woman," and she yields—vanquished in bewilderment. Devotion to her husband, the dread of " offending God," and the fear of the anathemas of a creed, combine to conquer her.

She resigns herself to her fate, and finally consents that her husband should take another wife. What a horrible ordeal! The night of gloom overhangs her path; life loses its charms; the sacred fireside circle is broken; she grieves; she mourns; and her once-gushing, affectionate heart withers and dies within her bosom.

Some women in Utah have for years lived in this torture, crucifying themselves in every thinking moment of their lives! Who can tell the bitter misery felt by such unhappy souls? What days of silent grief and bitter tears; what long, sleepless nights of harrowing thought; what terrible imaginings! Disconsolate, poor, lacerated hearts, desolate women; afraid of every coming hour; fearful of what they might see or hear of husbands who had sworn at the bridal-altar to be to them the undivided companions of their lives! The story of such women can never be told—but in two words their condition can be written: *Living martyrs!*

In its overburdened grief many a soul has craved the boon of death, and welcomed the thought of that hour when the cold grave would conceal them from the gaze of the living. And all this mourning comes from a "revelation of Jesus "Christ," commanding obedience to polygamy, with the terrible threat of damnation and cursing to the rebellious! How He must have changed!—He, who was to woman so gentle, so forbearing, so loving in His nature—now so fierce and unrelenting! But, it is claimed that the dread of polygamy is worse than its practical experience, and that women can "get "used to it," and become happy under its rule.

To assert that any true woman living in polygamy is in heart and soul satisfied and happy, is to simply libel her nature. A true wife craves the constant love of her husband, as naturally as the living body craves its daily food. His companionship is her little world. And the more affectionate and pure he is, the more she abhors his familiar association with another. Her instincts rebel against the institution, and he misrepresents all womanhood who charges her opposition to it, as is frequently done in Utah, to the baser motive expressed in the vulgar taunt of "desiring a man to herself."

The women are, however, not alone the sufferers by polygamy. The intelligent of the fair sex among the Mormons will readily admit this, and some even go so far as to pity their husbands, and to extend to them the genuine sympathy of their hearts, though his polygamy has been their own curse. Whatever else it has achieved, Polygamy has at least been impartial with the sexes, and while it has martyred the woman, it has not failed to enslave the men. Brigham openly avows the great trial of his soul when "the order" was first taught to him by Joseph Smith. Heber used to tell about his "shedding tears "enough to float a ship," when he was "commanded" to take another wife. The locks of another apostle are said to have silvered in a night, from mental anguish; and of another and another could be told tales of terrible struggles between love and duty. No intellectual man of soul and heart ever took a second wife without passing through "the valley of the "shadow of death." He would be dead to every impulse of manhood, who could gaze upon the sacrifice of his faithful wife, and the outrage to every sensibility of her nature, without sharing in her affliction. But it ends not with the second bridal-day.

From the day that Sarah turned Hagar from her door, and drove her into the wilderness with her offspring, there never was a time in woman's history when she desired to share her husband with another woman, and there never was a day when that husband could please two wives. The relationship is false. In their out-door occupations, cares of business, and obligations, the men have not the hours of mental suffering that the quiet domestic life induces; but they are seldom free from anxiety, even in the midst of business, and never will be, so long as manhood and appreciation of woman exist in their bosoms. With his first wife he has, it may be, grown from youth to hoary age, and the twain have become one. They have lived in each other's confidence, known each the other, and in everything were undivided. Another wife is added to the sacred union, and the happiness of life is fled. By the covenant of marriage, the second wife is to be to the husband another second self, and, desiring to be just, he seeks to avoid every appearance of partiality—but he fails. There are reminiscences clustering around the life of the first wife that are not yet

created around the other, though in name, profession, and intent, they are equal partners in the triple domesticity.   The
long, varied, and changing scenes of life's warfare that made
the first twain one in everything, still remain—affection is
very indivisible.

A youthful wife realizes that she too has affections that
crave a return of love : she is entitled to it—she demands it.
When, in the fickle fortune of marriage, three, four, five, or ten
hearts blend as one, greatly blessed are they ; but when their
individualities are distinct, the life of a patriarch is unenviable.

In the isolated life of the Mountains, the elders made no
concealment of their courtships.   To the Tabernacle, the theatre, and the ballroom, the maiden in her teens would be escorted by the already-married intended husband of three times
her years, with all the attention and delicacy of a romantic
youth.   From this charge, none of the brethren would claim
exemption.   There is conveyed in the institution a feeling of
man's superiority, and the more ignorant the intended patriarch the more vulgar is its parade.   Finally the day of sacrifice arrives, and is thus sketched by the apostle Pratt :

" When the day set apart for the solemnization of the marriage ceremony has arrived, the bridegroom, and his wife, and also the bride, together with their relatives, and such other guests as may be invited, assemble at the place which they have appointed.   The scribe then proceeds to
take the names, ages, native towns, counties, States, and countries of the
parties to be married, which he carefully enters on record.   The President,
who is the Prophet, Seer, and Revelator over the whole Church throughout the world, and who alone holds the " keys " of authority in this solemn
ordinance (as recorded in the 2d and 5th paragraphs of the Revelation on
Marriage), calls upon the bridegroom, and his wife, and the bride, to arise,
which they do, fronting the President.   The wife stands on the left hand
of her husband, while the bride stands on her left.   The President then
puts this question to the wife :

" ' Are you willing to give this woman to your husband to be his lawful and wedded wife for time and for all eternity ?   If you are, you will manifest it by placing
her right hand within the right hand of your husband.'

" The right hands of the bridegroom and bride being thus joined, the
wife takes her husband by the left arm, as if in the attitude of walking ;
the President then proceeds to ask the following question of the man :

" ' Do you, brother ' (*calling him by name*), ' take sister ' (*calling the bride by her name*) 'by the right hand, to receive her unto yourself, to be your lawful and wedded wife, and you to be her lawful and wedded husband, for time and for all eternity, with a covenant and promise, on your part, that you will fulfil all the laws, rites, and ordinances, pertaining to this holy matrimony, in the new and everlasting covenant, doing this in the presence of God, angels, and these witnesses, of your own free will and choice?'

" The bridegroom answers, 'Yes.'—The President then puts the question to the bride:

"' Do you, sister' (*calling her by name*), 'take brother' (*calling him by name*) 'by the right hand, and give yourself to him, to be his lawful and wedded wife for time and for all eternity, with a covenant and promise on your part that you will fulfil all the laws, rites, and ordinances, pertaining to this holy matrimony, in the new and everlasting covenant, doing this in the presence of God, angels, and these witnesses, of your own free will and choice?'

" The bride answers, 'Yes.' The President then says:

"' In the name of the Lord Jesus Christ, and by the authority of the Holy Priesthood, I pronounce you legally and lawfully husband and wife for time and for all eternity: and I seal upon you the blessings of the holy resurrection, with power to come forth in the morning of the first resurrection, clothed with glory, immortality, and eternal lives; and I seal upon you the blessings of thrones, and dominions, and principalities, and powers, and exaltations, together with the blessings of Abraham, Isaac, and Jacob; and say unto you, Be fruitful and multiply and replenish the earth, that you may have joy and rejoicing in your posterity in the day of the Lord Jesus. All these blessings, together with all other blessings pertaining to the new and everlasting covenant, I seal upon your heads, through your faithfulness unto the end, by the authority of the Holy Priesthood, in the name of the Father, and of the Son, and of the Holy Ghost. Amen.'

" The scribe then enters on the general record the date and place of the marriage, together with the names of two or three witnesses who were present." *

The reader will observe that, in this ordinance of polygamic sealing, the husband and the young bride are asked each the question, are you " doing this in the presence of God, an- " gels, and these witnesses, *of your own free will and choice.*" while the question put to *the wife* carefully avoids the issue that would instantly arise between her wounded, bleeding heart, and the falsehood that would be forced from her trembling lips if she essayed to utter that it was of her " own free " will and choice." That poor " victim " is but asked if she has been subdued and is " willing to give this woman " to her husband.

* *The Seer*, p. 32.

No man ever regained his senses after that act of sealing without feeling that he had fatally wounded the wife of his youth. It is a cruelty that he realizes as well as his wife, and he, the nominal but innocent cause of her wrong, seeks to assuage her sufferings by greater kindness and tenderness. But no smooth words, nor the soul-speaking affection of his eye, can heal that wound. It steals her life away, and in her true heart she curses the day she ever heard of Mormonism. For the man who realizes and shares the misery of his wife, the future life is but "a living lie." Were the man an angel, it would be impossible for him to act justly towards two or twenty wives, and divide to each the full measure of her rights.*

Brigham Young, with all the commanding influence of his position, could not silence the murmuring within his own domicile until he threatened to divorce all his wives, and told them, that, if they despised the order of Heaven, he would pray that the curse of the Almighty might be close to their heels, and follow them all the day long,† and even all that violent language has not attained the end ; their hearts revolt as much to-day, though they have schooled themselves into submission and silence.

Polygamy may be the marital relations of the sexes in heaven, it may be the "Celestial Law" of the gods—of that there is no discussion or dreaming ; but one thing is certain, that it is not the true marital relation of the sexes upon the earth. Thirty years of its practice under the most favourable circumstances have stamped it as a withering curse.

* It was the Author's intention when he commenced this work, to give a complete *exposé* of polygamy, exhibiting that institution in all its bearings and influences upon the social life of the people of Utah ; but an unlooked-for incident induced Mrs. Stenhouse to publish what she knew of polygamy. Had that book been written by any other authoress, reference would unquestionably have been made to it in this work ; the Author, therefore, sees no impropriety in acknowledging that his wife has produced a work which only a woman could write, and superior to anything which he himself could offer to the public, and he refers the reader to "A Lady's Life among the Mormons" (Russell Brothers, New York), as a full and unreserved "*Exposé* of Polygamy in Utah."

† Sermon, July 14, 1855, in the Bowery, Provo.

SHOOTING OF A RIVAL PROPHET

CHAPTER LI.

UTAH DURING THE REBELLION.—Change of Federal Officers—Brutal Attack
upon Governor Dawson by Mormon Rowdies—Three of them shot—A Rival
Prophet to Brigham—The "Morrisite" Community—They disregard a Writ of
Habeas Corpus—The Mormon Militia acting as a *Posse Comitatus*—Three Days'
Fighting—The Prophet Morris, his Counsellor Banks and two Women killed
after the Surrender—Arrival of new Federal Officers—An early Difficulty—Arrival
of the California Volunteers—Establishment of Camp Douglas—Brigham defies
the Law of Congress, and takes "an Elderly Young Woman" to Wife—The
Prophet afraid of Arrest—Citizens summoned to protect him—Chief-Justice
Kinney arrests the Prophet for violating the Anti-Polygamic Law—Brigham
gives Bail—The Grand Jury find no Evidence that Brigham had Married again
—Trouble with the Federal Officials—The Mormons invite them to leave the
Territory—The Tabernacle and Mormon Press rejoice in the Calamities of the
Union—General Connor and the Volunteers a Terror to Evil-Doers—A Midnight
Scare—Another False Prophecy—Brigham predicts another Four Years of War
only Four Days before General Lee surrendered.

THE governing principles of the Mormon faith, and the
chief features in the history of the Saints, have been placed
before the reader, but there yet remains much that is most interesting, which, however, must be briefly told.

Secretary Wooton, after the departure of Governor Cumming, had a very brief reign as "acting-governor." When the
first declaration of "secession" was announced, he sent in his
resignation to President Lincoln. John W. Dawson, of Indiana, was then appointed Governor; Frank Fuller, of New
Hampshire, Secretary; John F. Kinney replaced Chief-Justice
Eckles; and Associate-Justices Crosby and Flenniken succeeded Sinclair and Cradlebaugh. Fuller arrived before Dawson,
and, on the retirement of Mr. Wooton, he became " acting-
" Governor " as well as Secretary. This new batch of Federal
officers, together with the appointment of the Surveyor-Gen-

eral and the Superintendent of Indian Affairs, was an evident
"back-down," in order not to provoke Brigham at the outbreak of the war.

In due time Governor Dawson arrived; but there was mischief in store for him. He was almost immediately a victim
of misplaced confidence, and fell into a snare laid for his feet
by some of his own brother-officials. After a brief sojourn of
only a few weeks in Utah, he beat a hasty retreat from Zion,
and before he got well into the Wahsatch mountains, he was
dreadfully maltreated by some Mormon "rowdies," who assumed, "for the fun of the thing," to be the avengers of an alleged insult. Governor Dawson had been betrayed into an
offence, and his punishment was heavy.* Frank Fuller became a second time the "acting-Governor," and a few interesting pages of Utah history are associated with the period of
his governorship.

When Mr. Fuller assumed the duties of acting-Governor,
the Indians were reported troublesome on the Overland Mail
Route, and were threatening to stop the mail. Governor
Fuller, Chief-Justice Kinney, and six other gentlemen, connected with the mail and telegraph lines, joined in recommending to Secretary Stanton to authorize the Superintendent
of Indian Affairs, James Duane Doty, to raise, and put in service immediately, "a regiment of mounted rangers from inhab-
"itants of the Territory, with officers appointed by him," etc.
Brigham was then in his glory; it was the moment of his unchallenged reign. He could dictate at home, and he wanted
to teach the Governor and the Chief-Justice a lesson; and
he did so effectively. Three days later—April 14, 1862—the
Prophet telegraphed to the Utah Delegate at Washington,

---

* The Mormon authorities were dreadfully annoyed by this attack upon Governor Dawson, for they had a greater desire to disgrace the Government in his person than to see him "whipped." Immediate measures were taken to apprehend the
"rowdies," and two of them were secured. After they reached Salt Lake City, the
police, in taking them to the *cell-house*, said that the prisoners tried to escape, and
they shot them down. It was believed that the prisoners were walking in front of
the officers when the latter quietly put their revolvers to the back of their heads
and "stopped them." A third of these young men was related to Brigham by a
proxy marriage. He was pursued fifty miles west, and was likewise shot in an
attempt to make his escape with a stolen horse.

that the statements about the Indians in the telegram of those
gentlemen to the Secretary of War were wholly "without
"foundation in truth; besides," said the Prophet, "the militia
"of Utah are ready and able, as they ever have been, to take
"care of all the Indians, and are able and willing to protect
"the mail-line, *if called upon to do so.*"

Governor Fuller accepted the correction, and made a representation to President Lincoln harmonious with the Prophet's
wishes, and two weeks later he was authorized to call out
ninety mounted militia, properly officered, etc., for three
months' service between Forts Bridger and Laramie, and on
the same day the War Department telegraphed to "ex-Gov-
"ernor Young" to furnish supplies. Lieutenant-General Wells
had ninety of the "Nauvoo Legion" out in three days, ready
to march. Brigham triumphed, and Zion was safe. It never
would have done to have had "Colonel" Doty, and officers of
his choosing, command the "mounted rangers." Governor
Fuller, by this timely service, then laid the foundation of good
relations with the Prophet, but the Chief-Justice was, for the
moment, less fortunate.

When, on the 11th of April, the first telegram was sent,
the name of the Hon. John F. Kinney was being considered
by the Legislature of the "State of Deseret"—then in session.
It was thought by the Prophet that the moment was opportune for demanding the admission of Utah into the Union,
and the Hons. Wm. H. Hooper and John F. Kinney were to
be elected to carry the memorial and the constitution of the
proposed State from the Legislature to the seat of government. As soon as Brigham read the telegram, the name of
the Chief-Justice was ordered to be dropped, and a telegram
was instantly sent to Elder George Q. Cannon, in Liverpool,
directing him to immediately repair to Washington, and join
brother Hooper.

About this time a simple-minded, uneducated Welshman—
Joseph Morris, who had for a number of years previously been
the recipient of "impressions" and "revelations" which reflected unfavourably upon the course of Brigham Young—became an object of interest. Morris was one of the unfortunate
victims of "spirit-communication." After some years of wan-

dering in the States and in Utah, and opposing in a quiet way the Prophet Brigham, Morris got a "revelation" from "the "Lord," instructing him to warn Brigham of his sins. Brigham met the new prophet's revelation with a brief, filthy response, which perfectly upset poor Morris. He had no idea that any man could be so irreverent to Deity!

Thirty-five miles north of Salt Lake City—a short distance from where the Union Pacific debouches from Weber Cañon— Morris found listening ears. The bishop of Kington Fort, Richard Cook, and a number of intelligent men and women, received gladly the new prophet who had been raised up by "the Lord" to "deliver Israel from bondage." Numerous believers in a very short time gathered from various parts of the Territory, and Kington Fort, on the Weber, became an important place.

Morris abounded with revelations. His "gifts" exceeded in profusion those of all who had ever gone before him. The founder of Mormonism was nothing in comparison with his disciple from Wales. The adherents of the new prophet were perfectly overjoyed at the abundance of light that now shone upon their path, and some very intelligent men gathered to the Weber. Three English and three Danish clerks were daily employed in writing the heavenly communications from the mouth of the new prophet. Brigham had been barren—Morris was overflowing.

The new disciples "consecrated" all they possessed to a common fund—Christ was soon to descend among them, and their wants would only be of short duration. There was system, however, in this madness, and an inventory of every one's property "consecrated" was preserved, so that when there was any necessity for any particular portion of any person's possessions to be used, the chief controlling clerk had only to call for it, and the property not called for was retained by its original possessor; but over it he was only a steward.

As "the Lord" tarried, the enthusiasm of some of the converts rapidly cooled, and they retired from the Weber; and here began the difficulty that was to destroy Brigham's rival prophet. As the "apostates" withdrew, it became a question how much of their property they could reclaim. It had all been "consecrated," and, as it had occurred with Brigham before him, Morris could as reasonably have detained the whole of it. Morris's leading men, however, decided to let the "apostates" peacefully retire; but it was expected that they would honestly meet their share of the obligations of the little colony while they had been there among them. Some of the " rebels " were obstinate and dishonest, and picked from the general herd better cattle to take away than they had brought, and, where any of their property had not been called for, they would not make any allowance for the support that they had derived from the property of others. A feud arose, and the dissenters threatened a little war. They applied to the Mormon courts, and the latter were pleased enough with the opportunity of dealing with the Morrisites. Writs were issued, served, and repulsed. The dissenters from Morris waited for the chances of seizing the movable property of the Weber colony, and as wheat was sent to the mill they pounced upon it, and took the team and wagon as well. The " Morrisites " had to send more wheat, and a turbulent dissenter again awaited their appearance. Some of the former, however, had risen early in the morning and spread themselves over the country, keeping within view the advancing team and wheat. As the dissenter and two others pounced upon the convoy the second time, up sprung the Morrisites from their places of concealment, and took them prisoners. The dissenters were taken to Kington Fort, and put in a *calaboose* improvised for the occasion.

The friends of the captured sought their release ineffectually; the sheriff in that county could do nothing with the disciples under Morris. One (or two, as some affirm) of the wives of the prisoners went to Brigham, but he refused to interfere. He was too shrewd to meddle directly in that affair—it was clear enough to him that Morris could not last long. Many enthusiasts had been looking for the sudden appearance of " the Lord " among them, before Morris's day ; but the Weber prophet had the misfortune to fix the time, and, believing in his own revelations, he announced that there was to be no more ploughing and sowing, seed-time and harvest. They had already enough grain and cattle to sustain them till Christ came.

The importunate wife was referred to the courts, and Chief

Justice Kinney was visited. As judge of that judicial district, a petition was filed before him, setting forth that three men were unlawfully imprisoned, kept in close confinement, and heavily ironed by order of Joseph Morris, John Banks, and Richard Cook. On the 24th of May, 1862, a writ of *habeas corpus* was issued to the Territorial Marshal, and by his deputy served, but no attention was paid to it. On the 11th of June, a second writ was issued, and was also disregarded. There were men among the Morrisites who knew well enough that defiance of the law would involve them in serious trouble, but fanaticism was rampant, and reason was not listened to.

Chief-Justice Kinney was burning with indignation when his first writ was set aside; he now insisted upon the militia being called out as a *posse comitatus* to accompany the Territorial Marshal, and Acting-Governor Fuller issued the necessary order for the services of the militia.

For some time preceding this, the Morrisites had been warned by "the Lord" that the "Brighamites" were plotting their destruction, and they, accordingly, bought up all the rifles and ammunition that they could obtain. The Morrisites were well supplied when this judicial move was made, though they stoutly deny that they had any other intention, previous to this time, than to defend themselves against mobocracy.

Early on the morning of the 13th of June, the deputies of the marshal and an armed *posse* were seen on the South Mountain overlooking the Morrisite community. This was the first intimation the latter had of the coming war. When the *posse* had chosen their positions on the bench, the following proclamation was sent in to the Morrisites by one of their herd-boys:

"HEADQUARTERS, MARSHAL'S POSSE, WEBER RIVER, *June* 13, 1862.

"*To Joseph Morris, John Banks, Richard Cook, John Parsons, and Peter Klemgard:*

"WHEREAS, You have heretofore disregarded and defied the judicial officers and laws of the Territory of Utah; and whereas, certain writs have been issued for you from the Third Judicial District Court of said Territory, and a sufficient force furnished by the Executive of the same to enforce the laws, this is therefore to notify you to *peaceably* and *quietly* surrender yourselves and the prisoners in your custody forthwith.

"An answer is required in thirty minutes after the receipt of this document: if not, forcible measures will be taken for your arrest. Should you disregard this proposition and place your lives in jeopardy, you are hereby *required to remove your women and children ;* and all *persons peaceably dis-*

posed are hereby notified to forthwith leave your encampment, and are informed that they can find protection with this *posse*.

"H. W. LAWRENCE, Territorial Marshal, *per* R. T. BURTON and THEO-DORE McKEAN, Deputies."

For what afterwards transpired, the author is indebted to a gentleman who was then in the Morrisite camp, and who has furnished the following statement:

"Mr. Morris, a firm believer in the revelations he received, remarked, in answer to the inquiry: 'What shall be done?' that he would 'go and inquire of the Lord.' He was soon heard in solemn and earnest prayer. In the mean time, word was sent round the camp for the people to at once assemble in meeting, and consult on the question.

"Women and children came together hurriedly, yet there was no excitement, and soon the Bowery was well filled.

"Mr. Morris was seen to come out from his dwelling with a paper in his hand. This paper proved to be a *written revelation*. His council were awaiting him. The revelation was read to the council, and a peculiar document it was. It purported to be from God, who was represented as being pleased with His faithful people there, and as having brought the *posse* against them to show His own power in the complete destruction of their enemies. It also promised, that *now* the triumph of His people should come, their enemies should be smitten before them, *but not one of His faithful people should be destroyed;* not a hair of their heads should be harmed. The council at once stepped out into the Bowery, close to which lived all the leading men, and to save time, singing was omitted, and the meeting was opened briefly by prayer. Mr. John Parsons, in his clear, sonorous voice, then read the revelation. Mr. R. Cook arose to consult with the people as to which should be obeyed—the proclamation, demanding the surrender of the prisoners held in custody of Peter Klemgard, and four of the leading men of the church, or the revelation forbidding the surrender of these men. Before the people had a chance to speak, or vote, or do any thing at all in the matter, the booming sound of a cannon was heard, and screams from the third seat from the stand in the Bowery, and instantly two women were seen dead in the congregation, and the lower jaw, hanging only by a small strip of skin, was shot off a young girl of from twelve to fifteen years of age. It was the fearful and heart-rending screams of this girl that stopped the meeting. The people arose in utter confusion. Mr. Cook, still on his feet, suggested to all to go at once to their homes, and each man take care of his own family as best he could. Never was revelation more immediately falsified in the history of the world than then; for, scarcely had the promise of absolute safety been made, ere sudden destruction came.

"Men and women, panic-stricken, rushed hither and thither, some seeking safety in cellars, some in potato-pits—in short, anywhere or in any place in which security could be either reasonably or unreasonably hoped for.

"The first shot was in a few minutes followed by another, and still another, and the attack was continued. The *posse* drew nearer and nearer, and the firing was kept up incessantly, both with cannon and musketry.

"Had Colonel R. T. Burton, or Theodore McKean, had the pluck requisite to a common constable, they could have gone safely into the fort, served the summons, consulted with the authorities and people, and saved all effusion of blood. There was not a Morrisite in the fort that was armed, or that thought of arming. They met to consider the question, and to pray over it; for a more enthusiastically religious people never breathed: and while thus assembled, the first salutation they had was a cannon-ball in the assembly.*

"About an hour and a half after the firing commenced, the Morrisites got their arms, each man determining to defend his own family, if the *posse* came sufficiently near to attack them. From this was effected an organization, and a regular defence made. But at the time of the attack there was not a man armed."

After three days' fighting, the Morrisites raised the white flag, and ceased firing. Cautiously Colonel Burton and his *aides*, with a number of the men, entered into the Morrisite camp, and then transpired the bloody scene that has made "the Morrisite War" so famous in the West. Of that circumstance the following affidavit has been made:

"UNITED STATES OF AMERICA, TERRITORY OF UTAH, *ss.*

"Alexander Dow, of said Territory. being duly sworn, says:

"In the spring of 1861, I joined the Morrisites, and was present when Joseph Morris was killed. The Morrisites had surrendered, a white flag was flying, and the arms were all grounded and guarded by a large number of the *posse*.

"Robert T. Burton and Judson L. Stoddard rode in among the Morrisites. Burton was much excited. He said, 'Where is the man? I don't know him.' Stoddard replied, 'That's him,' pointing to Morris. Burton rode his horse upon Morris, and commanded him to give himself up in the name of the Lord. Morris replied, 'No, never, never!' Morris said he wanted to speak to the people. Burton said, 'Be d—d quick about it.' Morris said, 'Brethren, I've taught you true principles,'—he had scarcely got the words out of his mouth before Burton fired his revolver. The ball passed in his neck or shoulder. Burton exclaimed 'There's your prophet.' He fired again, saying, 'What do you think of your prophet now?'

* It is maintained by General Burton that the first two cannons fired were not loaded. But this statement is contested. The Morrisites are equally confident that they never heard a sound of cannon till the moment here referred to.

"Burton then turned suddenly and shot Banks, who was standing five or six paces distant. Banks fell. Mrs. Bowman, wife of James Bowman, came running up crying, 'Oh! you blood-thirsty wretch.' Burton said, 'No one shall tell me that and live,' and shot her dead. A Danish woman then came running up to Morris, crying, and Burton shot her dead also. Burton could easily have taken Morris and Banks prisoners, if he had tried. I was standing but a few feet from Burton all this time. And further saith not.   ALEXANDER DOW.

"Subscribed and sworn before me, this 18th day of April, A. D. 1863.
        "CHARLES B. WAITE, *Associate Justice*, U. T."

In the fight, two of the Marshal's *posse* were killed, six of the Morrisites and three of the latter wounded. Only one in the Morrisite camp was killed by the rifle-ball; it was the cannon at long range that did the damage. The first shot killed two women, and wounded a girl; another cannon-ball killed a woman and her child in the "wickiup." The mother-in-law of the new prophet was also killed in her "wickiup." A little infant had two narrow escapes for life. The first shot killed its mother, Mrs. Marsh, while it was in her arms, and it was in the arms of Mrs. Bowman when she was shot down.

After the surrender, the whole of the prisoners were marched to Salt Lake on the 17th, and on the 18th they were examined before Judge Kinney in chambers, and placed under bonds to appear at the next regular term of court.

In urging measures against the Morrisites, Judge Kinney feels satisfied that he only did his duty. It is difficult to see how he could long be passive when the order of his court was disregarded. Some also seek to deny the serious charges made in the affidavit of Dow against General Burton, but the prophet Morris and the women were killed after the surrender, and if not by Burton's revolver the greater was the crime—if difference there could be in such criminality. General Burton is not a blood-thirsty man, he is not a low blackguard, and is much respected as an honourable, good citizen ; if, therefore, he committed the atrocity of which he is accused, it was the work of a devoted fanatic, who, seeking, as he might suppose, to please the Prophet Brigham, did not hesitate to do so by ridding him of a troublesome rival. If General Burton did not shoot Banks and the women, then was he under obligation, as commander of the militia and chief deputy-marshal, to have brought the murderers to justice. Nothing of this kind was done, nor did the Chief-Justice or the acting-Governor make any inquiry. There might, perhaps, be some semblance of defence for General Burton's shooting; but, for any other, there could be none. To say that a second uprising was feared, as a justification for shooting Morris, is too trivial a statement to call for reply. There was not powder in the Morrisite camp to make further resistance possible, and their arms were piled upon the ground and were guarded by the Mormon militia.

That Elder John Banks was foully dealt with, there seems little room to doubt. He was wounded at the time of Morris's death, but not fatally. The manner of his "taking off" only is obscure. In the evening he was well enough to sit up and enjoy his pipe. Suddenly he died. Was he poisoned, shot, or "knifed," is the only query.* Those who could answer will not; the confidential statements of others are conflicting.

The bodies of Morris and Banks were brought to Salt Lake City, and placed where the people could see the dead prophet and his counsellor.

It is charged to Brigham Young that he inspired and fostered the indignation of Judge Kinney; but his defenders insist that *he did not interfere.*† Acting-Governor Fuller has

* Elder John Banks was among the first to receive Mormonism in England. He was soon ordained a high-priest, and during many years of labour among the Saints he had presided over the largest conferences in Britain, and at one time was one of the Presidency over the whole Church there. He was the most eloquent preacher that was ever in the Mormon Church. As his faith waned in Mormonism, he was painfully grieved and at times became intemperate. Before he was a Mormon, he had been a Chartist, and the "despotism" of the ruling priesthood was irksome to him. Years before he left England for Zion, he silently mourned over the One-Man power. His best life had been spent for Mormonism, he was then too far advanced in years to begin a new life, and he emigrated to Zion when ordered, hoping that his fears might be removed by better experience. Brigham Young was personally kind to him after he arrived at Salt Lake, and sought to help him over his material troubles; but there was in the heart of John Banks more than he could tell the Prophet. When he heard Morris, it was new hope to him; he believed that "the Lord" had again spoken, and he began life afresh.

† To say that Brigham Young could be indifferent to the Morrisite movement would be to belie his whole life's teaching. That such an action as that of Judge Kinney could take place without interesting him, or that Robert T. Burton and Theodore McKean could head a military *posse* without Brigham Young's approval, is simply ridiculous. A man who could, at that very time, tell the Government of the United States that he "would see it in hell first" before a man should march

also been charged with seeking the favour of the prophet Brigham by the readiness with which he called for the militia as a *posse* to aid the Marshal ; but Mr. Fuller declines all responsibility, and says that he only acted upon the urgent demand of the Chief-Justice, and that he had no option in the matter. An effort has also been made to bring in Major H. W. Lawrence, who was then Territorial Marshal, but now an "apos- "tate," for a share of the responsibility ; but he has proved that he informed the Chief-Justice and the acting-Governor that sending a military *posse* would certainly provoke armed resistance, and the innocent would suffer. He succeeded in delaying the execution of the writ, hoping that Morris and his advisers would surrender without compulsion. Major Lawrence left for the Eastern States, and some further complaint being made against the Morrisites, the writ was served during his absence, and the consequences were as have been here narrated.

Before the regular session of the Third Judicial District Court, at which the Morrisites were to be tried, an element was imported into Utah that was destined to trouble the happiness of the Prophet. A new Governor, in the person of Stephen S. Harding, of Indiana, was appointed to succeed Dawson, and Thomas J. Drake, of Michigan, and Chas. B. Waite, of Illinois, were appointed associate justices in the place of Flenniken and Crosby. At the same time a body of California volunteers, under command of Colonel Connor, were sent on to the Overland Mail Route to protect that and the telegraph-line across the plains, but the commander had also instructions to establish posts near Salt Lake City. The Tabernacle at that time was rejoicing in the fulfilment of the predictions concerning the overthrow of the Government, and the Mormon press was quite as indiscreet in the manifestations of its joy at the disasters that befell the Union army. Secretary Stanton had had his attention directed to Zion.

from Utah to aid in the suppression of the Rebellion, was not very likely to allow his brethren at the same moment to be summoned by Judge Kinney to engage in any unpleasant work. Besides, there were prominent and notorious men called to take part in the "Morrisite War," who had nothing whatever to do with the militia. The officers commanding that expedition did consult with Brigham Young, and he did instruct them, if fight it was to be, to "save the women and children, and be careful and not expose the boys"—i. e., the militia.

Governor Harding and Judge Waite were particularly agreeable to the Mormon leaders on their arrival; but, soon after, the sister of Judge Waite was unfortunate enough to pass some unpleasant strictures upon the Mormon women, and brother Heber, hearing some of the remarks of Miss Waite, repeated them in the Tabernacle in a Sunday sermon. Miss Waite had some kind of literary connection with an Eastern paper, and, during the summer of their arrival in Zion, her pen could not be too complimentary to the Mormons. In the winter after that unfortunate accident, that pen was dipped in gall.

Towards the middle of October, the California volunteers reached the former encampment of the United States troops at Camp Floyd, and there the Mormons hoped that Colonel Connor would establish his post; but that officer had a programme of his own, and the volunteers continued their march nearer to Salt Lake. Parties who would have been financially benefited by the volunteers occupying the vacated quarters at Camp Floyd tried to induce the colonel to remain there, and, failing that, they sought to intimidate him with the intelligence that the Mormons intended to dispute the passage of the Californians over the Jordan. At the same time, a story was current among the volunteers that Brigham Young, on hearing of their advance, had, out of contempt for them and the nation, cut down the United States flag-staff at Camp Floyd, and left it lying on the public road, over which they had to travel. There was no truth in this reported threat, for the Prophet had not taken down the flag-staff from any such considerations.[*] The reports, however, reached Colonel Connor through gentlemen whom he had reason to believe would tell the truth.

At the last encampment of the volunteers, sixty rounds of ammunition were issued to each man, the artillery was put in order, and the surgeons saw to their instruments. "If all hell "yawned beneath it," Colonel Connor was next day to cross "the Jordan."

There was not a sign of hostile preparation anywhere among the Mormons, nor any possibility of ambuscade in that barren, treeless country, yet so disloyal was the reputation of

* See page 422.

the Mormons that any act of contemplated hostility was easily credited.

On the 20th of October, 1862, with loaded rifles, fixed bayonets and shotted cannon, Colonel Connor marched the volunteers into Salt Lake City, and proceeded to " the bench " directly east of the city. There, at the base of the Wahsatch Mountains, they planted the United States flag, and created Camp Douglas.*

The unpleasant rumours of intended hostility, however unfounded, could but create prejudice on the part of the volunteers against the Mormons, and the readiness of the former to show fight gave birth to a feeling of uneasiness among the Saints.

The Governor's message to the Legislature, in December, was the tocsin of war, and was considered a very offensive document. He referred to the passage of the Anti-Polygamic law of July, of that year, and warned the people against the pernicious counsels of the apostles and prophets who had recommended it " to be openly disregarded and defied." The *manner* of the delivery of the message was worse than the matter, and probably no Legislature ever felt more humiliated and insulted. It was painful to observe the legislators, as they sat quiet and immovable, hearing their faith contemned. It was interpreted as an open and gratituous insult on the part of the Executive.

The Governor and the judges silently sought to secure some action of Congress that would enable the Federal courts to take cognizance of the Anti-Polygamy Bill, and other matters, and on this information coming to the knowledge of Brigham, a mass-meeting was called in the Tabernacle, on the 3d of March, 1863, to express the indignation of the people against the Governor and judges.

Very animated speeches were delivered by Brigham and the apostles, and a series of denunciatory resolutions against

---

* Colonel Connor could not possibly have selected a better situation for a military post, and certainly no place could have been chosen more offensive to Brigham. The artillery have a perfect and unobstructed range of Brigham's residence, and, with their muzzles turned in that direction, the Prophet felt awfully annoyed.

the offenders was approved by the audience, and a committee
appointed " to request them to resign their offices and leave
" the Territory." A petition asking their removal was sent to
President Lincoln. A counter-petition was sent by Colonel
Connor and his officers, asking their retention. Notwithstanding these troublesome times, Brigham had leisure for
a love affair, and, after a long siege of "an elderly young
" woman "—Amelia Folsom, from Council Bluffs—in which he
managed to make himself extremely ridiculous, the Prophet
violated the Anti-Polygamic law, and furnished his opponents
with an opportunity for proceeding legally against him.

Notwithstanding the open and avowed defiance of the law
of Congress, and the oft-repeated expression of willingness to
abide by the decision of the Supreme Court, Brigham, when
furnished with the opportunity which he had craved, took refuge from the issue in a most ungallant manner.

Colonel Connor had visited Judge Waite, and, on leaving
his house, one of the elders, who was loitering about, believed
that he overheard the colonel say : " These three men must be
" surprised." That was sufficient. Instantly the eavesdrop-
per flew to Brigham. The Prophet believed the story, hoisted
a signal to rally the militia, and in half an hour a thousand
armed men surrounded his premises, and within an hour another thousand were armed and on duty. The city was in
commotion, and rifles, lead, and powder, were brought out of
their hiding-places. On the inside of the high walls surrounding Brigham's premises, scaffolding was hastily erected in order
to enable the militia to fire down upon the passing volunteers.
The houses on the route which occupied a commanding position where an attack could be made upon the troops were
taken possession of, the small cannon were brought out, and the
brethren prepared to protect the Prophet.

There was no truth in the rumour of an intended arrest of
Brigham and his counsellors. The Mormon leaders, all the
same, believed it to be true, and they were cautious and watchful. A powerful telescope was placed on the top of Brigham's
" Bee-Hive" residence, and every move of the volunteers in
Camp Douglas was watched with great care. Night and day,
for several weeks, there was a body of armed men around the

Prophet, and signals agreed upon by which the whole people could be rallied by night or by day.

During this excitement Chief-Justice Kinney came to the Prophet's aid, and on the affidavit of a compositor—one of the brethren—accusing Brigham of an infraction of the law in taking to himself another wife, Judge Kinney issued a writ for his apprehension. This smart practice was adopted in order to render it impossible for Judge Drake or Judge Waite to arrest him if such was their desire. The U. S. Marshal waited upon Brigham, and in a friendly way told him that the Chief Justice required his presence in Chambers. Brigham comprehended the situation, and was soon there and under bail to await the action of the Grand Jury! This latter honourable body, composed of apostles, bishops, and elders, found no evidence to satisfy them that Brigham Young had married Amelia Folsom!!!*

The same Grand Jury found a true bill against the Morrisites for "armed resistance to the laws," censured Governor Harding, and voted Camp Douglas "a nuisance." †

* There was no act of Brigham's social life better known in Salt Lake City. He had been the talk and amusement of every circle of confidential friends for months. His gallantry was the theme of admiration! He had patted one rival quietly on the shoulder and conveyed to him enough in that way so that he understood that his future course was fortune if he retired gracefully; and when another young man sprang up and meant matrimonial business, he received a mission from "the Lord," that sent him out of the city. Miss Folsom could play the piano and sing "Fair Bingen on the Rhine." Such accomplishments, at that time, were rare and appreciated. Brigham had not taken to himself a wife for a goodly number of years, and "had got all the wives he wanted;" but Amelia attracted him. His carriage lingered by her mother's door for hours nearly every day. He got barbered and perfumed every morning, and replaced his homespun garments with broadcloth. Twice the Endowment House was warmed and made comfortable for the marriage ceremony: twice the prophet was disappointed. Finally the young woman was told that it was the will of "the Lord," but the Prophet would trouble her no more. Alarmed with the fear of possibly doing wrong, she sent for the Prophet, the Endowment House was again warmed, and the "sealing" was performed. That no one of that Grand Jury knew that Brigham Young had married Amelia Folsom, is very strange!

† It was currently reported that the water issuing from Red Butte Cañon was purposely fouled by the volunteers, in order to annoy the citizens in some of the wards, who used it for culinary purposes. With the Sunday sermons dinned into their ears, the Mormons could not but feel annoyed that the troops were stationed at the head of the stream; but of any intentional fouling of the waters there has

At the March session of the Third Judicial District Court, the Morrisites were tried. Ten of them were indicted for killing two of the *posse* during the fight; seven of these were convicted, one was "nolled," and two were acquitted. Sixty-six others were fined $100 each for resisting the *posse*. Of the seven convicted of "murder in the second degree," one was sentenced to fifteen years' imprisonment, one to twelve years, and five to ten years each. Governor Harding, regarding the prisoners as deserving of clemency, pardoned them all. Most of those who had professed the Morrisite faith, and who did not immediately leave the Territory, found employment and refuge at Camp Douglas. A month later, Colonel Connor took two hundred and fifty of them, and a company of the California Volunteers, to Soda Springs, where he established a post in Idaho, immediately beyond the northern Territorial limits of Utah, and this for a time ended the Morrisite secession.*

The volunteers were not numerous enough to "overawe" the Mormons, and their presence was, on that account, all the more irksome. To know that they "could use them up any "morning before breakfast," and yet be forced to tolerate their presence on the brow of a hill, like a watch-tower, was irritating to the Prophet's mind. The Tabernacle resounded with fierce denunciations every Sunday. Mischief-makers poured into the ears of the Prophet every story that could increase his prejudice against Colonel Connor; and the latter heard quite as much to incense him against Brigham. A collision for a long time seemed inevitable. The Prophet was then in his glory; the nation was engaged in war; the prophecies of the modern Seer were being fulfilled; and the republic was going to pieces—he had nothing to fear. Sometimes it seemed that

never been any reliable evidence. The story of passing the stream through the stables for that purpose is denied. Had the stream supplied Brigham Young, there might have been some ground for the charge; but, for the people, neither the commander nor his officers had any feeling but sympathy. Later in the year there was ground for complaint, as the water that irrigated the gardens was proportionally diminished by the camp, and was an injury to those wards.

* Five years later, one of the Morrisites, who had been a merchant-trader in Salt Lake City, recovered a valuable property that was sold at that time by order of the court to pay his fine. The property had been sold for "a mere song," and all about the transaction had the air of unnecessary persecution.

his better sense prevailed, and there would be hope of a permanent peace; but new rumours would reach him, and, on the following Sunday, he would go to the Tabernacle and open the phials of his wrath, and all again was excitement, and everybody was on the *qui vive*.

Providing for the possibility of a rupture at any moment, it was agreed that, if the struggle came by night, the citizens were to be summoned to arms by the firing of cannon from the hill-side, at the east of Brigham's residence; and, if the difficulty began during the day, the flag was to be hoisted over his Bee-Hive residence. To the latter signal the citizens had once responded; and it was believed that their readiness to fight for the Prophet had intimidated the commander of the volunteers, so that he would be unlikely to make an attack by day. At that time, it was believed that Colonel Connor, having been foiled in this first attempt,* entertained the idea of making a dash upon the Prophet's bedroom "in the dead of night," seizing him, and running him off to the States before the Mormons could learn of his situation, and render him any assistance.

On the night of the 29th of March, the citizens were aroused by the booming of cannon, and as hastily as garments could be thrown on, and arms could be seized, the brethren were seen hurrying from their homes towards the Prophet's residence. The struggle was apparently at hand. The signal cannon had been distinctly heard, and, as there was a gentle current of air from the east, those who lived west of the Prophet could hear the very music to which the volunteers were supposed to be marching into the heart of the city!

For his great victory over Bear-Hunter and other Indian chiefs, in a desperate battle in the depth of winter, two months

---

* General Connor never had orders to arrest Brigham Young, or he would have done so—or tried. At the time of the conversation with Judge Waite, already referred to, which created the panic and the assembling of the Mormons in arms, the prophet was not the subject of consideration. One of the brethren had married the three widows of a wealthy merchant within sight of Judge Waite's residence, and as that was an excellent case in which to try the application of the Anti-Polygamic Law, the General replied to the Judge that he would arrest him if the Court furnished the order. The anticipation that a difficulty would arise, from Judge Waite acting within Judge Kinney's Judicial District while the latter was present, was the only thing that prevented the arrest.

before, Colonel Connor had now been promoted to the rank of Brigadier-General, and the news had only just reached Camp Douglas! The military band had been called out to serenade the promoted commander, and the cannon was roaring over the mountains in honour of the victor!

MAJOR-GENERAL P. EDWARD CONNOR.*

Fortunately for those concerned, Elder A. O. Smoot, and not some mad fanatic, was mayor of the city of the Saints in those troublesome times. The Grand Jury had presented Camp Douglas as " a nuisance," and, following the municipal law, it should have been " abated." The camp annoyed Brigham, for

* General Connor raised the Third Regiment of California Infantry for the war, and was mortified to find himself sent " to watch Brigham Young." This forced detention in Utah was probably the prevailing cause of the first ill-feeling among the volunteers toward the Prophet. The General, however, made the most of his situation, and never missed an opportunity of making Brigham feel that he was there. He started a weekly paper—*The Vedette*—at Camp Douglas, in November, 1863, which was ably edited by Major C. H. Hempstead, and all the editorial work, composition, and delivery, were performed by the officers and soldiers. It became a " daily " in the following spring, and established itself in Salt Lake City, much to the annoyance of the faithful. In May, 1866, he was brevetted Major-General of Volunteers, for gallant conduct at the battle of Tongue River during the Powder River Campaign, Montana. It is believed, by the General, that Brigham once predicted that he would live to bury him head downward, and in his body plant a peach-stone, which would sprout, grow up, and bear fruit that would gratify the Prophet's taste!

he could never look out of his door without seeing it growing larger and larger, and every day more permanent. In the wrath of the moment he ordered the mayor to "move Connor and his men" out of the city limits.* But Mayor Smoot is a sober, calculating, brave man. He counted the cost of that task ; and after he had estimated how many men he would require, he informed the Prophet that he had sufficient, and that his plans were complete. Brigham's second thought had come, and his temper had passed away. He made no answer ; and the good sense of Abraham O. Smoot saved Mormonism. Had Brigham given that order to such a man as the present mayor, Daniel H. Wells, Camp Douglas would have been attacked, probably the garrison would have been "wiped out," many of the Mormons would have been killed, and, in the course of a few months, volunteers from the Pacific States and the Territories would have poured into Utah, and there would have been a bloody settlement of that passionate speech.†

Governor Harding, ‡ Secretary Fuller, and Judge Kinney, were removed ; James Duane Doty was appointed Governor ; Amos Reed, Secretary ; and John Titus, Chief Justice. The Government was striving to restore peace in Utah. Governor Doty had been in the Territory as Superintendent of Indian Affairs, and was a very discreet gentleman ; Mr. Reed was conservative ; Judge Titus was then unknown. Brigham regarded the removal of Judge Kinney as the result of the latter's devotion to the priesthood, and, by way of compensation, the honourable gentleman was sent Delegate to Congress in 1863.

Judge Waite resigned in 1864, and "left the Territory in

---

* Though the centre of the post is two and a half miles from the City Hall, a portion of the military reservation lapped over the nominal municipal boundary. It was this that furnished the ground for quarrel.

† After the General had heard of that order, he said to the Author: "I know, "sir, that Brigham Young could use up this handful of men ; but there are sixty "thousand men in California who would avenge our blood;" and to that was responded, "Yes ; and behind them there would be the whole nation." Nothing was more certain than, had that order been executed, there would have been no church, or prophets and apostles, in the Rocky Mountains to-day.

‡ There are no castle-walls high enough in Utah to conceal even *private life*, when the Saints are after an enemy ; and they were not long in discovering that S. S. H. was not the proper person to lecture them on the *immorality* of Polygamy. His removal did credit to the Government.

disgust;" Solomon McCurdy, of Missouri, was appointed his successor.

During the Southern Rebellion, when the Confederacy prevailed, the Spirit of "the Lord" was noisy; but, when the Union cause was in the ascendency, the preaching in the Tabernacle became more conservative.

The Church organ, the *Deseret News*,* was intensely "Copperhead," and chronicled the reverses of the Union arms with undisguised pleasure. By way of correction, General Connor established a Provost Guard in the city. As the war drew to a close, it was difficult to "quench the Spirit;" and, on the Sunday afternoon preceding the surrender of General Lee, Brigham predicted in the Tabernacle that there would be four more years of war.†

* When some leading men represented to Brigham that the course of the *News* would certainly provoke a difficulty with the troops—and it is true that at one time they seriously entertained the idea of "gutting out" the printing-office—the Prophet came out in "a card," and disclaimed his personal responsibility for anything in that paper but what carried his own signature. It was necessary, however, to sacrifice somebody, and the editor of the *News*, the Hon. Elias Smith, Judge of Probate, was selected for the victim. A violent letter from a sergeant in Camp Douglas had been published in the *News* without what Brigham considered a proper reply, and, under the pretext of righteous indignation, Judge Smith was removed. A more prudent, honourable gentleman than Judge Smith was not in Mormondom. He was not the "Copperhead," but the faithful exponent of the orthodox faith.

† Of course, Brigham has had to wriggle out of this prediction. He did not mean to say exactly that. He meant, he said, that there would be other four years of wrangling and fighting in the settlement of the controversy! Poor Brigham! He has twice put dates to his predictions, and in both instances he came to grief. Probably he won't venture a third.

CHAPTER LII.

AFTER THE WAR.—Grand Procession of Mormons and Gentiles—Prospective
Peace—The Federal Officers and Mormon Dignitaries wine together—The City
honours General Connor in the Social Hall—The Prophets and the Gentile
Ladies decline attending the Ball—Vice-President Colfax and Literary Friends
visit Zion—The Interview with the Prophet—The Hon. James M. Ashley sees
the Difficulty of convicting the Apostles for Polygamy—He tells Tom Corwin's
Story of the " *Eleven Jurors who had some of the Ham* "—A Gentile marries a
Mormon Elder's Second Wife—Mr. Brassfield assassinated—Great Excitement
among the Gentiles—General Sherman gives Brigham a Hint that he will send
Troops to Zion—Brigham hastens to assert his Innocence—Contention over the
Warm Springs—Dr. Robinson, the Contestant, is assassinated—A Foul and
Dreadful Murder—Brigham joins the Gentiles in offering a Reward for the Mur-
derers—No Detection—Years after, Brigham withdraws his Reward—Afraid of
tempting Men to Perjury—Three Apostates charged with stealing a Cow—
Arrested, confined, two murdered in " attempting to escape "—The Brethren
arrested for Murder, and escape—Chief-Justice Titus grossly insulted.

Wɪᴛʜ the closing of the war, there was some expectation
of peace in Utah; but peace there at any time can only be
temporary. The success of the Union arms was a suggestive
lesson; and, on the reinauguration of President Lincoln, the
Mormons were most loyal. On the 4th of March, 1865, there
was a grand Mormon and Gentile procession throughout the
principal streets of the city, and right in the centre of the main
street hustings were erected, and on the platform the Federal
officers—civil and military—met the Mormon apostles, city
dignitaries, and principal citizens. The past was to be forgotten, and there was evinced to the on-looker a feeling evidently
genuine and fraternal. General Connor was greatly moved at
the sight of the tradesmen and working-people who paraded
through the streets, and who cheered most heartily—and no

doubt honestly *—the patriotic, loyal sentiments that were uttered by the speakers. He wanted differences to be forgotten, and with gentlemanly frankness he approached the Author with extended hand, and expressed the joy he experienced in witnessing the loyalty of the masses of the people. The *Vedette* and the *Telegraph* had waged a fierce warfare, but peace for the future was resolved upon; and, as an evidence of good faith, the General proposed to immediately close the former journal.

At the end of the reinauguration services, the officers from Camp Douglas were entertained in the City Hall, and there met with apostles, bishops, and the chief men of the city, and they partook together of a cold collation and a glass of wine in the utmost friendship. The officers of the Nauvoo Legion escorted the officers of the California Volunteers back to their quarters, and every thing promised fair for the future.

A day or two after, the Author with a friend visited Camp Douglas, and with the General and his friend, Major Hempstead, passed a pleasant hour in contemplating and chatting over proposed changes. General Connor had been called to take command of the Department of the Platte, and he thought that, if the Mormon people were desirous of making " a new " departure," the silence of the *Vedette* was a proper thing.

A ball was soon after given by the city authorities at the Social Hall in honour of General Connor, preceding his departure for the Platte. It was conceived in kindness, but it was altogether a mistake. Brigham and his counsellors would not deign to be present; their wives and daughters, also, did not attend. The ladies of Camp Douglas, with a very few exceptions, would not accompany their husbands to meet " the Mor " mon women." Of the disposition of the Prophet and the ladies of Camp Douglas nothing was known until their absence from the Hall made everything palpably clear. The offending parties doubtless calculated upon the annoyance and mortification

* It is folly to charge the people with disloyalty to the Republic—it is only *the faith* that is disloyal. The Mormon community would be glad to-day to be in harmony with the nation. The native-born American naturally loves his country and her institutions, and the foreign-born population instinctively would render willing obedience to the laws of Congress. Disloyalty is not congenial to the people ; it is a burden to them.

that their absence would cause each the other; but on learning of the absence on both sides, conditions were changed, and the absent and the present alike felt insulted. The dance, however, went on; no one pretended to notice what all felt, and the night was pleasantly passed; but further reconciliation was at an end.

Two months later, Vice-President Colfax, ex-Governor Bross, of Illinois, Samuel Bowles, Esq., editor of the Springfield (Mass.) *Republican*, and Albert D. Richardson, Esq., of the New York *Tribune*, made their great overland trip to the Pacific. Their visit to the chief city of Zion afforded opportunities, both to the Mormons and the Gentiles, for exhibiting their devotion to the Government, and in a quiet way raking up again their local hostilities, and pouring their grievances and dislikes into the ears of the visitors. During their stay they had free intercourse with the Prophet, heard him preach, and frankly talked over the subject of Polygamy.*

At the first meeting of the Prophet and the Vice-President, in the hotel of the latter, Mr. Colfax, in a very good-natured way, expressed to Brigham the hope that " the Prophets of the " Church would have a new revelation on the subject [Polyga- " my], which would put a stop to the practice." In that friendly discussion the " biblical usage and authority " were pressed as a sanction for polygamy, and the question was asked the Mormon speaker, whether " the same usage and authority for " human sacrifice " would justify them in offering such sacrifices to-day. To the direct question, " Would you, if com- " manded by God, offer up your son or your enemy as a sacri- " fice?" he promptly replied, " Yes."

Brigham's sentiments on the Southern rebellion were in the course of the interview the subject of inquiry, and the Prophet is thus reported by Mr. Bowles:

---

* It has generally been charged that the very pleasant attentions shown to Vice-President Colfax and his friends, making them the guests of the city, and extending to them every courtesy and consideration, was a piece of the Prophet's diplomacy to parade his pretended loyalty, etc. This is not true. Brigham had not then begun to ask the good opinion of the world. The Hon. Wm. H. Hooper considered it proper that the city should show its respect " to the second officer of the Government," and with his suggestion Brigham acquiesced, possibly with some reluctance at first. Brigham was strong in those days; there was no bowing to Gentiles in his programme at that time.

" Now that peace is established, let all be pardoned ; but early in or
during the war he would have disposed of the rebel chiefs who fell into
the hands of the Government without mercy or hesitation.   Had he been
President when Mason and Slidell were captured, he would have speedily
put them ' where they never would peep,' and negotiated with England
afterwards.   He uttered this sentiment with such a wicked working of the
lower jaw and lip, and such an almost demon-like spirit in his whole face,
that, quite disposed to be incredulous on those matters, I could not help
thinking of the Mountain Meadows Massacre, of recusant Mormons, of
Danites and Avenging Angels, and their reported achievements." *

About two weeks later the Honourable Jas. M. Ashley, of
Ohio, then Chairman of the Committee on Territories, visited
Zion. Brigham met the gentleman frankly, and in the parlour
of Delegate Hooper there was a free conversation upon the
probable future relations between the Government and the
Mormons. The first question from Brigham was : " Well, Mr.
" Ashley, are you also going to recommend us to get a new
" revelation to abolish polygamy, or what are you going to do
" with us ? " . . . . " Now, Mr. President, I don't know what
" we can do with you. Your situation reminds me of an experi-
" ence of Tom Corwin. In the days of Tom's poverty, some-
" where in Ohio, he thought that he would hang out his law-
" yer's shingle, and catch a share of business. One day a
" smart fellow solicited his legal services ; he wanted Tom to
" defend him, and proposed to give him a fee of fifty dollars.
" That was a big sum to Tom then ; but when he heard the
" situation of his client he stated that he was under profes-
" sional obligations to say that he could be of no service to
" him. The client insisted that Tom should make a speech in
" court, and that was all he wanted. The case came on : the
" evidence was clear, witnesses had seen the prisoner steal some
" hams, carry them to a house, and there the hams were found
" in the client's possession. It was a clear case of theft ; the
" evidence was incontestable, and the prosecutor thought it
" needless to address the jury. The defendant, however, in-
" sisted that Tom should make his speech. A brilliant effort
" was made, the jury retired, and in a few minutes returned
" with a verdict of ' Not guilty.' The judge, the prosecutor,
" and Tom, were perfectly confounded. They glanced at each

* " Across the Continent," p. 113.

"other a look of inquiry. Nothing more could be done, and " the prisoner was discharged. As they retired from the court, " the lawyer said to the thief: 'Now, old fellow, I want you " 'to tell me how that was done!' 'Your speech did it,' was " the reply. 'No it didn't, and I want to know how *you* did " 'it.' 'Well, if you'll not speak of it till I get out of the " 'State, I shall tell you.' Tom accorded to this, and in perfect " confidence his client whispered : '*Well, eleven of the jurors* " '*had some of the ham.*'"

Brigham roared and laughed. With a Mormon jury, some of them doubtless polygamists, the institution was perfectly secure!

In the spring of 1866, a Gentile—O. N. Brassfield—was assassinated. Mr. Brassfield was married by Judge McCurdy, on the 20th of March, to the second wife of one of the brethren, who was then in Europe on mission, and on the evening of the 3d of April he was shot by some unknown person as he was entering his boarding-house. Every consistent Mormon in his faith sustained the deed, as the sentiment of the Church made it obligatory upon the "nearest of kin" to avenge the absent husband. Without any opinion upon Polygamy as an institution, it was an imprudent act to marry any woman who was the recognized "wife" of another man, and the mother of his children—until some formal separation had been made—even though that woman was before the law no "wife" at all. As an individual, Mr. Hill was wronged, but as a people the Mormons had no right to complain, for the example had been set Brassfield by the dignitaries of the Church. The conservative among the Gentiles took that view of the Brassfield marriage, but there were some among the Mormons who afterward deeply regretted the defence they had made of "the avenger," when they had reason to believe that the death of Brassfield was probably more an act of vindictiveness than the result of an enthusiast's conviction in carrying out the obligations which, it was asserted, the faith imposed. That the shooting was premeditated, and the intention known to others, there can be no doubt. No effort was made to arrest the perpetrator of the crime. The Gentile community was at first panic-stricken;

but, on recovering from the first stupor, they offered a reward of $4,500 for the arrest of the murderer, which, however, elicited no information. Orders had been given by the Secretary of War to disband the volunteers, but it was immediately countermanded till regular troops could relieve them.

General Sherman, then commanding the Department of the Plains, telegraphed to Brigham that he hoped to hear of no more murders of Gentiles in Utah, and he took that opportunity of assuring the Prophet that, though his language was not intended as "a threat," yet he might say that there were a great many soldiers who had just been mustered out of service, who would readily gather again and pay him a visit—should the lives of citizens be afterwards imperilled in the Territory. Brigham had a clear perception that W. Tecumseh Sherman was not a man of many words, and he hastened to inform him that there was a misrepresentation; that Brassfield had "seduced a man's wife;" and that life in Zion was as secure as elsewhere, if persons attended to their own business. The Prophet prepared a second telegram, that was signed by influential Gentiles, confirming that statement. Some of these gentlemen did regret that they were forced to do so; but the only choice then was between open hostility or quiet submission, and they were not prepared for the former.

In October of the same year, Dr. J. King Robinson was barbarously murdered.

Dr. Robinson was a native of Calais, Maine. He came to Utah from California in 1864, and was assistant-surgeon at Camp Douglas, till he was mustered out of the service in the beginning of the winter preceding his assassination. He then commenced the practice of his profession in the city, and in the spring of 1866 he married a very respectable young lady, the daughter of one who had in life been a prominent Mormon, but the widow and the family had outgrown the faith of the Prophet. The doctor was a man of excellent moral character, and had devoted much of his time to the children of the Gentile Sunday-school. He was the intimate friend of the Rev. Norman McLeod, who at that time was chaplain at the military post, and was preaching in Independence Hall in opposition to the Mormon faith. The doctor, doubtless, shared the sentiments of the minister, and both of them were thoroughly disliked by the prominent Mormons.

While in the United States service, the doctor and another surgeon formed the idea of taking possession of what is known as the Warm Springs to the north of the city, and intended at some time to erect there a hospital. A small board "shanty" was erected upon the ground, and other work was performed indicative of a purpose to hold possession of the property. The city Council claimed that the city owned the Springs and the land surrounding them, and the Marshal was ordered to remove the property of the doctor. He immediately brought an action against the city, and after a protracted trial Chief-Justice Titus decided against him. Three days afterwards he was assassinated.*

A large reward was offered for the apprehension of the murderers, and at the head of the list was the name of Brigham Young for $500; and very strangely indeed, about a year ago when several of the brethren had been arrested upon indictments found by the Grand Jury for that murder, Brigham gave public notice that he withdrew that portion of the offered reward, as he did not wish to be a party to any temptation to perjury !

The whole community was terribly excited. The Mormons felt that the murder was a great calamity to them. They saw at once that Dr. Robinson's contest with the city authorities would certainly be regarded as the cause of his "taking off." The Author well remembers meeting a prominent citizen the next morning, and learning the news from him. The first moment there was an ejaculation of painful surprise, and the first words uttered were the expression of Talleyrand, that it was "worse than a crime, it was a blunder." It was so fatal an error that it was with difficulty that the mind could be brought to conclude that Mormons had done it. Even after the lapse of several years it is hard to believe that the assassination of Dr. Robinson was either ordered or planned. Some of the

---

* As the dastardly and foul murder of this gentleman is an important feature in Utah history, and will yet occupy the attention of the public, as a *cause célèbre*, the speech of Governor John B. Weller, at the close of the examination of witnesses, is given entire in the appendix.

brethren who were arrested in 1871, on the indictment of a grand jury for the commission of the crime, were persons on whom such a suspicion would not have fallen, but for the assertion of some witnesses that they were seen in the locality.

About that time several acts of violence had occurred to unpopular Gentiles who had attempted to take and hold possession of what they claimed were unoccupied lands. The race-course on the west side of the Jordan had been looked upon with envious eyes, and some one had placed a "shanty" upon it and attempted to "jump" some one's title. The occupant and the shanty went into the Jordan together one night, and the former received a pistol-ball in one of his limbs after he reached the river. Two or three nights after, Lieutenant Brown and Dr. Williamson, formerly of the California Volunteers, had put up a tent upon a choice piece of land on the east side of the Jordan. One night they were suddenly pounced upon, wrapped up in an old tent-cover, and prepared for the same liquid grave. The lieutenant had had charge of the provost guard in the city, and was much respected, and so also was Dr. Williamson; their personal characters were irreproachable. The lieutenant begged of the attacking party to shoot him like a man rather than drown him like a dog. One of his assailants is said to have then recognized him, and, remembering some personal service rendered by the lieutenant, plead for him. This may have been only a part of a drama that was intended to frighten the occupants off the piece of land; Lieutenant Brown and Dr. Williamson, however, accepted the interference, and promised to immediately leave the country, which they did.

It has always appeared to the Author's mind that the Robinson murder was an accident and not premeditated. As one occurrence frequently suggests another of a similar character, it is very probable that the party attacking Dr. Robinson designed only to give him a beating and some rough usage. He was a young, athletic man, and when he first discovered so many men of evil purpose he very likely became alarmed, and in seeking to disengage himself from them, probably recognized some of them, and for their own protection and concealment the fatal violence was resorted to. From the angle of the wound upon the doctor's face the blow was evidently the work of a tall man, and from the direction the pistol-ball took, that was clearly the act of a short man. A tall and short man were not purposely selected as the victims of public suspicion; but, five years after the assassination, parties gave evidence before the grand jury against a number of persons whom they declared they had seen running away from the scene of the outrage, and, whether they were innocent or not, two of them were readily selected as being the two who killed the doctor. Had there been a settled purpose to kill him, it does not seem reasonable that seven men would have been intrusted with the work— they were too many to intrust with such a secret—neither would they have attacked him within seventy-five steps from his own door, and at a place surrounded by houses.

Assassination of Dr. J. King Robinson.

The inquest was held before Dr. Jeter Clinton, an alderman of the city, and the most perfect type of Dogberry (though without the simplicity of that worthy) that was ever seen in America. As a show of fairness, he at once associated with the city prosecuting-attorney a Gentile lawyer, Mr. C. H. Hempstead; then added Governor John B. Weller and Thomas Marshall, Esq., men of undoubted ability; and asked Chief-Justice Titus and Associate Justice McCurdy to sit on the bench with him. Probably nothing else could have been done then, but the eight days' examination was a waste of time. Upon the hypothesis that nothing of such grave importance is ever done in Utah without the order of Brigham Young, the labours of the

Gentile lawyers were evidently directed towards tracing the crime to the immediate order of some one in authority, and thereby bringing it home to the Prophet. It is very probable that, within thirteen hours after it was committed, Brigham knew something of how it occurred, but it is very doubtful whether he knew beforehand that it was contemplated. He knows too much of human nature to have confided that deed to so many men. One of those men will probably some day tell the story, just as some others are now seeking relief for their consciences by confessing to the Mountain Meadows massacre.

The funeral-procession of the murdered doctor rallied all the Gentiles. It was a grand sight. Probably there never was such a funeral before. As the procession moved slowly up the principal streets and along in front of Brigham's residence on the way to Camp Douglas Cemetery, there was a calm exterior, but any outrage then would have been met by men who were ready and willing to avenge the doctor's death. There was probably not a man in that long procession who did not feel the inspiration of vengeance. It was a public protest against the deadly influences that then ruled in Zion.

The death of Morris shook the faith of some; the assassina-ation of Robinson withered the faith of many more. Whether the ruling authorities had or had not any share in the deed, the fact remained the same, and painfully impressed the mind with the knowledge that so dreadful a crime could be committed and the perpetrators escape discovery. To make the matter worse, Brigham in the Tabernacle, to give the people something to think about, related that it was suggested that some of the soldiers who had been confined in the hospital and disliked the severity of the doctor's *régime*, had taken vengeance upon him when they got better! He stated that it was also surmised that the doctor might have been gambling and have quarrelled, and some one in anger had killed him! For neither story was there a particle of foundation. It never would do to let the people's minds be occupied with guessing for themselves, but never did Brigham Young seem so weak and ridiculous as when he uttered these silly stories. Some men, whom he saw almost hourly and heard their praises, winced terribly that day under the consciousness of shame.

With Chief-Justice Titus there had been no open rupture for a considerable time after his arrival, but they well knew that he held the leaders in detestation. Three apostates had been arrested in the country on the charge of stealing a cow: they were probably no great ornaments to society, but they had, however, a right to trial by jury. They were lodged in a place of confinement in Coalville—the first Mormon settlement on the line of the Pacific Railroad—and placed under the surveillance of an armed guard. The first that was heard of them afterwards was the story that "they had attempted to escape," and that the guard had been forced to fire upon them. Potter and Wilson were shot, and the former had his throat cut. Walker "dodged" the first shot of the guard, and was only slightly wounded. In his flight he was a second time hit, but managed to make good his escape and reached Camp Douglas. On his affidavit, Judge Titus caused the arrest of the parties whom he accused of the murders, but they soon after succeeded in escaping from the company of the Mormon marshal. The judge was dreadfully annoyed, and made no concealment of his sentiments. Walker soon after disappeared, and was never again seen.

In their foolish zeal and antagonism, one of the apostles and Brigham's agent got some silly women to make a very long night *chemise*, about ten feet in length—the judge is a very tall man—and tried to get a deputation of "sisters" to carry it to him with the compliments of the women of Utah. Several respectable ladies were invited to head this deputation, but declined (those ladies are now apostates), and the deputation motion was set aside, and finally an African was hired to carry the "present." The judge looked upon this incident as a threat as well as an insult, and considered that the lengthy night-garment was intended as *a shroud*. It was evidently in the mind of some one at that time to strike terror into the souls of all who were obnoxious in Zion.

* During October, 1872, Chief-Justice Titus had occasion to pass through Salt Lake City, and the Mormon papers were perfectly nauseating in their compliments to him. His Honour regarded the change of tone towards him as an attempt to injure the present Federal officers by way of contrast.

CHAPTER LIII.

THE DAWNING OF FREEDOM.—The Mercantile Struggle against Despotism—
"Freezing out the Gentiles"—Police Surveillance of Apostates' Stores—The
Walker Brothers—Brigham refuses a Check from them for $500—A Bishop told
to "cut away"—Handed over to the Buffetings of Satan—The Fight with Brigham—Fears of Violence—Gentile Merchants offer to sell out at a Great Loss and
leave the City—Brigham's Reply—The Gentiles and Apostates under the Ban—
Zion's Coöperative Mercantile Institution organized—Trouble among the Mormon Merchants—Ruin of the Small Traders—"The Seed of the Prophet Joseph"
go to Zion—The Reorganized Church—"Young Joseph"—Alexander H. and
David Hyrum Smith in Utah—Brigham's Jealousy—The Sons of Joseph meet
with Success—The "New Movement"—The *Utah Magazine*—Wonderful Revelations of Messrs. Godbe and Harrison—Voices from Heaven against Brigham—
The Beginning of the Great Apostacy—Godbe, Harrison and Kelsey expelled
from the Church—The *Magazine* opens its Batteries upon the Prophet—The Gentiles and Liberal Mormons encourage the "Rebels"—The "Reformers" start
a Newspaper—They preach and write themselves into Spiritualism—The Fetters burst and the Gentile Merchants triumph—Brigham's Power waning—His
Sceptre broken.

AT the departure of the Federal troops from Camp Floyd,
those who had there been engaged in business as merchants
came to the city and opened stores. Up to that time there
were few Mormon merchants—business was chiefly in the
hands of the Gentiles and a few Hebrews. Brigham Young
had discouraged the brethren from entering into commerce:
he hated the principal business street and called it vile names.
A few of the brethren, however, found "trading" profitable,
and others followed their example.

For a time efforts were made through the "teachers" to induce the Saints to deal exclusively with the merchants of "the
"household of faith;" but the priesthood could not control
everybody. Besides, the Gentile merchants, through having
contracts for supplying the troops and others, could often take

in exchange for their goods produce at better figures than the brethren could afford to give, and in other particulars the Gentiles had the preference with the people.

Preceding the assassination of Dr. Robinson, a large proportion of the Tabernacle sermons were devoted to "freezing " out" the Gentiles, and surveillance was offensively placed upon their stores, in order to discover who among the Saints would persist in trading with them. The police in sauntering to and fro could see the offenders and report them, and with these official eyes upon them, it took courage in the people to deal with a Gentile, Jew, or Apostate—especially with the latter.

Prominent and particularly exposed to this annoyance and injury were the Walker Brothers—four young men who "had " had the misfortune to have heard Mormonism in their youth " in England." They had been reared by parents who were in excellent circumstances in life; but who, in the confidence inspired by the enterprises of Hudson the "Railway King," risked and lost a fortune. The change from affluence to want did not, however, rob them of the teachings and morality that had been instilled into them by honest parents. The father could not at the moment leave England, but the mother and the four young boys sailed for America, stopped a short time in St. Louis, and ultimately reached Salt Lake City. They passed through all the poverty and labour that were known in Utah history. They toiled hard and honestly, ever keeping in their minds what they had been. On the arrival of the United States troops at Camp Floyd, in 1858, they entered into commerce on their own account. With untiring labour and close application to business, they began to accumulate property. They had long been dissatisfied with Mormonism—they had outgrown it, yet they were in a Mormon community, and they kept their thoughts to themselves. They contributed liberally to whatever was before the people, but they did not believe in paying a tithing of their annual incomes to the Church— they did not see evidence of its expenditure. A call was made upon them, and the leading member of the firm sent a check for $500 as " a contribution to the poor." The bishop of their ward took it to Brigham, but he would not accept it—"he would " make them pay their tithing, or he would cut them off from

" the Church." When the bishop returned the check, the brothers came to the conclusion that the issue might as well be met
then as at a later date. " Rob," as J. Robinson Walker is
familiarly called, took the check, tore it in pieces before the
bishop, and told him to " cut away." From that hour, Brigham waged against them unceasing warfare.

J. Robinson Walker.

The Walker Brothers never afterwards knew peace. Their
names were openly mentioned in Tabernacle sermons, and in
ward meetings, and the Saints were warned against dealing
with them ; but the " buffetings of Satan " did not break their
spirits. With all his machinery at work, Brigham is a heavy
enemy ; but the Walker Brothers were economical and tried
to please their customers, and while the policemen marched to
and fro before the front-door of their store, to see who did business with them, customers would slip in at the back-door.
Every scheme had to be resorted to. When Mormon traders
in the country purchased of the " Apostates," the goods would
be marked in such a way as to conceal that they had come
from the Walker Brothers, but finally Brigham got wind of that
also, and the bishops compelled the traders to produce their
invoices ! Some who had dealt for years with the Walker

Brothers had now to stop that commerce, or lose their fellow-ship with the Church!

After the assassination of Dr. Robinson, fears of violence were not unnatural, and many men, who had never before carried arms, buckled on their revolvers. Highly-respectable men in Salt Lake City forsook the sidewalks after dusk, and as they repaired to their residences traversed the middle of the public street, carrying their revolvers in their hands.

With such a feeling of uneasiness, nearly all the non-Mormon merchants joined in a letter to Brigham Young, offering if the Church would purchase their goods and estates at twenty-five per cent. less than their valuation, they would leave the Territory. Brigham answered them cavalierly that he had not asked them to come into the Territory, did not ask them to leave it, and that they might stay as long as they pleased.

It was clear that Brigham felt himself master of the situation, and the merchants had to " bide their time " and await the coming change that was anticipated from the completion of the Pacific Railroad. As the great iron way approached the mountains, and every day gave greater evidence of its being finished at a much earlier period than was at first anticipated, the hope of what it would accomplish nerved the discontented to struggle with the passing day.

The preaching did not, however, altogether succeed in preventing the Saints from " trading with the Gentiles." The country Saints would plead that they did not know a Gentile from a Mormon store, especially as some of the brethren were serving behind Gentile counters. To remedy this, Brigham called a meeting of the merchants in the City Hall, October, 1868, and there it was determined that the words " Holiness " to the Lord," over an all-seeing eye, should be written on every sign-board, and be put over the door of every Mormon store, so that " the wayfaring man, though a fool, might not err " therein." But even that did not suffice, and, later in the same year, the Prophet conceived the idea of uniting all the Mormon merchants in one grand coöperative * commercial

* One of the brethren, a small trader * * * *, claims that he went up to Brigham once to obtain his counsel and permission to start a coöperative scheme on a small scale throughout the Territory, and that Brigham told him to let it pass for the moment, and afterwards used it as the foundation of his grand mercantile institution.

scheme, by which he hoped finally to be able to "freeze out "the Gentiles" who were then in business, and discourage those who might have entertained the idea of coming there when the railroad was finished. For some months he laboured to this end, but the brethren saw the utter ruin of their commercial credit abroad if their stocks of goods were thrown together into one institution, to be controlled by other and irresponsible men, and as far as they dared they opposed the Prophet's coöperative scheme. His first project was for the merchants to deliver over their goods, and, if they did not find occupation in the institution, they could engage in some other branch of business or manufacture, and rent their stores for any other purpose, or, if they could do no better, close them and "go to farming." He contemplated one general wholesale coöperative store that would supply branch-stores in every ward in the city and in the country with all the goods that would be necessary for the people's consumption. The main business street in Salt Lake City was then to be left to the Gentiles, and they would soon have more stores than customers.

The Prophet was determined to succeed this time, and it was nothing to him if, in seeking the ruin of the Gentiles, his merchant brethren were sacrificed. The business that had been created by years of untiring labour was instantly to be abandoned. To one gentleman who represented that a merchant friend of his would be utterly ruined if forced into the coöperative scheme, and that he would probably have to sacrifice even his homestead in meeting his obligations at that time, while, if let alone, he could, with personal attention to his own affairs, maintain his credit, pay his debts, and preserve his property, Brigham answered heartlessly, that "he had no business "to get into debt, and if he loses his property it serves him "right."*

The organization was at length effected in the beginning of 1869, with a president, vice-president, and five directors. Brigham was president; Delegate Hooper, vice-president; the apostles George A. Smith, George Q. Cannon, Horace Eldredge,

---

* When the gentleman alluded to related this to the Author, he added: "I never "knew Brother Brigham till then. His words and manner opened my eyes."

Wm. Jennings, and Henry W. Lawrence, directors ; Wm. Clayton, secretary ; and H. B. Clawson, superintendent. This organization gave Brigham the controlling power should any such thing as opposition occur.

Mr. Jennings, a shrewd business man, who had rapidly amassed a fortune in commerce, saw that when the railroad was finished all goods would be depreciated by the change in freight, and, much as he might dislike closing the business that he had so successfully built up, he conceived very wisely that submission would be in this case profitable, and sold his stock to the coöperative, for about $170,000, and rented his store for three years, at an annual rental of $8,000. Eldredge and Clawson sold their stock also, and other merchants put in part of their goods, and in this way began " Zion's Coöperative Mer-" cantile Institution," and the Prophet became a merchant.

The Mormon merchants who did not join the Coöperative Institution and bring their goods there, and who did not put " Z. C. M. I." and the all-seeing eye over their doors, soon had a little of the Gentile experience. The police walked before their stores, and, by their presence, morally intimidated the Saints from buying of the rebellious brother.

In every ward a stock-holders' store was opened, and there the people were instructed to purchase their goods. But even all this did not accomplish the desired end—the people would find some excuse for coming into the principal business street, and Zion's Coöperative Mercantile Institution, that was created a wholesale establishment, opened retail stores in every branch of merchandise. A few of the wealthy merchants were able to survive this colossal competition supported by the teachings of the Tabernacle, and the all-pervading surveillance of the bishops throughout the Territory ; but the smaller merchants, both in and out of the Church, had to close business, and some of them, in the forced settlement of their affairs, lost nearly everything. The Walker Brothers, the Kahn Brothers, the Auerbachs, and a very few other wealthy Gentile and Hebrew merchants, were able to continue business, but at an immense daily sacrifice. The Walkers, who had before done a very extensive business, were greatly injured. Their commerce instantly fell from thousands of dollars per day to hundreds. They had valuable property at home, real estate elsewhere, U. S. bonds, and high commercial credit ; and they resolved to " see it out," and kept on their numerous staff of clerks, warehousemen, and book-keepers. When advised to close the business and leave the Territory, " Rob " answered that they had $120,000 which they could spare, and they would " hold on."

Most of the ward stores could not succeed, and the stockholders lost their money, but the grand experiment served the Prophet well. It made him at once the business associate of the leading Mormon merchants—the men of energy and success—and, without the toil and trouble of creating a business, he suddenly found himself a sharer in their profits,* and, in another particular, " Z. C. M. I. " was specially useful, for, in the varied branches of this commerce, his numerous sons, sons-in-law, and special friends have found permanent occupation.

While victory seemed to perch on the Prophet's banner, and the merchants appeared certain to be vanquished, silent and unseen influences were at work against the infallibility of the Prophet, and the divinity of his faith.

The " Reorganized Church of True Latter-Day Saints," under the presidency of the eldest son of Joseph Smith, very naturally had a longing after the spiritual welfare of the Rocky Mountain Saints. Two of their elders had been to Utah in 1862, and had been successful in turning some away from the faith in Brigham, and in laying the foundation for a still better work to be accomplished at a more convenient season. From the death of the founder of Mormonism, the Saints had had their attention riveted on " the seed " of the Prophet, and expected that some day the young man Joseph would be the head of the Church.

Brigham had fostered this faith in the Saints for some years, but when, in 1860, "young Joseph" was chosen President of the Reorganized Church, and publicly denounced Brigham and his Polygamy, it was evident that there was a mistake some-

---

* Very many years ago, before Brigham lost the characteristic innocence of poverty, he used to claim that, if he had not been a Prophet, he had at least been *Profit*-able to the Saints. Since his shrewd manipulation of the merchants, the Gentile papers now speak of the inspired head of the Church as " The Profit."

where. A younger brother—David Hyrum Smith—was then said to be "the coming man."

The second son of the Prophet, Alexander H. Smith, a good-looking, muscular Christian, had also, as a missionary, visited Utah. Brigham at first received him pleasantly, but would afford him no opportunity of addressing the Saints, and Joseph

Joseph Smith, the Prophet's Son.

F. Smith, one of Brigham's young apostles, and cousin of Alexander, gave him considerable public opposition.* The visit to Utah of this scion of the "royal house of Smith" added numbers to the new Church, and shook the faith of many more in Brigham. The success of his mission was satisfactory to him, and, after "casting his bread upon the waters," he returned to the States.

* The debate of the two Smiths was a curious spectacle for the Saints to witness. Here were the sons of Joseph and Hyrum Smith quarrelling over Brigham Young and Polygamy—Alexander H. maintaining that Brigham was a usurper, and that polygamy was from the devil, while Joseph F. was just as certain that Brigham was the true successor of "the martyred Joseph," and that polygamy was from heaven—and each "knew" that his position was true "by revelation," and "by the "Holy Ghost!" To make the wrangling still more interesting, Joseph F. made a malignant attack upon Mrs. Emma Smith, and called her a vile name before a public audience. Alexander H. was more a Christian than is admired by people generally, but he sprang up and warmly cautioned Joseph F. that, though they were cousins, he must not apply such an epithet to his mother again.

Another and an unlooked-for phase of Mormon experience was soon to demand public attention. Two elders were trying to establish a literary paper—*The Utah Magazine.* The proprietors were W. S. Godbe and E. L. T. Harrison; the latter was the Editor. Elder Harrison had essayed, once before, with his friend Edward W. Tullidge, to make literature a profession among the Saints, and had established the *Peep o' Day ;* but they met with insurmountable difficulties, and the paper stopped. The *Magazine,* with even Mr. Godbe's willing hand and ready purse to support it, realized that the effort to establish a purely literary paper in Utah was premature. The career of the *Magazine* was fast hastening to a close, and, by way of rest and recreation, the editor accompanied the merchant to New York. Both of them had struggled to preserve their faith in Mormonism, but the contents of the Book of Mormon, critically viewed, was a terrible test of credulity, and many of the revelations of " the Lord " savoured too much of Joseph Smith, and abounded with contradictions, and were very human at that. As for Brigham, " he was a hopeless case ; many of his measures were utterly devoid of even commercial sense, and far less were they clothed with divine wisdom—in all his ways, he was destitute of the magnanimity of a great soul, and was intensely selfish." To their developed intellects now, Mormonism seemed a crude jargon of sense and nonsense, honesty and fraud, devotion and cant, hopeless poverty to the many, overflowing wealth to the favoured few—a religion as unlike their conceptions of the teachings of Christ, as darkness is to light. Still, they had had pleasant associations in the Church. Mr. Godbe had been industrious and successful in business ; was kindly looked upon by the community, and had many friends, besides three wives, and a pleasant family of children ; everything dear to him was in Utah. It was painful to lose faith where there was everything to gain with it ; he was awkwardly situated. Mr. Harrison was an excellent writer, and was professionally an architect. He had been a missionary in Europe for many years, and had a respectable standing among the Saints, and he and Mr. Godbe were both presidents of Seventies, and the former was counsellor to his bishop.

Away from Utah, and travelling together over the Plains,

the old rumbling stage-coach afforded the two friends, as every
traveller in those days experienced, an excellent opportunity
for reflection. On the way they "compared notes" respecting
the situation of things at home, and spoke frankly together of
their doubts and difficulties with the faith. They discovered,
clearly enough, that they were—in the language of the orthodox—"on the road to apostacy," yet in their feelings they did
not want to leave Mormonism, or Utah. A struggle began in
their minds. With their conclusions that the faith was *not*
divine, they could not consistently and with a good conscience
continue to assume that it was so in future. To avow that
much was to be disfellowshipped, and incur the prospective
ruin of all earthly hopes while they remained among the
Saints; yet silence was hypocrisy. One proposition followed
another, and scheme after scheme was the subject of discussion, but not one of those schemes or propositions, when examined, appeared desirable; they were in terrible mental anguish.
Arrived in New York and comfortable in their hotel, in the
evening they concluded to pray for guidance. They wanted
light, either to have their doubts removed and their faith in
Mormonism confirmed, or, yet again, to have the light of their
own intellects increased that they might be able to follow un-
waveringly their convictions. In this state of mind the two
elders assert that they had an "extraordinary experience."

They claim that while they knelt and earnestly prayed, a
voice spoke to them and made some communication upon the
subject which most interested them. They were astonished
and bewildered, but instantly were calmed and self-possessed.
For three weeks, while, during the day, Mr. Godbe was purchasing goods in the busy marts of commerce, Mr. Harrison
was sitting quietly in the hotel preparing a series of questions
upon every subject of religion and philosophy that he could
think of; and in the evening, by appointment, "a band of
"spirits" came to them, and held converse with them, as
friends would speak with friends. One by one the questions
prepared by Mr. Harrison were read, and Mr. Godbe and Mr.
Harrison, with pencil and paper, took down the answers as
they heard them given by the spirits. This is their statement,
and they firmly believe it.

The reader may not care to follow their statements in detail, but in order to explain the work these Elders undertook, it may be added, that they maintain that during their experience in New York they had (but *not* by "table-rapping" or by "medi-"ums") a constant stream of communication by means of audible voices from a number of most distinguished historical personages.* Messrs. Harrison and Godbe have not paraded what is here stated, but, on the other hand, have been very reticent when speaking on the subject. These facts, however, are understood by their confidential friends, and Mr. Harrison is said to have in his possession intelligence assumed to have been given him by Humboldt, that will some day or other "upset" "the Darwinian theory," and which is as much beyond the speculations of Mr. Darwin, as the latter gentleman supposes his theory to be beyond the Genesis of Moses.

With these "communications" was given much information about Mormonism, how it originated, and how Joseph Smith had, by reason of his surroundings, his lack of education, the traditions of past ages, and the current ideas of Christendom, turned his "mediumistic" experience into the church-kingdom-building scheme that is known in Utah. What was true about Mormonism, they were told, should be preserved, and what was false should be rejected.

As a phenomenon, the story of Elders Godbe and Harrison will doubtless yet occupy the attention of the scientist and the spiritualist. They are men of unimpeachable veracity. They returned to Utah, and to a very small circle of friends confided what has here been only very briefly related, and their story was listened to. Elder Eli B. Kelsey, a Mormon of twenty-seven years' standing, and who was also a president of Seventies, was the intimate friend of Mr. Godbe, and Elder Edward W. Tullidge, another "Seventy," was the bosom friend of Mr. Harrison. Believing that Brigham had set out to build up a dynasty of his own, and that he, like David the king, looked upon the people as his "heritage," these four Elders resolved to sap the foundations of his throne, and to place before the people the

---

* These *séances* lasted about two hours every evening; "the voices were perfectly "audible, but only on one occasion could they see the forms of their visitors, and "these were indistinct in detail."

best intelligence they could command to enable them to realize their true position. Elder Henry W. Lawrence, a wealthy merchant, a bishop's counsellor, and a gentleman of the highest integrity, was early informed in confidence of this "New "Movement," and to his friend Mr. Godbe gave valuable material support. The *Magazine*, that had before this been hastening to an end, took a new lease of life, and became a brilliant, well-conducted paper.

Not a word was ever said against Brigham or the faith; no fault was found with any one or anything, but week after week the whole strength of four vigorous pens was let loose upon the ignorance and superstitions of the age. Brigham had instilled into the minds of the Saints that the world was degenerating to an end, propelled by lightning speed; Kelsey, without ever squinting at the Prophet, wrote the history of the past, and showed "How the World had Grown;" Tullidge resuscitated the "Great Characters" of the world, and without once alluding to Brother Brigham, the contrast was to his disadvantage; Harrison dwelt upon a philosophical faith, and Godbe exhibited the possibility of honest error. With such minds at work, and with such a field for labour, and innumerable subjects to handle, the writers had only to study caution and prudence. The *Magazine* was sought after by the reading portion of the community; soon its influence was felt, and the argus-eyes of the teachers were watchful to mark who "took it in."

No allusion had yet been made to the "experience" in New York, but in the midst of this preparatory literary work for the *dénoûment* that was sure to come, two of the sons of Joseph Smith—Alexander H. and David Hyrum—arrived in the city as missionaries. This afforded the *Magazine* writers their first opportunity of showing their intention of reaching Brigham's dynasty.

All the old women in the country wanted to see "David H." He was the child of prediction, and Brigham had now the opportunity of fulfilling his promise to "stand aside" when the sons of Joseph should come to Zion. Another experience, however, awaited the two brothers. They had not come up in "the right spirit. . . . If they were only on the right track, "he could almost embrace them." They had yet to learn that

to reach the upper seat the aspirant must come into the fold
humbly " by the door of the kingdom "—must be baptized by
one of Brigham's elders, receive the priesthood through him,
and acknowledge that Polygamy was divine; then he would
be introduced to the Church as its future leader, by right of
birth and by prediction.

The two brothers, though young, are intelligent men of
good address, with a liberal share of this world's experience.
They understood Brigham perfectly. In their interview with
the Prophet, he denied them the use of the Tabernacle, and
renewed his attack upon their mother. Alexander says:

" I, of course, differed from him, and told him so; and then he called
mother ' *a liar, yes, the damnedest liar that lives,*' * said that she tried to poison father, that she stole Uncle Hyrum's portrait and large ring. . . . After
our interview we returned to John's, and I vented my anger in biting my
food and swallowing it; but was nervous all the rest of the day—perhaps
from indigestion, as it did not sit well on my stomach." †

The two brothers were zealous, and resolved to preach
wherever they could obtain a hearing. Independence Hall
was obtained for their use, and there they held forth against
Polygamy. But Brigham was " too much" for them. The
bishops of the city wards were instructed to take with them
early the old Nauvoo Mormons and fill the room, to the exclusion of many others who wanted honestly to listen to them.
The apostle Joseph F., their cousin, continued to contend with
them that their father was truly the author of Polygamy among
the Mormons, and the meetings were often nothing but a
noisy wrangle.‡

* No man can be more suave in manner and soft in speech than Brigham Young
when he has an object in view, and wants to impress any one favourably; but when
he is the " Lion of the Lord," there is no expression too harsh for him to use, and,
if a lady is the object of his wrath, her sex is no protection to her.

† Alexander H. Smith's letter to the *Latter-Day Saints' Herald*, vol. xvi., p. 85.

‡ A correspondent of the San Francisco *Bulletin*, reporting one of the meetings
held by Joseph F., relates that this young apostle referred to the denial of polygamy
by his father (*see* p. 199), wherein he classified polygamy with *false and corrupt doctrines.* To this Joseph F. answered:

" It is said that I have proved my father a liar. I will show that he has not
lied. *There is a difference between telling a lie and not telling the truth* (!!!). Webster
says: ' Polygamy, a man having several wives, or a woman having several husbands.' *The latter part my father meant to deny,* and *not the former; therefore he did
not lie.*"

The *Magazine* modestly essayed the part of umpire between the belligerents, and, under the pretext of advising the young Smiths, seized the occasion to tell Brigham what the people felt respecting his dynasty project:

"If we know the true feeling of our brethren, it is that they never intend Joseph Smith's *nor any other man's son* to preside over them, simply because of their sonship. The principle of heirship has cursed the world for ages, and with our brethren *we expect to fight it till, with every other relic of tyranny, it is trodden under foot.*"

The writer of that paragraph, Elder Harrison, was immediately after appointed on a mission to England.

Neither Brigham nor the *Magazine* writers had cared as yet to show their hands to each other. The Prophet had, however, the advantage of position, and could force the others to yield or rebel. Besides appointing Mr. Harrison to England, Mr. Kelsey was appointed to go to the Eastern States, and another of the prominent elders, Mr. William H. Shearman, who was supposed to be in sympathy with them, also received a mission. They all declined to go. The ball was now in motion.

The Pacific Railroad had now been completed six months, and the hoped-for change and amelioration in the condition of the people of Utah through that influence had resulted in disappointment. The nearest point of the railroad to Salt Lake City was Ogden—over thirty-six miles distant—and it was only very rarely that the traveller passing from the river to the sea thought it worth his while to leave the comfort of a Pullman car to be jostled over a hideously rough road, in a Wells, Fargo stage, in order to hear Brigham in the Tabernacle and see the Saints at home.

The railroad had for the moment been a great injury to the Mormon people. Brigham had had the contract for building a large portion of the road, and sublet the work to responsible parties at ten per cent. less; these sub-contractors in their turn again let it to others; and whether the work paid the men who toiled, or not, Brigham and his friends were certain of their percentage and made large sums of money, while a great many of the small contractors and labouring men were utterly ruined. It was many months after the completion of the Pacific Railroad before the needy men could get their pay, and then it was in Utah Central bonds that did not at the time command more than forty-five cents on the dollar in Salt Lake City. The merchants who had credited the brethren during the building of the road, and who had to wait an indefinite period for the return of their money, were seriously injured by this forced delay. The railroad had its future mission, but something else was then wanted to break the bonds of theocracy.

Curiously enough, Godbe and Harrison claim to have been informed, in those remarkable *séances* in New York already referred to, that the only redemption possible for the people of Utah was through the development of the minerals in the mountains ; that, so long as they were poor, they were at the mercy of Brigham Young, and never could free themselves from the bondage into which they had been led through their confidence in the principles of faith taught by the elders. Knowing the opposition of the ruling priesthood to the discovery of the precious ores, it was a matter of serious consideration how they could convey that intelligence to the public, without coming in direct contact with Brigham, and bringing about an open rupture.

The subject had been considered for some time by that small circle of embryo " Reformers "—as one writer afterwards chose to designate them—and at last an article was written by Mr. Harrison. A few intimate friends had read it in manuscript before it went into the hands of the printer, and there was a general feeling that the hour of struggle was at hand. It was no slight matter for a few men who had given a score of years and more of zealous, devoted labour to build up Mormonism, and who had hitherto been as humble as children under the direction of the priesthood, to now contemplate a movement in opposition to a powerful hierarchy that had crushed everything that ever claimed attention without the Prophet's approval. It was a daring project, and was not undertaken without the most serious consideration of the consequences that it would and might involve. But men of revelation find a wonderful strength in their own convictions; and before their sense of duty there are no sacrifices too great to make.

These two elders—Godbe and Harrison—with their immediate friends who have been named, and a few brave women of spotless character, were ready " to walk into the jaws of " death," if it were necessary, in order to succeed in shattering that gigantic power that was crushing the manhood out of the people. This little band did not number altogether a dozen persons, and what they knew, or thought they knew, of the purpose of others, and the design among themselves, were matters secretly kept within their own bosoms.

Some very pungent articles had been published in the *Magazine*, that had awakened attention, and in some measure they had foreshadowed a purpose on the part of the writers to judge of the teachings and measures of Brigham Young as they would those of any other man ; but of the true nature of the " move-" ment " they were inaugurating, nothing had been fairly stated. The writers at first only aimed to provoke the people to thinking. " There is," wrote Harrison, " one fatal error, which pos-" sesses the minds of some, it is this : that God Almighty *in-*" *tended the priesthood to do our thinking.* . . . Our own opin-" ion is that, when we invite men to use free speech and free " thought to get into the Church, we should not call upon them, " or ourselves, to kick down the ladder by which they and we as-" cended to Mormonism. They should be called upon to think " on as before, no matter who has or has not thought in the " same direction. . . . Think freely, and think for ever, and, " above all, never fear that the ' Ark ' of everlasting truth can " ever be ' steadied ' by mortal hand or shaken."

This was very dangerous teaching to such a community. The Mormon people had never listened to that language in Zion. The elements of revolution were gathering, and everything seemed propitious for the rebellion.

Vice - President Colfax, ex-Governor Bross, and Sam. Bowles, Esq., were again to pay Zion a passing call. From the period of their first visit, they had, with their voice and pens, drawn the attention of the world's capitalists to that great enterprise, and they had in that given powerful aid to build the Pacific Railroad. The work was now fully achieved, and they had passed over it from Omaha to San Francisco, and since their return eastward they had some anxiety to see what it had done for Zion.

A day or two before they arrived, the Author's attention was accidentally drawn to a correspondence from Paris to the New York *Herald*, on the political condition of France and what French journalists assumed the people had suffered, through remitting all political power into the hands of Napoleon. It awakened thought upon Utah and Brigham Young, and an editorial upon "Progress" was published in the *Telegraph*. It was mild, impersonal, never once named the Territory or the Prophet—but it spoke of liberty. Under other circumstances it might have escaped the eyes of those who select the matter to be read to the Prophet.* Then, it was offensive, as it showed a harmony of thought with the *Magazine* writers, and they were now closely watched.

Mr. Colfax politely refused to accept the proffered courtesies of the city. Brigham was reported to have uttered abusive language in the Tabernacle towards the Government and Congress, and to have charged the President and Vice-President with being "drunkards and gamblers." One of the aldermen who waited upon Mr. Colfax, to tender him the hospitalities of the city, could only say that "he did not hear Brig- "ham say so." The weakness of the denial confirmed the impression obtained from so many sources that the Prophet had really said so, and Mr. Colfax followed his own programme during his stay. On the evening before his departure, he made a temperate yet firm speech, from a platform in front of his hotel, reviewing the situation of the Mormons towards the General Government, and especially in their preserving the institution of Polygamy against the law of Congress.

The Vice-President and his friends were made acquainted with the forthcoming opposition from members of the Church, and took much interest in the "Movement," believing as they did that the one-man-power and the infallibility of priesthood had seen their day.

Ten days after their departure, an article was published

---

* Brigham is not a reader in the ordinary sense of the expression. Captain R. F. Burton said of him that "his mind was uncorrupted by books." He probably never read a book, outside of the Mormon faith, in his life. His secretary, or Mr. Cannon, generally reads to him anything considered interesting or amusing. Their enlightenment of his mind is always in the direction of his own prejudices.

in the *Magazine* on " The True Development of the Territory "
—a very temperate statement of the difficulties of the people,
with some advice to them to devote attention to mining.

On the afternoon of the day on which that article was published, Brigham, in " the School of the Prophets," was furious.
The names of Godbe, Harrison, Tullidge, Stenhouse and three
others—not " rebels "—were called, and, as all these gentlemen were absent, Brigham, in his anger, moved that they all
be " disfellowshipped " from the Church, and the following
brief notification was sent to each :

"SALT LAKE CITY, *October* 16, 1869.

DEAR BROTHER : I hereby inform you that a motion was made, sec-   •
onded, and carried by a unanimous vote of the School of the Prophets to-
day, that you be *disfellowshipped* from the Church until you appear in
the School and give satisfactory reasons for your irregular attendance
there.   Your brother in the Gospel,

" GEORGE GODDARD, *Secretary.*"

For months, the events of that day had been anticipated,
and longed for. The accused were all well known to the public,
as well as to the Church, and, when the news was heard on the
street, it created great excitement. The Gentiles were jubilant.

On the Saturday following, the " rebels " appeared in the
School. Never before had there been such a scene in the " old
" Tabernacle." Mr. Godbe frankly stated his position, and
Brigham followed him with aggravating mimicry, turning
everything into ridicule. Mr. Harrison threw caution to the
winds, and answered the insinuations of the Prophet defiantly.
It was a squally time, and not without apprehension of danger.
The proprietors of the *Magazine* were finally notified that they
would be tried on the Monday succeeding, and, with the exception of ten or a dozen persons—friends of the writers—the
whole audience of about a thousand elders with uplifted hands
voted *not to read the Magazine!* The trial took place in the
City Hall, and the auditory was chiefly composed of the bishops, their counsellors, and faithful brethren ; a few friends of
the accused obtained admission. The apostle George Q. Cannon was selected to prefer the charge of apostacy.

Elders Godbe and Harrison had, as yet, no defined programme, but were ready for anything. They awaited the charges

of the apostle and manfully contended for *the right of private judgment* in all matters of faith or " counsel ; " but the apostle Cannon maintained that "*it is apostacy to differ honestly from* "*the measures of the President* [Brigham]—*a man may be* " *honest even in hell ;* " and counsellor Daniel H. Wells volunteered the extraordinary statement that the accused "*might as* " *well ask the question whether a man had the right to differ* " *honestly from the Almighty !* " Elders Cannon and Wells were faithful exponents of the Mormon Priesthood, and the Council could do no other than cut off the recusants from the Church.* When the vote of expulsion was taken, Elder Kelsey voted negatively, and, for the endorsement of the sentiments of his friends, he was immediately cut off, and with Godbe and Harrison was " turned over to the buffetings of Satan."

---

* Excommunication is not a mere use of words: it has a very practical application to the dissenter. There is an excellent illustration of this in the case of Elder John Hyde. When he was excommunicated, Brother Heber gave a very clear interpretation of that action in the following words:

" I want you," said he, to an audience of about three thousand persons, " to vote, " every one of you, either for or against, for there is *no sympathy to be shown unto* " *such a man*. Brother Wells has seconded the motion I have made. All that are " in favour that John Hyde be cut off from the Church of Jesus Christ of Latter-Day " Saints, and that he be delivered over to Satan to be buffeted in the flesh, will raise " their right hands. [All hands were raised.]

" A motion has been put and unanimously carried, that John Hyde be cut off " root and branch; that is, himself, and all the roots and branches that are within " him. This has no allusion to his family. He has taken a course by which *he has* " *lost his family*, and forfeited his priesthood; he has forfeited his membership. " The limb is cut off, but *the priesthood takes the fruit that was attached to the limb* " *and saves it, if it will be saved*. Do you understand me? His wife is not cut off " from this Church, but *she is free from him ; she is just as free from him as though* " *she had never belonged to him*. The limb she is connected to is cut off, and she must " again be grafted into the tree, if she wishes to be saved; that is all about it."— *Deseret News, January* 21, 1857.

Mr. Hyde loved his wife, a beautiful, well-educated young lady, and she was devotedly attached to him, but she had then less experience, and more faith in Mormonism, than her husband. He had left Utah on mission, and feared to return after he announced his apostacy, and he never saw his wife again. Mr. Hyde placed funds at the lady's disposal to enable her to leave Utah, but she was counselled to remain. and, afraid that Mormonism might be true, and that her husband might be wrong, she clung to Zion. In course of time, Mrs. Hyde, in the language of Brother Heber, was " again grafted into the tree," and is now entitled to the third share of the affections and protection of a good-natured brother, who, it is to be hoped, will never apostatize. Mr. Hyde applied for a divorce in an English court, and the case here stated became of public notoriety in that country. Mr. Hyde is now an eloquent and distinguished divine in the Swedenborgian Church in England, and has a very happy family. Respect for the lady in Utah suggests no further remark.

The trial was as fairly conducted as these things ever are. The accused were unmistakably guilty—all "reformers," "dis-"senters," must be guilty! Brigham, throughout, was calm and respectful. He had no interest in Mr. Harrison, but he was grieved to lose Mr. Godbe. Brigham called him "one of "his pets," whom he "would have carried around in his vest-"pocket." Mr. Godbe was a man of untiring energy, useful in many ways, liberal in contributions, and paid a heavy tithing. Brigham evidently regretted his ill-tempered mimicry of him in the Tabernacle. Then, he probably thought that he could bring the rebels to their knees. In the trial, he discovered that there was "method in their madness," and he could see by their de-fence, and by their protest against excommunication for differ-ing from him on matters of business and secular measures, that many would sustain them. It was then that he announced like Hildebrand that "as a man he was fallible, but he "was clothed with a priesthood that was infallible." As Brig-ham asserts that he is never without his priesthood, the rebels failed to see where fallibility ended and where infallibility began.

It was of no consequence to intelligent persons in Utah, whether Godbe and Harrison had received revelations or not; neither to these unbelievers was the character or the source of the revelations worthy of a moment's consideration; but here was an element that could reach the people of Utah. Men and women who had left Mormonism before and opposed the Church were easily overcome, as they had nothing to present to the Saints. Here were two elders, intelligent men, of no ordinary ability, and of strictly moral lives, claiming that they had had revelations from the highest circle of heavenly beings who were breathing anxiety for " humanity " and desirous of communicating with the Saints for their deliverance. The Gentiles, of course, took no notice of the sentiments of the revelations; but they saw in them the old influence of the original faith, and knew that it would affect those who were dissatisfied with the materialistic religion of Brigham Young. The Tabernacle sermons were almost wholly devoted to sec-ular interests—establishing coöperative stores, constructing canals, building tabernacles and temples, making big ditches, paying tithing, marrying young wives, manufacturing cloth, plaiting straw, raising fish, cultivating bees, planting mulberry-trees, and making silk; to which was added here and there, by way of variety, a tirade of abuse upon "the enemies of the "Saints," Congress, the Chief Executive, and the Gentiles in general, with a special *blessing* for the Federal judges in Utah! Occasionally there would be an attempt at a higher flight, but it was rare.   To all this, add that Elders Godbe, Harrison, Kelsey, Tullidge, Shearman, Lawrence, and others, had a living faith to preach—that which the people knew to be the original faith of the founder of Mormonism, and "the gifts" came back again. The converts of the apostles, too, could "speak in tongues" and prophesy, and could tell of visions, dreams, and the presence of angels!

Twenty-five years before that, one of the brethren had had a dream in Nauvoo—a wonderful dream! He saw the Saints enveloped in dark, heavy clouds, and saw Brigham and the apostles labouring indefatigably to keep them together. The Prophet and his aids were working like coopers, driving the hoops down with great force till the hoops burst, and the people rushed out of the circle, and ran in every direction, each one taking his own way. Of course, its interpretation was that "a grand apostacy" would some day take place. The "New Movement" was in a moment caught up as the fulfilment of Farnsworth's dream. The dreamer, however, had to add that Brigham's future after that was to be glorious! The latter portion, of course, was regarded by the "dissent-"ers" as an addendum. Farnsworth's dream, however, served a purpose, and thousands to-day in Utah believe that Brigham and the apostles have burst the hoops. They never can again drive them as tight as they did before.

The *Magazine*, now no longer restrained, reviewed the teachings of the infallible priesthood with great ability, but generally in respectful and temperate language. From all parts of the Territory the "reformers" were encouraged by letters of sympathy, and the Gentiles, who had long felt the lash of the Tabernacle, gave them liberal support. In less than two months from their expulsion from the Church, they dared to begin regular preaching, and, from the liberal contributions which

Mr. Godbe had given to the erection of the Thirteenth Ward Assembly Rooms, he forced the bishop to give him the use of the building on a part of every Sunday. On the morning of the 19th December, 1869, they preached for the first time, and the Assembly Rooms were literally packed. Notwithstanding the previous general apprehension of being "reported," a spirit of reckless indifference to consequences seized all classes, and "That's true," "Amen," could be heard throughout the addresses from all parts of the auditory. In the evening the Masonic Hall was occupied in the same way, the meetings were spirited and enthusiastic, and every good point made was greeted with the heartiest applause. The Walker Brothers gave noble support to the movement, and, in addition to liberal contributions, they fitted up one of their large stores in the centre of the main street, and gave the "apostates" its use gratuitously. There the "Movement" centred the opposing elements, and the leading elders preached every Sunday morning and evening, and one evening during the week.*

No one could have predicted the possibility of such a sudden change from fear to recklessness, and no one comprehended better than Brigham that it was the best policy to "let the "fire blaze away." At first, the bishops "cut off" all those who were tainted with apostacy, as soon as they gave any indication of the malady; but the cases became so numerous, and added so much to the influence of the "Movement," that "the cutting-"off" was not so very hastily pressed.

Of all the apostacies from the Mormon Church, this was the most formidable, and has done more damage to the position of Brigham Young than all of them put together. The preaching of the "reformers" first shook the people's confidence in the Prophet, and, as they travelled further, it has led many of them out of Mormonism altogether.

The "reformers" preached and wrote down Brigham's

* Soon after its inauguration, the "New Movement" received a very valuable accession to its numbers in the person of Elder Amasa M. Lyman, formerly one of the Twelve Apostles. He is a very eloquent preacher, and was the only member of the apostles who ever thought it worthy of his time to speak of "the love of Christ" and "the redemption of humanity." Amasa believed in intellectual Christianity, and is labouring throughout Utah now, appealing to the higher and better instincts of the people.

Mormonism effectively, and, to better support their cause, they started a weekly *Tribune*, then made it a daily *Tribune*,* and, with secular readers and secular hearers, they have written and preached themselves into modern spiritualism, and to-day maintain stoutly that the only truth about and in Mormonism has all the time been its spiritual experiences; that Joseph Smith was naturally a medium, and, glowing with magnetism, electrified everybody that ever came near him, and, believing that all his experiences came directly from a Divine source, he readily and honestly claimed that he was a prophet, seer, and revelator; and of Brigham Young they say also that he was an "impres- "sional medium," and by reason of his strong will-power, and the opportunities of such a formidable organization of priesthood, he has been able to rise to the dizzy height of claiming to be "the mouth-piece of God."

But for the boldness of the "reformers," Utah to-day would not have been what it is. Inspired by their example, the people who had listened to them disregarded the teachings of the priesthood against trading with or purchasing from the Gentiles. The spell was broken, and, as in all such life-experience, the other extreme was for a time threatened. Walker Brothers regained their lost trade, and, in one year from the time that this "New Movement" began, the stores of these merchants were so crowded during the Conference, that it was with difficulty their patrons could be served. The success of the Coöperative was for a time doubtful, and the Institution that was at first backed in commercial credit by such responsible names as Jennings, Hooper, Eldredge, and Lawrence, was changed into a stock company, where these gentlemen and their associates were protected by "limited liability."

It is gratifying to be able to add, that the Walker Brothers have fought the good fight for liberty, and have falsified the predictions of the Tabernacle, and exploded a powerful bugbear. According to Brigham and Amos M. Musser, they were to have become poor and destitute, and glad to get money enough to take them out of the Territory. They were roughly committed to the tender mercies of the devil many years ago,

* Another year later, and the *Tribune* passed into other hands, and became strictly a secular paper, with strong inclinations to pitch into "the Profit."

and his majesty was to buffet them with great severity.* They
certainly did have a heavy share of trouble for several years,
but Brigham was their Satan and Musser was their Buffeter.†
They had, however, the stamina that conquers, and to-day they
own more real estate, and more wealth in Zion, than any other
man or firm in the Mormon Church, except Brigham himself!
Godbe, Lawrence, and Kelsey, turned their attention to the
mineral industry of the country, and, to all appearance, they
have before them a wealthy future.   Elders who had devoted
all their lives to Mormonism had necessarily to come to grief,
when they quarrelled with Brigham, for, like Othello, " their
" occupation was gone," and Satan could handle them roughly ;
but it is worthy of mention that, notwithstanding this superstitious threat, it is indisputable that there are more wealthy
" apostates " than there are wealthy apostles and bishops all
put together.   Reference could be made to elders, some of
whom had to steal away from Utah, for fear of violent hands
being laid upon them, had their intended departure been
made known, who are, to-day, wealthy and respected gentlemen in the highest walks of life, both in the United States and
in Europe.

* So unrelenting was the persecution of that firm, that very few good Mormons
would even dare to work for the Walker Brothers, though the quality of " their pay "
to workmen was proverbially superior to what could be obtained from members of
the Church.   Those who ventured to enter their service as clerks, book-keepers,
salesmen, or warehousemen, were always suspected of being weak in the faith.

† Everybody was at liberty to take " a fling " at the Walker Brothers, but as a
general thing it was only done as a passing duty.   Brother Musser, however, made it
a special mission, and, as he was the agent of the Church, and was constantly travelling through the Territory, he was a most vindictive " Buffeter."   His defence for
pursuing them so relentlessly was : " Because they are becoming wealthy, and with
" wealth they gain influence, and there should be no influence among the Saints but
" that of the priesthood."

CHAPTER LIV.

BRIGHAM YOUNG.—His Father's Family—His Early Life and Occupation—Brigham's Faith—The "Gift of Tongues"—"Brother Brigham" opposed to Manifestations of the "Gift"—His Ideas of Unreasoning Obedience—The Prophet at Home—The "Trustee in Trust"—The Prophet's Wives—His Favourites—Brigham's Domestic Life—His Habits and Traits of Character—His Hours of Business —The Prophet in his Office—Extraordinary Influence with the People—Unheard-of Claims to Dictation in Secular Affairs—Lovers to ask Brigham's Permission to love—Troublesome Elders sent on Mission—Ordered to go to "Dixie"—Mission to the Indians—How the "Lamanites" were to be made a "White and Delight-"some People"—Heber's *Hint* to the Missionaries, and how they took it—Brigham on his Travels—The "Royal Blood of Young"—Reception of the Prophet among the Saints—"The Lion of the Lord" in his Glory—The Saints listen to the Prophet—His Style of Preaching—The Prophet's Successor—Brigham the Second—Founding a Dynasty—Nepotism greater than Birthright and Priesthood—The Precedent given by Brigham--George A. Smith, Brigham's Rightful Successor—Apostle George Q. Cannon—A Mission to Jerusalem—Influence of the Railroad—Influx of Gentiles—Brigham's Lost Opportunities—Great Wealth of the Prophet—How Brigham balanced his Account with the Church—How the Prophet got rich—The Probable Future of Mormonism at his Death.

THE engraving at the beginning of this work is a perfect representation of Brigham Young, on the seventy-first anniversary of his birth—June 1, 1872. His most intimate friends, and members of his family, pronounce it a faultless likeness. In a personal sketch of the man, there need be but little said of his early life ; the story of his later years is of more interest. A brief paragraph relative to his family, and furnished by himself, contains, probably, all that the reader will care to know :

"I was born in Whittingham, Windham County, Vermont, June 1, 1801. My father and mother removed to Smyrna, Chenango County, N. Y., when I was about eighteen months old. We lived in that place until 1813. Shortly after the commencement of the late war with Great Britain, my father and his family removed to the town of Genoa, Cayuga County,

BRIGHAM YOUNG ON HIS TRAVELS.

N. Y., in which county I lived until 1829. I then moved to Mendon, Monroe County, and in 1830 removed from thence to No. 9 Canandaigua, into a small house owned by Jonathan Mack, situated on the west side of the road, opposite to where Mr. Mack then lived. I helped to finish his new house, so that he moved into it before I left the place. I left Canandaigua in the first part of 1832, and returned to Mendon. April 14th, same year, I was baptized into the Church of Jesus Christ of Latter-Day Saints. . . . . After my return to Mendon, I removed to Kirtland, Ohio; from thence to Far West, Mo.; from thence to Nauvoo, Ill.; and from thence to the mountains. There are five brothers of us, in the following order: John, Joseph, Phineas H., myself, and Lorenzo D. The two former never lived in No. 9. Phineas H. and Lorenzo D. did live there, but removed long before I came. The five of us, with my two living sisters (I have three dead), are here."

Brigham was reared in the humblest walks of life; he "came "of poor but honest parents." By force of circumstances, he grew up in the practice of the strictest economy, and became early inured to hard work. The social position of his father's family may be judged from the boast of Brigham, in the days when the meek and the poor were to inherit the kingdom, that he had "only been eleven and a half days at school." He learned the trade of a painter and glazier, but, as that sometimes was insufficient for him, he tells that he "did many a "hard day's work for *six bits* a day." His "straitened circum- "stances" were not improved for some time after his first acquaintance with Mormonism, as he relates that he had to borrow some articles of clothing as well as a pair of boots to enable him to attend a conference of the Saints. The acceptance of Mormonism was, therefore, no sacrifice to him, and preaching "with- "out purse or scrip" was no lowering of his dignity. He was eminently suited to join the standard of the Prophet Joseph, which he did two years after the organization of the Church, when Sidney Rigdon was in the blush of his greatness in Ohio, and Oliver Cowdery was away in Western Missouri locating the New Jerusalem, where the kingdom was to be established "in "power and glory." Upon such a man, it was a proper thing for the first manifestation of "the gift of tongues" to fall. Rigdon was "learned in the Scriptures;" Cowdery had "seen angels;" Parley P. Pratt was an eloquent preacher; Orson Pratt was a Bible-reader and thinker; and, as in all these Brigham was deficient, it was highly proper that "the Lord" should take care

of him, and endow him with qualifications that rose above all
argument, and spurned contemptuously the logic of facts. It
was enough for Brigham Young to know that he had received
" the gift of tongues;" * with that he started to " bear testi-
" mony " that " the Lord " had raised up a prophet " in these lat-
" ter days," and that the Book of Mormon was necessarily true.

What Brigham Young *felt* in Kirtland exceeded in importance any thing that any one else would ever have to say.
Compared with his experience, learning, eloquence, and reason,
were but the snares of the evil one. He *only once* " felt a want
" of confidence in Brother Joseph Smith," and " the feeling did
" not last sixty seconds, and perhaps not thirty;" it gave him
" sorrow of heart," and he " clearly saw and understood, by
" the spirit of revelation," that if he " was to harbour a thought
" in his heart that Joseph could be wrong in any thing," he
would go from doubt to doubt, till, from " lack of confidence
" in his being the mouth-piece of the Almighty," he would
continue in a course of unbelief till he said, " there is no God."
Brigham says he repented of his unbelief " very suddenly . . .
" about as quickly as I committed the error." From this onward, " I never," says he, " had the ,feeling, for one moment,
" to believe that any man, or set of men, or beings upon the
" face of the whole earth, had any thing to do with him [Joseph],
" for he was superior to them all, and held the keys of salvation
" over them.† . . . He was God's servant, and not mine. He
" did not belong to the people, but to the Lord, and was doing
" the work of the Lord; and if he should suffer him to lead the
" people astray, it would be because they ought to be led astray.
" If he should suffer them to be chastised, and some of them de-
" stroyed, it would be because *they deserved it,* or to accomplish
" some righteous purpose. That was my faith, and *it is my faith*
" *still.*" ‡

With such a blind, unreasoning faith in the mission of Jo-

---

* It is a curious fact that Brigham Young is to-day the least desirous of listening to the exercise of this " gift." A lady tells that, one day, she was in the Prophet's
house, when one of his wives laid hands upon her to bless her, and she "spoke in
tongues." Another of his wives was present, and she had the " gift of interpretation." Before the lady left, they both requested her not to mention the circumstance, as " Brother Young" was opposed to such manifestations.

† " Journal of Discourses," vol. iv., p. 297.			‡ Ibid., p. 298.

seph Smith, and the abject slavery of mind that it involves, the key to Brigham Young's whole life is clear. No one had a right to sit in judgment upon Joseph; no one should now question his successor, Brigham! With such teachings, the Prophet is never wrong. When failure would close the argument with other men, he is still right ! But of the faith, more need not be added ; of the Prophet personally, the reader may expect some information.

Up to within a few years, Brigham had little intercourse with the outside world ; he was seldom seen by others than his own people, except on Sundays. There was nothing of the hermit about his disposition, but he always had "something to " see to "—a house building, a mill repairing, something was going on about his farm or his garden, the Temple-building, or the Tabernacle; his numerous family had some share of his time, and the Church affairs every day were brought before him.

Brigham Young's Home.

In this group of buildings the Prophet is understood to have his home, or that portion of it which a man with numerous wives can ever imagine that he possesses. The left building is called the " Lion-House," from the figure of a crouching lion over the portico—the work of a clever sculptor, now an "apostate." The next low building is the " Tithing-Office," where the clerks of the Trustee in Trust and the clerks of Brigham Young do the clerical service of the Church and the Prophet ; the smaller building beside it is Brigham's "private " office," where he is visited on business, and where he receives

distinguished strangers who feel honoured in calling upon
"Mr. President Young." The large building on the right is
the Bee-Hive House, and was the official residence of Governor
Young.

With fairness it may be said that his home is in the Bee-
Hive House, as it is there that he has his *chambre à coucher*,
gets his buttons fixed, and his hose repaired ; but, as the Prophet
is "master of his own actions," his whereabouts after business-
hours is very difficult to determine. The Lion-House is a long
building, with twenty rooms on the "living-floor," sleeping-
apartments for the children on the upper floor, and dining-
room, weaving-rooms, laundry, and other divisions, on the lower
floor. It was in that house that one of his dozen wives, residing
together, is reported to have rubbed off the chalk-mark from
her neighbouring sister's door, placing it on her own, and
thereby enjoyed the extra teachings of the Prophet without
his discovering the mistake.

East of the Bee-Hive House, the distance of a few hundred
yards, and on the hill-side, is the White House, an unpretentious building, where the legal Mrs. Young resides. The house
of his present favourite, Amelia, is about half a block and the
width of a street from the Prophet's office ; it is pleasantly and
conveniently situated. On the opposite side of the street, the
Nauvoo favourite lives quietly and undisturbed. Directly west
of Amelia, on the same block, Emmeline, the longest favoured
one, resides. A block and a half from the Prophet's office is
the residence of his last loved one, a very handsome young
lady, a "grass widow," who is said to have gained immensely
upon the affections of the Prophet. This lady added a little
cherub to the Prophet's kingdom, in his seventieth year, a
circumstance very much to his gratification, but not to Amelia's, as she makes no secret that she questions the paternity
of the little stranger ; but it is proper to add that Mrs. Cobb
Young is a lady of blameless life.

Brigham Young gave the revelation of Polygamy to the
world, and his own illustration of the patriarchal institution
can therefore with propriety be here given to the world without any violation of the rights of domestic privacy.

Adjoining his private office he had for many years his dormitory, which he is said to have strictly preserved unto himself. To that room, however, there were two doors; one opening into the Bee-Hive House, and another to a passage-way that terminated at the Lion-House. While Emmeline was the favourite, or years after, when Amelia was the honoured one, some of the less favoured sisters tell that the Prophet made frequent and very prolonged visits to the Lion-House after the hour of evening prayer. Heber, in his humourous and coarse way, used to make a singular and exceedingly practical application to his own children of I. Thessalonians v. 5; and with Brigham's children it was much the same.

It has generally been supposed that Brigham had an immense number of wives, and that everything around him and them was in the gorgeous Oriental style; but this is purely imaginative. There are probably *only* nineteen "sisters" who call him "husband," and, with the exception of Amelia and Mary—the rival favourites—they are all working-women, without any pretensions to being mere "ornaments." Brigham is not capable of appreciating much of that kind of thing. His early poverty and hard-working experience, sustained by a natural acquisitive disposition, have enabled him to eschew all extravagance. Speaking of his wives, he said, " He would " provide them comfortable homes, clothe them properly, and " give them what they wanted to eat; but Brigham Young was " master of his own actions." His wives have no idea, from their own experience, of the marital relations of husband and wife in the Christian sense. He sees them in the Lion-House, at the general dining-table, or at evening prayer in the parlour, where they are all collected at the ringing of the bell; but many of them he seldom sees elsewhere. He calls periodically upon a few of them, and inquires after their welfare, but there are others whom he rarely ever sees within their own particular habitations, unless in case of sickness, or when sent for. There is no romance about the lives of his wives: they are quiet, unobtrusive women, who have been sacrificed to their faith. There has been but a single instance of scandal associated with the name of one wife, many years ago, and that was evidently without foundation. When the penalty of certain death stares the transgressor in the face, few have the hardihood to brave it.

His attentions to his wives before the public are methodical and calculated. His first wife and Amelia will usually sit beside him on the sofa in the ballroom, and the other wives may find places elsewhere. When he goes on to the floor for the first cotilion, it is generally with Amelia; and the half-dozen others, who may be present, have the honour of dancing with the Prophet during the course of the evening. He is a lively dancer for a man of his years, evidently takes great pleasure in always being correct, and enjoys at times a thorough "brake-down" step at the close.

He is very regular in his habits. He generally rises between seven and eight in the morning, and dresses at once for all day. He steps into his office, at times, before breakfast, and takes a general survey of those who are there, and then he may, perhaps, saunter out and look at his premises; but, usually, he comes to the office about nine o'clock. The private secretary has his letters ready for his personal perusal, and also such items of business as may specially require his attention. He has, he says, schooled himself into the habit of never thinking twice upon any subject; and, when once it has received his attention, and he has pronounced his decision, he never wants to hear of it again. He is no scholar, and therefore never answers correspondence. As the autograph of all "great men" is sought after, the reader will probably peruse with interest the *fac simile*, on the opposite page, of a genuine letter, which the Prophet wrote over fifteen years ago. He has placed his name to so many letters and documents since that time, that his autograph on the steel engraving, at the beginning of this work, shows considerable improvement.

The barber is there about a quarter to ten, and shaves the Prophet in his office, no matter who may be present.

From ten to eleven he is to be seen on business.

The apostles, bishops, and leading citizens, have the *entrée* to his private office at any time, and enter without announcement, or even knocking at the door; but others have to pass through the Tithing-Office, and it is the duty of one of the clerks there to learn the visitor's business. Formerly the

to the Saints &c and a word from you city

Brethren, we would like to hand Bro.
Elias Smith to take charge of the Church
affairs in that place for the President and
for Geo. Bullock to assist him, till you
here from us

Gain had better keep your cattle
in proper halle that are there and get the
rest of your spare cattle there as soon
as you can.

Try to due right and never
faint in well doing, keep the faith of
the gospel, I pray the Lord to bless you

Brigham Young

chief clerk of the Trustee in Trust had that duty to perform, and if the business could be disposed of without carrying it to the Prophet, the visitor was so instructed. When the "sisters" have any complaints to make of their husbands, they run to the Prophet; but if the clerk can turn the visitor to "the "teachers," or to the bishop of her ward, it is done. When the aggrieved one is persistent, the clerk informs the Prophet, and he either sends an answer or grants an interview. To the humble, believing Saint, the answer or counsel has all the force of a revelation from heaven.

No one to-day, even in Utah, can form any idea of the thorough control that Brigham once had over the people. Nothing was ever undertaken without his permission—he knew of everything. No person could enter into business without consulting him, nor would any one ever think of leaving the city to reside in any other part of the country without first having his approval. Merchants who went East or West to purchase goods, had to present themselves at his office, and report their intention of going to the States at such a time—if he had no contrary orders to give them. Some, no doubt, may have sought his counsel on their proposed undertakings and journeys, believing that his superior wisdom could aid them, but in his own mind he claimed that the Saints should do nothing without his knowledge and approval. That oft-reiterated expression, that it was his right to dictate and control everything, "even to the ribbons that a woman should wear, or "to the setting-up of a stocking," was the truthful illustration of his feelings.

A ball even could not take place until he was consulted upon the propriety of dancing, then, and before the invitations were issued, the list of the invited was read to him, and he erased or added names at his pleasure. Before any of the married brethren could make love to a maiden with the view of making her a second, third, or tenth wife, he was expected to go and obtain Brigham's permission, and even the young men were instructed that properly they should do likewise. But the worst form of this surveillance, control, and dependance upon his will was the power which Brigham assumed in the most vital interests of every man's affairs. He not only sent

the missionaries abroad, when and whither he pleased, but
when he desired it, he sent the elders away for some cause of
offence, real or imaginary. He once told the best Mormon
lawyer in Zion, who had been a Federal judge, that if he came
again on to the platform where he stood, he would kick him
off it, and he appointed him to a mission in Van Diemen's
Land, and told him never to return—he never wanted to see
him there again. The lawyer went, performed his mission,
and returned to his family, and has since been of great service
to Brigham. Time after time he has called men living in Salt
Lake City to close their business, and go down to " Dixie "—
the southern part of the Territory, which has been regarded by
most people as a penal settlement, or place of banishment. Repugnance to such a country, or the inadaptability of the person
to any pursuits there, was nothing to him. Quite a number of
persons had to sacrifice property in the city in order to go to
" Dixie," and free tongues have not been slow to insinuate that,
in some instances, those persons were sent away for the very
purpose that the Prophet might the more easily purchase their
property. He sent at one time a mission to Fort Limhi, Sal-
mon River, to civilize the Indians. The brethren were counselled not to take their families with them, but they were to
live with the Indians, to educate and civilize them, and to
teach them various trades and farming. When Brigham and
Heber afterwards visited the missionaries to see how they were
succeeding, Heber, in his quaint way, told them that he did not
see how the modern predictions could well be fulfilled about
the Indians becoming " a white and delightsome people " without extending polygamy to the natives. The approach of the
United States army, in 1857, contributed to break up that mission, but not before Heber's hint had been clearly understood,
and the prophecy half fulfilled ! Heber was very practical, and
believed that the people should never ask " the Lord " to do for
them what they could do themselves, and, as all " Israel " had
long prayed that the Indians might speedily become a " white
" and delightsome people," he thought it was the duty of the
missionaries to assist " the Lord " in fulfilling his promises.
This was not the first time that a Mormon prophet attempted
to aid in bringing to pass the prophecies of " the Lord."   More

than one missionary appears to have thoroughly understood him ! *

The illustration at the beginning of this chapter is a perfect representation of the Prophet's style of travelling through the settlements. He tries to visit all the Saints once a year. His visit north occupies between three and four weeks, and his southern trip takes between five and six weeks.

The order of travel after leaving Salt Lake City is: first, the Prophet's carriage; next, the members of his family; then his counsellors, the apostles, chief-bishop, bishops generally ; then distinguished visitors. The latter take the first vacant place in the long suite, and remain there all through the journey. The only rank and aristocracy in Zion is priesthood, and precedence in every quorum is seniority of ordination. In these journeys, the last-ordained apostle is the last in the order of travel among the apostles; but if the youngest apostle should be a son of the Prophet he overtops them all—the " royal blood " of Young " is more honoured than the royal priesthood of Melchisedec !

Some miles before " the President's company " arrives at the first settlement to be visited, he is met by a company of mounted cavalry, bearing aloft the stars and stripes, and, as they near the settlement, the citizens turn out to greet the Prophet, and there is usually a procession of the school-children. If it is a very large settlement, and the bishop is a very " live man," the procession often embraces all the people. On such occasions there is a brass-band heading the citizens, the elderly brethren are arranged together, bearing in front of them a banner with the inscription, " Fathers in Israel ; " the elderly sisters have their banner, " Mothers in Israel ; " the young men carry their banner, " Defenders of Zion ; " the maidens their banner, " Daughters of Zion, Virtue ; " and the little, toddling school-children are, " The Hope of Israel." Those too young to walk are, as usual, in the arms of indulgent mothers, standing by the doors to make up the other part of the picture.

---

* One young man replied to Brother Heber that it was the teaching of the Church that the elders should always follow their " file-leaders," and that " if President Young and he should each take a squaw to wife and thus set the example, they would certainly follow suit." That ended the " bleaching " of the " Lamanites." There was no further instruction upon the fulfilment of the modern prophecies.

All along the procession may be seen banners bearing the devices, "Hail to Zion's Chief," "God Bless Brigham Young," and kindred sentiments of "Welcome." No doubt these honest, simple people truly and thankfully express on such occasions their kindly feeling for "Brother Brigham"—they see him but seldom!

On arrival, the Prophet is taken to the best accommodation in the settlement, his suite are distributed among the people, and every kind attention is extended to them all, and their horses and carriages no further require their care. The people are happy to see their "big brethren," and many of them strain their pockets to entertain their guests.

There is usually one or more "meetings" for preaching, and, as these visits occur in summer, "boweries" are improvised, and decorated with evergreens, flowers, and fruits, and oftentimes the homespun cloth and home-made coverlets are suspended through the Bowery to exhibit the manufactures of Zion.

The preaching is directed by the Prophet.* The people all

* As a preacher, Brigham is always listened to attentively—not so much either for style or the matter of his discourse, as from the expectation that he may "say something" that the auditor is anxious to learn. When he has moments of "great freedom" he can make himself interesting; but his utterance is the declamation of the unmethodical itinerant, and not the logical oratory of the thinker or reader. When he tries to make a set speech, he is a fearful failure. At the request of Vice-President Colfax and his friends, he spoke in the Bowery, and made astonishing havoc with history and Lindley Murray. On that occasion in support of Polygamy he brought up the very questionable charge against Martin Luther, that he countenanced Polygamy in acquiescing in the marriage of Philip, Landgrave of Hesse-Darmstadt, to a second wife while his first was still alive. Brigham was utterly ignorant of history, and the brethren in his office prepared him notes for this special occasion—the first he had ever tried to use—and he was perfectly confounded. On the paper before him were a few hard words about Philip, Landgrave of Hesse, and poor Brigham, innocent that the word "Landgrave" was a title of nobility, spoke of the supposed poylgamist as "*Mr. Philip Landgrave*"—a worthy example for the world to follow. The visitors could hardly contain their mirth, while the intelligent Mormons almost expired with mortification.

Of that occasion, Mr. Bowles wrote :

"There was every incentive for him to do his best ; he had an immense audience spread out under the 'Bowery' to the number of five or six thousand ; before him was Mr. Colfax, who had asked him to preach upon the distinctive Mormon doctrines ; around him were all his elders and bishops, in unusual numbers ; and he was fresh from the exciting discussion of yesterday on the subject of Polygamy. But his address lacked logic, lacked effect, lacked wholly magnetism or impressiveness. It was a curious medley of Scriptural exposition and exhortation, bold and bare statement, coarse denunciation, and vulgar allusion, cheap rant, and poor cant."—"Across the Continent," page 118.

want to hear him; but in such long journeys he calls upon every one of the visitors to speak to the Saints. The addresses are usually upon some general policy of the time, and exhorting the Saints to faithfulness. Frequently there is a dance in the evening, or a serenade-party of singers at the Prophet's headquarters, and before his door and around the house where he sleeps there is a vigilant armed guard walking all the night. Next morning he is escorted by the cavalry till another body of cavalry meets him, and thus he travels from settlement to settlement until his return to Salt Lake City. These visits are exceedingly pleasant to those who accompany the Prophet, and exhibit clearly his influence over the people for weal or woe.

The Prophet usually takes his favourite wife with him on such occasions, and of late years his second son, Brigham, Junior, has always accompanied him, and here occurs the thought: Who shall succeed him in all this?

The Apostle George A. Smith.

By right of rank it should be his first counsellor, George A. Smith, a nephew of the Prophet Joseph Smith, and an apostle.

At the death of Joseph, Brigham claimed that the Quorum of the First Presidency—composed of Joseph and Hyrum Smith and Sidney Rigdon—was dissolved by the assassination of the

first two named, and that the ruling authority then devolved
upon the Quorum of the Twelve Apostles, of which he was
the President. Had Hyrum Smith lived, he would have been
the President at the death of Joseph, and by that same order
George A. Smith should now succeed Brigham Young as President of the Mormon Church ; but few, if any, believe that, if
he outlives Brigham, such will be the case.

The Apostle Brigham Young, Junior.

An apostle once asked Brigham, in a disinterested way [for,
at that time, that apostle was certainly free from guile], who
would be his successor. It was an ill-timed question, for Brigham had only just then taken a young wife, and was looking
after others ; besides, it was exceedingly unpleasant to suggest
to a newly-married man, that there would be a pair of empty
slippers in his house some day. The Prophet answered, very
curtly, that "the Lord" would manifest that in due time.
"The Lord's" due time has evidently come, and "Young
"Brig," as he is called, is the manifestation.

Wherever the Prophet goes, the junior accompanies him,
and the people are getting used to his presence. The junior is
learning how the senior manages the bishops, and is garnishing
his mind with useful information ; and there is no doubt that,

by this training and constant association of the son with the father before the people, the latter will clearly get into their minds what " the Lord " has set his hand to do.*

Personally, Brigham Young, Junior, is not a popular man with the Saints ; he is not their choice for president ; but the Prophet his father has determined to build up a dynasty, and preserve his name to the world, and Brigham, Junior, is a fortunate accident. *Brigham the Second* will always suggest to the memory Brigham the First. Further, no one could imagine Brigham Young, Senior, so excessively foolish as ever to leave such an inheritance to the Smith family ! George A. Smith, by favour with the people, as well as by rank, is the legitimate successor of Brigham Young, according to Brigham's own precedent, but he will never attain to that position, except by revolution, and there is nothing of that character in him. Brigham, in this, however, shows to the Saints that he will permit nothing to stand in the way of his own ambition ; that rank in George A. Smith, and birthright in his own son, Joseph A., are nothing when his purposes are considered. All the past preaching of the rank and birthright of the priesthood is negatived in the successorship of Brigham Young, Senior, by Brigham Young, Junior.†

* Several years ago, Brigham secretly ordained his three sons apostles—Joseph A., Brigham, and John W.—with the intention that Brigham, Junior, should subsequently be the President of the Church, and his two brothers be his counsellors. This gave terrible offence to Brother Heber, who was the first in the line of succession ; but Brigham shrewdly asked Heber to join him in the ordination of the three sons. To have refused would have caused an open rupture, and for Heber to comply, and take part in the ordination, for ever closed Heber's lips—almost.

Joseph A., the eldest son, is the most popular of the Young family, but he has far too much sense to desire to be a prophet. John W. has, of late years, become engrossed in secular affairs, and has quite a clinging respect for the world that now is. " Briggy " is by no means a dunce, but he is, under the circumstances, the most capable of the three of filling his father's shoes. Joseph A. and John W. are both smart young men, and can get well enough through the world ; but Brigham, Junior, will find the Tithing-Office a great convenience.

† The doctrine of inheriting priesthood has ever been held sacred in the Mormon Church ; hence John Smith, the eldest son of Hyrum Smith, was ordained Patriarch over the whole Church, *solely* because he was the eldest son. Brigham looked upon him as a very unfit person for the office, but the right of succession was inherent in him, and he could not be set aside without offending the Smith family, and it has been Brigham's policy to show respect to those members of the " royal family of Smith " whom he can control.

The most promising man among the Mormons for the successor of Brigham, at one time, was the young apostle George Q. Cannon.

The Apostle George Q. Cannon.

He is by far the ablest young man among the apostles. He has the education of travel, is a reader, a writer, and a man of pleasant manners. When he returned from his mission in Europe, several years ago, he spoke like a thinker, and showed, for a time, a capacity that commanded respect; but he soon learned that there was but one leader in " Israel," and he gradually settled down to the level of the other apostles, and, while Brigham sends George A. Smith on a mission to Jerusalem, he sends George Q. Cannon delegate to Congress, to let the Saints feel and realize that the Church affairs can do without them both : and meantime " Briggy " is being initiated into the mysteries.

The public generally are looking forward to the death of Brigham Young for the utter disintegration of Mormonism, but in this there will be disappointment. There will, doubtless, be many changes and some opposition,* and, with the removal

* There has been some expectation that neither Orson Pratt nor John Taylor will submit to the presidency of Brigham Young, Junior. Of late years Orson has so sunk his individuality of character, that little confidence can now be placed in his doing anything, but Brother John has within him a manacled giant that may then,

of Brigham's iron hand, there will be an independence never before realized since he ruled the Church; but it will take a long time to educate the people out of the system. As railroads are built, mines developed, and enterprise grows up in the Territory, the influx of Gentiles, and the establishment of Christian schools and institutions, will soon break in upon the doctrine of exclusive salvation.

Had Brigham Young been a great man, he had the best opportunity that mortal ever possessed of showing it. There never was a people more willing to do what they were told than the Mormons, and he could have swayed them whither he pleased. He could have left behind him imperishable records of his care for the poor, the aged, and the infirm ; but, while there is not a single hospital or institution, worthy the name, founded in Zion, he has himself become immensely rich. Having control of the tithing, and possessing unlimited credit, he has added "house to house and field to field," while every one knew that he had no personal enterprises sufficient to enable him to meet anything like the current expenses of his numerous wives and children. As Trustee in Trust he renders no account of the funds that come into his hands, but tells the faithful that they are at perfect liberty to examine the books at any moment. He is charged with having, in 1852, balanced his account with the Church to the modest sum of $200,000, by directing the clerk to place to his credit the same amount "*for* "*services rendered;* " and, in 1867, he further discharged his obligations, amounting to the small sum of $967,000, in a similar manner.*

perhaps, burst forth into freedom. There are few more powerful men than this apostle, and, had not Brigham made it a point to hedge him round, and arrest his development, he would have been a great man in Zion. That he should ever submit to the dictation of young Brigham does not seem possible.

* It is due to a gentleman who was once the chief clerk of the Church, and with whom the Author was on very intimate terms, to state here that it was not from him that this information was obtained. Throughout this work, the Author has observed a strict reticence upon everything that was at any time communicated to him in confidence. Furthermore, though he had daily intercourse with Brigham Young, his family, and his immediate friends, not a single thing that ever transpired in Brigham's office or house, in his presence, has been alluded to. On all that he saw or heard while Brigham's guest, or when with him in the capacity of friend, a studied silence has been maintained.

For several years past, the agent of the Church, A. M. Musser, has been engaged in securing legal deeds for all the property
the Prophet claims, and by this he will be able to secure in his
lifetime to his different families such property as will render
them independent at his death. The building of the Pacific
Railroad was said to have yielded him about a quarter of a
million; the Utah Central Railroad brought him also a very
large sum of money, and, altogether, "the Lord" has dealt
liberally with his servant Brigham.

The actual wealth of the Prophet will never be known.
There is probably not a county in Utah where he has not some
valuable property. Whenever new settlements have been laid
out, he has not been the last to "place" his name upon the
records. With his "opportunities," a man of his characteristics could not fail to become a great landed proprietor. Heber
used to preach that Brigham and he would one day "own the
"people," and had the Tabernacle predictions about "famines,
"and wars, and rumours of wars," received the terrible fulfilment that they expected, there was quite a possibility of Heber's words coming true. Brigham took up great tracts of
land, and the Legislature gave him grants of all he coveted.*
With these constantly accumulating in value, and a tithing-
office at the Prophet's command, in a time of great scarcity,
when the Gentiles were to come to Zion begging for bread, it
is not difficult to imagine the facilities which Brigham would
have had for realizing Heber's boast.

* It is not strange that a man of his prominence should have had many favours
shown to him; in any new community in the West any man with a hundredth part
his influence could not fail to receive many advantages; but the complaint is, that
Brigham was never satisfied with the lion's share of anything, but was for ever wanting to "gobble up" *everything* that promised immediate value. The Legislative records of Utah are the proofs of the immensity of his organ of acquisitiveness. All the
Twentieth Ward "Bench" to the north of the city, and lying east of his premises,
was given to him. He had it surveyed into lots half the ordinary size, and from that
alone he has derived an excellent revenue. A few years ago, Mayor Wells tried to
get the City Council to give Brigham a large tract of land on the west of the city,
and he wanted the Council also to improve it for the Prophet; but some members
protested, on the ground that the city was unable to do so. "Squire" Wells was
very indignant, and tried to encourage the brethren to "have faith in the Lord,"
and illustrated the advantages of "trusting in the Lord," by stating that when he
went on a mission to England he had to sell some land to pay his expenses, but
that, on his return, Brigham had handed him the deeds of his city property! To
the credit of the City Council, they still remained weak in the faith

The report has been circulated that Brigham was the third largest depositor in the Bank of England; but, though George Peabody has been mentioned as confirming this story, it does not seem possible. A wealthy Gentile, who called upon the Prophet some years ago, assured the Author that Brigham voluntarily stated to him that he really had several millions deposited there. In seeking to fathom Brigham's reasons for such a communication, the gentleman could only account for it by the Prophet's own statement that "he had not "asked him concerning the number of his family, or tried to "pry into anything." Brigham was rather charmed with his visitor on this account, and was very frank and communicative. The Prophet's sermons have long established for him the reputation of a boaster; and, as he will be second to no man, it is quite likely that he took some pleasure in informing this gentleman that he had a bank-account which could not be despised. Some years later—in 1871—a New York journalist visiting the Prophet, referred to the rumour about his having a deposit of $17,000,000 in the Bank of England ; and Brigham is said to have regretted that it was untrue, and that he had not a dollar outside of Utah, but that the Church * had some small amount abroad for its use. That Brigham Young has money "salted "away," that he will not touch under the pressure of any necessity but that for which it was "salted," is most assuredly believed by some who have had excellent opportunities of knowing his business. A man of his shrewdness, with so many threatenings of forced removal from Utah, and the possible contingencies of the application of law, never would permit himself to be caught penniless. Brigham has money—plenty of it.

Of his income from his numerous and vast estates, his theatre, the Coöperative business, his railroad-bonds,† mills, farms, rents in the city, and from all sources, the Internal Revenue Office at Washington has on record the following statement : For 1867, $18,400 ; for 1868, $20,005 ; 1869, $28,584 ; 1870, $25,500 ; 1871, $111,680 ; 1872, $39,592. Of

---

* Louis XIV. said, "*L'État, c'est moi.*" Brigham could as truthfully say, "*L'Église, c'est moi.*"

† Brigham is the President of the Utah Central Railroad, but has *only six shares* in that property; he has, however, managed to possess $600,000 of its bonds!

course, no one believes that these are anything like the correct figures. *

Brigham, though of a "long-lived family," is not a strong man physically. He has flattered himself with the hope that he would live to the age of Moses, but he is not likely to "drag out" to a hundred and twenty years. It is to be hoped, however, that the limit of his days may not yet arrive. Enlightening agencies now at work in Utah are quietly telling upon the first faith of the people, and the formerly unchallenged authority of Brigham to dictate in all things is being set aside. He should live on till the issue of Mormonism with Christianity has been fairly reached ; and when the barbarism of the worst phases of the Jewish polity revived has given place to civilization and development, Mormonism, having abandoned its Theocracy, will take its place among the innumerable sects of the day. This can be better achieved in his lifetime.

The early death of Brigham Young would make the fight with his successor the more difficult, as the latter would then feel it incumbent upon him to contend for the idiosyncrasies of his predecessor. If Brigham lives but a few years longer, much that is now tottering will be cast down and disappear for ever. But die when he will, and succeed him who may, the "one-man power" can never be inherited. Brigham succeeded Joseph when the people were in trouble and consternation, and they threw their individuality at his feet, and gave him absolute dictatorship—they needed a deliverer. Now, all this is changed, and hundreds who hailed with acclamation the sceptre in the hands of Brigham in Nauvoo, are fatigued, tired, and weary of it in Salt Lake City, and never would endure it in the hands of Brigham Young, Junior. The experiment of Theocracy will die out with Brigham's flickering flame of life ; and, when he is laid in the tomb, many who are silent now will curse his memory for the cruel suffering that his ambition caused them to endure.

* It is a curious fact that one Gentile—Mr. Warren Hussey, the banker—paid last year to the Government, within a few hundred dollars, twice as much as the whole amount of revenue-tax paid by the entire Mormon people, including Brigham Young and all the Mormon merchants !

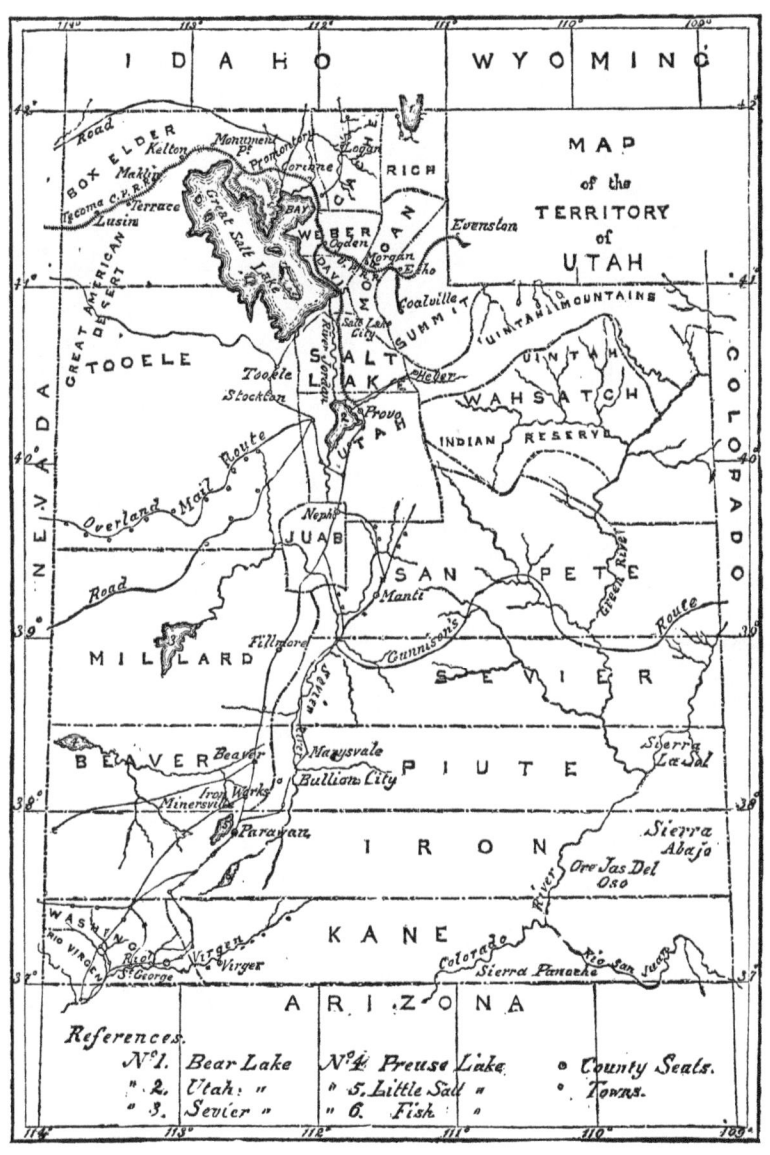

MAP OF UTAH TERRITORY.

CHAPTER LV.

THE TERRITORY OF UTAH.—Its Boundaries and Character—The Lakes—Superficial Area—The Settlements—Population—Excess of Male Inhabitants—Mules voting for Delegates to Congress !—"Getting up" Petitions—The Militia—The Nauvoo Legion—The Federal Governors—A Stormy Political Meeting—Governor Shaffer's Difficulties—Change of Officers—A Proclamation—Resolute Conduct of the Governor—His Last Official Act—Conflict between Mormon Officials and Federal Officers—Delegate Hooper justifies Polygamy in Congress—Dr. Newman discusses Polygamy with Orson Pratt—Appointment of Chief-Justice McKean—His Legal Decisions—The Hawkins Case—Decisions reserved by the Supreme Court—Brigham's Anxiety for a State Government.

GEOGRAPHICALLY, Utah lies between 109° and 114° west longitude and 37° and 42° north latitude, less a tract equal to 1° of latitude and 2° of longitude taken from the northeast corner by act of Congress, July, 1868, and attached to Wyoming Territory.

When the Territory of Utah was created, in 1850, its western boundary extended to the eastern limits of California, and embraced politically the country now known as the State of Nevada. The Territories of Idaho and Montana to the north, Colorado and Wyoming to the east, and Arizona to the south, were then uncreated. The organization of these Territorial governments changed the boundaries of Utah, but left ample space for the growth and development of a large population. The area of the Territory at the present time is 84,476 square miles, or 54,065,075 acres.

The Territory is almost divided into two parts by a magnificent range of mountains—the Wahsatch—that enters its eastern limits, traverses the country in a southwesterly direction a distance of four hundred miles, and extends beyond its borders into the adjoining Territory of Arizona.

That section of Utah lying east of the Wahsatch range consists of an elevated plain five thousand feet above the level of the sea, with here and there separate and distinct ranges of mountains. Although comparatively unexplored, it is ascertained that deposits of a superior quality of bituminous coal exist there in several localities, while reports have been occasionally circulated of placer gold mines of great richness and extent being found in those mountain ranges.

Aside from its future importance as a mineral region, and as affording a range for stock, it is probable that but little of that section, beyond the Uintah Indian reservation, will prove of much value to the farmer, in consequence of its sterility.

In the western and lesser division of Utah, a series of beautiful valleys is found, extending throughout the entire length of the Territory.

Saline and fresh water lakes are numerous. The most extensive are Great Salt Lake and Lake Utah.* The former is one hundred miles in length in a southeasterly and northwesterly direction, by fifty miles in width, showing sixty feet of water at its deepest soundings, and holding in solution twenty per cent. of salt. Lake Utah is situated forty miles south, and is connected with Great Salt Lake by the river Jordan. It contains fresh water, and is twenty-four miles long by twelve miles wide. These lakes will be most useful in the future as sources of internal communication; but, aside from this, Lake Utah is now invaluable for purposes of irrigation.

The rivers formed in the mountains from the melting of the snow are numerous, but of no great length—Bear River in the north, and the Colorado and its tributaries, the Green and Grand, which drain the eastern division, excepted.

The Government surveys commenced in the year 1855, by the establishment of an independent base and meridian at the southeast corner of Temple Block, in Salt Lake City, latitude 40° 46′ 2″ north, longitude 111° 53′ 30″ west, and continued

---

* Bear Lake, or the northern boundary line, is a beautiful azure sheet of water, twenty-five miles long and six wide. The rugged mountains on the eastern side of the lake are magnificent, and look the very counterpart of the towering peaks of Savoy that environ the blue waters of the Lake of Geneva. No tourist in Europe ever gazed upon a prettier mountain country than that of northern Utah, between Bear Lake and the Pacific Railroad.

until 1857. Utah was subsequently attached to Colorado for surveying purposes, and, by act of Congress, approved July 16, 1868, it was again constituted a separate surveying district, and a land office was established in Salt Lake City.

The surveys extended, in the beginning of 1872, over 4,016,825 acres, of which 92,637 acres were embraced in vacated Indian reservations, and at that date no lines had been carried eastward beyond the base of the Wahsatch Mountains.

The land office was opened March 15, 1869, and from that date declaratory statements under the Preëmption Act of September 4, 1841, had been filed for 400,000 acres. Of that extent of land, 68,315 acres had been paid for with cash, mainly at the minimum price of $1.25 per acre. In addition, 20,480 acres had been located with military bounty land-warrants, and 23,200 acres with Agricultural College scrip.

Homestead entries, covering 167,250 acres, have been made under the act of May 29, 1862.

Estimating that there are 2,000,000 acres, or the one twenty-seventh part of the Territory, susceptible of cultivation, there yet remain 1,500,000 acres unappropriated for future settlement.

The Mormon settlements extend to the full limits of the Territory in every direction, but the necessity in the beginning of guarding against the incursions of the Indians induced the founders of new homes to keep within supporting distance; and following the natural sweep of the valleys at the base of the mountains, the principal settlements are found near to each other, almost in a direct line from north to south. Brigham's policy was, to occupy as fast as possible the best lands, and, though there is doubtless good land still unclaimed, the Prophet may be said to have made his point, and Utah Territory may truthfully be regarded as " the inheritance of the Saints," and no justly thinking person can grudge them possessions for which they have fought so bravely and so long through many years of discouragement and privation.

The first settlement founded was Salt Lake City; and, just as soon as the pioneers could save seed from their first harvests, they were urged to go out and settle in every direction.

The Prophet, of course, had the control of everybody, and the men whom he deemed the best suited to intrust with the task of founding cities were appointed to that mission. Scores of others were called to accompany them, and volunteers were permitted to join their ranks. The settlements have thus grown in number, till there are now thirty incorporated cities and about fourscore towns and villages regularly organized, with a bishop or acting-bishop over each.

There are numerous mining cities springing into existence in the cañons, but, properly speaking, there is but one Gentile commercial city in the Territory—Corinne, a very enterprising town, situated on the Central Pacific Railroad, about sixty-five miles north of Salt Lake City.

The population of Utah for several years was reported to be about 125,000 souls, but with the recent large influx of Gentiles added, there are probably not more than that number of inhabitants at the present time. The last census reports (1870) fix the population at 88,374, but there were probably then about 100,000.*

From the first effort to obtain admission for Utah into the Union, the population of the Territory has always been greatly overstated. One of the persons last engaged in taking the census related to the Author that one of the Mormon sisters, in the southern part of the Territory, in reporting to him the

---

* The following is a table of the counties in Utah, and their population (Census Report, 1870):

Box Elder	4,754	Millard	2,754	Tooele	2,177
Beaver	2,008	Piute	257	Utah	13,385
Cache	8,229	Rich	2,087	Weber	7,880
Davis	4,460	Salt Lake	18,406	Wahsatch	1,252
Iron	2,141	Sevier	365	Washington	3,063
Juab	2,251	San Pete	6,884		
Kane	1,513	Summit	2,536	Total	88,374
Morgan	1,972				

The principal cities and towns, with a population of over 500, may be of interest by way of reference:

Brigham City	1,075	Grantsville	755	North Ogden	684
Bountiful	1,517	Gunnison	520	Ogden City	3,127
Beaver City	1,209	Heber City	663	Provo City	2,720
Corinne	873	Kaysville	1,423	Payson	1,571
Cedar City	522	Kanosh	521	Parowan	862
Centreville	544	Logan	1,800	Salt Lake City	12,846
Coalville	642	Moroni	646	Slaterville	508
Ephraim City	1,216	Mount Pleasant	1,360	St. George City	1,442
Fillmore City	905	Manti	1,154	Sugar House Ward	651
Farmington	976	Minersville	510	Tooele City	953
Fairview	540	Mill Creek	920	Washington	515
Fountain Green	590	Nephi City	1,358		

number of the family in her domicile, was somewhat surprised
that he did not take the names of the deceased members who
had once lived there, and innocently added : " That is the
" way we used to do it ! " A good story is also told of a limb
of the law who named his pair of mules, and then cast their
votes for the delegate to Congress. The Apostle Benson used
to say on the Sunday evening preceding the election : " Now,
"brethren, let us have a good vote ; the President wants a rous-
" ing vote ; we must have so many ! " Not long ago, some of
the teachers engaged in obtaining signatures to a sisters' petition to Mrs. Grant, asking her influence with the President to
favour the non-interference of Congress with Polygamy, took
down the name of one lady, who reports the circumstance, and
the names of all her daughters, including a little girl of a dozen
summers, and then asked her whether she had not some children who were now no longer living. She replied in the
affirmative, and was then told that her *dead* daughters' names
ought to be added, as petitioners, to the list, as " they were
" certain to be polygamists in heaven ! "

However much such proceedings might be deprecated from
a moral stand-point, the priesthood who favour such questionable doings have no idea of responsibility save to " the Lord,"
and all is fair that is done for his service and for " the king-
" dom's sake ; " " any thing to beat "—the Gentiles !

One-fifth of the entire population of the Territory is in
Salt Lake City, and singularly enough for a polygamic Territory, in all the counties save three—Cache, Iron, and Salt
Lake—there is a preponderance of male inhabitants ; in one
county—Washington—the sexes are equal in number. According to the census, there are two thousand and fifty-six more
males than females in Utah !

All able-bodied citizens between the ages of eighteen and
forty-five are enrolled in the militia of the Territory, and form
part of the organization called the "Nauvoo Legion." The
Governor of the Territory is commander-in-chief of the militia,
and such was Brigham Young, in the fullest meaning of that
term, while he was the chief Executive ; but since his deposi-
tion, no Governor has felt that he was more than a "figure-

"head," and that virtually the militia was still in the hands of the Prophet.

The "Legion" has a thorough organization, and numbers about thirteen thousand men, who are well armed and equipped, and well drilled. The chief of the Legion is Daniel H. Wells, the second counsellor of Brigham Young, who bears the title of lieutenant-general. There are two major-generals, nine brigadier-generals, twenty-five colonels, and one hundred and twelve majors, with their respective staff-officers.

The Mormons have a great deal of pride in being soldiers, and on muster parade they make a good show. During the early occupation of the Territory, Brigham tried to obtain arms for the militia from the Government, but "fortunately he was "unsuccessful," and now the arms with which the Saints are equipped are their own property. The reader may remember that, after Governor Ford made a demand for the State arms in Nauvoo, the Mormons, when shortly afterwards hastily summoned to protect the city, were found to be as well armed as before. For many years it has been rare for a Utah missionary in England to return to Zion without taking back to the mountains a sword, the best rifle he could obtain, and the latest improved revolvers.

One-fifth of the "Nauvoo Legion" is enrolled in the cavalry, and better and more daring riders than the Utah boys would be difficult to find anywhere. The "Legion" has only a few pieces of artillery, and those of very ancient manufacture. In former years, the Church was little able to buy ordnance; it was difficult to transport heavy guns secretly, and, as there was no commercial avarice to be gratified by the possession of a few pieces, Zion is to-day very badly supplied with this important arm of the service. With all the bombast of prediction to sustain it, there is not in "the kingdom of "God upon earth" twenty-four hours' defence against Grant, Sherman, or Sheridan.

With these distinguished generals of the Republic the Author has had the honour of speaking upon Utah affairs, and he is much gratified at being able to state that, while the priesthood have, in their folly, laboured to array the Church against the Government, these soldiers of the nation have breathed only forbearance and kindly consideration for the men and women who have braved the labours of the desert and the howling wilderness, and they have expressed the wish that the Mormons could learn without bitter and sad experience that they were a part of the Republic, and a valuable connecting link between the decaying past and the budding future of the world's history. But, between the military glory that the most devoted Saint might legitimately crave, and that obedience to the "powers that be," which a faithful representative of the nation should demand, there has been a continual strife. It is natural for Brigham Young, with his religious faith, to desire the conservation of all civil, judicial, and military authority among the Saints, but it is as natural for the representatives of the Government to insist that the Federal authorities be acknowledged in any legitimate sphere of action to which they may have been appointed. The Governors who succeeded Alfred Cumming have, each and all, in their annual message to the Legislature, asked to be properly acknowledged commander-in-chief of the militia, but the legislators, by purposed delay and circumlocution, manage to pass over, session after session, any action that would disturb the organization of the Nauvoo Legion. To the annual drills the Governor would be invited, and before him, if he attended, the militia would parade, and some of the brethren would make speeches and compliment the chief Executive, but the latter would quietly smile to his friends, and make some remark that might be interpreted: "Well, we can't help it, and there's no use in "making trouble."

It has been generally understood that the Secretary of War, General Rawlins, had, during his visit to Utah, in 1868, been much dissatisfied with what he saw of Mormon Theocracy, and, on his return to Washington, had asked the appointment of " Wills " Shaffer, of Illinois, for Governor. "The reconstruction of the South " was then thought to be enough for the Government to deal with, but, on the retirement of Governor Durkee, General J. Wilson Shaffer was appointed to Utah. His appointment was regarded as the precursor of a different line of policy from that which had previously prevailed.

Between the time of Governor Durkee's resignation and

the arrival of Governor Shaffer, at the end of March, 1870,
Secretary S. A. Mann had been acting-Governor. Mr. Mann
had outdistanced even Secretary and Acting-Governor Fuller
in his pliant services to the Prophet and the Legislature.

After the arrival of the new Governor a change was soon
apparent. Every one—Mormon and anti-Mormon—felt that
there was a man of energy in the Executive chair. Governor
Shaffer was sick and dying, but he meant to be Governor
de facto as well as de jure. The New Movement orators and
writers were then in the heat of their little battle with Theocracy, and had allied to their revelations a determination to
be political. A few weeks before Governor Shaffer arrived
among the Saints, a political meeting of "Liberals" had been
broken up by prominent men of the community. The rough-
and-ready brethren from several of the wards had been invited,
who rushed in and filled the hall, and nothing but the utmost
coolness and prudence on the part of the Liberals prevented
the effusion of blood. "The brethren" were armed, and when
the plot of the priesthood was discovered,* there were few of
the Gentiles present who did not expect that a massacre would
take place before the meeting was finally dispersed.

* Brigham Young sent his chief clerk the next morning to assume responsibility
for the damage done to the hall, and it was very fortunate that only broken benches
had to be settled for, as there was evidence direct as to who gave the instructions
to overwhelm the Liberals. If an investigation of this occurrence had taken place,
it would have revealed that dozens of men sat and stood in that hall the whole
of the evening, with their hands upon their revolvers, watching for the first blow.
Two notorious "Minute men" were seated behind one of the leading Liberals, apparently there as other citizens, without any show of purpose; but, if a fight had
begun, it was believed that he would have been their victim. He knew of their
presence, and sat unmoved with his revolver under his coat, while one of his friends
stood close by, apparently unconcerned, but with his revolver also ready, watching
the other two. There were dozens in similar positions throughout the hall, expecting every moment that some unguarded word might begin the trouble. That meeting was held in Zion.

It is affirmed that, at a meeting of the "School of the Prophets," a short time
previous to this, one of the leading men, speaking of Godbe, Harrison, and Kelsey,
said that "the best thing that could occur to them was, to *put them out of the way*."
Seeing that the sentiment was not received with favour, but created quite a feeling
of horror, he arose and said that "the School should understand that that was not
"counselled." A number of the members of the School threw down their tickets
of membership on the ground when they left the building, and trampled them under
their feet, and never returned to the School again.

The New Movement had caused considerable excitement, and the principal leaders had good reasons for believing that they owed the safety of their lives to their own ability to defend them, and to nothing else. Their steps were dogged at night, and for some months dangerous characters were seen prowling around their houses, evidently seeking their opportunity. The "Reformers" never went out of doors without arms, and every precaution was taken at home by fixing an extra supply of bolts and bars to doors and windows. Godbe, Harrison, and Kelsey, were never permitted by their brethren to be out after sunset without a friendly escort. And this dread of assassination was not the unfounded apprehension of cowardice. Men who were brave enough to attack the Prophet and Theocracy in the chief city of Zion, with at the same time a knowledge of the desperate deeds that had already been committed, were men not to be frightened by shadows.

It was in the midst of this trouble that Governor Shaffer arrived among the Mormons, and no man of his intellect and nerve could assume the duties of that office without being at once forced to the determination of adopting such legal measures as were within his reach, to give protection to those whose persons were endangered.

Before he left Washington, he doubtless had the assurance of the Government that he would be sustained in everything that was legitimate and proper to do in affording protection to all citizens irrespective of faith. Representations were made of the insecurity felt in the country, as well as in the city, wherever there was dissent from the Prophet, and a few companies of United States troops were asked for. Lieutenant-General Sheridan visited Utah, and made himself acquainted with the actual situation of affairs. This distinguished soldier expressed the kindliest sentiments for the people, admired the work they had accomplished, and hoped that nothing would occur to disturb them in the peaceful possessions of their homes. His visit was at the finest season of the year, and he was truly charmed with the appearance of the city. Troops, whenever wanted, would, however, be forthcoming, not as a menace to the community, but that at their camp the oppressed might find beneath the stars and stripes the protection of the Govern-

ment. Governor Shaffer is dead; he cannot answer his tra-
ducers; but these were his sentiments, and almost his words
to the Author, as well as the words of the great cavalry-soldier
of the Republic.

The constant division among the Federal officers of the Territory had not only been advantageous to the priesthood, but
it had also been a scandal to the Government, and that condition of affairs Governor Shaffer was charged to bring to an
end. A new Secretary soon succeeded S. A. Mann, and the
Hon. James B. McKean, of New York, was appointed Chief-
Justice; there was also a new marshal in the person of Colonel
M. T. Patrick, of Omaha.

Governor Shaffer believed that the Mormon leaders had
been disloyal to the Government, and were determined to preserve within their own hands the military power of the Territory, and to practically ignore him as commander-in-chief, as
they had his predecessors. As the annual three days' drill was
about to take place, he issued the following proclamation:

EXECUTIVE DEPARTMENT, SALT LAKE CITY, U. T., *September* 15, 1870.

Know ye, that I, J. Wilson Shaffer, Governor of the Territory of Utah,
and Commander-in-Chief of the militia of the Territory of Utah, do hereby
forbid and prohibit all musters, drills, or gatherings of any nature, kind,
or description of armed persons, within the Territory of Utah, except by
my order, or by the order of the United States Marshal, should he need
a *posse comitatus* to execute any order of the Court, and not otherwise.
And it is hereby further ordered, that all arms and munitions of war belonging to either the United States, or the Territory of Utah, not in possession of United States soldiers, be immediately delivered by the parties
having the same in their possession, to Colonel Wm. M. Johns, Assistant-
Adjutant General.

And it is further ordered, that should the United States Marshal need
a *posse comitatus* to enforce any order of the Court, he is hereby authorized
and empowered to make a requisition upon Major-General P. E. Connor
for such *posse comitatus*, or armed force, and Major-General P. E. Connor
is hereby authorized to order out the militia, or any part thereof, as of my
order for said purpose or purposes, and no other.

Witness my hand, and the Great Seal of said Territory, at Salt Lake
City, this 15th day of September, A. D. 1870.   J. W. SHAFFER, *Governor*.
Attest.

VERNON H. VAUGHAN, Secretary of Utah Territory.

This was an extraordinary document. It was the desperate
act of a man driven to the assertion of a right and duty of

office that had been practically denied him. The Lieutenant-General had proceeded with his usual indifference towards the Governor, and issued his military orders for mustering and drilling the troops as if he had had no superior. The Governor had had no previous opportunity of calling him to account, and it was now necessary that he should do so, or quietly take his place with his predecessors who had been known in this capacity only in name.

Governor Shaffer was unhappily situated when he resolved to assert his position as commander-in-chief of the militia, for he had no choice of persons whom he could appoint to aid him in the work that he undertook to accomplish. It was necessary that he should appoint some one to take command of the militia, and that one—Major-General P. Edward Connor—though in every way qualified as an officer, was the last person in the Territory whom the militia would at that time have desired to see placed over them.

Could Governor Shaffer have found an officer who had had no controversy with the leaders, the Mormons might have objected all the same to his appointment, but in the appointment of General Connor to be " major-general of the Utah militia," they had argument on their side. Governor Shaffer had the other argument, that they had forced him to that appointment—he had no alternative. The lieutenant-general, through the adjutant-general, had remonstrated, and asked that the musters be permitted to take place, as the orders had been issued, but the Governor was inexorable, and sent a scorching letter of reply, in which he related to the lieutenant-general his treasonable proceedings and the disloyalty of the Mormon leaders. That was the last official act of Governor Shaffer, and it was solely his own, and not the emanation of "a ring," as charged by the Mormons. He was dictating the last words of the letter as the Author entered the Executive office, and there he was lying upon his couch, weak, exhausted, and scarcely able to speak. "I have answered their letter, Sten-"house," he said.

" And I expect, Governor, after the acknowledgment of "your authority, you have granted them permission."

" You think I would! Stenhouse, if I were not dying, I

"would get up and whip you. They are traitors, and I only "regret that I shall not live to help to bring them to justice. "Brigham Young has played his game of bluff long enough. "I will make him show his hand."

The country was excited. On the one side it was persistently asserted that the drill would be held in spite of the Governor; and those who were acquainted with the latter knew well that he would maintain the spirit and letter of his proclamation. Had the lieutenant-general persevered, the Governor would have sent the marshal to arrest him and the chief officers. The marshal would have been walked out of camp, the Governor would have telegraphed for five thousand regular troops, they would have been sent, and the looked-for collision would have taken place. The muster, however, did not take place in Salt Lake county, but in distant parts of the Territory; the militia were assembled and drilled, but no mention was made of the fact in the Mormon papers.

The Governor died on the last day of October—six weeks after the difficulty had begun; the militia trouble did not end with his life.

The return of the Fourth of July afforded another opportunity for a difficulty. "Lieutenant-General" Wells issued an order for a portion of the militia to take part in the procession on the nation's birthday. Governor George L. Woods was absent from the Territory, and George A. Black, who had been Governor Shaffer's private secretary, was now Secretary of the Territory and acting-Governor. He immediately issued a proclamation, forbidding "the said military parade under the "said order of the said Daniel H. Wells," as "no such office "or officer (was) recognized by the commander-in-chief of the "militia of this Territory as that of lieutenant-general." Wells was furious, and threatened to bring out the militia; and "he "would see if a boy should interfere with them."

Age not being considered in points of law and military rule, acting-Governor Black paid no attention to sneers or threats, and called upon the commander of the United States military at Camp Douglas to be present in the city on the morning of the Fourth, with all his available command, to await further requisitions. The commandant of the United States troops had had a newspaper difficulty with Governor Shaffer. He had dined with Brigham Young and a few of his wives, was charmed by the prophetic *entourage*, and thought "*le Presi-* "*dent Young est un très gentil homme, et ses femmes sont très* "*comme-il-faut.*" He was on the side of Brigham for no other reason than that he was profoundly ignorant of the question at issue between the Republic and the Theocracy, and the instinct of his nationality inclined him to the side of courtesy. General R. De Trobriand was, however, a soldier, and when interrogated by the Mormons as to what he would do on the order of the Governor, he answered: "I would shoot you down." Before such a matter-of-fact reply the threatening of Daniel H. Wells succumbed, and he countermanded the military parade in time to save a collision.

From these incidents the reader will perceive the inevitable and interminable contest that must for ever exist on this subject between the Mormons and the Federal Governor. The militia have rights, as citizens, to elect their officers; and undoubtedly, if left to their own selection, their chief would have been Daniel H. Wells, simply because Brigham had nominated him to that post; and the Governor must be commander-in-chief, because Congress had appointed him to that position. Throughout this controversy, it was evident that Theocracy and Republicanism were naturally antagonistic, and that the representatives of neither theory would yield to the other. The militia of Utah are Brigham's brethren; they have enlisted on the side of "the Kingdom," and the Republic is a Gentile institution. The Federal officers, however, reverse the *status* of the parties—the Republic is everything, Brigham and his "kingdom" are but an "ism."

On that Fourth of July (1871), the Saints and the Gentiles had separate processions in honour of the day, and all passed off peaceably; but, from that time to the present, the Utah militia has never been mustered. Gospel and law were now to mingle in the interesting history of Utah.

In the spring of 1870, Delegate Hooper delivered a very carefully prepared speech in the House of Representatives in

defence of his constituents practising polygamy, upon the
ground that the Bible sanctioned that institution, and that the
Constitution of the United States forbade any interference
with religious worship. To this speech, the Rev. J. P. Newman, then pastor of the Metropolitan Church at Washington,
and Chaplain of the Senate, delivered a reply. ' A Salt Lake
paper, noticing this, intimated that the reverend gentleman
had delivered the sermon in the wrong place, and that the
Mormon Tabernacle was the place where it should be heard.
Regarding this as a challenge, Dr. Newman announced his
purpose of visiting Utah. Early in August he arrived among
the Saints, accompanied by the Rev. Dr. Sunderland, of the
Congregational Church, at Washington, and, immediately on
his arrival, he notified Brigham Young that he was there in
compliance with his challenge, and was ready to discuss with
him the subject of Polygamy on Biblical grounds.

Brigham informed the Doctor that he had never challenged
him, and disavowed all responsibility for the utterances of the
journal in which he deemed himself invited to come to Utah.
But the reverend gentleman was determined not to be put off,
and several letters passed between him and the Prophet. Finally, the apostle, Orson Pratt, was appointed by Brigham to
take the affirmative in the discussion upon the subject—"Does
"the Bible sanction Polygamy?" The Doctor was desirous
of a thorough and exhaustive discussion; but the arrangement
finally agreed upon was, that the argument should extend over
three days, and that the speeches should be of one hour each.
The Tabernacle on the Friday and Saturday was well filled,
and on the Sunday it was crowded. The debate was published
in full, and in it the best arguments were set forth that could
be adduced from opposite stand-points. Dr. Newman exhibited
at least one important fact to the Mormons, namely, that the
greater portion of the renowned characters mentioned in the
Bible were monogamists, and not polygamists. He denied
that Abraham was a polygamist: "At no time did he have
"more than one wife; his connection with Hagar was an offence
"against God, who commanded him to put her away. Jacob
"had nothing to do with the evil after his conversion at Jabbok.
"Isaac, Joseph, Moses, Aaron, and Joshua, were all monoga-

"mists.   David lived eleven years after he had put away his "wives.   Solomon was too wicked for either party to be proud "of.   The great Bible law is : 'Let every man have his own "'wife, and let every woman have her own husband.'   The "claims of the Mormons to sustain Polygamy under the reli- "gious liberty guaranteed by the Federal Constitution was "false in principle, for the religious liberty of the American "citizen is limited in respect to decency and morality, and "does not extend to license which would be subversive of the "well-being of society and the perpetuity of the national life."

Had the reverend gentleman succeeded in securing a discus- sion with the apostle Pratt, upon the relative merits of polyg- amy and monogamy, and exhibiting which was harmonious with Christianity and the civilization of the nineteenth century, the discussion would doubtless have been of more permanent value in Utah ; but, so long have the people there had drilled into them the names of Abraham, Isaac, and Jacob, David and Solomon, associated with polygamy and the favour of " the Lord," that it would take a thorough and lengthened im- mersion in the waters of Lethe to prepare them to listen to anything to the contrary.

The appointment of Chief-Justice McKean had been flatter- ingly noticed by the Mormon press, and the Saints were grati- fied with the assurance that he was " both a lawyer and a "gentleman."   On the morning after his arrival, a Mormon met with him in the company of other gentlemen, and in- tently surveying the new arrival, after the fashion of Western freedom, he burst out with his opinion : " Judge, in three " months you will be the best-abused man that was ever " in Utah."   The personal bearing of Judge McKean im- pressed the belief that he was an honourable, intellectual man.*

* When Chief-Justice Titus went to Utah, seven years before, a Mormon gentle- man, who had travelled with him across the plains, gave an entertainment to the Judge shortly after his arrival.   That Mormon gentleman was then a good Saint, high in the confidence of the Prophet.   After dinner he said to the Author : " How long will it be before we make the Judge our enemy ? "   In his mind no honourable, independent man could fill the office of Federal judge, and be long on good terms with the priesthood.   Before the three months expired, Judge McKean was anathe- matized, and the cursings of the priesthood have ever since largely increased upon his devoted head.

The associate-justices then and now in Utah—Obed F. Strickland and Cyrus M. Hawley—had revived the controversy of Judge Stiles [*see* p. 282], and maintained that the United States Marshal was the proper officer of the District Court, and that it was he who should empanel the juries of those courts. Chief-Justice McKean held the same opinion. Soon one important case and then another and another was brought up in the Third District Court, over which Judge McKean presided, and his Honour's rulings were against the laws of the Utah Legislature regulating the selection of jurors through the County Court and the Territorial Marshal. The three Federal judges, forming the Supreme Court of the Territory, were united in that decision. The Mormon lawyers filed exceptions, and appealed to the Supreme Court of the United States.

Pending the reference of this question to the highest tribunal, the Third District Court proceeded with its business. On the resignation of the United States District Attorney * for the Territory, Judge McKean appointed R. N. Baskin, Esq., acting-prosecutor, and the latter appointed General George R. Maxwell his assistant. Mr. Baskin was the counsel for Dr. Robinson, when the latter gentleman was assassinated, and General Maxwell was a brave and fearless soldier during the rebellion. Maxwell regarded the Mormon leaders as disloyal to the Government. Baskin regarded them as the aiders and abettors of murderers.

During the September [1871] term of this court, indict-

---

* It is customary for Mormon writers to array Federal officers against each other ; hence the apostle Geo. A. Smith, in his " Answer to Questions," p. 69, says : " C. H. Hempstead, Esq., U. S. Attorney, being unwilling to prosecute under the rulings of the court, resigned." It is fair to Judge McKean and Mr. Hempstead to state that, whatever might be Mr. Hempstead's opinion of the rulings of Judge McKean, he had sent in his resignation at least one year before the date referred to, and had only " held over " at the special request of President Grant. Mr. Hempstead, on his resignation of the office of Prosecuting Attorney, immediately became one of the counsel for Brigham Young—an act for which no one could reproach him. No gentleman of Mr. Hempstead's ability would retain the office of Prosecuting Attorney—the salary being nominal. Mr. Baskin had refused it several times, and only accepted it *pro tem.* to aid in the prosecution for the murders, and during that prosecution Mr. B., it is stated, was offered a fee of $25,000 as a retainer on the part of some of the accused.

ments were found against leading Mormons for murder, and among the number were Brigham and Wells. The latter was apprehended, and bail accepted for his appearance when wanted. Brigham, when arrested, was permitted to remain a prisoner in his own house under the charge of a United States deputy-marshal; the others were sent to Camp Douglas for safe-keeping. The arrest of such prominent persons created great excitement, and for a time it was uncertain if the Mormons would not resist the officers of the law, and deliver their brethren. In the midst of this trouble, George C. Bates, Esq., of Illinois, was appointed United States Attorney for Utah, and soon his influence was perceptibly felt in favour of the indicted Mormons. It should be added, however, that Mr. Bates claims that he did not believe in the rulings of the judges.

It was during this term of court that a Mormon, Thomas Hawkins, was tried " for living in adultery " with two " wives " in addition to his legal wife. It was on the affidavit of the latter that the prosecution was commenced, and Hawkins was finally convicted, and sentenced to three years' imprisonment, and a fine of $500. This was regarded as a test case, and showed clearly to the Mormons that, with the United States marshal to select the jurors, their own Territorial laws against " lewd and lascivious conduct " could convict all polygamists,* whenever the legal wives chose to make complaint. The press and pulpit were let loose on Judge McKean, and he was represented as everything evil that rancour could suggest. He was a second Jeffreys, and, compared with him, Nero was a Christian gentleman.

To give the arguments and the authorities *pro et con*, in this long and bitter controversy, would fill a volume. The Federal judges claimed that their rulings were harmonious with the past decisions of the United States Supreme Court, and that they could not recognize the right of the Legislature to create a Territorial marshal, and to place him in their courts. In this

---

* While Chief-Justice Eckles was at Fort Bridger, in the winter of 1857–8, and held his court within the military encampment of General Albert S. Johnston, he charged the grand jury upon this same Territorial law, in almost the same language as did Chief-Justice McKean upwards of twelve years later. The charge, therefore, that the latter gentleman originated the idea, and tortured the Territorial statute to suit his purposes, is not correct. (See *Atlantic Monthly*, April, 1859.)

they were sustained by the opinion of the then United States Attorney-General, and when the appeal was made to the United States Supreme Court, they were fully satisfied that they would be sustained. The attorneys for the Mormons laboured assiduously at Washington, and, contrary to the usual custom in the Supreme Court, the forthcoming decision had been whispered to some grateful ears! The Mormon anniversary conference, beginning on the 6th of April, was continued over, without adjournment, awaiting that decision. On the 15th of that month, Chief-Justice Chase delivered a decision reversing the ruling of the Federal judges in Utah, and sustaining the Legislature of the Territory in the "whole matter of selecting, "empanelling, and summoning jurors." This ended the long and troublesome controversy, and all the Mormons indicted for murder by the grand jury empanelled by the United States marshal were immediately liberated, and "Brother Brigham" attended the conference, and the prolonged session closed.

The winter of 1871–2 was a remarkable epoch in Mormon history, both at home and abroad. Brigham fully realized his weakness. Years before he had boasted that he would "send "to hell across lots" the man who dared to arrest him. When, however, the time came for making good his threat, he quietly submitted to the United States Marshal, and was for some time a prisoner in his own house under the surveillance of that officer. In his service, men whom he had despised went to Washington, and proffers were made to them of senatorial and congressional honours, if they could only get Utah admitted into the Union as a State. He who had before-time spurned all Gentile influences and defied "the powers that be," consented to accept the aid of both men and women at the seat of Government, in order to avert the threatening doom. Richard, at Bosworth Field, shouting : "My kingdom for a horse," evinced no greater anxiety than did the Prophet for the admission of Utah into the Federal Union. Everything failed him abroad, except the decision of the Supreme Court; but with that rendering of the law respecting the powers of the Territorial legislature, the Probate Courts of Utah gathered new life, and the Federal Courts were again powerless to prosecute the Church leaders for any crimes of which they might be accused.

SALT LAKE CITY, FROM THE NORTH.

CHAPTER LVI.

SALT LAKE CITY.—Its Situation and Beauty—Its Railway Communication—
Water Supply—Great and Increasing Improvement—The Tabernacle—Brigham
the Architect of Zion—Inspiring the Prophet with an Idea—The Great Organ
—The Tabernacle Services—Results of the Influx of Gentiles—Brigham's Com-
mercial Street—Christian Churches in Utah—Their Work and Influence—The
Episcopal Church—Christian Schools—Brigham's Opinion of Gentile Instruc-
tion—The Methodist Teacher's Difficulties—Polygamy opposed by Mr. Mc-
Leod—The Liberal Institute—Lectures in Zion—Evidences of Prosperity—
Progress of Civilization in Utah.

THERE is no city in the United States, with a population of
only twenty thousand inhabitants, so universally known as Salt
Lake City. It is the chief city of Zion—the dwelling-place of
the Prophet—the habitation of the Saints—and the grand centre of "the Kingdom of God upon earth." It is the city of
prediction, "beautiful for situation, and the joy of the whole
"earth."

But, setting aside prediction, and the innumerable verses of
poetry that have been dedicated to

"The city I love so well,"

the uninspired visitor to Utah, as well as the enthusiastic disciple, cannot fail to be pleased with the first glimpse of this
oasis in the desert. When the journey to Utah from the East
was made by the mule overland stage in twenty days, or by the
slow ox-team in ninety days, the weary and exhausted pilgrims
would burst out into expressions of rapturous delight at beholding a city of gardens stretching miles away—east and west,
north and south.

The entrance to the Valley at that time was through the
cañons of the Wahsatch range of mountains on the east, and,

these being still comparatively high on the rim of the basin, the eye of the traveller could take in at a glance almost the whole extent of the city that lay nestling at the base of the mountains on the northern side of the Valley. It was a charming picture of city and farm, lake and mountain, seldom to be seen in any country. But all the enthusiastic experience of by-gone days is now greatly modified. The city "stands where "it did," and is improving greatly every year, but the low lands on which the railroad, entering the Valley from the north, has been constructed, render the first view of it rather disadvantageous than otherwise. Besides, the comfort and luxury of a Pullman palace car, and the hasty journey of sixty hours from the Missouri river, unfits the *voyageur* for appreciating the delights that the hope of visiting the city once inspired. It is one thing to look out upon a desert country from behind the rich damask curtains of a sleeping-car; and it is another thing to have travelled over that same desert, exposed to the vertical rays of a burning summer's sun, or the pitiless storm that threatened to blow everything into shreds, or to have felt the drenching rains pouring through the wagon-covers as if they were sieves, while underneath might be seen the kind mother holding tight to her bosom her last loved one, and paterfamilias cowering beneath the bows of the wagon, with umbrella in hand, attempting to divert at least a little of the deluge from their devoted heads. Add to that the enchanting experience of herding cattle by night, hunting for water miles distant from camp, gathering "buffalo-chips" for the fires of the *cuisine;* and to all that throw in the possibility of a stampede of the cattle, or an Indian attack, and the reader will have no difficulty in understanding the enthusiasm that inspired the early pilgrims to Zion when they reached the goal of their hopes.

The attention of every visitor to Zion in summer is attracted by the excellent arrangement for the distribution of water through all parts of the city. The melting snows rush down City Creek Cañon on the north, and dash and foam over the rough boulders, and clear the natural obstructions of the rugged and tortuous windings of the mountain-gorge with all the impetuosity of the cataract and fall, but before the water reaches the city boundary it is controlled by the will of man, and conducted to the extremities of the city east and west, and by an admirable system of ditching it flows gently down each side of the wide streets, serving the poorer inhabitants with all the water they require for household use. Every garden-lot has its own private ditch, through which, at a fixed hour, the water is conducted, in measured quantity, according to the extent of the parched soil that needs the magic life that springs from irrigation.

In the spring of the year, when the fruit-trees around the dwellings are in blossom, and the young leaves are in their freshest green, the view of the city is very beautiful; but all the romance that once hung around that picture is gone. Israel is no longer isolated from the rest of the world; the " un- " godly Gentiles " have gained a foothold among the brethren, and other men than Saints take unto themselves wives of " the " daughters of the Lord."

In the building of Western cities there are always three very marked stages of progress—the log-house, the adobe, and the rock or brick building. The great majority of the homes of the Saints in the city are now in the transition state between the two extremes. Many very fine private residences have been built within the last few years, and, with the increasing development of the mines, and the extension of commerce, improvement is observable in every direction.

The passing visitor will find but very little to occupy his attention—there are very few places of immediate interest; but the student who can make a lengthened sojourn with the Saints, will find the Prophet and the institutions of Zion remarkably interesting.

The first object—after Brigham—that every visitor should see is the new Tabernacle.* It is the most uncomely edifice that

* The traveller to Zion who wants to see polygamy within the inner threshold of the homes of the Saints, will be disappointed if he expects any such gratification, and very properly so. A lady visitor to Brigham's office, after being courteously received by the Prophet, expressed the wish that she might see his wives; to which he politely answered: " They are not on exhibition, madam." His answer was very proper. No lady or gentleman is denied admittance to his office, on simply sending in a card; but the better way to secure a pleasant interview is to ask some well-to-do brother to give a personal introduction, and the visitor should

was ever erected for a place of worship, but it holds a great many
persons—twelve thousand. As seen from a distance, it looks
like a huge turtle. From east to west it measures two hundred
and fifty feet; from north to south, one hundred and fifty; and
from the floor to the ceiling, eighty. It is oval in shape, and
without a column to obstruct the vision; but, in compensation
for that advantage, as "the Lord" had everything to do with
its construction, an utter disregard for what Gentile experience
could have suggested might have been expected, and the massive building grew up and was finished free from every taint of
the science of acoustics. When it was dedicated and opened
for preaching, not one-third of the audience could hear any
speaker distinctly, and the rest of the auditory heard only a
rumbling noise, and were left to guess the subject from the
gestures of the preacher. Of course, the ungodly considered
those who heard the least were the most favoured!

Brigham is architect enough for everything in Zion; he
knew just "exactly what was wanted," and had it constructed
according to his own views. No one could advise him. If
any friend can possibly get into his "inspired" head clear ideas
upon any subject, and be dexterous enough to have it appear
that it is the Prophet who is imparting to him the information,
and does not let it be seen even to himself that he is teaching
the Prophet, all is well, and the intelligence will be acted upon.

"I think it is your idea, President, that it should be done
"in this manner?"

"Let me look at that again;—yes, I think so, don't you?"

"Yes."

"Well, go ahead and do it."

When the Tabernacle was nearly finished, and much glory
was anticipated, there were a number of claimants for honour.
Brother Grow, brother Angel, and brother Folsom, wanted
each the major share of glory, if Brigham should leave any for
distribution: but, when the building was found to be a magnificent failure, even the apostle, Orson Hyde, hesitated to

make sure that the brother is in good relations with the Prophet. Brigham is very
human, and he can button himself up to an unwelcome visitor in a style that the
stranger is not likely to forget; but, when he is in excellent humour, he is a perfect Chesterfield.

credit it to " the Lord." After many weeks of hard labour,
and endeavouring to arrive at some conclusion, Brigham finally
discovered that there was " no echo in the building—the voice
" only reverberated ! "

Interior of the Mormon Tabernacle.

The organ is a handsome piece of work, and reflects great
credit upon the Mormon builder and mechanics.   The Boston
organ, and that in the Plymouth Church, Brooklyn, are both
larger, but they are of foreign manufacture.   This organ is
said to be the largest that has been built in the United States.

The Tabernacle should, if possible, be visited on a Sunday
afternoon—the " spirit " is hardly warmed up in the morning
assembly.   The organ plays better, the choir sing better, and
" the spirit " flows better.   Everything is better on a Sunday
afternoon.

The choir occupy the upper seats round the organ, and directly in front sit the Prophet and his two counsellors.   In
front of them, there is a long seat for the twelve apostles, and
before these is the " President of the Stake " and his two coun-

sellors. On the lower range, directly facing the audience, sit the chief bishop and his counsellors, together with the other bishops and their counsellors, who may be appointed to administer the sacrament.

The Mormon assembly has nothing of the character of "worship" in the sense of that term as used by the old established churches, and is as far distant from the intellectual addresses of the modern pulpit as it can well be. There is no preparation for anything. The service was in the first days of the Church expected to be directed by the Spirit;—probably that may be the expectation now.

In every Stake of Zion there is a president and two counsellors, who preside over the spiritual affairs of the Church in that particular locality. Utah is a "Stake." The present president is Elder John W. Young, the younger of Brigham's three prominent sons. The twenty bishops of Salt Lake City have each two counsellors, and are the presiding element in all the ward assemblies; but in the Tabernacle assembly on Sunday mornings and afternoons, when all the Saints are expected to be there in order to be refreshed by "the droppings of the "Sanctuary," the authority of the bishops is unrecognized, and either the President of the Stake or one of his counsellors presides. He announces the number of the hymn. At the elevation of the conductor's wand, a very excellent choir starts into position. A few touches of the organist, and a great volume of human voice is well directed in the rendering of some familiar air, or it may be some Mormon adaptation of a new popular melody.

After the hymn some brother, or apostle, a bishop, or some elder who is conspicuous on the platform, is invited to pray. If it should fortunately be "George A." [the apostle Smith], who is invited, the audience listens to a brief, manly petition, with a great deal of satisfaction. "George A." is no weeping worshipper, and, when he has told "the Lord" his story, the congregation utter vigorously, "Amen," and sit down prepared to hear another hymn.

It may appear invidious to make such a distinction among the Mormon praying elders; but no visitor to the Tabernacle can listen to the lengthy confusion of utterances that often are inflicted upon that long-suffering people without appreciating the terse, brief, and hard-sense petitions of the elder named. When one of those fearfully long-praying elders "lets loose," he forgets nothing, and will " run half an hour." He generally begins with Brigham, who is to be blessed in his basket and in his store ; his wives, his families, his flocks and his herds are to be multiplied ; his houses and his lands are to be increased ; he is to be made the wisest man in the world, is to confound all his enemies, and those who rise up against him are to fall into every conceivable snare, and finally reach the nether regions. After he gets through with the chief, he passes on to his counsellors ; then he groups the apostles, and is very particular that the blessings be proportionate to their rank ; the bishops are next in order, and, as they are numerous, the favours solicited for them are very general ; then he comes to the Saints at large, and they need the greatest care and protection against the inroads of the Gentiles and the attacks of the Indians ; and here he remembers with peculiar unction that the red-skins are to become a "white and delightsome people," and are to turn unto "the Lord," in fulfilment of the predictions of the "Book "of Mormon." The sermons need not be described here ; the quotations already cited in this work are amply sufficient to enlist the sympathy of the world in behalf of the people. At the close of the sermon there is a doxology, and the people are dismissed with a brief blessing.

On the same block, near the Tabernacle, the visitor will see the foundation of the great Temple. On the northwest corner from the Tabernacle, there stands the "Endowment House," an unpretentious building externally, but within its portals are performed all the rites and ceremonies that hold Mormonism together.

The promise of the "Endowments" in that small building has drawn thousands of disciples from the nations of the Old World to Zion, and the teaching of the priesthood concerning the blessings of the Endowments has done more to inspire the sacrifices made by European Saints than everything else put together But what a terrible disappointment has followed all those bright hopes ! An intelligent gentleman, who had for many years looked forward to the time when he would receive his Endowments, was interrogated shortly after having "passed through "the House," by another who had been there before him, about what intelligence he had received. His answer was expressive of the general experience : "I went in expecting everything; "I came out with nothing."

The Mormon leaders have always asserted that Free-Masonry was a bastard and degenerate representation of the order of the true priesthood. The reader needs, therefore, no other statement than that of the leaders, to form an estimate of the signs, grips, passwords, rites, and ceremonies of the Endowment House.* When the Temple is finished, in that edifice the ordinances, according to the fulness of the priesthood, will be administered : thither the angels will come, and there "the "Lord" will find a place of rest upon the earth. The anxiety of the Saints for "the Lord's" rest is now apparently not very urgent. The erection of the Temple has been so very slow that its completion is to many a matter of much doubt.

Ecclesiastically, the city is divided into twenty wards, over each of which are placed a bishop and two counsellors. The bishop may be a merchant, a farmer, or mechanic. Education, talent, or refinement, has nothing to do with the selection for office. They are generally reliable men,† who can be depended upon to do as they are told, and see that the Saints do their duty and pay their tithing regularly. In each ward the bishop holds a meeting every Sunday night. Under this divisional supervision, the city, if twenty times larger, would be under the same complete control.

---

* In "The Mormon's Own Book," by T. W. P. Taylder, pp. 139–147, a singular resemblance is pointed out between the ceremonies in the *Eleusinia*—a festival among the Cretans—and the mysteries of the Mormon Endowment, as set forth by Van Dusen.

† Governor Cumming often related that when loving swains and their lasses used to come in from the country and seek his services to unite them in wedlock, he would invariably send them to the nearest bishop. When directing them to the residence of that ecclesiastic, the Governor enjoyed hugely the instructions which he gave: "Go up two blocks, then turn to the right, and go about three blocks farther ; wherever you see a good house and a large wood-pile, that's where the bishop lives, and if he does not suit you, go on to the right or left until you see another great wood-pile, and thereabouts you will find another bishop's residence." In those days a good wood-pile was a certain evidence of comfortable circumstances. With the railroad and the Gentile coal, the old landmarks have passed away.

DESIGN OF SALT LAKE TEMPLE.

The civil government of Salt Lake City is nominally like that of city governments elsewhere—with a mayor, five aldermen, nine councillors, a recorder, treasurer, and marshal, all apparently the choice of the people; but there the Church rules as much as in the Tabernacle.

All elections in Utah are dictated by the priesthood. Brigham Young as directly selects or approves of the brethren who are to be elected, as he does of the brethren to be sent on missions to preach the gospel. A caucus of a few apostles and leading men is generally held in the historian's office a few weeks before the election, and if none of the old city council have apostatized or disgraced themselves they continue in office. When a vacancy has to be filled a name is suggested and that is submitted to "brother Brigham." He approves it, and the next day the announcement is made of "the people's ticket." There is to be no "scratching" of that ticket. On one occasion Dr. Jeter Clinton deservedly fell into universal disfavour, and even Mayor Wells could no longer hold up "brother Jeter" for reëlection as an alderman. A nephew of Brigham's was to be substituted. On the day of election, Brigham was at Provo, and the liberal Mormons wanted to elect Bishop Woolley instead of the Prophet's nephew. This desire was so general and so well supported that Mayor Wells and the apostle George Q. Cannon, who had charge of the election, consented to the "scratching" off of the nephew's name. The Bishop was overwhelmingly elected. At the next meeting of "the school of "the Prophets" Brigham was furious. He was mad with rage; he stormed and cursed, and, in the paroxysms of his wrath, he announced that the anger of "the Lord" was kindled against them for "scratching" the ticket. The apostle was melted to tears, and the Mayor was speechless with emotion. When he regained a little control over his organs of speech, the Mayor humbly confessed his sins, and told how he realized that the anger of "the Lord" had pierced him through as Brigham's eyes met his! He felt that he had sinned grievously in "scratching" the name of the Prophet's nephew off the ticket. The bishop, too, who had been honoured by the majority of votes, came in for a share of the Prophet's anger, and he consequently declined to accept the election, and Jeter "held

" over," and continued in office, to the great annoyance of the respectable inhabitants of the city.

A still better illustration of the people's voting was exhibited on the reëlection of a popular delegate to Congress. The delegate, as is usual on such occasions, was thanking a public audience for the renewed expression of their confidence in sending him to the seat of Government to represent them. Brigham sprang up after the delegate-elect, stroked his beard, shrugged his shoulders, and mimicked the voice and gestures of the delegate, and repeated his thanks to the people. Then he raised himself to his full height, and, in his own sarcastic way, asked : " Does not brother X. Y. Z. know *who* sent him to " Congress ? He thanks the people for their expression of con- " fidence in him. The Saints have no confidence in him, and " if he had not been sent by the priesthood, he would not have " received twenty votes throughout the whole Territory, and " half of these would have been from hickory Mormons." That delegate—an honourable gentleman—took the snubbing, and ever afterwards fully realized that he represented the priesthood at the seat of Government.*

The city had at one time the reputation of being the most orderly in the Union, and it probably well deserved that reputation. Every person was taxed to the uttermost to procure the necessaries of life, and there was no room for the idler, and a man without visible means of support was unknown. With the change from the quiet life of an agricultural population to a life amidst the busy marts of commerce and speculation, there has been as significant a change in Zion as in any mining Territory in the West, and no one bears so singular a relation to the worst features of the change as the Prophet himself.

By way of speculation, Brigham constructed a street through some of his property, parallel with the principal thoroughfare, and rented the ground to parties who wished to

---

* The pretended freedom of the ballot in Utah is a perfect farce. Every ballot is numbered, and the number placed against the name of the voter, and in this way those who dare to vote contrary to the published ticket are known to the priesthood. In other parts of the Union, the numbering of the tickets might be of no moment, but in Utah, where the slightest opposition is branded as rebellion, and is treated accordingly, it is of the last importance, as it practically precludes all free voting.

build for commercial purposes. Curiously enough, after the
buildings were erected, it was there that the *demi-monde* con-
gregated, and followed their profession. In " Brigham's Com-
" mercial Street " no lady would venture to be seen. But,
while the reputation of a part of the city has changed for the
worse in morals, it is gratifying to state that other elements
are at work for the benefit and elevation of the people, and

St. Mark's Church.

...ristian churches, schools, and associations, are being firm
founded in Zion. For many years there was no place where
anything but Mormonism could be heard, and the stranger
who could not accept the new Prophet and his revelations was
entirely cut off from all religious communion. All this is past,
and there are now the places of worship of several denomina-

tions of Christians, who are all of them increasing in influence and numbers. But a few years ago no one would have dreamed that such a change could be so rapidly effected. The Roman Catholics have erected a neat little church; the members of the Methodist Episcopal Church are building a commodious meeting-house; * and a very handsome edifice has recently been completed by the Episcopal Church, at a cost of $48,000. When the first ministers of this Church arrived in the city, in 1867, they found only two communicants. They now number about 120 highly-respectable citizens, with about 130 members of families attendant.† In their parish-school they have about 250 children. The work of their ministry has been conducted by Bishop Tuttle, assisted by the Revds. T. W. Haskins and R. M. Kirby—gentlemen universally respected.

The labours of these Christian teachers are mainly directed to the education of the young, though not a few parents likewise, in different parts of the Territory, have returned to their "first love in the Gospel." Many a mother greets the missionary with a welcome salutation, and bids him God-speed. These women do not desire to see their children involved in the same labyrinth of confusion and barren materialism into which they have themselves been led. At the last conference held in Salt Lake City, the apostle Richards, in the interest of the children, kindly warned parents to be on their guard against the labours of these missionaries. Brigham, with his usual Machiavellianism, corrected the apostle, and said he differed from him. This was purely for outside effect. With the general reader the Prophet's remarks would have passed for liberality; with the Mormons they were nothing but dust for the eyes of the Gentiles. Brigham was sarcastic and facetious: " *Our friends* who have *such care* for us . . . . " I say to you, *I do thank you. I thank you sincerely* for your " kindness [he bowed too lowly], and you shall receive your " reward for *all the good* that you do. . . . . If these schools can

---

* Since the arrival in Utah of the Rev. G. M. Pierce—Superintendent of the Missions—in May, 1870, the Methodist Episcopal Church has expended $30,000. Eight ministers are engaged in preaching and teaching, and there are four day-schools and six Sunday-schools sustained by their efforts. The preachers are energetic men, and meet with encouraging success.

† This handful of Christians have established the first free hospital in Zion.

" receive our children—and they are receiving many—and
" teach them *without money and without price, send your chil-*
" *dren there.*" Brigham well knew that no Christian societies
proposed to educate the children of the Saints " without money
" and without price "—though some very poor children had
been picked up—and to the Mormon people that very condition stated was virtually a prohibition of their children being
sent to the Gentile schools.

The priesthood in Provo have since illustrated how they
understood Brigham. The Rev. J. P. Lyford had been preaching very successfully in that town, had been kindly received
and treated with social politeness by the people who came
and listened to him. Some sent their children to his Sunday-
school, and that gave offence to the leaders. To remove all
excuse for sending them there, the Mormon teachers opened
school at the same hour. The Methodist teacher, perceiving
the purpose for which this was done, changed the hour of his
school from the morning to the afternoon. The children then
again attended school, and, perceiving this, the Mormon teachers changed theirs to the same hour. Of course, the Methodist
teacher will return to his former hours of attendance.

Elder Franklin D. Richards, when he instructed the Saints
not to send their children to the Gentile schools, was speaking
as an honest, consistent apostle, and representative of the Mormon Church. He knew well enough what he was saying. The
people who heard him also knew, and Brigham knows full well
that scores of times he has publicly forbidden the bishops to
engage Gentile teachers in their schools; and when such men
as Bishop Woolley have done so against his orders, they have
always had trouble with the Prophet. Whenever a Gentile
teacher has been permitted to follow his or her profession,
there have always been special and peculiar reasons for the
rare exception.

While the agencies of the Churches are quietly accomplish-
ing much good in many ways—by teaching, example, and
kindness to the poor—the Rev. Norman McLeod, the former
intimate friend of Dr. Robinson, is lecturing again in Independence Hall, and exposing polygamy, theocracy, and all the
evils charged to the Mormon priesthood. The new-movement

"Reformers," in their first zeal, erected a building, and dedicated it to the "Church of Zion;" but, with the change in their sentiments, they have rechristened it "the Liberal In- "stitute," and there lecturers, male and female, of every shade of opinion in religion, politics, or science, can hold forth for the edification of Saint and sinner. The Liberal Institute is the Faneuil Hall of Utah, and from its platform will go forth facts of history and science that will work in a few years a grander revolution among the Saints than would the presence of ten thousand troops, or any other movement that could possibly be construed into "persecution."

In the gradual disintegration that is now going on, and whose progress is being daily accelerated, the Churches will find a few Saints seeking communion again within the folds in which they once rejoiced in their Redeemer; and a much larger number of the dissatisfied will repudiate all religious associations for the remainder of their lives; but the great bulk of the Mormon people, who are tired of Brigham and Polygamy, and who have still the remembrance of their past experience, without the change of thought that the present light of the world might bring, will turn their eyes towards young Joseph Smith as the successor of his father, and the head of the Mormon Church.

The building of the Utah Central Railroad, from the junction of the Union and Central Pacific Railroads at Ogden to Salt Lake City, was completed in January, 1870, and from that time the city has much improved in appearance and in its commerce. The exorbitant charges for overland freight no longer heavily tax the pockets of the poor nor cool the ambition of the rich for the improvement of their homesteads; and the Municipal Council, too, has shown some ambition to add to the comfort and security of the city. Water and gas-works are being introduced, and the steam fire-engine is to be seen in the streets of Zion. Cars are now running through the streets, from the depot past the hotels, and everything has the air of progress and not of retrogression. There have always been several good hotels in the city, both Gentile and Mormon, and to their number has been added this year the Walker House, which will do much to make the chief city of Zion a pleasant resting-place for the tourist who is visiting Utah.

Numerous elegant private residences have recently been built, that tell of wealth, and the appreciation of a better life than that predicted by the Prophet.* The wealthy proprietors of city property vie with each other in the erection of elegant stores, and the past poverty and rough building are fast passing away. Some conception of the energy and enterprise of both Mormon and Gentile merchants may be gleaned from the fact that edifices are now being erected with brick from Philadelphia, and iron fronts from New York. The First National Bank has met with rare prosperity, and very properly has taken the lead in inaugurating the "iron age" in building.

With such indications of the stability of commerce, and the inevitable growth and development of the Territory, how strangely read the prophecies of the Tabernacle! Twenty-five years ago, when the exiles were poor and

The First National Bank of Utah.

needy, and but a little higher in the scale of social life than the Indians, it was natural enough for Brigham to prophesy of the dissolution of all society. The end seemed near enough to him then, but he has since become wealthy, and his name is found to railroad bonds, whose redemption is dated later than the time when he professes to believe the second coming of Christ will be!

* For several years the Tabernacle sermons abounded with predictions about famine and desolation.

43

Whatever follies have been committed by enthusiasts in fixing the date for the reappearance of the Son of Man, Brigham is fully resolved that the whispering of the "Spirit" to Joseph Smith * shall in no way interfere with his own mundane affairs. Instead of preparing for this great event, which was, in the beginning of Mormonism, a matter of faith with all the Saints, Brigham is bent on the accumulation of everything of worldly value, as if this "wicked world" were to "wag" on for ever. Every act of his life shows that he has no faith in the predictions of his predecessor.

Had Brigham Young been a man of benevolence, intellect, refinement, and consistency, and had he cultivated the better qualities of the human nature that he once had in his power to mould, the present age would have seen recorded in the history of the world the establishment of another powerful sect—a sect which would probably have become one of the distinctive religions of the ages yet to come. As it is, Brigham has shorn the faith of the Saints of its strength, and robbed it of the charm of its early days ; and the lesson left indelibly inscribed upon his work, and upon that of the latter days of his predecessor, is that the civilization of the world is progressive, and that the whisperings of that still, small voice from the Mount opposite Jerusalem, and not the thunders from the Mount in the Wilderness, will influence and direct the advancing mind of the nineteenth century.

* In his Autobiography, Joseph Smith says :

"I was once praying very earnestly to know the time of the coming of the Son of Man, when I heard a voice repeat the following: 'Joseph, my son, if thou livest *until thou art eighty-five years old*, thou shalt see the face of the Son of Man ; therefore, let this suffice, and trouble me no more in this matter!'"

Joseph was born in 1805, consequently the great event is fixed for 1890.

[WINNEMUCCA MINES.]   B I N G H A M   C A Ñ O N .   [KELSEY TUNNEL.]

CHAPTER LVI.

THE MINES OF UTAH.

THE POTOSI OF THE WEST.—Early Anticipations of the Treasures of Utah—Ore discovered in the Mountains—First Discovery of Argentiferous Galena—Enterprise of General P. E. Connor—The United States Soldiers "prospect" for Mines—Mr. Eli B. Kelsey lectures on the Wealth of Utah—Incorporation of the West Jordan Mining Company—First Smelting-Furnace erected at Stockton—Rush Valley Smelting Company formed—Waiting for the Railroad—First Shipments of Ore—The Utah Central Railroad—Rich Ores in Ophir District—Silveropolis—Valuable Mines in East Cañon—Colonel E. D. Buel's Works in Cottonwood—Numerous Furnaces erected—Results of Inexperience—First Mill in Utah—Extraordinary Success—Large Shipments of Bullion and Ores—The Emma Mine—Formation of Veins of Ore—The Action of Water and Volcanic Force—Statistics of the Emma Mine—Its Immense Value—*Bonanzas*—Extraordinary Dividends to Proprietors—Southern Mines—True Fissure-Veins—Their Importance—Solfataric Action—The Mineral Springs—The Staples of the Utah Mines—Silver and Lead—Gold in Bingham Cañon—Gold in Sevier River—Quartz Mines—Gold near Ogden—Iron and Lead Ores—Supply of Fuel—Gradual Improvements—Scarcity of Wood—Discoveries of Coal—Building Material—Importance of a Valid " Title "—Development of Locations—Contested Claims—Commissioner Drummond's Decision—The Vast Mineral Resources of Utah—Importance of the Territory—Its Beauty, Wealth, Capabilities, and Claims to Attention.

IN launching the timber logs down the mountain sides, occasionally a piece of lead ore, that had been disintegrated from ledges of that mineral, would be revealed to the sight of " the brethren," and from these accidental circumstances arose the impression among the Saints that there were valuable minerals in the mountains. It was also seriously believed that there were large numbers of gold ledges somewhere ready to be revealed for " the building up of Zion," the embellishment

of the Temple, and the general comfort and pleasure of the
Saints, whenever they had gained the experience necessary to
make a prudent use of the precious ore.

When the *furore* created by the discovery of gold in California attacked the Saints and was drawing some of them away
to the Pacific coast, the Prophet used to hold the victims of
that fever up to ridicule in his sermons, and promised the Saints
who stayed at home greater wealth there in the harvest-fields,
and a far greater amount of wealth in the time to come, for he
knew where the article was in such great abundance that he
could "go out and bring in a wagon-load of gold" if it were
necessary to do so. But "the Lord" wanted the Saints to
build themselves homes, make themselves farms, and, when
they had been well tried in poverty, He would reveal to
them "the hidden treasures of His storehouse."

Many years ago, the Author stood by the side of Brigham
at his office door when he told a prominent bishop of the Methodist Church, who was passing through the city, that, from
where they then stood and chatted, he could see where there
was more gold than ever the Saints would want to use, unless
it were in the manufacture of culinary vessels, ornamentation,
or for "paving the streets of the New Jerusalem." Brigham
doubtless believed what he said. He could from his office
door look to a range of mountains where a "great discovery
"of pure *gold*" had been made, but its locality was to be sacredly kept a secret which no one knowing would divulge.
Years later, the "pure gold" turned out to be a large body of
pyrites of iron in a crystallized form, which to the inexperienced
eye had all the appearance of gold! The belief that large
quantities of gold exist in the mountains still remains; and
that "the Lord" would not permit the Gentiles to discover it,
was a frequent theme in the Tabernacle.

Many a time Brigham has ridiculed, in Sunday sermons,
the Gentile prospectors, and told them that they were blind
and could not see the precious metals when they were even
lying before their eyes, and frequently they would "stub their
"toes" against the ores and knew not what hurt them; and
then, with a dash of inspiration, he would comfort them with
the assurance that they would never discover them until he

[Brigham] was willing that they should be discovered. "If ever "they discover them, *it shall be over my faith.*"

While confidence was entertained that "the Lord" would guard the treasures of the mountains for His Saints, and the Prophet was mocking the would-be miners, the first discovery of a ledge of argentiferous galena was made by a lady—the wife of a surgeon of the California Volunteers, under the command of Colonel Connor.

A portion of the horses of the California Volunteers had been sent to Bingham Cañon to graze, and with them a company of men as a guard. A picnic party of officers and their wives from Camp Douglas was improvised, and Bingham was selected, as the troops were there. During the rambles of the party on the mountain-sides, this lady, who had a previous acquaintance with minerals in California, picked up a loose piece of ore. The Volunteers immediately prospected for the vein, discovered it, stuck a stake in the ground, made their location, and from that hour Utah has been known to the world as a rich mining country.

Colonel Connor, elated by this discovery, published to the world that there were minerals in Utah upon the domain of the United States; and all were free to prospect; and that his troops should afford all necessary protection to the prospector and miner. He had had no occupation for his troops—they were eating the bread of idleness, and were discontented at being detained in Utah, and not taking part in the war. The discovery in Bingham was opportune, to favour prospecting, and it would appease the men and give them the chance of possibly enriching themselves and the country. An order was promulgated that a certain number of men would be furloughed to prospect, and every facility afforded them to travel within certain boundaries. Wearing the blue, and the honourable sign "U. S.," they could enter what cañons they pleased. Thus to Colonel Connor, and the California Volunteers under his direction, is the honour due for the first discoveries in Utah.

Mr. Eli B. Kelsey, thoroughly breaking off from Mormonism, and believing that the hour had fully come to develop the mineral resources of the Territory, started out in the old missionary style to lecture upon Utah in the Atlantic and Pacific States, in the summer of 1870. He wrote to the papers, spoke to "boards of trade," published a pamphlet, and created quite an interest among capitalists, and was the means of sending into the mining districts a hundred thousand dollars in the fall of 1870. The first of Eastern capitalists who, at this time, was converted, was an enterprising merchant of New York, William M. Fliess, Esq., who joined Mr. Kelsey, and advanced the "working capital" required to develop some valuable mines. From that time capital has flowed into Utah, and wealth has been dug out of the mountains in such abundance —in proportion to the capital and labour employed—as to justify the hope that Utah will yet be the first mining country in the world.

The following article has been written and compiled expressly for this work by a gentleman well acquainted with mining work, who visited and studied the

MINES OF UTAH.*

On the 17th of September, 1863, Captain A. Heitz, with a number of soldiers, found the first vein of argentiferous lead ore in Bingham Cañon. The first mining record is that of the West Jordan mine, in favour of one Ogilvie, and some others. In the following December, a mining district was formed and named the West Mountain Mining District. It covered all the Oquirrh range of mountains, from Black Rock at the southern end of Salt Lake, south of the 40th parallel of latitude. But little work was done in the new discovery until the following spring. In the interim two other ledges had been discovered, namely, the Galena mine (on the 26th of January, 1864), and the Empire (February 6, 1864) ; both contiguous to the original discovery.

In the month of March following, a military post was established, known as Camp Relief, near the present site of the town of Stockton, in Rush Valley, Tooele County, and several companies of cavalry were posted there, who, excited to a high pitch by the recent successes of some of their comrades in arms in mineral discoveries, availed themselves of every possible opportunity when off duty to explore for ledges, or to develop such mines as they had already located. On the 11th of June following, at a miners' meeting held at the camp, the Rush Valley Mining District was formed, embracing all the western slope of the Oquirrh range from its northern to its southern limits. The eastern side, sloping into Salt Lake

* Colonel E. D. Buel kindly placed at the Author's disposal a voluminous and valuable manuscript on the " Mining Districts of Utah," from which much information has been taken for this article.

Valley, still retains the original name of West Mountain District. In the summer of 1864, the West Jordan Mining Company was incorporated under the laws of California, and work by a tunnel was commenced on the mine, at a cost of sixty dollars per foot, which could now be done for ten dollars. Blasting-powder was at that time $25 a keg; now it is less than one-sixth of that price, and labour is also more abundant.

The first smelting-furnace in the Territory was erected at Stockton, in 1864, by General Connor. He at this time became aware of the importance of having the mineral interest developed to the fullest possible extent, and induced a large number of his California friends to enter into the enterprise. The Rush Valley Smelting Company was organized at the same time, by the military officers at Camp Douglas; and a furnace was built by them at Stockton.

General Connor followed, with his second furnace, on the reverberatory plan, with an inclined flue, one hundred and fifty feet long. During the summer and fall of 1864, furnaces were built by the following parties, in and around Stockton and Rush Valley (mining prospects innumerable having by that time been located in the neighbourhood), viz.: The St. James; Finnerty; J. W. Gibson; Nichols & Brand; Hartnet; Davids & Company; and one cupola blast-furnace by Johnson, Monheim & Company. A cupelling furnace was also built by Stock & Weberling, in the same year.

But the treatment of ores by smelting was a task new to these Californians, and their experience in milling the gold ores of their State was of no service to them in this task. This disadvantage was increased by the fact that charcoal was not abundant, that rates of transportation were excessively high, and both the materials of which the furnaces were built, and those used in the daily operations, were very dear. These are circumstances which would tax the ability of the most experienced; and the Californians, unused to the work, failed entirely. A good deal of money was spent, with no result, excepting the establishment of the fact that the ores were easy to treat. During this time of trial, the usual history of new mining-fields was repeated, and companies which were organized with high hopes spent large sums, and became bankrupt.

The Knickerbocker and Argenta Mining and Smelting Company was organized in New York, to operate in Rush Valley, and expended about one hundred thousand dollars in the purchase of mines and the material for working them. But, owing to the impossibility of making medium and low-grade ores pay, at such a distance from the market, the company lost their money, and abandoned the enterprise. Thus, after two years of steady, earnest, hopeful toil—from the time of the first discovery in 1863, to the same month in 1865—the business of mining had to be suspended to await the advent of the "iron horse," which was to bring renewed vitality to the occupation of the miner.

With the failure to work the mines profitably, came the disbanding of the volunteer troops, in the latter part of 1865-6. Their places could

now be filled by the regulars—the rebellion by this time having been suppressed—and, as the owners and locators (who were principally military
men) could not subsist on non-paying mines, the question arose as to how
their rights could be secured while they were seeking employment elsewhere. Their method of solving the difficulty has resulted in the greatest
injury to the cause which had its rise in their energy and determination.
They called miners' meetings, and amended the by-laws of the district in
such a manner as to make claims perpetually valid, which had had a certain but very small amount of work done upon them. For the performance of this work, a certificate was given by the district recorder. This
certificate prohibited all subsequent relocation of the ground. In consequence of this provision, the mines of Stockton long lay under a ban,
and it is only since the wonderful discoveries made in neighbouring
cañons, that mining has been energetically resumed there. While the
operations, detailed above, drew attention chiefly to the Rush Valley
mines, discoveries were gradually becoming numerous in other districts.

The first discovery of silver-bearing lead ore had been made in the
Wahsatch range, in Little Cottonwood Cañon, and in Mountain Lake, in
the summer of 1864, by General Connor, but nothing was done towards
development until the district was organized, in the fall of 1868 ; when,
for the first time, operations of any extent were begun on the mines by
Messrs. Woodhull, Woodman, Chisholm, Reich, and others. The first
shipments of galena ore from the Territory were made in small quantities
by Messrs. Woodman & Co., Walker Brothers, and Woodhull Brothers, of
Little Cottonwood ore, in July, 1868, being the first products of the Emma
mine. Several other shipments were made, in the fall of that year, by
the same parties. The completion of the Utah Central Railroad to Salt
Lake City, in January, 1870, presented the long-looked-for opportunity
of embarking with certainty in the business of mining.

During the fall of 1868, and the spring of 1869, mining was taken hold
of with "a will," and it was soon proved, beyond a question, that the
mines of Utah were possessed of real merit. What better proof can be
looked for than the fact that from their first discovery they were not only
self-sustaining, but highly remunerative ? The first shipment of ore to
market having proved a success, work was pushed on with the utmost
vigour on the mines already discovered. This was especially the case
in Little Cottonwood district, on such mines as the Flagstaff, Emma,
North Star, Savage, Magnet, Monitor, and others. Thus an impetus was
given to the business of prospecting for mines all over the Territory ; and
this led to the innumerable discoveries subsequently made. The export
of ores has increased from a few irregular weekly shipments, as in the fall
of 1868, and throughout 1869, to that of a regular and constant stream,
during the summer months, of from four hundred to six hundred tons
weekly. In one month the Walker Brothers shipped 4,000 tons. In the
two months—August and September, 1872—2,458 tons of ore, and 1,363
tons of silver-bearing lead and iron, were sent out of the Territory. The

ALTA CITY, LITTLE COTTONWOOD.

[ORIGINAL SKETCH, BY A MISER, 1875.]

latter item shows what progress has been made in smelting the ores within the limits of the Territory itself.

It was during the excitement produced by the very rich developments made on the Emma and other mines of Little Cottonwood, that "horn," or chloride silver ores, of a very rich character, were discovered in East Cañon—now known as Ophir District. The first location in this district was made on the 23d of August, 1870, and was named Silveropolis. This location was soon followed by many others of a similar kind of mineral, all proving, at the surface, to be very rich—such as the Tampico, Mountain Lion, Mountain Tiger, Petaluma, Zella, Silver Chief, Defiance, Virginia, Monarch, Blue Wing, and many others, with promising prospects. All were found on what is known as Lion and Tiger Hills, immediately south of Ophir City; and the ores (unlike those of Cottonwood) are adapted to mill treatment alone.

At the same time, prospecting was going on upon the north side of Ophir, where many very extensive ledges of lead ore, carrying silver, were found; which ores are adapted to the smelting-process only. A remarkable distinction is to be noticed in the character of the ores on either side of the cañon, the bottom of which appears to be the dividing-line. On the north side, at the distance of not more than one-third of a mile, is found a combination of sulphides of iron, lead, arsenic, antimony, and zinc —the iron predominating, and carrying silver in appreciable quantities, with fifteen per cent. to forty per cent. of lead. On the south side, distant from the cañon about one mile, in a direct line, the silver occurs as chloride, with little or no base metal. But, small as the quantity of the other minerals is, they contain lead, molybdanum, antimony, and zinc, and therefore few of the mines yield ore that can be *well* treated without roasting. Probably fifty or sixty per cent. may be taken as the average yield of those ores in the mill, when they are treated raw. But a proper roasting increases this to eighty-five and even ninety per cent., and upwards. Some mines yield a remarkably pure chloride-ore—a dolomitic limestone containing true chloride of silver in a very pure condition.

It was at the time of these discoveries that the district now known as "Ophir" was formed in that part of the Oquirrh range known as East Cañon, and originally included in the Rush Valley district. Some forty locations had been made as early as 1864 and 1865. The conditions under which the ore exists in these mines is somewhat peculiar. It is in concentrations, which are often small and exceedingly rich, or larger and less concentrated, though still very rich. Mines were opened, which, when the overlying earth was removed, disclosed a narrow vein, exhibiting along its length a number of "boulders" highly impregnated with chloride of silver. These frequently assayed from $5,000 to $20,000 a ton; * though their value would vary very much in different parts of the same mass. As

---

* The Walker Brothers shipped west from the Silveropolis 40 tons of ore, which netted $24,000, of the first workings of that mine.

a rule, the ore of East Cañon may be estimated at $80 to $150 per ton in value, though considerable quantities run much higher. But the marvellous stories of the $10,000 and $20,000 ore, found in boulders, attracted the attention of prospectors in other parts of the West; and these discoveries in Ophir, together with the wealth of the "Emma," have probably done more than any thing else to bring about that strong tide of immigrating prospectors which has so rapidly raised Utah to the position of a first-rate mining-field. At all events, they would probably have been sufficient for the work, had the other discoveries been of less importance than they really are.

The working of these mines not only opened new districts, but revived the activity of those which had suffered partial abandonment, and at present there is not one district where important works are not going on. Great encouragement was also received from Eastern and foreign capitalists. Important sales were made, and a great deal of money brought in as working capital. At the same time a number of smelting-works were built. The amount of ore which these were capable of treating is variously estimated at from 200 to 400 tons per day; but few of them are now running. In June, 1870, the Woodhull Brothers built a furnace eight miles south of Salt Lake City, at the junction of the State road with Big Cottonwood Creek. It did some service in testing practically the ores of the Territory, and from these works was shipped the first bullion produced from the mines of Utah. It was smelted from ores of the Monitor and Magnet, and other Cottonwood mines.

These works were soon followed by the Badger State Smelting Works, about four miles south of the city of Salt Lake, on the State road, which were commenced in August, 1870. They produced their first bullion on the 18th of March, 1871. The next works were those of Jennings & Pascoe, immediately north of the city, at the Warm Springs. They contained reverberatory furnaces, which are not well adapted to the average ores of Utah, but are useful for the preparation of galena ore for the blast-furnace. A cupola or blast-furnace has since been added to these works, increasing their value greatly.

The next, and best designed works of any built in the Territory until a late period, were those of Colonel D. E. Buel, at the mouth of Little Cottonwood Cañon. The smelting-works of Buel & Bateman, in Bingham Cañon, which followed, were built on the same plan as those in Little Cottonwood.

During the winter of 1870–1, Messrs. Jones & Raymond built furnaces in East Cañon for the purpose of treating the lead-ores of that district. A renewal of operations also took place in Stockton, and the works there have suffered greater vicissitudes than any others in the Territory. Tintic, a new district, saw the next establishment built. But, during the year 1871, furnaces were erected in all quarters : in Little Cottonwood, by Jones & Pardee ; in Big Cottonwood, by Weightman & Co. ; in Bingham Cañon, by Bristol & Daggett ; in American Fork, by Holcombe, Sevenoaks

THE PIONEER MILL, OPHIR DISTRICT, EAST CANON.

& Co., and others. These were nearly all shaft-furnaces, rather rude in construction, though with some well built furnaces among them. The only works which deserve notice, for the introduction of good metallurgical models, are those of Robbins & Co., who built a large reverberatory furnace for reducing the ore by charcoal, after preliminary roasting ; and the works of Colonel Buel, in Little Cottonwood, where the later constructions of German metallurgists were introduced with good judgment and effect. The furnaces which Colonel Buel placed in his Cottonwood and Bingham Cañon works have been repeatedly copied in later-erected establishments, and have proved themselves as serviceable in this country as abroad.

Thus, sixteen furnaces were built in as many months, and the number has since been increased more than one-half; but it cannot be said that great success has attended them. Few have continued in active operation, and fewer still work with the regularity necessary to success. It is impossible to doubt that a history like this must be the result of inexperience. It is but a repetition of the course of affairs in Nevada, where men accustomed to the amalgamation of gold undertook to treat silver ores, which require a very different process. They at first ascribed their failures to some peculiarity of the ores, which were thought to be different from any others in the world; but, now, they confess that the cause of their difficulties was simply ignorance. Undoubtedly, that is the real secret of the trouble experienced by smelters in Utah; and doubtless, when they have become more experienced, they will not hesitate to acknowledge that ignorance of the work was the cause of their first failures, instead of giving the numerous excuses that are now current.

In addition to the foregoing means of reduction, there was built in Ophir District, East Cañon, a first-class crushing and amalgamating mill, in May and June, 1871, by the Walker Brothers, of Salt Lake City. It is known as the Pioneer Mill. It has fifteen stamps, and was built by the firm to work the ores of the Silveropolis, Tiger, Rockwell, Zella, Silver-Chief, and other mines—the mill-process alone being adapted to the ores of that section of Ophir known as Lion Hill, where horn chloride silver ores are found. There are also four or five "Mexican arastas" in successful operation in East Cañon. The mill-men have met with better success in Utah than the smelters, for they are engaged in a task familiar to them ; the process being the same as that in use in Nevada and some parts of California.

Notwithstanding all the discouragement which has been met with hitherto by the smelters, the progress of mining in Utah has been wonderful. Remembering that the first really practical work done towards the development of the mining interests was commenced only in the fall of 1868, and making due allowance for the inclement season then at hand, which the miners had to pass through in such high altitudes as those where the mines are situated, it will be understood how it was that the summer of 1869 had progressed so far before work to any appreciable amount was done. Considering the shortness of the time, the record of what has been done is most extraordinary.

From the summer of 1869 to the 25th of September, 1871, there were shipped from the Territory 10,000 tons of silver and gold ores, of the gross value of $2,500,000; of bullion, or pig-lead, containing gold and silver, 4,500 tons, of the gross value of $1,237,000; copper ores, 231 tons, of the gross value of $6,000. Salt also has been exported to the extent of 1,100 tons, of the value of $4,000 ; and silver bars, obtained by milling chloride ores, have produced $120,000. The annual product of gold from Bingham Cañon, by improved appliances for washing and sluicing, has been increased from $150,000 to $250,000. The number of districts by exploration and location have grown from two, as in 1868, to thirty-two in 1871. Since June, 1870, there have been erected eighteen smelting-furnaces, built at an aggregate cost of $200,000, several of which are producing bullion.

If this were a professional mining work, it would be an error to single out a few of the most remarkable mines in Utah for description, to the exclusion of the great number of lesser mines. As it is not intended to offer here a guide, either to the miner or the speculator, but, on the contrary, to present the average disinterested reader with information about the great works of nature in the Territory, as well as the history of the people who have settled it, no impropriety will be committed in discussing the character of the famous Emma mine, that has attracted especial attention.

Nature has formed her mineral deposits in various ways. Sometimes volcanic forces have opened a cleft in the rocks, which has been filled by minerals introduced either in solution or in a gaseous form. Sometimes the mass of ore has been withdrawn, by means which are still mysterious to us, from the neighbouring rocks. Other veins, again, are merely cracks in the rock, formed by contraction as the mass became more and more dense, or more and more dry, examples of which action may be constantly seen in clay beds lying in the sun, and these cracks have been filled from the surface. But the method to which the student of geology in the West is forced chiefly to give his attention is, the formation of veins by hot waters. There is a lively and constant circulation of water within the bowels of the earth, and, little as the ancient alchemists imagined it, water is *the* "universal solvent." The action of these subterranean waters is greatly increased by various substances which they already hold in solution, and also in many instances by their high temperature. A hot spring bursting through the narrow crevice in the rock will not only wear away a larger channel, but it will enlarge its path by taking the solid rock into solution and bearing it also away. It is supposed that this action has been enormously intensified in the case of vein formation, from the fact that frequently the waters, springing from a great depth, are under immense pressure, and at a temperature which is very much above that of boiling water, as it is known on the surface of the earth.

Under these circumstances, the magnitude of the caverns, whose ex-

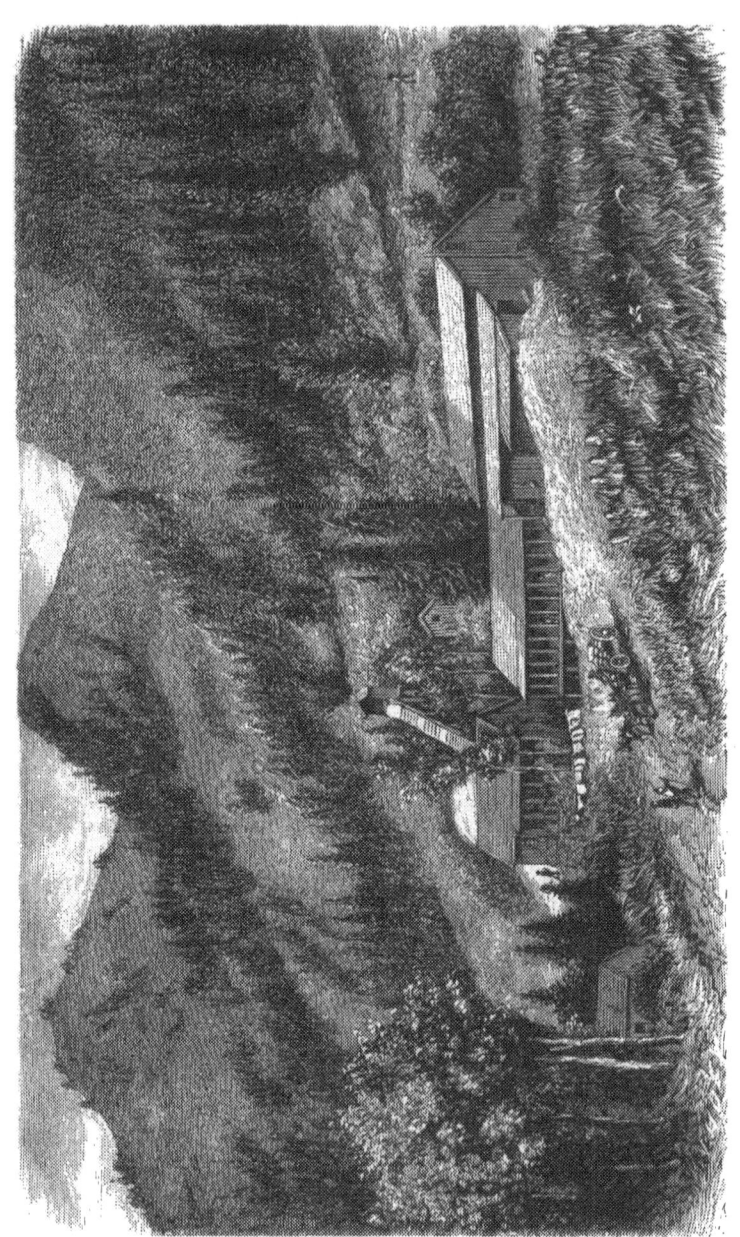

THE EMMA MINE, LITTLE COTTONWOOD.

cavation we can ascribe to no other cause than the action of water, appears less marvellous. The same description of caverns are found in the East, though usually empty, or else filled with some other substance than ore, as clay and other minerals. But it is in the West that the manifestations of this action are most widely found. The theory just mentioned, respecting the origin of most of our mines, may be regarded as the most probable one, as we not only find almost innumerable hot springs throughout the whole mountain-region of the Territories, and springing up even in our very mines themselves, when, in our efforts to obtain the ore, we remove the rock that has choked their passage, but we also have in this country springs which are still forming mines. In Georgia there is a hot spring which deposits gold quartz, and we have only to imagine a time of volcanic disturbance, leaving behind it a period of intense solfataric activity, covering the whole Western country, to see this action, so feebly illustrated in Georgia, become the source of many thousands of mineral deposits. The word 'solfataric,' used to describe the process by which these mines are formed, is derived from the name of a volcano near Naples, and means all the forces of a volcano which are not included in the actual eruption of lava.

In every mine it is an important question to ascertain its extent, and, since we cannot penetrate the earth with our eyes, no resource is left but to determine the mode in which the vein was formed. If we can make sure that a given mine is in a great cleft formed by forces far below, and afterwards filled from the same source, we may feel confidence in the long continuance of our supply of ore. But the difficulty with veins which are formed by hot waters, or by any sort of solfataric action, is that we can never ascertain except by actual trial how far below the surface the sources of the deposits are to be found. Some mines, like the Comstock, are vast in every direction—length, depth, and breadth; but the Comstock is a true fissure-vein, the crevice having been formed by volcanic force, and afterwards filled by hot waters which deposited the ore. Others are so shallow as to be nearly worthless as mines.

The Emma in many respects rivals the Comstock, and in some excels it. Of less remarkable length, its width is enormous, and it has been explored for 230 feet in depth, with every prospect of much longer continuance. The history of this important mine can be given in a few words; its discovery has already been mentioned. Since the great body of ore was opened, it has been developed until the work done and its results are as follows:

Depth of workings,	. . . .	. 230 feet.	
Breadth "	. . . .	. 6 to 40 "	
Length "	. . . .	. 475 "	
Cubic feet excavated, .	. . .	about 500,000	
Tons of ore,	. . . . .	. about 30,000	
Tons of waste and third-class ore,	.	about 15,000	
Value of sales (September, 1872), about		$3,000,000	

The profit on these sales has been immense, and probably bears a greater proportion to the expenses than that of any other large mine in the country. The cost of mining and raising the ore for a period of time had been only about eight per cent. of its value, a proportion remarkably low, and due to the soft nature of the ore, which rarely requires blasting. Its value per ton, at that time, averaged about $190 or $200, and in some of the later workings ore having a value of more than $200 has been found, but the general average of the Emma first-class ore ranges about $150 per ton, and second class $80. At present, about 100 tons of ore are extracted daily.

The distinctive peculiarity of this mine is not its size, for many are larger, but it is what is called in mining language a *bonanza* of very unusual dimensions. In every mine there are alternations of ore and rock— the latter worthless. When the mass of ore reaches an unusual size, it is called a *bonanza*. Some of these form the wonders of mining history, as, for instance, that great *bonanza* of Potosi, in South America, from which scores of millions of dollars were taken. Attention was first attracted to the Comstock lode by the great *bonanza* of the Gould & Curry mine. The Poorman lode in Idaho contained a *bonanza* which yielded the largest masses of silver sulphide that have ever been seen. As yet the workings on the Emma have been confined to this great *bonanza*, with the exception of some casual trials of the vein, outside its limits, and, until the great deposit begins to show some signs of exhaustion, this course will probably be continued. There will then remain the prospect of finding paying bodies of ore in the vein, as well as the chance of a second large mass. But the importance of that which is already under exploration may be judged from the fact that the ore removed, with that remaining, is said to be worth fifteen million dollars. There is nothing in this to indicate the approaching end of the works. It is quite within the power of nature to have formed there an ore-mass which may continue to the greatest depths. The geology of the district has not yet been sufficiently well studied to enable a judgment to be formed of the future prospects of the mine, but so far as is known there is nothing to indicate a discontinuance of this *bonanza* at a less depth than five to ten times that which has been reached.

Remarkable success has attended the mine from the hour the great deposit was reached. The dividends, since it was placed on the London market [November, 1871], have been $75,000 per month, and still, owing to continued developments, it shows much larger reserves of ore to-day than it did a year ago ; the nett value of the ore in one portion of the mine alone being estimated by reliable experts at over $10,000,000. No signs of exhaustion are apparent, but, on the contrary, the workings are steadily sinking lower, and developing at every foot still larger quantities of ' metal' increasing in value.

Active mining has not been in progress in this deposit for more than two and a half summers, but in that time the profits have, as before stated, amounted to about three million dollars. Dividends to the amount of one and a half per cent. a month on the capital [$5,000,000] have already been paid. The present earnings are double that amount.

On the same hill are a number of very rich mines, leading to the conclusion that the Emma Hill is a grand repository of argentiferous ore. Noticeably there is the Flagstaff higher up and west of the Emma, which has shown great richness. Again, almost due north, about 700 feet higher up the hill, a cluster of four mines—the Last Chance, Hiawatha, Montezuma, and the Savage—covering a lineal measurement of over 7,000 feet, which are said to have developed ores equal in richness to the Emma. The Emma was sold to English capitalists, in the spring of 1872, for £1,000,000 sterling. The Flagstaff was sold in the same market for £300,000. The group of mines—Last Chance, Hiawatha, Montezuma, and Savage, were sold to Detroit and New York capitalists in the fall of 1872, for $1,500,000, and incorporated under the laws of the State of New York, under the title of the Winsor-Utah Silver Mining Company. These three great companies are sanguine that their mines are inexhaustible—during this generation, at least.

South of this cañon is the American Fork; north of it is Big Cottonwood; both of which are worthy neighbours. In fact, the whole district, composed of these three cañons, and perhaps also those over the range to the east of them, is one of the most remarkable collections of mineral deposits in the world. It is, however, in no way remarkable that such concentrations of mineral wealth should occur. On the contrary, it is quite in accordance with the conclusions formed from experience in other quarters of the world. There is no region of the globe where every mountain-peak in a long range is a volcano. Only one or two are active, and about these are found the evidences of disturbance. In the same way the lesser volcanic forces, which have been the origin of the mines, have broken forth at intervals, and left nests of ramifying veins.

Parley's Park is the name given to a district east of the Cottonwood, and just over the range. A new mine—the McHenry—just discovered there, is said to be one of the wonders of mining.

South of the Cañons which are at present the principal centres of activity, are a number of others which are known to contain deposits of ore, and it is highly probable that the mineral district reaches far southward, perhaps to Mexico. Some of these cañons have been hastily examined. In others a good deal of work has been done; important mines have been opened, and they are only waiting for the railroad to reach them, to rise into importance equal to that of the neighbouring cañons which have enjoyed better opportunities. Camp Floyd, forty miles west of Salt Lake City, is one of these, and there the Mormon Chief, Sparrowhawk, Silver Cloud, and other mines, have been opened and worked with great success. Tintic is another promising district, and Star district, nearly 200 miles from Salt Lake City, is another, while the mines in Sevier district have attracted a great deal of attention. In truth, these districts are important in proportion to the nearness of the railroad, and, as that progresses southward, district after district may be expected to assume its proper position as a source of mining activity.

When a vein is formed in a fissure already existing in the rock, and
formed from below, the probabilities are that the body of ore continues
for more than four thousand feet in depth, which is the present limit of
ability to penetrate the crust of the earth by machinery. Such veins are
called *true fissure-veins*, and are held in such esteem that every miner
labours to prove his own vein to be of this class. But it is probable that
the number of this kind of vein is comparatively small in the West. This
rule holds good in other countries besides America, and it is a remarkable
fact that the buyers of mines expend their energies in seeking a class of
veins which the history of mining does not prove to be of first importance. It would be a discovery of great value if we could learn to judge
of the depth from which the veins of any particular district were filled;
but, not usually having that knowledge in our power, we must trust, for
the present, to the evidences of the miner's pick and drill. It is for this
reason that the discovery of a great deposit, like the Emma, draws such
numbers of ore-seekers to its neighbourhood. Not the least noticeable
fact, in connection with the Utah mines, is, that nearly every cañon shows
at least several of these greater productions of nature. In Little Cottonwood, the Emma, Flagstaff, Davenport, the Winsor-Utah mines, and North
Star, are the leading mines on one side; in American Fork, there are
the Miller and the Pittsburg; in Bingham, the Winnemucca, West Jordan, and Buel and Bateman mines take the lead for magnitude; and, in
East Cañon, on one side, the Last Chance, Silver Shield, Velocipede,
Chicago, Erie, and other mines; and on the other are the Tiger, Zella, Lion,
Silver Chief, Silver Exchange, Sunnyside. In Dry Cañon, adjoining East
Cañon, there are also good paying mines—of which the Mono is the most
prominent.

As has been already observed, many remnants of the solfataric action,
which produced the mineral deposits, remain in Utah; near Salt Lake
City are hot springs used as public baths. The water is strongly impregnated with sulphur, and contains numerous salts. Similar springs, and
of a still higher temperature, are at a little greater distance. In Oneida
County are the Soda Springs, so called; and, in fact, these springs are
found in great numbers in the Territory. On the road to East Cañon,
there is a spring which supplies water so slightly tinctured with sulphur
that its taste is unperceived until after it has been drunk. Then a delicate flavour, far from unpleasant, remains in the mouth; and in other
respects this water is delicious.

Some of the mineral waters are not hot, but are rather of an icy cold-
ness, a number of such springs being found about seventy miles northeast
of Salt Lake City. But it would be a tiresome task to enumerate all the
mineral springs of Utah. Like all the Western regions, it has many a
"mountain-tap" whose refreshing and pungent waters have been drunk
by the trapper in fond remembrance of the cider from which he was separated by a thousand miles of wilderness.

The staples of the Utah mines are silver and lead; but gold is also found, and, in one cañon—Bingham—it has been mined for years with great profit. About one million dollars' worth of the precious metal is said to have been washed out of the gravel, and the sands are still very remunerative. Gold is also found in some of the lead mines, but whether it exists there as auriferous galena, or combined with the iron, which is also one of the constituents of the lead ore, can only be surmised. Auriferous galena has been found in other countries, but it is not common, and it is noticeable that the mines which show most gold contain also most iron. But Bingham Cañon is not the only spot in Utah where this metal is found. Many streams give evidence of the presence of gold in their sands, and, were the thorough means so well known in California applied to their working, Utah would be a gold-producing country of no mean order.

Gold-sands were worked in the Sevier River, in Juab County, as early as 1861, and, in a very rude way, paid two dollars to five dollars per man. Quartz-mines were also found in the same region in 1868–9, and the approach of the railroad will, perhaps, permit these ledges to be worked. The discovery of gold near Ogden, on the line of the Pacific Railway, in 1871, made a good deal of stir; but the importance of silver-mining in the Territory overshadows all other discoveries.

Copper has not yet been worked in the Territory. Deposits of the ore are reported, but thus far they do not seem to have authorized the investment necessary for mining-works. Tin and mercury ores are also reported, but in neither case with reasonable proof.

Next in importance to the mines of silver and lead are those materials which are necessary for the utilization of the ore. Chief of these are iron ore and fuel. Iron ore is put down as valuable in its relation to the lead ores, rather than for its possible use as a source of iron. Furnaces for smelting this ore for its metal have been erected in Iron County, about two hundred and thirty miles south of Salt Lake City, but that was before the railroad was finished. Fuel is not sufficiently abundant, and labour is too high, to make it at all certain that iron can yet be made in the Territory cheaper than it can be brought from the East.

But iron ore, or some product containing iron, is an absolute necessity in the treatment of lead ores. Utah has seen many furnaces built, but with an almost unceasing round of failures. It is impossible to give any other reason for the ill-success of so many adventurers, except the general one that they were ignorant of the work they undertook. But, if there is any one of their errors which is especially prominent, it is their failure to seek a cheap supply of iron ore. Instances have been known where the smelting of ore cost less than twenty dollars a ton for all expenses but the iron ore used; that alone amounted to fifteen dollars more. The reason of this heavy expense is, that the ore is mined in Wyoming Territory, and carted to the Pacific Railroad, on which it is carried to Salt Lake Valley, where another cartage of twenty or twenty-five miles farther increases the expense. For all this there is no need whatever. Utah contains a great number of

44

iron ore deposits which might be opened. Some are on the line of the railway, as in Weber Cañon, much nearer Salt Lake City than those from which ore is now drawn. Others are reported in other parts of the Territory, and there is strong probability that ore could be found within twenty miles of the principal mining cañons. A mine of this material convenient to the smelting-works would be of the greatest value, not only to its owners, but to the future of the Territory. It would decrease the cost of smelting, in many cases one-third, and would contribute so much to thorough work in the furnace that the furnace-owners of Utah would find it to their interest to combine for the purpose of seeking iron ore in their valley. Their dilemma will be greatly lessened when the Utah Southern Railroad finds its way to the great deposits of the southern counties; but it is needless to wait so long.

As to localities at present known, magnetic ore is reported at Devil's Gate, on the Weber River; specular ore on Church Island, in the Lake; hematite ore at Farmington, between Salt Lake City and Ogden, and at other places, in the Oquirrh Range, and to the southward.

Coal is really of secondary importance to iron, as to cost, but of course it is a *sine qua non* in smelting. The character of Utah ore is such that much of it requires twice the amount of iron ore as of coal, and at about the same or a greater cost per ton. Utah is not well wooded. It lies so far inland that it receives but little moisture from either ocean. Nothing but the intense cold of winter enables it to arrest what few vapours escape condensation on the Sierra Nevada and Rocky Mountains, and even in winter the dryness of the air is such during the intervals between the storms that the thick coating of snow evaporates with wonderful rapidity. These conditions are not favourable to the growth of timber, and Utah has little or no timber except in the mountain gorges, where it can be had in considerable abundance for mining purposes when roads are constructed. Fortunately, considerable deposits of coal are near at hand, and, though it is not of the best description, being a cross between lignite and bituminous coal, its value to the Territory is beyond expression. It can be used, and there is no fear that the mines will outlast it. Its price, too, is such that the enterprising metallurgist who undertakes the task of utilizing it in the right way will find himself greatly profited. As yet nothing is known of the exact extent of the coal-beds. They are found for more than one hundred miles along the line of the railroad, and other beds are known in the southern, or, more properly, the central part of the Territory. It is by no means impossible that other deposits will be found in the heart of Utah, and it is absolutely certain that the day is not far off when the smelters of the Territory will be forced to solve the problem of how to use their coal.

Of building-material Utah offers many sorts. The first houses of the Mormons were built of adobes or sun-dried bricks, a material which makes an admirably close shelter. Excellent clay, both for common and for fire bricks, is found. Of stone, there is quartzite, a hard, durable sandstone,

in almost every cañon.   Its colour is lighter than that used in the East, and
it is also of a livelier red.   Probably, in its numerous beds of limestone,
some good building-varieties will be found, but the rock in the neighbourhood of the mines has been so much altered by metamorphic action as to
destroy its usefulness as a building-material.   For the same reason, the
softer rocks discovered in the Plains are absent, or at least have not yet been
discovered in any quantity.   For building-lumber it is at present for the most
part dependent upon the great forests of the Nevada Mountains, though
its mining-lumber is cut near the mines in which it is to be used.   For
works which will bear a heavy cost, an excellent granite, light in colour
and wearing well, is at hand, and has been used in the foundations of the
Mormon Temple.

The great desideratum in a mining country is the assurance of being
in possession of a clear and valid title to property.   Without it, the rich-
est mine in the world is nothing but a source of interminable litigation
and most aggravating annoyance.   Owing to the peculiar difficulties which
beset the first mining prospectors in Utah, many were unable to work locations that were then made, and left the country.   Till work had been
performed sufficiently to develop the presence of ore, such "locations" of
course had no actual value, and not infrequently the "location," made one
week, would be abandoned for a better "prospect" the following week.
In this way, some untiring, hopeful men spread their names over many
pages of record, and ultimately retired, disgusted and broken in spirit,
from the further pursuit of the buried wealth.

In all mining countries, the hill-sides are honeycombed with such abandoned locations, and, in some of the now regularly organized mining-dis-
tricts of Utah, they had, at one time, a very serious aspect; but, fortunately, a contest over interests of considerable importance has led recently
to an important decision by the Commissioners of the Land-Office, that
sets at rest the question of unworked and undeveloped ancient claims, and
gives assurance and protection both to the honest miner and the enterprising capitalist.

Two discoveries had been made—the Last Chance and Hiawatha—in
Little Cottonwood Cañon, in the summer of 1870, almost in a direct line
with the Emma.   When the work on these discoveries developed to the
satisfaction of their owners, they were duly recorded, in the usual legal
way, both in the mining-district and with the County Recorder.   In January, 1872, application was made, by Colonel E. A. Wall, at the United
States Land-Office, for a patent covering the two mines.   Before the ninety
days' notice had expired, another party, J. W. Haskin, filed a sworn protest against the patenting of said claims, and averred that, "for the sum
"of one dollar," he had purchased certain prior-located claims, with which
the Last Chance and Hiawatha—for which the patents were then asked—
would come in contact to his injury.   Commissioner Drummond, after
maturely reviewing the claims of the protesting party, not only in the case

of the mines named, but in other similar claims, set aside the protest, and rendered a decision that must give great satisfaction to miners in general. He says :

"Old abandoned locations appear upon the records of every mining-district, which, provided the whereabouts of the locators can be ascertained, may be purchased for a mere trifle : this being true not only of Utah, but in the other mineral-producing States and Territories.

"In the great majority of these cases, these old locations were described upon the records in such a vague and indefinite manner that the *locus* could not by any possibility be determined with any degree of certainty from such record.

"To allow the interposition of the record of these abandoned, unoccupied claims to be a bar to proceedings for patent by *bona-fide* claimants of an actual well-defined vein or deposit, of which they have actual possession, and upon which they have made substantial improvements, without the clearest and most unquestionable proof of identity and actual conflict, would result in a virtual nullification of the Mining Act : these paper locations of undefined lodes, the *locus* of which cannot be determined, with any degree of certainty, from such records, being conveniently floated around so as to be made to conflict with any valuable mines in the same district, which confliction is usually discovered immediately after the *bona-fide* claimant has found his lode to be of value, and has applied for patent. . . . The records of all districts show almost innumerable 'locations' of claims as lodes where sufficient work was never done to test the fact whether such lode really had any existence or not.

"These locations were usually made years ago by various parties, who recorded a lode for almost every hole dug by them while out prospecting, whether any ore was found or not ; and to treat such records as valid adverse claims to property actually worked and occupied by *bona-fide* claimants would put it in the power of a few enterprising individuals to suspend, in a great measure, the execution of the mining statutes."

Though it may have been both unpleasant and expensive, to the parties directly interested in these and other great mines in Utah, to have been forced into litigation, their temporary misfortune, calling forth this decision, will be of lasting benefit to the future mining development of the country.

From what has been said, the reader will gather that Utah has great mineral resources. It is fully able to house and support any number of people. As a field for the tourist it offers attractions to be found nowhere else. Different from Nevada on the one hand, and from Colorado on the other, its scenery is most like that of the Austrian Alps, but on a far grander scale. Instead of valleys five or ten miles across, its mountains lie twenty or thirty miles apart, stretching a hundred miles away before they are lost to sight. The peculiar clearness of the air makes a vista of sixty miles appear like a day's walk, and more than one unsuspecting Eastern traveller has attempted to reach the mountains which lie so plainly in sight from Salt Lake City, in a walk before breakfast ! In one case, after two hours' walk, the gentleman found that he was still twelve miles from the foot of the mountain which he had expected to reach in half an hour. Utah deserves a visit. To the Eastern man the change is usually beneficial, and many a man overworked, but unable to find the right place to recuperate in, could purchase health by riding and driving through the sage-bush valleys of Utah, with just enough interest in the mines to give him occupation.

APPENDIX.

I.

[See page 617.]

THE following is the speech of Gov. John B. Weller, at the close of the examination of witnesses relative to the assassination of Dr. J. King Robinson :

"Gentlemen of the Jury, let us look for one moment at the circumstances connected with this case, as disclosed by the testimony : Doctor Robinson (aged 31 years) had resided in this city for three years, having previously been attached to the military forces as a surgeon. He was an amiable, quiet Christian, universally loved and respected. In March last he was married to a young lady of 18 years, of one of your most estimable families. Ascertaining that certain property, upon which the Warm Spring is found, near this city, was wholly unoccupied, and believing it to be a portion of the public domain, locates on it and proceeds to make improvements. Without any previous notice whatever, an armed force of the police is sent out by order of the city authorities, who destroy his buildings and eject him from the premises. He appeals, as was the bounden duty of a good citizen, to the organized tribunals of justice for redress. During the progress of the case his counsel raise the question before the Chief Justice of the Federal Court, that the city, because of the non-performance of certain acts, had no legal existence. This question was fully argued, and on the 19th day of October the Judge decided in favour of the city. Dr. Robinson gave notice of his intention to appeal. On the 11th day of October, a bowling-saloon, owned by the doctor, was destroyed by a gang of twenty or thirty men, part of whom were disguised. For this act, performed at midnight, a number of persons were arrested, and on the 13th day of October examined before the District Court. The Chief of Police and two of his subordinates were identified as parties in this affair, and bound over by the Chief Justice—the first in the sum of $2,000, and the other two in the sum of $1,500 each. On Saturday, the 20th, Dr. Robinson, under the advice of his counsel, goes to the house of the Mayor, to give notice that he intends to hold the city responsible for the damages which he had sustained by the wanton destruction of his property. The Mayor, as soon as he ascertained who he was, ordered him to leave his house. Great care is taken by the *Telegraph* newspaper to chronicle this act the next morning in the following terms:

" ' As Well Trained.—The admiration for Zebra, Napoleon, and Leopard, on Friday night, was "snuffed out" by the greater admiration for Dr. Ball-alley, as he cleared from the Mayor's house yesterday afternoon. His Honour had only to open the door, direct his finger, and the man of pills and bluster vamosed with a grace that fairly eclipsed little Leopard under the admirable direction of Bartholomew.'

" On the very next day after this publication, between the hours of 11 and 12 p. m., a man goes to the house of the doctor, after he had retired to bed, wakes him up, tells him that a brother of his (Jones) had broken his leg by the fall of a mule, that he was suffering very much and required his professional services immediately. The doctor hastily throws on his clothes and proceeds with this man upon what he regarded a mission of mercy. At a distance of 175 steps from his dwelling he was struck over the head two blows with some sharp instrument, and then immediately shot through the brain. The shriek of the doctor when he was struck, and the report of the pistol, were heard by a number of witnesses. Two gentlemen in a boarding-house (distant from the scene of murder about 150 steps), who had not yet retired to bed, hearing the noise, stepped to the window and saw three men running to the east at full speed. They went down-stairs, and in a very few minutes found the murdered man. One remains on the ground, and the other goes to the City Hall for the police. He finds the Chief and five of his men sitting by the stove, all of whom had shortly before returned from the circus. The Chief directs his men to go down at once and investigate the matter, and then retires to bed. Arriving at the scene of the murder, one policeman goes for Dr. Ormsby (a distance of some 300 yards), who is too much indisposed to go out. Three other physicians are sent for, who arrive in due time. The body is removed to Independence Hall, some fifty yards. In the meanwhile the poor wife is informed of the murder. She wildly rushes to the Hall and insists upon the removal of the body to the house. He is carried to the house, and in an hour expires. Previous to this the police return to the City Hall and retire to bed.

" One witness saw one of the assassins running from the spot towards the northwest; two witnesses saw three men running towards the east; three witnesses saw three men running south—making in all seven men at least engaged in the murder. Some of the witnesses saw the assassins at a distance of four or five feet. The spot selected for the deed was on the corner of one of the most public streets in the city. The moon was at its full and shining brightly. One witness says 'it was light enough to find a pin on the ground.' Between the place of murder and the house from which he was decoyed is, as I have said, 175 steps. Between these two points, on the same side of the street, there are five dwelling-houses, all occupied by families, and on the opposite side the same number. The nearest dwelling-house to the murder is forty feet.

"The shriek which preceded the report of the pistol was heard at a distance of 250 steps.

"The Chief of Police goes down to the scene of the murder the third day after. The Mayor is informed of the murder at 10 o'clock the day after it occurred.

"And upon this evidence I have a few plain questions to propound, which I will leave you and others to answer. I do not propose to discuss them, simply because I could not do so without increasing the excitement which already exists, and producing an exasperated state of feeling, which could not at the present time result in any public good:

"1. If my associate Judge Stout, the City Attorney, had been murdered under the circumstances Dr. Robinson was, would the police have exhibited a greater degree of vigilance and energy ?

"2. Would the attention of the 4,000 people who assembled at the 'Tabernacle' (where secular affairs are often discussed), on the succeeding Sabbath, have been called to the crime, and they exhorted to use every effort to ferret out the assassins?

"3. Could any prominent Mormon be murdered under the same circumstances, and no clew whatever found to the murderer ?

"4. Would any portion of the 500 special police have been called into requisition or ordered on duty ?

"5. Would any of the numerous witnesses who saw the assassins fleeing from their bloody work have been able to recognize and name them ?

"6. Have we not utterly failed to prove, after full investigation, that Dr. Robinson had a personal enemy in the world, and have we not proved that he had had difficulties with none except the city authorities ?

"7. Is there any evidence that he had done anything to make personal enemies, unless it was having the Chief of Police and two others bound over to answer a charge of riot ?

"8. Would he have been murdered if he had not by his land-claim raised a question as to the validity of the city charter ?

"9. Would the ten-pin alley have been destroyed if it had not been his property, and that he had a suit pending against the city ?

"10. Would the Mayor of the city have ordered him out of his house two days before he was murdered, if he had not understood that he claimed damages from the city for the wanton destruction of his property ?

"11. Is it not remarkable that a gang of men could go to a bowling-alley, nearly surrounded by houses, within 60 steps of the most public street of the city, between the hours of 11 and 12 at night, demolish the windows and break up with axes and sledges the alley, and no witnesses found to identify the men, or who knew anything whatever about the perpetrators of the act ?

"12. Are not the Jury satisfied that some witnesses have withheld evidence calculated to fasten guilt upon certain parties, because they feared personal violence?

"13. Is there not an organized influence here which prevents the detection and punishment of men who commit acts of violence upon the persons or property of ' Gentiles ?'

"14. If a Mormon of good standing had been murdered, would the Mayor, to whom the Chief of Police reports, have been informed of the act before 10 o'clock the next day ?

"15. Would the Chief of Police have gone to bed as soon as he heard of the crime, and waited three days before he visited the scene of the murder ?

"16. Was the murder committed for the purpose of striking terror into the ' Gentiles,' and preventing them from settling in this Territory ?

"17. Is it the settled policy of the authorities here to prevent citizens of the United States, not Mormons, from asserting their claims to a portion of the public domain in the regularly-organized judicial tribunals of the country ?

"18. Are all legal questions which may arise in this city between ' Mormons ' and ' Gentiles ' to be settled by brute force ?

"19. Do the public teachings of the ' Tabernacle ' lead the people to respect and obey the laws of the country, or do they lead to violence and bloodshed ?

"And now, gentlemen of the Jury, I have a few general remarks to submit upon some of the incidental questions alluded to in the course of the examination :

"I came here, as many persons well know, with no prejudices against the people who control this city and Territory. When they were driven out of Illinois and Missouri, I may have been familiar with the circumstances which led to the act, but I do not choose to go back and review them. It is enough to say that a strong impression was left upon my mind that they had been persecuted because of the peculiarities of the religion which they professed. Under these circumstances, it is scarcely necessary to say that my sympathies accompanied them in their weary pilgrimage over barren and desolate plains and stupendous mountains into these now pleasant valleys. Here they established settlements which, without their labour and industry, would have remained in the undisturbed possession of savages and wild beasts. The discovery of gold in California, the establishment of an Overland Mail, passing through this city, and the subsequent discovery of rich minerals, in Nevada on the west and Idaho and Montana on the north, afforded the people of Utah a ready market, and at high prices, for all the products of their labour. Without this the people would have remained isolated and their whole commerce would have consisted in a simple exchange of commodities amongst themselves, and this city would have been an inconsiderable town.

"I have said that I have no prejudices whatever against these people. I did not come here as a missionary or a moral reformer. I have endeavoured to obey the laws, respect the rights and opinions, and what I may regard as the prejudices of the people. The religion which they profess I have neither by argument, ridicule, nor otherwise attempted to change. Under the Constitution, which of course is the supreme law of the land, they have a right to worship God in their own way and according to the dictates of their consciences. I never war against anything that is constitutional. Nor have I attempted in any way whatever to interfere with any peculiar institutions which they claim to have adopted (and which now exist amongst them) upon Divine revelation. I have nothing, therefore, to say about their religion or customs, but I have a few observations to submit touching the public teachings of those who are recognized as the leaders in this community :

"As a general principle, there can be no security for either person or property in a community where any of the laws are openly disregarded. I have been taught from my infancy to regard the Constitution, and the laws of Congress passed in pursuance thereof, as the supreme law of the land. To these, as an American citizen, I owe implicit obedience. Laws might be passed which I may regard as unconstitutional or in derogation of the rights of the people, but so long as they remain upon the statute-book it is my duty to respect and obey them. If the people of this Territory consider any laws of Congress arbitrary, unjust, or unconstitutional, they can only resort to the legislative power for a repeal, or to the Courts for a judicial decision. Resistance to their execution, by force of arms, is treason. Are not the people of this Territory exhorted by those who direct and control their minds to disregard a law of Congress and obey the behests of their spiritual advisers? Have not sentiments been promulgated upon many occasions, in the 'Tabernacle,' calculated to inflame the minds of the people against the 'Gentiles' and lead to acts of violence? Is he not a dangerous teacher who advises the people to avenge their own wrongs by taking the law into their own hands? It is moral treason against the Government and destructive of the best interests of society. Here we have a large number of young men, the sons of the early Mormons who migrated to this country twenty years ago, who have been taught from their childhood that the 'Gentiles' are their enemies, and that it is a duty they owe to their God to wage unceasing warfare against them. This has been from year to year impressed upon their minds and by men whom they regard as prophets. Here, as elsewhere, there are many persons not overburdened with wisdom, but filled with fanaticism, who are apt to believe from these teachings that it is lawful to strike down those who stand in the way of spreading their creed.

"The great body of the people here believe that certain leaders in the Church are inspired of God, as were Abraham, Isaiah, and the other prophets of old, to declare His will; and is it a matter of surprise that murders are committed? How different were the principles inculcated by the founder of the Christian religion! He preached peace and good-will amongst men, instead of calling into action the worst passions of the human heart. 'Blessed,' said He, 'is the peacemaker.' Did He not teach obedience to the laws and respect for the powers that be? Did He not say, 'Thou shalt love thy neighbour as thyself?' Did He not say, 'Love your enemies and pray for those who despitefully use and persecute you?' Why, when surrounded by his enemies and nailed to the cross, He extended His eyes towards heaven, and with His dying breath exclaimed, 'Father, forgive them; they know not what they do!' How utterly inconsistent are these sentiments, promulgated by our illustrious Saviour, with the doctrines taught by our modern Prophet in the 'Tabernacle!'

"Whilst following the practices of some of the patriarchs of old, they have also adopted the creed, 'An eye for an eye, and a tooth for a tooth.'

"What has been the result of these teachings upon society here?

"There are a number of respectable men in this city, some of whom have families, who dare not go upon your streets at night! Nor are they men who are afraid of shadows. They have shown their courage upon the field of battle in defence of the honour of the country, and would not shrink from meeting any of them single-handed in the light of day. But they do not choose to meet an organized band of assassins at midnight. They dare not go to your theatre or other places of amusement. Is it not hard that here, in an American Territory, supposed to be under the protection of our national flag, citizens who have perilled their lives to sustain the supremacy of our laws and the integrity of the Government, are compelled to remain in their houses at night to escape the hands of murderers?—men who have violated no law, trespassed upon the rights of no one, but have simply incurred the displeasure of the dominant party? Can this state of things be tolerated on American soil? A government which habitually fails to give protection to its people must soon cease to command their confidence or respect. But I do not choose to pursue this subject any further.

"In this connection, however, I feel called upon to notice the extraordinary efforts which have been made and are still being made at the 'Tabernacle,' as well as by the press, to destroy the confidence of the people in the courts established by the Federal Government in this Territory. Judges, selected by the Government because of their legal attainments and sterling integrity, have been sent out here to administer the laws and preserve the peace and order of society. If, in the faithful performance of their duties under the oath they have taken, they make a decision in conflict with the interests or the opinions of the dominant party, they are bitterly denounced and every effort made to impair their power and lessen their influence. To effect this, slang and ridicule are generally employed. If a Federal Judge will decide every question which arises between a Mormon and 'Gentile' in favour of the former, he can have an easy and quiet time. He can have as much fulsome praise as he desires. But, if he decides in favour of the latter, 'uneasy lies the head that wears a crown.' In the meanwhile, lawyers are denounced as thieves and plunderers. Why this constant denunciation of a profession that has furnished many of the ablest and best men that ever lived? It is because lawyers in every civilized country have been considered indispensable in the administration of justice, and, as a part of the judicial system of the country, must also be prostrated; it is because they believe that disputes as to the ownership of property should be settled by the courts, and not by brute force.

" And now, gentlemen of the Jury, my task is done. In the name of the people, whom I represent, I thank you for the patience you have exhibited during this protracted examination. I have laboured zealously and to the best of my humble ability to unravel the mystery, but I confess I have failed. We have not been permitted to lift the veil, and show you the perpetrators of this horrible murder—a murder most atrocious in its inception, brutal and cowardly in its execution—a crime which in many respects stands without a parallel. But the blood of a pure and honourable man, shed in the streets of your city, calls aloud to Heaven for vengeance, and I trust the cry will be heard and answered; for is it not written that ' whoso sheddeth man's blood by man shall his blood be shed?' "

II.

WRITERS ON MORMONISM.

THE following is a list of some of the authorities—books, pamphlets, essays, etc.—which, with innumerable private letters and valuable documents in MS., have been consulted in preparing this work for the press:

ADAMS, G. J.—Letter to his Excellency John Tyler. New York, 1844.
Address by a Minister of the Church of Jesus Christ of Latter-Day Saints to the People of the United States. Printed while the Mormons were at Nauvoo.
AMBERLEY, VISCOUNT—The Latter-Day Saints. *Fortnightly Review*, Nov., 1869.
Authentic History of Remarkable Persons, etc. New York, 1849.

BEADLE, J. H.—Life in Utah; or, The Mysteries and Crimes of Mormonism. Philadelphia, 1870.
BENNETT, JOHN C.—History of the Saints; or, An Exposé of Joe Smith and Mormonism. Boston, 1842.
BRADFORD. W. J. A.—The Origin and Fate of Mormonism. *Christian Examiner*, Sept., 1852.
BREWSTER, JAMES COLIN—An Address to the Church of L. D. S. Springfield, Ill., 1848.
BRIGHAM, WM. J.—The Church of Latter-Day Saints. *Old and New*, Sept. and Oct., 1870.
Brighamism, its Promises and their Failures. Plano, Ill.
Brigham Young and his Women. *Galaxy*, Dec. 1, 1866.
BROWN, ALBERT G.—The Utah Expedition. *Atlantic Monthly*, March, April, and May, 1859.

BULFINCH, Rev. STEPHEN G.—The Mormons. *Christian Examiner*, 1858.
BURTON, RICHARD F.—The City of the Saints. New York, 1862.
Burton's City of the Saints. [Review.] *Edinburgh Review*, Jan., 1862.

CAMPBELL, ALEXANDER, and JOSHUA V. HINES—Delusions; An Analysis of the
    Book of Mormon. Boston, 1832.
CASWELL, Rev. H.—The City of the Mormons; or, Three Days in Nauvoo. Lon-
    don, 1843.
——, The Prophet of the Nineteenth Century. London, 1843.
——, Joseph Smith and the Mormons. [Chap. xiii. of "America and the American
    Church."] London, 1851.
——, Mormonism and its Author, etc. London, 1858.
CHANDLESS, WM.—A Visit to Salt Lake. London, 1857.
CLARK, Rev. JOHN A.—Gleanings by the Way. Philadelphia, 1842.
CLARKE, F. W.—The Mormon Widow's Lament. *Galaxy*, May 1, 1871.
Concordance and Reference Guide to the Book of Doctrine and Covenants. Plano,
    Ill., 1870.
CONYBEARE, W. J.—Mormonism. *Edinburgh Review*, April, 1854.
CORRILL, JOHN—A Brief History of the Church of Jesus Christ of Latter-Day
    Saints. St. Louis, 1839.

Defence of Polygamy by a Lady of Utah [Mrs. Belinda Pratt], to her Sister in
    New Hampshire. Great Salt Lake City, 1854.
Demoralizing Doctrines and Disloyal Teachings of the Mormon Hierarchy. New
    York, 1866.
Deseret News, Salt Lake City.

Epitome of the Faith and Doctrines of the Reorganized Church of Jesus Christ of
    Latter-Day Saints. Plano, Ill.

FAULCONER, M.—Fulness of the Atonement. Plano, Ill.
——, M. A.—Questions for the Use of Scholars in the Latter-Day Saints' Sunday-
    Schools. Plano, Ill., 1869.
FERRIS, BENJ. G.—Utah and the Mormons. New York, 1856.
——, Mrs. B. G.—The Mormons at Home. New York, 1856.
FORD, Governor THOMAS—History of Illinois.
FULLER, METTA VICTORIA—Mormon Wives; a Narrative of Facts stranger than
    Fiction. New York, 1856.

Gospel, The—[broadsheet]. Plano, Ill.
GRANT, J. M.—Three Letters to the *New York Herald*. New York, 1852.
GREEN, NELSON WINCH.—Fifteen Years among the Mormons. Narrative of Mrs.
    Mary Ettie V. Smith. New York, 1860.
——, Mormonism, its Rise, Progress, and Present Condition. Hartford, 1870.
GREENE, JOHN D.—Facts relative to the Expulsion of the Mormons from the State
    of Missouri. Cincinnati, 1839.
GUNNISON, J. W.—The Mormons, or Latter-Day Saints in the Valley of the Great
    Salt Lake. Philadelphia, 1852.

HAY, JOHN.—The Mormon Prophet's Tragedy. *Atlantic Monthly*, Dec., 1869.
HICKMAN, WM. A.—" Brigham's Destroying Angel," Life of. Edited by J. H. Bea-
dle. New York, 1872.
History of the Mormons.—Chambers, Edinburgh.
—— and Ideas of the Mormons. *Westminster Review*, Jan., 1853.
HOOPER, WM. H.—Extension of Boundaries. Speech in the House of Representa-
tives. Washington, Feb. 25, 1869.
——, The Utah Bill. . . . Speech, etc. March 23, 1870. With Remonstrance of
the Citizens of Salt Lake City. Washington, 1870.
HOWE, E. D.—Mormonism Unveiled. Painsville, 1834.
HYDE, JOHN, Jun.—Mormonism ; its Leaders and Designs. New York, 1857.
Hymns, A Collection of Sacred. Voree, 1850. Second edition.
——. A Collection of Sacred. New York, 1838.
——, Sacred and Spiritual Songs. 14th edition. Salt Lake City, 1871.
——, The Saints' Harp, etc. Plano, Ill., 1870.

Idolatry. Plano, Ill.

JAQUES, JOHN.—Catechism for Children. Salt Lake City, 1870.
JENKINS, H. D.—The Mormon Hymn Book. *Our Monthly*, Dec., 1870.
JOHNSTON, JAMES F. W.—Joe Smith and the Mormons. *Harper's Magazine*, June,
1851.
Journal of Discourses. Vols. 4. Liverpool.

KANE, THOMAS L.—The Mormons. A Discourse. Philadelphia, 1850.
KENDALL, HENRY, D. D.—A Week in Great Salt Lake City. *Hours at Home*, May,
1865.
KIDDER, DANIEL P.—Mormonism and the Mormons. New York, 1842.

Life among the Mormons—*Putnam's Monthly*, August to December, 1855.
LOSSING, BENSON J.—The Mormons. *Harper's Magazine*, April, 1853.
LUDLOW, FITZ-HUGH.—Among the Mormons. *Atlantic Monthly*, April, 1864.
——, The Heart of the Continent, etc. New York, 1870.
LYON, JOHN—The Harp of Zion. Liverpool, 1853.

McCARTHY, JUSTIN—Brigham Young. *Galaxy*, Feb., 1870.
McCHESNEY, JAMES—An Antidote to Mormonism. New York, 1838.
MAC, R. W.—Mormonism in Illinois. *American Whig Review*, April, June, and
December, 1852.
MARSHALL, CHARLES — Characteristics of Mormonism. *Transatlantic Magazine*,
Aug., 1871.
MARTIN, MOSES—A Treatise on the Fulness of the Everlasting Gospel. New York,
1842.
MAYHEW, HENRY—The Mormons, etc. 3d edition. London, 1852.
Memoir of the Mormons. *Southern Literary Messenger*. Nov., 1848.
Millennial Star, Liverpool.
Memorial to Congress. Plano, Ill., 1870.
Mormonism Past and Present. *North British Review*, Aug., 1863.

Mormons, The—History of their Leading Men. *Phrenological Journal*, Nov., 1866.
—— in Utah. *Bentley's Miscellany*, June, 1855.
——'s Wife, The. *Putnam's Monthly*, June, 1855.
MORRIS, ANNIE—A Week among the Mormons. *Lippincott's Magazine*, July, 1870.
Mountain of the Lord's House. Plano, Ill.

New American Religions. *London Quarterly Review*, April, 1867.

Olive Branch. Kirtland, Ohio, and Springfield, Ill.
Origin and History of the Mormonites. *Eclectic Magazine*, Nov., 1850.

PAGE, JOHN E.—The Spaulding Story, etc., Exposed. Plano, Ill., 1866.
Pearl of Great Price. Liverpool, 1851.
PRATT, ORSON—Remarkable Visions. New York, 1841.
——, A Series of (16) Pamphlets. Liverpool, 1851.
——, Divine Authenticity. Liverpool.
——, The Kingdom of God. Liverpool.
——, PARLEY P.—A Voice of Warning. New York, 1837.
——, Late Persecution of the Church. . . . Written in Prison. New York, 1840.
——, Key to Theology.
——, The Millennium and Other Poems. Treatise on the Regeneration and Eternal
    Duration of Matter. New York, 1840.

REID, MAYNE. The Mormon Monsters. *Onward*, Nov., 1869.
Rejection of the Church. Plano, Ill.
REMY, JULES—A Journey to Great Salt Lake City. London, 1861.
Report of Three Nights' Public Discussion in Bolton. Liverpool, 1851.
RICHARDS, FRANKLIN D.—A Compendium of the Faith and Doctrines of the Church.
    Liverpool, 1857.
Rise and Progress of the Mormon Faith and People. *Southern Literary Messenger*,
    Sep., 1844.

SEELEY, R. H.—The Mormons and their Religion. *Scribner's Monthly*, Feb., 1872.
Seer, The. Washington, D. C., and Liverpool.
Senate Document—Trial of Joseph Smith, Jun., and others, for high treason and
    other crimes against the State of Missouri. Feb. 15, 1841.
SHEEN, ISAAC—The Narrow Way. Plano, Ill.
——, The Plan of Salvation. Plano, Ill.
Sketches of Mormonism, as Drawn by Brigham Young and the Elders. *Western
    Literary Messenger*, July, 1856.
SMITH, ALEXANDER H.—Polygamy, etc. Plano, Ill.
——, DAVID H.—The Bible *versus* Polygamy. Plano, Ill.
——, GEORGE A.—The Rise, Progress, and Travels of the Church, etc. Salt Lake
    City, 1869.
——, JOSEPH—Book of Doctrine and Covenants. Liverpool, 1849.
——, The Book of Mormon. Palmyra, 1830.
——, Book of Mormon, Completely Revised by the Translator. Nauvoo, Ill., 1840.
——, Book of Mormon. Salt Lake City, 1871.
——, The Holy Scriptures, Translated and Corrected **by the** Spirit of Revelation.
    Plano, Ill., 1867.

APPENDIX. 745

SMITH, JOSEPH—Reply to Orson Pratt. Plano.
——, " Who then Can be Saved ? " Plano.
——, LUCY (Mother of the Prophet)—Biographical Sketches of Joseph Smith the
Prophet, and his Progenitors for Many Generations. Liverpool.
——, T. W.—Spiritualism Viewed from a Scriptural Stand-point. Plano.
——, The " One Baptism," etc. Plano.
——, The " One Body." Plano.
SNOW, ELIZA R.—Poems, Religious, Historical, and Political. Liverpool, 1856.
SPAULDING, SAMUEL J.—Spaulding Memorial: A Genealogical History, etc. Bos-
ton, 1872.
SPENCER, ORSON—Patriarchal Order; or, Plurality of Wives. Liverpool, 1853.
——, Letters. Liverpool, 1848.
STENHOUSE, Mrs. T. B. H.—A Lady's Life among the Mormons. New York, 1872.
STURTEVANT, J. M.—Review of Mormonism in All Ages. American Biblical Reposi-
tory, Jan., 1843.
Successor in the Prophetic Office, etc. Plano.
SUNDERLAND, LA ROY—Mormonism Exposed. New York, 1842.

TAYLDER, T. W. P.—The Mormon's Own Book. London, 1855.
——, The Mormon's Own Book . . . Also a Life of Joseph Smith. London, 1857.
TAYLOR, JOHN—The Government of God. Liverpool, 1852.
——, Three Nights' Public Discussion at Boulogne-sur-Mer. Liverpool, 1850.
——, Truth Defended, etc. Liverpool, 1840.
THOMPSON, CHARLES—Evidences in Proof of the Book of Mormon. Batavia, New
York, 1841.
Tithing. Plano, Ill.
Trial of the Witnesses to the Resurrection of Jesus. Plano, Ill., 1870.
True Latter-Day Saints' Herald. Cincinnati, and Plano, Ill., 1860–1872.
Truth Made Manifest: A Dialogue. Plano.
Truth by Three Witnesses; A Warning Voice. Plano.
TUCKER, POMEROY—Origin, Rise, and Progress of Mormonism. New York, 1867.
TULLIDGE, E. W.—Brigham Young and Mormonism. Galaxy, Sept., 1867.
——, Leaders in the Mormon Reform Movement. Phrenological Journal, July,
1871.
——, The Mormon Commonwealth. Galaxy, Oct. 15, 1866.
——, The Mormons: Who and What they are. Phrenological Journal, Jan., 1870.
——, The Reformation in Utah. Harper's Magazine, Sept., 1871.
——, The Utah Gentiles: Who and What they are. Phrenological Journal, May,
1871.
——, Views of Mormonism. Galaxy, Oct. 1, 1866.
——, Wm. H. Hooper, of Utah. Phrenological Journal, Nov., 1870.
TURNER, J. B.—Mormonism in All Ages. New York, 1842.
——, O.—Origin of the Mormon Imposture. Living Age, Aug. 30, 1851.

Utah. Beadle's Monthly, July, 1866.

Valley Tan. Salt Lake City.
VAN DUSEN, INCREASE, and MARIA, his Wife.—Spiritual Delusion. New York, 1854.

VAN DUSEN, INCREASE McGEE, and MARIA, his Wife—Startling Disclosures. New York, 1849.

——, INCREASE McGEE, and MARIA, his Wife—Sublime and Ridiculous Blended. New York, 1848.

Visit to the Mormons. *Westminster Review*, Oct., 1861.

Voice of the Good Shepherd. Plano, Ill.

WAITE, Mrs. C. V.—The Mormon Prophet and his Harem. Chicago, 1857.

WARD, AUSTIN N.—The Husband in Utah. New York, 1857.

——, MARIA—Female Life among the Mormons. New York, 1855.

WATERS, ——, Life among the Mormons, etc. New York, 1868.

WELLS, SAMUEL R.—Our Visit to Salt Lake City. *Phrenological Journal*, Dec., 1870.

——, The Mormon Question. *Phrenological Journal*, Dec., 1871.

WESTBROOK, G. W.—The Mormons in Illinois. St. Louis, 1844.

WHITTIER, JOHN G.—A Mormon Conventicle. *Living Age*, Dec. 4, 1847.

WINCHESTER, B.—A History of the Priesthood. Philadelphia, 1843.

Yankee Mahomet, The. *American Whig Review*, June, 1851.

INDEX.

AARONIC PRIESTHOOD, 476, 556.
Abraham, 682, 683 ; seen in a vision,
64 ; his equivocation pleaded, 192.
— Book of, 507.
Across the Continent (by Samuel Bowles),
614, 660.
Adair, John W., 441.
— Samuel, 441.
Adam, 485, 489 ; seen in a vision, 63.
Adam-Deity, 202, 185, 188, 492, 494, 558,
561.
Adam-Ondi-Ahman, 77, 85, 86.
Adultery, strange confession of, 295.
Affinity, 184.
Africans, 561.
Abrahamsen, an emigrant, 314.
Aldrich, M., 175.
Alexander, Colonel, 365.
Allen, Captain Ira, 240, 244.
Allyer, 175.
Alma, 544.
Alton, 215.
Alvin (brother of Joseph Smith), seen in
a vision, 64.
Amelia (Folsom), 653.
America, Ancient, 518.
American Fork, 132.
Amos, David, 225.
Anderson, Kirk, 102. (Vide Valley Tan.)
Anthon, Professor, his story of the Book
of Mormon, 25.
Anti-Mormons, 16, 80, 132, 215, 218, 220,
284.
Anti-Polygamy Act, 197.
Apostacy, cause of, 1, 67 ; spirit of, 361 ;
very great in England, 202.
— Brigham Young on, 502 ; of Walker
Bros., and others, 623, 631, 637. (Vide
New Movement)
Apostates, 61, 622, 627, 641 ; arrested,
621 ; murder of, 621 ; cut off, 640 ;
successful, 645.
Apostles, Twelve, 75, 127, 146, 263, 612 ;
chosen, 60 ; seniority of, 61.
Appendix of Doctrine and Covenants, 192.
Appendix, 737.
45

Archer of Paradise (P. P. Pratt), 128.
Argus, Open Letters of, 430, 439, 442,
415, 461.
Arizona, 669.
Arkansas, emigrants to, 424, 428, 430,
435, 414, 449, 452.
Army of the Lord, 50, 56 ; disbanded, 58.
— The Standing (in Utah), 453.
— The United States, in Utah, 369, 371,
396, 415, 417.
Ashley, 100.
— James M., 614.
Assassination of Joseph and Hyrum
Smith, 166-176.
Assembly rooms, Salt Lake City, 643.
Atchison, General D. R., 82-84, 99, 100,
103, 116.
Atlantic Monthly, The, 401, 685.
Atwood, Millen, 314, 328.
Atwood, W., 316.
Auerbachs, merchants of Salt Lake City,
627.
Austin, Dr., 84.
Authorities elected, 566, 567.
Autobiography of Joseph Smith, 26, 65,
125.
Autograph of Brigham Young, 654.
Avard, Dr. Sampson, originator of the
Danite Band, 91, 93.

BABBITT, Almon W., Secretary of
Utah, 247, 270, 280.
Bachelor, Origen, 190.
Baker, Colonel, 214.
Baldwin, Caleb, 112.
Ball, 244, 249.
Ballot in Utah, 702.
Bank, Kirtland Safety Society, 72.
— First National, of Utah, 707.
Bankers, Joseph Smith and Rigdon as, 70.
Banks, John, 594, 599, 600.
Banner of the Gospel [W. Woodruff],
128.
Baptism, first Mormon, 28 ; for the dead,
475 ; by immersion, 475.
Baptiste, 336.

Baptiste, Jean, a grave-digger who robbed the dead, 482.
Barbarism, Slavery and Polygamy twin relics of, 308.
Baron, David Le, 225.
Baskin, R. N., District Attorney, 681.
Bateman, Wm., 444.
Bates, George C., United States Attorney for Utah, 685.
Battalion, Mormon, 240–249, 259, 268, 273, 274.
Battle Creek, 432.
Baurak Ale [Joseph Smith], 50, 51, 56.
Beadle, J. H., 452.
Bear River, 670.
— Lake, 670.
Bee-Hive House, 604, 607, 652, 653.
Bennett, John C., General of Nauvoo Legion, etc., 129, 134–136, 144, 145, 183, 184, 198.
Benson, Elder Ezra T., 553, 673.
Benton, Senator, 249.
Bernhisel, Honourable J. H., 213, 386.
Bible, The, Book of Mormon compared with, 533, 540.
— New translation of, 41.
Bidamon, Major L. C., 188, 225.
Big Cottonwood Lake, 349, 397.
Big Elk, 250.
Big Fishing River, 55.
Big Mound, The, 225.
Bingham Cañon, 712.
Bird, William, 466.
Bishop, Gladden, 212, 305, 306.
Bishops (Mormon), 295, 698, et al.
Black, Adam, 81, 82, 111.
— George A., 680.
— Jeremiah S., Attorney-General, 408.
Blackburn, Bishop, 302.
Black's Fork, 366, 370.
Blair, Seth M., United States Attorney in Utah, 275, 282.
Blessings, 563, 564.
Blood-shedding for love, 299.
Boarding-house at Nauvoo, 128; revelation on, 129.
Bogart, Captain, an anti-Mormon, 81, 94–96.
Boggs, Governor of Missouri, 82, 111, 116, 137, 140, 217, 248; letter of, 96.
Bollwinkel, J. M., 502.
Bolton, Major-General Lewis, 83.
Book of Abraham, 182, 507.
Book of Covenants, 192. (Vide Doctrine and Covenants.)
Book of Mormon, 29, 74, 123, 197, 206, 489, 547, 555, 630, 650, 697.
Boston, prediction of its destruction, 5.
Boulogne-sur-Mer, Apostle Taylor at, 194.
Bowery, 588, et al.
Bowman, Mrs., a Morrisite, 599.

Bowles, Samuel, editor of the Springfield Republican (Mass.), 613, 637.
Boyle, 444.
Boynton, John F., 69, 76.
Brandebury, Chief-Justice of Utah, 277.
Brannan, Elder Samuel, 256; takes 600 emigrants to San Francisco, 238; interviews the President, 259.
Bassfield, O. N., assassination of, 615, 616.
Breckinridge, Senator John C., 348.
Brewer, murder of, 418.
Brewster, Elder, 212.
Bridger, Fort, 302, 330, 357, 370, 376, 380, 384, 385, 401, 404, 428, 593, 685.
Bridger, Jim, 256.
Brigham Young, 5, 44, 52, 60, 68, 79, 113, 123, 127, 128, 175, 186, 187, 193, 205, 223, 243, 244, 247, 253, 263, 264, 268, 269, 272, 275, 281, 289, 292, 295, 300–305, 313, 322, 331, 335, 336–339, 342, 346, 349, 350, 355, 358, 367, 371, 376, 382, 390, 398, 410, 411, 416, 422, 435, 442, 446, 448, 459, 460, 463, 464, 472, 487, 490, 494, 500, 557, 560, 562, 566, 573, 588, 593, 596, 600, 604, 608, 610, 620, 626, 628, 632, 638, 640, 649, 650, 652–659, 660, 661, 664–668, 673–677, 680–686, 693–698, 701, 708, 711.
Brigham, Junr., 662.
British Government, Mormon Memorial to, 222.
British Missions, 9, 135, 201, 266, 271, 310, 458; statistics of, 202.
Brocchus, Perry E., Associate Justice of Utah, 275–279.
Brockman, Thomas A., a Campbellite preacher and leader of the anti-Mormons, 226, 227.
Bross, Lieut.-Governor of Illinois, 612.
Brown County, 153.
— Captain James, 268.
— Hyrum, 199.
— Lieutenant, 618.
— Sam, 80.
Browne, Albert G., 401.
Buchanan, President James, 346, 348, 352, 381, 382, 391, 393, 395, 413, 416, 423.
Buckmaster, Colonel, 174.
Buffington, Joseph, Chief-Justice of Utah, 275.
Bullock, T., clerk to Brigham Young, 271.
Buncombe, 89, 94.
Bunker, 314.
Buren, President Martin Van, 123.
Burlington, Iowa, 123.
Burns's poem "Holy Willie," 76.
Burr, General, 298.
Burton, Captain R. F., on Brigham Young, 638.

Burton, Colonel [now General] R. T., 367, 595, 598–600.
Butler, John L., 80.

CACHE County, 673.
Cache Valley, 397.
Cahoon, Thyrza, 191.
— Reynolds, 191.
Caldwell County, 69, 82, 85.
Calhoun, Honourable J. C., 147.
California, 146, 244, 248, 256, 269, 306, 405, 416, 434, 444, 452, 462, 669; emigration to, 424, 432; Volunteers, 422, 602, 606, 612, 712; gold discovered in, 273.
— Upper, 236, 240, 243, 360; taken by the United States, 239; bounds of, 284.
— Southern, Mormon settlement in, 353.
Calvin Sorrow, John, 450.
Camp Douglas, 604, 608, 609, 620, 621, 680, 685.
— Douglas Cemetery, 620.
— Floyd, 110, 411, 602, 622, 623.
— Scott, 379.
— U. S., in Utah, 397.
— of Death, 370.
Cannon, Apostle George Q., 626, 639, 640, 664, 701.
Carey, a Mormon, 105.
Carlin, Governor of Illinois, 134, 137.
Carolina, 420.
Carroll County, 69, 82, 93, 94, 100, 102.
Carson Valley, 284, 285.
— City, 353, 410.
— River, 353.
Carter, Simeon, 113.
Carthage, 149, 150, 156, 164, 169, 172.
— Grays, 155, 165.
— Jail, 163, 204.
Cartwright, Thomas, 444.
Cass County, 47.
Caswell, Rev. H., 106.
Catechism (Reformation), 295.
Cedar City, 397, 404, 431, 439, 440, 443–445, 451, 452, 455, 459.
Celestial Marriage, 176.
Central Pacific Railroad, 672, 706.
Champion of Right [Apostle John Taylor], 128.
Chandler, Michael H., 509.
Chariton County, 102.
Charter of Nauvoo, 133, 134.
Chase, 112.
Chenango County, N. Y., 21.
Chicago, 355; Mormon elders at, 354; wagons, 333.
Chicago Tribune on the Mormon Battalion, 248.
Chihuahua, 106.

Child's Corner, 465.
China Creek, 199.
Chislett, Mr. John (writer of the Hand-Cart Story), 312, 314, 332, 417, 485.
Christ, mode of His incarnation, 485; a polygamist, 485; appears in America, 535.
Christian Churches in Utah, 703, 704.
Christianity, influence of, 460.
Church, The Mormon, 6, 91, 148, 645, 696; organization, 7; in Britain, 202;
— difficulties in, 205; first organized, 30; leaders of, 461; funds of, 667. (Vide Missions and Mormons.)
— The Reorganized, 263.
— of Zion, 706.
Cincinnati, 348.
City Creek Cañon, 692.
Clara Crossing, 435.
Clark, John B., first division of Missouri militia, 83, 96, 99, 100, 108, 110, 111.
Clawson, H. B. (son-in-law of Brigham Young), 422, 627.
Clay County, 47, 80, 89, 112, 147.
Clayton, William, 189, 255, 627.
Cleveland, Sarah M., 191.
Clinton, Dr. J., 619, 701.
Coalville, 621.
Cobb, Mrs. Van Cott, 652.
Cold, sufferings of the army from, 370.
Colfax, Vice-President, 613, 637, 638, 660.
Colorado, 448, 669, 671.
Colorado River, 269.
Columbia River, 269.
Commander-in-Chief of Militia, 432, 435; of the "Armies of Israel," 50.
Commerce, Hancock Co., Illinois, 123.
Commissioners, United States, to Utah, 396, 399, 450.
Committee on Territories, 614.
Comstock, Captain Nehemiah, 100, 101.
Confederate Army, 377.
Confederate States, 499.
Conference, the first Mormon, 36; at Nauvoo, 211, 221, 238, 421; of the Church, 255, 258, 276, 566, 644, 704.
Confession (during the "Reformation"), 294.
Congress, Memorial to, from sons of Joseph Smith, 197; act of, 669; Mormon petition to, 214; slavery before, 420; committees of, 456; Delegates to, 609;
Connor, Colonel [now General], 601, 604, 606–608, 610–612, 679, 712.
Contract, mail, 348; fraudulent, 416.
Contractors' War, The, 416.
Contracts: Brigham Young's, 635.
Converts, how made, 8.
Cook, Bishop Richard, 596.
Cooke, Philip St. George, Major-General, 241.

Coöperative [Zion's Coöperative Mercantile Institution], 625–628, 644, 667, 672.
Copley, Lemon, 196.
Corinne, 672.
Corinne *Reporter*, 450.
Corn Creek, 433, 434.
Cott, Elder John Van, 333, 336.
Council, 165; in Nauvoo, 204.
Council Bluffs, 225, 250, 262–265, 382, 477, 604.
Counterfeit money, 218.
— plates, 410–412.
— United States drafts, 410.
Court, Supreme, 684, 686.
Courts, United States, 110, 278, 282, 284, 285, 402, 406, 408, 415, 594, 597, 601, 606, 684.
Courts, Circuit, 111, 155; of Illinois, 218; of Hancock County, 175.
Covenants and Commandments, 40, 192. (*Vide* Doctrine and Covenants.)
Cowdery, Oliver (Joseph Smith's scribe, etc.), 26; baptized, 28–30; see (with J. S.) a great vision, 65, 75, 112, 190–194, 255, 649.
Cowdery, Lyman, 76.
Cox, Mr., of Indiana, 101.
Cradlebaugh, Judge John, 352, 401, 403–410, 411, 445, 463, 591.
Creation, The, Brigham Young on, 4–7; new story of, 488.
Crickets in Utah, 270; destruction of crops by, 270.
Crimes, confession of, during the "Reformation," 296.
Crooke, Father, 557.
Crooked River, 91, 95.
Crosby, Associate-Justice, 594, 601.
Cumming, Alfred, Governor of Utah, 352, 334, 377, 383, 389, 391–398, 400; policy of, 402; 407–413, 434, 445, 676, 697, 698.
Cutler, Elder Alphaeus, 191, 212.
— Lois, 191.

DALLAS, Hon. Vice-President Geo. M., 238.
Dame, Colonel Wm. H., 434, 437, 440, 441, 454, 461.
Daniels [testifies to the murder of Joseph Smith], 160.
Danites, 79, 91–93, 614.
Darwin's Theory and Mormonism, 632.
Davies County, 69, 80, 82, 83, 93, 96, 97, 102, 112, 268.
Davis, Bishop, 451.
— Jacob C., 175.
— William, 175.
Dawson, J. W., Governor of Utah, 591, 601; attack upon, 592.

Dayton, 553.
Deacon, 556.
Dead, robbing the, 482.
Declaration of Independence, Brigham's, 365.
Denning, General, 154.
Democratic Convention, 348.
Democrats, 126.
Department of the Plains, 616.
Deseret, State of, 269, 274–276, 363, 554–557, 455, 593; boundaries of, 269.
— Currency, 412.
— News, 94, 302, 305, 307, 347, 362, 406, 504, 506, 567, 610, 610.
Desperadoes in Utah, 417.
Destruction Company, the, 89.
Detroit, 213.
Devil, out in of, 490, 491; devils, 574; casting out, 34.
Devil's Gate, 336, 358.
De Witt, 85.
Diagram of the Celestial Kingdom, 506.
Dick Wedding, 80.
Disfellowshipping, 639, 645.
Divine authenticity, 523.
Divine Plan, 314, 333, 338, 341, 523.
Dixie, 658.
Doctrine and Covenants, 27, 39, 165, 190–196, 206.
Don Carlos Smith, 86.
Doniphan, General, 83, 85, 99, 166.
Dotson, Peter K., 352.
Doty, Jas. Duane, Governor of Utah, 592, 595, 601.
Douglas, Camp, 605, 606, 612, 680, 685, 712. (*Vide* Camp.)
— Judge and Senator, Stephen A., 127, 138, 117, 316–318.
— Hon. John, 113.
Dow, Alexander, affidavit of, 599.
Doniphan in Kansas, 366.
Drake, Thos. J., Associate-Justice, 601, 605.
Dream, Farnsworth's, 612.
Drummond, Judge W. W., ill conduct of, 285, 307.
Drummond, Mrs., 285.
Beulah, extraordinary Mormon song, 370, 372.
Dunbar, Elder W. C., 319, 560.
Dunklin, Governor of Missouri, 55, 77.
Dunn's Company, 155.
Durfee, 463, 466.
Durkee, Governor, 675.
Durphy, Perry, 80.

EAGLE VALLEY, 358.
Earl, W. J., 465.
Eastern States, Jesse C. Little presides over, 237.
Echo Cañon, 362, 363, 369, 390, 393, 414.

Eckles, Chief Justice, 352, 377, 389, 391, 685.

Edmonds, Judge John W., 31.

Edmunds, George, 225.

Elang Joseph, 111.

Eldridge, Elder, 625, 614.

Elect Lady [Emma Smith], the, 21, 183.

Elections in Missouri, 159.

Elections in Utah, 701, 702.

Elkhorn Wood River, 316.

Ellsworth, Edmund, 311.

Emigrants, Mormon, 578; hard-cart, 311; sufferings of, 320; story of, 321; horrible distress of, 325; loss of, 331; miserable death of, 356.

Emigration, 265, 291; to California, 273.

Emigration Cañon, 306.

Emma (Hale), wife of Joseph Smith, 21. (Vide Elect Lady.)

Emma Smith's Year Book, 653.

Emmett, Elder James, 206, 212.

Endowment promised, 54; given, 63; 175, 697, 698.

Endowment House, 297, 305, 697.

English Saints, 303. (Vide Missions and British.)

Enoch, 50.

Enoch, Order of, 502, 503.

Ensign Peak, 266.

Entablature of Truth [George A. Smith], 123.

Entablature on the Temple at Nauvoo, 223.

Episcopal Church in Utah, 703.

Epistle, a general, 265.

Equivocation in the Marriage Ceremony, 193.

European Saints, 307.

Evans, David, 12.

Evening and Morning Star, 12, 13.

Excommunication, 202; of Apostates, 640.

Expedition to Utah, 175, 421.

Exposé of Polygamy, 283.

Expositor, The Nauvoo, 118, 155, 157, 163, 164, 283.

Express, The B. Y., 315.

Expulsion of the Mormons from Missouri, 112.

Extermination of the Mormons resolved on, 95, 96, 104.

FAITH of the Mormons in Joseph Smith, 114.

Farnsworth's Dream, 612.

Far West, 69, 71, 88, 91, 103, 108.

Fearnought, Captain [David Patten], 93, 94.

Federal Army, 396, 397.

— Court, 686. (Vide Courts.)

— Judges, 685, 686.

Federal Officers, 678, 681.

— Troops, 410, 421, 428; leave Camp Floyd, 622.

— Appointments, 282.

Felt, N. H., 319.

Ferguson, James, 283, 109.

Ferris, Secretary, 279.

Festivities at Big Cottonwood Lake, 319.

Fillmore, Millard, 274, 482, 483, 459, 460.

First Presidency, 264, 265, 268.

Flag staff, presentation of, to Brigham Young, 122.

Flenniken, Chief Justice, 591, 601.

Florence, Neb. [Winter-Quarters], 316, 317, 331, 381.

Florida, 361.

Floyd, Camp, 346, 397, 408, 410, 412, 413, 416, 419, 422, 445, 452.

Floyd, John B., Secretary of War, 352, 397.

Fobbs, assassination of, 405.

Folsom (Young), Amelia, 604, 605, 652.

Forbes, Mr., 167.

Ford, Governor of Illinois, 142, 143, 117, 118, 152, 163, 165-169, 170, 172, 171, 181, 185, 198, 211, 222.

Ford's History of Illinois, 135, 143, 149, 150, 153, 157, 170, 150, 151.

Forney, Jacob, 401, 402, 450.

Fort Bridger, 625.

Fort Limhi, Mission to, 658.

Foster, Robert D., 129.

Fourth of July, 286, 311, 123, 680, 681.

Fox, Jesse W., "consecration" of his goods, 502.

Francher, Charles, 150.

Freedomism threatened, 184, 185.

Freeman, Columbus, 111.

Fremont, John C., 249.

Frontier cities, 250.

Frontiers, the, 312.

Fuller, Frank, Secretary of Utah, 591-594, 600, 609.

Funeral of Joseph and Hyrum Smith, 174.

Funerary Disk. (Vide Book of Abraham.)

GALLAGHER, Wm., 175.
Galland, Dr Isaac, 129.

Gallatin, Davies County, 80.

Garden of Eden, in Missouri, 77.

Garden Grove, 250.

Gauge of Philosophy [Orson Pratt], 128.

Gazelam [Joseph Smith], 50.

Gee, Lysander, 406.

Gentiles, 622, 642, 665, 693, 697.

Gibbs, Luman, 112.

Gifts, 551, 612, et al.

Gila River, 269.

Giles, Old, an emigrant, 335.
Glaze, Mr., 102.
God, Heber C. Kimball declares that Brigham Young is as, 486; Mormon ideas of, 484.
Godbe, Wm. S., 342, 562, 630, 636, 639, 640, 641, 643, 645, 676, 677. (*Vide* Harrison and New Movement.)
Goddard, Geo., 639.
Gold, discovery of, in California, 273.
Golden's Point,165.
Gold plates found by Joseph Smith, 21.
Goodyier, an Indian trader, 268.
Gospel, a new, 60.
Governor of Utah, proclamation by, 358; Brigham Young. 366.
Grand River, 77, 86, 670.
Grant, President U. S., 671; letter to, from Author, 241.
— G. D., 317, 319, 326.
— Thos. D., 83.
— J. M., Apostle, 278; originates the "Reformation," 293; 303, 305, 497, 561.
Great Britain, 420. (*Vide* Missions and Britain.)
Great Plains, 334.
Green, John P., 44.
— Plains, 215.
— River, 367, 670.
Greenwood, 451.
Grover, Thos., 113.
Grover, Wm. H., 173, 175.
Guadaloupe Hidalgo, 269.
Gulls in Utah, 270.
Gunnison. Lieutenant, 173, 189, 273, 464.
Guyman, N. J., 464, 665.

HAIGHT, President, engaged in Mountain Meadows Massacre, 435, 437, 440, 441, 444, 447-449, 451-454.
Hale family, the, 21. (*Vide* Emma Smith.)
Halley, Wm., 244.
Halliday, George, 335.
Ham's Fork, 336, 338.
Hamlet, plagiarism of, 543.
Hamlin, Jacob, 448, 450.
Hamlin's Ranche, 441.
Hampton, Ben, 337.
Hancock, Solomon, 113.
Hancock County, 143, 153, 199, 213, 214, 217.
Hand Cart Emigration, 311; plan divinely inspired, 313; song, 333.
Hardin, J. J., Brigadier-General, 214, 217.
Harding, Stephen S., Governor of Utah, 601, 602, 605, 606, 609.
Harmony, Susquehanna Co., 21, 440, 451, 459.

Harney, Brigadier-General, 352, 365, 412.
Harris, Martin, amanuensis to Joseph Smith, 22, 26, 29, 75, 76.
— Mrs., 26.
— B. D., Secretary of Utah, 275, 277.
Harrison, E. L. T., 444, 562, 630, 631, 633, 636, 637, 639-642, 676, 677; revelations to, 631, 632.
Hartnett, John, 352.
Haskins, Rev. T. W., 704.
Hatch, Ira, 444, 451, 456.
Haun, 101.
Haun's Mill, 100; massacre of Mormons at, 102.
Hawkins, Thos., trial of, for polygamy, 685.
Hawley, Cyrus M., Associate-Justice, 684.
Hawn, Francis, 450.
Healing, gifts of, 8, 9.
Heber C. Kimball. (*Vide* Kimball.)
Heitz, Captain A., 713.
Hempstead, Major C. H., U. S. Attorney, 608, 612, 684.
Hendrick, Elder, 212.
Herald, New York, 116, 278, 386, 412, 658.
Hewett, Richard, 199.
Heywood, Joshua L., U. S. Marshal, 275.
Higbee, Sarah, 191.
— Judge Elias, 123, 145.
— Bishop John M., 444, 448, 451.
— Francis M., 145.
High Council at Nauvoo, 222. (*Vide* Council.)
High-Priests, 295. (*Vide* Priests, etc.)
Hill, 615. (*Vide* Brassfield.)
Hillman, Sarah, 191.
Hinckle, Colonel, 84, 85, 94, 104, 105.
Historical Society of New York, 413.
History of Illinois (*Vide* Ford), 106, 217, 248.
Hoge, Mr., 142.
Holland, Simpson, 368.
Hollman, District Attorney, 281.
Holy Ghost—*a man!* 361.
Hooper, Hon. W. H. [Delegate], 593, 613, 614, 626, 644, 684.
Hopkins, Chas., 444.
Horse-Head, 450.
Hospital, Salt Lake City, 704.
Hudson, Frederick, 386.
Huff, Mary, 450.
Human Sacrifices, 613. (*Vide* Reformation.)
Hunt, John A., 335.
Hunter, Ann, 191.
Hurd, Dr. Garland, an Indian agent, 413.
Hussey, Mr. Warren [banker], Salt Lake City, 668.
Hyde, Elder John, 391, 393, 545, 546, 560, 640.

Hyde, John, Mrs., 640.
— Orson [Olive-Branch of Israel], 46, 52, 60, 68, 88-90, 94, 128, 146, 205, 263, 264, 284, 353, 476, 483-485, 505, 506, 573, 574, 694.
Hymns. Mormon, 371, 374, 498, 499; inspired, 2; Montgomery's, 165, 166; by Taylor, 360.
Hyrum Smith, death of, 177. (*Vide* Smith.)

ICARIANS, French, at Nauvoo, 223.
Idaho, 606, 669.
Illinois, 123-127, 133, 139, 142, 147, 181, 211, 285, 350, 405; Governor of, 141-144; militia of, 112; history of, 181, 198, 248; Saints in, 120, 284. (*Vide* Ford.)
Income, Brigham Young's, 666-668.
Indemnity to Mormons, and people of Davies and Caldwell Counties, 113.
Independence, Jackson County, 88, 108, 319.
— Brigham Young's Declaration of, 351.
— Sidney Rigdon's Declaration of, 91. (*Vide* Salt Sermon.)
— Hall, 616.
Indiana, 120, 181.
Indian affairs, 359, 366, 401, 432, 450, 451.
Indian Agent, 413, 419; country, 186, 250, 401, 428; farm, 464; superintendent, 286; interpreter, 289.
Indians, 243, 255, 272, 273, 283, 351, 377, 409, 421, 434, 435, 437, 416-448, 450, 431, 457, 458, 593, 670, 697; prisoners, 409; Utah, 448; mission to, 658.
Indians, "White," 401.
Infallible Priesthood, 14, 286, 644.
Ingram, 444. (*Vide* M. M. Massacre.)
Inspired Hymn, 2.
Investigation of murders, 405, 463.
Iowa, 214, 215, 225, 314, 316, 317; Saints journey through, 222, 315.
— Camp, 314.
— City, 333, 391.
Iron County, 410, 673.
Iron Creek, 435, 440.
Isaiah (quoted), 25.

JACK Mormons, 214.
Jack's Valley, 353.
Jackson County, 108, 119, 268; inheritance in, 49; 448.
Jacksonville, 217.
Jacobs, H., 90.
Jail, Two Minutes in, 170, 171.
James, an old emigrant, his death, etc., 327-329.
Jarvis, 297.

Jeddy [Jededah M. Grant], his mule, 293, 295; 300, 301.
Jennings, Elder Wm., 625, 644.
Jerusalem, the new, 37, etc. (*Vide* Zion.)
Jim Bridger, 256.
"Joab, a General in Israel," 127.
John, Uncle, 563.
Johns, Colonel Wm. M., 678.
Johnson, Bishop A., 191, 463-465.
Johnson, Luke, 60, 69, 76.
Johnson, Lyman E., 60, 69, 76.
Johnston, General Albert Sidney, 366, 369, 376, 377, 388, 389, 392, 395, 407, 411, 412, 417, 445, 510, 685.
Johnston, Joaquin, 418.
— Polly Z., 191.
— Mrs., 466.
— County, Arkansas, 456.
— Nephi, 444.
Jones, Mr., a Pittsburg banker, 71-73. (*Vide* Kirtland Bank.)
— Captain Dan, 335, 387.
— Henry, 405.
Jordan River, 298, 396, 431, 432, 670.
Joseph A. (Young). (*Vide* Young.)
— Smith. (*Vide* Smith.)
— "the young," consecrated, 204; 555, 628, 706.
Journal of Discourses, 277, 280, 303, 305, 306, 650.
Judd, Rebecca, Miss, 101.
Judges, Federal, 100.
July 24th in Salt Lake Valley, 423.
Juries, Mormon, 408.
Jurors, story of the eleven who "had some of the ham," 615.

KAHN Bros., 627.
Kane, Thomas L., Colonel (now Major-General), 238, 211, 217, 275, 382-389, 391, 412, 413.
Kanesville, 250, 264.
Kanosh, an Indian chief, 404, 436.
Kansas, 112, 315, 364.
Kearney, Colonel (now General) S. W., First Dragoons, 240, 243, 244.
Kearns, H. H., 466.
Keeper of the Rolls [Apostle Willard Richards], 128.
Kelsey, Eli B., 632, 633, 640, 642, 645, 676, 712, 713.
Kesler, Bishop, 298.
Keys restored, 33.
Kimball, H. C., Apostle, 44, 52, 60, 68, 69, 123, 186, 205, 263, 277, 291, 295, 300, 301, 306, 331, 330, 376, 379, 485, 517, 560-562, 573, 632, 640, 653, 658, 659, 666; and the "Reformation," 291; prophecy of, 274.
— H., Captain, 230, 329.

Kimball, Vilate, Mrs., 506.
— W. H., 317, 314, 326.
Kinderhook, ancient plates found at, 518.
King, Judge Austin A., 83, 111, 117.
Kingdom, the, 495, 496, 498, 500, 502, 681, 691; an earthly, 1; of God, 506.
Kingdom, Celestial, diagram of, 505.
Kington, Port, Bishop of, 261.
Kinney, Chief Justice John F., 280, 281, 591, 593, 594, 599-601, 605, 607, 609.
Kirby, Rev. R. M., 704.
Kirtland, Ohio, 39, 43, 44, 60, 64, 74, 78, 182, 650; Joseph Smith flies from, 70, 73; return to, 119.
— Temple, dedication of, 64.
— Safety Society Bank, 72, 274.
Klemgard, Peter, 597.
Knight, Newel, 33, 552, 553.

LADIES' Relief Society, 190, 191.
La Fayette, 47.
La Harpe, 255.
Lake Utah, 670.
Lamanites preached to, 37. (Vide Book of Mormon.)
Lamentation, the, of Parley P. Pratt, 5.
Land-Office (Salt Lake City), 671.
Land of promise, 299.
Landon, 298.
Lapeer County, Michigan, 199.
Laramie, Fort, 319, 322, 323, 500.
La Roy Sunderland, 5.
Latter-day Saints, Brigham Young the head of Church of, 265. (Vide Mormon.)
— Messenger and Advocate, 49, 208.
Law, William, 113, 129, 130, 198.
— Wilson, 118, 191.
— Jane, 191.
Lawrence, Major H. W., 595, 601, 627, 633, 642, 644, 645.
Leavenworth, Fort, 211, 249, 345, 348, 365, 366.
Le Clerc [Pied Riche], 250.
Lee, Major John D., 434, 450, 419-449, 451, 454-456, 461.
— General, 610.
— County, Iowa, 259.
Legion, The Nauvoo, 133, 134, 139, 149, 150, 153, 157, 168, 612.
Letter of Joseph Smith to the Saints, 113, 118.
— to President Grant from the Author, 241.
— from P. St. George Cooke, 213.
— from a lady, 378, 379.
— of President Buchanan, 382.
— to Brigham Young, 146.
Lewis, Samuel, 111.
— Samuel, Junior, 434.
Lexington, 95.

Liberal Institute, Salt Lake City, 706.
Liberals, those of Utah, 676, et al.
Liberty, 89, 112.
Lions, 215.
Lincoln, President, 318, 591, 604, 611.
Lindorth, James, 335.
Lion House, 651, 653.
Lion of the Lord [Brigham Young], 128, 273, 374, 385, 500, 631.
Literary and Musical Society, 306.
Little, Elder J. Esse C., 207, 210, 211, 217.
Liverpool, emigration from, 205, 512, 514, 516; missionaries, 511, 512.
Livingston County, 102.
Log Tabernacle, 261.
Los Angeles, 213, 452.
Loveridge, Alexander, 414.
Lucas, General S. D., 83, 99, 101, 106, 109, 110.
Lyford, Rev. J. P., 705.
Lyman Wight 212.
Lyman, Apostle Amasa M., 263, 613.

MACK, Jonathan, 649.
— Massenia, Utah, 633. (Vide Utah.)
Mann, Mrs. John [Vide M. M. M.], 444.
Martin, S. A., Secretary of Utah, 676, 678.
Manuscript of Book of Mormon stolen, 26.
Maps, 115.
Marcy, Captain R. B., 389, 390, 396.
— Hon. W. L., Secretary of State, 210.
Mariposa County, 96.
Marks, Rosannah, 191.
— Sophia E., 191.
— William, counsellor to "young Joseph," 198.
Marriages, 190-194, 504; in Utah, 187.
Marsh, Thomas B., President of the Twelve Apostles, 57, 88-91, 94, 205.
Marsh, Mrs., a Morrisite, 599.
Marshall, Thomas, 273.
Martin, Leader of a Hand-cart Company, 331.
Martin's company [hand-cart], 330-332.
Mason and Slidell's case, Brigham Young on, 611.
Massacre of Mormons at Haun's Mill, 101.
Massacre at Mountain Meadows, 357, et seq.
Matheney, Sims, 441.
Matty, a nickname for President Van Buren, 124.
Maxwell, General George R., 684.
McAllister, Major, 367.
McArthur, Daniel, 311.
McBride, 101.
McCord, Alexander, 247.
McCulloch, Peace Commissioner, 384.
McCurdy, Solomon, Judge, 610, 615.
McDonald, A. F., 462, 465.

McDonough County, 149, 150.
McDulange, F. C., 444.
McEwan, Henry, 502.
McFarlan, Daniel, 444.
McFarlan, John, 444.
McGaw, James, 384.
McKean, James B., 442, 678, 683, 684.
McKean, Deputy-Marshal L., 597, 600.
McKinzie, George, 165.
McLean, Hector, 129.
McLellin, Wm. E., 60, 76.
McLeod, Rev. Norman, 616, 705.
McRae, Alexander, 442.
Medium, Joseph Smith a, 14.
Melchisedec Priesthood, 176, 556, 559.
Memorial to Congress from sons of Joseph Smith, 197. (45th Congress.)
Merrick, Me., 104.
Merriman, Colonel, 214.
Message, alleged, from Brigham, ordering Mountain Meadows Massacre, 448.
Methodist Episcopal Church, Salt Lake City, 704.
Mexican War, 248.
Mexico, California a part of, 269.
— New, 269.
— Gulf of, 269.
Michael, seen in a vision, 64.
Migration to Salt Lake Valley, 267.
Militia, Mormon, 366, 412, 673, 680.
Millennial Star, 5, 185, 201, 211, 248, 265, 270, 291, 307, 313, 342, 505.
Miller, Eleazar, foreman of jury, 285.
— George, 191.
— Mary C., 191.
— P. B., 412.
Mills, W. G., 331.
Mines in Utah, 670, 709-734; prophecies of, 636, 710.
Minute-Men, 676.
Miracle, the first Mormon, 33.
Mission to Carson Valley, 283.
— British, 185, 201.
— of reorganized Church, 629.
Missions, Mormon, 9, 38, 41, 68, 312, 175, 479, 494.
Missionaries, Mormon, called in, 353; arms brought from England by, 671.
Missionary Elders, absurd fears of, 354.
Missionary work, 11, 568-572, 658.
Mississippi, 123, 577; baptisms in, 476.
Missouri, 74, 87, 90, 112, 123, 125, 127, 133, 138, 139, 141, 142, 244, 350, 577; Upper, 82, 88; troubles in, 48, 78, 80, 81, 116, 117; emigrants from, 424, 428, 430; Saints in, 107, 124, 281; militia, 109.
— River, 255, 265, 311, 334, 348, 382, 692.
Mobbers, 55, et seq.
Mobs cause trouble, 46, et seq.

Mohammed, Joseph Smith compared to, 24, 203.
Mojave River, 434.
Montana, 669.
Montgomery's Hymn, 166.
Montrose, 151.
Morality, revelations on, 40.
Mormon, derivation of name, 43; 348, predictions, 597; leaders, 397; faith, sketch of, by Joseph Smith, 474; first sermon, 3; militia, 109; troubles, beginning of, 15; church organization, 6; missionary work [see Missions], 10.
— Book of, 25, 189, 423, 526.
Mormonism, 668.
— primitive, 1; grounds of faith in, 2, et seq.
Mormons, sufferings of, 230, 225; trials of, 111; cruelties to, 228; social position of, 115; confidence in, 71; arrive in Salt Lake Valley, 260; loyalty of, 611, 612.
— the,—work by Mackay, on the Saints, 173.
— Own Book, 698.
— Church, 643, 645.
— war, the, 312, 355, 557.
— The, a religious publication, 317, 354.
Moroni, an ancient American prophet, 450.
Morris, Joseph, a prophet among the Mormons, 520, 595-600, 620.
Mountain Meadows Massacre, 357, 403, 404, 406-410, 422, 437, 439, 446, 448, 455, 460, 461, 611, 620.
Mule, Jeddy's, 293.
Murders, 615-620.
— secret, 353, 117, 439, 441.
— of apostates, 621.
Musser, Amos M., 582, 611, 645, 666.

NAUVOO ["The Beautiful"], founded, 129; flourishes, 130; 125, 126, 129, 133, 111-113, 147, 152-156, 169, 170, 172, 201, 205, 215, 226, 361; Joseph Smith brought back to, 141; Mormon tactics at, 112; Common Council of, extraordinary ordinances, 152; Mayor and Common Council of, surrender, 162; troubles in, 162; Apostles go to, on Joseph Smith's death, 219; High Council at, 221; attack on, by anti-Mormons, 226; cruelties to Saints in, 228; population of, 252; evacuation of, 242; exiles from, their order of travel, 272; Mormons from settlements flee to, 265; conference at, 421; municipal court, jurisdiction of, 150; court sets aside writ on Joseph Smith, 155, 160.

Nauvoo, Charter, 133, 139; Governor Ford on, 140.
— House, 136. (*Vide* Boarding-House.)
— *Expositor*, 148, 159.
— Legion, 673–675; called out, 139, 147, 165, 187, 593.
— Temple, festivities at the foundation of, 143, 205; cost of, 232; building of, 238; completed and destroyed, 241.
— Recorder's office, 158.
— a citizen of, his account of the Mormons, 148.
Navajo Indians, 450.
Negroes, origin of, 490, 492.
Nelson, Abraham, 80.
— Hiram, 80.
Nephi, Book of, 27, 189, 526. (*Vide* Book of Abraham.)
Nevada, 353, 410, 669.
New England States, 120.
— Mexico, 380.
— Orleans, 265, 429.
— Testament, inspired translation of, 44.
— York, 713; prophecy of destruction of, 5, 457; Saints in, 120; Elders in, 355, 356; Joseph Smith in State of, 21; apostates in, 630–634.
Newman, Dr. J. P., discussion with Orson Pratt on Polygamy, 682.
New Movement, 631–638, 643–645, 676, 677.
Nomlen, Jabez, 441.
North Platte, 331.
— Bluff Fork, 319.

OBEDIENCE, unquestioning, required, 212; Brigham Young's idea of, 650; H. C. Kimball on, 650.
O'Fallon's Bluff, 335.
Officers, Federal, 376; U. S., in Utah, 411; appointed, 591; manipulated, 287–413, *et seq.*
Ogden City, 268, 706.
— Junction, 635.
Ohio, Saints gather to, 39, 40, 120; apostacy in, 68, 184.
Old man in Israel, 200.
Olive Branch of Israel [Orson Hyde], 128.
Omaha, Nebraska, 250, 316, 334, 637.
Open Letters to Brigham Young, by Argus, 431, *et seq.*
Oquakee, 285.
Oquirrh Range, 397.
Order, Brigham Young's, for the Mountain Meadows Massacre, 448.
— of Enoch, 502.
Oregon, 146, 117, 222; appointment of Governor of, 248.
Osborne, Dr. [Colonel Kane], 381.
Osiris, 513. (*Vide* Book of Abraham.)

Outrage in San Pete, 301.
Ox-teams, 312.

PACIFIC RAILROAD, 621, 625, 666.
Page, John E. [The Sun-Dial], 128.
Pappan, 336.
Parks, Brigadier-General, 84, 99.
Parowan, 135–137, 410, 444, 459, 461.
Parrish, 361, 366, 403–406, 424, 426, 437, 462, 503. (*Vide* Potter.)
Parsons, John, 597.
Patriarch, The [Hyrum Smith], 130, 212, 503.
Patriarchal David's Staff [William Smith], 128.
Patrick, Colonel M. T., 678.
Patten, Captain David, 60, 93–95, 128, 205, *et seq.*
Pay of the Mormon Battalion, Brigham Young draws, 217.
Payson, 405, 432.
Peabody, George, 667.
Pearl of Great Price, 26, 507.
Pep o' Day, 630.
Peniston, Colonel, 80, 458.
Penn, 120.
Pennsylvania, Saints in, 120, 124.
Penrose, "C. W. P.," 673.
Perpetual Emigration Fund, 340, 577.
Persecution of Apostates, 645.
Petition of Ladies to Mrs. President Grant, 673.
Petty, Catherine, 191.
Phelps, W. W., 42, 46, 112, 128, 174, 182.
Pied Riche, Chief of Pottowattamies, 250.
Pierce, President, 281, 307.
— Harrison, 411.
— Rev. G. M., 704.
Pike, Sergeant, 419.
Pinto Creek, 435, 440, 443, 459.
Pioneers, 261, 319.
Pisgah, Mount, 244, 250.
Pittsburg bankers visit Joseph Smith, 71, 72.
— Sidney Rigdon at, 205.
Plains, journey across the, 317, 630.
Plates, gold, discovered by Joseph Smith, 21.
Platte, Department of, 612.
— River-crossing, 335, 336.
— Bridge, 338.
Point of the Mountain, The, 397.
Police, captain of Salt Lake City, 466.
Polk, President, 222, 238, 239, 247–249, 361.
Pollock, Samuel, 444.
Polygamy, revelation on, 145, 176; origin of, 182; first publicly taught, 183, 201; painful results of, 186; extraordinary facts of, 186; repudiated, 190, 192–196, 199–201; in England, 201,

202; in Nauvoo, 225 301, 582–585, 588; in Utah, 613, 615, 621, 629, 634, 638, 652, 660, 673, 682, 683, 685, 693, 706.
Polytheism in Nauvoo, 159, 160.
Pond Town, 405.
Pony Express, 420.
Pope, Judge N., 140.
Post-Office Contracts, 345.
Potomac, Army of, 421.
Potter [and Parrish], murder of, 301, 403–405, 463, 464.
Pottowattamies, 250.
Potts, John, 243.
Powder River, 608.
Powell, L. W., United States Commissioner, afterward Governor, 391, 394.
Pratt, Apostle Orson [Gauge of Philosophy], 128 ; 5, 9, 11 ; conversion of, 36 ; 52, 60, 123, 205, 263, 264, 353, 425, 483, 492–498, 545, 552–555, 586, 649, 664, 682.
— Apostle Parley P. [Archer of Paradise], 128, 455; debate with La Roy Sunderland, 4, 5; converted, 36 ; 52, 61, 94, 104, 112, 123, 128, 196, 205, 263, 270, 351, 352, 429, 432, 492–494, 649.
Preachers [Methodist, Baptist, etc.] take arms against the Mormons, 105.
Predictions, 42 ; fulfilled, 348 ; false, of Brigham Young, 376, 610.
Preëxistence, of souls, 486.
Presidency of United States, 348.
— the First [in Mormon Church], 204, 560.
President of the United States, Joseph Smith candidate for, 174.
— of Stakes of Zion, 695, 696.
Press, Associated, the, 413.
Preuss, map designed by, 269.
Price, Colonel Sterling G., 110.
— James, 444.
Priesthood, 63, 637, 678 ; Aaronic, 28 ; Melchisedec, 28, 659 ; infallible, 11, 342 ; High, Joseph President of, 42 ; gradations of, 62 ; in Zion, 556.
Priests, 558.
Probate Courts of Utah, 686. (Vide Courts.)
Processions through Salt Lake City, 611, 620.
Proclamation of Brigham Young, 358; of Governor Shaffer, 678.
Progress, an article in Salt Lake Telegraph, 638.
Promised Land, 481.
Prophecies of Brigham Young, 376, 610. (Vide Brigham.)
— of Joseph Smith, 420. (Vide Smith.)
Prophet of the Nineteenth Century [Work by Caswell], 106.

Prophets, School of, 41. (Vide School.)
Prospect Hill, 337.
Provo City, 399, 403–407, 432, 444, 450; Mayor of, 407, 701, 705.
Proxy wives, 187.
Prudence, Angeline, 150.
Public discussion, 195 ; in England, 483, 682.

QUEEN of England, Memorial to, 576. Quincy (Ill.), Joseph Smith flees to, 117, 123, 143, 169, 215.
Quorums, 61, 205, 295 ; of apostles, 559; of Three, 560; of Twelve, 204, 262, 662.

RAY County, Mo., 89, 94, 100, 110.
Rawlins, General, 675.
Rebecca, 450.
Rebellion, the Utah, 336, 337.
Red Butte Cañon, 336, 605.
Reed, Chief-Justice, 279, 609.
Rees, 96.
Reformation in Utah, the, 286, 292, 409, 410, 461, 464, 467, 473.
Reformed Egyptian, 123, 489.
Reformers, 636, 642, 677, 705, 706. (Vide New Movement.)
Reichau, 336.
Reign of Terror in Utah, 407.
Reorganized Church, 221, 554, 658.
Republican party, 307, 348.
Resurrection, Mormon theories of the, 470, 480–483, 487.
Revelation, 50, 51, 107, 108, 253, 254, 631 ; a new, proposed by Vice-President Colfax, 613.
Rhode Island, letter to, from a lady, 378.
Rich, C. C., 95, 353.
Richards, Franklin D., Apostle, 108, 313, 329, 333, 335, 339, 340, 411, 442, 542, 704, 705.
Richards, Willard, Doctor and Apostle [Keeper of the Rolls], 128, 163, 169, 170, 171, 241, 255, 263, 278.
Richardson, Albert D., of New York Tribune, 613.
Richmond, Ray County, 89, 95, 100, 110; jail, 109.
Rigdon, Sidney, 36, 41, 69, 72, 74, 78, 86, 87, 91, 104, 112, 123, 124, 137, 204–206; cut off, 207, 208, 210, 562, 649.
Rigdon, Nancy, daughter of Sidney, 205.
Riggs, William, 444.
Robinson, Angelina, 191.
— Dr. J. King, 616–618, 623, 705.
— Quartermaster Lewis, 366.
— George W., 104.

Robinson, Cornet, 136.
Rockwell, Orrin Porter [a "Danite"], 140, 141, 367.
Rocky Mountains, 146, 221, 237, 379; Zion in, 175.
Rocky Ridge, 327.
Rogers, Mr., of Davis County, 101.

SACRAMENT, the first Mormon, 37.
Sacrifices, Human, 613.
Sacrifices, human, commended, 304, 410.
Safety Society Bank, at Kirtland, 70, 387.
Saint Louis, 215, 244, 266, 285, 596, 597, 623; U. S. Treasurer at, 119.
Saints persecuted, 47. (Vide Mormons.)
— to be avengers, 57.
— scattered, 120. (Vide Mormons.)
Salt Creek, 432.
— dearth of, in the U. S. army in Utah, 377.
— Sermon, Sidney Rigdon's, 78, 79.
Salt Lake, 259, 670.
— Valley, 259, 260, 347, 691, 692.
— City, 102, 144, 183, 185, 260, 644, 623, 625, 626, 645, 661, 668, 670, 672, 676, 691–698, 701, 706, 707; its climate, 291; poverty in, 304, 314, 315, 382; troops passing through, 396; 382, 397, 428, 606.
— County, 673.
Salter, Job, 208.
Sam, an ancient American Prophet, 550.
San Bernardino, 353, 434, 444.
San Francisco, 354, 615, 687.
— Bulletin, 634.
Sanhedrim, 75.
San Pete, 301, 302.
Santa Clara, 447, 448, 451.
Savage, 517.
Savage, Levi, 444, 328, 329.
School of the Prophets, 639, 701.
School, Sunday, in Salt Lake City, 701, 705.
Schuyler County, 149, 150.
Scott, Camp, 376–379, 383, 384, 389, 396, 417.
Scott, Lieutenant-General, 380, 396.
Sealing, 504.
Secretary of War, the U. S., 380.
Seer, the, 557.
Seminole Indians, 336.
Sermon, the first Mormon, 33.
Seth, 50.
Settlements, Mormon, 671.
Seventies, 61, 295, 559.
Shaffer, Governor J. Wilson, 675–679, 681.
Sharpe, Thos. C., editor of the Warsaw Signal, 165, 172, 173.
Shaver, Judge, 279, 281.

Shearer, Norman, 112.
Sherman, Wm. H., 635, 642.
Sheridan, General, 674.
Sherman, General, 616.
Shiloh, 377.
Shoal Creek, 100, 101.
Sierra Nevada Mountains, 269.
Signal, the Warsaw, 172.
Sinclair, Chas. E., the Hon. Associate Justice, 283, 352, 404–408, 591.
Singleton, Captain, 153.
Slade, William, 444.
Slavery, 308.
Smith, Alexander H., 629, 633, 634.
— Albert, 395.
— Captain of Carthage Grays, 153.
— David Hyrum, 213, 629.
— E., 502.
— Elias, Judge, 610.
— Emma [his Elect Lady], 175, 186, 188–191, 629, 634.
— Eva, 429.
— George A. [Entablature of Truth], 52, 123, 124, 154, 185, 560, 626, 661–664, 684, 696.
— Hyrum, 30, 52, 73, 108, 112, 120, 152, 153, 155, 166, 167; funeral of, 171, 188, 190, 192 of, 350, 573, 601, 603, 605.
— Joseph, the Prophet of the Lord, 13; tarred and feathered, 41, 42; 30, 41, 60, 61, 68, 72, 76, 81, 82, 88, 89, 90, 104–108, 110, 111, 117, 120, 124, 129, 136, 137, 138, 147, 172, 173, 175, 178, 181–176, 182, 183, 204, 206, 304, 306–384, 382, 172, 487, 506, 507, 508, 521, 540, 547, 630, 632, 644, 649, 661; early life of, 16; baptized by Oliver Cowdery, 28, 29; he prophesies of Brigham Young, 68; in Missouri, 69; flees from Kirtland, 70; surrenders, 104; in prison, 115; his trial, 118; troubles of, 123; becomes Lieutenant-General, Mayor, etc., 135; character of, 157–175; death of, 168; character summed up, 175; funeral of, 174; posterity of, 185, 186, 188; and polygamy, 186; his prediction of Senator Douglas, 517; prophecy of, 120; the first to be "resurrected," 480; prediction of, 499; faith of, 555.
— Joseph, 444.
— Joseph, Jr., 329, 634.
— Klingon, Bishop, 439, 442–151.
— General Persifer F., 565.
— Lucy [mother of Joseph], her book, 14.
— Robert J., justice of the peace, 155.
— William B. [Patriarchal David's Staff], 211.
— Don Carlos, 86.
— Samuel H., 30.

Smoot, Elder A. O., Mayor of Salt Lake City, 349–352, 608, 609.
Snow, Eliza R., Secretary of Ladies' Society. and poetess, 191.
— Zerubbabel, Associate-Justice, 275, 278.
— Erastus, 333.
Social Hall, Salt Lake City, 286.
Soda Springs, 368, 606.
Sophronia [or Mary] Huff, 450.
Sorrow, John Calvin, 455.
South, the, 46, 212, 307; prophecy of rebellion in, 44; rebellion, 610.
South Pass, 330.
Southern California, 353.
Southey, Robert, the poet, strange passage from, 89.
Spanish Fork, 432, 464.
Spaulding, Solomon, 208, 508, 513.
Speech extraordinary of General Clark, 110.
Spencer, Augustine, 155.
— Orson, 266.
— Daniel, 333, 335, 339, 341, 342.
Spiritualism and Joseph Smith, 66, 508, 520–522, 546, 551, 552, 631, 632, 636, 641.
Springfield, 119, 215.
Springfield, speech of Senator Douglas at, 347.
Spring Hill, 77.
Springville, 301, 403, 404, 407–409, 432, 462–463, 465.
Springville, murder at, 459.
Squatter sovereignty, 317.
Staines, Elder W. C., Superintendent of Emigration, 301.
Stakes of Zion, 645, 696. (Vide Zion.)
Stanley, Mr., 102.
Stansbury, Captain Howard, 272.
Stanton, Secretary, 592, 601.
Star office destroyed, 46, 49.
Star. (Vide Millennial.)
Stenhouse, Elder T. B. H., disfellowshipped, 639.
Steptoe, Lieutenant-Colonel E. J., 364.
Stewart, J. M., 463, 465, 467.
— William, 444.
— Riley, 80.
Stiles, Judge George P., 280, 282, 283, 285, 307.
Stoddard, Judson L., 598.
Stores destroyed, 422.
Strang, Elder James, 185, 212.
Strickland, Obed, Associate-Justice of Utah, 112, 684.
Sunday-Schools in S. L. C., 704, 705.
Sunderland, La Roy, 351.
Sunderland, Dr., of Washington, 682.
Sun-Dial, the [John E. Page], 128, 273.

Surveys in Utah, 671.
Sweetwater, the, 320, 329, 331, 337, 368.

TABERNACLE, Salt Lake City, 125, 182, 280, 294, 299, 300, 303, 305, 332, 333, 372, 374–376, 379, 380, 384, 392, 397, 400, 415, 420, 462, 473, 485, 486, 546, 561, 586, 601–610, 627, 634, 638, 641, 642, 644, 651, 666, 693–697, 701; discourses in, 359, 361, 610, 624, 611, 695–697, 711; O. Pratt in, 493; discussion in, 682.
Table Mountain, 273.
Taggit, William, 450.
Taos, 380.
Taylder, T. W. P., author of "The Mormon's Own Book," 603.
Taylor [Champion of Right], Apostle John, 128, 150, 157, 166, 169, 170, 174, 191, 195, 204, 235, 241, 248, 263, 264, 333, 339–341, 357, 359, 364, 365, 664.
— Leonora, 191.
— Steve, 336.
— President Zachary, 249, 276, 277, 280, 361, 557.
Telegraph, The Salt Lake, 612, 638.
Temple, The, 108, 266, 478; to be reared, 38; revelation on, 38; at Independence, 120; in Kirtland, 49, 61–63; dedication of, 63; in Nauvoo, 123; foundation of, 136, 137, 140–146, 174; completing of, 217, 224; finished, 223; dispute whether finished, 224–226, 480, 505; in Salt Lake City, 670, 697, 698.
— Block, 260.
Tenant, Mr., an emigrant, 335.
Territorial Legislature, 276, 282.
— Marshal, 684.
Territory of Utah, Organic Act of, 281.
Terry, Parshal, 405.
Testament, Old, inspired translation of, 45.
Texas, 364.
Theocracy, Mormon, 668, 675, 681.
Theodule Devéria, 516. (Vide Devéria and Book of Abraham.)
Theological Institute, 390.
Thompson, Robert B., 129.
Thornton, 444.
Times, The London, 324.
Times and Seasons, 79, 136, 137, 190, 199, 200, 211, 212, 474, 519.
Timpanogos, 272.
Tithing, 266, 416, 456, 578, 623, 698.
— Office, 651, 654.
Titus, Chief-Justice, 617, 621, 683.
Tom Corwin's story, 614.
Tompkins, Judge, 117.
Tongues, gift of, 650. (Vide Gifts.)
Tooele, 268.
Trains, United States, burning of, 368.

Transmigration of souls, 481, 488.
Treason charged against Joseph Smith, 112.
Trial of Joseph Smith (vide Smith); of assassins of Smith, 175.
Trial of Mormons for murder and polygamy, 685.
Tribune, Salt Lake, 641.
— The New York, 34, 301.
— The Chicago, 248.
Trobriand, General R. De, 681.
Troubles in Missouri, 46.
True Latter-Day Saints' Herald, 225, 634.
Trustee in Trust, 502, 578, 651, 657, 965.
Truth for the Mormons, 278.
Tullidge, Elder Edward W., 342, 630, 632, 633, 639, 642.
Tullis, David, 451.
Tuttle, Bishop, 704.
Twelve Apostles, 162; Brigham Young President of, 210. (Vide Apostles.)
Tyler, Elder, 334, 336, 444.

UNITED Brethren, 573.
  Union Pacific Railroad, 268, 363, 635, 637, 706.
United States Army in Utah, 417, 658, 677.
— Marshal, 686.
Urim and Thummim, 28, 29.
Utah Territory, organized, 274; boundaries of, 274, 669; crops in, 270; difficulties in, 279, 407; murders in, 418; population of, 672; statistics of, 691, 706.
— County, 268.
— Central Railway, 636, 667, 706.
— Expedition, 365.
— Lake, 272.
— Magazine, 630, 635, 637, 639, 642.

VALLEY, Salt Lake, 396. (Vide Salt Lake.)
— Tan, 402, 409, 418.
Van Buren, 47.
Vaughan, Vernon H., 678.
Vedette [newspaper], 612.
Vic [Queen Victoria], Rigdon threatens to pull the nose of, 207.
Vision of Joseph Smith, 15, 16, 18; of Joseph Smith and Oliver Cowdery, 28, 63; at dedication, 63, 64; of apostates, 642.
Vleit, Major Stewart Van, 353; in Salt Lake City, 356, 358, 362, 364, 385.
Volunteers, 604, 612, et al.
Vorhee, 185.

WAHSATCH Mountains, 377, 592, 669, 670, 673, 691.

Waite, Associate-Justice Charles B., 599-602, 605, 609.
— Mrs., her book, 247, 279, 453.
— Miss, 602.
Walker Brothers, merchants of Utah, 417, 623, 627, 643-645.
— J. Robinson, 621, 623-628.
— Cyrus, candidate for Congress, 142.
— House, 706.
Wallock, Major-General, 96.
War, in Utah, preparing for, 353.
— The Civil, 421.
Warm Springs, 617.
Warren, Major, 217.
Warsaw, 154, 169, 215.
Washington, a Latter-Day Saint, 481.
— Monument, 276.
— County, 459.
— City, 436.
Washoe Valley, 353.
Watt, George D., 573.
Weatherford, 214.
Webb, C. G., 319, 333.
Weber Cañon, 593, 594.
— County, 268.
— Station, 393.
Weld, Dr., 225.
Welding, Dick, 80.
Weller, Governor John B., 617.
Wells, General Daniel H., 272, 367, 368, 371-376, 412, 593, 609, 640, 666, 680, 681, 685, 701.
Western Standard, 354.
Wheelock, Elder C. H., 321, 335, 336.
White, Captain Joel, 443.
Whitmer family, 29; David, 30, 75, 112; John, 112; Peter, 30.
Whitney, Bishop, 5, 6.
— Eliza Ann [counsellor], 191.
— N. K., 191.
Wife, spiritual, 193.
Wight, Colonel Lyman [Wild Ram of the Mountains], 81, 82, 86, 104, 111, 112, 123, 206, 263.
Wild Cats, Missouri, 424, 428.
Wiley, Mr. R., 548.
Williams, Colonel Levi, 149, 165, 172, 175 203-205, 209, 314, 319, 320.
— Frederick G., counsellor of Joseph, 69.
Williamson, Dr., 618.
Willie, Captain James G. [Hand-cart Company], 314, 319, 320, 323-329.
Willis, John, 175, 439, 441, 444.
Willow Creek, 329.
Wilson, Alexander, District Attorney, 401.
— General, 106.
— an apostate, 621.
Winter-Quarters [Florence], 250, 255, 261, 264, 316; log-cabin at, 262.
Witnesses to Book of Mormon, 29, 76, 112, 508.

Wood, William, 243.
— River, 318.
Woodruff, Apostle Wilford [Banner of the Gospel], 128, 52, 79, 191, 263.
— Phœbe, 191.
Woods, Satchel, 94.
— Governor George A., 680.
Woodward, William, 314, 317, 328.
Woolley, Bishop, 701, 705.
Wootton, Secretary, 445, 591.
Word and Will of the Lord, 253.
Works, Abigail, 191.
Wyoming, 669.

YOUNG. (Vide Brigham.)
— Bishop L. D., 379.
— John, 649.
— John W., 696.
— Joseph, 649.
— Lorenzo D., 649.
— Phineas H., 649.

Young, Joseph, 100.
— Joseph A., 319, 322, 336, 663.
— Mrs. Mary Ann Angel, 652.

ZACH, Old. (Vide Taylor.)
Zion, the New, 39, 120, 217, 259, 355, 363, 371, 375, 379, 396, 120, 423, 428, 452, 601, 613, 633, 637, 691, 692; emigration to, 313, 316, 333, 341; Stake of, 297; defence of, 353; in Kirtland, 100; in Jackson County, 268, 554; the Rocky Mountain, 276; predicted by Joseph Smith, 146; crimes in, 620; terror in, 621; Stakes of, 695, 696.
— Daughters of [Danites], 93.
Zion's Camp, 52, 55, 57, 58.
— Songs of, 349.
— Coöperative Mercantile Institution, 625, 627, 628. (Vide Coöperative.)
Zion's Watchman [La Roy Sunderland's paper], 5, 351.

THE END.

www.ingramcontent.com/pod-product-compliance
Lightning Source LLC
Chambersburg PA
CBHW020327020726
47475CB00068B/18